Microsoft®

Core Reference

MICROSOFT® .NET COMPACT FRAMEWORK

Andy Wigley
Mark Sutton

PUBLISHED BY
Microsoft Press
A Division of Microsoft Corporation
One Microsoft Way
Redmond, Washington 98052-6399

Library of Congress Cataloging-in-Publication Data
Wigley, Andy.
Microsoft .NET Compact Framework / Andy Wigley, Stephen Wheelwright.
p. cm.
Includes index.
ISBN 0-7356-1725-2
1. Microsoft .NET Framework. 2. Application software--Development. 3. Pocket computers. 4. Mobile computers. I. Wheelwright, Stephen. II. Title.

QA76.76.M52 W54 2002
005.2'768--dc21 2002038655

Printed and bound in the United States of America.

1 2 3 4 5 6 7 8 9 QWT 8 7 6 5 4 3

Distributed in Canada by H.B. Fenn and Company Ltd.

A CIP catalogue record for this book is available from the British Library.

Microsoft Press books are available through booksellers and distributors worldwide. For further information about international editions, contact your local Microsoft Corporation office or contact Microsoft Press International directly at fax (425) 936-7329. Visit our Web site at www.microsoft.com/mspress. Send comments to *mspinput@microsoft.com*.

Acquisitions Editor: Anne Hamilton
Project Editor: Dick Brown
Technical Editor: Donnie Cameron

Body Part No. X08-82212

To Caroline, my love and my best friend.

Table of Contents

Part III Common Programming Tasks

Part V Advanced Mobile Application Development

Acknowledgments

A large number of people at Content Master and at Microsoft Press have been involved in producing the book before you. Particular thanks is due to my colleagues at Content Master: Rob Burbidge, Rory MacLeod, Graeme Malcolm, John Sharp, Mark Sutton, and Stephen Wheelwright, who shouldered much of the task of writing it, and David Glanville, who managed the book for Content Master.

At Microsoft Press, thanks is due to all the people who worked on the book: technical editor Donnie Cameron, project editor Dick Brown, copy editor Holly M. Viola, electronic artist Michael Kloepfer, compositor Dan Latimer, proof coordinator Patricia Masserman, and Web page creator Tess McMillan. Thanks also to Danielle Bird and Anne Hamilton, acquisitions editors, who oversaw the commencement of this project and gave me the opportunity to write the book.

Thanks to the following people in the .NET Compact Framework product group and other parts of Microsoft who gave their support to the book, gave their help and advice, and reviewed chapters: Miller Able, Paul Appleby, Jamie De Guerre, Mark Gilbert, Craig, Neable, Kent Sharkey, and Theresa Venhuis. In the wider developer community, the following people were particularly helpful and answered technical queries or supplied code samples: Ralph Arvesen, Neil Cowburn, Michael Scott Heydt, and Michael Wittenburg.

Finally, away from the computing world, particular thanks to my wife, Caroline, with whom I share love, adventures, and dreams, and to my wonderful daughters, Frances and Clêr.

Introduction

There are two main factors driving increased usage of handheld devices in the enterprise. The first is the ever-decreasing cost of hardware. In the week that I write this, Dell is launching its first Pocket PC at a price that is intended to undercut rivals, Hewlett Packard has announced new low-end and high-end iPaqs, and Microsoft and Samsung announced the availability of a new Pocket PC concept design that "dramatically lowers costs and reduces product development time for mobile device OEMs and original device manufacturers." All this competition among suppliers drives prices lower and makes it more likely than ever that enterprises will consider it a worthwhile investment to issue smart devices to large numbers of their employees.

The devices are becoming more capable as well. Processors are getting faster, and the devices at the low end of the market now come with 32 MB of RAM, compared to 16 MB a short while ago. Higher-end devices routinely come with Bluetooth and 802.11 wireless networking built in, and phone-PDA hybrids such as the Pocket PC phone edition are able to use General Packet Radio Service (GPRS) or CDMA2000 packet-switched data communications over mobile phone operators' networks.

The second key ingredient driving uptake is improved software architectures. The .NET Compact Framework is an example of a managed execution environment. The runtime engine sits on the device and is responsible for managing the execution of .NET applications. This functionality yields a number of benefits, such as memory management, cross-language interoperability, and improved error handling. The .NET Compact Framework also implements a unified, object-oriented, hierarchical, and extensible set of class libraries that encapsulates common and not-so-common tasks into classes that can be called by any application written in any .NET language.

The most significant benefit is that the programming model for .NET Compact Framework devices is identical to that used by the developer using .NET to build applications for desktop PCs and servers. The .NET Compact Framework implements a compatible subset of the functionality of the full .NET Framework, so developers use the same techniques to achieve similar tasks, using the same developer tools, such as Visual Studio .NET. Prior to .NET, developing applications for Windows CE required a different toolset and programming techniques that were similar to Win32 development for the desktop but different enough to cause many companies to shy away from making the necessary investment in training development staff. Now desktop developers can easily transfer their .NET development skills over to developing applications for handheld devices, reducing developer training costs.

Some "fundamentalist" software developers have complained that .NET "dumbs down" the development process for Windows. That's not right. .NET certainly makes it very much easier to do the simple things, but it also makes it much easier to do some quite complex things, such as accessing Web services or building components. But that just frees your time to develop more innovative software solutions. Some of the most innovative solutions will be distributed systems built with rich client applications running on handheld devices working with enterprise data accessed using XML Web services or the data integration capabilities of SQL Server CE. With their lower cost, better performance, and improved software development process, handheld devices are ready to take their place as key components of enterprise applications.

System Requirements

You'll need the following software to work through the samples in this book:

- Microsoft Visual Studio .NET 2003
- Microsoft Windows 2000, Microsoft Windows XP, or Microsoft .NET Server

The minimum hardware specification for your development PC is a Pentium II-class processor, 450 MHz with a minimum of 128 MB (Windows 2000) or 256 MB (Windows XP or Windows .NET Server) of RAM. You'll need around 5 GB of free hard disk space to install Visual Studio .NET 2003.

Visual Studio .NET 2003 includes emulators of a Windows CE .NET and a Pocket PC 2003 device, so a real handheld device is not essential. However, if you want to test applications on a real device, you'll need the following hardware and software:

- A Pocket PC 2000 or 2002 device or a Windows CE .NET 4.1 or later device
- ActiveSync 3.6 or later (download from *http://www.microsoft.com/mobile/downloads*)

- Serial/USB synchronization cable or infrared to synchronize to the desktop PC. Once the device has set up a partnership with your development PC, you can use Ethernet (or wireless Ethernet), if your device supports it.

Sample Code

Most of the sample code in this book is written in C#. Many readers will prefer to use Visual Basic, so we have implemented most of the samples in Visual Basic .NET as well and made all of them, both the C# and the Visual Basic .NET samples, available for download from the Web site supporting this book. We hope that Visual Basic .NET developers will download the samples and refer to those when reading the text. Fortunately, in .NET, the differences between languages are not as pronounced as they used to be. C# and Visual Basic .NET applications are structurally identical and only the language syntax changes, so passages in the text that describe how to use a programming technique in C# should be understandable to someone referring to the Visual Basic .NET version of a sample.

You can get to the samples from *http://www.microsoft.com/mspress/books/5960.asp*. Click the Companion Content link in the More Information box on the right side of this page to bring up the Companion Content Web page. The Companion Content Web page has instructions for installing the sample code on your own PC. Check the Support: Book And CD link for corrections and updates to the book as well.

Support

Every effort has been made to ensure the accuracy of this book and the companion content. Microsoft Press provides corrections for books through the World Wide Web at the following address:

http://www.microsoft.com/mspress/support

To connect directly to the Microsoft Press Knowledge Base and enter a query regarding a question or an issue that you might have, go to

http://www.microsoft.com/mspress/support/search.asp

If you have comments, questions, or ideas regarding this book or the companion content, or questions that aren't answered by querying the Knowledge Base, please send them to Microsoft Press by e-mail to

mspinput@microsoft.com

or by postal mail to

Microsoft Press
Attn: Microsoft .NET Compact Framework Editor
One Microsoft Way
Redmond, WA 98052-6399

Please note that product support is not offered through the preceding mail address. For product support information, please visit the Microsoft Support Web site at: *http://support.microsoft.com*.

Part I

.NET Compact Framework Architecture

1

Introducing the .NET Compact Framework

Microsoft .NET is often referred to in the press as "Microsoft's platform for Web services." The .NET Framework does make it very easy to build applications that make use of XML Web services, but that wasn't the reason for creating it. It just happened that XML Web services became established as an industry force at about the same time that Microsoft was devising its next-generation application runtime environment and developer tools. As Bill Gates put it at the launch of Visual Studio .NET on February 13, 2002: "The .NET vision incorporates more than just Web services. It talks about how people use these things, being able to get their information at any time, any place, on any device, pocket-sized devices, tablet-sized devices, in the car, or the TV set, you name it, all connected up to these capabilities."

As you can see, this vision encompasses a variety of mobile devices, including handheld computers. Today, not everyone wants or needs the facilities that handheld computers offer. However, as they get cheaper, designs improve, and battery life increases, handheld computers are becoming more and more appealing to many companies and individuals. But the key to the usefulness of these devices is, as always, the availability of good applications. Until now, developing software to run on handheld devices required special skills that were different enough from the skills required to develop applications for the desktop that most companies declined to meet the costs of training staff and diverting them from mainstream development activities.

Developing applications for handheld devices will require special skills for some time yet; the resource-constrained nature of handheld devices and the special design skills required to build good applications that work with a small screen size ensure that. However, with the .NET Compact Framework and Smart Device Extensions (SDE) for Visual Studio .NET, Microsoft has provided a consistent software development experience for desktop and mobile developers. Developers who have gained experience working with the full .NET Framework in Visual Studio .NET can develop for handhelds using the same development environment, the same programming languages, and class libraries that are a subset of the full libraries. This capability adds up to lower development costs, more versatile developers, and (we hope) more numerous and better-quality applications available on handheld devices!

A Brief History of Smart Mobile Computing Devices

The .NET Compact Framework is for devices that have the following characteristics:

- A capable CPU
- RAM for program and data storage
- Persistent storage, such as a disk drive or RAM disk

These are the characteristics of what have become known as smart devices. Although there's no authoritative definition, broadly speaking, smart devices are small-form, mobile devices that are capable of running programs and connecting to a computer network. Some mobile phones offer messaging and the ability to access mobile Web content through a Wireless Application Protocol (WAP) or i-mode microbrowser, but these phones offer little or no support for running custom applications. The smart devices that the .NET Compact Framework targets are more capable than these mobile phones. Version 1 of the .NET Compact Framework is specifically for Pocket PCs and embedded solutions running Windows CE .NET. However, the .NET Compact Framework has been designed with portability in mind, and it is possible that we will eventually see implementations for other device-form factors and other operating systems.

Beginnings of Portable Computing

The first portable computer was the Osborne 1, which appeared in 1981. Describing it as *portable* seems laughable now, but it met the design criteria of Adam Osborne, a well-known publisher of technical books in the early days of the personal computer, who wanted a computer with a built-in screen that could fit under an airplane seat. The unit boasted a small 5-inch CRT, which displayed 52 characters but could be shifted left or right to display longer lines of text. (See Figure 1-1.) The Osborne was introduced at the West Coast Computer Faire in April 1981, and it was also notable for being the first machine to come bundled with a suite of software that included BASIC, WordStar, and SuperCalc. The unit retailed for $1,795 and had brisk sales of about 10,000 machines a month.

Figure 1-1 The Osborne-1, the first portable computer.

The Osborne 1 enjoyed its status as sole portable computer for only a short time. In 1982, a brash new startup released its first product onto the market, which was a compact personal computer. The company even derived its name from the compact nature of this product, and so Compaq computer was born. The Compaq Portable weighed 28 pounds and was the size of a sewing machine. It can be considered compact only in comparison to its main competitor in 1982, the IBM-PC. However, it possessed a major advantage over the Osborne 1 in that it ran MS-DOS and claimed 100% compatibility with programs written for the IBM-PC. The Compaq Portable was similar in performance to the IBM-PC with an 8088 processor, 128 KB of RAM, a single 5.25-inch floppy disk, and a built-in 9-inch green monochrome monitor. The complete system sold for $3,000.

Many other portable computers came and went over the next few years, including the Epson HX-20 and the Commodore SX-64, but the next interesting development along the path to handheld computers was the Radio Shack TRS-80 Model 100. This was essentially the first notebook-size computer that had a built-in display, used a regular keyboard, and could run on AA batteries. The unit had an 8-line by 40-character LCD display and came with BASIC and a word processor built into ROM. It initially sold for $800 in an 8 KB version and $1, 000 in a 24 KB version.

PSION Invents the Personal Organizer

It is generally accepted that UK technology company Psion defined the personal digital assistant (PDA) genre with the launch of its first organizer back in 1984. The Psion 1 was based on 8-bit technology, came with 10 KB of non-volatile character storage in cartridges, two cartridge slots, a database with a search function, a utility pack with math functions, a 16-character LCD display, and a clock/calendar. The optional Science Pack turned the Psion into a genuine computer capable of running resident scientific programs and being programmed in its own BASIC-like language, Psion Organizer Programming Language (POPL).

The Psion 1 was superseded by the Psion II, and between the mid-1980s and the early 1990s, 500,000 Psion IIs were produced. Many of these were commercial point of sale (POS) versions that did not include the standard built-in organizer functions but ran specialized applications.

The Series 3a, launched in 1993, broke new ground with its ability to link to a desktop PC and transfer, convert, and synchronize data between the two environments. For a couple of years, Psion's domination of the PDA market was assured, and the success of the 3a was built upon by the more powerful Series 3c and the third generation 32-bit Series 5, launched in 1997. However, in 2001, after years of being squeezed by Palm and Windows CE, Psion announced that they were pulling out of the PDA market and concentrating on their Symbian software joint venture with Nokia and Sony-Ericsson.

PDA Market Expands

The name *Personal Digital Assistant* was first coined by then Apple CEO John Sculley in a speech at the Winter Consumer Show in January 1992. The *Free Online Dictionary of Computing (http://foldoc.doc.ic.ac.uk/)* describes a PDA as a "small handheld computer used to write notes, track appointments, and otherwise keep your life in order. PDAs provide all the functionality of a cheap pad of paper at hundreds of times the cost, and with far less storage capacity." Hmmm, for early PDAs, that's probably a fair description. The first device that offered rather more than the equivalent of an expensive pad of paper was Apple's Newton MessagePad, which came out in August 1993. (See Figure 1-2.) This innovative device used pen-input and handwriting recognition, Personal Information Management (PIM) features, and communications capability. The Newton was an instant success, and soon there were a number of competitors, including the Amstrad PenPad, the Casio and Tandy Zoomer, the Sony MagicLink, and the IBM/Bell South Simon.

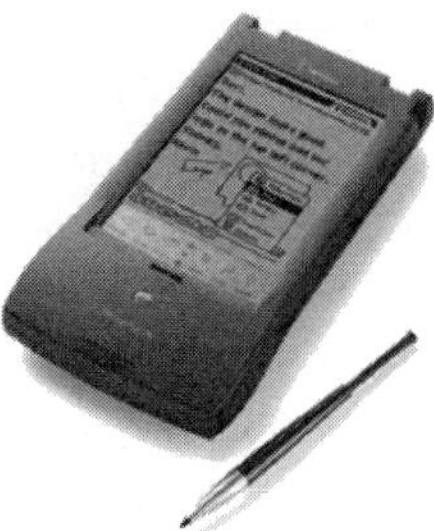

Figure 1-2 Apple Newton featuring handwriting recognition.

All these early devices, though impressive enough, drew criticism because the handwriting recognition just wasn't accurate enough. The handwriting technology in the Apple Newton was very sophisticated and attempted to learn an individual user's handwriting and convert it to text. Although a brave attempt, this approach proved to be unreliable. It was not until March 1996 that industry pundits finally agreed that someone had gotten it right, when Palm Computing Inc. released its first Palm Pilot PDAs. These devices use their own "language" of letter shapes called Graffiti that the user must learn (which typically takes around 20 minutes), which is easier for the device to recognize and results in more accurate data entry. The Palm Pilot swiftly outstripped sales of any competitors, and by the end of 1999, Palm boasted a staggering 70 percent of the worldwide PDA market; 20,000 developers were employed in writing applications for the device.

Microsoft and Handhelds

Sensing an opportunity that was too good to miss, Microsoft entered the fray in fall 1996 with its first embedded operating system, Windows CE, supported by around 40 companies who promised to develop CE-compatible hardware and software. However, the first two major releases of this operating system did not meet with universal acclaim. Early devices were too battery hungry, and the GUI tried too hard to mimic that of the Windows desktop, resulting in a complicated interface that was not appropriate for handheld devices.

Pocket PC 2000, which is a specific implementation of Windows CE version 3, appeared in April 2000 and featured a brand new GUI layout that answered much of the criticism directed at earlier versions. Pocket PC devices, led by the hugely successful Compaq iPaq, quickly became a major competitor to Palm in enterprise, high-end PDA accounts. An update, Pocket PC 2002, followed in late 2001. Figure 1-3 shows devices that use Windows CE–derived operating systems. Market research published in April 2002 from Canalys (*www.canalys.com*) analyzing mobile shipments during Q1 of 2002 in the Europe and Middle East markets put devices running Palm OS at 43 percent, with Windows CE at 34 percent. However, the Windows CE device share was up 33 percent from a year earlier, while Palm was down 44 percent. (See *http:/ /www.canalys.com/pr/r2002041.htm.*)

Windows CE .NET was officially released on January 8, 2002. It is the fourth major release of the operating system.

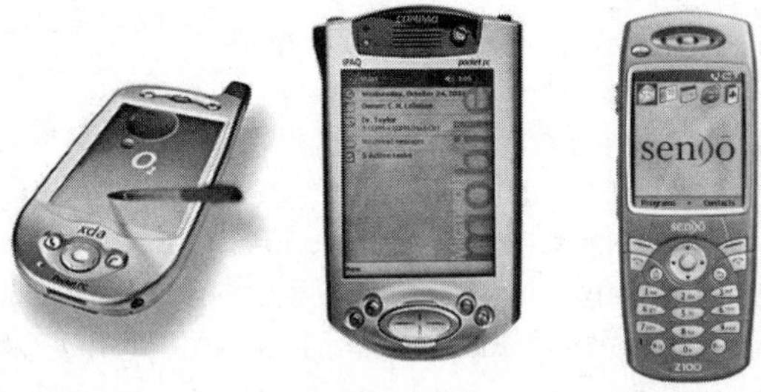

Figure 1-3 Three of the most recent devices running Windows CE–derived operating systems: O2 XDA, Compaq iPaq H3870, and Sendo Z100.

Microsoft .NET

What is .NET, and what benefits does it bring to Windows CE developers? The benefits of .NET have been written about hundreds of times since it was first announced. So rather than repeat the list of good points all over again, let me give a practical example.

Before .NET

The following code listing is some of the source code for an incredibly useful (!) COM component called HelloWorldProvider, created using eMbedded Visual C++ 3 and Active Template Library (ATL). This component returns the string "Hello, World" to a caller. What isn't shown are the various other files such as HelloWorldProvider.cpp and .def, and StdAfx.cpp and .h, all files that are necessary to implement COM "plumbing." (The full implementation is available in this book's sample files for those who are interested.)

HelloWorldProvider.idl

```
// HelloWorldProvider.idl : IDL source for HelloWorldProvider.dll
//

// This file will be processed by the MIDL tool to
// produce the type library (HelloWorldProvider.tlb)
// and marshalling code.

import "oaidl.idl";
import "ocidl.idl";
    [
        object,
        uuid(1D781DA4-A0AE-4F87-97A4-E8D67678B5FC),
        dual,
        helpstring("IHelloWorld Interface"),
        pointer_default(unique)
    ]
    interface IHelloWorld : IDispatch
    {
        [propget, id(1), helpstring("property Message")]
            HRESULT Message([out, retval] BSTR *pVal);
    };

[
    uuid(E0829B73-C513-4509-936D-D905376F4B0C),
    version(1.0),
    helpstring("HelloWorldProvider 1.0 Type Library")
]
library HELLOWORLDPROVIDERLib
{
    importlib("stdole32.tlb");
    importlib("stdole2.tlb");

    [
        uuid(BE71BAA4-7E78-4178-B00C-4E0D53886989),
        helpstring("HelloWorld Class")
    ]
    coclass HelloWorld
    {
        [default] interface IHelloWorld;
    };
};
```

HelloWorld.h

```
// HelloWorld.h : Declaration of the CHelloWorld

#ifndef __HELLOWORLD_H_
#define __HELLOWORLD_H_

#include "resource.h"       // main symbols

/////////////////////////////////////////////////////////////////////////////
// CHelloWorld
class ATL_NO_VTABLE CHelloWorld :
    public CComObjectRootEx<CComSingleThreadModel>,
    public CComCoClass<CHelloWorld, &CLSID_HelloWorld>,
    public IDispatchImpl<IHelloWorld, &IID_IHelloWorld,
&LIBID_HELLOWORLDPROVIDERLib>
{
public:
    CHelloWorld()
    {
        m_MessageTxt= SysAllocString(L"Hello, World");
    }

DECLARE_REGISTRY_RESOURCEID(IDR_HELLOWORLD)

DECLARE_PROTECT_FINAL_CONSTRUCT()

BEGIN_COM_MAP(CHelloWorld)
    COM_INTERFACE_ENTRY(IHelloWorld)
    COM_INTERFACE_ENTRY(IDispatch)
END_COM_MAP()

// IHelloWorld
public:
    STDMETHOD(get_Message)(/*[out, retval]*/ BSTR *pVal);
private:
    BSTR m_MessageTxt;
};

#endif //__HELLOWORLD_H_
```

Admittedly, when you create a project such as this one, the wizard generates most of the code listed here, but nonetheless, as you can see, it's a complicated beast! An eMbedded Visual Basic client program that uses this server is fortunately much simpler. A Visual C++ client, however, which is not shown here, shares some of the complexity of the server. The following code is from the application HelloWorldClient_COM, available with this book's sample files.

HelloWorld.cpp

```
// HelloWorld.cpp : Implementation of CHelloWorld
#include "stdafx.h"
#include "HelloWorldProvider.h"
#include "HelloWorld.h"

/////////////////////////////////////////////////////////////////////////////
// CHelloWorld

STDMETHODIMP CHelloWorld::get_Message(BSTR *pVal)
{
    CComBSTR tbstr;
    tbstr=m_MessageTxt;
    *pVal=SysAllocString(tbstr);
    return S_OK;
}
```

HelloWorldClient.bas

```
Option Explicit

Dim comServer As Object

Sub Main()
    Dim aMsg
    Set comServer = CreateObject("HelloWorldProvider.HelloWorld")
    aMsg = comServer.Message
    MsgBox aMsg
End Sub
```

.NET Is a Better COM

Now let's do the same thing in .NET—in fact, let's improve upon it. In eMbedded Visual Tools, you cannot create a COM server using Visual Basic, but here is the code for a .NET class library written in Visual Basic .NET, which does the same thing as the COM server listed previously.

HelloWorldProvider.vb

```
Namespace HelloWorldProvider
    Public Class HelloWorld
        Public ReadOnly Property Message() As String
            Get
                Return "Hello, World"
            End Get
        End Property
    End Class
End Namespace
```

Here are two clients, one in C# and one in Visual Basic .NET:

Client.cs

```
using System.IO;

namespace ClientCsharp
{
    class Client
    {
        static void Main(string[] args)
        {
            HelloWorldProvider.HelloWorld myServer;
            myServer = new HelloWorldProvider.HelloWorld();
            string aMsg = myServer.Message;
            // Write the greeting to a file
            StreamWriter sr = File.CreateText(@"\My Documents\Greeting.txt");
            sr.WriteLine(aMsg);
            sr.Close();
        }
    }
}
```

Client.vb

```
Imports System.IO

Module Client

    Sub Main()
        Dim myServer As HelloWorldProvider.HelloWorld
        myServer = New HelloWorldProvider.HelloWorld()
        Dim aMsg As String = myServer.Message
        ' Write the greeting to a file
        Dim sr As StreamWriter
        sr = File.CreateText("\My Documents\Greeting.txt")
        sr.WriteLine(aMsg)
        sr.Close()
    End Sub

End Module
```

The most significant benefit of .NET is exposed in this example—it's a *simpler programming model.* You can write components using any language supported by .NET, and it is extremely simple to write a component that is usable from any other language compatible with .NET. The simple reason for this is that all these languages are built on top of the same type system. In other words, at the lowest level, object types in each language compatible with .NET are the same. A *String* in Visual Basic .NET is the same type of object as a *string* in C#. This compatibility makes it easy to call components written in different languages—in fact, you can write classes in one language that inherit from a parent class written in another.

The other thing to notice from this example is that both the Visual Basic and the C# client use the *StreamWriter* and *File* classes to output the message to a file. *StreamWriter* and *File* are .NET Framework classes in the *System.IO* namespace. All languages can use the same .NET Framework classes, so if you do switch languages, you don't have to learn a whole new set of runtime functions. This consistency lies throughout Visual Studio .NET as well. The same Windows Forms Designer, for example, is available from whichever programming language you choose.

This simple example suggests that COM is about only cross-language software components, but COM is more than that. An enhanced version called Distributed COM (DCOM) allows remote COM calls via any network to another PC. The full .NET Framework includes .NET Remoting, which is a substantial improvement over DCOM. However, .NET Remoting is not supported for the .NET Compact Framework. However, XML Web services are a viable alternative to .NET Remoting, and the .NET Compact Framework does make it easy to build first-class Web service client applications for mobile devices.

Is That It?

Of course not! .NET is not just about easy-to-implement components. What cannot be shown in a simple code listing such as the previous one is the greater reliability of code built on .NET. .NET applications run under the control of a runtime called the common language runtime (CLR). The CLR performs a just-in-time compilation of all code at run time; allocates memory when you create new objects; and does garbage collection of objects that are no longer required, which automatically frees up memory no longer needed by .NET objects.

Because the CLR compiles all code at execution time, it implements strict type checking. Errors such as unsafe casting of one object type to another, addressing an array out of bounds, or writing past the end of a buffer are just not possible. The common language runtime also manages security, allowing much finer control over the functions that a piece of code is allowed to perform and the resources it may access.

.NET and Mobility

The power of the .NET Framework gives Microsoft the perfect platform on which to create new software products that target mobile devices. These products complement each other to solve the problems faced by enterprises when implementing mobility solutions.

.NET Compact Framework

The .NET Compact Framework is a "lite" version of the full, desktop .NET Framework. It includes a compatible subset of the base class libraries of the full .NET Framework, and it throws in a few new ones that are specifically designed for mobile devices. The .NET Compact Framework also has a new implementation of the common language runtime, built from the ground up to run efficiently on small devices that are constrained in both memory and CPU power and which must conserve battery power.

The first release of the .NET Compact Framework is for Pocket PC 2000 and 2002 devices and devices using Windows CE .NET version 4.1 or later. You can expect to see it appear in many other devices, such as smart phones, in the near future. Network operators might provide their own libraries, allowing developers to create applications that make use of service offerings unique to that network operator. The .NET Compact Framework has been designed with portability in mind, so it is possible that it will be available on other operating systems, although at the time of this writing, Microsoft has not announced any specific plans. As a developer, I would be very happy if I were able to create .NET Compact Framework applications that run on Windows CE .NET and also devices running on the EPOC, Linux, or Palm operating systems!

Visual Studio .NET 2003 includes the software and tools you need to create applications that run on devices where the .NET Compact Framework is installed. The components necessary to install the .NET Compact Framework on a handheld device install onto your desktop computer when you install Visual Studio .NET 2003.

Like the .NET Compact Framework, ASP.NET mobile controls (formerly known as the Microsoft Mobile Internet Toolkit (MMIT)) allows you to build applications for mobile devices. However, .NET Compact Framework applications run on the device as "rich clients" with access to the resources of the device, such as storage and other hardware components. In ASP.NET applications, the only software running on the device is a Web browser. Figure 4 illustrates the difference.

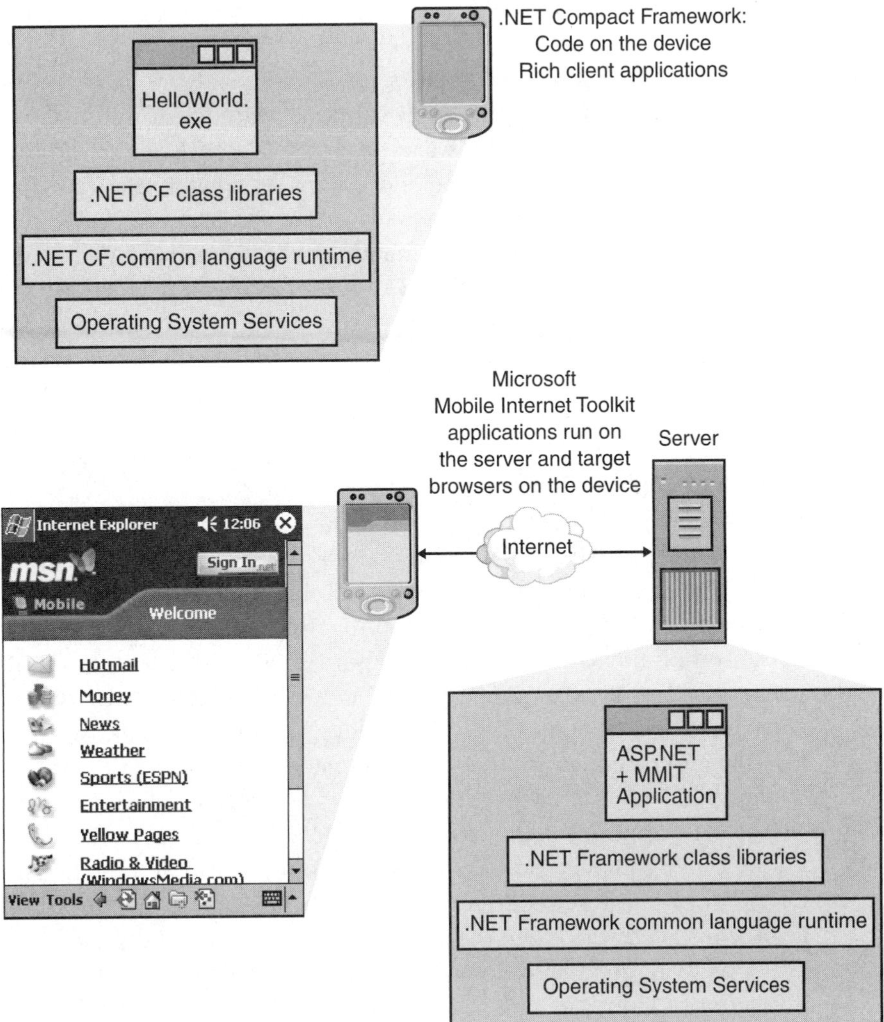

Figure 1-4 **Figure 1-4** .NET Compact Framework applications run code on the device; ASP.NET mobile Web applications use only the Web browser.

SQL Server CE

SQL Server CE is a compact relational database that runs on Windows CE devices. It was first released in 2000 and has already proven its popularity with Windows CE developers prior to the appearance of the .NET Compact Framework. It is upwardly compatible with SQL Server, using compatible data types, and it has a small footprint of only around 800 KB on an ARM processor, which is suitable for constrained devices.

Version 2 of SQL Server CE supports many more intrinsic functions than the earlier release (functions such as *ABS*, *LOG*, *PI*, *SUBSTRING*) and features such as parameterized queries and unions. However, the most significant new feature is the *System.Data.SqlServerCe* managed data provider, which allows a SQL Server CE database to be manipulated from .NET Compact Framework applications. The classes in the *System.Data.SqlServerCE* namespace give access to data stored directly in the database and allow use of the powerful Remote Data Access (RDA) or of merge replication, which are two powerful techniques for replicating data from an enterprise SQL Server down to SQL Server CE on the device for use in mobile applications.

ASP.NET Mobile Controls

ASP.NET mobile controls allow you to use Visual Studio .NET to develop mobile Web applications targeting microbrowsers on PDAs, smart phones, WAP, and i-mode phones. The ASP.NET mobile controls and developer tools were formerly called the Microsoft Mobile Internet Toolkit (MMIT), which was released on the same day as Visual Studio .NET 2002 as an add-on component that you download separately from *msdn.microsoft.com/downloads*. With the release of Visual Studio .NET 2003, development of mobile Web applications is a fully integrated part of the IDE (Integrated Development Environment) and no longer a separate product. The emphasis with this product is "reach, rather than rich." One application developed using MMIT version 1 works with browsers on 160+ different handheld devices, with support for more coming all the time.

Applications execute on an IIS Web server that has the full .NET Framework installed, but .NET is not required on the handheld device. MMIT applications work great with Pocket Internet Explorer found on Pocket PC and other Windows CE devices, but in contrast to .NET Compact Framework applications, no application code downloads to execute on the device. (See *Building .NET Applications for Mobile Devices* by Andy Wigley and Peter Roxburgh Microsoft Press, 2002, ISBN 0-7356-1532-2, for more details on building Web applications with the Microsoft Mobile Internet Toolkit.)

Mobile Information Server

Mobile Information Server (MIS) comes in two flavors—the carrier edition used by network carriers, and the enterprise edition. You use MIS to allow mobile users with Pocket PCs or WAP phones to synchronize with a Microsoft Exchange server to send and receive e-mail and alerts. It also offers powerful client authentication features. During 2003, MIS will lose its identity as a separate product and its functionality will be merged into Exchange and into Microsoft ISA Server (Internet Security and Acceleration Server).

.NET Compact Framework Target Platforms

The first version of the .NET Compact Framework supports Windows-powered Pocket PCs and embedded solutions built on Windows CE .NET.

Platforms That Run It

.NET Compact Framework version 1 is supported on the following Microsoft platforms:

- **Pocket PC 2000** These devices were available from a number of manufacturers and used ARM, MIPS, SH3 or SH4 processors. .NET Compact Framework is supported on all these processors.
- **Pocket PC 2002** This update to the Pocket PC operating system was released late in 2001. Pocket PC 2002 was released only for ARM processors.
- **Pocket PC 2002 Phone Edition** This is the Pocket PC 2002 operating system with additions to support telephony functions. At the time of this writing, no additional libraries have been announced to access telephony functions from a .NET Compact Framework application.
- **Pocket PC .NET** This new update to the Pocket PC operating system is built on a kernel of Windows CE .NET.
- **Windows CE .NET version 4.1 or later** Windows CE .NET is targeted at the embedded market. Any custom operating system image that you create with Platform Builder can also include the .NET Compact Framework, and you can develop applications for your embedded solution using Visual Studio .NET 2003.

And Platforms That Don't

.NET Compact Framework is not supported on these Microsoft platforms:

- **Windows CE versions 3 and earlier** Note that Pocket PC 2000 and 2002 are built on a Windows CE version 3 kernel. However, Pocket PC 2000 and 2002 are the only derivatives of Windows CE 3 that are supported.

- **Handheld PC 2000 and earlier** Handheld PCs have larger screens than Pocket PC devices, small but usable keyboards, and longer battery life. Handheld PC 2000 is also built on a Windows CE version 3 kernel, but this and earlier versions of Handheld PC are not supported.
- **Microsoft Smartphone 2002** This long-awaited product, much trailed using its code-name Stinger, is appearing in the market at roughly the same time that this book is published. Smartphone 2002 is based on the Pocket PC 2002 operating system, but with changes to support the smaller device size and button navigation, rather than the touch-sensitive screen of Pocket PCs. Although this device is not supported in the first release of the .NET Compact Framework, expect to see support for it follow fairly soon.

Developer Tools

There are currently three different toolsets available to developers building applications for Pocket PC and Windows CE.

Visual Studio .NET 2003

Visual Studio .NET 2003 includes capabilities that allow you to write and debug applications for the .NET Compact Framework. You use exactly the same tools and techniques that you use to develop applications for the full .NET Framework, but you use the .NET Compact Framework base class libraries, which are a subset of those in the full Framework. When testing, you deploy to a real handheld device or to an emulator and debug remotely enjoying the use of full Visual Studio .NET debugging facilities.

Both the full .NET Framework and the .NET Compact Framework provide an abstraction of the facilities offered by the underlying operating system—Windows 95, Windows 98, Windows NT, Windows 2000, and Windows XP for the .NET Framework; Windows CE and Windows CE .NET for the .NET Compact Framework. In the past, you worked more directly with the Win32 API of the underlying operating system, so inevitably, developing for Windows CE became something of a specialist area. Now you achieve similar tasks on both platforms using the same .NET classes, using the same methods and properties, and you do that using the same tools. Never before has developing for handheld devices been so similar to "mainstream" development, which is an attractive feature for enterprises concerned about the cost of training specialist staff. When skills are transferable, development costs decrease.

Having said that, developing applications for handheld devices will always require some specialist skills. Many of these relate to design decisions involving the physical dimensions of the display, the special challenges of getting data to and from a handheld device, and the security implications of exposing valuable enterprise data on a device that is on a wireless network and that is easily lost or stolen. The section "Unique Challenges Facing Mobile Developers" later in this chapter looks into this in more detail.

There are a number of situations in which developers will have to work outside of the .NET Compact Framework.

- To have direct access to the underlying Win32 API to carry out functions not provided through the .NET Compact Framework class libraries. An example of this is to call the *sndPlaySound* Win32 function to play audio. This is easily achieved using P/Invoke, which is described in Chapter 22.
- To access COM objects. There is no COM Interop in the .NET Compact Framework, so transparent access to COM objects is not possible. You can still use COM objects, but you must use eMbedded Visual C++ to create a flat wrapper around the object implementing sufficient function calls to use the COM object. You use P/Invoke to call functions in the dynamic link library (DLL) containing your wrapper. This technique requires knowledge of COM and C++.
- To interact with DLLs provided by peripheral suppliers, such as a barcode scanner. In time, peripheral suppliers will undoubtedly offer .NET libraries allowing developers to use their peripheral device directly from managed code. However, in the short term, it is possible that you might need to use a peripheral device for which there is only a DLL interface available. You will have to use P/Invoke to call functions in the library to communicate with the peripheral equipment.

eMbedded Visual Tools Version 3

eMbedded Visual Tools version 3 is a stand-alone development environment that gives something of the look and feel of Visual Studio 6. The eMbedded Visual Tools include eMbedded Visual Basic and eMbedded Visual C++ (shown in Figure 1-5), including SDKs for the Pocket PC, Palm-size PC, and Handheld PC.

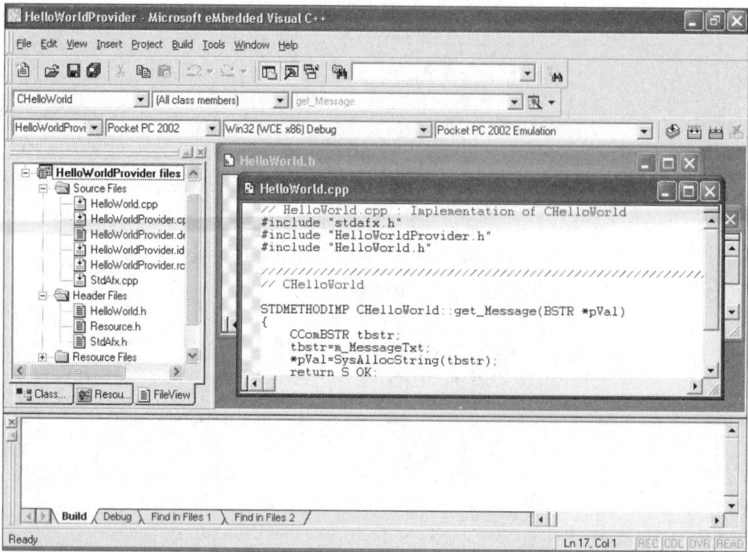

Figure 1-5 eMbedded Visual C++ IDE.

Use eMbedded Visual Tools to build applications for devices that the .NET Compact Framework does not support. You should also consider using eMbedded Visual C++ to build the best performing native code applications or where you need to have direct control over device hardware and operating system services. Although the .NET Compact Framework runtime provides excellent performance for .NET applications, for applications requiring pure speed, eMbedded Visual C++ with its direct access to the underlying operating system will still outperform .NET.

eMbedded Visual Basic provides quick development time, but applications do not perform as well as those built with eMbedded Visual C++ or the .NET Compact Framework. It's actually more akin to VBScript and is interpreted on the device, not compiled to native code. Older eMbedded Visual Basic applications will still run on Windows CE .NET, and no plans have been announced to phase out runtime support. However, the recommended approach for existing developers skilled in eMbedded Visual Basic is to move to the .NET Compact Framework. Table 1-1 lists the compelling reasons why Visual Basic .NET is a better choice for mobile development than eMbedded Visual Basic.

Table 1-1 Comparison of eMbedded Visual Basic to Visual Basic .NET

Feature	eMbedded Visual Basic	Visual Basic .NET
Full, strongly typed language	Script-based, limited type support, and type checking	Full, strongly typed, object-oriented language
Rich error handling	Limited *On error goto*	Full .NET exception handling, consistent with all other .NET languages
Binary executable	Script interpreted at runtime	Full .NET executable, compiled to native code at execution time
Visual Studio IDE	Custom development environment	Development tools fully integrated into Visual Studio .NET
Compatibility with desktop development	Custom APIs loosely based on Visual Basic 6	Compatible subset of the full .NET Framework libraries with .NET Compact Framework class libraries

eMbedded C++ Version 4

eMbedded C++ version 4 is the latest update and is targeted at Windows CE .NET embedded solutions. As with its predecessor, this is a stand-alone IDE that allows you to develop native applications using the Win 32 API, the Microsoft Foundation Classes (MFC), and ATL. Version 4 works with Windows CE .NET only.

Getting Started with Smart Device Projects in Visual Studio .NET

You use Visual Studio .NET 2003 to develop applications for the .NET Compact Framework. This new release of Visual Studio .NET adds the capability to develop applications using the .NET Compact Framework and has the advantage of allowing experienced .NET Framework application developers to use their skills to develop applications for smart devices.

Differences between Smart Device and PC Application Projects

Although you use the same environment to create Smart Device projects as you would use to create desktop projects, there are a number of differences that you should be aware of.

- Additional tools are provided for connecting to and debugging on a remote device.
- When debugging your application, you must select a device to run your application on. You may either use a device emulator running on the development computer or a physical device connected to the development computer either directly (by serial or USB) or via a network connection.
- You can generate the CAB file used to distribute your application from within your device project rather than having to create a separate deployment project.
- The classes available to you differ from those available for projects built with the full .NET Framework. The classes available can be found by using the integrated help system or the Visual Studio Object Browser from within your device project. Visual Studio .NET IntelliSense lists only the classes and class members that you may use.

Creating a Smart Device Application Project

You create a project for smart devices the same way that you create a desktop project. The main difference is that you cannot choose the Project Type (for example, Windows Application or Class Library) until you have chosen a target platform for your project.

You create a Smart Device Application project by clicking the New Project button on the Start Page or by selecting New from the File menu and then choosing Project. You will see the New Project dialog box displayed, as shown in Figure 1-6. You select the language that you will use for your project from the left pane of the New Project dialog box. The right pane of the dialog box lists the Project Templates available for the selected language. You select the Smart Device Application template to create a Smart Device Application project.

> **Note** Visual Studio .NET 2003 supports either the Visual Basic .NET or the C# programming language for Smart Device Application projects.

You must enter a name for your project and the location to use for the files that compose your project in the lower section of the New Project dialog box.

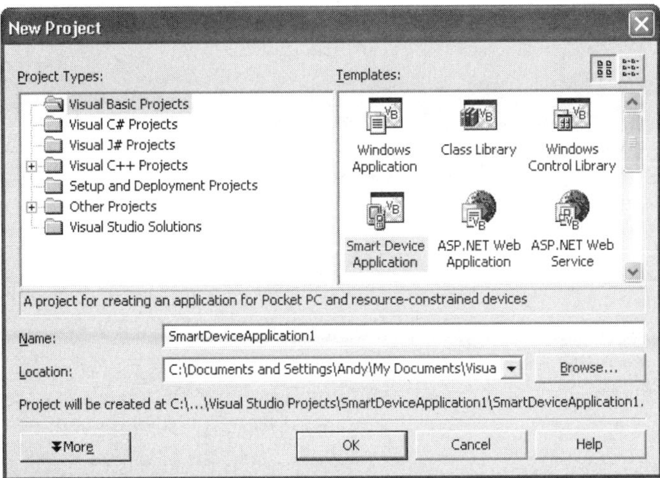

Figure 1-6 Visual Studio .NET New Project dialog box.

Smart Device Application Wizard

After you click the OK button in the New Project dialog box, you choose the target platform and project type for the application using the Smart Device Application Wizard, as shown in Figure 1-7. The upper-left section of the dialog box lists the available platforms. The right side of the dialog box lists the currently installed devices that will run the application targeting the selected platform type.

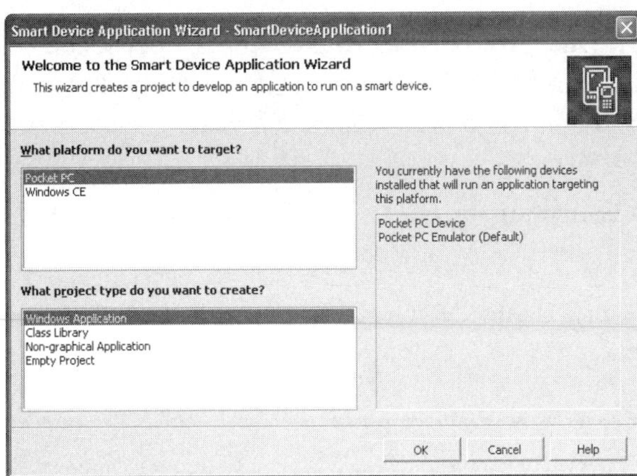

Figure 1-7 Visual Studio .NET Smart Device Application Wizard.

The lower section of the dialog box lists the project types available for the select target platform, as described in Table 1-2.

Table 1-2 Smart Device Application Project Types

Project Type	Description
Windows Application	Used to create an application with Windows Forms for information entry and display
Class Library	Used to create a library of classes for use by developers in their projects
Non-Graphical Application (Pocket PC only)	Used to create a project that has no graphical elements and could be used to create a background task that has no need for any user interaction
Console Application (Windows CE only)	Used to create a project that has no graphical elements, but that can be called from the Windows CE command console
Empty Project	Creates a project that contains no files

Desktop vs. Device Projects

Certain features that are available to desktop application projects are not available to device application projects. The following is a list of the major differences between desktop and device projects:

- **File Input/Output for Visual Basic .NET projects.** Device projects support only the .NET *System.IO* namespace. The use of the Visual Basic .NET *Microsoft.VisualBasic.FileSystem* namespace is not supported on devices.
- **COM interop is not supported.** You'll learn more about alternative techniques to use COM objects in Chapter 22.
- **The use of Visual Basic .NET late binding is not supported in device projects.**

The wizard creates the project files for the selected project type and displays the default project environment. Figure 1-8 shows the default project environment for a Windows Application project.

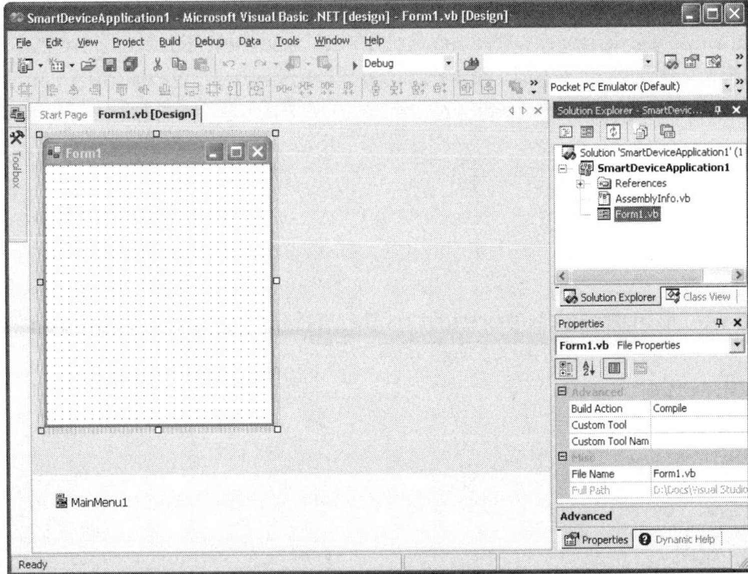

Figure 1-8 Visual Studio .NET Smart Device Windows Application project.

Managing Your Project

The Visual Studio .NET development environment looks and acts very much as it does when you develop desktop applications.

SDE projects do not have access to all the controls that you would find in a standard desktop project. Figure 1-9 shows the standard toolbox for a Windows Application SDE project.

Figure 1-9 Visual Studio .NET Smart Device Extensions toolbox.

Table 1-3 shows the supported controls in an SDE project. The .NET Compact Framework does not support all the members for the controls listed. For a full list of the supported controls and the members supported for each control, see the "System.Windows.Forms" page in the ".NET Compact Framework Classes" section of the .NET Compact Framework documentation, which you can access as described in the following "Help System" section. Chapter 3 and Chapter 4 will cover the use of each of these controls and how they differ from their counterparts in the full .NET Framework.

Table 1-3 Controls Supported in the .NET Compact Framework

Button	NumericUpDown
CheckBox	OpenFileDialog
ComboBox	Panel
ContextMenu	PictureBox
Control	ProgressBar
DomainUpDown	RadioButton
Form	SaveFileDialog
DataGrid	StatusBar
HScrollBar	TabControl
ImageList	TextBox
InputPanel	Timer
Label	ToolBar
ListBox	TrackBar
ListView	TreeView
MainMenu	VScrollBar

Help System

You can find interactive help through the Dynamic Help window, as shown in Figure 1-10, and via Visual Studio .NET IntelliSense technology, which displays the syntax for the command that you are typing using pop-up windows and drop-down lists.

The main help system within Visual Studio .NET is extended to include the .NET Compact Framework and SDE. On the Content, Index, and Search pages of the help system, the Filter By drop-down list now has .NET Compact Framework as one of the filter options available. Figure 1-11 shows an example of the Filter By drop-down list. When this filter is applied, it will filter the general .NET Framework libraries to show only the classes available in the .NET Compact Framework.

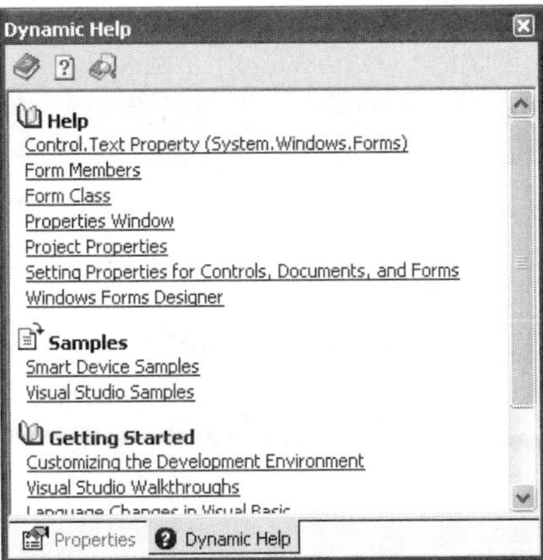

Figure 1-10 Visual Studio .NET dynamic help.

You access the complete online documentation for the .NET Compact Framework by selecting Contents from the Help menu, then Visual Studio .NET – Developing with Visual Studio .NET – Designing Distributed Applications – Developing for Devices – Smart Device Projects.

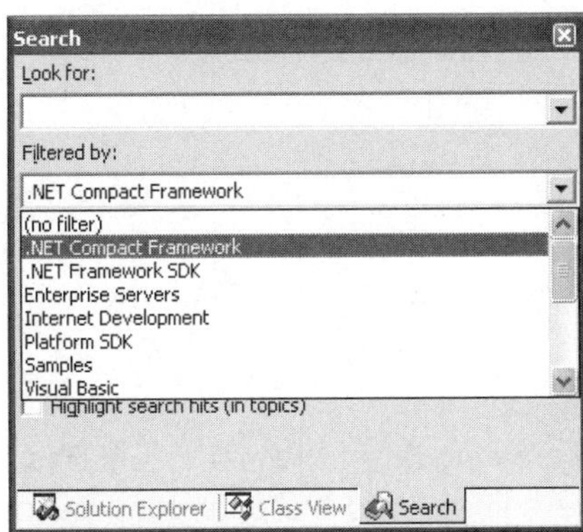

Figure 1-11 Visual Studio .NET help page Filter By drop-down list.

Creating a Hello World Application

It is traditional to write a Hello World application as an introduction to a new language or system, and I do not intend to break with this tradition. You will have a chance later in this book to use some of the more advanced features of the .NET Compact Framework.

Create a Smart Device Application Project

To create your Smart Device Application, start Visual Studio .NET. Select New from the File menu, and then select Project. The New Project dialog box, as shown in Figure 1-12, is displayed. Select Visual C# Projects in the Project Types pane on the left, and then select Smart Device Application in the Templates pane on the right.

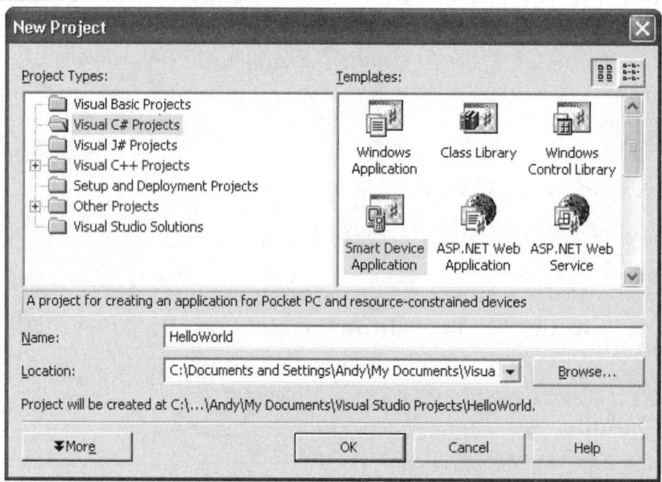

Figure 1-12 Visual Studio .NET New Project dialog box.

Enter **HelloWorld** as the name of your project in the Name text box at the bottom of the New Project dialog box. Leave the project files location as the default location or enter a new location if you want. Click the OK button.

> **Note** The steps involved in creating this project in Visual Basic .NET differ only in the line of code entered into the command button click event.

The Smart Device Application Wizard displays, as shown in Figure 1-13. Choose Windows CE as the target platform. This will allow us to test the application against both Windows CE and Pocket PC devices later in this chapter. Choose Windows Application as the project type, and click the OK button.

Visual Studio creates the project files and displays the default project view. Form1.cs displays in design mode, sized to the dimensions of a typical Windows CE .NET device screen. Since we want to run this application on both Windows CE .NET and Pocket PC, we must resize the form. In the Properties window, scroll down to the *Size* property, and enter **246, 295**. After you press Enter, the form resizes and displays as shown in Figure 1-14.

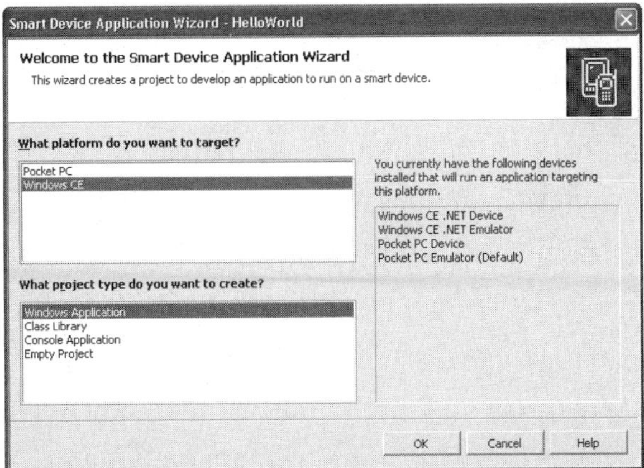

Figure 1-13 Visual Studio .NET Smart Device Application Wizard.

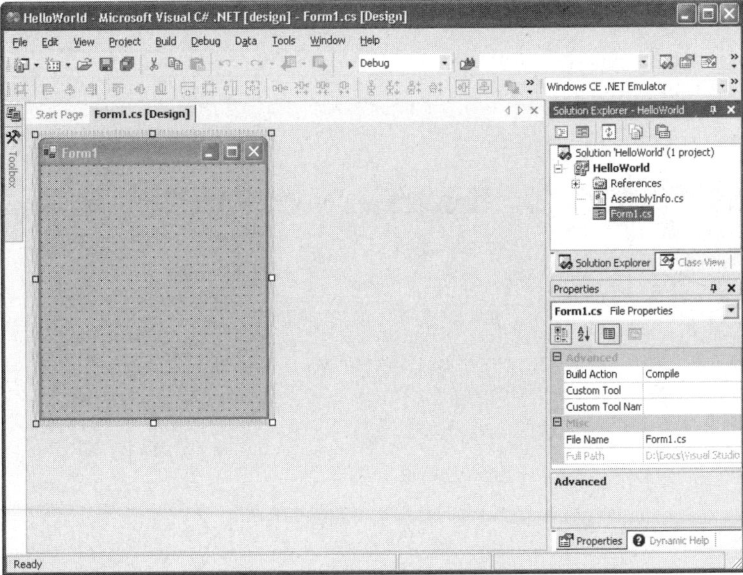

Figure 1-14 Visual Studio .NET HelloWorld project.

Modify the Project

Using the toolbox, add a label to *Form1*. Expand the label to cover the top half of Form1. With the label selected, change the Font Size property to 48 and delete the text from the Text property.

Using the toolbox, add a button control to the bottom center of *Form1*. Change the button's *Size* property to **100, 50** and its *Text* property to **Say Hello**. The form should look like the one shown in Figure 1-15.

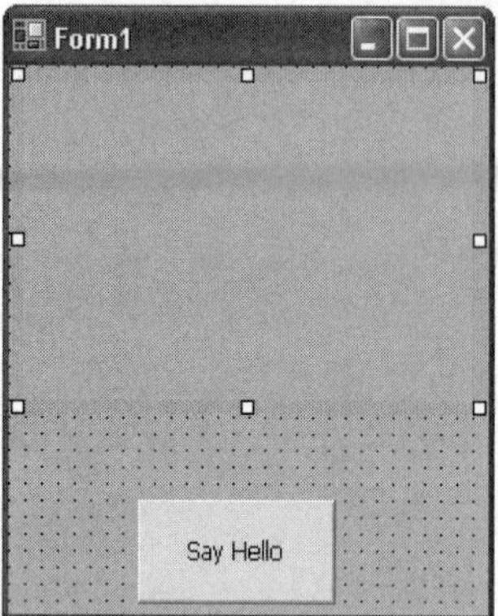

Figure 1-15 Visual Studio .NET HelloWorld application *Form1*.

Double-click *button1* to create a click-event procedure, and enter the following line of code into the editor:

```
label1.Text = "Hello World";
```

Figure 1-16 shows what the source code view of Form1.cs will look like after you enter the code.

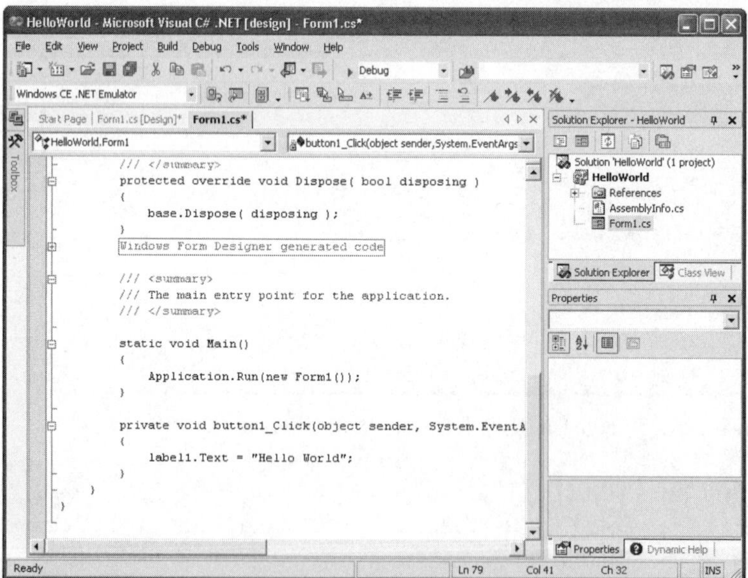

Figure 1-16 Visual Studio .NET HelloWorld application button1_Click event handler.

Save your project. You will test your application using the emulator in the next section.

Using the Emulator

To test your application, you can use a physical device connected to the development computer directly or via a network connection. If you do not have access to a physical device, you can use the emulator, which is included in Visual Studio .NET 2003. The emulator emulates a Pocket PC device or a Windows CE .NET device. Nevertheless, your finished application should be tested against a physical device before deploying it to customers.

The first time you use the emulator, the .NET Compact Framework deploys before your application. Normally, this only happens the first time you use the emulator, but if you shut down the emulator without choosing the Save Current State option or if you select the emulator's File menu then choose Hard Reset, you will find that the .NET Compact Framework deploys again the next time you test an application.

You can emulate of a Pocket PC device, as shown in Figure 1-17, or a Windows CE device, as shown in Figure 1-18.

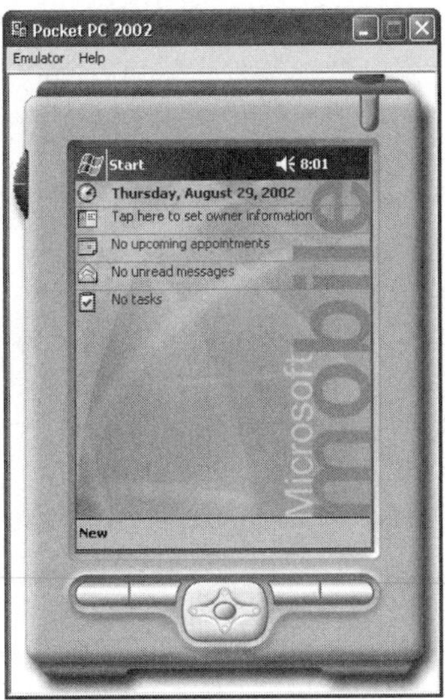

Figure 1-17 Emulation of a Pocket PC device.

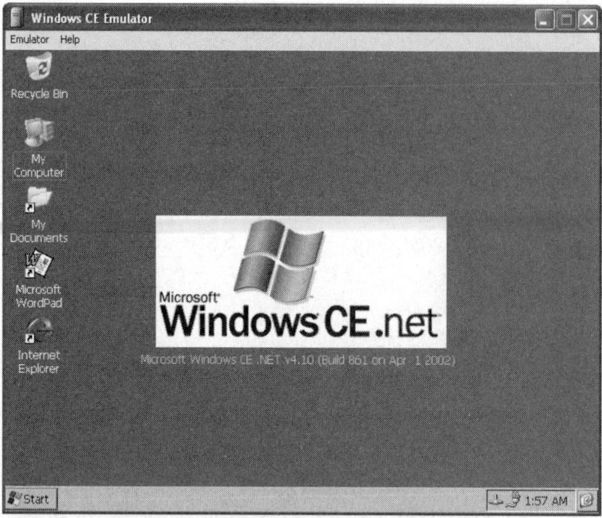

Figure 1-18 Emulation of Windows CE device.

Requirement for Development PC to Be on a Network

For your application to be deployed to the emulator, the development computer must have an active network connection. If no network connection is active, the deployment of your application will fail with a Connection Failed error message.

If you do not have an active network connection, either because you do not have a network card or are not connected to a network, you can install the Microsoft Loopback Adapter to simulate a network connection.

The emulator is a real Pocket PC or Windows CE .NET operating system running within a Windows process on the development machine. Logically, it is a separate computer, and the emulator and Visual Studio .NET communicate with each other using network protocols. This cannot work if your development computer does not have a valid TCP/IP address, which it gets when it connects to a network or if the Microsoft Loopback Adapter is installed.

To add the Loopback Adapter, open the Control Panel and follow these steps:

1. In the Add Hardware Wizard, click Next until the wizard asks if you have already connected the hardware to this computer. Select Yes, I Have Already Connected The Hardware, and then click Next.

2. In the Installed Hardware list, select Add A New Hardware Device and then click Next.
3. Select Install The Hardware That I Manually Select From A List (Advanced), and then click Next.
4. In the Common Hardware Types list, select Network Adapters and then click Next.
5. In the Manufacturer list, select Microsoft. In the Network Adapter list, select Microsoft Loopback Adapter and then click Next.
6. Continue to click Next through the Add Hardware Wizard as it installs the Microsoft Loopback Adapter.

Using the Pocket PC Emulator

To test the HelloWorld application in the Pocket PC Emulator, select Start from the Debug menu. The Deploy dialog box shown in Figure 1-19 is displayed. This dialog box lists the available devices that support the current project type.

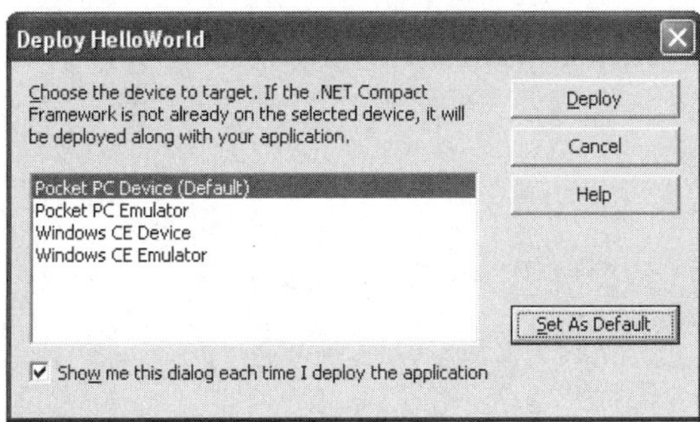

Figure 1-19 Deploy dialog box.

Select Pocket PC Emulator, and click the Deploy button. Visual Studio will now build your application and start the emulator. Once the deployment is successful, Visual Studio will start your application on the emulator. Click the Say Hello button in the emulator window, and the Hello World message will be displayed, as shown in Figure 1-20.

Figure 1-20 Pocket PC emulator.

Using the Windows CE .NET Emulator

The process of running your application on the Windows CE .NET emulator is identical to running it on the Pocket PC emulator. Figure 1-21 shows your application running on the Windows CE emulator.

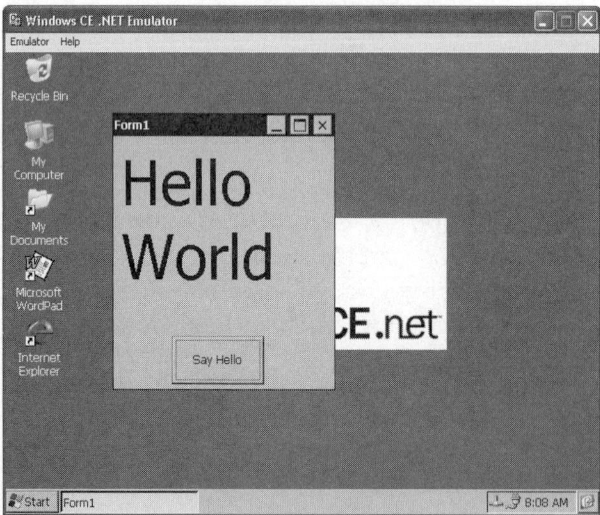

Figure 1-21 Windows CE emulator.

Unique Challenges Facing Mobile Developers

The .NET Compact Framework opens up mobile development to many more developers than before, by virtue of its consistent programming model with developing for the desktop. However, there remain unique design considerations requiring special skills of mobile developers and designers.

Get Data to Your Device

Handheld devices such as Pocket PCs offer Personal Information Management synchronization facilities that give you mobile access to e-mail, contacts, and appointments. Useful though that is, it's not very interesting. Nor is a disconnected handheld device very interesting! Where they become interesting, particularly to developers, is when you get data to the device and make use of that data in mobile applications. If you have a device capable of wireless connectivity, the possibilities for data transfer to and from the device make many interesting applications possible.

However, application mobility involves more than just being wireless. Truly mobile applications are able to go anywhere. This simple statement implies different factors that you must consider when designing a mobile application.

- How often is data transferred to and from the device? Only when the device synchronizes with a desktop host once a day, or is the device connected at all times to a wireless LAN giving always-on connectivity? Or does the device use a wide-area wireless connection that gives connectivity when the device has strong signal strength from a base station, but which might be out of range, for example, in mountainous regions?
- If network connectivity is unreliable, it might be necessary to cache data on the device for use by an application while the device is disconnected.

A clever developer using good design practices can make the state of connectedness at any one time transparent to the user.

The .NET Compact Framework was designed from the ground up with connectivity in mind and offers many facilities for implementing applications in any one of these scenarios. In particular, it allows a handheld device to be a first-class XML Web services client.

XML Web Services

XML Web services are redefining the way that distributed computer systems work together. Built on common standards such as XML and HTTP, XML Web services offer a lightweight model for exposing services across a network, allowing any enterprise server running on any software platform to connect easily with services elsewhere on the network. By extending XML Web services to devices, you make the devices more useful. As long as the device has a connection to the Web, applications on the device can connect to multiple sources of data and services on the Web, aggregating them in order to present valuable applications to the mobile user. XML Web services also serve as an excellent way of passing data back to the enterprise back-end servers. Mobile users can carry out functions in the field and then connect to a Web service to pass data back to the enterprise to update master data stores. Thus, the results of the mobile user's work are immediately available to everyone in the enterprise.

If network connectivity is not guaranteed, the .NET Compact Framework allows you to cache data easily on the device, either as XML or custom format data files, or in a SQL Server CE database. When connectivity resumes, an application reads the cached updates to transfer them to the back-end servers.

SQL Server CE

XML Web services provides one solution to the problem of data transfer. SQL Server CE provides two others. Again, needing no more than an Internet connection on the device, .NET Compact Framework applications can make use of classes in the *System.Data.SqlServerCE* namespace to access remote SQL servers to pull data to the device and push back changes or to download a replicated data store to the device.

Resource-Constrained Devices

This is so obvious that it hardly needs saying, but in case it hasn't dawned on you: handheld devices are small, have limited display area and limited memory, and must run on battery power for long periods of time.

Unless your application will run on a device that has a keyboard, your users will have to enter data using a stylus. This requirement has interesting implications for GUI design, such as always using easy-selection techniques such as drop-down lists and designing to limit the amount of textual input required of a user. Figure 1-22 shows a good example of screen layout that makes maximum use of the available display area.

Always keep in mind the memory requirements of your application, and if you need to hold large objects in memory, release them as early as possible. Remember that on Pocket PCs you do not normally have an Exit button. An application tends to run continuously, and its window is pushed to the back when other applications are in use. How you design for this situation is covered in Chapter 4.

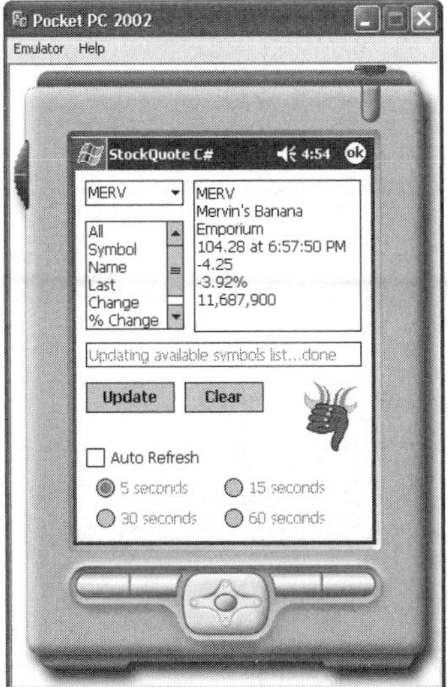

Figure 1-22 Small screen display and different input techniques test the design skills of the mobile developer.

Security Implications

Finally, it's a well-known fact that the majority of applications have security added as an afterthought, rather than being designed up front with security in mind. It's particularly important that security in mobile applications is considered right from the start. Security is usually touted as the number one concern of any enterprise considering the rollout of mobile applications, and with good reason. There are many possibilities for security breaches where mobile devices are involved.

- Devices hold information about contacts that you might not want falling into the hands of a competitor.
- Applications on a mobile device require data. Sensitive corporate data stored on a device might be at risk if the device is lost or stolen. Data might need to be encrypted when transferred over the Web, through XML Web services, and data might need to be encrypted and password protected (or perhaps even secured by biometric methods such as fingerprint recognition) while on the device.

- Client devices must be authenticated when accessing private resources exposed through IIS, such as Web services or SQL Server data.

Chapter 12 explores how to design and build safe and secure mobile applications.

Summary

This chapter introduced the .NET Compact Framework and explained how it provides an improved development experience compared to previous development tools. Two of its major strengths are its strong compatibility with the full .NET Framework and that the development tools are a fully integrated part of Visual Studio .NET 2003.

We walked through the development of a simple project to explain how to use the developer tools integrated into Visual Studio .NET 2003. We also positioned the .NET Compact Framework against other Microsoft software products for mobility, such as ASP.NET mobile controls and eMbedded Visual Tools.

The rest of this book goes into the details of each part of the .NET Compact Framework and explains how you use it to develop effective smart-device applications.

2

.NET Framework Fundamentals

As a developer, you write application code using your preferred .NET language, such as Visual Basic .NET or Visual C# .NET. When you build the application, the .NET compilers output Microsoft Intermediate Language (MSIL), which is a representation of your code that is independent of the target platform. Then the linker packages the output in a Portable Executable (PE) file. Generally, these PE files contain no native code and execute on any platform for which there is a .NET common language runtime (CLR), as long as the .NET Framework class libraries that the application references are available on that platform as well.

When you build applications targeted at devices equipped with the .NET Compact Framework, you use the same compilers used with applications intended for the full .NET Framework. Both the full .NET Framework CLR and the .NET Compact Framework CLR execute files in the same PE file format. The .NET Compact Framework CLR is not, however, a direct port of the desktop version targeted at the CPUs found on Windows CE devices. Instead, it is a new implementation, built from the ground up, that is a compatible subset of the full implementation and that is optimized for devices that are constrained in CPU power, memory, and input/output capabilities. Mercifully, despite this new implementation, the programming differences visible to the developer are relatively few.

This chapter explains how the .NET Compact Framework CLR works, delves into many of the basic types found in the class libraries, and highlights the primary areas where the compact implementation differs from the full .NET Framework.

.NET Compact Framework Execution Environment

When you develop applications for smart devices using Visual Studio .NET 2003, you work on a Windows development PC to write the code. Your Smart Device Application project references the language-specific libraries for your chosen language, Visual Basic .NET or C#, and also the .NET Compact Framework class libraries that your application needs. When you debug your application, it does not run on your development machine. Visual Studio .NET deploys your compiled executable and the required libraries onto the target Windows CE device, which is either a real Pocket PC or Windows CE .NET device, or to one of the emulators. An emulator is not a *simulator*; it's not an x86 process running on your Windows workstation that simulates the behavior of a Windows CE device. It's an actual Windows CE .NET or Pocket PC operating system image compiled for an x86 processor, which runs within a container that is a Windows process.

On the target device, your application runs within an instance of the CLR, which is the execution environment responsible for executing .NET applications.

Common Language Runtime

The CLR is the most important part of the .NET Framework. It is responsible for taking a .NET assembly that has been compiled to MSIL, setting up an application domain for it to run in, using its just-in-time (JIT) compiler to compile methods to native code so that they execute on the host processor, and managing memory allocation, garbage collection, and class loading. The CLR also manages the security structure in which the application operates.

The CLR actually consists of two distinct parts, the execution engine, which interfaces with the underlying operating system services, and the class libraries, which are the basic building blocks of any .NET application. We explore the class libraries in the section ".NET Compact Framework Class Libraries" later in this chapter.

Managed Code and Native Code

.NET applications run under the control of the CLR, which is to say they are *managed* by it. This management extends to managing memory, garbage collection, exception handling, interacting with underlying runtime services, and guaranteeing type safety, so .NET code is known as *managed code*. Code that runs unfettered by the control of the CLR and which has direct access to underlying operating system services is called *unmanaged* or *native* code.

Figure 2-1 shows the basic layout of the .NET Compact Framework execution environment. Applications, device-specific class libraries, and the majority of the base class libraries are all compiled to MSIL and run under the control of the CLR, so they are all managed code. The execution engine itself is a native executable, as is the Platform Adaptation Layer (PAL), which is an abstraction layer between the execution engine and the underlying operating system. The PAL and the execution engine are packaged together into a single executable, Mscoree.dll.

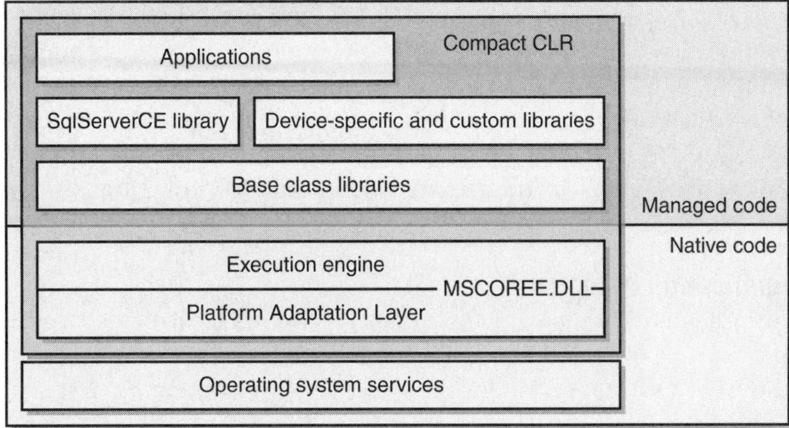

Figure 2-1 .NET Compact Framework execution environment structure.

Portable Execution Environment?

The .NET Compact Framework is designed to be portable. To port the execution engine to a new platform, implementers need only write new versions of those parts of the architecture that are processor-specific, that is, the JIT compiler and the PAL. No execution engine changes are necessary because that part is written in ANSI C. The PAL is there specifically to aid the porting of the .NET Compact Framework to a new platform; it encapsulates most of the platform-specific functionality. This architecture makes it easier for Microsoft to port the .NET Compact Framework to new and modified platforms in the future. Microsoft doesn't ship a "porting kit" with the .NET Compact Framework, nor does the company distribute the PAL APIs.

In .NET Compact Framework version 1, there is one implementation of Mscoree.dll for each supported CPU (ARM, MIPS, SH3, SH4, and so on) for target devices running the Windows CE 3 operating system (Pocket PC 2000 and Pocket PC 2002) and one implementation for each of the processors you might encounter in devices running Windows CE .NET. A different PAL was implemented for the Windows CE 3 and the Windows CE .NET adaptations.

Application Domain Hosts

The regular Windows CE shell application loader is updated on platforms where the .NET Compact Framework is installed so that when you start an application in the normal way (from the Start menu or by clicking a .exe file in Windows Explorer), the application loader recognizes that the application should be run by the .NET Compact Framework. This application loader, which is of course native code, is an *application domain host*. An application domain host loads the CLR into a process, creates the application domains within the process, and loads application code into the application domains.

Future versions of the .NET Compact Framework might include an unmanaged C application programming interface (API) called the Hosting API, which will allow you to load the compact CLR into a process. See the topic "Hosting the Common Language Runtime" in the Programming with the .NET Framework book in the online documentation for a discussion of how to achieve this with the full .NET Framework.

Application Domains

An *application domain* is an entity analogous to a regular operating system process, except that the application domain is completely under the control of the CLR, rather than under the control of the operating system. Every .NET application runs inside an application domain, and the CLR ensures that all resources used by the application during operation are released when the application ends. A single operating system process hosts an instance of the CLR, and that CLR can manage multiple application domains. Each application domain executes a single application.

Application domains offer the following advantages for isolating applications at runtime compared to using separate processes:

- Managed code must be passed through a verification process before it is allowed to run. (See "Verifiable Type-Safe Execution" later in this chapter.) The verification process guarantees that one application cannot access invalid memory addresses that might affect another; in other words, the verification process guarantees that the application's code is type-safe. Because the CLR is able to verify managed code as being type-safe, it is able to offer as great a level of application isolation as if the applications were running in separate processes, but at a much lower cost. Memory faults cannot happen, so failure of one application cannot affect another.

- You can start a new application in a new application domain, and you can stop an application in an application domain without starting or stopping a process. Application activation and termination are much cheaper than if each application were to run in its own process. Note, however, that the current implementation of the Windows CE shell loader spins up a new process and CLR for each application, rather than looking to see if a process running the CLR exists, creating a new application domain within it, and running the application there.
- The CLR prevents direct calls between objects in different application domains.

By default, there is one application domain per process. An application running in one application domain might start another application domain (use the *System.AppDomain.ExecuteAssembly* class). Note that this process is synchronous, so execution of the first application domain suspends until the new application domain terminates. However, an application might start a new thread and create an application domain in that thread, allowing concurrent operation of the two application domains. In most applications, you will not need to create a new application domain.

> **Note** Unlike the full .NET Framework, the .NET Compact Framework does not currently support loading assemblies into a domain-neutral code area for use by multiple application domains.

Verifiable Type-Safe Execution

One of the most important parts of the .NET runtime is the verifier, which ensures that code is safe to run, leading to improved reliability. Before any method in a .NET assembly can execute, the JIT compiler must compile it to native code; the verifier is part of the JIT compiler.

Scripting and interpreted languages allow variables to be used without explicitly declaring their types. (The Visual Basic 6 *Variant* type gives similar flexibility.) This flexibility can lead to unintended behavior in a program and mysterious program crashes. In compiled languages such as C or C++, the language allows you to take a pointer to an object and copy any bytes of data there. Usually, the programmer has the skill to ensure that the program copies the intended data to the target address, but bad use of pointers and buffer overruns are a major source of hard-to-fix bugs in programs written in these languages.

.NET is very strict on the usage of types. The verifier ensures that all types in the code are declared properly and are used correctly. This means that .NET code cannot fail because of any of the following:

- Uninitialized variables
- Bad use of pointers
- Unsafe casts
- Buffer overruns
- Array indexing out of bounds

JIT Compilation Not Interpreted!

.NET compiles MSIL code to native code before execution. It doesn't compile the whole assembly as you might think, but instead it compiles on a method-by-method basis, only when the method is called. Once compiled, the runtime caches the native code for the method in memory for the duration of program execution, so compilation occurs only once. The garbage collector clears up cached code after the program terminates. This gives good performance at runtime because only the code required by that particular run of the application compiles and it runs directly as native code. Figure 2-2 shows the process.

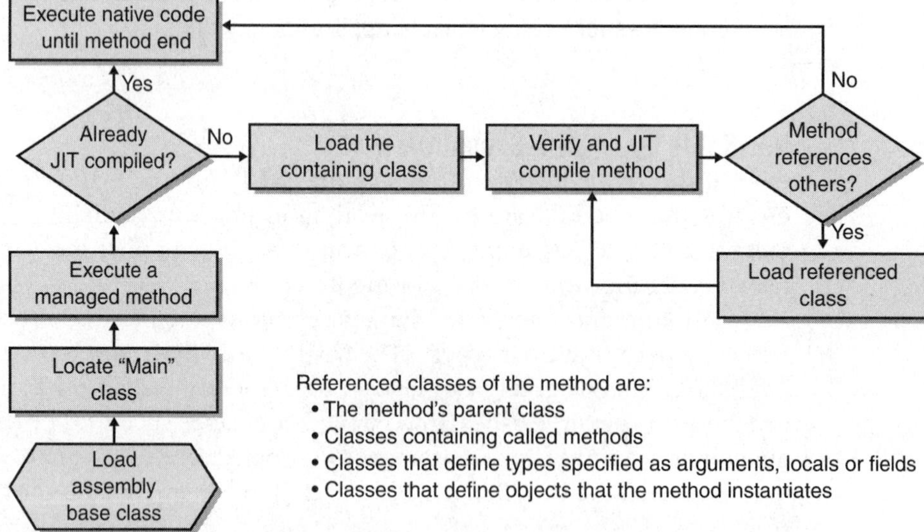

Figure 2-2 JIT compilation process.

A further benefit of this approach is that it reduces the need for program storage on the device. Applications and class libraries compiled to MSIL are much smaller than those compiled to native code. Code compiled to native code by the JIT compiler is cached in memory only as long as it is needed, and then it is discarded.

Garbage Collection

In Visual C++ before .NET, you had to manually delete all objects that you instantiated. When using COM objects, you had to take great care to increment the object's reference count when you added a reference to the object and decrement it again when you removed the reference. This was difficult to do, even for experienced developers, leading to many applications leaking memory while they executed, resulting in eventual failure.

With .NET, you don't have to worry about these problems. All objects are instantiated while under the control of the managed runtime, and the code is verifiably type-safe. As a result, bad practices or oversights that could cause an application to leak memory and fail are generally not possible; the runtime easily detects when an object is no longer required.

The garbage collector runs at intervals to free the memory taken up by objects that no program references anymore and by native code, held in the JIT compiler's cache, of applications that have completed execution. You do not have to explicitly delete objects because the garbage collector will do that for you sometime later. If your application uses an object that employs unmanaged or scarce resources and you want to explicitly free the resources the object holds in your code, implement the *IDisposable* interface in the object. See the section "Releasing Resources with *IDisposable*" later in this chapter.

Rich Exception Handling

The CLR implements a standard way of handling and reporting runtime errors across all .NET languages. Visual Basic .NET gets new *Try*, *Catch*, and *Finally* keywords, and C# has similarly named keywords. To raise an exception in code, Visual Basic .NET has the *Throw* keyword; in C#, it's *throw*.

In the following Visual Basic .NET snippet, the statements to execute follow the *Try* statement. If the creation of the *FileStream* object fails because the file is not there, the *FileStream* object throws an exception of type *FileNotFoundException*, which the first *Catch* block traps. Any other exception falls through to the second *Catch* block. Note that the second *Catch* block traps exceptions of type *Exception*, which is the parent class of all exceptions, so the second *Catch* block traps all exceptions that have not been trapped by the more-specific *Catch* block before it. The *Finally* block executes whether or not the operation in the *Try* block is successful.

```
Imports System.IO
⋮
Module MyModule
    ⋮
    Sub Main()
        Dim myFileStream As FileStream
        Try
            myFileStream = New FileStream("myfile.txt", FileMode.Open)
        Catch fnfexc As FileNotFoundException
            'Take action if the file isn't there
            ⋮
        Catch general As Exception
            'Take action on other error
            ⋮
        Finally
            'Finally block is optional, but if you specify it
            'it executes whether or not the operation succeeds
            ⋮
        End Try
        ⋮
    End Sub
    ⋮
End Module
```

Note that the base class libraries don't contain any exception error strings, to reduce the footprint of the files deployed to the device. For debugging, or on systems where space is not at a premium, you must add a reference to System.SR.dll to your project so that it deploys to your device along with your application. The System.SR.dll assembly contains the full set of exception strings.

Remote Debugging

One of the crucial components of the .NET Compact Framework runtime for the developer is the support for remote debugging. Without it, you would not be able to develop on your development workstation, deploy your application to the target device, be it an emulator or a real device, and debug your application from within Visual Studio .NET running on your development workstation. Remote debugging support allows you to set breakpoints to halt operation while your application is running on the target device so that you can examine variables and structures, step through code a line at a time, and set watches on data. SDE remote debugging operates over TCP/IP, Serial, USB, or infrared connections. The process is outlined in Figure 2-3.

You should always debug .NET Compact Framework applications working from Visual Studio .NET on a development workstation. There's no debugger on the device to debug programs while disconnected from your development machine. Without remote debugging, you'd have to liberally sprinkle Visual Basic .NET *MsgBox* or Visual C# .NET *MessageBox* statements throughout your application to inspect variables in your program.

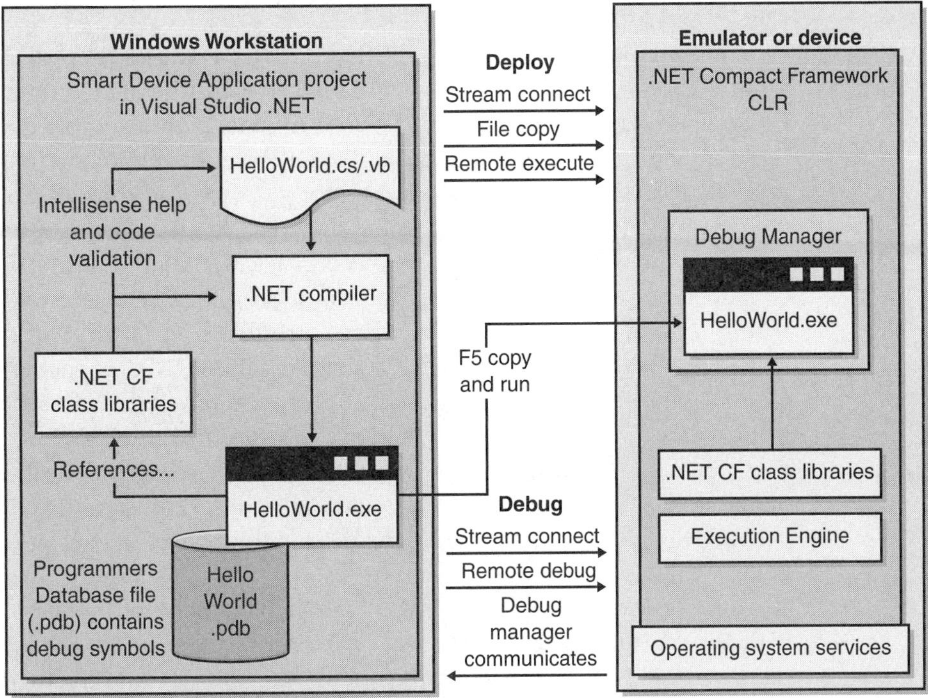

Figure 2-3 .NET Compact Framework remote debugging, with support for F5 copy and run.

Assemblies

As with the full .NET Framework, the unit of execution in the Compact Framework is the assembly. An assembly is a dynamic-link library (.dll) or an executable (.exe), and it is the result of compiling and linking your code. An assembly contains not only the MSIL for your application code, but also *metadata*, which is additional information containing instructions to the runtime that tell it how the code must be executed. Metadata is an important ingredient of .NET applications and is a new concept for Microsoft developers. Along with the code, you can declare attributes on methods, on classes, or on assemblies, defining things such as the security requirements for the module. These attributes are written into the assembly executable as metadata. The most obvious examples of attributes are those defined in the file AssemblyInfo.cs (AssemblyInfo.vb in Visual Basic projects), which is a file that Visual Studio .NET automatically adds to your project. This file defines attributes for the version number of the assembly, its description, the company that created it, and whether the assembly conforms to the Common Language Specification. (See the section "Common Language Specification" later in this chapter.) You can also define attributes for classes and for methods.

Assemblies for the .NET Compact Framework and the full .NET Framework are in the same format; they're created with the same compilers, which produce the same MSIL. However, you cannot take an assembly created for the desktop and run it directly on the other, although in certain circumstances, it is possible to take an application created for a device and run that application on the desktop. An important part of the metadata in an assembly is the *manifest*, which records, among other items, the exact identities of the assemblies that contain the base classes that your application references. These identities—or *strong names*, to use the correct term—are different in the two frameworks. However, you can recompile code written for the .NET Compact Framework in a desktop project and, in most cases (unless you have used classes such as *SqlCECommand* or *IrDaClient*, which are unique to the .NET Compact Framework), the application will compile and run unchanged on the full .NET Framework. The same cannot be guaranteed going in the opposite direction because the .NET Compact Framework is a compatible subset of the full .NET Framework.

In version 1.1 and later of the full .NET Framework (version 1.1 shipped with Visual Studio .NET 2003), the desktop CLR does allow applications compiled against .NET Compact Framework assemblies to run directly on the desktop without recompilation. The desktop CLR recognizes that the .NET Compact Framework assemblies that your application references are compatible subsets of the same-named assemblies in the desktop .NET Framework, and it redirects assembly references to the full .NET Framework equivalents. Chapter 23 looks into cross-framework interoperability in more detail.

Working with Class Objects

The .NET Framework is entirely object-oriented. There are some points worth reinforcing about working with class objects within the .NET Framework, chiefly object construction and destruction, how callbacks work, and using delegates and events.

Constructors and Finalizers

In most cases, you create objects by creating new instances of a class using the new keyword, and you do not explicitly delete those objects. Instead, you rely on the .NET Compact Framework garbage collector to detect when the object becomes unreferenced and to delete the unreferenced object, freeing up memory. An object becomes unreferenced when no other classes or applications need the object. Consider the following C# example:

```
Public void MyMethod()
{
    MyCustomClass aClassInstance = new MyCustomClass();
    aClassInstance.DoSomethingWithMyClass();
}
```

In this example, the instance of the *MyCustomClass* called *aClassInstance* is in scope only while *MyMethod* executes. When program flow moves beyond this method, the *aClassInstance* object might be removed during the next run of the garbage collector.

This might worry C++ developers, who are used to explicitly deleting objects. In fact, a C# class might have a method that looks identical to a C++ destructor, but in .NET Framework parlance, it is called a *finalizer*.

```
public class MyFinalizerClass
{
    public MyFinalizerClass()
    {
        // TODO: Add constructor logic here
    }
    ~MyFinalizerClass()
    {
        // TODO: Add finalizer logic here
    }
}
```

Finalizers give you the opportunity to run some clean-up code before an object is garbage collected, but they have a number of limitations and shouldn't be used much. It is much better to explicitly release resources held by the object, by implementing something like a *Close* method or the *IDisposable* interface (described in the next section). Even then, a finalizer method would be a good place to put code to release resources in a tidy way, in case the developer forgets to call the *Close* or *Dispose* method. In Visual Basic .NET, you declare a finalizer using the following syntax:

```
Public Class Class1

    Public Sub New()
        ⋮
    End Sub

    Protected Overrides Sub Finalize()
        MyBase.Finalize()
    End Sub
End Class
```

If a class has a finalizer, when you create a new instance of that object, the runtime adds it to a list of objects that will require finalization. When a garbage collection occurs, if the object is found to have no references to it but it is on the finalization list, it is marked as ready for finalization. When the garbage collector completes, it starts the finalizer, which goes through the marked objects and executes their finalizers. This removes the object from the list of objects requiring finalization, and they will be cleaned up on the next garbage collection.

Finalizers should be used with care because they have the following limitations:

- There is no guaranteed order for finalization, so be careful if object *a* holds a reference to object *b*; object *b* might not be around if object *a* tries to make use of object *b* during finalization.
- Finalization occurs on a different thread to execution.
- Objects with finalizers stay around on the system for longer and impose a higher overhead on the system.

Releasing Resources with *IDisposable*

It is particularly important on resource-constrained devices such as handhelds to release resources as early as possible if the resources that an object holds are scarce. When the garbage collector deletes an object, it releases all managed resources held by the object. However, the garbage collector has no conception of how to release unmanaged resources that the object might hold, such as window handles or open files. In such a case, implement the *IDisposable* interface in the object. This interface consists of the *Dispose* method, which interacts with the *Finalize* method of the class, as shown in the following annotated example:

```
// This class implements IDisposable
public class ClassUsesScarceResources: IDisposable
{
    // Pointer to an external unmanaged resource
    private IntPtr handle;
    // Other managed resources this class uses
    private Component Components;
    // Track whether Dispose has been called.
    private bool disposed = false;

    // Constructor
    public ClassUsesScarceResources()
    {
        // Your constructor code
    }
```

```
// Implement IDisposable.
// A derived class should not be able to override this method,
// so do not make this method virtual.
public void Dispose()
{
    Dispose(true);
    // Instruct the GC to remove this object from the
    // Finalization queue to prevent finalization code
    // from executing a second time.
    GC.SuppressFinalize(this);
}

// Dispose(bool disposing) executes in two distinct scenarios.
// If disposing equals true, the method has been called directly
// or indirectly by a user's code. Managed and unmanaged resources
// can be disposed.
// If disposing equals false, the method has been called by the
// runtime from inside the finalizer and you should not reference
// other objects. Only unmanaged resources can be disposed.
protected virtual void Dispose(bool disposing)
{
    // Check to see if Dispose has already been called.
    if(!this.disposed)
    {
        // If disposing equals true, dispose all managed
        // and unmanaged resources.
        if(disposing)
        {
            // Dispose managed resources.
            Components.Dispose();
        }
        // Release unmanaged resources. If disposing is false,
        // only the following code is executed.
        CloseHandle(handle);
        handle = IntPtr.Zero;
    }
    disposed = true;
}

// This finalizer will run only if the Dispose method
// does not get called.
// It gives your base class the opportunity to finalize.
// Do not provide finalizers in types derived from this class.
~ClassUsesScarceResources()
{
    // Do not re-create Dispose clean-up code here.
    // Calling Dispose(false)is optimal in terms of
    // readability and maintainability.
```

(continued)

```
            Dispose(false);
        }

        // Allow your Dispose method to be called multiple times,
        // but if you call any method of this class after it has been
        // disposed then throw an exception.
        // Add this check to see if it has been disposed to all methods.
        public void DoSomething()
        {
            if(this.disposed)
            {
                throw new
                        ObjectDisposedException("ClassUsesScarceResources");
            }
        }
    }
```

If you create an instance of a class built according to this model, your application should call the object's *Dispose* method when you want to release the object's managed and unmanaged resources prior to garbage collection, as shown here:

```
myObject.Dispose();
```

This has the effect of running all the objects' finalization code.

Note the call to *GC.SuppressFinalize* in the *Dispose* method in this example. It's important to call the *SuppressFinalize* method of the garbage collector to instruct the system to remove this object from the finalization queue. As a result, the garbage collector does not try to run the object's finalizer when the time comes for disposal and simply removes it on the next garbage collection.

The C# *using* Statement

C# offers a useful statement designed for use with classes that implement *IDisposable*. It takes a new instance of such a class, executes some statements on it, and then automatically calls the object's *Dispose* method to remove it. For example, using an ADO.NET SqlConnection object:

```
using (SqlConnection myconn = new SqlConnection(connString))
{
    myconn.Open();
    ⋮
}
```

is the same thing as

```
SqlConnection myconn = new SqlConnection(connString);
try
{
    myconn.Open();
```

```
    ⋮
}
finally
{
    if (myconn != null) ((IDisposable)myconn).Dispose();
}
```

Visual Basic .NET does not have an equivalent statement, so you must use the *Try/Finally* syntax.

Delegates and Events

A .NET event is a kind of callback from one class to one or more others. A class publishes an event, and one or more other classes subscribe to that event. You find yourself working with events over and over in .NET, particularly when working with GUI classes such as the Windows Forms classes. When you write some code that executes when a button is pressed, you actually write code in an event handler method in your Windows Forms class. The button class publishes a *Click* event, and it also defines a *delegate* method, which defines the method signature of any event handlers for that event. Your event handler method conforms to the signature defined in the delegate by using the same number and type of parameters. Your class subscribes to the button class's *Click* event so that when that button class fires a *Click* event, it calls your class's event handler code and the event handlers of any other subscribers.

A delegate is like an interface, but whereas an interface might consist of a number of methods that implementers of the interface must provide, a delegate defines the signature of a single method.

Consider the following class called *Incrementor*, which has a simple *_number* field. What we want to do is implement an *Increment* event, such that when the value of *_number* increments, the class notifies any clients subscribed to the *Increment* event.

```
using System;

namespace NETCFDevelopersReference
{
    public class Incrementor
    {
        private int _number = 0;

        public void AddOne()
        {
            _number++;
        }
    }
}
```

Not very interesting so far! The first stage in implementing an event on this class is to define the class that is passed in the event to inform subscribers about the event. In this example, this class is called *IncrementorEventArgs*, and we want to use it to inform clients what the new value of the number field of the *Incrementor* object is. Therefore, it has a public read-only property named *Value* that we use to pass the new value of the number field, and it also has a constructor that we use to set the *Value* property when the *IncrementorEventArgs* class is built. This class must descend from *System.EventArgs*.

```
using System;

namespace NETCFDevelopersReference
{
    public class Incrementor
    {
        ⋮
    }

    public class IncrementorEventArgs : EventArgs
    {
        private int _value;

        public IncrementorEventArgs(int newValue)
        {
            _value = newValue;
        }

        public int Value
        {
            get
            {
                return _value;
            }
        }
    }
}
```

Now, in the *Incrementor* class, declare the event and the delegate. The delegate defines the required signature of an event handler method, so any event handler methods that we write in client classes must take the same type and number of parameters and must return the same type. By convention, an event handler always takes two parameters. The first parameter is the object that is the source of the event. The second parameter is an object that contains the event arguments—in this case an instance of *IncrementorEventArgs*.

```
public class Incrementor
{
    private int _number = 0;

    public void AddOne()
    {
        _number++;
    }

    // Declare the signature required of event handler methods
    public delegate void IncrementEventHandler(
        object sender, IncrementorEventArgs e);
    // Declare the event and link it to the delegate
    public event IncrementEventHandler Increment;
}
```

When the *Incrementor* class needs to raise its event—when its value is incremented—it must determine if there are any subscribers to the event by checking that *Increment* is not null. If subscribers exist, it must create an instance of *IncrementorEventArgs* and send out the event to the subscribers, as shown in the following code:

```
public class Incrementor
{
    private int _number = 0;

    public void AddOne()
    {
        _number++;
        // Increment event is not null if there are any subscribers
        if (Increment != null)
        {
            // Create new IncrementorEventArgs to send to subscribers
            IncrementorEventArgs e = new IncrementorEventArgs(_number);
            Increment(this, e);
        }
    }

    // Declare the signature required of event handler methods
    public delegate void IncrementEventHandler(
        object sender, IncrementorEventArgs e);
    // Declare the event and link it to the delegate
    public event IncrementEventHandler Increment;
}
```

The client program for this class is a Windows CE console application named EventClient. It declares a method that matches the delegate—this is the event handler. It subscribes to the event by adding its event handler to the *Incrementor.Increment* event, as shown here:

EventClient.cs

```
using System;

namespace NETCFDevelopersReference
{
    public class EventClientClass
    {
        static void Main(string[] args)
        {
            EventClientClass thisclass = new EventClientClass();
            thisclass.DoStuff();
        }

        public void DoStuff()
        {
            Incrementor myInc = new Incrementor();
            // Subscribe to the event
            myInc.Increment += new Incrementor.
                IncrementEventHandler(myIncrementEventHandler);
            myInc.AddOne();
            myInc.AddOne();
            myInc.AddOne();
            Console.ReadLine();
        }

        void myIncrementEventHandler
            (object sender, IncrementorEventArgs e)
        {
            Console.WriteLine("My event handler got called!" +
                " The value is {0}.", e.Value.ToString());
        }
    }
}
```

You'll find the *Incrementor* class, the *IncrementorEventArgs* class, and the EventClient application within the Incrementor solution included with this book's sample files. Figure 2-4 shows the output from the EventClient application on the Windows CE emulator.

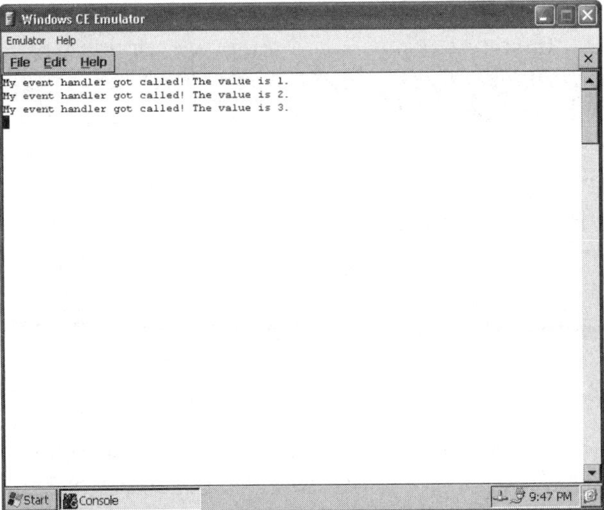

Figure 2-4 Output of the test console application showing execution of an event handler.

Note The C# compiler in the full .NET Framework supports asynchronous delegates, which allow a synchronous method to be called in an asynchronous manner. Instead of invoking the delegate method directly, your code calls the *BeginInvoke* method, which starts execution of the delegate method on another thread, allowing execution to continue on the calling thread. The *EndInvoke* method returns the results.

The .NET Compact Framework does not support asynchronous delegates. If you try to implement asynchronous delegates in the .NET Compact Framework, you'll get compile-time errors because the *AsyncResult* class is not defined in the .NET Compact Framework libraries.

.NET Compact Framework Class Libraries

From the developer's point of view, the interesting parts of the .NET Compact Framework are the class libraries. This huge selection of classes and APIs are the building blocks of any .NET application. They provide an abstraction from the operating system services, allowing developers to add functionality to programs in a consistent manner, regardless of the programming language or operating environment. Before .NET, the Windows developer chose between a bewildering array of different technologies, such as Visual Basic, or Visual C++ with the Win32 API, with MFC, or with ATL. All these approaches had different ways of achieving even fairly basic things, such as file I/O. With the .NET Compact Framework, regardless of your choice of language, be it Visual Basic .NET, Visual C# .NET, or any other .NET language that might be available in the future, you use the same .NET Framework classes in a consistent manner to achieve the same functionality.

Class Library Structure

The .NET Compact Framework class libraries contain less than 50 percent of the classes in the full .NET Framework. This sounds like a huge disparity and probably leads you to think that the functionality of the .NET Compact Framework libraries is seriously limited compared to the .NET Framework libraries. However, the .NET Compact Framework contains all the basic classes, together with the majority of the more commonly used classes, in the full .NET Framework. The .NET Compact Framework's design goal of providing a programming model that is consistent with that of the full .NET Framework has been largely achieved. Much of the disparity can be attributed to the absence of the ASP.NET classes in the *System.Web* namespace and the absence of COM Interop. The .NET Compact Framework doesn't support running a Web server on your handheld device or the direct use of COM objects from within a .NET Compact Framework application.

The basic layout of the .NET Compact Framework class libraries is similar to the layout of the class libraries in the full .NET Framework. However, the *System.Web* namespace contains only classes that enable a .NET Compact Framework application to act as a Web services client, and not those classes concerned with serving Web content using ASP.NET. The basic class structure is shown in Figure 2-5.

Figure 2-5 groups the .NET Compact Framework classes as follows:

- **Base** Contains the basic data types, collection classes such as queues, arrays, and hash tables, classes to perform file and network I/O, classes to support the .NET Compact Framework security architecture, and classes for application globalization.

- **Data and XML** Contains the ADO.NET classes and classes for parsing and formatting XML data.
- **XML Web services** Contain classes to allow operation as an XML Web service client but not (at least in this release) to serve XML Web services.
- **Windows Forms** Contains all the classes you use to build rich client graphical interfaces.

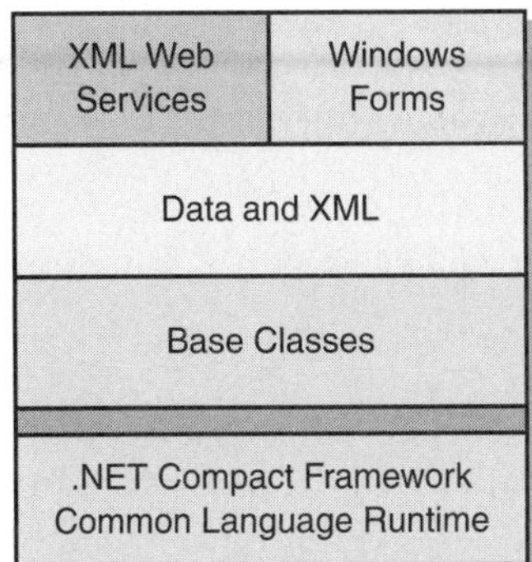

Figure 2-5 Organization of the .NET Compact Framework base class libraries.

Appendix A describes all the classes in the .NET Compact Framework libraries.

System.Object

In the .NET Compact Framework, only single inheritance is allowed. Languages such as unmanaged C++ allow a child class to inherit from more than one parent, which can cause complications. In .NET, a child has only one parent. If you take any type/object in .NET and move up through the inheritance hierarchy, eventually you end up at *System.Object*. This type is the granddaddy of them all and sits right at the top of the .NET Compact Framework family tree. If you create a new class and do not state a parent class, it implicitly inherits from *System.Object*.

Every type in the .NET Compact Framework inherits the following public methods from *System.Object*.

- ***Equals*** The expression *object1.Equals(object2)* returns *true* if two objects are considered equal. For a value type, the two objects are equal if they have the same value. For reference types, they are equal if they both reference the same object.
- ***GetHashCode*** This method returns a hash value for the type, useful in hashing algorithms or hashtables.
- ***GetType*** The expression *object1.GetType()* returns an instance of *System.Type*, which represents the exact runtime type of *object1*.
- ***ToString*** This method returns a string representation of the object and is useful when debugging code, as a quick way of confirming the value of an object.

Note that C# has the language keyword *object*, which is a synonym for *System.Object*.

Value and Reference Types

The *System* namespace of the .NET Compact Framework contains structures and classes that define all the basic data objects that you work with, such as integers, floating point numbers, and so on. There are two types of object in the .NET Compact Framework, *value* types and *reference* types.

Value types are small data items that are allocated on the stack for performance reasons and include the elementary data types such as *System.Byte*, *System.Char*, *System.Short*, *System.Int32*, and so on. In the .NET Compact Framework, a value type is a structure, which inherits from the *System.ValueType* structure. You can create your own lightweight objects that behave like value types by declaring them with the *struct* (C#) or *Structure* (Visual Basic .NET) keyword. You call the appropriate constructor of your structure using the *new* keyword. You do not have to use the *new* keyword when you declare a value type. If you don't call *new*, the runtime creates an instance of the value type with all its fields zeroed. If you do, for value types, *new* creates an object on the stack and then calls the constructor if your structure has one.

In Visual C# .NET, the *class* keyword (*Class* in Visual Basic .NET) is used to declare a reference type, and instantiation of a reference type requires the use of the *new* keyword. Reference types are allocated on the heap and are cleared up by the garbage collector when no longer required. One potential cause of confusion arises when you declare an array of value type elements. An array is actually a *System.Array* object, which is a reference type, so you must declare it using the *new* keyword. But each element of the array is a value type and doesn't need to be declared with the *new* keyword, as shown in the following Visual Basic example:

```
Dim aSingleInt As Integer
Dim anArrayOfInts() As Integer = New Integer(8) {}
```

Here is the C# version:

```
int aSingleInt;
int[] anArrayOfInts = new int[5] {};
```

What happens when a method requires a reference type and you want to use a value type? The way that the .NET Compact Framework handles this is called *boxing*. Take the following statement:

```
Console.WriteLine("Value Type is {0}", 7);
```

The {0} in the string is a string formatting placeholder and indicates that the first parameter following it should be inserted in its place. String format syntax expects the parameter to be a reference type, but the integer 7 is a value type on the stack. .NET boxes it, which means to allocate a box on the heap and copy the value of the value type into the box. The box reference is then used in the method call. Boxing happens implicitly when a value type is passed in a call requiring a reference type.

You can box value types yourself to convert them to a reference type. Simply create an object and copy the value in, as shown in this example:

```
int vtype = 7;
object o = vtype;    // Box the value.
```

To retrieve a value type from a box, you unbox it. However, the runtime doesn't know the original type of the value type, so you must cast the object back to the same type it was originally, as shown here:

```
int newvtype = (int)o;    // Unbox the value.
```

Elementary Data Types

In the .NET Framework, all the elementary types that you work with, such as integers, doubles, and so on, are structures defined in the *System* namespace. Even something as common as a 32-bit integer is a type defined in the *System* namespace—namely *System.Int32*. You could code your applications describing all your integers as *System.Int32* types, but doing so doesn't lead to readable code. Instead, each .NET programming language retains the language keywords for a type, but these actually are synonyms for the .NET Framework type, as shown in Table 2-1.

Table 2-1 Elementary Types and Language Mappings

Framework Type	Description	Visual Basic Keyword	Visual C# Keyword
System.Boolean	Boolean value	*Boolean*	*bool*
System.SByte	Signed byte	-	*sbyte*
System.Byte	Byte	*Byte*	*byte*
System.Char	Unicode character	*Char*	*char*
System.DateTime	Date and/or Time	*Date*	-
System.Int16	Signed short	*Short*	*short*
System.UInt16	Unsigned short	-	*ushort*
System.Int32	Signed integer	*Integer*	*int*
System.UInt32	Unsigned integer	-	*uint*
System.Int64	Signed big int	*Long*	*long*
System.UInt64	Unsigned big int	-	*ulong*
System.Single	Single-precision floating point	*Single*	*float*
System.Double	Double-precision floating point	*Double*	*double*
System.Decimal	Fixed-precision number	*Decimal*	*decimal*
System.String	Unicode string	*String*	*string*

> **Note** Where a programming language does not offer a language keyword for a type, it does not mean that you cannot use it. You must simply reference the full name of the type as defined by the .NET Framework class libraries. For example, use *System.DateTime* for a date type in C#.
>
> The other thing to note is that *System.String* is the only one of the types listed in Table 2-1 that is a reference type and not a value type. *System.String* is a .NET class, so you must use the *new* keyword when you instantiate one in your code.

Language Interoperability

The fact that all types used in any .NET programming language descend from the same structures and classes is the reason for one of the biggest benefits of the .NET Framework. You can write classes and methods using one language and call them from programs written in another. You can catch an exception thrown by a module written in one language in a different module written in another and be able to understand and act on that exception. You can even define classes in one language and create derived classes in another, as the following example illustrates:

SmartDeviceVBbaseClass.cs

```
Namespace SmartDeviceVBbaseClass
    Public Class aVBclass
        Private _basename As String

        Public Property Basename() As String
            Get
                Return _basename
            End Get
            Set(ByVal Value As String)
                _basename = Value
            End Set
        End Property

        Public Sub New()
            _basename = "Base Class"
        End Sub
    End Class
End Namespace
```

SmartDeviceCsChildClass.cs

```
using System;

namespace SmartDeviceCsChildClass
{
    public class CsChildClass: SmartDeviceVBbaseClass.aVBclass
    {
        public CsChildClass() : base()
        {
            ChildClassName = "Child class name";
        }

        private string _childClassName;
        public string ChildClassName
        {
            get
            {
                return _childClassName;
            }
```

(continued)

SmartDevicesCsChildClass.cs *(continued)*

```
            set
            {
                _childClassName = value;
            }
        }
    }
}
```

In use, a program such as this one in Visual Basic does not care which language the classes were written in.

VBClient.vb

```
Module VBClient
    Sub Main()
        Dim oneOfThoseChildClasses As SmartDeviceCsChildClass.CsChildClass _
            = New SmartDeviceCsChildClass.CsChildClass()

        Console.WriteLine("Basename: " & oneOfThoseChildClasses.Basename)
        Console.WriteLine("Childname: " & _
            oneOfThoseChildClasses.ChildClassName)
        Console.ReadLine()
    End Sub
End Module
```

This program demonstrates cross-language inheritance producing the following simple output:

```
Basename: Base Class
Childname: Child class name
```

You'll find the code for this application in the CrossLanguageInheritance solution included with this book's sample files.

Common Language Specification

The common language runtime provides the foundation for language interoperability by providing the common type system that all languages use. However, each language uses the common type system and metadata to define its own specific language features, some of which might still be incompatible with other languages. For example, if you define a method that takes an unsigned 32-bit integer as a parameter, that method will be unusable from a language that has no notion of unsigned 32-bit integers.

To ensure complete language interoperability, Microsoft defined the Common Language Specification (CLS), which defines only those language features that are common to all languages. If you write your own class libraries and ensure that they are CLS-compliant, your library is usable from all .NET languages.

You can mark an assembly and a class as being CLS-compliant to make the compiler flag any noncompliance, as the following C# code illustrates.

```
using System;
// Assembly marked as compliant
[assembly: CLSCompliantAttribute(true)]
// Class marked as compliant
[CLSCompliantAttribute(true)]
public class MyCLSclass
{
    ⋮
}
```

For more details on the CLS, look up the topic "What is the Common Language Specification?" in the .NET Framework online help.

Primary Differences from the Full .NET Framework

The .NET Compact Framework is a compatible subset of the full .NET Framework. Classes were excluded from the .NET Compact Framework for three main reasons:

- Because they expose Windows system services available on desktop versions of Windows but not in Windows CE. For example, ASP.NET classes, which require IIS in the underlying operating system services, are excluded from the .NET Compact Framework.
- Because they implement functionality that does not make sense in a handheld application, such as printing. However, watch third-party suppliers move swiftly in with .NET Compact Framework class libraries to offer this functionality for those developers who need it!
- Because they are too large in footprint or too computationally expensive to implement, and alternatives exist. A major design goal for the .NET Compact Framework was to keep the footprint as small as possible and to limit demands on the CPU and hence battery power. Consequently, the .NET Compact Framework excludes functionality such as Remoting and XML Path Language (XPath) and Extensible Stylesheet Language Transformations (XSLT).

The result is a footprint for the core execution engine, base classes, and ADO.NET of around 1.5 MB (compiled for an ARM processor). SQL Server CE classes require an additional 1 MB on the device, not including the space required for databases.

Figure 2-6 shows a high-level overview of the namespaces in the full .NET Framework with those that are not present in the compact implementation shown grayed out.

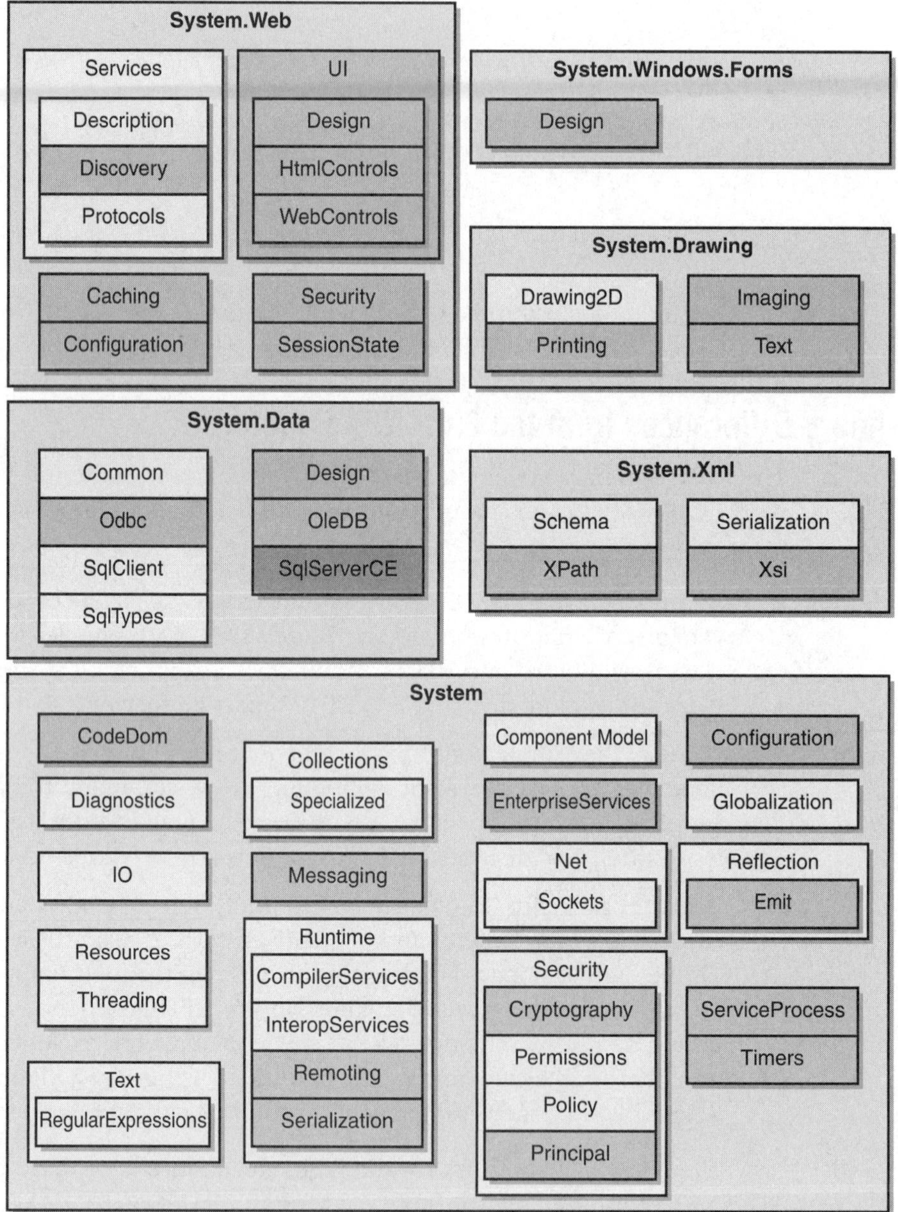

Figure 2-6 .NET Framework namespaces, identifying those absent from the .NET Compact Framework.

In Figure 2-6, the *System.Data.SqlServerCE* namespace is specific to the .NET Compact Framework, so no equivalent exists in the full .NET Framework. The presence of a namespace in both implementations does not mean that all the classes, methods, enumerations, and interfaces are found in both. The .NET Compact Framework namespaces contain fewer classes, and the classes that exist might not include exactly the same methods as the corresponding classes in the full .NET Framework. The *System.Net* and *System.Net.Sockets* namespaces contain classes to enable infrared communication that are found only in the .NET Compact Framework.

Where the .NET Compact Framework has a class of the same name as a class in the full .NET Framework, the .NET Compact Framework class is designed to be semantically compatible with the full .NET Framework class. Where methods and classes are found in both frameworks, the techniques to use those methods and classes remain the same in both frameworks.

Application Configuration Files

In the full .NET Framework, the *System.Configuration* namespace contains classes that allow an application to fetch constants from an XML configuration file. Storing constants in an external file rather than embedded into the code allows for easier reconfiguration later on. For example, a typical usage might be to define a connection string to a database in the application configuration file. If the assembly name is MyAssembly.dll, the configuration file name will be MyAssembly.dll.config, which will be in the same directory as the assembly.

If the configuration file contains the following data

```
<?xml version="1.0" encoding="utf-8" ?>
<configuration>
    <appSettings>
         <add key="Connection String"
        value="Integrated Security=true;Server=(local);Database=MyDB;" />
    </appSettings>
</configuration>
```

the code to retrieve the *Connection String* setting in an application for the full .NET Framework is:

```
using System.Configuration;
:
// Connection string for user data (in config file)
private string connString = System.Configuration.
    ConfigurationSettings.AppSettings["Connection String"];
```

There is no support built in to the .NET Compact Framework for accessing configuration files. However, you can easily write your own. For example, the following class is an example of how you can access application settings in your .NET Compact Framework applications in a similar manner to full .NET Framework applications:

ConfigurationSettings.cs

```
using System;
using System.Collections;
using System.IO;
using System.Reflection;
using System.Xml;

namespace Custom.Configuration
{
    /// <summary>
    /// Custom class that simulates the operation of
    /// System.Configuration.ConfigurationSettings.AppSettings
    /// </summary>
    public class ConfigurationSettings
    {
        const string sectionTag = "appSettings";

        public static Hashtable AppSettings
        {
            get
            {
                Hashtable settings = new Hashtable(5);

                // Get path to config file as URI
                string assemblyPath =
                    Assembly.GetCallingAssembly().GetName().CodeBase;
                string configFileUrl = assemblyPath + ".config";

                // Parse config file
                XmlDocument cfgDoc = new XmlDocument();
                FileStream fs = new FileStream(configFileUrl,
                    FileMode.Open, FileAccess.Read);
                cfgDoc.Load(new XmlTextReader(fs));
                fs.Close();

                // Get descendant nodes within the 'sectionTag' tags
                XmlNodeList nodes =
                    cfgDoc.GetElementsByTagName(sectionTag);
```

(continued)

ConfigurationSettings.cs *(continued)*

```
                foreach(XmlNode node in nodes)
                {
                    foreach(XmlNode childnode in node.ChildNodes)
                    {
                        XmlAttributeCollection attributes =
                            childnode.Attributes;
                        settings.Add(attributes["key"].Value,
                            attributes["value"].Value);
                    }
                }
                return settings;
            }
        }
    }
}
```

Note that this class is declared to be in the *Custom.Configuration* namespace. If you're porting full .NET Framework applications to the .NET Compact Framework and you don't want to change the code that accesses application settings, you might feel justified in changing the namespace declaration to *System.Configuration*. Normally, you should not declare custom classes in the *System* namespaces because they are reserved for .NET Compact Framework classes. It is better practice to declare this class in a custom namespace and modify the source code.

A test application, which we will call TestAppSettings, has an XML configuration file called TestAppSettings.exe.config. Add this file to your Visual Studio .NET project, and set its Build Action property to Content so that it copies to the target device when you deploy. The file contains the following data:

TestAppSettings.exe.config

```
<?xml version="1.0" encoding="utf-8" ?>
<configuration>
    <appSettings>
        <add key="TestString" value="This is a test string"></add>
    </appSettings>
</configuration>
```

In your .NET Compact Framework applications, you can now use the same syntax you use in a full .NET Framework application. *AppSettings* is a static property of this *ConfigurationSettings* class (*Shared* in Visual Basic .NET), so you do not need to instantiate an instance of the class to use the *AppSettings* method. The Windows CE .NET console application that follows shows the usage.

TestAppSettings.cs

```
using System;
using Custom.Configuration;

namespace NETCFDevelopersReference
{
    class TestAppSettings
    {
        static void Main(string[] args)
        {
            Console.WriteLine("TestString: " +
                ConfigurationSettings.AppSettings["TestString"]);
            Console.ReadLine();
        }
    }
}
```

You'll find the listings for ConfigurationSettings.cs, TestAppSettings.exe.config, and TestAppSettings.cs in the TestAppSettings solution included with this book's sample files.

A word of warning: this *ConfigurationSettings* class parses the whole configuration file every time you read a single setting, so it will be inefficient with large numbers of settings. You should write your own code to read configuration settings in a more efficient manner if you make heavy use of them.

COM Interop

Because of size constraints, the .NET Compact Framework does not include COM Interop classes, which allow managed applications to call COM objects, such as ActiveX controls, directly. So the bad news is that you cannot use any ActiveX controls that you might have used with eMbedded Visual Tools 3 applications directly from the .NET Compact Framework. A large part of the full .NET Framework is concerned with making COM interoperation seamless, but the footprint on a resource-constrained device is just too large.

If you want to access a COM object from a managed application, you must use eMbedded Visual C++ or eMbedded Visual Basic to create a native wrapper, a native DLL, which allows you to interact with the COM object. You then use P/Invoke to call the DLL entry points from within managed code.

You call an unmanaged DLL by using P/Invoke, with the *Declare* statement in Visual Basic or with the *DLLImport* attribute in Visual C#. For example, the Web site *http://www.gotdotnet.com/team/netcf/samples* includes a sample that accesses the Pocket Outlook Object Model (POOM) from within managed code. The native DLL, which wraps the POOM COM objects, has methods such as *IPOutlookApp_Logon*, *IPOutlook_CreateAppointment*, and many others that expose the POOM functionality. In managed C# code, you make these methods callable using the following syntax:

```
[DllImport("PocketOutlook.dll", EntryPoint=
        "IPOutlookApp_Logon")]
private static extern int do_Logon
        (IntPtr self, int hWindowHandle);
```

Now in managed code, you call do_Logon to call out to the method in the native DLL and hence interact with the COM object. For more information on this, study the POOM sample and read Chapter 22 in this book.

Although the .NET Compact Framework does not include COM Interop, it does include some built-in support that facilitates accessing COM objects in the way described here. On startup, every .NET Compact Framework application domain registers into a COM Single-Threaded Apartment (STA), so should you choose to use COM objects, your application is prepared to do so.

For the application designer, there are two main scenarios for creating a native DLL wrapper for COM objects and providing a managed class as an interface to that object.

- To use legacy COM objects, perhaps for accessing particular add-on hardware on the device. This allows you to retain your COM code but hide the complexity from your managed code developers.
- Third-party control developers who want to make sure their controls are as easy to use from managed code as they were from eMbedded Visual Basic or eMbedded Visual C++. New controls could be developed in COM to support eMbedded Tools, with a managed wrapper for .NET Compact Framework code. However, it is recommended that new control development be done in managed code, not only for ease of development but also to ensure the highest performance for the control in managed code.

Internet Deployment

The full .NET Framework allows you to deploy a simple stub program on target computers whose only function is to download a .NET assembly from a URL. The downloaded assembly contains the actual code to be executed for the application. This approach has the added advantage that the .NET runtime on the client system saves the downloaded assembly in a download cache. Thereafter, every time the application starts on the client system, the runtime checks the version of the assembly at the download URL. If the version has not changed, the cached version runs. Otherwise, the runtime downloads the new version. This is a powerful way of ensuring that large numbers of client systems always run updated code.

Unfortunately, you cannot use this technique with the .NET Compact Framework. Internet deployment requires a consistent network connection so that the runtime can verify the version of the downloaded assembly each time the application runs. Handheld devices are assumed to have an unreliable connection, and applications should be able to run when disconnected from the network. There is no download cache in the .NET Compact Framework. Chapter 6 discusses deployment with the .NET Compact Framework in more detail.

Ngen.exe

Ngen.exe is a tool used with the desktop CLR to precompile assemblies to native code at installation time, also known as install-time JIT. Of course, this leads to faster execution. This option is not available with the .NET Compact Framework, mainly because the size of assemblies compiled to native code far exceeds the size of the same assembly in MSIL. Handheld devices do not in general possess a large quantity of storage for program files. Pocket PC devices do not have a physical disk drive and must store all program code that is not preinstalled into ROM in virtual storage in RAM, which is typically 32 MB or 64 MB, with some of that space required for program execution.

Reflection Emit

The *System.Reflection.Emit* namespace contains classes that allow a compiler or tool to emit metadata and MSIL and optionally generate a PE file on disk. The users of these classes are compilers and script engines.

.NET Compact Framework developers write applications using Visual Studio .NET on a development workstation, so the target device does not need any source code compilation facilities. However, the lack of these classes does mean that you cannot use .NET languages such as JScript .NET or Python .NET for .NET Compact Framework applications. These languages require the ability to generate MSIL at runtime to support certain language features. (Note that Visual Studio .NET 2003 supports smart device application development only with Visual Basic .NET or Visual C# in any case, although support for development in other languages should be forthcoming from Microsoft and third parties in the future.)

Remoting

The .NET Compact Framework does not support .NET Remoting. If you need to communicate with .NET components situated on a remote machine, you should implement an XML Web services façade for the component and access it that way.

Serialization

Because of size and performance considerations, the .NET Compact Framework doesn't support the use of the *BinaryFormatter* class or the *SoapFormatter* class. The *BinaryFormatter* class is used for binary serialization of objects, and the *SoapFormatter* class is used for SOAP serialization.

In the full .NET Framework, you apply the *SerializableAttribute* class to a type to indicate that instances of the type can be serialized, as the following example illustrates:

```
//An object that may be serialized
[Serializable()]
public class ASimpleClass
{
   ⋮
}
```

Then you use the *Serialize* and *Deserialize* methods of either a *BinaryFormatter* or *SoapFormatter* object to save to and retrieve from persistent storage.

Although the *SoapFormatter* class is not available in the .NET Compact Framework, there is still support for transmitting data using SOAP in XML Web services. You can also still convert ADO.NET datasets to and from XML format in order to save those datasets on disk or some other persistent storage device. For other types of objects, you will have to write your own custom methods for saving and restoring data to and from persistent storage. See Chapter 10 for details of how to serialize class objects in the .NET Compact Framework.

System.CodeDom Namespace

The *System.CodeDom* and *System.CodeDom.Compiler* namespaces are concerned with generating and compiling source code dynamically. These classes are of most interest to tool vendors who produce developer tools that generate source code. This is not supported by the .NET Compact Framework.

Support for Printing

Printing support is something that has been of interest to only a minority of handheld developers. Handheld applications tend to be for information retrieval or gathering and rarely involve a requirement for printed output. However, a printed receipt to support a doorstep sale is one scenario where printing can be of value. There is no support for printing in the Pocket PC operating system, and so far, support for this functionality has been left to third-party suppliers.

Support for printing from managed code is not in version 1 of the .NET Compact Framework. If you want to use an infrared, Bluetooth, or serially connected printer from a managed application, you will need to use P/Invoke to call out to the supplier's native DLL. Undoubtedly, third parties will not be slow in producing managed libraries to access their hardware.

Visual Basic File I/O

The Visual Basic .NET runtime offers language keywords for file access that are similar to those used in Visual Basic 6, such as the *FileOpen* function. However, the recommended approach for .NET is to use the classes in the *System.IO* namespace, such as *Directory*, *FileStream*, and *FileInfo*.

In order to reduce the size of the Visual Basic .NET runtime for the .NET Compact Framework, Visual Basic 6–style file I/O is not available. You must use the *System.IO* classes, as shown in this example:

```
Try
    Dim fstream as IO.FileStream  = _
        New IO.FileStream("\netcfapps\myfile.txt", IO.FileMode.Open, _
            IO.FileAccess.Read, IO.FileShare.Read)
Catch fnfexcept As IO.FileNotFoundException
    Console.WriteLine("File not found")
Catch exc As Exception
    Console.WriteLine("Exception: " & exc.Message)
End Try
```

Chapter 10 describes Input/Output in more detail.

Web Forms

The *System.Web* namespace in the full .NET Framework contains all the ASP.NET classes (*System.Web.UI.**), as well as those classes that serve and consume XML Web services. Serving Web content is not a common function for a handheld device, so this part of the .NET Framework is not implemented in the .NET Compact Framework. Windows CE devices might act as a client for ASP.NET applications (or any other Web server technology) using the Pocket Internet Explorer browser bundled into the handheld package, but this does not require the presence of any additional runtime components such as the .NET Compact Framework on the handheld device. On the Web server, you might use ASP.NET mobile controls to develop Web applications targeted at Pocket Internet Explorer.

The .NET Compact Framework includes classes necessary for the device to act as an XML Web services client. It is possible to conceive an application scenario where it would be useful for a handheld device to be able to act as an XML Web services server—for example, other applications could call in to the device to get an up-to-date picture of the device owner's calendar appointments. If you need this kind of functionality, implement a Web service on a server that acts as a proxy for the handheld device. An application on the device calls an XML Web service, passing updates that the application on the server uses to update records held on the server. This same server application exposes an XML Web service that makes this information available to callers.

XPath/XSLT

There is no support for XPath queries into XML documents. It was too expensive in CPU and memory to implement for the .NET Compact Framework. There is support for Simple API for XML (SAX) parsing with the *XmlTextReader* class and for Document Object Model (DOM) parsing with *XmlDocument*. With the *XmlDocument* class, you can use methods such as *GetElementsByTagName* to locate specific nodes in the document tree as an alternative to XPath queries.

XSLT is another area that is computationally too expensive to provide within the .NET Compact Framework. More often than not, XSLT is used to transform an XML document into HTML for display. Because the primary method of presenting output with the .NET Compact Framework is Windows Forms rather than Pocket Internet Explorer (which is difficult to use anyway because of the lack of direct support for invoking ActiveX controls), the lack of this functionality on a handheld device is not a serious restriction.

Heavy XML document processing, such as XSLT document transformations should be offloaded to a remote server. Sending formatted data from the server to the device when possible is considered good application design. Sending the data in a form that is appropriate for the handheld application using XML Web services is better than sending raw data to the device and trying to perform computationally expensive processing on the device.

Summary

We covered a lot of topics in this chapter. We started by describing the architecture of the .NET common language runtime and how your application code is compiled at the point of execution to native code. We looked at the basics of how types are defined in the .NET Framework and how the common type system leads to easy cross-language interoperability.

We looked at classes in a little more detail, at how you use events and delegates, and at how to dispose of objects properly releasing their resources, a topic that has particular relevance on constrained devices.

Finally, we highlighted the major areas where the .NET Compact Framework differs from the desktop implementation of the .NET Framework.

Part II

Developing Applications with the .NET Compact Framework

3

GUI Development with Windows Forms

One of the most important features of any application, and particularly an application intended to run on a mobile device, is the look and feel of its user interface. No matter how effective or well designed your application is, if you do not provide an interface that is easy to interact with, people are unlikely to use the application.

When designing a user interface, you need to bear in mind the differences between the devices that it might be displayed on. Mobile devices are not simply miniature PCs and cannot be treated as such. You must remember that as well as having a smaller viewable area, mobile devices can often display only a limited number of colors. You should ensure that you design your applications to make the best use of available screen real estate. Some handheld devices provide a small keyboard, but on the majority of devices, a stylus is the input device, so you cannot expect a user to enter large amounts of data.

This chapter focuses on graphical user interface (GUI) development using the .NET Compact Framework. You will learn about the *System.Windows.Forms* namespace, the controls that a developer can exploit in a user interface, and the differences between the .NET Compact Framework and the full .NET Framework.

Introducing the *System.Windows.Forms* Namespace

The *System.Windows.Forms* namespace in the .NET Compact Framework is a subset of the full .NET Framework *System.Windows.Forms* namespace. The implementation in the .NET Compact Framework is optimized for performance and size. Features of the full *System.Windows.Forms* namespace that are resource intensive or that are not appropriate for device applications have not been implemented in the compact *System.Windows.Forms* namespace. The following list shows the main restrictions:

- No drag-and-drop support
- No printing capabilities
- No support for ActiveX controls
- Limited graphics support
- Support for only a subset of the properties, methods, and events

It is important that you understand the features, restrictions, and standards of your selected target device before you start to develop your application. You can examine the Software Development Kit (SDK) of the target device to learn the best practices for developing a GUI on that device. You should take a look at other applications on the device to analyze the way in which the GUI works and incorporate the good points into your own applications.

Creating Windows Forms

You can create Windows Forms applications for smart devices using Visual Studio .NET in much the same way that you can create Windows Forms applications for the desktop. Most of the commonly used controls are available in the .NET Compact Framework, and examples of these are shown later in this chapter. You can also create your own custom controls with the .NET Compact Framework by inheriting from the *System.Windows.Forms.Control* class or from one of the other Windows Forms controls in the *System.Windows.Forms* namespace. For more information on creating custom controls, see Chapter 18.

The Forms Designer

The Forms Designer allows you to add controls to the form by dragging them from the toolbox, to position controls on the form, and to set properties at design time.

You write code for the form in the Code View window. You can display this window by right-clicking the form in Designer View and selecting View Code from the shortcut menu, or by selecting Code from the View menu. You can access the events that a control publishes by selecting the control and clicking the Events button in the Properties window.

Windows Forms Target Platform Differences

The Pocket PC and the Windows CE .NET devices provide different user interfaces, so they have different requirements when you are designing a form. Therefore, Visual Studio .NET asks you to choose the target device when you start building your application.

Pocket PC Projects

Selecting the Pocket PC target platform when creating a Smart Device Extensions (SDE) application automatically adds a *MainMenu* component to the main form of the application. (Because it is a component rather than a graphical control, it appears in the control area beneath the Form layout display.) At run time, this menu is at the left of the bottom menu bar with the soft input panel (SIP) icon on the right. If you don't want a menu in your application, delete the *MainMenu* control from your form in the Forms Designer.

At design time, the form has a control box containing Minimize, Maximize, and Close buttons and a fixed single border. On a Pocket PC, forms generally display full screen, regardless of the size you set at design time, and the *MaximizeBox* property is ignored. You must set the *MinimizeBox* property to *false* if you want a form with an OK button at the top that terminates the application when the user clicks it. If *MinimizeBox* is *true*, the form displays at run time with an X icon in the taskbar, which (unlike with a desktop Windows application) minimizes the application, leaving it running in the background. See Chapter 4 for more information on how to create applications that conform to Pocket PC behavioral guidelines.

Windows CE .NET Projects

If you choose Windows CE .NET as the target environment when you create your project, Visual Studio .NET creates a form sized at 640 x 450, which is appropriate for many Windows CE .NET devices. There is no menu on the form by default, so you must drag one from the toolbox if you want one. Unlike Pocket PC projects, the form's control box contains Minimize, Maximize, and Close buttons that operate in the same way as they do in a desktop project. You can remove the control box by setting the *ControlBox* property to *false*, or you can remove the Minimize or Maximize buttons within the control box by setting the *MinimizeBox* or *MaximizeBox* properties to *false*.

The form has a fixed single border. You can set the *FormBorderStyle* property to *Sizable*, but this setting is not observed. Forms are always fixed size and are not user resizable, apart from toggling between full screen and the design size by clicking the Maximize button.

Comparing Forms Behavior in the .NET Framework and the .NET Compact Framework

Apart from the Maximize and Minimize buttons, there are some other specific differences between the behaviors of Windows Forms in the .NET Framework compared to those in the .NET Compact Framework. These differences are summarized in the following sections.

AcceptButton and *CancelButton*

Forms in the .NET Compact Framework don't support the *AcceptButton* and *CancelButton* properties. A desktop Windows application interprets pressing the Enter key as being equivalent to clicking the button that the *AcceptButton* property references; the application executes the button's *Click* event handler. Typically, you would set the *AcceptButton* property to reference the OK button of a dialog-box form. The *CancelButton* property is similar, except that it indicates which button's code should be executed if the user presses the Esc key.

AutoScroll

A form in a smart device application does not have an *AutoScroll* property. In the full .NET Framework, this property enables you to specify that scroll bars should appear automatically if controls are positioned outside the form's visible client area (usually because the user has resized the form). To emulate this behavior in the .NET Compact Framework, you can use the HScrollBar and VScrollBar controls as described in the "The HScrollBar and VScrollBar Controls" section later in this chapter.

Anchor

Controls placed on a form in a smart device application do not support the *Anchor* property. In the full .NET Framework, this property allows you to make a control's position or size relative to a side or sides of a user-resizable form. If the user resizes the form, anchored controls will move with respect to the borders of the form.

IsMdiContainer

You cannot create Multiple Document Interface (MDI) applications with the .NET Compact Framework, so the *IsMdiContainer* property is not available.

KeyPreview

There is no *KeyPreview* event for a form in a .NET Compact Framework application. In the full .NET Framework, you can use this event to enable a form to receive keyboard events before they are received by the active control.

TabIndex and *TabStop*

Forms created using the .NET Compact Framework do not support the concept of tabbing between controls like you can in a desktop Windows application. Pocket PCs do not have a keyboard in any case, but for Windows CE .NET devices that do have a keyboard, this is a significant restriction.

Keyboard Events

Very few controls in the .NET Compact Framework receive *KeyDown* and *KeyUp* keyboard events. The TextBox control, the form itself, and custom controls you create yourself that inherit from *System.Windows.Forms.Control* are the only ones that do.

Paint and *Resize* Events

The *Paint* and *Resize* events are raised only by the Form, Control, Panel, and PictureBox controls, which means that, in general, you cannot create custom controls that derive from an existing control and simply override the *OnPaint* method to achieve different rendering. You can override *OnPaint* only in custom-controls classes derived from *Form* or *Control*. You can override *OnResize* only for control classes derived from *Form*, *Control,* or *Panel*. See Chapter 18 for more details on creating custom controls.

Supported and Unsupported Controls

All controls derive from the *System.Windows.Forms.Control* base class. The *Control* class itself supports a subset of the methods, properties, and events of the equivalent class in the full .NET Framework, as shown in Table 3-1. Windows Forms controls for the .NET Compact Framework inherit properties, methods, and events from the base class, but they are not always implemented in the descendant control for performance reasons. For example, the .NET Compact Framework calls the *Paint* and *Resize* events only for the *Form*, *Control*, *Panel*, and *PictureBox* classes, as previously noted. See the description of each control later in this chapter for more details about the specific functionality of each control.

Not all controls are supported in the NET Framework and the .NET Compact Framework. Table 3-2 lists the full .NET Framework controls that are not available in the .NET Compact Framework.

Table 3-1 Supported Events, Properties, and Methods of the *System.Windows.Forms.Control* Base Class

Supported Events	Supported Properties	Supported Methods
Click	*Bounds*	*BringToFront*
Disposed	*ClientRectangle*	*Dispose*
EnabledChanged	*Capture*	*CreateGraphics*
KeyDown	*ClientSize*	*Focus*
KeyUp	*ContextMenu*	*Hide*
MouseDown	*Controls*	*Invalidate*
MouseMove	*DataBindings*	*PointToClient*
MouseUp	*Enabled*	*PointToScreen*
Paint	*Focused*	*Refresh*
ParentChanged	*Font*	*SendToBack*
Resize	*Location*	*Show*
TextChanged	*MouseButtons*	*Update*
	Parent	
	Size	
	Text	
	Visible	

Table 3-2 Unsupported Controls in the .NET Compact Framework

GroupBox	RichTextBox
NotificationBubble	Print controls
CheckedListBox	ColorDialog
ErrorProvider	HelpProvider
LinkLabel	NotifyIcon
ToolTip	Splitter
FontDialog	

Graphics Support

A sophisticated GUI often consists of a combination of Windows Forms controls and graphical content drawn onto the form or controls using classes in the .NET Compact Framework *System.Drawing* namespace, which is a subset of *System.Drawing* in the full .NET Framework. Some of the graphics features available to desktop applications are not supported in smart device applications. These features include GDI+ support, transparency, and the GDI functions for arcs, paths, imaging, and 2-D and 3-D drawing. Chapter 21 describes graphics support in more detail.

Exploring Windows Forms Controls

The .NET Compact Framework provides a subset of the controls available in the full .NET Framework. Furthermore, for the controls that the .NET Compact Framework does implement, not all of the methods, properties, and events supplied in the .NET Framework are available. The description of each control later in this chapter explains the most significant differences from the full .NET Framework. However, for a complete list of the supported methods, properties, and events of each control, see the Appendix of this book and the Class Library Comparison Tool. You can find the latter in the MSDN documentation by navigating to the section "Developing with Visual Studio .NET," then "Designing Distributed Applications," "Developing for Devices, "Smart Device Projects," ".NET Compact Framework," and finally ".NET Compact Framework Classes."

Creation of Controls

The Forms Designer allows you to drag and drop controls from the toolbox directly onto a form. You can then change the size, position, and other properties of those controls. You can also instantiate controls at run time using code. The following example shows the code you might use in a form to create a button at run time, setting its position relative to its container (which is a form) and adding it to the form's *Controls* collection so that it displays:

```
System.Windows.Forms.Button submitButton = new Button();
submitButton.Location = new Point(100,100);
submitButton.Text = "Submit";
this.Controls.Add(submitButton);
```

Members of Controls

Because the controls in the .NET Compact Framework are a strict subset of the controls in the full .NET Framework, most of the properties, events, and methods are identical in use. However, there are exceptions to this rule. Some of the features of the controls have been excluded from the .NET Compact Framework, either because of resource limitations or because the feature is not applicable for a smart device application.

Properties

You can set the properties of a control using the Properties window at design time or using code at runtime. Setting properties at design time is just a matter of clicking the control on the form, selecting the property you want to change, and then either typing in the new value or selecting it from a drop-down list, as appropriate.

Methods

You can use methods of controls in the .NET Compact Framework in the same way that you use them in the full .NET Framework. Again, you will find that some methods are not supported.

Events

Event handling in the .NET Compact Framework is no different from that used in the full .NET Framework. However, you will find that some events are not supported. To handle a particular event, you create a method containing the code to be executed when the event occurs and attach the method to the event.

You can create an event method for a control simply by double-clicking the control in the Forms Designer. This action wires up the *primary* event for that control, which is the event you are most likely to want to use. For example, the primary event for a Button control is the *Click* event. You can create event handler methods for any of the events that a control supports, not just the primary event, using the Properties Window in the Forms Designer. Click the Events button in the Properties Window, and select the particular event from the list displayed, as shown in Figure 3-1. If you have an existing method that you want to use to handle the event, you can choose it from the drop-down list. If you want to create a new event method, double-click the event handler's name field to create a method with the default name, or type in your preferred name.

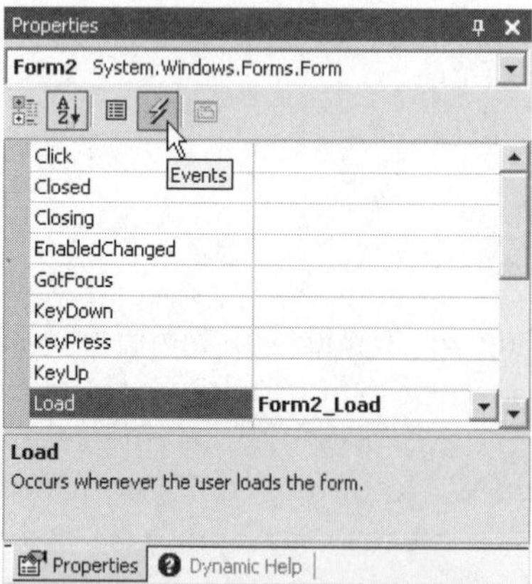

Figure 3-1 Access all events through the Events button in the Properties window.

Whichever of these techniques you use, Visual Studio .NET generates code in the *InitializeComponent* method to wire-up the event to the specified method. (The *InitializeComponent* method is part of the Windows Forms Designer–generated code, created and maintained automatically by Visual Studio .NET, and it is described in the next section.) For example, double-clicking on the background of a Form control called *Form1* creates the *Form1_Load* event handler and adds the following code to the *InitializeComponent* method:

```
this.Load += new System.Eventhandler(this.Form1_Load);
```

You can also write similar code yourself if your application needs to dynamically attach a method to an event.

Property and Event Settings

Whenever you drag a control from the toolbox onto a specific position on a form, drag the boundaries of a control to resize it, set properties of a control in the Properties window, or double-click a control to define an event handler, Visual Studio .NET generates code that performs the same task in the *InitializeComponent* method. When the application starts up, this method is executed, causing the form and controls to appear as you have laid them out. This method is held in a special region of code that is collapsed by default, so you usually do not see its contents as you work on the code in your form. The region is labeled "Windows Form Designer generated code," as shown in Figure 3-2.

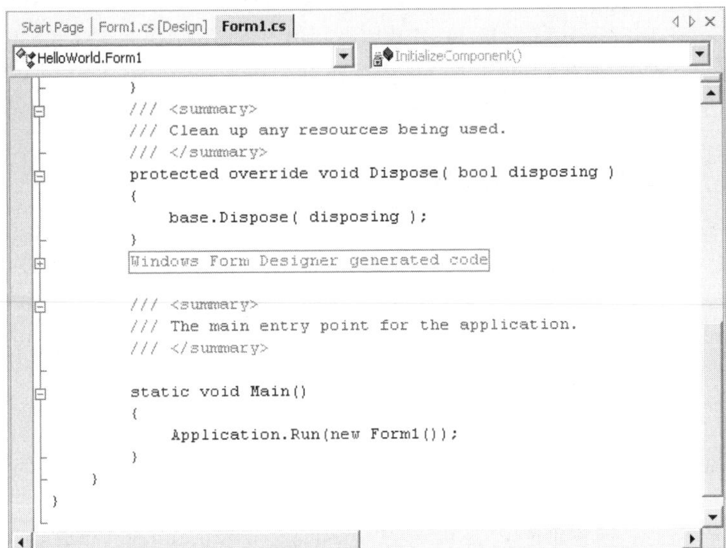

Figure 3-2 Windows Form Designer–generated code region.

If you click on the plus sign at the left margin to expand it, you will see code similar to that shown below, which is for a simple form that contains a Label control:

```
#region Windows Form Designer generated code
/// <summary>
/// Required method for Designer support - do not modify
/// the contents of this method with the code editor.
/// </summary>
private void InitializeComponent()
{
    this.label1 = new System.Windows.Forms.Label();
    //
    // label1
    //
    this.label1.Location = new System.Drawing.Point(32, 96);
    this.label1.Text = "Enter your Name: ";
    //
    // Form1
    //
    this.ClientSize = new System.Drawing.Size(394, 295);
    this.Controls.Add(this.label1);
    this.Text = "Form1";
}
#endregion
```

If you examine the code for any application you create with Visual Studio .NET, you will see that the *InitializeComponent* method is called from within the constructor for the form. At run time, the constructor executes and calls *InitializeComponent* to create controls and set their location and other properties to the same values you defined when you designed the form.

.NET Compact Framework Controls

In this section, you will find descriptions and code samples for all the standard controls available in the .NET Compact Framework.

The Button Control

The Button control is one of the most commonly used controls in a Windows application. A button can be clicked with the mouse or stylus. This causes the control to raise the *Click* event.

Buttons in smart device applications cannot be visually customized; they do not support the *BackColor*, *BackGroundImage*, *Font*, *ForeColor*, or *Image* properties. To work around these limitations, you can create your own button control derived from the *Control* class and add these operations to the *OnPaint* event. For more information on creating custom controls, see Chapter 18.

The CheckBox Control

The CheckBox control is commonly used to present a Yes/No or True/False option to the user. The *Checked* property indicates the current state of the control, *true* or *false*. The *CheckedState* property records the same thing, as *CheckState.Unchecked* or *CheckState.Checked*, but there is a third state for this property, *CheckState.Indeterminate*, which is only available if you set the *ThreeState* property to *true*. If the *CheckedState* property of the control is *CheckState.Indeterminate*, the control appears checked but grayed out. In this state, the control does not respond to the user clicking on it, as long as the *AutoCheck* property is *false*.

```
checkBox1.ThreeState = true;
checkBox1.CheckState = CheckState.Indeterminate;
checkBox1.AutoCheck = false;
```

If *AutoCheck* is *true*, the control reenables when the user clicks on it.

The CheckBox control provides two events that can be raised when the state of the control changes: *CheckStateChanged* and *Click*. If the *AutoCheck* property is *true*, the check box automatically changes state when the user clicks on the control. Otherwise, you must trap the *Click* event and change the state explicitly in code. Note that if you change the state of the control programmatically, the control raises a *CheckStateChanged* event but not a *Click* event.

Figure 3-3 shows two CheckBox controls. The second control is initially set to *CheckState.Indeterminate* until the user clicks on the first check box. You'll find the code behind this figure in the CheckBoxSample project, available with this book's sample files.

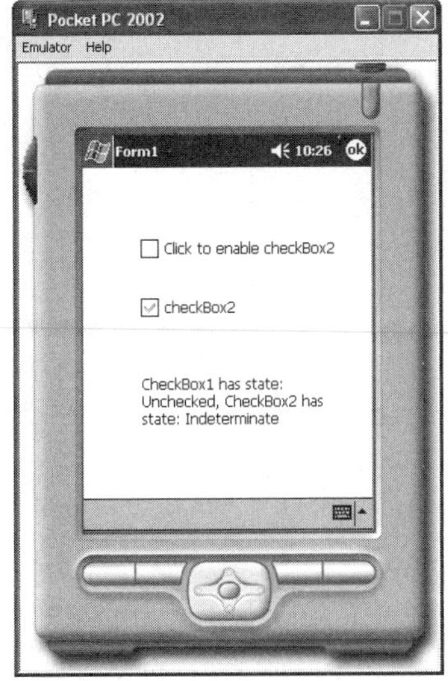

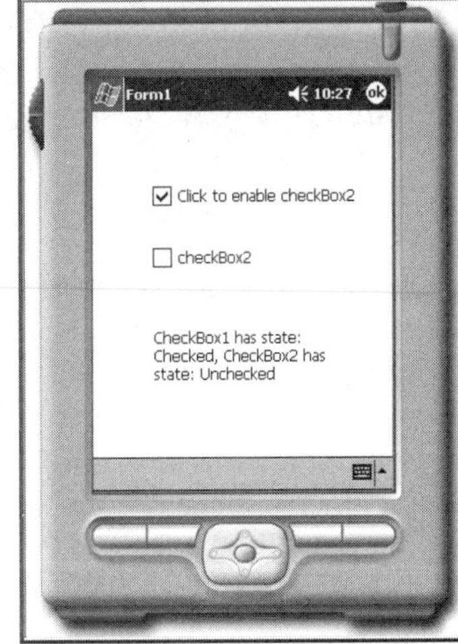

Figure 3-3 Checkbox controls.

The ComboBox Control

The ComboBox control is a good way of presenting choices to a user, while conserving screen space. The user clicks the control, and a list of options drops down.

> **Note** In the ComboBox control in the .NET Framework, you can set the *ComboBox.DropDownStyle* property to *ComboBoxStyle.Simple*. This allows users to enter new text values into the control that are not in the list. *ComboBoxStyle.Simple* is not available in the .NET Compact Framework. Only *ComboBoxStyle.DropDownList* is available, which means that when the user enters text into the control, the text is used to match an entry in the list and users can select only entries from the list. (The *DropDownStyle* property of the ComboBox control defaults to *ComboBoxStyle.DropDownList*, and this property is not even displayed in the Properties window because it cannot be changed.)
>
> The Compact .NET Framework ComboBox control does not support the *Sort* property. You must sort the data prior to adding it to the control.
>
> Also unsupported are the methods *FindString* and *FindStringExact*. These methods locate a matching string in the list of items. The workaround is to iterate through the *Items* collection of the control to locate an entry.

You can add items to a ComboBox control at design time by setting the *Items* property in the Properties window, or in code by using the *Add* method of the *Items* collection, as shown below:

```
// Add Items to a ComboBox
comboBox1.Items.Add("Item 1");
comboBox1.Items.Add("Item 2");
```

The *SelectedIndex* property indicates the index of the selected list item. (The list is zero-based.) If you set this property in code, the selected item displays in the control. If no item is selected, this property returns -1 when it is queried. The *SelectedItem* property is similar, but it returns a reference to the selected item.

```
// Get selected item with SelectedIndex
label1.Text = (string)comboBox1.Items[comboBox1.SelectedIndex];
// Get selected item with SelectedItem
label2.Text = (string)comboBox1.SelectedItem;
```

You can also bind this control to a collection. Set the *DataSource* property to the collection name, and set the *DisplayMember* property to the name of the property in the source data item to display in the list. You'll find the full code for the following program in this book's ComboBoxSample sample project.

ComboBoxSample.cs

```
using System;
using System.Drawing;
using System.Collections;
using System.Windows.Forms;

namespace ComboBoxSample
{
    public class Form1 : System.Windows.Forms.Form
    {
        private System.Windows.Forms.ComboBox comboBox1;
        private System.Windows.Forms.Label label1;
        private System.Windows.Forms.Label label2;
        private System.Windows.Forms.MainMenu mainMenu1;

        public Form1()
        {
            InitializeComponent();
        }

        protected override void Dispose( bool disposing )
        {
            base.Dispose( disposing );
        }
        #region Windows Form Designer generated code
        /// <summary>
        /// Required method for Designer support - do not modify
        /// the contents of this method with the code editor.
        /// </summary>
        private void InitializeComponent()
        {
            this.mainMenu1 = new System.Windows.Forms.MainMenu();
            this.comboBox1 = new System.Windows.Forms.ComboBox();
            this.label1 = new System.Windows.Forms.Label();
            this.label2 = new System.Windows.Forms.Label();
            //
            // comboBox1
            //
            this.comboBox1.Location = new System.Drawing.Point(56, 64);
            this.comboBox1.Size = new System.Drawing.Size(100, 21);
            this.comboBox1.Text = "comboBox1";
```

(continued)

ComboBoxSample.cs *(continued)*

```
        this.comboBox1.SelectedIndexChanged += new
            System.EventHandler(this.comboBox1_SelectedIndexChanged);
        //
        // label1
        //
        this.label1.Location = new System.Drawing.Point(56, 128);
        this.label1.Text = "label1";
        //
        // label2
        //
        this.label2.Location = new System.Drawing.Point(56, 176);
        this.label2.Size = new System.Drawing.Size(100, 48);
        this.label2.Text = "label2";
        //
        // Form1
        //
        this.ClientSize = new System.Drawing.Size(240, 270);
        this.Controls.Add(this.label2);
        this.Controls.Add(this.label1);
        this.Controls.Add(this.comboBox1);
        this.Menu = this.mainMenu1;
        this.MinimizeBox = false;
        this.Text = "Form1";
        this.Load += new System.EventHandler(this.Form1_Load);

    }
    #endregion

    static void Main()
    {
        Application.Run(new Form1());
    }

    private void Form1_Load(object sender, System.EventArgs e)
    {
        comboBox1.DropDownStyle =
            ComboBoxStyle.DropDownList; // Only option!

        State[] states = new State[] {
                                  new State("Alabama", "AL"),
                                  new State("California", "CA"),
                                  new State("Texas", "TX")
                                };
        comboBox1.DataSource = states;
        comboBox1.DisplayMember = "LongName";
```

(continued)

ComboBoxSample.cs *(continued)*

```
            SetLabels();
        }

        private void comboBox1_SelectedIndexChanged(
            object sender, System.EventArgs e)
        {
            SetLabels();
        }

        private void SetLabels()
        {
            label1.Text = "Selected Index: " +
                comboBox1.SelectedIndex.ToString();
            label2.Text = "Selected Item: " +
                ((State)comboBox1.SelectedItem).LongName;
        }
    }

    public class State
    {
        private string shortName, longName;

        public State(string longName, string shortName)
        {
            this.longName = longName;
            this.shortName = shortName;
        }

        public string ShortName
        {
            get { return this.shortName; }
        }

        public string LongName
        {
            get { return this.longName; }
        }
    }
}
```

The ContextMenu Control

The ContextMenu control allows you to build pop-up menus that are associated with a control and are activated by tap-and-hold on a Pocket PC or by right–clicking a control in Windows CE .NET. Figure 3-4 shows an example.

> **Tip** If you are developing with the Pocket PC Emulator, you simulate tap-and-hold by pressing and holding down the left mouse button.

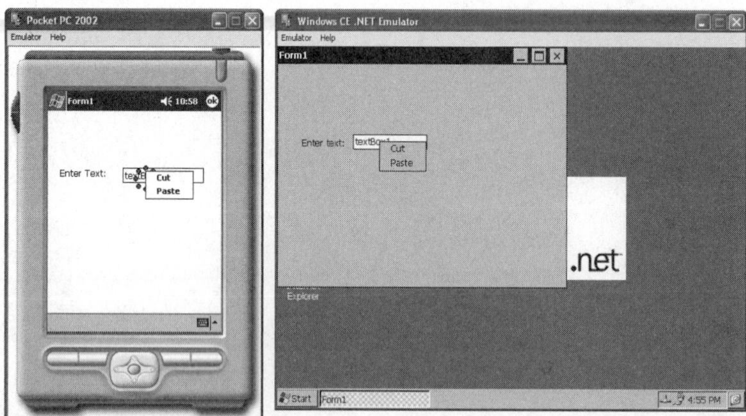

Figure 3-4 ContextMenu representation on Pocket PC and on Windows CE .NET.

The ContextMenuSample and ContextMenuCENETSample projects, available with this book's sample files, illustrate the use of the ContextMenu control.

When you drag a ContextMenu control from the toolbox onto a form, it positions in the components area at the bottom of the designer. Click the ContextMenu control in the components area to select it, and then type in the required menu items just as you would for a MainMenu control. Although the designer positions a ContextMenu control in the same position as a MainMenu control, at run time, the ContextMenu control displays next to the control that initiates it. To display a ContextMenu when a user taps and holds on a control, set the *ContextMenu* property of that control to the name of the ContextMenu control.

You can also create a *ContextMenu* instance in code. You add *MenuItem* objects to it and then set the *ContextMenu* property of a control to the *ContextMenu* object to activate it for that control, as shown in the following example:

```
// Create Context Menu Object
System.Windows.Forms.ContextMenu ConMenu = new ContextMenu();

// Create Menu Items
System.Windows.Forms.MenuItem menuItem1 = new MenuItem();
```

```
menuItem1.Text = "&Paste";
System.Windows.Forms.MenuItem menuItem2 = new MenuItem();
menuItem2.Text = "&Cut";

// Add menu items to context menu
ConMenu.MenuItems.Add(menuItem1);
ConMenu.MenuItems.Add(menuItem2);

// Assign context menu to textbox
textBox1.ContextMenu = ConMenu;
```

When a user invokes a context menu, the *Popup* event fires. You can handle this event to customize the menu options shown or to enable or disable menu options as appropriate. When a user selects an item in a context menu, the *Click* event of that *MenuItem* object fires.

> **Note** The ContextMenu control in the full .NET Framework has the *ContextMenu.SourceControl* property. If a *ContextMenu* object is used by more than one control, you can find out which control was used to invoke the *ContextMenu* object by querying this property. This property is not available with the .NET Compact Framework. The easiest workaround for this is to use a different *ContextMenu* object for each control.

The following code fragment shows how to handle the *Popup* event to disable the Cut command if there is no text in the control and how to handle the *Click* event for the Paste and Cut menu items from the previous example:

```
public class Form1 : System.Windows.Forms.Form
{
    private System.Windows.Forms.TextBox textBox1;
    private System.Windows.Forms.Label label1;
    private System.Windows.Forms.MainMenu mainMenu1;
    private System.Windows.Forms.ContextMenu ConMenu;
    private string TextClipboard = "";

    ⋮
    // Other code not shown
    private void Form1_Load(object sender, System.EventArgs e)
    {
        // Create Context Menu (as shown previously)
        ConMenu = new ContextMenu();
        ⋮
```

(continued)

```
            // Wire up the Popup event handler
            ConMenu.Popup +=
                new System.EventHandler(this.MyPopupEventHandler);
            // Wire up Click events for the MenuItems
            menuItem1.Click +=
                new System.EventHandler(this.MyCutMenuItemEventHandler);
            menuItem2.Click +=
                new System.EventHandler(this.MyPasteMenuItemEventHandler);
        }

        protected void MyPopupEventHandler(
            System.Object sender, System.EventArgs e)
        {
            // Disable Cut if no text in control
            ConMenu.MenuItems[1].Enabled = (textBox1.TextLength > 0)
                ? true : false;
            // Disable Paste if no text in our Clipboard
            ConMenu.MenuItems[0].Enabled = (TextClipboard.Length > 0)
                ? true : false;
        }

        protected void MyCutMenuItemEventHandler(
            System.Object sender, System.EventArgs e)
        {
            // Cut the text in the TextBox and save to our Clipboard
            TextClipboard = textBox1.Text;
            textBox1.Text = "";
        }

        protected void MyPasteMenuItemEventHandler(
            System.Object sender, System.EventArgs e)
        {
            // Paste any text on our Clipboard to the TextBox
            textBox1.Text = TextClipboard;
        }
    }
```

The DataGrid Control

The DataGrid control displays data from a data table or a collection. The developer can select which data columns to display from the source data table, customize the column width and the header text, and handle the events that are raised when the user selects a row or a cell.

The .NET Compact Framework implementation of the DataGrid control offers a subset of the features found in the DataGrid control of the full .NET Framework. The following list describes the main differences:

- You can bind this control only to a single *DataTable* object or *DataView* object. The full .NET Framework DataGrid control displays a hierarchical view so that, if the source *DataSet* object contains two or more *DataTable* objects linked by a *DataRelation* object, the user can expand each row in the list to display related records in the child tables. The .NET Compact Framework DataGrid control displays rows from a single table or view only, and each row is not expandable.
- The DataGrid control does not have built-in editing support, unlike the full .NET Framework version of the control. You must implement your own support for editing records by trapping user selections (described in the next section) and displaying your own user interface to support editing.
- You can customize the appearance of the DataGrid control, but only a subset of the underlying class's properties and methods found in the full .NET Framework version are available in the .NET Compact Framework.

You set the *DataSource* property to the object that functions as the data source. This can be

- A *DataTable* object.
- A *DataView* object.
- An *ArrayList* object. (All items in the list must be of the same type as the first item in the list; otherwise, an exception is thrown.)
- Any component that implements the *IListSource* or *IList* interfaces.

You can use a *DataTable* object contained in a *DataSet* object. In a full .NET Framework application, you would set the *DataSource* property to the *DataSet* object and the *DataMember* property to the name of the required *DataTable* (or use the *SetDataBinding* method, which sets both of these properties in one statement). However, the *DataMember* property is not supported in the .NET Compact Framework. Instead, set the *DataSource* property to the required table inside the *DataSet* object directly, as shown here:

```
// myDataSet may contain more than one DataTable
DataTable myDataTable = myDataSet.Tables["Customers"];
dataGrid1.DataSource = myDataTable;
```

By default, the *DataGrid* object displays all the rows and columns in the source data, and the columns display with a header that is the column name. Columns and rows can be resized by clicking and dragging a column-divider bar, and the control has built-in scroll bar support if the data to be displayed doesn't fit in the control's display area.

Determining the User's Selection Users can select a whole row by clicking or tapping in the left column, or they can select a single cell. You can detect when the user clicks or taps anywhere on the control by trapping the *MouseUp* event. You pass the X and Y coordinates where the user clicked (from the *MouseEventArgs* object associated with the *MouseUp* event) into the *DataGrid* class's *HitTest* method. This method returns a *HitTestInfo* object, which has *Type*, *Row*, and *Column* properties returning information about the cell that the user clicked. The *HitTestInfo.Type* property returns a member of the *DataGrid.HitTestType* enumeration, which contains the values *Cell*, *ColumnHeader*, *ColumnResize* (the divider line between two columns), *RowHeader*, *RowResize*, or *None*. The row and column indices are zero-based. If the user clicks on the column header or row marker, the cell index returned is -1.

The following sample code writes to the console the type, row, and column of the area where the user clicks. If the user clicks a cell, the code displays the cell's data value displays.

```
private void dataGrid1_MouseUp(object sender, MouseEventArgs e)
{
    // Get the DataGrid by casting the event sender
    DataGrid myGrid = (DataGrid)sender;
    // Create a HitTestInfo object using the HitTest method
    DataGrid.HitTestInfo myHitInfo = myGrid.HitTest(e.X, e.Y);
    Console.WriteLine(myHitInfo.Type);
    Console.WriteLine(myHitInfo.Row);
    Console.WriteLine(myHitInfo.Column);

    if (myHitInfo.Type == DataGrid.HitTestType.Cell)
    {
        // Write out cell data
        object celldata = myGrid[myHitInfo.Row, myHitInfo.Column];
        Console.WriteLine(celldata.ToString());
    }
}
```

The *CurrentCell* property sets or gets the cell that has the focus. You cannot set this property at design time, but if you set it in code at run time, the grid will scroll to display the cell if it's not already visible.

```
// Set focus to cell 3,5
myGrid.CurrentCell = new DataGridCell(3,5);
```

You can get this property to return a *DataGridCell* object to find out which cell has the focus. The *CurrentCell* property has one curious characteristic that makes the property unreliable for determining exactly which cell is clicked: If the user clicks on a cell in a new row, for example the cell at row 1, column 2, the *DataGridCell* object returned by the *CurrentCell* property correctly reports that the cell is the one at row 1, column 2. If the user then clicks on another cell in the same row, say the cell at row 1, column 1, the *DataGridCell* object returned by the *CurrentCell* property continues to report that the cell is at row 1, column 2.

Formatting DataGrid Output You format the output of the DataGrid control by setting properties of the control. You can set the display colors using the *BackColor*, *ForeColor*, *GridLineColor*, *HeaderBackColor*, *HeaderForeColor*, *SelectionBackColor*, and *SelectionForeColor* properties. The *ColumnHeadersVisible* and *RowHeadersVisible* properties determine whether the column titles and the row-indicator column display. (They are both *true* by default.) Other style properties found in the *DataGrid* class in the full .NET Framework are not supported in the .NET Compact Framework.

The style properties of the *DataGrid* class allow you to define colors, but they don't allow you to set column titles or widths. To do so, you must create an instance of the *DataGridTableStyle* class, add an instance of *DataGridColumnStyle* to it for each column you want to display, and then add the *DataGridTableStyle* instance to the *TableStyles* property of the *DataGrid* class. For example, consider a *DataGrid* that displays records from the Customers table. To format the columns, first create an instance of *DataGridTableStyle* and set its *MappingName* property to the name of the table, as shown here:

```
DataGridTableStyle ts1 = new DataGridTableStyle();
ts1.MappingName = "Customers";
```

Next create an instance of *DataGridColumnStyle* for each column. *DataGridColumnStyle* is an abstract class, so you must create an instance of *DataGridTextBoxColumn*, which is the only concrete descendant class supplied with the .NET Compact Framework. (The full .NET Framework also has the *DataGridBoolColumn* class, which is not supported in the .NET Framework.) You then set *MappingName* to the column name to display, and you set the *HeaderText* and *Width* properties to control the formatting.

```
/* Add a GridColumnStyle and set its MappingName
to the name of a DataColumn in the DataTable.
Set the HeaderText and Width properties. */
DataGridColumnStyle boolCol = new DataGridTextBoxColumn();
```

(continued)

```
boolCol.MappingName = "Current";
boolCol.HeaderText = "IsCurrent Customer";
boolCol.Width = 150;
ts1.GridColumnStyles.Add(boolCol);

// Add a second column style.
DataGridColumnStyle TextCol = new DataGridTextBoxColumn();
TextCol.MappingName = "CustName";
TextCol.HeaderText = "Customer Name";
TextCol.Width = 250;
ts1.GridColumnStyles.Add(TextCol);
```

The *DataGridTextBoxColumn* class doesn't support all of the formatting options found in the full .NET Framework *DataGridTextBoxColumn* class, such as *Format*. Instead of using *DataGridTextBoxColumn*, you can write a custom class that inherits from *DataGridColumnStyle* and implements your own custom formatting for the column. Finally you add the *DataGridTableStyle* instance to the table styles collection of the *DataGrid*.

```
/* Add the DataGridTableStyle instance to
the GridTableStylesCollection. */
dataGrid1.TableStyles.Add(ts1);
```

> **Tip** If you create a *DataGridTableStyle* instance and add it to the table styles collection before adding any *DataGridColumnStyle* objects to the instance, *DataGridColumnStyle* objects are automatically generated for you for each column in the data source. If you want to change only a few columns out of many or hide some columns, it might be quicker to use an automatically generated collection and then programmatically alter or remove the *DataGridColumnStyle* objects for those columns.

Figure 3-5 shows two screen shots with output from a simple application. The first screen shot shows the default output of the DataGrid control. The second screen shot shows the control's output after the Change Appearance button is pressed, which causes the application to create and apply some column styles. The application also sends details about the cell the user clicks to the console. You must run this sample on a Windows CE .NET emulator or device to view console output. The code for this sample is shown in the following listing, DataGridForm.cs, and is included with this book's sample files, in the DataGridSample project.

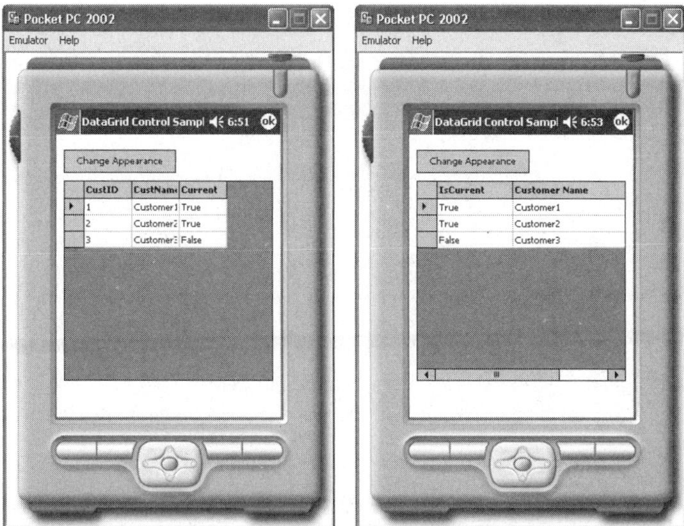

Figure 3-5 Default DataGrid presentation, reformatted using column styles.

DataGridForm.cs

```
using System;
using System.ComponentModel;
using System.Data;
using System.Drawing;
using System.Windows.Forms;

public class DataGridForm : System.Windows.Forms.Form
{
    private Button button1;
    private DataSet myDataSet;
    private DataTable myDataTable;
    private System.Windows.Forms.DataGrid dataGrid1;
    private bool TablesAlreadyAdded;

    public DataGridForm()
    {
        // Required for Windows Form Designer support.
        InitializeComponent();
        // Call SetUp to bind the controls.
        SetUp();
    }

    /// <summary>
    /// Clean up any resources being used.
    /// </summary>
```

(continued)

DataGridForm.cs *(continued)*

```
protected override void Dispose( bool disposing )
{
    base.Dispose( disposing );
}
#region Windows Form Designer generated code
/// <summary>
/// Required method for Designer support - do not modify
/// the contents of this method with the code editor.
/// </summary>
private void InitializeComponent()
{
    this.button1 = new System.Windows.Forms.Button();
    this.dataGrid1 = new System.Windows.Forms.DataGrid();
    //
    // button1
    //
    this.button1.Font = new System.Drawing.Font
        ("Microsoft Sans Serif", 8F, System.Drawing.FontStyle.Regular);
    this.button1.Location = new System.Drawing.Point(8, 16);
    this.button1.Size = new System.Drawing.Size(120, 24);
    this.button1.Text = "Change Appearance";
    this.button1.Click += new System.EventHandler(this.button1_Click);
    //
    // dataGrid1
    //
    this.dataGrid1.Location = new System.Drawing.Point(8, 48);
    this.dataGrid1.Size = new System.Drawing.Size(224, 208);
    this.dataGrid1.Text = "dataGrid1";
    this.dataGrid1.MouseUp +=
        new System.Windows.Forms.MouseEventHandler(this.Grid_MouseUp);
    //
    // DataGridForm
    //
    this.ClientSize = new System.Drawing.Size(240, 270);
    this.Controls.Add(this.dataGrid1);
    this.Controls.Add(this.button1);
    this.MinimizeBox = false;
    this.Text = "DataGrid Control Sample";

}
#endregion

public static void Main()
{
    Application.Run(new DataGridForm());
}
```

(continued)

DataGridForm.cs *(continued)*

```
private void SetUp()
{
    // Create a DataSet with two tables and one relation.
    MakeDataSet();
    /* Bind the DataGrid to the DataTable.*/
    myDataTable = myDataSet.Tables["Customers"];
    dataGrid1.DataSource = myDataTable;
}

protected void button1_Click(object sender, System.EventArgs e)
{
    if(TablesAlreadyAdded) return;
    AddCustomDataTableStyle();
}

private void AddCustomDataTableStyle()
{
    DataGridTableStyle ts1 = new DataGridTableStyle();
    ts1.MappingName = "Customers";

    /* Add a GridColumnStyle and set its MappingName
    to the name of a DataColumn in the DataTable.
    Set the HeaderText and Width properties. */
    DataGridColumnStyle boolCol = new DataGridTextBoxColumn();
    boolCol.MappingName = "Current";
    boolCol.HeaderText = "IsCurrent Customer";
    boolCol.Width = 80;
    ts1.GridColumnStyles.Add(boolCol);

    // Add a second column style.
    DataGridColumnStyle TextCol = new DataGridTextBoxColumn();
    TextCol.MappingName = "CustName";
    TextCol.HeaderText = "Customer Name";
    TextCol.Width = 200;
    ts1.GridColumnStyles.Add(TextCol);

    /* Add the DataGridTableStyle instance to
    the GridTableStylesCollection. */
    dataGrid1.TableStyles.Add(ts1);

    // Sets the TablesAlreadyAdded to prevent executing
    // more than once.
    TablesAlreadyAdded=true;
}
```

(continued)

DataGridForm.cs *(continued)*

```
private void Grid_MouseUp(object sender, MouseEventArgs e)
{
    // Get the DataGrid by casting sender.
    DataGrid myGrid = (DataGrid)sender;
    // Create a HitTestInfo object using the HitTest method.
    DataGrid.HitTestInfo myHitInfo = myGrid.HitTest(e.X, e.Y);
    Console.WriteLine(myHitInfo);
    Console.WriteLine(myHitInfo.Type);
    Console.WriteLine(myHitInfo.Row);
    Console.WriteLine(myHitInfo.Column);

    if (myHitInfo.Type == DataGrid.HitTestType.Cell)
    {
        Console.Write("Data: ");
        object celldata = myGrid[myHitInfo.Row, myHitInfo.Column];
        Console.WriteLine(celldata.ToString());
    }
}

// Create a DataSet with two tables and populate it.
private void MakeDataSet()
{
    // Create a DataSet.
    myDataSet = new DataSet("myDataSet");

    // Create a DataTable.
    DataTable tCust = new DataTable("Customers");

    // Create three columns, and add them to the  table.
    DataColumn cCustID = new DataColumn("CustID", typeof(int));
    DataColumn cCustName = new DataColumn("CustName");
    DataColumn cCurrent = new DataColumn("Current", typeof(bool));
    tCust.Columns.Add(cCustID);
    tCust.Columns.Add(cCustName);
    tCust.Columns.Add(cCurrent);

    // Add the table to the DataSet.
    myDataSet.Tables.Add(tCust);

    // Create three customers in the Customers Table.
    DataRow newRow1;
    for(int i = 1; i < 4; i++)
    {
        newRow1 = tCust.NewRow();
```

(continued)

DataGridForm.cs *(continued)*

```
            newRow1["custID"] = i;
            // Add the row to the Customers table.
            tCust.Rows.Add(newRow1);
        }
        // Give each customer a distinct name.
        tCust.Rows[0]["custName"] = "Customer1";
        tCust.Rows[1]["custName"] = "Customer2";
        tCust.Rows[2]["custName"] = "Customer3";

        // Give the Current column a value.
        tCust.Rows[0]["Current"] = true;
        tCust.Rows[1]["Current"] = true;
        tCust.Rows[2]["Current"] = false;
    }
}
```

The DomainUpDown Control

The DomainUpDown control is very similar to a ComboBox or ListBox control, but it takes up very little space, so it is ideally suited to Pocket PC applications. It allows the user to select from a list of objects; the control calls the *ToString* method of each object to provide the text that displays. Visually, it is rendered as a text box with a pair of buttons for moving up or down the list, as shown in Figure 3-6 (positioned above two labels). The disadvantage over the ComboBox or ListBox control is that the user is unable to see the whole list of items.

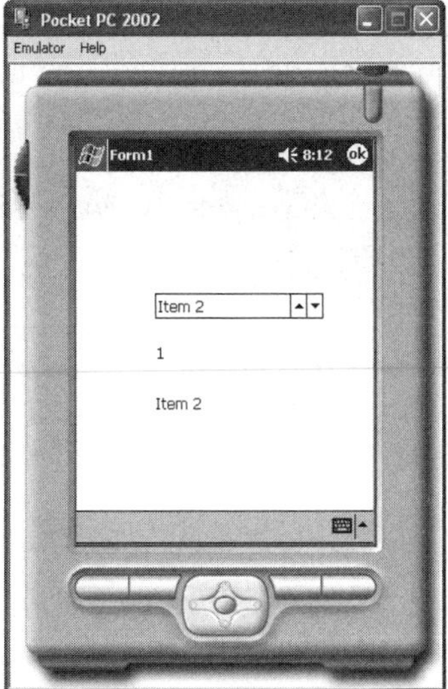

Figure 3-6 The space-efficient DomainUpDown control.

Users select items from this control by:

- Clicking on the Up or Down Arrow buttons.
- Pressing the Up or Down Arrow key. Many Pocket PC devices have a large button for navigation, which acts as a joystick for games. Pressing the top or bottom of this button is equivalent to pressing the Up or Down Arrow key.
- Typing the name of an item in the list.

If you set the *ReadOnly* property to *true*, only items in the list can be selected. If you set the *ReadOnly* property to *false*, the user can type text that is not in the list.

> **Note** Unlike the DomainUpDown control in the full .NET Framework, this control does not perform input validation when a user types directly into the control. The *SelectedItemChanged* event does not occur when a user types directly into the control. You must validate user entry elsewhere in your code before using a user-entered value.
>
> This control does not support the Boolean *Sorted* property found in the full .NET Framework control. When *true*, the *Sorted* property sorts the underlying collection in alphabetical order; when *false*, it keeps the items in the order in which they were added. If you want to sort the underlying collection of objects in the .NET Compact Framework control, use the *DomainUpDown.Items.Sort* method. However, once sorted, the items cannot be unsorted, so if you require this functionality, you will have to retain a copy of the unsorted collection and use that to reload the DomainUpDown control to return to the original order of entry. (The DomainUpDownSample project, available with this book's sample files, demonstrates this process.)

On startup, the *SelectedIndex* property has the value -1, indicating that no item is selected. If you want to preselect an item, set the *SelectedIndex* property to the required index.

The following code sample shows how to add items to the list and how to handle the *SelectedItemChanged* event that fires when the user selects an item:

```
private void Form1_Load(object sender, System.EventArgs e)
{
    domainUpDown1.Items.Add("Item 1");
```

```
    domainUpDown1.Items.Add("Item 2");
    domainUpDown1.Items.Add("Item 3");
    domainUpDown1.Items.Add("Item 4");
       domainUpDown1.ReadOnly = true;
    }

private void domainUpDown1_SelectedItemChanged(
    object sender, System.EventArgs e)
{
    label1.Text = domainUpDown1.SelectedIndex.ToString();
    label2.Text =
        domainUpDown1.Items[domainUpDown1.SelectedIndex].ToString();
}
```

The HScrollBar and VScrollBar Controls

Most controls that need scroll bars already provide them when the content exceeds the dimensions of the control. However, if you want to achieve the same effect when using other controls, you must use the HScrollBar and VScrollBar controls.

The *Minimum* property defines the position when the scroll box is at the left end (HScrollbar) or top (VScrollBar) of the control. The *Maximum* property defines the other end of the scroll bar. The *SmallChange* property defines the increment to use when the user presses one of the arrow keys (the navigation pad on a Pocket PC) or clicks one of the arrow buttons at either end of the scroll bar. The *LargeChange* property defines the increment for when the user presses the Page Up or Page Down keys, or when the user clicks on the scroll bar track outside of the scroll box.

You should consider setting *SmallChange* and *LargeChange* to a percentage of the *Height* (VScrollBar) or *Width* (HScrollBar) values so that the scroll bar moves in proportion to its size.

The *ValueChanged* event fires when the scroll bar has been scrolled. In the event handler, you can query the *Value* property to find out the current scroll position.

> **Tip** When you scroll to the end of the scroll bar, the *Value* property has the value (*Maximum* – *LargeChange*). For example, if *Minimum* = 0, *Maximum* = 100, and *LargeChange* = 20, when the scroll bar is fully scrolled, *Value* will be 80.

For an example of coding with the VScrollBar control, see the example accompanying the description of the Panel control later in this chapter.

The ImageList Control

The ImageList control is a component that acts as a container for images. The *Images* property of an ImageList control exposes the images collection. In the Forms Designer, you add images to the control by clicking the ellipsis button shown against the Images property in the Properties window. This opens the Image Collection Editor window, which allows you to select images and add them to the control. Images that you add in this way are stored in the resource file for the form and deploy to the target system as resources embedded inside the application assembly.

Alternatively, you can add an image to the control at run time using *ImageList.Images.Add* method. Note that this adds a new image at the beginning (position 0) of the collection, rather than at the end. When working with graphics files, you should add them to your project and either set the Build Action property for each graphic to Embedded Resource so that the graphics are included in the application assembly, or set the Build Action to Content so that the graphics files deploy to the device as separate files.

All images in an ImageList control have the same size, which is (16, 16) by default. You can set the *ImageSize* property to specify a different size.

The ListView, TreeView, and Toolbar controls can use images held in an ImageList control. When using the ListView control, you can set the control's *LargeImageList* and *SmallImageList* properties to instances of an ImageList control. When the *ListView.View* property is set to *View.LargeIcon*, images from the *ImageList* object pointed to by *LargeImageList* will be displayed alongside the list items. Similarly, when the *ListView.View* property is set to *View.Details* or *View.SmallIcon*, images from the *ImageList* object pointed to by *SmallImageList* will be displayed alongside items. When the *ListView.View* property is set to *View.List*, no images will be displayed. To specify which image will be displayed alongside each item, set the *ImageIndex* property of each list item using code such as this:

```
ListView.Items[n].ImageIndex = indexOfImageInImageList;
```

> **Note** In the full .NET Framework, the Button, Checkbox, RadioButton, and Label controls can also use images from an ImageList. This is not supported in the .NET Compact Framework.

The following example is part of a Visual Studio .NET project that includes four graphics files. The *Form_Load* method constructs a new instance of an *ImageList* class and adds the graphics to it. The code then adds list items to a ListView control and sets the control's *ImageIndex* property to the correct index in the *ImageList* instance.

```
using System;
using System.Drawing;
using System.Collections;
using System.Reflection;
using System.Windows.Forms;
⋮
private void Form1_Load(object sender, System.EventArgs e)
{
    ImageList imgList = new ImageList();
    // Add the four images that were inserted into the app assembly
    // as embedded resources
    Bitmap bmp = new Bitmap(Assembly.GetExecutingAssembly()
        .GetManifestResourceStream("NETCFDevelopersReference.pic01.jpg"));
    imgList.Images.Add(bmp);
    bmp = new Bitmap(Assembly.GetExecutingAssembly()
        .GetManifestResourceStream("NETCFDevelopersReference.pic02.jpg"));
    imgList.Images.Add(bmp);
    bmp = new Bitmap(Assembly.GetExecutingAssembly()
        .GetManifestResourceStream("NETCFDevelopersReference.pic03.jpg"));
    imgList.Images.Add(bmp);
    bmp = new Bitmap(Assembly.GetExecutingAssembly()
        .GetManifestResourceStream("NETCFDevelopersReference.pic04.jpg"));
    imgList.Images.Add(bmp);
    imgList.ImageSize = new Size(64, 64); //These are 4x  default size

    // Display in the ListView
    listView1.SmallImageList = imgList;
    listView1.View = View.List;
    // Define the List items - the image appears alongside
    // CAREFUL - Images get added to the ImageList at the top
    // Last added image has index 0
    listView1.Items.Add(new ListViewItem("Andy"));
    listView1.Items[0].ImageIndex = 3;
    listView1.Items.Add(new ListViewItem("Pyrenees"));
    listView1.Items[1].ImageIndex = 2;
    listView1.Items.Add(new ListViewItem("Jess"));
    listView1.Items[2].ImageIndex = 1;
    listView1.Items.Add(new ListViewItem("Caroline"));
    listView1.Items[3].ImageIndex = 0;
```

The full code for this listing is in ListViewSample.cs, available with this book's sample files. The sample generates the output shown in Figure 3-7.

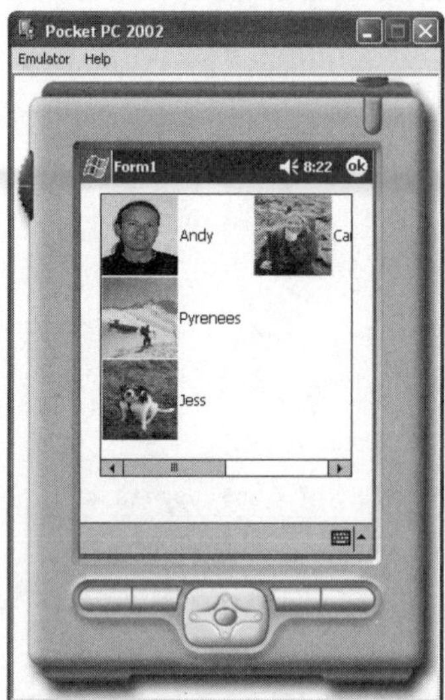

Figure 3-7 ListView control displaying images stored in an ImageList.

The Label Control

The Label control needs very little explanation. You use this control to display text, specified by the *Text* property. If the text is too large for the control area, it will be truncated, so be sure to size it appropriately. You can use the *TextAlign* property to align text within the control to one of the following *System.Drawing.ContentAlignment* values: *TopLeft* (the default), *TopCenter*, or *TopRight*.

Unlike the full .NET Framework, the Label control in the .NET Compact Framework does not support the *Click* event. Chapter 18 describes how to create a custom control that implements a clickable label.

The ListBox Control

The ListBox control displays a list of items from which a user can make a choice. It has built-in scroll bar support, and if the number of items exceeds the display area, a vertical scroll bar appears automatically.

The properties and methods of the ListBox control are almost identical to those of the ComboBox control. The main difference between these two controls is that the ComboBox control displays the list of items only when the user clicks on the Down Arrow button on the right of the control. The ListBox displays as many items as it can within the size you allocate to it when you add it to a form, with a vertical scroll bar if necessary, as illustrated in Figure 3-8.

> **Note** The ListBox control in the .NET Compact Framework differs from the version in the full .NET Framework in the following two significant ways:
>
> 1. It does not support multicolumn lists, so there is no *MultiColumn* property, nor will a horizontal scroll bar appear if the list's items are wider than the control display area.
> 2. It does not support multiple selections. The user can select only a single item.

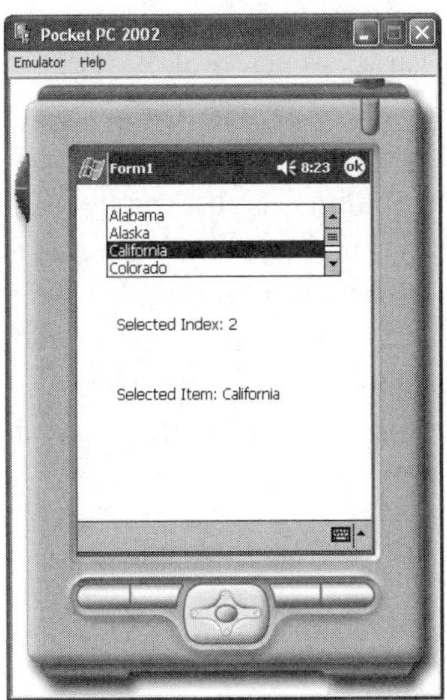

Figure 3-8 ListBox control adds a vertical scroll bar if necessary and supports single item selection.

You add an item to a ListBox control in code using the *Add* method of the *Items* collection, and you can remove an individual item with the *Remove* method of the *Items* collection, as the following code illustrates:

```
// Add Items to a ListBox
listBox1.Items.Add("Item 1");
listBox1.Items.Add("Item 2");
```

You can clear the *Items* collection with the *Clear* method.

Another way to populate a ListBox control is by editing the *Items* property in the Properties window at design time. The *SelectedIndex* property indicates the index of the selected list item. If you set this property in code, the selected item displays in the control. If no item is selected, this property returns -1. The *SelectedItem* property is similar but returns a reference to the selected item. Obtaining an index or a reference to the selected item of a ListBox control is exactly like obtaining an index or a reference to the selected item of a ComboBox control.

You can also bind the ListBox control to a collection. Set the *DataSource* property to the collection name, and set the *DisplayMember* property to the name of the property in the source data item to display in the list. See the example code for the ComboBox control earlier in this chapter; the code used there applies equally well to the ListBox. You'll find code that uses the ListBox control in this book's ListBoxSample.cs sample file.

The ListView Control

ListView controls are used to display a list of items, with an optional icon that can help to visually identify the item. An example of an application that can display items in this way is Windows Explorer. The items in a list view can be displayed in one of four ways: large icons, small icons, list, or details.

The ListView control can display additional text, or subitems, for each item in the Details view. The first column displays the item text, for example, a contact name. The second, third, and subsequent columns display the first, second, and subsequent associated subitems. The following sample adds items to a ListView control named *ContactsList* and adds subitems to the main items to hold different phone numbers for each contact:

```
// Show items in report style view
ContactsList.View = View.Details;
// Display a checkbox against each item row
ContactsList.CheckBoxes = true;
// Select entire row when any sub item selected
ContactsList.FullRowSelect = true;
// Show Grid lines
ContactsList.GridLines = true;

// Create Items for List View
ListViewItem Contact1 = new ListViewItem("Darren");
Contact1.SubItems.Add("0293 4839 499");
Contact1.SubItems.Add("0238 3827 399");
Contact1.SubItems.Add("0739 2938 202");

ListViewItem Contact2 = new ListViewItem("Peter");
Contact2.SubItems.Add("0574 8478 498");
```

```
Contact2.SubItems.Add("0902 0923 098");
Contact2.SubItems.Add("0983 4898 493");

ListViewItem Contact3 = new ListViewItem("Lin");
Contact3.SubItems.Add("0263 3874 498");
Contact3.SubItems.Add("0465 5947 594");
Contact3.SubItems.Add("0938 2833 309");

// Create list view columns
ContactsList.Columns.Add("Name",-2, HorizontalAlignment.Left);
ContactsList.Columns.Add("Work",-2, HorizontalAlignment.Left);
ContactsList.Columns.Add("Home",-2, HorizontalAlignment.Left);
ContactsList.Columns.Add("Mobile",-2, HorizontalAlignment.Center);

// Add items to list view
ContactsList.Items.Add(Contact1);
ContactsList.Items.Add(Contact2);
ContactsList.Items.Add(Contact3);
```

Figure 3-9 shows a ListView control displaying information using the detail view as coded in the previous example.

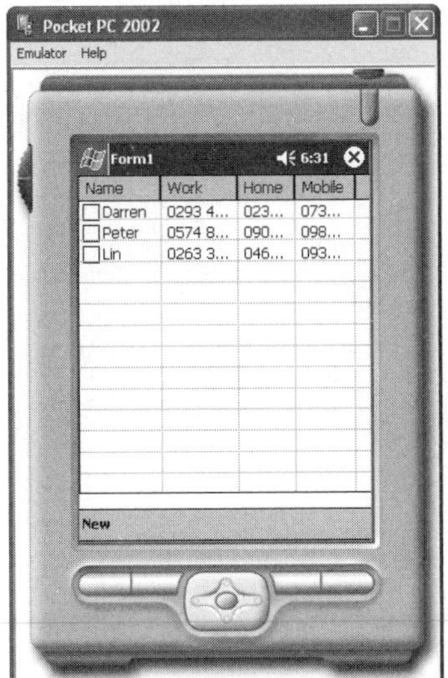

Figure 3-9 ListView control.

You can query the Items collection, iterate through the list, and examine the *Checked* property of each item to determine which items the user has selected.

```
foreach (ListViewItem chkItem in ContactsList.Items)
{
    if (chkItem.Checked)
```

```
        {
            // Do something with checked item
        }
}
```

To access the row with current focus, you can use the *FocusedItem* property of the control, and to retrieve the text of a subitem, you can use the *SubItems* collection.

```
MessageBox.Show(ContactsList.FocusedItem.SubItems[0].Text);
```

See also the "The ImageList Control" section earlier in this chapter for details of how to use a ListView control to display graphics from an ImageList control.

The MainMenu Control

As we have previously stated, a Pocket PC application contains a MainMenu control by default. On a Pocket PC, menus are displayed at the bottom of a form. In a Windows CE application, you must add a MainMenu control to the form yourself, and the control will be displayed at the top of the form, in the same way as for a standard desktop application.

Figure 3-10 shows a MainMenu control at the bottom of the window in a Pocket PC application.

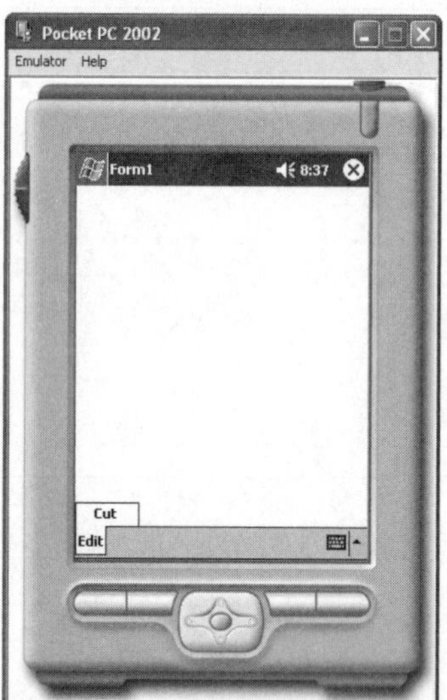

Figure 3-10 MainMenu control in a Pocket PC application.

Keep in mind that adding a menu to the form will reduce the client area available to the form. However, it is often an efficient way of presenting multiple user options.

You can add items to a MainMenu control at design time using the menu designer or at run time through code. The following sample code shows how to add a menu item with one submenu to a MainMenu control, called *mainMenu1*, at run time:

```
MenuItem SubItem1 = new MenuItem();
MenuItem Item1 = new MenuItem();
SubItem1.Text = "Cut";
Item1.Text = "Edit";
Item1.MenuItems.Add (SubItem1);
mainMenu1.MenuItems.Add (Item1);
```

The NumericUpDown Control

The NumericUpDown control is similar to the DomainUpDown control, but it works with integer values, rather than objects. You can set the *Minimum* and *Maximum* properties to the upper and lower limits, and you can set the *Increment* property to the size of the step for when the user clicks the Up or Down buttons. The *Value* property returns the current selected value.

When the user clicks the Up or Down Arrow button, the step is always of the *Increment* value, unless a step of that increment would cause the value to exceed the maximum or be less than the minimum value. For example, if the *Increment* property is set to a value of 3, *Minimum* to 0, and *Maximum* to 100, the steps are 0, 3, 6, 9, and so on. When the control reaches the value 99, the next step up sets the value to the maximum value, which is 100. If the user now clicks the Down arrow, you might expect the control to take the value 97, but in fact, it continues to decrement to the next value that is a multiple of the *Increment* value, so the value is set to 96!

The NumericUpDown control accepts only integers. Decimal values are truncated. (For example, 4.34 becomes 4.) The Pocket PC implementation can't handle values beyond that of a 16-bit signed integer.

As with the DomainUpDown, you can set the *ReadOnly* property to *true* to limit users to values selected through the Up or Down buttons. If it is set to *false*, users can type any value into the control.

> **Note** Unlike the NumericUpDown control in the full .NET Framework, the .NET Compact Framework NumericUpDown control does not perform input validation when a user types directly into the control. The *ValueChanged* event does not occur when a user types directly into the control. You must validate user entry elsewhere in your code before employing a user-entered value.

If a user types in a value that falls between the *Minimum* and *Maximum* values, both the *Value* and *Text* properties of the control take that value. If the entered value is outside the allowable range, the *Text* property takes the entered property, while the *Value* property returns the *Maximum* value. You'll find code that illustrates how to use this control in this book's NumericUpDownSample.cs sample file.

The OpenFileDialog and SaveFileDialog Controls

These two controls represent two commonly used dialog boxes in Windows applications. They are components, so when you drag them from the toolbox, they appear in the components area at the foot of the design window. To make either of these dialog boxes visible, call the *ShowDialog* method. This method returns a *DialogResult* enumeration. *DialogResult.OK* means the user pressed the OK button, and you can determine the full path and filename of the filename the user selected by accessing the *Filename* property. *DialogResult.Cancel* means the user pressed the Cancel button to quit the dialog box. On the Pocket PC, the dialog box displays full screen, but on Windows CE .NET, it is a pop-up dialog box window, as on the desktop.

The *Filter* property sets the different file types that are valid with either of these dialog boxes and the associated file extensions. You represent each file type by a string containing a description, then a vertical bar (|), and then the filename format. To specify further filters, put them all together in one string separated by a | character.

```
saveFileDialog1.Filter =
    "Jpeg image|*.jpg|Bitmap image|*.bmp|GIF image|*.gif"
```

Each file filter you specify appears in the File Types drop-down list box in the Open or Save dialog box. The *FilterIndex* property gets or sets the currently selected file filter. This index is 1-based, not zero-based as you might expect. It defaults to 1.

One significant limitation of these dialog boxes is that they restrict users to the My Documents folder and one level of subdirectories below that. You can use the *InitialDirectory* property to specify the path to a subdirectory under My Documents; if the name you specify does not exist, the folder used is My Documents.

The following code sample creates a folder called Andy's Files under My Documents and then displays a SaveFileDialog control so that the user can enter a filename. The sample creates a file with the user-specified filename and writes the contents of a TextBox control to the file. The sample creates a SaveFileDialog control dynamically, but you can also drag this control from the toolbox and set the control's properties using the Forms Designer.

```
include System.IO;
include System.Windows.Forms;
⋮
private void button1_Click(object sender, System.EventArgs e)
{
    // Create the folder
    Directory.CreateDirectory("\\My Documents\\Andy's Files");

    SaveFileDialog dlg = new SaveFileDialog();
    dlg.Filter = "Text File|*.txt";
    dlg.FileName = "andy.txt";
    dlg.InitialDirectory = "\\My Documents\\Andy's Files";

    if (dlg.ShowDialog() == DialogResult.OK)
    {
        StreamWriter sw = new StreamWriter(dlg.FileName, false);
        sw.Write(textBox1.Text);
        sw.Close();
    }
}
```

In the sample files for this book, you'll find the OpenFileDialogSample and SaveFileDialogSample projects, which demonstrate how to use these controls.

The Panel Control

The Panel control acts as a container for other controls. At design time, you place other controls onto the panel. If you move the panel, the controls it contains move with it. A Panel control provides a visual cue to the user that the controls in the panel are related. The Panel control is a good alternative to using a GroupBox control (which is not supported by the .NET Compact Framework)—for example, when grouping RadioButton controls. The Panel control supports the *BackColor* property.

The .NET Compact Framework Panel control has some differences from the full .NET Framework implementation, which are summarized in the following list:

- The *BorderStyle* property is not supported. Panels display without a border. To give a panel a border, you must use the drawing classes to add one manually.
- The *AutoScroll* property is not supported. In the full .NET Framework, this property allows the user to scroll to any controls placed outside the Panel control's visible boundaries. You can work around this using HScrollBar and VScrollBar controls.
- The *BackGroundImage* property is not supported.

You can work around the absence of *AutoScroll* in the *Form* and *Panel* classes in the following way:

1. First choose the control that defines the scrollable viewing area. This could just be a Form control if you want the scrollable viewing area to fill the form, or position a Panel control onto the form if you want the scrollable viewing area to be less than the form's entire client area.
2. Drag a VScrollBar or HScrollBar control and a Panel control into the control that defines the viewing area. If the control that defines the viewing area is a Panel control, you'll be dragging a second Panel control into the Panel control that defines the viewing area. Size the interior panel to be larger than its container and big enough to contain all the items you want to show.
3. Set the *Minimum* property of the scroll bar to zero and the *Maximum* property to the difference in size between the interior panel and its container. Set the *LargeChange* and *SmallChange* properties as appropriate (perhaps 20 percent of the value in the *Maximum* property for the *LargeChange* property and 10 percent for the *SmallChange* property, or values to suit your own application).
4. Write a *ValueChanged* event handler. In the event handler for a vertical scroll bar, set the *Top* property of the interior panel. In the event handler for a horizontal scroll bar, set the *Left* property of the interior panel to be -1 times the scroll bar value. In other words, the interior panel is positioned to a negative location relative to its container.
5. The interior panel is seen to scroll inside its container.

The code that follows shows the use of the Panel and VScrollBar controls, and Figure 3-11 shows the output generated by this sample. The PanelSample project is available with this book's sample files. The containing Panel control, *panel1*, has a height of 160, and *panel2*, which is contained within *panel1*, has a height of 270. The *panel2* control contains seven Label controls as a simple example to illustrate the technique.

PanelSample.cs

```
using System;
using System.Drawing;
using System.Collections;
using System.Windows.Forms;
```

(continued)

PanelSample.cs *(continued)*

```
namespace NETCFDevelopersReference
{
    public class Form1 : System.Windows.Forms.Form
    {
        private System.Windows.Forms.VScrollBar vScrollBar1;
        private System.Windows.Forms.Panel panel1;
        private System.Windows.Forms.Panel panel2;
        private System.Windows.Forms.Label label1;
        private System.Windows.Forms.Label label4;
        private System.Windows.Forms.Label label3;
        private System.Windows.Forms.Label label2;
        private System.Windows.Forms.Label label5;
        private System.Windows.Forms.Label label6;
        private System.Windows.Forms.Label label7;
        private System.Windows.Forms.Label label8;

        public Form1()
        {
            InitializeComponent();

        }

        protected override void Dispose( bool disposing )
        {
            base.Dispose( disposing );
        }
        #region Windows Form Designer generated code
        /// <summary>
        /// Required method for Designer support - do not modify
        /// the contents of this method with the code editor.
        /// </summary>
        private void InitializeComponent()
        {
            this.mainMenu1 = new System.Windows.Forms.MainMenu();
            this.vScrollBar1 = new System.Windows.Forms.VScrollBar();
            this.panel1 = new System.Windows.Forms.Panel();
            this.panel2 = new System.Windows.Forms.Panel();
            this.label4 = new System.Windows.Forms.Label();
            this.label3 = new System.Windows.Forms.Label();
            this.label2 = new System.Windows.Forms.Label();
            this.label1 = new System.Windows.Forms.Label();
            this.label5 = new System.Windows.Forms.Label();
            this.label6 = new System.Windows.Forms.Label();
            this.label7 = new System.Windows.Forms.Label();
            this.label8 = new System.Windows.Forms.Label();
            //
```

(continued)

PanelSample.cs *(continued)*

```
// vScrollBar1
//
this.vScrollBar1.Location = new System.Drawing.Point(224, 16);
this.vScrollBar1.Maximum = 91;
this.vScrollBar1.Size = new System.Drawing.Size(13, 160);
this.vScrollBar1.ValueChanged +=
    new System.EventHandler(this.vScrollBar1_ValueChanged);
//
// panel1
//
this.panel1.Controls.Add(this.panel2);
this.panel1.Location = new System.Drawing.Point(8, 16);
this.panel1.Size = new System.Drawing.Size(216, 160);
//
// panel2
//
this.panel2.BackColor = System.Drawing.Color.LightGray;
this.panel2.Controls.Add(this.label8);
this.panel2.Controls.Add(this.label7);
this.panel2.Controls.Add(this.label6);
this.panel2.Controls.Add(this.label5);
this.panel2.Controls.Add(this.label4);
this.panel2.Controls.Add(this.label3);
this.panel2.Controls.Add(this.label2);
this.panel2.Controls.Add(this.label1);
this.panel2.Size = new System.Drawing.Size(216, 268);
//
// label4
//
this.label4.Location = new System.Drawing.Point(8, 112);
this.label4.Text = "label4";
//
// label3
//
this.label3.Location = new System.Drawing.Point(8, 80);
this.label3.Text = "label3";
//
// label2
//
this.label2.Location = new System.Drawing.Point(8, 48);
this.label2.Text = "label2";
//
// label1
//
this.label1.Location = new System.Drawing.Point(8, 16);
this.label1.Text = "label1";
```

(continued)

PanelSample.cs *(continued)*

```
        //
        // label5
        //
        this.label5.Location = new System.Drawing.Point(8, 144);
        this.label5.Text = "label5";
        //
        // label6
        //
        this.label6.Location = new System.Drawing.Point(8, 176);
        this.label6.Text = "label6";
        //
        // label7
        //
        this.label7.Location = new System.Drawing.Point(8, 208);
        this.label7.Text = "label7";
        //
        // label8
        //
        this.label8.Location = new System.Drawing.Point(8, 240);
        this.label8.Text = "label8";
        //
        // Form1
        //
        this.ClientSize = new System.Drawing.Size(240, 270);
        this.Controls.Add(this.panel1);
        this.Controls.Add(this.vScrollBar1);
        this.Menu = this.mainMenu1;
        this.MinimizeBox = false;
        this.Text = "Form1";
        this.Load += new System.EventHandler(this.Form1_Load);

    }
    #endregion

    /// <summary>
    /// The main entry point for the application.
    /// </summary>
    static void Main()
    {
        Application.Run(new Form1());
    }

    private void Form1_Load(object sender, System.EventArgs e)
    {
        vScrollBar1.Minimum = 0;
```

(continued)

PanelSample.cs *(continued)*

```
            // Set the scrollbar maximum to the overlap size.
            vScrollBar1.Maximum = panel2.Height - panel1.Height;
            this.vScrollBar1.LargeChange = this.vScrollBar1.Maximum / 5;
            this.vScrollBar1.SmallChange = this.vScrollBar1.Maximum / 10;
            // Adjust the Maximum value to make the raw Maximum value
            // attainable by user interaction.
            this.vScrollBar1.Maximum += this.vScrollBar1.LargeChange;
        }

        private void vScrollBar1_ValueChanged(
            object sender, System.EventArgs e)
        {
            // Reposition the interior Panel depending on scrollbar value.
            panel2.Top = -1 * vScrollBar1.Value;
        }
    }
}
```

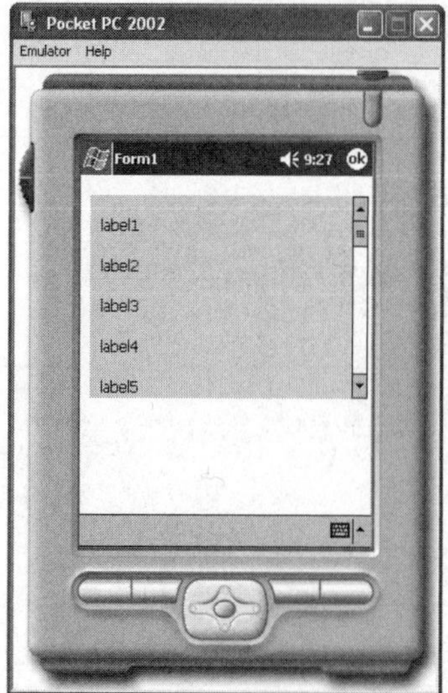

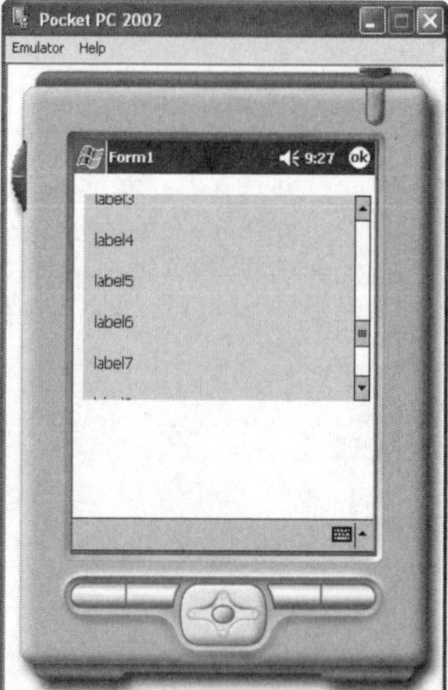

Figure 3-11 A scrollable panel built using a VScrollBar control and one Panel control contained within another.

The PictureBox Control

You use the PictureBox control to display an image. You load an image into the PictureBox control using the control's *Image* property. Two of the most commonly used techniques for including images in an application are:

- Load an image from disk, for example:

```
Bitmap imageFromFile = new Bitmap(@"\Program Files\graphic1.bmp");
pictureBox1.Image = imageFromFile;
```

> **Tip** An easy way to deploy an image file along with your application is to add the file to your Visual Studio project and set its Build Action property to Content. When your application is deployed during debugging or if you build a CAB file for later deployment, the graphic file is included with it.

- Include the image file as an embedded resource inside the assembly. To do this, add the graphic file to your project and set the Build Action property to Embedded Resource in the Properties window. At run time, load the file using the following code:

```
Bitmap bmp = new Bitmap(Assembly.GetExecutingAssembly()
    .GetManifestResourceStream(
        "namespace.filename.jpg")); // or .bmp, .png, etc
```

The PictureBox control in the full .NET Framework is capable of resizing images (*PictureBox.SizeMode = PictureBoxSizeMode.StretchImage*), resizing the control to match the image size, positioning images at the upper left in the control, or centering images. None of these options are available in the .NET Compact Framework. If you need to resize your image, you must use methods of the graphics classes in the *System.Drawing* namespace to resize the image before adding it to the PictureBox control. Images are always positioned at the upper left of the control.

The PictureBox control in the .NET Compact Framework does not support the *Click* event. You can derive a custom control that has this functionality by creating a control that derives from *System.Windows.Forms.Control*, overriding the *OnPaint* method, and using the *DrawImage* to draw your picture.

The PictureBoxSample project, available with this book's sample files, illustrates these techniques.

The ProgressBar Control

The ProgressBar control allows you to give a visual cue to a user regarding how close a long-running procedure is to completion. Visual cues such as these are essential to reassure users that something is still happening while background processing is going on so that they don't mistake a lengthy period of inactivity on the screen for a program crash! As shown in Figure 3-12, the bar moves from left to right under the control of your program. The *Minimum* and *Maximum* properties define the minimum and maximum values of the progress bar, and the *Value* property indicates how much of the progress bar is filled in. When the *Value* property equals the *Maximum* property, the progress bar control is completely filled. Note that if you set the *Value* property in code multiple times within the same method (for example, while looping through a lengthy series of operations), the progress bar repaints immediately each time you set it, so you do not need to call the *Application.DoEvents* method after setting *Value* in order for the display to update.

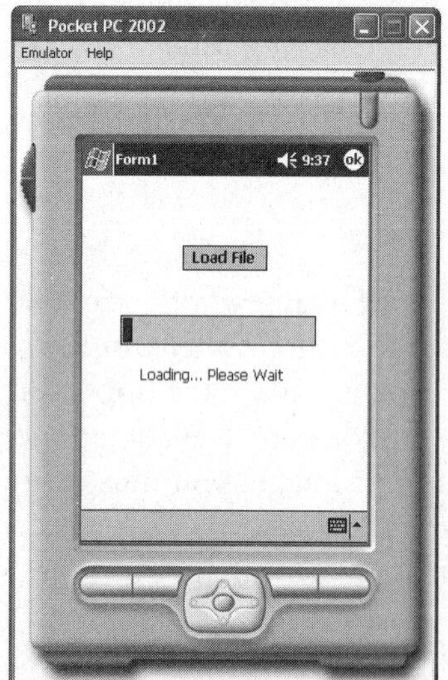

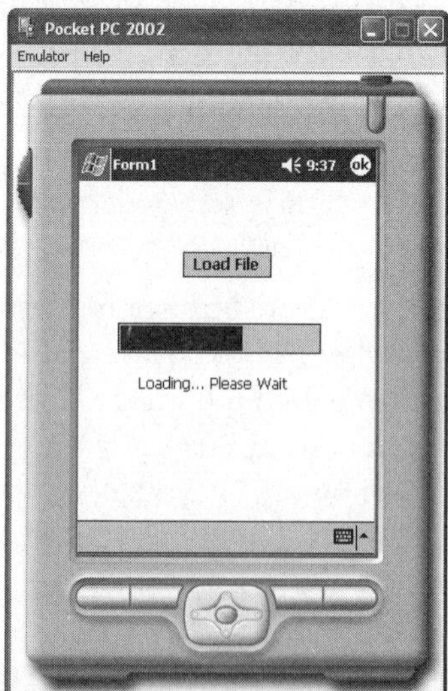

Figure 3-12 ProgressBar control updating to show how much progress the program has made through a lengthy procedure.

The following code is taken from the ProgressBarSample application in this book's sample files. The program uses an *XmlTextReader* object to read in a large file, and it updates the progress bar after every 100 reads from the file.

The form contains a ProgressBar control, a Label control used to report what is happening, and a Button control that the user can click to start the file loading.

ProgressBarSample.cs

```
using System;
using System.Drawing;
using System.Collections;
using System.IO;
using System.Windows.Forms;
using System.Xml;

namespace NETCFDevelopersReference
{
    /// <summary>
    /// Summary description for Form1.
    /// </summary>
    public class Form1 : System.Windows.Forms.Form
    {
        private System.Windows.Forms.Button button1;
        private System.Windows.Forms.ProgressBar progressBar1;
        private System.Windows.Forms.Label label1;

        public Form1()
        {
            InitializeComponent();
        }

        protected override void Dispose( bool disposing )
        {
            base.Dispose( disposing );
        }

        #region Windows Form Designer generated code
        /// <summary>
        /// Required method for Designer support - do not modify
        /// the contents of this method with the code editor.
        /// </summary>
        private void InitializeComponent()
        {
            this.button1 = new System.Windows.Forms.Button();
            this.progressBar1 = new System.Windows.Forms.ProgressBar();
            this.label1 = new System.Windows.Forms.Label();
            //
            // button1
            //
            this.button1.Location = new System.Drawing.Point(84, 56);
            this.button1.Text = "Load File";
```

(continued)

ProgressBarSample.cs *(continued)*

```
            this.button1.Click += new System.EventHandler(this.button1_Click)
;
            //
            // progressBar1
            //
            this.progressBar1.Location = new System.Drawing.Point(32, 112);
            this.progressBar1.Size = new System.Drawing.Size(164, 24);
            //
            // label1
            //
            this.label1.Location = new System.Drawing.Point(48, 152);
            this.label1.Size = new System.Drawing.Size(136, 20);
            this.label1.Text = "label1";
            //
            // Form1
            //
            this.ClientSize = new System.Drawing.Size(240, 270);
            this.Controls.Add(this.label1);
            this.Controls.Add(this.progressBar1);
            this.Controls.Add(this.button1);
            this.MinimizeBox = false;
            this.Text = "Form1";
            this.Load += new System.EventHandler(this.Form1_Load);

        }
        #endregion

        static void Main()
        {
            Application.Run(new Form1());
        }

        private void Form1_Load(object sender, System.EventArgs e)
        {
            label1.Text = "File not loaded";
        }

        private void button1_Click(object sender, System.EventArgs e)
        {
            label1.Text = "Loading... Please Wait";
            // Force form to display label text change
            Application.DoEvents();

            // Assume this file is about 25000 nodes
```

(continued)

ProgressBarSample.cs *(continued)*

```
            progressBar1.Minimum = 250;
            progressBar1.Maximum = 25000;
            progressBar1.Value = progressBar1.Minimum;

            // Get path to XML file - in same directory as this program
            string path = System.Reflection.Assembly.
                GetExecutingAssembly().GetName().CodeBase;
            string xmlFileUrl = new FileInfo(path).DirectoryName
                + @"\progressbarsample.xml";
            XmlTextReader xmlrdr = new XmlTextReader(xmlFileUrl);
            int readcount = 0;
            while (xmlrdr.Read())
            {
                // Do something ...

                // Update progressbar every 100 reads.
                if ((++readcount % 100) == 0)
                {
                    if (progressBar1.Value < progressBar1.Maximum)
                        progressBar1.Value += progressBar1.Minimum;
                }
            }
            // Complete
            progressBar1.Value = progressBar1.Maximum;
            label1.Text = "Complete!";
        }
    }
}
```

The RadioButton Control

RadioButton controls are used to offer mutually exclusive options to users. If you place two or more RadioButton controls on a form, they are automatically mutually exclusive with respect to each other. However, if you want two or more separate groups of mutually exclusive RadioButton controls on the same form, place a Panel control onto the form and drag the RadioButton controls onto the Panel. RadioButton controls housed on one panel will operate as a separate group, independent of RadioButton controls placed on another panel.

The *Checked* property defines whether a RadioButton control is selected. When the user clicks any RadioButton control, any other RadioButton controls that are part of the same group will be automatically deselected. (The value of the *Checked* property will be set to *false*.) The *CheckedChanged* event fires when the *Checked* property of a RadioButton control changes.

Figure 3-13 shows RadioButton controls in use. You'll find the code for this application in this book's PictureBoxSample sample project.

Figure 3-13 RadioButton controls to select between loading an image from a disk file or from the embedded resource in the assembly.

> **Note** The RadioButton control in the full .NET Framework allows you to display an image directly or to link the control to an ImageList control. This functionality is not supported in the .NET Compact Framework. The *Appearance* property, which allows you to choose how the radio button is rendered, is also unavailable. Only the traditional presentation style is supported on mobile devices.

The StatusBar Control

The status bar is an area that displays at the bottom of a form, usually used to display status information. The StatusBar control allows you to manipulate the status bar from application code. The StatusBar control in the .NET Compact Framework is quite limited in its functionality compared to the version in the full .NET Framework. The version in the .NET Compact Framework does not support multiple panels or the *Click* event, and you can use it only to display a text message. The StatusBar control is a useful alternative to a ProgressBar control for displaying information messages during a long-running procedure. For an example of the appearance of the StatusBar, see Figure 3-15 in the following section.

The TabControl Control

The TabControl control displays multiple overlaid views, rather like file dividers in a ring binder or tab dividers in the drawer of a filing cabinet. It is a very useful control on handheld devices because it makes efficient use of the screen display area. Users can click on a tab to bring it to the front, and you can do the same thing in code.

When you drag a tab control onto a form, initially it has no tabs. You can add or remove tabs in code, or use one of the following three ways in the Forms Designer:

- Right-click the tab control, and choose Add Tab or Remove Tab from the context menu, as shown in Figure 3-14.
- Click the ellipsis button (…) shown in the *TabPages* property in the Properties window to display the TabPage Collection Editor.
- Click the Add Tab or Remove Tab link displayed below the Properties window when the tab control is selected.

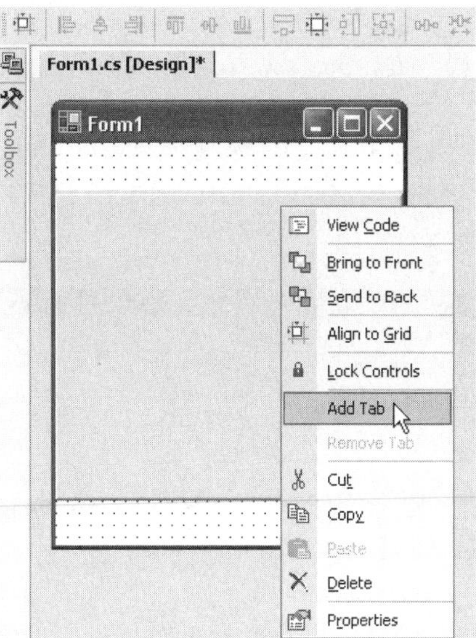

Figure 3-14 Adding tabs using the Forms Designer in Visual Studio .NET.

The *TabControl* object can't be linked to an *ImageList* object as it can in the full .NET Framework.

At design time, you can click on any tab to select it, and the Forms Designer brings that tab to the front. You can drag other controls onto the tab control just as you would with a form or a panel. Note that the tabs display along the top of the tab control at design time, which is how the control renders at run time on a Windows CE .NET device. However, on a Pocket PC, the tabs render along the bottom of the control at run time to suit Pocket PC design standards.

The Forms Designer allows you to set the location of a tab control to somewhere other than (0, 0). You can also set the location of the control arbitrarily in code. However, in a Pocket PC device, at run time, a tab control is always relocated to (0, 0), that is, the upper-left corner of the containing control. The containing control is usually a form, so if you do not want the tab control to be positioned at the upper left of your form, first drag a Panel control onto the form to the required position and then drag the tab control onto the panel.

The *SelectedIndexChanged* event fires when the user clicks a tab in the tab control or when you change the displayed tab in code by setting the *SelectedIndex* property. The *Click* event fires when the user clicks the background of a tab in the tab control.

The following listing is from the TabControlSample project, available with this book's sample files. It loads details of films playing at a cinema from an XML file. (In a real application, this data would come from an XML Web service.) This data is used to populate a ListView control on the first tab page.

While the data loads, a StatusBar control on the main form informs the user what is happening. After the data has loaded, the StatusBar is made invisible. When the user clicks on a film in the list, the second tab page appears, to show more details of the film. An example of the output for this sample is shown in Figure 3-15.

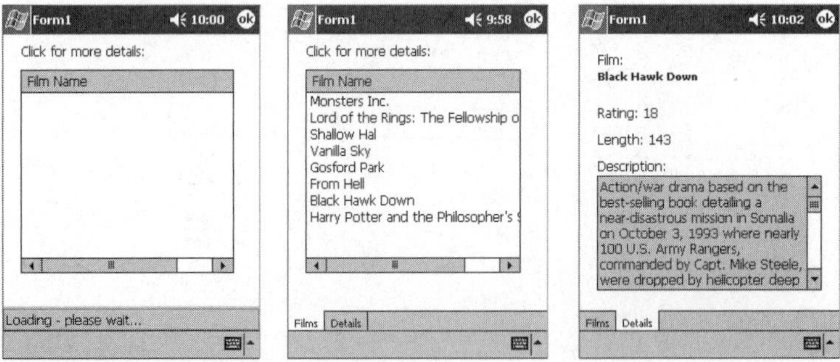

Figure 3-15 TabControl sample showing a list of films on the first tab and details on the second.

TabControlSample.cs

```
using System;
using System.Drawing;
using System.Collections;
using System.Windows.Forms;
using System.Data;

namespace TabControlSample
{
    /// <summary>
    /// Summary description for Form1.
    /// </summary>
    public class Form1 : System.Windows.Forms.Form
    {
        private System.Windows.Forms.TabControl tabControl1;
        private System.Windows.Forms.TabPage tabPage1;
        private System.Windows.Forms.TabPage tabPage2;
        private System.Windows.Forms.Label label1;
        private System.Windows.Forms.ListView listView1;
        private System.Windows.Forms.ColumnHeader columnHeader1;
        private System.Windows.Forms.Label label2;
        private System.Windows.Forms.Label label3;
        private System.Windows.Forms.Label label4;
        private System.Windows.Forms.Label label5;
        private System.Windows.Forms.Label label6;
        private System.Windows.Forms.TextBox textBox1;
        private System.Windows.Forms.StatusBar statusBar1;
        private System.Windows.Forms.MainMenu mainMenu1;

        public Form1()
        {
            InitializeComponent();
        }

        protected override void Dispose( bool disposing )
        {
            base.Dispose( disposing );
        }

        #region Windows Form Designer generated code
        /// <summary>
        /// Required method for Designer support - do not modify
        /// the contents of this method with the code editor.
        /// </summary>
        private void InitializeComponent()
```

(continued)

TabControlSample.cs *(continued)*

```
        {
            this.statusBar1 = new System.Windows.Forms.StatusBar();
            this.tabControl1 = new System.Windows.Forms.TabControl();
            this.tabPage1 = new System.Windows.Forms.TabPage();
            this.listView1 = new System.Windows.Forms.ListView();
            this.label1 = new System.Windows.Forms.Label();
            this.tabPage2 = new System.Windows.Forms.TabPage();
            this.textBox1 = new System.Windows.Forms.TextBox();
            this.label6 = new System.Windows.Forms.Label();
            this.label5 = new System.Windows.Forms.Label();
            this.label4 = new System.Windows.Forms.Label();
            this.label3 = new System.Windows.Forms.Label();
            this.label2 = new System.Windows.Forms.Label();
            this.columnHeader1 = new System.Windows.Forms.ColumnHeader();
            //
            // statusBar1
            //
            this.statusBar1.Location = new System.Drawing.Point(0, 248);
            this.statusBar1.Size = new System.Drawing.Size(240, 22);
            this.statusBar1.Text = "Loading - please wait...";
            //
            // tabControl1
            //
            this.tabControl1.Controls.Add(this.tabPage1);
            this.tabControl1.Controls.Add(this.tabPage2);
            this.tabControl1.SelectedIndex = 0;
            this.tabControl1.Size = new System.Drawing.Size(280, 272);
            //
            // tabPage1
            //
            this.tabPage1.Controls.Add(this.listView1);
            this.tabPage1.Controls.Add(this.label1);
            this.tabPage1.Location = new System.Drawing.Point(4, 22);
            this.tabPage1.Size = new System.Drawing.Size(272, 246);
            this.tabPage1.Text = "Films";
            //
            // listView1
            //
            this.listView1.Columns.Add(this.columnHeader1);
            this.listView1.FullRowSelect = true;
            this.listView1.Location = new System.Drawing.Point(16, 32);
            this.listView1.Size = new System.Drawing.Size(200, 184);
            this.listView1.View = System.Windows.Forms.View.Details;
            this.listView1.SelectedIndexChanged +=
```

(continued)

TabControlSample.cs *(continued)*

```
        new System.EventHandler(this.listView1_SelectedIndexChanged);
        //
        // label1
        //
        this.label1.Location = new System.Drawing.Point(16, 8);
        this.label1.Size = new System.Drawing.Size(128, 20);
        this.label1.Text = "Click for more details:";
        //
        // tabPage2
        //
        this.tabPage2.Controls.Add(this.textBox1);
        this.tabPage2.Controls.Add(this.label6);
        this.tabPage2.Controls.Add(this.label5);
        this.tabPage2.Controls.Add(this.label4);
        this.tabPage2.Controls.Add(this.label3);
        this.tabPage2.Controls.Add(this.label2);
        this.tabPage2.Location = new System.Drawing.Point(4, 22);
        this.tabPage2.Size = new System.Drawing.Size(272, 246);
        this.tabPage2.Text = "Details";
        this.tabPage2.Visible = false;
        //
        // textBox1
        //
        this.textBox1.Location = new System.Drawing.Point(16, 128);
        this.textBox1.Multiline = true;
        this.textBox1.ReadOnly = true;
        this.textBox1.ScrollBars =
            System.Windows.Forms.ScrollBars.Vertical;
        this.textBox1.Size = new System.Drawing.Size(208, 104);
        this.textBox1.Text = "textBox1";
        //
        // label6
        //
        this.label6.Location = new System.Drawing.Point(16, 112);
        this.label6.Text = "Description:";
        //
        // label5
        //
        this.label5.Location = new System.Drawing.Point(16, 88);
        this.label5.Size = new System.Drawing.Size(200, 16);
        this.label5.Text = "label5";
        //
        // label4
```

(continued)

TabControlSample.cs *(continued)*

```
        //
        this.label4.Location = new System.Drawing.Point(16, 64);
        this.label4.Size = new System.Drawing.Size(200, 16);
        this.label4.Text = "label4";
        //
        // label3
        //
        this.label3.Location = new System.Drawing.Point(16, 32);
        this.label3.Size = new System.Drawing.Size(200, 32);
        this.label3.Text = "label3";
        //
        // label2
        //
        this.label2.Location = new System.Drawing.Point(16, 16);
        this.label2.Text = "Film:";
        //
        // columnHeader1
        //
        this.columnHeader1.Text = "Film Name";
        this.columnHeader1.Width = 250;
        //
        // Form1
        //
        this.ClientSize = new System.Drawing.Size(240, 270);
        this.Controls.Add(this.statusBar1);
        this.Controls.Add(this.tabControl1);
        this.MinimizeBox = false;
        this.Text = "Form1";
        this.Load += new System.EventHandler(this.Form1_Load);

    }
    #endregion

    static void Main()
    {
        Application.Run(new Form1());
    }

    private DataSet ds;

    private void Form1_Load(object sender, System.EventArgs e)
    {
        statusBar1.Visible = true;
        Application.DoEvents();
```

(continued)

TabControlSample.cs *(continued)*

```
            ds = new DataSet();
            //Load from XML file
            string path = System.Reflection.Assembly.
                GetExecutingAssembly().GetName().CodeBase;
            string Xmlfname = new System.IO.FileInfo(path).DirectoryName
                + @"\TabControlFilmData.xml";
            ds.ReadXml(Xmlfname);

            //Load the listview
            int filmscount = ds.Tables[0].Rows.Count;
            foreach(DataRow row in ds.Tables["Films"].Rows)
            {
                this.listView1.Items.Add(
                    new ListViewItem(row[1].ToString()));
            }

            statusBar1.Visible = false;
        }

        private void listView1_SelectedIndexChanged(
            object sender, System.EventArgs e)
        {
            if (listView1.SelectedIndices.Count > 0)
            {
                int selectedIndex = listView1.SelectedIndices[0];
                label3.Text =
                    ds.Tables[0].Rows[selectedIndex][1].ToString();
                label4.Text = "Rating: "
                    + ds.Tables[0].Rows[selectedIndex][2].ToString();
                label5.Text = "Length: "
                    + ds.Tables[0].Rows[selectedIndex][3].ToString();
                textBox1.Text =
                    ds.Tables[0].Rows[selectedIndex][5].ToString();
                //Switch to Details tab
                tabControl1.SelectedIndex = 1;
                tabPage2.Visible = true;
            }
        }
    }
}
```

The TextBox Control

You use the TextBox control to accept user input. It is one of the few controls in the .NET Compact Framework that supports the *BackColor* and *ForeColor* properties. It also receives *KeyPress*, *KeyUp*, and *KeyDown* events. However, it does not support the *Click* event.

The *PasswordChar* property behaves differently in the .NET Compact Framework than in the full .NET Framework. Regardless of the character you enter for this property at design time, asterisks will appear to mask the user input at run time.

The TextBox control in the .NET Compact Framework does not support the *CharacterCasing* property, which in the full .NET Framework allows you to automatically convert all the text (both existing and entered) into either uppercase or lowercase characters. A workaround for this is to subclass the TextBox control and override the *OnKeyPress* event, as shown in the following code:

```
public class myTextBox : TextBox
{
protected override void OnKeyPress(KeyPressEventArgs e)
    {
        if(Char.IsLetter(e.KeyChar))
        {
            // Save the current caret position
            int pos = this.SelectionStart;

            // Insert the upper case character
            this.Text = this.Text.Insert(
                this.SelectionStart, Char.ToUpper(e.KeyChar).ToString());

            // Setting the Text of the text box resets the selection
            // so we need to manually set the new caret position
            this.SelectionStart = pos + 1;
            e.Handled = true;
        }
    }
}
```

The Timer Control

The Timer control is optimized for use in Windows Forms applications and allows you to execute event handler code repeatedly at a user-defined interval for as long as the Timer control is enabled. There are alternative timers in the *System.Threading* namespace that you should use outside of a window. Use the Timer control where processing occurs in a single thread.

When you drag a Timer control from the toolbox onto a form, it is not displayed on the form but appears in the component area underneath, alongside any menu controls. At run time, you start the timer by setting the *Enabled* property to *true* (in code), and you stop it by setting the *Enabled* property to *false*. The *Interval* property determines the length of time in milliseconds between

Tick events. The Timer control raises the *Tick* event every *Interval* milliseconds as long as it is enabled.

In the following example, the application assembly includes an image as an embedded resource. This image is displayed as a splash screen logo when the application starts running. The Timer is enabled in the *Form_Load* method, and the timer interval is set to 100 ms. Every time the *timer1_Tick* event handler executes, it executes *Graphics.DrawImage()* to write the graphic to the form. Each time the *Tick* event is raised, the *timer1_Tick* method resizes the graphic so that the user sees a simple animation effect, as illustrated in Figure 3-16.

Figure 3-16 Timer used to redraw a graphic so that it appears larger each time.

TimerSample.cs

```
using System;
using System.Drawing;
using System.Collections;
using System.Reflection;
using System.Windows.Forms;

namespace NETCFDevelopersReference
{
    public class Form1 : System.Windows.Forms.Form
    {
        private System.Windows.Forms.Timer timer1;

        private struct ImageSize
        {
            public int Width;
            public int Height;
            public int incWidth;
```

(continued)

TimerSample.cs *(continued)*

```
        public int incHeight;
    }
    public Form1()
    {
        InitializeComponent();
    }
    protected override void Dispose( bool disposing )
    {
        base.Dispose( disposing );
    }
    #region Windows Form Designer generated code
    /// <summary>
    /// Required method for Designer support - do not modify
    /// the contents of this method with the code editor.
    /// </summary>
    private void InitializeComponent()
    {
        this.timer1 = new System.Windows.Forms.Timer();
        //
        // timer1
        //
        this.timer1.Tick += new System.EventHandler(this.timer1_Tick);
        //
        // Form1
        //
        this.ClientSize = new System.Drawing.Size(240, 270);
        this.MinimizeBox = false;
        this.Text = "Form1";
        this.Load += new System.EventHandler(this.Form1_Load);

    }
    #endregion

    private Bitmap logo;
    private ImageSize imageSize ;

    static void Main()
    {
        Application.Run(new Form1());
    }

    private void Form1_Load(object sender, System.EventArgs e)
```

(continued)

TimerSample.cs *(continued)*

```
        {
            imageSize = new ImageSize();
            imageSize.Width = 0;
            imageSize.Height = 0;
            logo = new Bitmap(Assembly.GetExecutingAssembly()

                .GetManifestResourceStream(
                    "NETCFDevelopersReference.logo.bmp"));
            imageSize.incHeight = logo.Height/ 10;
            imageSize.incWidth = logo.Width / 10;

            timer1.Interval = 100; // Interval in milliseconds
            timer1.Enabled = true;
        }

        private void timer1_Tick(object sender, System.EventArgs e)
        {
            if (imageSize.Width <= logo.Width)
            {
                Graphics g = this.CreateGraphics();
                // Increase size of graphic each time
                imageSize.Width += imageSize.incWidth;
                imageSize.Height += imageSize.incHeight;
                // Destination Rectangle - new dimensions and centered:
                int left = (this.Width - imageSize.Width) / 2;
                int top = (this.Height - imageSize.Height) / 2;
                Rectangle destRect = new Rectangle(
                    left, top, imageSize.Width, imageSize.Height);
                // Draw it
                g.DrawImage(logo, destRect,
                    new Rectangle(0, 0, logo.Width, logo.Height),
                    GraphicsUnit.Pixel);
            }
            else
                timer1.Enabled = false;
        }
    }
}
```

The ToolBar Control

A toolbar contains buttons that are, by convention, shortcuts to commonly used menu items. For the user, clicking a toolbar button is often quicker than navigating to the appropriate menu item. The ToolBar control provides a mechanism for implementing a toolbar in a .NET Compact Framework application.

A toolbar consists of one or more graphical buttons. You cannot put text on these buttons, so you must use the ToolBar control with an ImageList control to supply the graphics. In Pocket PC devices, ToolBar buttons appear along the bottom line of the screen to the right of any menu options you define for your application in a MainMenu control. In Windows CE devices, ToolBar buttons appear along the top of the form and, as in Pocket PC devices, to the right of any menu options.

To use the ToolBar control, first drag an ImageList control onto your form. Then click the ellipsis button against the *Images* property, and use the Image Collection Editor to add images to the ImageList control. These images automatically resize to the appropriate size for a toolbar button (16 x 16 pixels), and they get loaded into the resource file for the form, so you do not need to deploy the images separately to the target system. Then, drag a ToolBar control from the toolbox onto your form and set the *ImageList* property to the name of the ImageList control. Click the ellipsis against the Buttons property to open the ToolBarButton Collection Editor, and add the required buttons to the ToolBar control. You can choose from the following four types of buttons, determined by the *Style* property:

- **PushButton** A simple single push button. If you set the *Pushed* property to *true*, the button has the appearance of being pushed in all the time, but it works just the same as when *Pushed* is *false*.
- **ToggleButton** A push-in, push-out button. The *Pushed* property sets or gets a value indicating whether the button is currently in or out.
- **Separator** Inserts a small area of blank space between buttons. You can also display a graphic in place of the default blank space.
- **DropDownButton** Appears on the toolbar with a small arrow to indicate that pressing the button reveals more options. You must set the *DropDownMenu* property of this type of button to reference a ContextMenu control.

You must set the *ImageIndex* property of each button to the index of a graphic in the associated ImageList control, unless the button is a separator and you want to display blank space rather than a graphic. Figure 3-17 shows a simple application that demonstrates how each button style appears; this sample also has a regular main menu to the left of the toolbar.

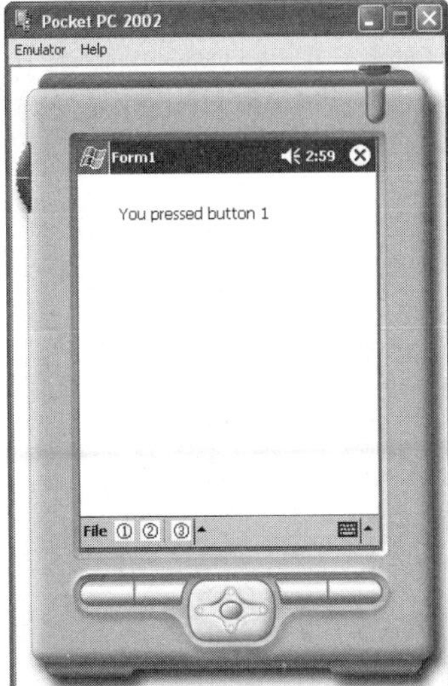

Figure 3-17 Toolbar buttons using the PushButton, ToggleButton, Separator, and DropDownButton styles.

To detect when a user presses the image, trap the *ButtonClick* event of the toolbar. The event handler receives a *ToolBarButtonClickEventArgs* object, which identifies which button was pressed, as shown in this example:

```
private void toolBar1_ButtonClick(object sender,
    System.Windows.Forms.ToolBarButtonClickEventArgs e)
{
    if (e.Button.Equals(this.toolBarButton1))
    {
        label1.Text = "You pressed button 1";
    }
    else if (e.Button.Equals(this.toolBarButton2))
    {
        label1.Text = "Button 2 is clicked " +
            (e.Button.Pushed ? "in" : "out");
    }
}
```

The TrackBar Control

The TrackBar control appears as a slider, which the user can move in order to select a value. A typical application is to select a user-configurable setting, for example, a refresh rate or timeout value. In Figure 3-18, which shows the appearance of a TrackBar control, the numbers underneath the TrackBar control are in a separate Label control, and the background is gray thanks to the enclosing Panel control.

Figure 3-18 A TrackBar control in use.

You can set the *Minimum* and *Maximum* properties to define the extents of the TrackBar control, and you set the *TickFrequency* property to the required value between tick marks along the slider. The *SmallChange* property defines the increment to use when the user presses one of the arrow keys. (Arrow keys are the navigation pad on a Pocket PC.) The *LargeChange* property defines the increment when the user presses the Page Up or Page Down keys, or when the user clicks the TrackBar control on either side of the slider.

The TreeView Control

The TreeView control presents a hierarchical view of a collection of objects. The TreeView control has the *Nodes* property, which is a collection of *TreeNode* objects. You add one or more nodes to this collection, and these nodes are the root nodes of the tree. You set the *Text* property of each *TreeNode* object to determine the text that displays at that node. Each *TreeNode* object has a *Nodes* property as well. You can add further *TreeNode* objects to each root node, and you can add child *TreeNode* objects to each of those, and so on.

The *TreeView* class gives you a lot of control over the presentation of the tree. The following properties of the *TreeView* class dictate how the tree displays:

- The *ShowRootLines* property gets or sets a value indicating whether lines are drawn between the tree nodes that are at the root of the tree.
- The *ShowLines* property gets or sets a value indicating whether lines are drawn between each node.
- The *ShowPlusMinus* property gets or sets a value indicating whether + and - buttons are drawn next to nodes that have child nodes, allowing the user to expand and contract the view of child nodes.
- The *ImageList* property gets or sets an ImageList control on your form that supplies icons for the nodes to display. The *ImageIndex* property is the index of the icon in the ImageList control that displays next to all nodes by default. You can override the default icon displayed for a particular *TreeNode* object by setting the *ImageIndex* property the *TreeNode* object.
- The *SelectedNodeIndex* property gets or sets the index of an icon in the ImageList control that displays next to a node the user has selected, which the user does simply by clicking the node. The user can select only a single node at any one time. When the user selects a node, the *AfterSelect* event fires.
- The *CheckBoxes* property causes a check box to be displayed next to each node. The *Checked* property of the *TreeNode* object sets or gets whether a particular node is checked. When the user checks a node, the TreeView control fires the *AfterCheck* event.

Figure 3-19 shows an example Grocery Order application that displays three different categories of grocery product and a number of products within each category. The user can check a product to order it. The TreeView control automatically displays scroll bars if the size of the tree exceeds the display area.

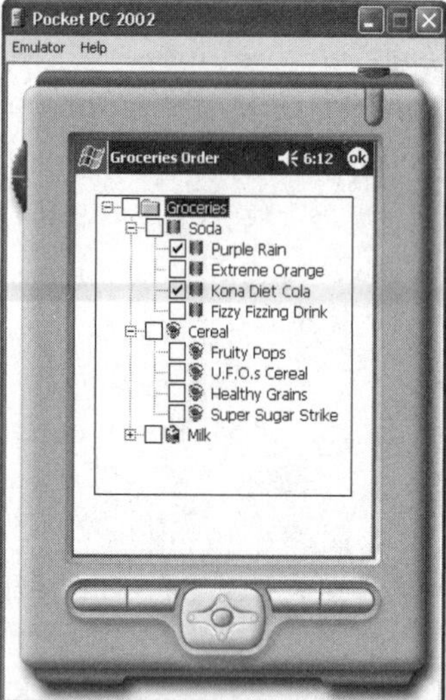

Figure 3-19 TreeView control displaying lines, check boxes, plus and minus buttons, and icons from an *ImageList* object.

The data for this example loads from an XML file for simplicity, but it could easily come from an XML Web service. The root node Groceries was created with Forms Designer, but in *Form1_Load*, we load the dataset from the file and then walk the Categories table to create the next level of nodes. Then the code walks the Products table and adds product nodes below the appropriate category node. As an optimization, the category nodes are saved in a *ListDictionary* collection, keyed on the *ProductID*, which makes identifying the correct parent node more efficient.

TreeViewSample

```
using System;
using System.Drawing;
using System.Collections;
using System.Collections.Specialized;
using System.IO;
using System.Reflection;
using System.Windows.Forms;
using System.Data;

namespace NETCFDevelopersReference
{
    public class Form1 : System.Windows.Forms.Form
```

(continued)

TreeViewSample *(continued)*

```
{
    private System.Windows.Forms.ImageList imageList1;
    private System.Windows.Forms.TreeView treeView1;

    public Form1()
    {
        InitializeComponent();
    }

    protected override void Dispose( bool disposing )
    {
        base.Dispose( disposing );
    }
    #region Windows Form Designer generated code
    /// <summary>
    /// Required method for Designer support - do not modify
    /// the contents of this method with the code editor.
    /// </summary>
    private void InitializeComponent()
    {
        System.Windows.Forms.TreeNode treeNode1 =
            new System.Windows.Forms.TreeNode();
        System.Resources.ResourceManager resources =
            new System.Resources.ResourceManager(typeof(Form1));
        this.treeView1 = new System.Windows.Forms.TreeView();
        this.imageList1 = new System.Windows.Forms.ImageList();
        //
        // treeView1
        //
        this.treeView1.CheckBoxes = true;
        this.treeView1.ImageList = this.imageList1;
        this.treeView1.Location = new System.Drawing.Point(16, 16);
        treeNode1.Text = "Groceries";
        this.treeView1.Nodes.Add(treeNode1);
        this.treeView1.Size = new System.Drawing.Size(208, 232);
        //
        // imageList1
        //
        this.imageList1.Images.Add((
            (System.Drawing.Image)(resources.GetObject("resource"))));
        this.imageList1.Images.Add((
            (System.Drawing.Image)(resources.GetObject("resource1"))));
        this.imageList1.Images.Add((
            (System.Drawing.Image)(resources.GetObject("resource2"))));
        this.imageList1.Images.Add((
            (System.Drawing.Image)(resources.GetObject("resource3"))));
```

(continued)

TreeViewSample *(continued)*

```
        this.imageList1.ImageSize = new System.Drawing.Size(16, 16);
        //
        // Form1
        //
        this.Controls.Add(this.treeView1);
        this.MinimizeBox = false;
        this.Text = "Groceries Order";
        this.Load += new System.EventHandler(this.Form1_Load);

    }
    #endregion

    static void Main()
    {
        Application.Run(new Form1());
    }

    private void Form1_Load(object sender, System.EventArgs e)
    {
        // Load the Dataset from XML
        DataSet ds = new DataSet();
        string path = Assembly.GetExecutingAssembly()
            .GetName().CodeBase;
        ds.ReadXml(new FileInfo(path).DirectoryName
            + @"\GrocerToGo.xml");

        // Add Nodes to root for each Category in the Categories table
        ListDictionary categoryNodeLookup = new ListDictionary();
        foreach(DataRow row in ds.Tables["category"].Rows)
        {
            TreeNode tn = new TreeNode();
            tn.Text = (string)row[1]; // Category name
            // Image from Category ID
            int categoryID = Int32.Parse(row[0].ToString());
            tn.ImageIndex = categoryID;
            treeView1.Nodes[0].Nodes.Add(tn);

            // Save a dictionary lookup of category tree nodes
            categoryNodeLookup[row[0].ToString()] = tn;
        }

        // Add Products to each Category node
        foreach(DataRow row in ds.Tables["product"].Rows)
        {
```

(continued)

TreeViewSample *(continued)*

```
                TreeNode tn = new TreeNode();
                tn.Text = row[2].ToString(); // Product name

                // Search for correct node in next level up
                string categoryID = row[1].ToString();
                TreeNode parentNode =
                    (TreeNode)categoryNodeLookup[categoryID];
                parentNode.Nodes.Add(tn);
                // Give it same Image as its parent
                tn.ImageIndex = parentNode.ImageIndex;
            }

            treeView1.CheckBoxes = true;
            treeView1.ShowRootLines = true;
        }
    }
}
```

Summary

In this chapter, we looked into how Windows Forms operates in the .NET Compact Framework and highlighted some of the key differences from the full .NET Framework. We described all of the standard controls in the .NET Compact Framework and showed how to use them in an application. Third-party control vendors have many other controls available that you can purchase for use in your applications.

In the next chapter, we will look at some additional factors you must consider when designing a GUI application, such as how to ensure that your application runs correctly on a Pocket PC and conforms to the expected behavior on that platform. We will examine an example application, which uses many of the Windows Forms controls covered in this chapter. You should also visit Chapter 18 to discover how you can create custom Windows Forms controls that exhibit different characteristics and behavior than the standard controls described here.

4

Building Windows Forms Applications

Although we have seen that building a Windows form and its associated code for the .NET Compact Framework is very similar to the way it is done in the full .NET Framework, the design of the form is very different. This is especially true for Pocket PC applications. Whereas Windows CE is designed to emulate the look and feel of the Windows desktop, the Pocket PC operating platform is designed with a smaller form factor, a touch screen, and a stylus input.

This means that when you design an application that targets the Pocket PC platform or any Windows CE device with limited screen size, you should plan the number, size, and layout of the controls for each form.

An example application, DVD Catalog, will be used throughout this chapter to illustrate the points that are being made. The full DVD Catalog application is available with this book's sample files.

Working with Forms

The *Form* class you use in a Windows CE project and the one you use in a Pocket PC project are identical; they have the same properties, methods, and events. However, the values of some of the properties will depend on the physical device the application is targeting. The maximum height and width of the form will be determined by the physical size of the device the form will be used on. When certain properties of the form are set, the behavior of the form varies depending on whether the form is part of a Windows CE project or a Pocket PC project.

Setting Properties of the *Form* Class

The values that control the form's border style, as well as the ones that control the appearance of the form's control box and the form's minimize, maximize, and close buttons, differ between a Windows CE project and a Pocket PC project. This section discusses setting properties that relate to the form's appearance and how those settings affect the form depending on the target platform.

- **The *FormBorderStyle* property** controls the style of the border of the form. This property can be set at design time using the Microsoft Visual Studio Properties window or at run time using code. The settings that can be used for this property are the same in both Windows CE and Pocket PC projects, although the results are different in a Windows CE and a Pocket PC project. The default setting for a form is *FormBorderStyle.FixedSingle.*

  In a Pocket PC project, setting the property to *FormBorderStyle.None* creates a form with no border and no caption. The form can be moved and resized using code. Setting the property to any other value will cause the form to expand to fill the desktop area and will prevent the form from being moved or resized. The desktop area is the entire screen minus the Start menu bar and the main menu bar of the application, if present.

  In a Windows CE project, setting the property to *FormBorderStyle.None* or *FormBorderStyle.FixedDialog* creates a form with no border or caption. The form can be resized and moved using code but not by the user. All other settings create a form with a border and a caption that can be moved using code or by the user, but the form can be resized only using code.

- **The *WindowState* property** accepts two settings only: *FormWindowState.Normal* or *FormWindowState.Maximized.* No setting to minimize a window exists for this property.

  In a Pocket PC project, the form will fill the desktop area when its *WindowState* property is set to *FormWindowState.Normal.* Setting the property to *FormWindowState.Maximized* will make the form fill the entire screen, obscuring the Start menu bar while still displaying the form's main menu if one is present.

  In a Windows CE project, setting the WindowState property to *FormWindowState.Normal* will cause the form to display according to the *Size* property. Setting the form to *FormWindowState.Maximized* will cause the form to expand to fill the entire desktop area.

- **The *ControlBox* property** can be set to *true* to display the form's control box or *false* to prevent the form's control box from displaying. In a Pocket PC form, the control box contains only one button: a close button or a minimize button. The *MinimizeBox* property controls which button is displayed. In a Windows CE form, the control box always contains a close button, and the minimize and maximize buttons are displayed depending on the settings of the *MinimizeBox* and *MaximizeBox* properties of the form.

    - The *MinimizeBox* property controls the display of the minimize button. In a Pocket PC form, the *MinimizeBox* property can be set to *true* to display the minimize button, which looks like an X on the Pocket PC, or it can be set to *false* to display a close button, which looks like an OK button on the Pocket PC. In a Windows CE form, the *MinimizeBox* property can be set to *true* to display the minimize button or it can be set to *false* to hide the minimize button.

    - The *MaximizeBox* property controls the display of the maximize button. In a Pocket PC form, this property has no effect; forms have no maximize button on Pocket PC devices. In a Windows CE form, the *MaximizeBox* property can be set to *true* to display the maximize button or it can be set to *false* to hide the maximize button.

    - The *Size* property is used to set the form's width and height. In a Pocket PC form, this property is used only if the *FormBorderStyle* property is set to *FormBorderStyle.None*. In a Windows CE form, the *Size* property sets the height and width of the form just as it does in a full .NET Framework form.

    - The *Location* property specifies the placement of the form on the screen, using *x* and *y* coordinates relative to the upper left of the screen. In a Pocket PC form, the *Location* property has no effect unless the form's *FormBorderStyle* property is set to *FormBorderStyle.None*. In a Windows CE form, the *Location* property sets the position of the form on the screen just as it does in a full .NET Framework form.

Keeping to Form Display Guidelines

Pocket PC user interface guidelines recommend that all forms should always be the full size of the desktop area (the full screen, excluding the Start menu), but it's possible to create a form that's smaller than the desktop area. If you create a form that is smaller than the physical screen, the form should be centered vertically and horizontally on the screen, taking into account the Start menu, the main menu, and, if visible, the soft input panel (SIP). (See the section "Working with the Soft Input Control" later in this chapter.)

Creating Custom Dialog Boxes

Custom dialog boxes are dialog boxes that you create yourself, using forms, for your application. The *ShowDialog* method is used to display your dialog box form. This method disables the parent form while the dialog box is shown. The dialog box returns a result to the calling form, but the public members of the dialog box are also available to the parent form after the call to *ShowDialog* has returned. The following code shows an example of calling a full-screen dialog box and testing the returned value:

```
AddDVDForm addForm = new AddDVDForm();

if (addForm.ShowDialog() == DialogResult.OK)
{
    // Add DVD to summary Table
}
```

If you need to, you can use the *FormBorderStyle* and *Size* properties of the *Form* class to size a dialog box so that it's smaller than the screen size of the device. If you size a dialog box like that, you should also use the *Location* property to place your dialog box in the most convenient position on the screen. One possible use for a dialog box form that is smaller than the screen size is to present a Logon dialog box on top of the main form the first time the application is launched.

A common task for an application that uses sensitive data is to require the user to log on before the data is accessed. It's important to make sure that an application that contains sensitive data is secure. For more information about securing your application, see Chapter 12.

The problem with having a logon screen, rather than a logon dialog box, appear first in your application is that the logon screen will function as the main form of the application. This might not seem like a problem, until you close the form to free resources. Because the form is your application's main form, closing it will close your application. The solution is to have your main form call a logon form as a dialog box and continue or exit depending on the result of the dialog box.

The DVD Catalog example application uses a logon dialog box to protect the user's DVD data. The application has a form called *MainForm*, as shown in Figure 4-1, which lists the DVDs in the user's collection.

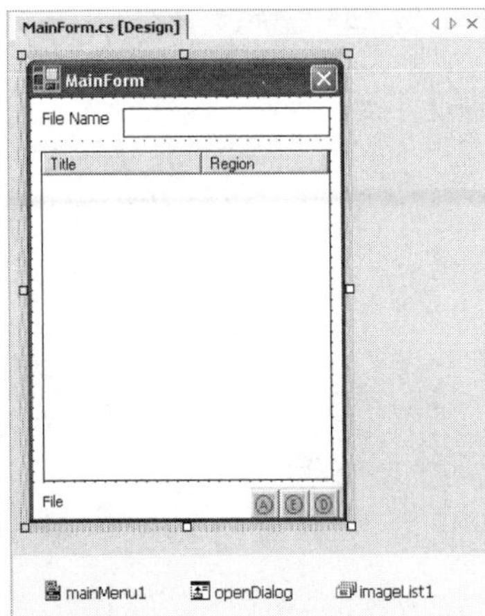

Figure 4-1 DVD Catalog application: *MainForm.*

The application uses another form, called *LogonForm*, to request the user's logon details. Figure 4-2 shows what *LogonForm* looks like.

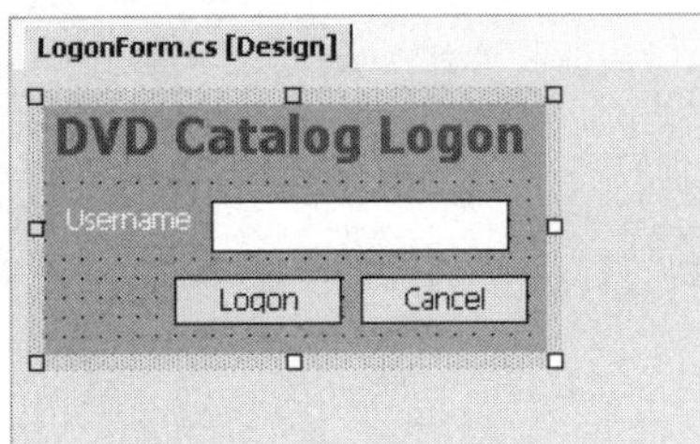

Figure 4-2 DVD Catalog application: *LogonForm.*

The following code is the *Load* event handler for *MainForm*. In this event handler, we need to create a new instance of the *LogonForm* object and call it as a dialog box. The logon form will return *DialogResult.Ok* or *DialogResult.Cancel*, depending on whether the user entered a valid user name or simply closed the logon form. If the user's details are valid, the main form will continue with its normal processing. If the user closes the logon form without entering a valid user name the main form will close the application.

> **Note** To have a dialog box's control available to the calling form, declare the control with the *public* access modifier.

```
private void MainForm_Load(object sender, System.EventArgs e)
{
    LogonForm LogonFrm = new LogonForm();

    if (LogonFrm.ShowDialog() == DialogResult.Cancel)
    {
        LogonFrm.Dispose();
        this.Close();
    }
    else
    {
        this.Text+= " - " + LogonFrm.Username.Text;
        LogonFrm.Dispose();
        OpenCatalogFile(DataFile);
    }
}
```

The *Click* event handler for the Logon button of *LogonForm*, shown in the following example code, checks the user's logon credentials, using the *CheckUser* routine defined elsewhere in the application. The event handler returns a dialog box result of *DialogResult.OK* if the user enters a valid user name.

```
private void LogonButton_Click(object sender, System.EventArgs e)
{
    if (CheckUser(Username.Text))
    {
        this.DialogResult = DialogResult.OK;
    }
    else
    {
        MessageBox.Show("Username not valid. Please Try Again",
            "Logon Error");
    }
}
```

If the user closes the form without entering a valid user name, the logon form's *CancelButton_Click* event handler returns *DialogResult.Cancel* to the main form, which will then close the application.

```
private void CancelButton_Click(object sender, System.EventArgs e)
{
    this.DialogResult = DialogResult.Cancel;
}
```

Using Built-In Dialog Boxes

The built-in dialog boxes are encapsulated in the *OpenFileDialog* and *SaveFileDialog* classes. These dialog boxes can be used for opening and saving files in the device's file system.

Both of these classes have a *Filter* property, which allows you to specify which file types will be displayed in the file list of the dialog box. Like custom dialog boxes, built-in dialog boxes return a *DialogResult* value to specify whether the results of the dialog box were successful.

The following code sample shows the use of the *OpenFileDialog* class, and Figure 4-3 shows the code running in a Pocket PC environment:

```
OpenFileDialog openDialog = new OpenFileDialog();
openDialog.Filter = "XML Files|*.xml";

if (openDialog.ShowDialog() == DialogResult.OK)
{
    OpenCatalogFile(openDialog.FileName);
}
```

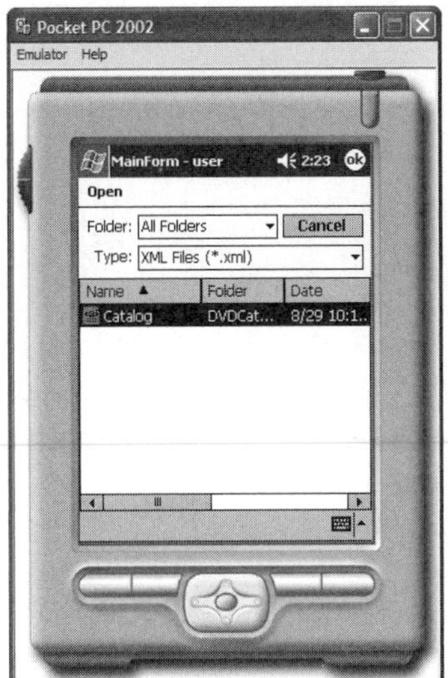

Figure 4-3 The *OpenFileDialog* class in action on a Pocket PC device.

The following code sample shows the use of the *SaveFileDialog* class, and Figure 4-4 shows the code running in a Pocket PC environment:

```
SaveFileDialog saveDialog = new SaveFileDialog();
saveDialog.Filter = "XML Files|*.xml";

if(saveDialog.ShowDialog() == DialogResult.OK)
{
    SaveCatalogFile(saveDialog.FileName);
}
```

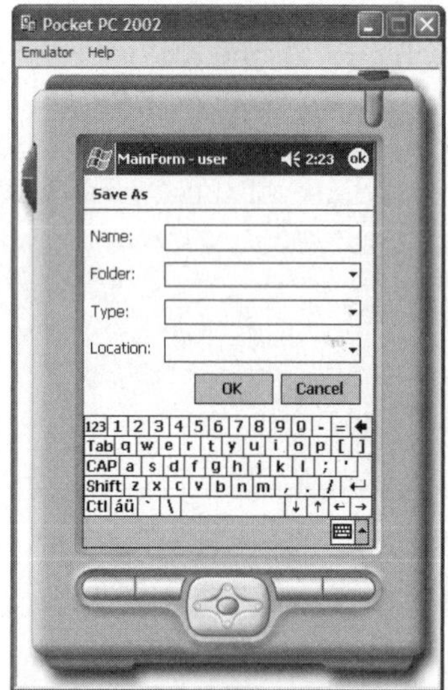

Figure 4-4 The *SaveFileDialog* class in action on a Pocket PC device.

Working with the InputPanel Control

The InputPanel control allows the user of a Pocket PC to enter textual information by using either an on-screen keyboard or a handwriting recognition panel. The InputPanel control appears at the bottom of a form whenever the form contains a MainMenu control or a ToolBar control.

When the InputPanel control is available for use by the user, it is important to design the form so that the InputPanel control obscures no important controls when it is raised. This is especially true for controls that require text input. The two techniques to use in designing your forms are to have all the text-input controls above the top of the raised InputPanel control and to move controls on the form to make room for the InputPanel control. Remember to include scroll bars on the form if you opt for the second technique. This will allow the user to keep the InputPanel control raised and still have complete access to all the controls on your form.

The code below demonstrates how to show the InputPanel control when a TextBox control receives the focus and hide the InputPanel control when the TextBox control loses the focus:

```
private void textBox1_GotFocus(object sender, System.EventArgs e)
{
    // When the user selects this field, automatically raise SIP
    inputPanel1.Enabled = true;
}

private void textBox1_LostFocus(object sender, System.EventArgs e)
{
    // Automatically lower SIP
    inputPanel1.Enabled = false;
}
```

As has already been stated, it is important to be mindful of the use of the InputPanel control by the user when designing your forms. Remember to place any text-input controls above where the InputPanel control will be displayed or to move controls up when the InputPanel control is displayed.

The *EnabledChanged* event is triggered when the InputPanel control is raised or lowered by the user or programmatically. Text-input controls that will be obscured when the InputPanel control is raised should be placed inside a Panel control. When the InputPanel is raised, you can reposition the Panel control at the top of the screen.

The following code shows the *EnabledChanged* event handler moving a Panel control above the InputPanel control when the InputPanel control is raised, and moving it to the back to its original position when the InputPanel control is lowered.

```
private void inputPanel1_EnabledChanged(object sender, System.EventArgs e)
{
    // Trap whenever the InputPanel is raised or lowered
    // whether by user action or programmatic control

    // The Bounds property returns the size and location of
    // Input Panel.
    // Set the top of the Panel that is inside the Form to
    // -1 * the height of the input panel to ensure SIP
    // never obscures controls
```

(continued)

```
    if (inputPanel1.Enabled == true)
        this.panel1.Top = 180 - inputPanel1.Bounds.Height;
    else
        this.panel1.Top = 180;

}
```

Figure 4-4 in the previous section shows the InputPanel control with the on-screen keyboard selected.

Using the MainMenu Control

The MainMenu control is added to the first form in a Pocket PC Windows application by default, but you will have to add it manually to any additional forms. Windows CE supports the MainMenu control but does not add it to any forms automatically. As mentioned, in a Pocket PC application, if you want the user to be able to choose to use the SIP or to choose which SIP to use, you will need to add a MainMenu or ToolBar control to the form.

To add menu items to the MainMenu control, click the menu bar and type in the menu items your application requires. Figure 4-5 shows the MainMenu control in Windows Forms Designer.

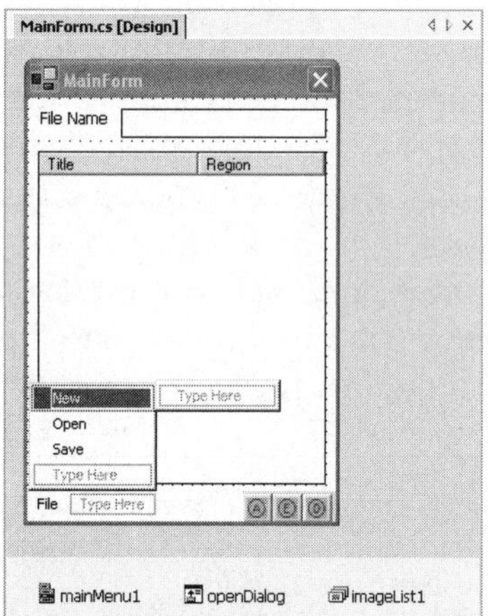

Figure 4-5 MainMenu control in Windows Forms Designer.

Figure 4-6 shows the menu expanded showing the New, Open, and Save commands that have been added to the MainMenu control of the DVD Catalog sample application.

Figure 4-6 The MainMenu control as it appears in a Pocket PC application.

You can create a cascading menu structure with the MainMenu control, but a cascading menu should be used on a Pocket PC application only when it will not clutter the screen. A Windows CE application can be less conservative in the use of its menus because a Windows CE device generally has a larger screen and a more Windows-like appearance.

The MainMenu control of a Pocket PC application should include functions that are necessary for the use of the application but not functions that will be used frequently by the user. You should place frequently used functions on a toolbar to allow the user easier access to them.

Functions should not be duplicated between the main menu and a toolbar. This is different from the recommendation for desktop applications, where you should provide the user with several different approaches to accessing any of the application's functions. With a Pocket PC application, you need to be aware of the limited space available to your application and place access to the application's functions in the most appropriate location. Do not hide a function in a menu when the function is likely to be used every time your application is run.

Using the ToolBar Control

The ToolBar control is a useful way of adding frequently used commands to a form. The ToolBar control is available for use in both a Windows CE project and a Pocket PC project. In a Pocket PC application, the toolbar is displayed at the bottom of the form. In a Windows CE application, the toolbar is displayed at the top of the form.

As is the case with the MainMenu control, when a toolbar is added to a form, the SIP control is available to the user, so you should take care to design your forms with the SIP in mind.

The toolbar acts as a container for buttons that the user can click to perform functions in your application. Each button can have a different image assigned to it from an ImageList control to help identify the button's function. The default image size is 16 by 16 pixels, but the image size can be changed to suit the images you want to use. Image size guidelines are provided in the section "General Design Guidelines" later in this chapter. The style of each button can be set to *DropDownButton*, *PushButton*, *ToggleButton*, or *Separator*. The *DropDownButton* style causes the button to display a pop-up menu when clicked. The *PushButton* and *ToggleButton* styles cause the buttons to look like standard buttons, but the *ToggleButton* style causes the button to stay down when clicked. The *Separator* style displays a space or a line between buttons, allowing clearer definition between button groups.

When you have added a ToolBar control to your form, you add buttons to the ToolBar control using the ToolBar Button Collection Editor. With the ToolBar Button Collection Editor, you can define the type of buttons that appear on your ToolBar control by setting ToolBar button properties such as *Style*, *DropDownMenu*, and *ImageIndex*. The *ImageIndex* property accepts an index into the list of images in the ImageList control associated with the ToolBar control. Figure 4-7 shows the ToolBar Button Collection Editor for the ToolBar control in the DVD Catalog sample application.

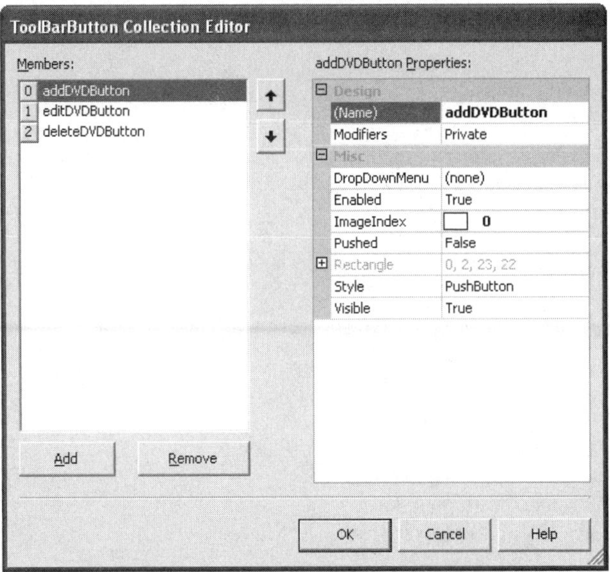

Figure 4-7 ToolBar Button Collection Editor.

The following code shows an example of adding a ToolBar control to a form programmatically:

```
// Create ImageList object for use by the toolbar
ImageList imageList = new ImageList();

// Load bitmaps into ImageList from the application's embedded resource
Bitmap bmp;
bmp = new Bitmap(
    Assembly.GetExecutingAssembly().
        GetManifestResourceStream(
            "NETCFDevelopersReference.Add.bmp"));
imageList.Images.Add(bmp);

bmp = new Bitmap(
    Assembly.GetExecutingAssembly().
        GetManifestResourceStream(
            "NETCFDevelopersReference.Edit.bmp"));
imageList.Images.Add(bmp);
```

(continued)

```
bmp = new Bitmap(
    Assembly.GetExecutingAssembly().
        GetManifestResourceStream(
            "NETCFDevelopersReference.Delete.bmp"));
imageList.Images.Add(bmp);

// Associate ImageList object with the toolbar
DVDToolbar.ImageList = imageList;

// Add the New button to the Toolbar
ToolBarButton btn = new ToolBarButton();
btn.ImageIndex = 0;
DVDToolbar.Buttons.Add(btn);

// Add the Edit button to the Toolbar
btn = new ToolBarButton();
btn.ImageIndex = 1;
DVDToolbar.Buttons.Add(btn);
DVDToolbar.Buttons[1].Enabled = false;
DVDToolbar.Buttons[1].Visible = false;

// Add the Delete button to the Toolbar
btn = new ToolBarButton();
btn.ImageIndex = 2;
DVDToolbar.Buttons.Add(btn);
DVDToolbar.Buttons[2].Enabled = false;
DVDToolbar.Buttons[2].Visible = false;

// Add toolbar to form
this.Controls.Add(DVDToolbar);

// Add the event-handler delegate.
DVDToolbar.ButtonClick += new ToolBarButtonClickEventHandler(
    this.DVDToolbar_ButtonClick);
```

The preceding code first creates an *ImageList* object and then loads three bitmaps using the *GetManifestResourceStream* function to retrieve the images from the embedded resources of the application. The toolbar will use these bitmap images to display the three buttons that will be added to the ToolBar control.

Then the code sets a reference to the *ImageList* object in the ToolBar control. Three *ToolBarButton* objects are created, made to reference an image in the *ImageList* object, and then added to the ToolBar control.

The ToolBar control is then added to the current form. Finally an event-handling routine is associated with the *ButtonClick* event of the ToolBar control. This allows you to detect when the user taps a button in the toolbar and to take whatever action is required for the tapped button. An example of an event handler for the toolbar's *ButtonClick* event, from the DVD Catalog example application, is shown here:

```
protected void DVDToolbar_ButtonClick(object sender,
    ToolBarButtonClickEventArgs e)
{
    // Evaluate the Button property to determine which button was clicked.
    switch(DVDToolbar.Buttons.IndexOf(e.Button))
    {
        case 0: // Add
            MessageBox.Show("Add DVD Button clicked");
            break;
        case 1: // Edit
            MessageBox.Show("Edit DVD Button clicked");
            break;
        case 2: // Delete
            MessageBox.Show("Delete DVD Button clicked");
            break;
    }
}
```

This code example displays a message specifying which button was clicked. The button that was clicked is identified by inspecting the *ToolBarButtonClickEventArgs* parameter, which includes a reference to the button that was clicked. The *IndexOf* method of the *Buttons* collection in the toolbar returns the zero-based index of the button, which is numbered from the left side of the toolbar. Note that if you have used separator buttons in the toolbar, the number of functioning buttons will not be consecutive. Figure 4-8 shows how the toolbar should look. It shows the three buttons—Add, Edit, and Delete—in the finished application.

Figure 4-8 DVD Catalog toolbar example.

Programming Form Activation and Deactivation on Pocket PC

The Pocket PC user interface guidelines have been created to ensure that applications running on these devices give good ergonomics and behave in a consistent manner. There are two significant recommendations relating to applications that differ from a desktop Windows PC. The first is that there should be only a single occurrence of an application running at any time. When you start an application from the Start menu, if the application is already running, that copy is reactivated. If it's not already running, a new copy is started. The .NET Compact Framework runtime automatically ensures that there is only a single occurrence of your application; there is no need to write any code to look for another occurrence of your application.

The second significant recommendation for an application on a Pocket PC is that once started the user should not be able to close it. When a user switches to another application, the window for the new application fills the screen and hides your application in the background; it is *deactivated*. When the user selects your application again from the Start menu or by clicking the application's icon on the Most Recently Used (MRU) bar on the Today page, your application is *activated* once more.

Programming Activate and Deactivate

When an application is deactivated on a Pocket PC device, the application should release as many resources as possible to conserve the limited resources of the device. It might be required to run in the background for a very long time, perhaps as long as days, until the user reactivates the application or resets the device, so you should try to design your application to use a minimum of resources while it is deactivated.

When an application is deactivated, the .NET Compact Framework automatically performs a garbage-collection process to release memory resources that the application no longer needs. Garbage collection in the .NET Compact Framework has been optimized for the lower memory specification of the device rather than for speed and scalability, as in the full .NET Framework. All memory allocations are taken from a single pool so that it's easy to free up memory resources if the device starts to run low on memory.

You will still need to specifically release resources such as open database connections, large objects in memory (such as datasets), and connections to COM ports. Two *Form* events are provided by the .NET Compact Framework to enable you to detect when your application is moved to the background or restored to the foreground of the system display windows. The *Form.Deactivate* event is used to detect when your application is minimized, and the *Form.Activate* event is used to detect when your application is brought back to the foreground of the system. The following code example shows event handlers in C# for both of these events:

```
private void Form1_Activate(object sender, System.EventArgs e)
{
    // Put code here to restore any database or COM port connections etc…
}

private void Form1_Activate(object sender, System.EventArgs e)
{
    // Put code here to free up application resources
    // (i.e. Database or COM port connections etc…)
}
```

Programming Form Close

If your application conforms to Pocket PC user interface guidelines, you must not allow users to close the main form of your application. You must not put a *Close* option on the menu, and you must ensure that the form toolbar displays only the X icon (equivalent to Form Minimize on Windows CE .NET and desktop PC windows) and not the OK icon (which is the Form Close button).

In a Pocket PC form, set the *MinimizeBox* property to *true* to display the minimize button (the X icon) or set the property to *false* to display a close button (the OK icon). The main form of your application should not be closeable. All dialog box forms that your application displays should be full screen and should be closeable through the OK icon to return to your main application form.

Closing of Applications by the Pocket PC Shell

When the system becomes low on memory, Pocket PC developers using eMbedded Visual C++ have to respond to a *WM_HIBERNATE* message sent to the main window of an application by releasing memory and other resources. Developers using the .NET Compact Framework don't have to worry about this. There is no event an application receives to indicate that the operating system has requested the application to hibernate. Instead, the .NET Compact Framework runtime responds to this condition by garbage collecting and releasing cached JITted code.

If resources on the device become low, the operating system will start to close applications that are running in the background. Because your application might be closed by the operating system while it is minimized, it is important that the application write any changes to data immediately or in response to the *Deactivate* event. If the application doesn't write data changes immediately or during the *Deactivate* event, there is a risk of leaving the data in an inconsistent state.

Handling the Tap-and-Hold Event

Because a Pocket PC device does not have a mouse, users cannot right-click a control. Instead, they must tap the control with the stylus and then hold the stylus in place until the context-sensitive menu is displayed. To provide context-sensitive menus for your controls, you use the ContextMenu control. The ContextMenu control is described in Chapter 3.

If you want to provide functionality other than a context-sensitive menu to the tap-and-hold action on a control, you must trap the action manually. You should create a timer control on your form and set its interval to the amount of time you want the user to hold the stylus for before triggering your function. Capture the *MouseDown* event to start the timer and the *MouseUp* event to stop the timer. Capture the timer's *Tick* event to execute the code for the tap-and-hold action. You should also capture the *MouseMove* event if you want to allow the user to move the control without triggering the tap-and-hold action. The following code shows the technique just described to provide a custom tap-and-hold event for *Form1*:

```
private void timer1_Tick(object sender, System.EventArgs e)
{
    // Your action code should go here
}

private void Form1_MouseDown(object sender,
    System.Windows.Forms.MouseEventArgs e)
{
    // Start Timer control
    timer1.Enabled = true;
}

private void Form1_MouseUp(object sender,
    System.Windows.Forms.MouseEventArgs e)
{
    timer1.Enabled = false;
}
```

Handling Pocket PC Hardware Keys

A Pocket PC does not have a keyboard and relies on the use of a stylus and the SIP for most of the input from the user. A Pocket PC device does have some hardware keys available to it. Figure 4-9 shows a typical example of the hardware keys on a Pocket PC device.

Figure 4-9 Pocket PC device hardware keys.

It is possible to capture these keys in the *KeyDown* event that occurs when the user presses these keys.

The Compaq iPAQ has a central pad that generates the following five different types of key codes:

- *Keys.Up* is triggered when the top of the pad is pressed.
- *Keys.Down* is triggered when the bottom of the pad is pressed.
- *Keys.Left* is triggered when the left side of the pad is pressed.
- *Keys.Right* is triggered when the right side of the pad is pressed.
- *Keys.Return* is triggered when the center of the pad is pressed.

The following code example shows a *KeyDown* event handler. The code uses the *KeyCode* of *KeyEventArgs* to detect which key has been pressed.

```
private void Form1_KeyDown(object sender,
    System.Windows.Forms.KeyEventArgs e)
{
    switch (e.KeyCode)
    {
        case Keys.Up:
            MessageBox.Show("UP key pressed");
            break;
        case Keys.Down:
            MessageBox.Show("DOWN key pressed");
            break;
        case Keys.Left:
            MessageBox.Show("LEFT key pressed");
            break;
        case Keys.Right:
            MessageBox.Show("RIGHT key pressed");
            break;
        case Keys.Return:
            MessageBox.Show("key pressed in");
            break;
    }
}
```

Giving an Application Its Final Touches

Once you've finished coding your application's functionality, you'll want to give your application an icon and provide a shortcut to the application in the Start menu of the Windows CE or Pocket PC device.

Associating an Icon with Your Application

To associate an icon with your application, open the project Property Pages dialog box, select the General section, and enter the path to the icon in the Application Icon property. Figure 4-10 shows the project Property Pages dialog box.

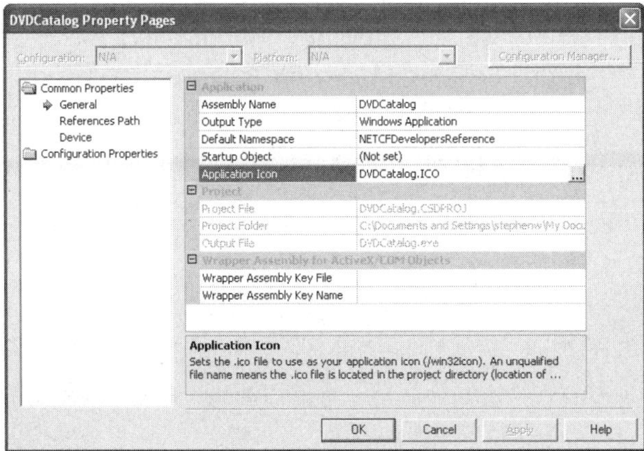

Figure 4-10 Project Property Pages dialog box.

Adding a Shortcut to the Start Menu

Adding a shortcut to the Start menu will allow the user to launch your application more easily. To add a shortcut to the Start menu, place the shortcut in the \Windows\Start Menu folder on the device.

The configuration file used to build your application's CAB file is used to define the shortcut that will be created for your application when it's installed on the device. If you use Visual Studio .NET to create your application's CAB file, a shortcut section will be included in the configuration file. The following section describes which sections of the configuration file need to be changed to create a shortcut for your application if you build the configuration file manually.

Three sections of the configuration file are affected. The first section that you need to change is the *DefaultInstall* section. You use the *CEShortcuts* keyword to point to the section that will create the shortcuts for your application. The following code is an example of the *DefaultInstall* section from the configuration file of the DVD Catalog application:

```
[DefaultInstall]
CopyFiles = Files.Common
CEShortcuts = Shortcuts
```

After pointing to the section that will define your shortcuts, you add that section into the configuration file. The format of the entries in this section are *shortcut_filename*, *shortcut_type_flag*, and *target_file*.

- *shortcut_filename* is the name of the shortcut. It will appear in the Start Menu.
- *shortcut_type_flag* defines whether the shortcut is to a file or a folder. Empty or 0 represents a shortcut to a file; a non-zero numeric value represents a shortcut to a folder.
- *target_file* specifies the target file or folder of the shortcut.

The following listing shows the *Shortcuts* section of the configuration file of the DVD Catalog application:

```
[Shortcuts]
DVD Catalog, 0, DVDCatalog.exe
```

The third and final section that you will change is the *DestinationDirs* section. This section defines the paths to use for various other sections. You enter the shortcut's section name followed by the path to your shortcuts. The following listing below is taken from the configuration file for the DVD Catalog application:

```
[DestinationDirs]
Shortcuts = 0, %CE17%
Files.Common=0,%InstallDir%
Files.ARM=0,%InstallDir%
Files.SH3=0,%InstallDir%
Files.MIPS=0,%InstallDir%
Files.X86=0,%InstallDir%
```

This topic will be covered in more detail in Chapter 6.

General Design Guidelines

The "Designed for Windows for Pocket PC" logo program has some detailed requirements for applications written for the Pocket PC. The logo program specifies the usage of such things as icons, menus, toolbars, and the input panel. A handbook is available that details the design requirements for meeting the "Designed for Windows for Pocket PC" logo program criteria. The handbook can be downloaded from the Web site *http://www.qualitylogic.com/certprograms/pocketpc_spec.html.*

On a Pocket PC device, there is no keyboard, so all text input needs to be done using the SIP. If you compare the use of the SIP and a keyboard, you will find that the SIP is time-consuming and error-prone. When you design your input forms, reduce the need to enter textual information by providing drop-down lists of the most common entries for each input. For example, the Task Input Form on a Pocket PC device uses drop-down list boxes to provide the user with the most common subjects for the task. Figure 4-11 shows the Task Input Form with the Subject drop-down list box displayed.

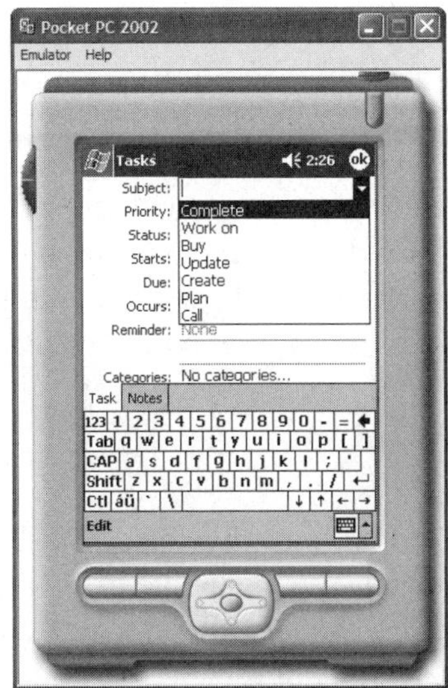

Figure 4-11 Task Input Form showing the Subject drop-down list box.

Remember that the user is using a stylus instead of a mouse to select items on your form. To aid the user in selecting items, make controls sufficiently large to avoid target misses. The recommended size for a button on a Pocket PC device is 5 millimeters (21 by 21 pixels) for a stylus target and 9 millimeters (38 by 38 pixels) for a finger target. Also provide sufficient space between controls to reduce the risk of a missed hit. This is particularly important if the commands perform cut or copy functions.

As a general rule, you should consider the way the user is going to use your application. Minimize the distance between common controls and tasks so that the user is not constantly moving the stylus back and forth across the screen.

Consider the way the device is held. The most frequently used or most important information should be positioned so that it's not obscured by the user's hands when he or she is entering data or selecting items.

Group related controls together for ease of access. You should reduce the movement the user needs to make to perform the most common functions of your application.

On a Pocket PC device, the screen's height is greater than its width. This is different from the standard desktop screen, which has a width greater than its height. You must be aware of this narrower display when you design your application's forms. Controls should be arranged vertically rather than horizontally to avoid making the user scroll the display horizontally to see all the controls. Forms should be designed to fit all the required controls onto one form without scrolling. This allows the user to see all the information that he or she requires without having to scroll the display. If a form can't be designed to display all the required controls without scrolling, the most important controls should be displayed first and secondary controls should be displayed in the area of the form that will need to be scrolled into view. Avoid overlapping forms and controls, especially in a Pocket PC application.

Feedback to the user should be provided for the actions he or she performs. This feedback can be in the form of a sound or a change in the appearance of the form or controls. The use of graphics to enhance your applications is covered in Chapter 21.

> **Note** The Pocket PC SDK has comprehensive guidelines on all aspects of Pocket PC application design. You can find and download a copy of the Pocket PC SDK by going to *http://msdn.microsoft.com/downloads*, expanding Software Development Kits in the table of contents, and then selecting Pocket PC 2002 SDK.

Summary

In this chapter, we covered properties of the *Form* class, using custom and built-in dialog boxes. We showed how to use InputPanel, MainMenu, and Toolbar controls. We covered how to detect when your application was activated and deactivated, and we explained what happens when your application is deactivated on a Pocket PC and how your application should respond to deactivation. We also looked at adding the finishing touches to your application, such as a shortcut in the Start menu and associating an icon with your application. Finally we covered some general guidelines for creating a user interface for your applications.

5

Testing and Debugging

It is a fact of life that programmers make mistakes. Although the compilers and other tools of the .NET Compact Framework have been designed to find as many errors as possible, it is not possible for a computer to find all problems in advance. In this chapter, we examine some techniques and tools that you can use to deal with various kinds of problems that an application might encounter.

Detecting and Correcting Programming Errors

The easiest error to fix is the syntax error, which occurs when the programmer writes code that is not valid in the programming language being used. Syntax errors are found at compile-time and are reasonably easy to resolve. Other kinds of errors occur when the application compiles successfully but does not work as expected. The application might produce incorrect results, or it might run successfully at first and then crash with some kind of error message. Errors of this kind are called run-time errors, semantic errors, or logic errors.

As well as programmer errors, the environment in which an application is executing can cause problems. For example, someone might unplug a data cable right after your application opens a network connection to a remote computer using Ethernet. Or perhaps your application is running out of memory because the user is trying to run too many applications concurrently with yours. In circumstances such as this, the .NET Compact Framework throws an exception. By default, when an exception occurs, the run-time system will display a message to briefly explain the error and then terminate the process. Terminating a program with a cryptic error message, however, is rarely acceptable. Robustness is important. You might not be able to control every aspect of the environment that your application is executing in, but you can at least make sure that you handle errors in a user-friendly and appropriate manner. The languages of the .NET Compact Framework allow you to catch some or all exceptions and handle them within your application.

Using the Debugger

The .NET Compact Framework debugger is a powerful tool for fixing problems in application programs. Specifically, you can use the debugger to

- Set breakpoints in programs on a line or a program condition.
- Single-step the application or run it to another breakpoint.
- Examine the values of expressions and modify the contents of variables.
- Alter the execution sequence of your program.

Debugging an Example Application

To illustrate the debugger, the example application shown in Figure 5-1 will be used. Quadratic Equation Solver is a simple Pocket PC application that solves quadratic equations.

Figure 5-1 Quadratic Equation Solver application.

The user enters three floating-point numbers that represent the three coefficients of a quadratic equation. When the Solve button is pressed, the two roots are calculated. The code for QuadraticSolver.cs, available with this book's sample files, follows.

QuadraticSolver.cs

```
using System;
using System.Drawing;
using System.Collections;
using System.Windows.Forms;
using System.Data;

namespace QuadraticSolver
{
    public class Quadratic : System.Windows.Forms.Form
    {
        private System.Windows.Forms.Label lblA;
        private System.Windows.Forms.TextBox txtB;
        private System.Windows.Forms.Label lblB;
        private System.Windows.Forms.TextBox txtC;
        private System.Windows.Forms.Label label1;
        private System.Windows.Forms.Button cmdSolve;
        private System.Windows.Forms.TextBox txtRoot1;
        private System.Windows.Forms.TextBox txtRoot2;
        private System.Windows.Forms.TextBox txtA;

        // Visual Studio generated code
        ⋮

        private void cmdSolve_Click(
            object sender,
            System.EventArgs e)
        {
            // Coefficients of quadratic
            double a = 0.0, b = 0.0, c = 0.0;

            // Convert user input
            a = double.Parse(txtA.Text);
            b = double.Parse(txtB.Text);
            c = double.Parse(txtC.Text);

            // Calculate results
            double temp = Math.Sqrt((b*b)-(4*a*c));
            double root1,root2;

            // Calculate the two roots
            root1 = (-b + temp) / (2 * a);
            root2 = (-b - temp) / (2 * a);

            // Display roots
            txtRoot1.Text = root1.ToString();
            txtRoot2.Text = root2.ToString();
        }
    }
}
```

The form contains three text input fields (*txtA*, *txtB*, and *txtC*) that are used to input the three coefficients of a quadratic equation. It also contains two text fields (*txtRoot1* and *txtRoot2*) that are used for output of the two results. The event handler *cmdSolve_Click* will be studied for the purposes of this chapter. This method can be split into three sections: conversion of text input into floating-point numbers, calculation of the results, and conversion of floating-point results into textual form for output.

Understanding Default Exception Handling

In the example application, if the user enters invalid text such as *cat* into any of the three input fields, the *double.Parse* method will raise an exception because the input field's *string* value cannot be converted into a *double*.

Run the application as stand-alone code (without the debugger) by selecting Start Without Debugging from the Microsoft Visual Studio .NET Debug menu or by pressing Ctrl+F5. Enter invalid text such as *cat* into the first text input control, and then click the Solve button. A message box similar to the one shown in Figure 5-2 will appear.

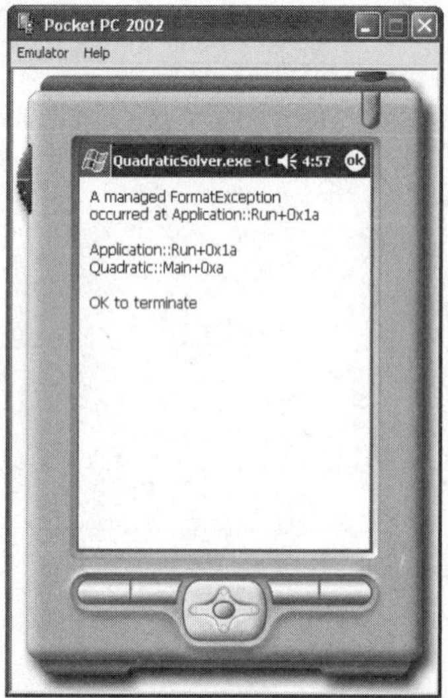

Figure 5-2 Default exception handling in the stand-alone environment.

The default behavior when an exception is raised is to display a message such as the one shown in Figure 5-2 and to terminate the application when the user presses the OK button. Press the OK button to terminate the application.

Handling Exceptions in the Debugger

Run the Quadratic Equation Solver application again, but this time use the debugger by selecting Start from the Debug menu or by pressing F5. Enter invalid data as before, and click the Solve button. The same exception occurs, but this time the debugger detects it and displays the dialog box shown in Figure 5-3 on the development workstation.

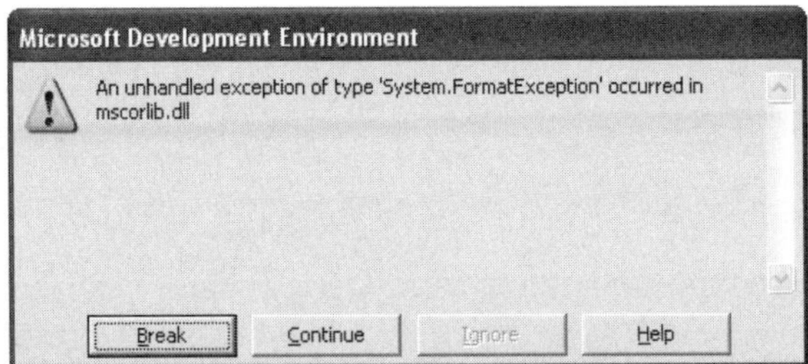

Figure 5-3 Default exception handling in the debug environment.

At this point, you have two main options. You can click the Break button, which hands control to the debugger, or you can click the Continue button, which will return control back to the Quadratic Equation Solver application. Click the Continue button. The application continues with its default exception handling, which is to terminate the application.

Drawing on Debugger Features

Debugging applications in the .NET Compact Framework is conceptually just like debugging applications in the full .NET Framework. The main difference when debugging .NET Compact Framework applications is that the debugger is running in one environment (the Windows desktop) and the application being debugged is running in a different environment (the .NET Compact Framework, either on a real device or an emulator). If you have used .NET Remote Debugging, you'll see that the principle is very similar.

Many of the core features of the debugger will be familiar to users of Visual Studio .NET and also to users of other debugging environments such as those supplied with Microsoft eMbedded Visual Tools, Microsoft eMbedded Visual Basic, and Microsoft eMbedded Visual C++. Debugging works with both the emulators and the actual devices.

Entering Break Mode

When the application is operating in the debugging environment, it is in one of two states: it either running, or it is in break mode. In break mode, program execution is suspended and you can examine the state of the application. Most of the debugger features that allow you to examine the program's state are available only in break mode. There are several ways for the debugger to enter break mode, as listed here:

- When an exception is encountered (as in the previous example)
- When a breakpoint is reached
- When the debugger user forces an interruption of the program

You can break execution manually at any time by choosing Break All from the Debug menu. Alternatively, you can press Ctrl+Alt+Break on the keyboard, which has the same effect.

Creating a Breakpoint

When execution reaches a line containing a breakpoint, execution of the program is suspended and the debugger enters break mode. To demonstrate this, load the Quadratic Equation Solver project into Visual Studio .NET and locate the *cmdSolve_Click* method. Select the line containing the first call to *double.Parse*, and press the F9 key to set a breakpoint. To indicate that a breakpoint has been set, a red circle will appear in the left margin of the code editor and the text of the line containing the breakpoint will be highlighted in red, as shown in Figure 5-4.

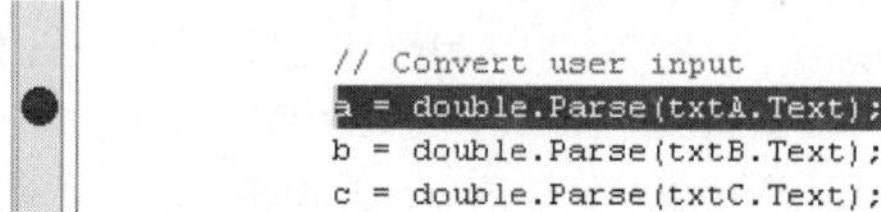
// Convert user input
a = double.Parse(txtA.Text);
b = double.Parse(txtB.Text);
c = double.Parse(txtC.Text);

Figure 5-4 Displaying a breakpoint.

Run the application using the debugger (by pressing F5). The application will be deployed and will start. Enter **6** in the first text input field of the application, and click the Solve button. The breakpoint will then be reached and will interrupt program execution immediately before execution of the first call to *double.Parse*. The line that is about to execute is highlighted in yellow, with an arrow in the left margin, as shown in Figure 5-5.

```
// Convert user input
a = double.Parse(txtA.Text);
b = double.Parse(txtB.Text);
c = double.Parse(txtC.Text);
```

Figure 5-5 Reaching a breakpoint.

Watching Variables and Expressions

The watch facility allows the developer to evaluate variables and expressions. With the Quadratic Equation Solver application in break mode, it is possible to examine the input data in the *Text* property of *txtA* in various ways.

Command Window

In Visual Studio .NET, you can switch to the Command Window pane and enter **? txtA.Text** to cause the debugger to evaluate and display the value of *txtA.Text*, as shown in Figure 5-6. If the Command Window pane is not visible, you can access it by selecting Other Windows from the View menu and then selecting Command Window.

Figure 5-6 Displaying data in the Command Window pane.

Watch Window

You can also open the QuickWatch window by selecting QuickWatch from the Debug menu or pressing Ctrl+Alt+Q. If you enter **txtA.Text** in the expression field and press the Recalculate button, the QuickWatch window will evaluate and display the value of *txtA.Text*, as Figure 5-7 shows.

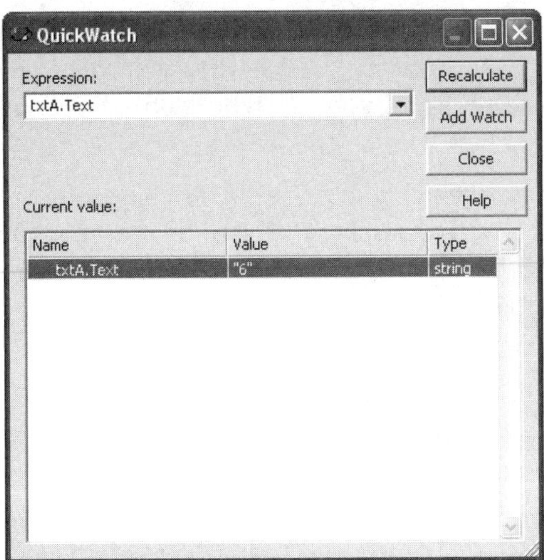

Figure 5-7 Displaying data in the QuickWatch window.

If you want a permanent display of the expression, you can press the Add Watch button, which adds the expression to a list in the Watch window, shown in Figure 5-8.

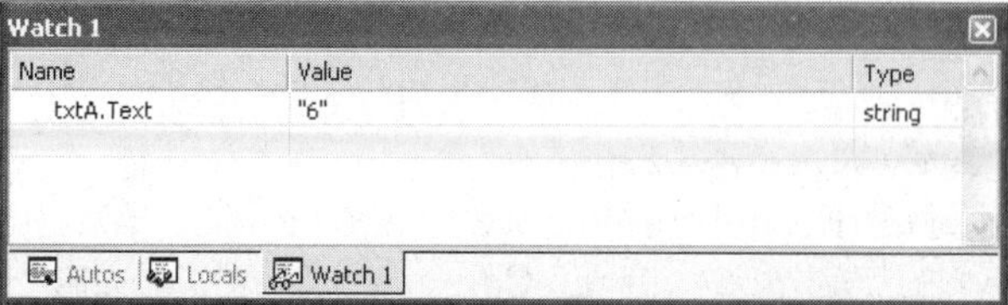

Figure 5-8 Displaying data in the Watch window.

DataTips

While in break mode, the Visual Studio .NET debugger also displays the value of a variable when you place the mouse pointer over that variable in the code editor window. The value is shown in a floating DataTip window, as seen in Figure 5-9.

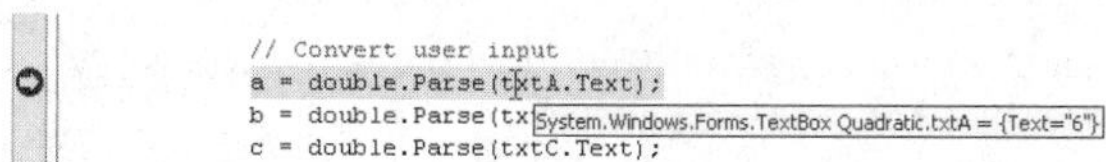

Figure 5-9 Displaying data using a DataTip window.

Stepping Through an Application

Single-stepping allows you to run a program one step at a time.

- The Step Over command, which you can access by selecting Step Over from the Debug menu or by pressing F10, executes one complete statement before returning to the caller. Method calls are executed completely.
- The Step Into command, which you can access by selecting Step Into from the Debug menu or by pressing F11, is similar to the Step Over command, but if the line being debugged is a method for which source code is available, the execution reaches the first statement of the method and then returns the debugger to break mode. This is useful if you wish to debug code inside a method call.
- The Step Out menu selection in the Debug menu (also accessible via the Shift+F11 keyboard shortcut) executes the current method until its final statement before returning the debugger to break mode.

Continuing a Program from Break Mode

You can resume execution of a program from break mode using the Continue command, which you can access by selecting Continue from the Debug menu or by pressing F5.

Terminating a Program

To force a program to terminate and unload from memory, select Stop Debugging from the Debug menu or press Shift+F5.

Removing Breakpoints

The F9 key acts as a toggle and will remove a breakpoint if one already exists on the current line. To remove all breakpoints, select Clear All Breakpoints from the Debug menu or press Ctrl+Shift+F9.

Setting More Complex Breakpoints

Using F9 to set a breakpoint is a convenient shortcut to create a simple breakpoint. The New Breakpoint dialog box, accessible from the Debug menu and shown in Figure 5-10, allows the developer to create more complex breakpoints that are associated not only with a location in the program code, but also with additional conditions or hit counts.

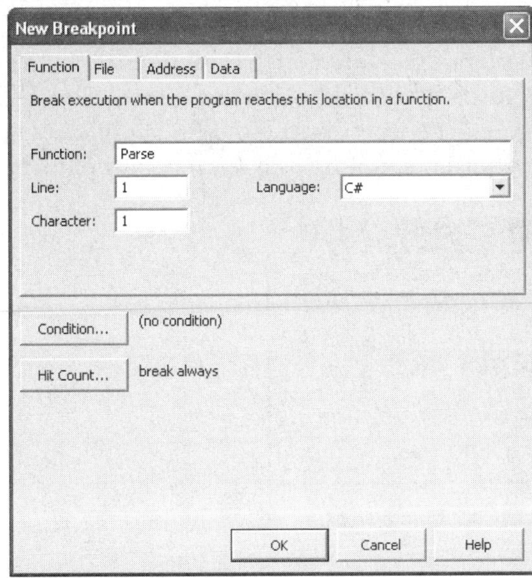

Figure 5-10 New Breakpoint dialog box.

A similar dialog box can be reached by selecting Breakpoint Properties from the context-sensitive menu when the line of code in the code editor already contains a breakpoint. This allows the developer to change settings for an existing breakpoint.

Breakpoints with Conditions

Clicking the Condition button brings up the Breakpoint condition dialog box, which allows you to attach a condition to a breakpoint; the breakpoint takes effect only if the condition evaluates to *true*. Figure 5-11 shows the Breakpoint Condition dialog box.

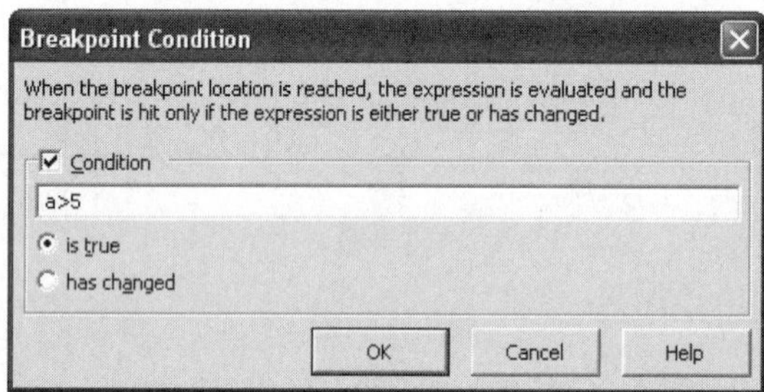

Figure 5-11 Breakpoint Condition dialog box.

Breakpoints with Counters

A breakpoint without a hit count causes program execution to break each time the breakpoint is reached. If you want to make a breakpoint active only after the breakpoint has been reached a specified number of times, you can specify a hit count for the breakpoint. Clicking the Hit Count button in the Breakpoint Properties dialog box causes the Breakpoint Hit Count dialog box to be displayed, as shown in Figure 5-12. You can use the Breakpoint Hit Count dialog box to configure a variety of hit count options for the current breakpoint.

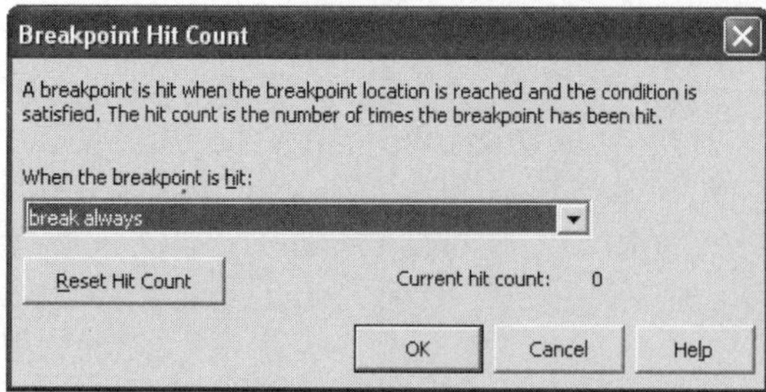

Figure 5-12 Breakpoint Hit Count dialog box.

The current selection in the When The Breakpoint Is Hit drop-down list determines how the breakpoint should behave when it is hit. That drop-down list contains the following options:

- **Break always** This setting, which is the default setting, causes the debugger to ignore the breakpoint's hit count.
- **Break when the hit count is equal** This setting causes the breakpoint to take effect when the breakpoint's hit count is equal to a specified hit count.
- **Break when the hit count is a multiple of** This setting causes the breakpoint to take effect when the breakpoint's hit count is a multiple of the specified hit count.
- **Break when the hit count is greater than or equal to** This setting causes the breakpoint to take effect when the breakpoint's hit count is greater than or equal to the specified hit count.

If you select any option other than Break Always, the Breakpoint Hit Count dialog box displays an additional field for you to specify a hit count. Unless you select Break Always, the debugger keeps track of the number of times the breakpoint has been hit during the current session. Hit counts have an effect on program performance in the debugger, since the debugger has to check the current hit count against the hit criteria each time the breakpoint is reached.

While the debugger is in break mode, the Breakpoint Hit Count dialog box allows you to view the current hit count for the current breakpoint. The Reset Hit Count button of the Breakpoint Hit Count dialog box sets the current hit count for the current breakpoint to zero.

> **Tip** If you want to break every time the breakpoint is hit but also want to keep track of the hit count in the dialog box, choose the option to break when the hit count is a multiple of the specified hit count and specify a count of 1.

Disabled Breakpoints

During debugging, there are times when you don't want all the breakpoints to be active all the time. Breakpoints can be removed, as shown earlier, but it might be more convenient to temporarily disable one or more breakpoints.

When a breakpoint is disabled, the debugger remembers its location but the breakpoint has no effect. To disable a single breakpoint, right-click the line that contains the breakpoint and then select Disable Breakpoint from the shortcut menu that appears.

A disabled breakpoint is indicated by a circle in the left margin as before, but the circle is no longer filled in solid red. You can enable or disable all the breakpoints at once by selecting Enable All Breakpoints or Disable All Breakpoints from the Debug menu.

Starting Applications Without Debugging

Sometimes, you might want to run the program you're developing without using the debugger at all. This can be useful if you want to perform a quick test of the application and do not want the overhead of establishing a debugging session between the development environment and the target environment. Selecting Start Without Debugging from the Debug menu will deploy the application and cause the target device to execute the application just as if it were started from the target device's Start menu. You will not, however, be able to debug the application. You will not be able to break the application's execution, and if the application crashes, you will not be able to handle the application's exceptions in the debugger.

Unsupported Debugger Features

Compared to debugging applications for the desktop environment, the following limitations apply when debugging applications that target a Pocket PC or a Windows CE device:

- Native code disassembly, register dumps, and stack dumps are not available.
- The ability to change source code while the program is in break mode and apply the changes without leaving the debug session is not supported.
- It is not possible to attach the debugger to an existing process or application domain that was previously running outside the debugging environment. Users can debug only those processes or application domains that have been started for debugging.

Tracing Output from an Application

The *System.Diagnostics* namespace contains the *Debug* class. In the full .NET Framework, the *Debug.Write* method can be used to send application-specific information to any registered listener applications, such as debuggers. If the application is running under the debugging environment, output from *Debug.Write* is sent to the output window of the Visual Studio .NET debugger.

```
using System.Diagnostics;
⋮
Debug.Write("The value of x is " + x.ToString());
```

The initial release of the Visual Studio. NET debugger for the .NET Compact Framework does not implement this feature. However, you can define your own listener classes within your application to handle debug messages. The DebugTrace application included with this book's sample files demonstrates how to handle debug messages.

If you use methods in the *Debug* class to print debugging information, you can make the application easier to debug without impacting the performance and code size of your shipping product. Operations on the *Debug* class are ignored when an application is built and deployed using a release build. (See the *Conditional* attribute explained later in this chapter.)

Using Assertions Within an Application

The .NET Compact Framework also supports a *Trace* class, which is in effect for both debug and release builds. In the .NET Compact Framework, this class supports only the *Assert* method and does not support full tracing the way the full .NET Framework counterpart does.

```
using System.Diagnostics;
⋮
Trace.Assert(bean.IsMagic, "This is not a magic bean");
```

In this example, if the assertion is *true*, nothing is displayed. If *bean.IsMagic* is *false*, the dialog box shown in Figure 5-13 appears.

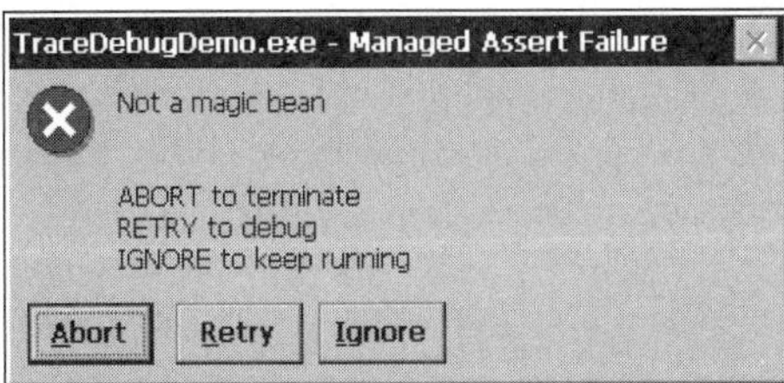

Figure 5-13 Managed Assert Failure dialog box.

The Abort button terminates the application. The Retry button will try to connect to the debugger, and the Ignore button will attempt to continue the application. Assertion failures cannot be trapped and handled using *try* and *catch*.

Handling Exceptions in the Debugger

The .NET runtime has a comprehensive exception handling facility, and both C# and Visual Basic .NET are able to take advantage of it. Chapter 2 describes exception syntax in more detail. When an application is being debugged, the developer can configure the debugging environment to handle exceptions in a number of different ways. For each exception (or group of exceptions), you can specify how the debugger should behave both when the exception is thrown and when the exception is not handled.

- When the exception is thrown, the application can break into the debugger or it can continue running. Breaking into the debugger when the exception is thrown will allow you to catch an exception before any exception handling code is executed.
- If the exception is not handled, the application can break into the debugger or it can continue running.

Changing the settings so that the application breaks into the debugger when the exception is thrown allows you to trap an exception whenever it occurs regardless of whether an exception handler is active at the time of the call. This can be particularly useful if you want to debug exception handlers.

The setting for what to do when the exception is not handled allows you to manage an unhandled exception on the "second try," after the debugged application has tried to handle the exception and failed.

To reach the Exceptions dialog box that controls exception handling for the debugger, choose Exceptions from the Debug menu. The Exceptions dialog box is shown in Figure 5-14.

The Exceptions dialog box contains a tree control, with each root node representing a category of exceptions. If you expand a category, you will see the names of individual exceptions or subcategories of exceptions.

The node icon for each exception or category name indicates the current setting for what to do when the exception is thrown. A large red ball with an *X* on it signifies that the exception will cause a break into the debugger. A large gray ball signifies that execution will continue. A small gray ball indicates that the the node inherits the settings from its parent node. If a category is selected in the Exceptions dialog box, the chosen option affects all the exceptions in that category that are set to inherit settings from the parent node.

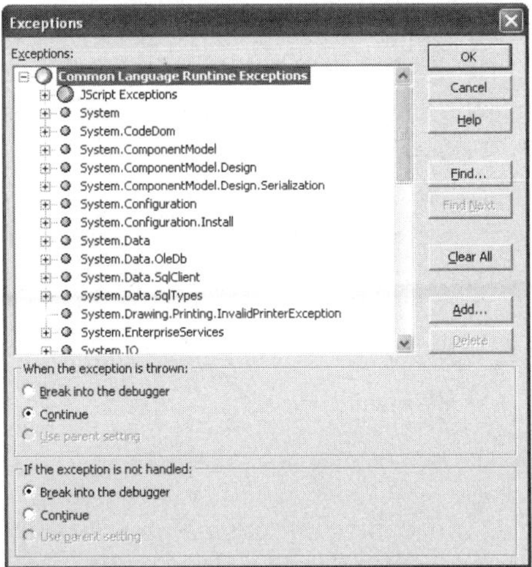

Figure 5-14 The Exceptions dialog box—exception-handling options for the debugger.

Tip If you know the name of the exception for which you want to control the debugger's behavior but do not know in which category that exception is to be found, use the Find button to enter a string and search for the exception by name. After you have found the first occurrence of an exception with a name that contains the string you entered, use the Find Next button to find another exception with a name that contains the same string.

If your application has its own exception classes, you can use the Add button to add a developer-defined exception to a selected category. The Delete button will delete it, and the Clear All button will delete all developer-defined exceptions from the list.

Controlling Release Code Size

It is quite common for a developer to write code that is of interest only during development and is of no concern to the end user. When working in a resource-constrained environment such as Windows CE, you might want the power of such diagnostic code when developing the application, without having to include the extra code in the final product. There are two useful techniques that you can use if your application has code that is required only for the debug build. When Visual Studio .NET builds a debug version, it sets the *DEBUG* compile-time constant. This constant is not set for the release build.

You can use the *#if* preprocessor directive to conditionally compile code based on the value of a compile-time expression. Program code between *#if DEBUG* and *#endif* is compiled only for the debug build. This is the traditional technique, which has been inherited from the C programming language.

```
:
#if DEBUG
MessageBox.Show("WARNING - this is the debug build");
#endif
:
```

In the preceding example, the call to *MessageBox.Show* and the string associated with that call are included in the output assembly for the debug build only. This ensures that the release assembly is as small as possible. However, conditional compilation can be awkward to use if there are many separate blocks of code subject to conditional compilation.

The *Conditional* attribute can be used to make the assembly loader ignore calls to a specified method if a compile-time expression is *false*. Methods with the *[Conditional("DEBUG")]* attribute are always compiled, but if *DEBUG* is not set, calls to the methods are not made at run time.

```
public class SomeClass
{
    // Calls to this method are ignored
    // in the release build
    [Conditional("DEBUG")]
    public void DebugInfo()
    {
        :
        // The method body is always compiled
        // for both debug and release builds
        :
    }
    :
    DebugInfo(); // For release build, this call is ignored
    :
}
```

Using the *Conditional* attribute at the start of a method ensures that the processor overhead of calling the debugging code is not required for the release build (when the *DEBUG* symbol will not be defined). It is also more convenient because the *Conditional* attribute appears only once. Unlike conditional compilation, the body of the method is always compiled, so there is no effect on the size of the output assembly.

You might want to use a combination of these two techniques. For example, you could put all your debug and trace code in methods marked with the *Conditional* attribute and enclose the bodies of each of those methods with *#if* and *#endif* directives.

Generating Longer Error Messages in Exceptions

In the full .NET Framework, a descriptive text message is associated with each exception. For reasons of space, the .NET Compact Framework DLLs do not contain this extensive text. Instead, the text of exceptions is contained in a separate resource assembly that can be downloaded with the application only if you require it. For the core classes of the *System* namespace, the text messages are found in System.SR.dll.

If you add a reference to your projects to System.SR.dll in the .NET Compact Framework directories, you get the full text of error messages in your exceptions. No other action is required; adding the assembly to a project will cause that assembly to be deployed.

This DLL is relatively large (around 80 KB), and you might not want to deploy it in environments where file and memory space are at a premium. However, it is a useful asset during the development process because it allows exception handlers to provide more comprehensive error messages.

Adopting Strategies for Testing and Debugging

The emulation environment is certainly useful, especially if you have restricted access to real hardware on which to test the applications. The startup options for the emulator allow you to try out applications in various configurations and allow you to get a feel for how an application will perform on platforms with different amounts of free memory, video devices, and so on.

This kind of facility is useful if you are developing a generic application to run on a wide variety of Pocket PC or Windows CE .NET devices. Testing your application on as many platforms as possible before releasing it can be very beneficial, and the emulator is a powerful tool to do this. If you develop a customized version of the operating system using Microsoft Platform Builder, you can run the custom operating system image in the emulator to develop applications, even if the real embedded device is not available.

On the other hand, the emulator might be relatively slow compared to a real device. The difference in speed between real and emulated hardware is difficult to quantify, but it is generally noticeable, especially if the host system is relatively slow or if the emulator has to compete with other applications on the host for processor time. Any application that is processor-intensive will necessarily run slowly under the emulator. In particular, a time-critical application might have problems running on the emulator and might show erratic or inconsistent performance.

Also, the emulator is not (and does not claim to be) an exact emulation of all hardware. Although you can "connect" the emulator serial and parallel ports to the real ports on your desktop PC, and Ethernet connectivity can also be emulated, no other hardware devices are supported under emulation. If your application relies on such hardware, emulation will not give you all the functionality you require. Consequently, the emulator will be of limited use unless it's a close match to your target platform. However, the emulator can often be used to build prototypes in the early stages of development, and it will often be useful if you're experimenting with different user interfaces.

You might also find it useful to design your application in layers or tiers. At the simplest level, this could be achieved by separating the user interface from the rest of the application. For larger applications, you might find it useful to separate the business logic into separate layers. This approach has several benefits, not the least of which is the ability to design and test the layers in isolation.

You might find it helpful to design the user interface using the full .NET Framework and port the application to the .NET Compact Framework afterward. This gives you the full power and convenience of the .NET environment at the outset. Be aware, however, that the .NET Compact Framework does not have all the capabilities of the full .NET Framework.

Configuring the Emulator from Visual Studio

To configure the way the emulator behaves, select Options from the Tools menu in Visual Studio .NET. In the Options dialog box, select the Device Tools folder and then the Devices item in the tree view on the left of the dialog box. Figure 5-15 shows the Options dialog box.

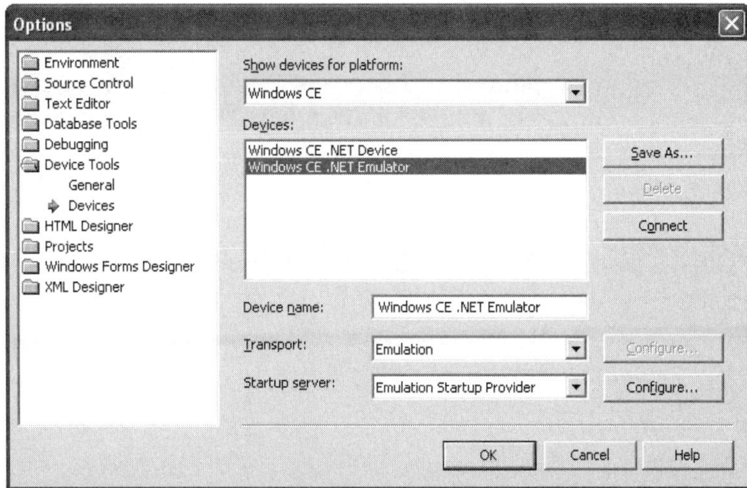

Figure 5-15 The Options dialog box showing device configuration options.

Select the emulator you want to configure in the Devices list, make sure Emulation Startup Provider is selected in the Startup Server drop-down list, and press the Configure button to bring up the Configure Emulator Settings dialog box, shown in Figure 5-16.

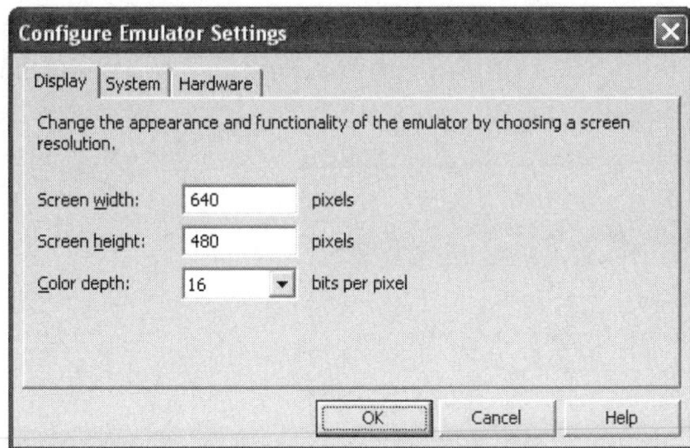

Figure 5-16 The Display tab of the Configure Emulator Settings dialog box.

The Display tab of the Configure Emulator Settings dialog box allows you to specify a size for the emulator display. The minimum size is 80 by 64 pixels, and the maximum is 1024 by 768 pixels. Both width and height must be an exact multiple of 8. You can specify a color depth of 8, 16, or 32 bits per pixel.

The System tab (shown in Figure 5-17) allows you to set the amount of memory that is emulated, in units of megabytes. The Host key, which is the single key on the development computer that activates menu shortcuts, can be changed. You can select the Left or Right Alt, Ctrl, Shift, or Windows logo key.

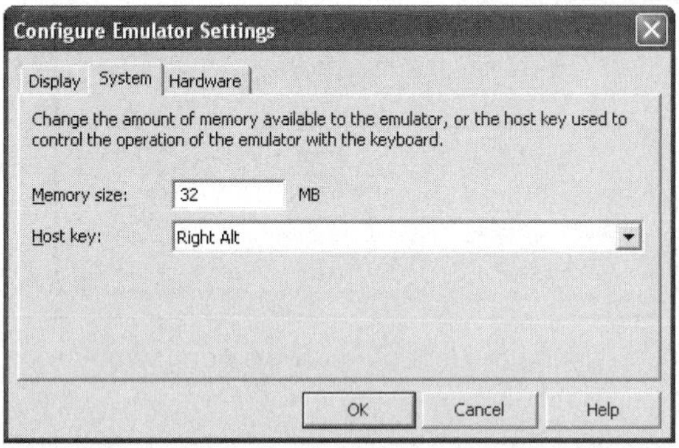

Figure 5-17 The System tab of the Configure Emulator Settings dialog box.

The Hardware tab (shown in Figure 5-18) allows you to set up mappings between the emulator's serial and parallel ports and the actual hardware of your development workstation. By default, the emulator simulates an environment with no serial or parallel ports, but you can map either or both serial ports onto the COM ports of the development workstation, and you can map the emulated parallel port onto the development workstation's printer port.

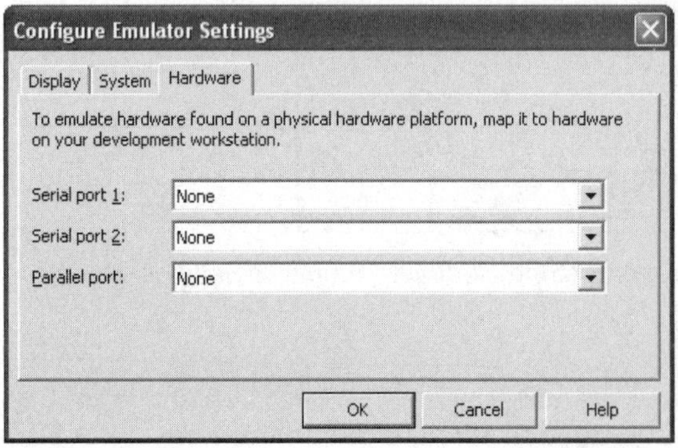

Figure 5-18 Hardware tab of the Configure Emulator Settings dialog box.

Tip The emulator requires your development workstation to have a configured network adapter. If your development machine does not have a network adapter (or if it is disconnected, a situation which often happens when a laptop is on the move), you will need to install the Loopback Adapter. Chapter 1 describes how to install the Loopback Adapter. Refer to your operating system help for further details of installation.

In some configurations, network operations from the emulator might not work correctly if the host computer has multiple IP addresses. This can occur if the host computer has multiple network adaptors, but it can also occur if you have the Loopback Adapter installed alongside a real network card. In such cases, you might have to disable or uninstall one adapter to perform network operations from the emulator.

Starting the Emulator Manually

If you want to start the emulator manually, without loading Visual Studio .NET, you can run the emulator as a stand-alone Windows application. The program, Emulator.exe, is found by default in the C:\Program Files\Microsoft Visual Studio .NET\CompactFrameworkSDK\ConnectionManager\bin directory. Emulator.exe supports the following command-line options:

- **Image File** The emulator requires an image file that defines the emulated operating system image. The supplied image files are found in the Images subdirectory of the directory where Emulator.exe is found. Generic Pocket PC 2002 and Windows CE .NET images are supplied with Smart Device Extensions; the exact images available to you will also depend on whether you have installed localized versions of Windows CE. The image file used by the emulator is defined with the /CEImage option.

- **Ethernet** The Emulator has support for a simulated Ethernet adapter, using the /Ethernet command-line option, which can have values of true or false. If Ethernet support is enabled, it takes the form of a single adapter using the IP protocol emulating a DEC 21040 Ethernet card. You can actually use any Ethernet card that is supported by your development workstation.

- **Video** The /Video option allows the screen configuration to be set, using the format /Video *WidthxHeightxDepth*.
- **Skin** The /Skin option allows you to specify a custom skin for the emulator's GUI. See the section "Using Emulator Skins" for a detailed discussion of this option.

You might want to create a batch file similar to StartEmulator.bat, shown here, to start up stand-alone emulation.

StartEmulator.bat

```
C:
cd "\Program Files\Microsoft Visual Studio .NET\CompactFrameworkSDK\→
  ConnectionManager\bin"
start emulator /CEImage images\windowsce\webpad\1033\wce4webpad.bin
```

The *cd* command changes the current directory to the directory in which the emulator is installed. If you have installed the Visual Studio .NET and Smart Device Extensions files in a directory other than the default, you will need to make corresponding changes to the batch file. The *start* command on the second line ensures that the command shell does not wait for the emulator to terminate before continuing.

Using Emulator Skins

The GUI for the emulator can be customized by creating a skin. A custom skin gives the emulator the look and feel of a specific hardware platform. Skins are not essential, but you might find them helpful if you want to customize the emulator appearance. Skins are defined in an XML file, as shown in the following example code.

Oval.xml

```
<?xml version="1.0"?>
<skin>
  <view
    titleBar ="Oval Emulator Skin"
    displayPosX="72"
    displayPosY="72"
    displayWidth="336"
    displayHeight="216"
    displayDepth="8"
    normalImage="Oval.bmp"
```

(continued)

Oval.xml *(continued)*

```
    mappingImage="OvalButtonMap.bmp"
    downImage="OvalButtonDown.bmp"
  >
    <!-- Red button -->
    <button mappingColor="0xFF0000" toolTip="Left"  onClick="Key_Left"/>
    <!-- Green button -->
    <button mappingColor="0x00FF00" toolTip="Up"    onClick="Key_Up"/>
    <!-- Blue button -->
    <button mappingColor="0x0000FF" toolTip="Right" onClick="Key_Right"/>
    <!-- Yellow button -->
    <button mappingColor="0xFFFF00" toolTip="Down"  onClick="Key_Down"/>
  </view>
</skin>
```

All XML elements and attribute names are case-sensitive, and all attribute values must be enclosed in quotation marks.

The *<skin>* XML element defines a skin. This element contains a *<view>* element, which defines the overall appearance of the skin and zero or more *<button>* elements, each of which defines the action of a button.

The *<view>* element contains the main attributes for the view of the skin. The attributes are described in Table 5-1.

Table 5-1 Attributes for *<view>* Element

Attribute Name	Meaning
titleBar	The text that appears in the emulator window's title bar.
displayPosX, *displayPosY*	The coordinates of the upper left of the emulated display window within the emulator client area, measured in pixels.
displayWidth, *displayHeight*	The size of the emulated display window, measured in pixels. For width, choose an integer between 80 and 1024. For height, choose an integer between 64 and 768. Sizes must be multiples of 8.
displayDepth	The display's color depth (8, 16, or 32 bits per pixel).
normalImage	A file containing a bitmap with all buttons up (unselected).
mappingImage	A file containing a bitmap whose colors define the button positions.
downImage	A file containing a bitmap with all buttons down (selected).

Each *<button>* element defines a simulated hardware button. The attributes for the *<button>* element are described in Table 5-2.

Table 5-2 Attributes for *<button>* Element

Attribute Name	Meaning
toolTip	Text that will appear above the button when the mouse hovers over it.
onClick	A string that defines what happens when the button is pressed.
onPressAndHold	A string that defines what happens when the button is pressed and held.
mappingColor	The color used in the *mappingImage* bitmap to define the button. All pixels in the mapping image that are found of this color are considered to be part of the button on the emulator screen.

Using Image Files

For a simple emulator skin that defines no hardware buttons, the only image file that is required is *normalImage*. This is a bitmap file that defines the look of the emulator screen.

If you want your emulator to support buttons, the *normalImage* bitmap must contain a representation of the buttons in the up or unselected state, and two additional bitmaps (specified via the *mappingImage* and *downImage* attributes) are required to specify the location of the buttons and their appearance when down or selected.

Consider the following example files. For the skin defined in the Oval.xml file, the Oval.bmp file appears as shown in Figure 5-19.

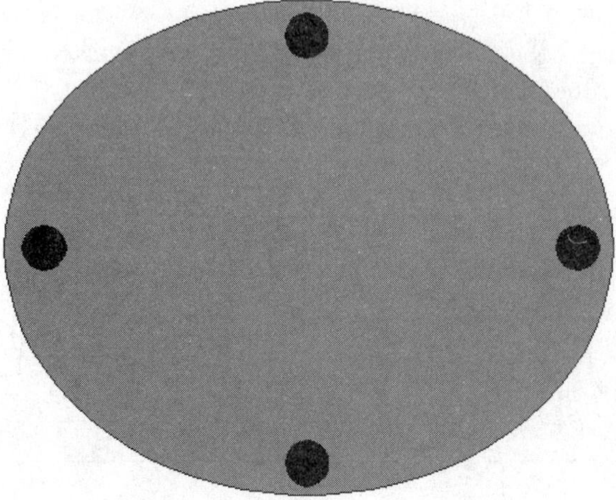

Figure 5-19 Main skin image.

Notice the four circles at top, left, bottom, and right. Each of these defines the appearance of a hardware button in the up state.

The OvalButtonMap.bmp file has four areas picked out in different colors to indicate the location of the buttons. In this case, the colors used are red for the left button, blue for the right button, green for the top button, and yellow for the bottom button, as shown in Figure 5-20.

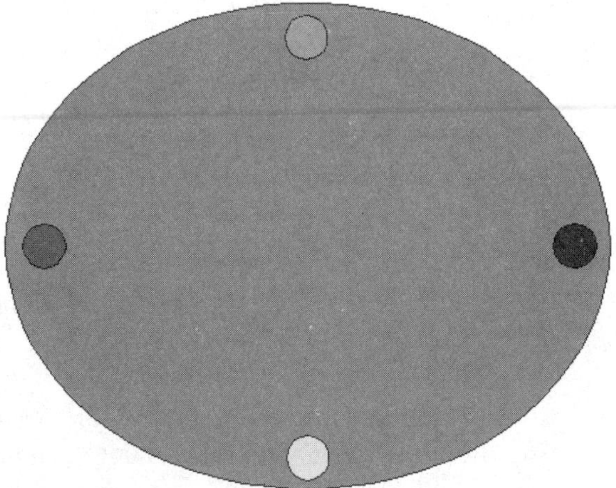

Figure 5-20 Skin image—button map.

Finally the OvalButtonDown.bmp button shows the state of the emulator when all the buttons are depressed. In this example, the buttons are white when down, as shown in Figure 5-21.

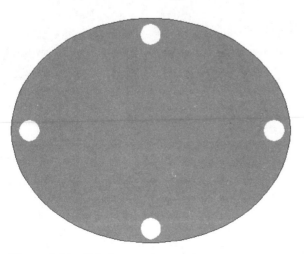

Figure 5-21 Skin image—button-down map.

Emulating Hardware Buttons

The *onClick* attribute of the *<button>* element is a string that specifies the key presses that the emulated application receives when the button is clicked. You can specify a hexadecimal or decimal value corresponding to a raw keyboard scan code, or you can choose from predefined symbols, such as *Key_F1* for the F1 function key, *Key_7* for the number 7, *Key_Escape* for the escape key, or *Key_Z* for the letter Z. A complete list of key symbols can be found in the online help for the emulator. Note that these symbols are case-sensitive.

The emulator also provides the following three special key codes:

- DOWN:
- UP:
- SHUTDOWN

The *DOWN:* key code provides the effect of keeping pressed in the keyboard key corresponding to the key code that follows the *DOWN:* key code. The *UP:* key code provides the effect of releasing the keyboard key corresponding to the key code that follows the *UP:* key code. For example, the following entry means that a button will send the keystrokes for Left+Shift+Z when the button is depressed, followed by Left+Shift+A when the button is released.

```
onClick=
"DOWN:Key_LeftShift Key_Z UP:Key_LeftShift  Key_A"
```

The *SHUTDOWN* key code simulates a shutdown hardware button, displaying a dialog box that allows the user to shut down the emulator.

Starting the Emulator with a Skin File

To use a skin file with the emulator, the following steps are required:

- Define the bitmaps as required.
- Create an XML file as outlined above, with *<skin>* and *<view>* elements and a button element for each button.
- Start the emulator with the /skin command line option followed by the full path name of the XML skin definition file.

Here's a sample batch file used to start the emulator using the ppc2002.bin image and the Oval.xml skin definition file. You'll have to place the XML file and all the bitmaps in the C:\skins directory to try this example. Running the OvalEmulator batch file will produce the result shown in Figure 5-22.

OvalEmulator.bat

```
setlocal
rem Change these directories to match your development system
set EMDIR=C:\Program Files\Microsoft Visual Studio .NET\¬
  CompactFrameworkSDK\ConnectionManager\bin
set SKINDIR=C:\Skins
start "" "%EMDIR%\emulator" /CEImage "%EMDIR%\images\pocketpc\¬
  2002\1033\ppc2002.bin" /skin "%SKINDIR%\Oval.xml" /Ethernet true
```

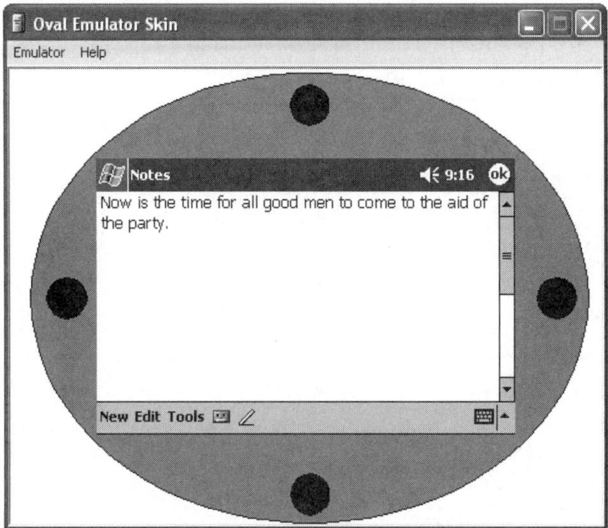

Figure 5-22 Emulator in action.

You'll find this example's files in this book's sample files, in the CustomSkin directory for this chapter. Using custom skins in this way can make your emulation environment match your target platform or platforms more closely.

> **Tip** Although you can use skins to customize the appearance of the emulator, they cannot be used to change the feature set of the emulated environment. The Windows CE .NET and Windows CE 3 operating systems are both modular and highly configurable. The emulators that ship with the Visual Studio .NET environment are intended to represent typical configurations that match common off-the-shelf consumer hardware such as PDAs. If you're targeting a specific device, the vendor of the device might provide you with an emulator that is more specific to the device.

Summary

In this chapter, you have seen how the powerful debugging features of the full .NET Framework have been implemented for the .NET Compact Framework environment. In keeping with the design philosophy of the .NET Compact Framework, some features of the full .NET Framework are not implemented entirely. Notwithstanding these limitations, most common debugging and testing requirements are provided. The emulation environment can also be customized to match your target environment.

6

Completing and Distributing Your Application

You've written your application, tested it, and debugged it, and now you're ready to add the finishing touches to it and distribute it as a completed application to your user base.

This chapter explains how to create an installation package you can deliver to your users, describes different techniques for deploying applications to devices, and explains how to store shared assemblies in the Global Assembly Cache (GAC).

Choosing Project Settings

Settings you make in your Visual Studio .NET project affect the files that deploy to the target device, the directory where the application deploys, and the icon that displays in File Explorer.

Using the File Build Action Property

In a Visual Studio .NET project, you can use the Build Action property to specify the action that Visual Studio .NET takes for a file when you build your application.

The Build Action property has four settings:

- **None** Specifies that the file is not included in the build output group. An example of a file that needs this setting is a text file that contains documentation for the project.
- **Compile** Specifies that the file is compiled and included in the build output. This is the default setting for code files such as forms and modules.

- **Content** Specifies that the file is included in the build output group. This is the default setting for Web files, XML files, and graphics files. The file deploys to the target directory as a separate file.
- **Embedded Resource** Specifies that the file is included in the main build output file, which can be an executable or a DLL. This setting can be used to provide graphic and other resource files. In your applications, you access embedded resources using the following code:

```
Assembly.GetExecutingAssembly()
.GetManifestResourceStream("namespace.filename.extension")
```

The default setting for the Build Action property depends on the type of file that you add to your project. For example, if you add a form to your project, the default setting for the Build Action property is Compile.

Associating an Icon with Your Application

You can associate an icon with your application by using the project's Property Pages dialog box. Select the General section from the Common Properties folder in the tree view on the left of the dialog box. Then select the Application Icon field, and enter the path to the icon you want to associate with your application. You can also click the Browse button that appears when the Application Icon field is selected. Figure 6-1 shows the project's Property Pages dialog box with the Application Icon field selected.

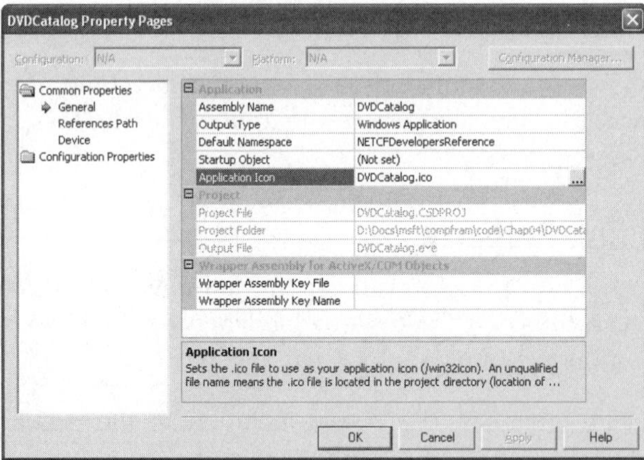

Figure 6-1 General page of the project's Property Pages dialog box.

The icon you associate to your application displays in the top line of the Start menu on a Pocket PC when the application is running, and it appears in the Start Menu if you create a shortcut to your application there. For details of how to create a shortcut, see the section "Usage of the *CEShortCuts* Section" later in this chapter.

Setting the Deployment Directory

The default deployment directory is \Program Files\<*Application name*>. You change the default installation location of your application by selecting the project in the Solution Explorer window and then changing Output File Folder in the Properties window. As shown in Figure 6-2, you can also change the default installation location in the project's Property Pages dialog box. In the Device section, select the Output File Folder field and enter the destination directory for your application.

The Benefits of Application-Private Assemblies

One benefit of the .NET Framework deployment model is that by default each application has its own private copies of other assemblies that it references. The exceptions to this rule are shared assemblies stored in the GAC. (See the section "Installing Assemblies into the Global Assembly Cache" later in this chapter.)

When you create a Visual Studio .NET project to build a class library, the project compiles into an assembly. In another project, which we'll call *AppA*, you can add a reference to that class-library assembly in order to make use of it. When you do this, Visual Studio .NET copies the class-library assembly you referenced into the bin\debug directory, and when you build a CAB file (discussed in the section "Packaging Your Application" later in this chapter), Visual Studio .NET includes the copy of the class-library assembly along with the AppA assembly.

If you update the class library to add new functionality or fix bugs and then create a new application, AppB, which also references the class library, the new application takes its own private copy of the updated class library.

You can see that as long as AppA and AppB deploy to different directories, each application has its own copy of the class library and each application runs using the exact same version of the class library with which it was developed. If both applications used the same copy of the class library at run time, the updates to the class library that happened after AppA was built could inadvertently break AppA. But with application-private assemblies, this cannot happen.

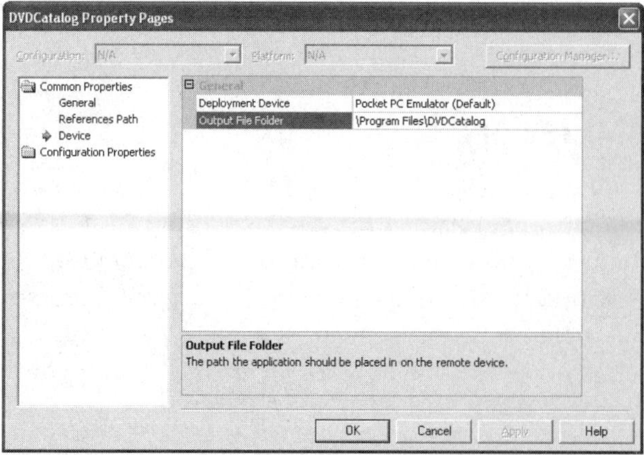

Figure 6-2 Device page of the project's Property Pages dialog box.

Packaging Your Application

You package your applications into self-extracting .cab (CAB) files. CAB files deliver all files needed by your application in one file, thus preventing the risk of partial installation of your application.

You build a CAB file for your application in one of two ways. You can either generate the CAB file from Visual Studio .NET, or you can use the CAB Wizard application (Cabwiz.exe) at the command line.

Both methods have their advantages and disadvantages. Using Visual Studio .NET to create the CAB file is quick and easy but is not very flexible in configuring installation options for your application. Using CAB Wizard will take longer because it requires you to set up the configuration file, but you have complete control over the installation of your application on the target device. For example, Visual Studio .NET doesn't allow you to specify the shortcut to your application in the target device's Start menu. To specify the shortcut, you'll need to create or modify a configuration file to include the *CEShortcut* key and you'll need to generate the CAB file using CAB Wizard.

You can use both methods to create your custom CAB file. First create the CAB file using Visual Studio .NET, and then modify the configuration file that Visual Studio .NET creates to include any custom settings you require. Visual Studio .NET also creates the file BuildCab.bat, which you use to rebuild your application's CAB file.

Creating Processor-Specific CAB Files

Code that you write for the .NET Compact Framework compiles to Microsoft Intermediate Language (MSIL). MSIL is a binary format that the common language runtime reads and compiles at run time, but MSIL itself is platform- and processor-independent. Despite this, Visual Studio .NET creates a CAB file for each processor type supported by the .NET Compact Framework. For example, if you build the application HelloWorld for the Pocket PC platform and then create CAB files for that application, Visual Studio .NET creates four files: HelloWorld_PPC.arm.cab, HelloWorld_PPC.mips.cab, HelloWorld_PPC.sh3.cab, and HelloWorld_PPC.x86.cab.

The only difference in the CAB files will be if you have used native components that do not support all the processors supported by the .NET Compact Framework. Visual Studio .NET creates CAB files only for the processors that are supported by all the components used in your project. For example, if you build a HelloWorld application that uses a native component that does not support the MIPS processor and then create CAB files for that application, Visual Studio .NET creates only three files: HelloWorld_PPC.arm.cab, HelloWorld_PPC.sh3.cab, and HelloWorld_PPC.x86.cab.

Building CAB Files Using Visual Studio .NET

To create your CAB files from Visual Studio .NET, select the Build CAB File option from the Build menu. This menu option is available in Visual Studio .NET only when you have your application project open.

Visual Studio .NET saves the CAB files it generates to the folder *project*/cab/*buildmode*, where *project* is the name of your project and *buildmode* is either Debug or Release. It also creates a batch file, a configuration file, and a dependencies file. You use the batch file, called BuildCab.bat, to rebuild your application's CAB files if you make changes to the configuration file. You customize the creation of your CAB file by changing settings in the configuration file, which Visual Studio .NET names according to the project and the target system, such as *project_targetsystem*.inf. For a project named HelloWorld that targets a Pocket PC device, Visual Studio .NET will name the configuration file HelloWorld_PPC.inf. The dependencies file, Dependencies.ppc, records the dependencies for your application's CAB file. Generally, the principal dependency is the CAB file for the .NET Compact Framework runtime. At installation time, the CAB installer checks that named dependencies have already been installed on the device.

When the CAB files are built, Visual Studio .NET moves them to your project folder's bin/release or bin/debug folder, depending on the current build mode.

Building CAB Files Using CAB Wizard

To use CAB Wizard, you must provide a configuration file for it to process. See the section "Understanding the Configuration File" later in this chapter for details on the format of the configuration file.

The syntax for using the CAB Wizard from the command line is:

```
Cabwiz.exe inf_file [/dest dest_directory] [/err error_file]
    [/cpu platform_label [platform_label]]
```

Here's the detail for each parameter:

- ***inf_file*** The full path and filename for the configuration file to be used to create the CAB file.
- ***dest_directory*** The absolute destination directory for the CAB files. If no directory is specified, the *inf_file* directory is used.
- ***error_file*** The absolute path and filename of the file that CAB Wizard will use to log errors that might occur during the creation of the CAB files. If no file is specified, error messages are displayed in message windows. If a file is specified, CAB Wizard can run without creating windows, which is useful for creating automated builds.
- ***platform_label*** These parameters cause CAB Wizard to create CAB files for each platform specified. The platform labels are the labels defined in the configuration file. The /cpu option must be the last option on the command line.

The following example creates a CAB file for the ARM and MIPS processors for an application called DVDCatalog:

```
Cabwiz.exe "c:\DVDCatalog\DVDCatalog.inf" /err DVDCatalog.err /cpu arm mips
```

> **Note** The path to Cabwiz.exe is not shown in the preceding example for clarity, but unless you add Cabwiz.exe to your *PATH* environment variable, the program must be called with its full path to run correctly.
>
> The default installation path for Cabwiz.exe is C:\Program Files\Microsoft Visual Studio .NET 2003\CompactFrameworkSDK\v1.0.5000\bin\.

Using the Resource File Generator

The Resource File Generator (CFResgen.exe) command-line utility allows you to convert .txt (text) files and .resx (XML-based resource format) files into common language runtime .resource files. These .resource files can then be embedded into your run-time executable file or satellite assembly. The CFResgen.exe utility can also convert .resource files into .txt or .resx files.

The syntax of the command is

```
cfresgen [/compile] filename.extension [outputfilename.extension]
```

The /compile option allows you to specify multiple .txt or .resx files to be converted into .resource files. If the /compile option is not used, only one file can be converted.

See Chapter 19 for more information on resource files and how to use them in your applications.

Understanding the Configuration File

The configuration file tells Cab Wizard how to build CAB files for your application. For example, the following code is the configuration file for the DVDCatalog application:

```
[Version]
Signature="$Windows NT$"
Provider="My Company"
CESignature="$Windows CE$"

[CEStrings]
AppName="DVDCatalog"
InstallDir=%CE1%\%AppName%

[CEDevice]
VersionMin=3.00
VersionMax=3.99

[DefaultInstall]
CopyFiles=Files.Common
CEShortcuts = Shortcuts

[DefaultInstall.ARM]
CopyFiles=Files.ARM
CESetupDLL=vsd_setup.dll

[DefaultInstall.SH3]
CopyFiles=Files.SH3
CESetupDLL=vsd_setup.dll
```

(continued)

```
[DefaultInstall.MIPS]
CopyFiles=Files.MIPS
CESetupDLL=vsd_setup.dll

[DefaultInstall.X86]
CopyFiles=Files.X86
CESetupDLL=vsd_setup.dll

[Shortcuts]
DVD Catalog, 0, DVDCatalog.exe

[SourceDisksNames]
1=,"Common1",,"C:\Documents and Settings\stephenw\My Documents\➘
    Visual Studio Projects\DVDCatalog\obj\Debug\"

[SourceDisksNames.ARM]
2=,"ARM_Setup",,"C:\Program Files\Microsoft Visual Studio .NET\➘
    CompactFrameworkSDK\v1.0.3300\Windows CE\wce300\ARM\"

[SourceDisksNames.SH3]
3=,"SH3_Setup",,"C:\Program Files\Microsoft Visual Studio .NET\➘
    CompactFrameworkSDK\v1.0.3300\Windows CE\wce300\SH3\"

[SourceDisksNames.MIPS]
4=,"MIPS_Setup",,"C:\Program Files\Microsoft Visual Studio .NET\➘
    CompactFrameworkSDK\v1.0.3300\Windows CE\wce300\MIPS\"

[SourceDisksNames.X86]
5=,"X86_Setup",,"C:\Program Files\Microsoft Visual Studio .NET\➘
    CompactFrameworkSDK\v1.0.3300\Windows CE\wce300\X86\"

[SourceDisksFiles]
DVDCatalog.exe=1

[SourceDisksFiles.ARM]
vsd_setup.dll=2

[SourceDisksFiles.SH3]
vsd_setup.dll=3

[SourceDisksFiles.MIPS]
vsd_setup.dll=4

[SourceDisksFiles.X86]
vsd_setup.dll=5

[DestinationDirs]
Shortcuts = 0, %CE17%
```

```
Files.Common=0,%InstallDir%
Files.ARM=0,%InstallDir%
Files.SH3=0,%InstallDir%
Files.MIPS=0,%InstallDir%
Files.X86=0,%InstallDir%

[Files.Common]
DVDCatalog.exe,,,0

[Files.ARM]
vsd_setup.dll,,,0

[Files.SH3]
vsd_setup.dll,,,0

[Files.MIPS]
vsd_setup.dll,,,0

[Files.X86]
vsd_setup.dll,,,0
```

The following sections first describe the macro strings you use for Windows CE directories and then each section of the configuration file.

Configuration File Directory Identifiers

You use directory identifiers in the configuration file for your application to identify standard Windows CE directories. Table 6-1 lists the macro strings that can be used and the directory that they point to.

Table 6-1 Standard Windows CE Directory Identifiers

Macro String (Directory Identifier)	Windows CE Directory
%CE1%	\Program Files
%CE2%	\Windows
%CE4%	\Windows\StartUp
%CE5%	\My Documents
%CE8%	\Program Files\Games
%CE11%	\Windows\Start Menu\Programs
%CE14%	\Windows\Start Menu\Programs\Games
%CE15%	\Windows\Fonts
%CE17%	\Windows\Start Menu

Description of the *Version* Section

The *Version* section of the configuration file is used to specify the creator of the file. Other relevant information is also defined in this section. The *Version* section of the configuration file is a required section; if it is not included, errors will occur when you try to rebuild your application's CAB file.

The following three keys in this section must be present for the CAB file build to be successful:

- ***Signature* key** Must be set to either "$Windows NT$" or "$Windows 95$". It does not matter which of these settings you choose.
- ***Provider* key** Should be set to the name of your company. The name you enter here appears on windows that display during installation.
- ***CESignature* key** Must be set to "$Windows CE$".

Applying the *CEStrings* Section

The *CEStrings* section of the configuration file provides string substitutes for the application name and default installation directory. The *CEStrings* section of the configuration file must be present when you build your application's CAB file; errors will occur if it is not present.

The following two keys are required in this section:

- ***AppName* key** Set to the name of your application.
- ***InstallDir* key** Contains the default installation location for your application on the target device. Directory identifiers are used in the *InstallDir* string to identify the various directories on the target device. See the "Configuration File Directory Identifiers" section earlier in this chapter for more information. In the following example, if your application's name is DVDCatalog, *InstallDir* translates to \Program Files\DVDCatalog:

  ```
  InstallDir = %CE1%\%AppName%
  ```

  Any further occurrences of *%AppName%* and *%InstallDir%* in the configuration file will be replaced with the strings set up in the *CEStrings* section.

Using the *Strings* Section

The *Strings* section of the configuration file is an optional section and is used to provide string substitution for your own requirements. Any number of custom keys can be defined in this section.

```
[Strings]
string_key = string_value
```

Any occurrences of *%string_key%* in the configuration file will be replaced by *string_value*, which consists of a string of printable characters.

Description of the *CEDevice* Section

The *CEDevice* section is an optional section of the configuration file that defines the supported devices for the CAB file. This section is of little relevance for a .NET Compact Framework application. For more information, please refer to the Windows CE .NET SDK documentation.

Specifying the *DefaultInstall* Section

The *DefaultInstall* section of the configuration file defines the default installation for your application. The *DefaultInstall* section is a required section in the configuration file, and the creation of your CAB file fails if this section is missing. Additional *DefaultInstall* sections can be specified for the various processor types supported. For example, the section *DefaultInstall.ARM* would define the default installation for the ARM processor.

The following five keys can be used in this section, but only the *CopyFiles* key is required for a successful CAB file build:

CopyFiles Defines the file copy sections of the configuration file; see the section "Usage of the *CopyFiles* Section" later in this chapter for more details. More than one file copy section can be defined with this key by separating the section names with commas.

For example, this *DefaultInstall* section defines the following two file copy sections:

```
[DefaultInstall]
CopyFiles = ARM.Files, MIPS.Files
```

AddReg Defines the name of the section of the configuration file for adding entries to the registry; see the section "Description of the *AddReg* Section" later in this chapter for more details. More than one section for adding entries to the registry can be defined using the *AddReg* key by separating the section names with a comma.

CEShortcuts Used to define the shortcut sections in your configuration file that define the shortcuts to your application. You can define more than one shortcut section by separating the shortcut section names with a comma. For more information on shortcuts, see the section "Usage of the *CEShortCuts* Section" later in this chapter.

CESetupDLL Specifies the Setup.dll file to provide for the installation and removal of your application. This is always vsd_setup.dll for .NET Compact Framework applications. You must also list vsd_setup.dll in the *SourceDisksFiles* section of the configuration file.

CESelfRegister Used for self-registering components. Unless your CAB file installs new COM objects, you will not need to use this key.

Defining the *SourceDisksNames* Section

The *SourceDisksName* section of the configuration file is required and defines the location of the files for your application. A different *SourceDisksName* section can be defined for each processor your application supports. This is achieved by suffixing the processor identifier to the section name. For example, to define a *SourceDisksName* section for the ARM processor, you would define the section as *SourceDisksName.ARM.*

The format for entries in this section is *disk_id* = *,comment,,path*.

- ***disk_id*** Identifies the disk in the set.
- ***comment*** Denotes a text comment.
- ***path*** Identifies the path to your application's files. This path can be absolute or relative and can contain directory identifiers.

Defining the *SourceDisksFiles* Section

The *SourceDisksFiles* section defines the name and path of the files for your application. A different *SourceDisksFiles* section can be defined for each processor that your application supports. For example, to define an ARM *SourceDisksFiles* section, you would define the section as *SourceDisksFiles.ARM.*

The format of the key entries for this key is *filename* = *disk_id*, *subdir.*

- ***filename*** Denotes the name of the file you are installing.
- ***disk_id*** Identifies the disk in the set.
- ***subdir*** Is optional and defines the subdirectory where the files for your application are located.

Specifying the *DestinationDirs* Section

The *DestinationDirs* section of the configuration file defines the destination directories for your application. This section of the configuration file must exist for a successful CAB file build. The keys in this section consist of the section names containing the lists of files that will be copied to the target device. The key values define the destination path for the files.

The format for entries in this section is *file_list_section_name* = 0, *sub_dir_name*.

- ***file_list_section_name*** Identifies the name of the file section for which a destination path is being defined. See the section "Usage of the *CopyFiles* Section" later in this chapter for a definition of the file section.

- ***sub_dir_name*** Defines the destination directory location of the files in the specified file section. The path can contain an absolute path, the *%InstallDir%* substitution string, or a directory identifier from Table 6-1.

Usage of the *CopyFiles* Section

At least one *CopyFiles* section must exist in the configuration file. These sections describe the default files that will be copied to the device when your application installs. You can define as many *CopyFiles* sections as you require for your application. Within each *CopyFiles* section, you can define multiple files that need to be copied during installation.

Each *CopyFiles* section is defined as follows:

```
[DefaultInstall]
CopyFiles = copyFileSectionName

[copyFileSectionName]
destinationFilename, sourceFilename, ,flags
<;$VE>
```

Here's the detail for each parameter:

- ***copyFilesSectionName*** Defines the name of the *CopyFiles* section.
- ***destinationFilename*** Identifies the destination filename.
- ***sourceFilename*** Identifies the source filename. This parameter is optional if it is the same as *destinationFilename*.
- ***flags*** The optional *flags* parameter defines any actions to be taken during the copying of the file. Please refer to the Windows CE SDK for a full list of the values supported by Windows CE.

Description of the *AddReg* Section

The *AddReg* sections are optional sections of the configuration file. These sections are defined by the *AddReg* key under the *DefaultInstall* section of the configuration file. Each section defines the registry keys, and values are added to the registry when your application is installed. For more information, see the device's SDK.

Usage of the *CEShortCuts* Section

The *CEShortcuts* sections are defined using the *CEShortcuts* key under the *DefaultInstall* section of the configuration file. The *CEShortcuts* key and *CEShortcuts* sections are optional. The *CEShortcuts* sections define the shortcuts that will be created on the target device during installation.

The format for defining the *CEShortcuts* sections is as follows:

```
[DefaultInstall]
CEShortcuts = shortcuts_sec_name

[shortcuts_sec_name]
file_name, type, target, destination
```

- ***shortcuts_sec_name*** Defines the name of the *CEShortcuts* section.
- ***file_name*** Defines the name that the shortcut will be saved to the device with.
- ***type*** Defines the type of shortcut. Zero or empty defines a shortcut to a file, and a nonzero defines a shortcut to a folder.
- ***target*** Defines the destination file or folder for the shortcut. If a file is specified, it must also be specified in the *CopyFiles* section. Use a *file_list_section_name* as defined in the *DestinationDirs* section or the *%InstallDir%* substitution string.
- ***destination*** Optional and defines the destination path for the shortcut file. A directory identifier from Table 6-1 or *%InstallDir%* can be used. If no value is present, the default directory destination, as defined in the *DestinationDir* section, is used.

Below is a section of the configuration file for the DVDCatalog application as an example of the *CEShortcuts* section in use:

```
[DefaultInstall]
CopyFiles = Files.Common
CEShortcuts = Shortcuts

[Shortcuts]
DVD Catalog, 0, DVDCatalog.exe

[DestinationDirs]
Shortcuts = 0, %CE17%
Files.Common = 0,%InstallDir%
Files.ARM = 0,%InstallDir%
Files.SH3 = 0,%InstallDir%
Files.MIPS = 0,%InstallDir%
Files.X86 = 0,%InstallDir%
```

Distributing Your Application

Once you have built the CAB files for your application, you can distribute the application to your users using one of the following methods:

- A Web site
- A file share
- Another device
- Memory storage cards
- Server or desktop PC using ActiveSync

In addition to the CAB file for your application, you might also need to distribute other CAB files to support your application. The following is a list of the CAB files you should include in your distribution:

- CAB file for the .NET Compact Framework (unless it is already installed)
- CAB file for your application
- CAB files for components that your application uses that are not part of the standard .NET Compact Framework

Because the CAB files contain all the information needed to install your application, the user only needs to tap the CAB file to begin the installation process. The installation process begins by extracting the application files into the installation directory specified in your application's CAB file. Normally, the CAB file will be removed after the installation process is complete. To prevent a CAB file from being removed after installation, right-click the CAB file in Windows Explorer, select Properties from the shortcut menu, and then check Read-Only under Attributes.

Installing the .NET Compact Framework

In future versions of Windows CE .NET, the .NET Compact Framework runtime and base class libraries will be fully integrated into the operating system, and you will not have to take special steps to install them on the device. Currently however, if you try to install an application onto a new device, you will see an error such as that shown in Figure 6-3.

By default, you'll find the CAB files for the .NET Compact Framework runtime in the C:\Program Files\Microsoft Visual Studio .NET 2003\CompactFrameworkSDK\V1.0.5000\Windows CE folder. Two more folders are located in that folder: wce300 contains CAB files for Windows CE 3 and Pocket PC 2000 and 2002 devices, and wce400 is for Windows CE .NET and Pocket PC .NET. In each of those folders are the processor-specific folders, such as ARM, MIPS, SH3, and x86 for Pocket PC platform. (Note that devices with the Intel XScale processor use ARM binaries.)

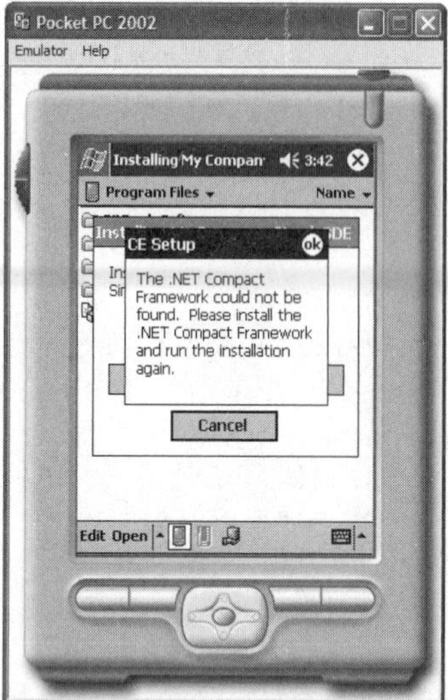

Figure 6-3 Attempting to install a .NET Compact Framework application on a device that doesn't have the common language runtime.

The file netcf.cjk.ppc3.*{proc}*.cab is the installation file for the .NET Compact Framework for Pocket PC platform, where *{proc}* is the processor type. For Windows CE .NET platforms, the file is netcf.all.wce4.*{proc}*.cab. Transfer one of these files to the target device using the same techniques you would use for an application installation file, and install that before your application.

> **Note** You do not have to manually install the .NET Compact Framework on a device you use for testing during development. Visual Studio .NET automatically installs the .NET Compact Framework runtime and base class libraries on your target device (which includes the emulators) when you debug an application.

Deploying from a Web Site

The CAB file for your application can be made available for download on a Web site. Users start Pocket Internet Explorer and either enter the URL for the CAB file in the address bar or visit a Web page, which you provide, that contains links to the CAB files.

You can carry out a simple test to see how this works. Create a simple smart device application, and then choose the Create Cab Files option to build the CAB files. Create a folder anywhere on your development computer—call it something like NETCFDeploy—and copy all the CAB files for the application into it. In Windows Explorer, right-click the NETCFDeploy folder, select Sharing and Security from the shortcut menu, and then in the Properties dialog box, click the Web Sharing tab. Select the Share This Folder option button, and in the Edit Alias window that appears, type the Web site name you want—this could be NETCFDeploy again, or any other name you want. Click OK. You have now created a Web page containing the CAB files for your application. For example, if your development machine is called MyPC, you can use the URL *http://mypc/netcfdeploy/mysimpleapp_ppc.arm.cab* to fetch the CAB file for the application mysimpleapp for ARM processors, such as the Compaq iPaq Pocket PC.

Now, on your device, make sure you are connected to your development machine through ActiveSync, or connected to your LAN by a wireless or wired connection. In Pocket Internet Explorer, select Address Bar from the View menu if the address bar is not visible, and then enter the URL to the correct CAB file for the processor type of your device. You will see a window asking you to confirm the download, such as that shown in Figure 6-4. NETCFSelect Open File After Download and click Yes to download the application and start it.

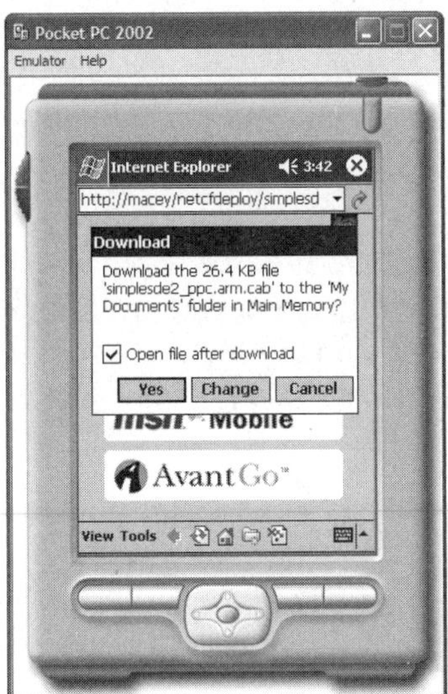

Figure 6-4 Using Pocket Internet Explorer to install an application deployed through a Web site.

Deploying from a File Share

You can place the CAB files for your application on a network share. From a cradled device or a device that is connected to the LAN using 802.11b wireless or an Ethernet wired connection, your users can use File Explorer to access files on the network share.

Deploying from Another Device

This is not a serious option for wide-scale deployment, but in some circumstances, you could use an infrared connection to distribute your application from one device to another. If you use File Explorer to navigate to an application on your device and then tap and hold, one of the context menu options is Beam File. The recipient starts the Infrared Receive application to accept the file transfer.

Deploying with Memory Storage Cards

If you use memory storage cards and are deploying to a Pocket PC, you can take advantage of the Autorun feature of the Pocket PC. This feature allows the Pocket PC to run an application when a memory storage card is inserted into or removed from the device. When a memory storage card is inserted into a Pocket PC device, the system will search the root directory for a subfolder with the same name as the processor type of the device. For example, a device with an SH3 processor will search for a subfolder with the name SH3. When a subfolder with a matching name is found, the subfolder is then searched for an Autorun.exe file. If this file is found it is copied to the \Windows folder. The system then executes the Autorun.exe file with the *install* parameter. When the memory storage card is removed, the system will execute Autorun.exe with the *uninstall* parameter. You can use the Autorun.exe file to install one or more applications. An example of an Autorun.exe application is provided in the Windows Platform SDK for Pocket PC.

Deploying Through ActiveSync

You can deploy your application to the user's device using ActiveSync in two ways. Your first option is to use the Explore feature of ActiveSync to copy the CAB file to the device. Then the user must use File Explorer on the device to find and tap the CAB file to start the installation process. The second option is to use Application Manager to manage the installation of your application. Application Manager is a desktop application that is installed on the user's desktop computer. You can use Application Manager to install and uninstall applications from your Windows CE device.

To use Application Manager to install your application, you must create an Application Manager initialization (.ini) file. This file provides the information that Application Manager requires to install your application. You must also create a desktop setup application. This setup application must check to make sure that a current version of Application Manager is installed and then call Application Manager passing the .ini file as a parameter.

The following Visual C++ code, from the Setup application in this book's sample files, checks the registry key HKEY_LOCAL_MACHINE\Software\Microsoft\Windows\CurrentVersion\AppPaths\CEAppMgr.exe. If the key does not exist, the code displays an error and aborts the setup process.

```
HKEY hkey

if(RegOpenKeyEx(HKEY_LOCAL_MACHINE,
    TEXT("software\\Microsoft\\Windows"
        "\\CurrentVersion\\App Paths\\CEAppMgr.exe"),
    0, KEY_READ, &hkey) != ERROR_SUCCESS)
{
    MessageBox(NULL, TEXT("Unable to find Application Manager"),
        TEXT("Error"), MB_OK);
    return 1;
}
```

If the key exists, the code retrieves the current path to Application Manager from the registry key using the following Visual C++ code. Again, an error is displayed if the registry value cannot be found.

```
DWORD dwDataSize = MAX_PATH + 1;
DWORD dwType = REG_SZ;
TCHAR szPath[MAX_PATH + 1];
TCHAR szCurPath[MAX_PATH + 1];
TCHAR szParams[MAX_PATH * 2 + 2];

if(!RegQueryValueEx(hkey, NULL, NULL, &dwType,
    (PBYTE)szPath, &dwDataSize) == ERROR_SUCCESS)
{
    MessageBox(NULL, TEXT("Unable to find Application Manager "),
        TEXT("Error"), MB_OK);
    return 2;
}
```

Once the path to Application Manager is available, the setup application needs to pass the .ini file to Application Manager as a parameter. The setup application prepares the .ini file, Setup.ini in this example, to be used as a parameter.

```
szParams[0] = TCHAR(0);
_tcscat(szParams, TEXT("\""));
_tcscat(szParams, szCurPath);
_tcscat(szParams, TEXT("\\Setup.ini\""));
```

The code then creates a *SHELLEXECUTEINFO* construct to hold the information required by the *ShellExecuteEx* function.

```
SHELLEXECUTEINFO exinfo;

exinfo.cbSize = sizeof(exinfo);
exinfo.fMask = 0;
exinfo.hwnd = NULL;
exinfo.lpVerb = NULL;
exinfo.lpFile = szPath;
exinfo.lpParameters = szParams;
exinfo.lpDirectory = NULL;
exinfo.nShow = SW_SHOWDEFAULT;
exinfo.hInstApp = hInstance;
```

The setup application then calls Application Manager using the *ShellExecuteEx* function and displays an error message if there is any problem with the call.

```
if(!ShellExecuteEx(&exinfo))
{
    MessageBox(NULL, TEXT("Unable to Launch Application Manager"),
        TEXT("Error"), MB_OK);
    return 3;
}
```

Creating an Application Manager Initialization File

You register your application with Application Manager using the information contained in the Application Manager initialization file. The initialization file has the following format:

```
[CEAppManager]
Version       = 1.0
Component     = component_name

[component_name]
Description   = descriptive_name
[Uninstall    = uninstall_name]
[IconFile     = icon_filename]
[IconIndex    = icon_index]
[DeviceFile   = device_filename]
CabFiles      = cab_filename [,cab_filename]
```

Here's the detail for the strings:

- ***component_name*** Defines the name of the section for your application.
- ***descriptive_name*** Defines what will appear in the description field of Application Manager when a user chooses the application.
- ***uninstall_name*** Defines the application's Windows Uninstall registry key name. This name must match the application's registered Windows Uninstall key name, which is found in the HKEY_LOCAL_MACHINE\Software\Microsoft\Windows\CurrentVersion\Uninstall registry key. This will allow Application Manager to remove the application from the desktop computer and device.
- ***icon_filename*** Specifies the desktop icon file. This string is used to display an icon with the filename specified by *device_filename* when the filename is viewed in ActiveSync.
- ***icon_index*** Is a number used to display an icon with the filename specified by *device_filename* when the filename is viewed in ActiveSync. If this key is nonexistent, the first icon in the file specified by *icon_filename* is used.
- ***device_filename*** Identifies the filename that will display with the icon specified by *icon_filename* and *icon_index* when the filename is viewed in ActiveSync.
- ***cab_filename*** Identifies the filename of the available CAB files, relative to *install_directory*. Use commas to separate multiple *cab_filenames*.

The following code example shows a typical .ini file:

```
[CEAppManager]
Version      = 1.0
Component    = DVDCatalog

[Games]
Description  = Catalog your DVDs
Uninstall    = DVDCatalogUninstall

IconFile     = DVDCatalog.ico
IconIndex    = 0
DeviceFile   = DVDCatalog.exe

CabFiles   = SH3\DVDCatalog.cab,MIPS\DVDCatalog.cab
```

Using Trickle-Feed Deployment

One of the headaches for anyone deploying an application to a number of clients is ensuring that all of them keep up to date with the latest version of your application. One technique you can use with the full .NET Framework is *trickle-feed*, or Internet, deployment. In this technique, you create a small application that functions as a bootstrap loader and loads an assembly from a URL, using the *System.Reflection.LoadFrom* method. The bootstrap loader stores the assembly in a download cache. Every time you run that application on the client, the bootstrap loader checks if a newer version of the application exists on the server. If a newer version exists, the program downloads the newer version of the application automatically. Otherwise, it runs the version in the download cache.

The .NET Compact Framework does not support the *System.Reflection.LoadFrom* method and a download cache, but you can write an application that works in a similar fashion. To achieve this, you need to use a loader application. When your device connects to synchronize with your desktop or connects to your LAN in some other way, this loader application checks for a newer version of your application on a network share. If your application is up to date, the loader starts your application normally, but if there is a newer version of your application the loader application copies the updated assemblies for your application to the device before starting your application.

The following code listing shows the code from an example loader application. The example contains two routines that check for a newer version of the application and that copy the newer version of the application if one is found.

The *EnsureApplicationUpToDate* method uses the *FileInfo* object to check that a file for the application exists, and the *NewAssemblyAvailable* method checks whether the application needs updating. *File.Copy* copies the new application file if required.

The *NewAssemblyAvailable* method checks the dates on the installed application file and the application file on the network. It returns a value of *true* or *false* depending on the dates of the two files.

```
private void Start_Click(object sender, System.EventArgs e)
{
    // Name of assembly to check
    string Application = @"\Windows\TrickleFeedApplication.exe";
    //
    // Make sure the application is up to date
    //
    EnsureApplicationUpToDate(Application);
    this.Hide();
```

```
        //
        // Create a new application domain and execute the main
        // application in that domain.
        //
        AppDomain Domain = AppDomain.CreateDomain(
            "Trickle Feed Application", null);
        Domain.ExecuteAssembly(Application);
        // This app now waits until loaded one exits
        this.Close();
    }

    private void EnsureApplicationUpToDate(string Application)
    {
        FileInfo finfo = new FileInfo(Application);
        if (File.Exists(Application) == false ||
            NewAssemblyAvailable(finfo) == true)
        {
            MessageBox.Show("Updating application");
            // N.B. you might get a FileNotFound exception if you
            // are using the emulator. In the emulator,
            // go to Start - Settings - System tab - About - Device ID tab
            // and change the name to something other than 'POCKET_PC'.
            File.Copy(appNetworkPath + finfo.Name, Application, true);
        }
    }

    private bool NewAssemblyAvailable(FileInfo finfo)
    {
        if (File.Exists(finfo.Name) == false )
            return false;

        DateTime onDevice = File.GetLastWriteTime(finfo.Name);
        DateTime onServer = File.GetLastWriteTime(appNetworkPath + finfo.Name);

        return !onDevice.Equals(onServer);
    }
```

It is possible to adapt this technique to create a loader application that uses the *HttpWebRequest* and *HttpWebResponse* classes to update your application over a HTTP connection.

Installing Assemblies into the Global Assembly Cache

The GAC is a store for assemblies that are shared among several applications that are installed on the device. You use the GAC to install a custom control library or common class library that you have written that will be used by several applications. The .NET Compact Framework base class library assemblies are in the GAC. The GAC is a memory-resident cache of shared assemblies.

Files that install in the GAC go in the \Windows directory. If you examine the \Windows directory on a device where the .NET Compact Framework has been installed, you will see a number of files with names beginning with GAC, such as GAC_mscorlib_v1_0_5000_0_cneutral_1.dll. At run time, the common language runtime uses the Cgacutil.exe utility to update the GAC with the information about an assembly that is a part of the GAC. Cgacutil.exe installs as part of the .NET Compact Framework.

You install your assembly into the GAC by signing it with a strong name and including a .gac file with your CAB file. The .gac file is a text file that lists the absolute path and filename for each of the files that you want to be installed into the GAC. The list of assemblies to be installed into the GAC (the .gac file) can be either ANSI or UTF-8, but not Unicode. The following listing is an example of a .gac file:

```
\Program Files\SampleApplication\Assembly1.dll
\Program Files\SampleApplication\Assembly2.dll
\Program Files\SampleApplication\Assembly3.dll
\Program Files\SampleApplication\Assembly4.dll
```

The .NET Compact Framework will update the GAC with the files listed in your .gac file the next time you run your application. Each time your application runs, the .NET Compact Framework reads the .gac file for your application and updates the GAC with any changes that have been made. If the .gac file is deleted from the \Windows directory, the files that were listed in the .gac file are deleted from the GAC the next time your application runs. The .NET Compact Framework maintains a set of registry entries to reference-count the shared assemblies in the GAC. When the .gac file is uninstalled, the application's references to the shared assemblies are subtracted from the reference count, and if no references remain, the shared assembly is removed from the GAC.

> **Note** Unlike the full .NET Framework, files that install to the GAC are verified at run time, not at the time they're installed. Verification consists of using the digital signature that is part of the assembly's strong name to verify that the file has not been tampered with since it was signed.
>
> Another difference from the full .NET Framework is that assemblies cannot be precompiled in the .NET Compact Framework because there is no NGen.exe tool.

Understanding Strong-Named Assemblies

A strong-named assembly is an assembly that has been signed with a strong name, which consists of the assembly's text name, version number, culture information, public key, and a digital signature.

An assembly that has been signed with a strong name has the following attributes:

- Strong names guarantee name uniqueness. The private-public key pairs used to generate the strong name are unique; no one could create the exact same key pairs as you use, so no one could create an assembly that could successfully masquerade as your assembly.
- Version lineage is protected. Because the strong name used on your assembly can be generated only by you, users can be sure that any new version they install is from you.
- The strong name guarantees that the contents of the assembly have not been altered. The strong name is applied to the file in an assembly that contains the assembly manifest. The assembly manifest contains a hash of the contents of each file in the assembly, and these hashes form part of the content that goes into the digital signature. When a strong-named assembly is referenced later on, the runtime extracts the hash from the digital signature and compares it to a new hash it generates of the assembly's files. If they match, the runtime is satisfied that the contents of the assembly have not been tampered with since the assembly was built.

To sign your assembly with a strong name, you edit the AssemblyInfo file for your project. The following three lines appear toward the bottom of the AssemblyInfo file when it is generated by Visual Studio .NET:

```
[assembly: AssemblyDelaySign(false)]
[assembly: AssemblyKeyFile("")]
[assembly: AssemblyKeyName("")]
```

Here's the detail for each attribute:

- ***AssemblyDelaySign*** An advanced option that allows an assembly to be partially signed at development time and fully signed at a later date. This is useful if the key that will be used for signing the assembly is not available at development time.
- ***AssemblyKeyFile*** Points to the file that contains the key to use for signing this assembly.

- ***AssemblyKeyName*** The name of a key in the cryptographic service provider (CSP) on your computer that is to be used to sign the assembly.

If both an *AssemblyKeyFile* and an *AssemblyKeyName* are specified and the key name specified can be found in the CSP, that key is used to sign the assembly. If the key name is not found in the CSP, the key in the key file specified is installed into the CSP and used to sign the assembly.

Signing an Assembly with a Strong Name

The first step in signing an assembly with a strong name is to generate the key pair. To generate a key pair, start the Visual Studio .NET Command Prompt (accessible from the Visual Studio .NET Tools group on the Start menu) on your development machine and run the Strong Name Tool (sn.exe) by entering the command *sn –k keyfilename*. The *keyfilename* string specifies the location and filename of the file that sn.exe creates, which contains the two keys. By convention, the key file extension is .snk. If the path and filename of the output file includes spaces, remember to put it in quotes, as shown in Figure 6-5.

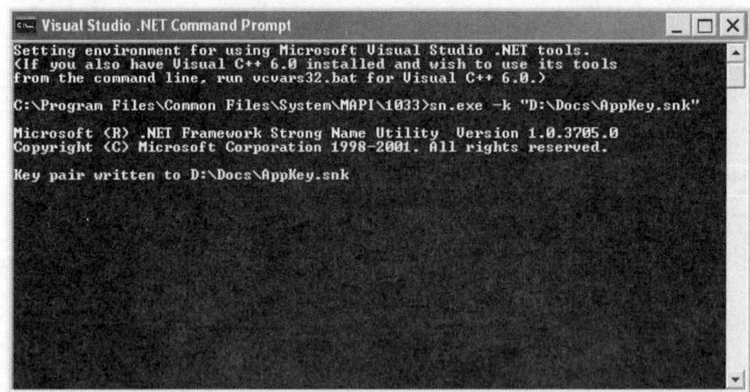

Figure 6-5 Using the Strong Name Tool (sn.exe) to generate a key pair.

The resulting file must be placed in a directory accessible to the project, and then you must edit the AssemblyInfo file and set the *AssemblyKeyFileAttribute* so that the assembler knows where to find the key file. Be aware that the default location for the key file differs between Visual Basic .NET and C#. For Visual Basic .NET, the path you specify for the key file is relative to the directory containing the Visual Studio .NET Solution. For C#, the path is relative to the directory containing the binary. The following examples are for a key file placed in the main project directory:

```
' Visual Basic:
<Assembly: AssemblyKeyFile(?cl1Key.snk?)>

// Visual C#:
[Assembly: AssemblyKeyFile(@?..\..\cl1Key.snk?)]
```

When you build your project, the result is an assembly with a strong name. If you use MSIL Disassembler (Ildasm.exe), a tool provided with the .NET Framework SDK, you can confirm this. At the command prompt, type **Ildasm**. Select Open from the File menu, browse to the executable, and click the Open button. If you double-click Manifest, you can see the public key that is embedded within it, as shown in Figure 6-6.

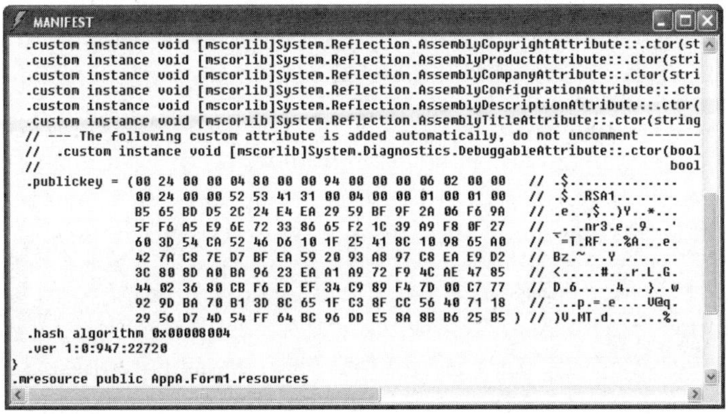

Figure 6-6 Using Ildasm.exe to examine the manifest of an assembly.

Using Side-by-Side Versioning

Side-by-Side versioning is supported in the .NET Compact Framework. In the GAC, you can store different versions of the same assembly. Applications store the exact identity of the assemblies that they were built against in the assembly manifest, so they continue to run with that same version forever, even if a newer version is installed. You can examine which versions of shared assemblies an application references using the MSIL Disassembler tool shown in Figure 6-6.

Three attributes determine the identity of an assembly: name, version, and culture. You set the version and culture through declarative attributes in the source code of the assembly. The compiler sets the assembly name when the assembly is created. In Visual Studio .NET, the assembly name is one of the project properties.

In the case of shared assemblies, these three attributes—name, version, and culture—together with a strong name define the identity of an assembly. The *AssemblyVersionAttribute* attribute is assigned a numeric value in the format *major.minor.build.revision*, for example, 1.2.0.0. The value you assign has particular significance in the case of strong-named assemblies and is used by the runtime for versioning. The four parts of the version number map logically to three specific meanings.

- ***Major.minor*** The first two parts of the version number are the primary identification of the current release of the assembly. Change these numbers when the version of the assembly is known to be incompatible with the previous release of the assembly, such as a major new release.
- ***Build*** A version of an assembly that differs from a previous release by its build number is considered to be *Maybe Compatible* with the previous release. Typical examples are a service pack or an incremental daily build during development.
- ***Revision*** An assembly that differs from another version of the same assembly only by its revision number is considered a *Quick Fix Engineering* (QFE) update to the previous release. An example would be an emergency update that users must upgrade to.

During development, it is usual to express the *build.revision* part of the version number with just an asterisk (*), for example, 2.1.*, indicating that default values should be assigned for build and revision. In this case, the assembly linker sets the build to be equal to the number of days since January 1, 2000 in local time, and the revision to be equal to the number of seconds since midnight, January 1, 2000 divided by two.

The *AssemblyCultureAttribute* attribute is an enumerated field that defines the culture the assembly supports. If this value is null, this defines the neutral culture and is the default value. Assemblies that contain code must have this attribute set to null, and by definition also contain resources for the neutral culture. In Visual Studio .NET, you add support for multiple locales in an application by adding Assembly Resource File items to your project to contain culture-specific resources. Assembly Resource Files are compiled into assemblies where the *AssemblyCultureAttribute* attribute has a value indicating the culture it supports.

In Visual Studio .NET, you record assembly attributes in the AssemblyInfo.cs (or AssemblyInfo.vb) file. The *AssemblyVersionAttribute* attribute defaults to a value of 1.0.* in Visual Studio .NET projects. To provide an assembly with an identity that ensures that each incremental build is numbered differently from its predecessors, you need to declare the following attributes (example in Visual Basic):

```
' Set Version Number for the assembly
<System.Reflection.Assembly:AssemblyVersionAttribute("1.0.*")>
' Neutral culture
<System.Reflection.Assembly:AssemblyCultureAttribute("")>
```

In C#, you declare the following attributes:

```
[assembly: AssemblyCulture("")]
// Version information for an assembly consists of the following
// four values:
//      Major Version
//      Minor Version
//      Build Number
//      Revision
//
// You can specify all the values or you can default the Revision
// and Build Numbers by using the '*' as shown below:
[assembly: AssemblyVersion("1.0.*")]
```

Version Policy

Applications record the identity of referenced assemblies in their assembly manifest and always execute using the same versions of those referenced assemblies. With the full .NET Framework, you could override this behavior using version policy files and force applications that were compiled against one version of a shared assembly to use an updated version of the shared assembly instead. The current release of the .NET Compact Framework does not support the use of policy files, so this behavior cannot be changed. You would need to recompile your application using the new assembly to enable your application to use the new version.

Summary

In this chapter, we looked at the project settings that you use for configuring your project for deployment. We then examined the options for packaging your application using Visual Studio .NET and the CAB Wizard application. We also detailed the contents of the configuration file that CAB Wizard uses to build your CAB files.

We looked at the different ways that you can distribute your application's CAB files to your users. We talked about installing the .NET Compact Framework and distributing your application in a number of ways, from using the Web to using memory storage cards. We also discussed trickle-feed deployment, where you want your application to be updated over a network connection.

We covered the GAC and how to install your components in the GAC. We showed how to sign your project with a strong name and how to implement side-by-side versioning in the GAC.

Part III

Common Programming Tasks

7

Working with Collection Classes

The .NET Compact Framework includes a number of classes designed to allow you to work with collections of objects. Most applications work with arrays or more complex collections of objects, and .NET languages include features specifically designed to help you access those objects. C#, for example, has the *foreach* keyword, and Visual Basic .NET has the similar *For Each* statement.

This chapter looks at how you use arrays and other collection classes in the .NET Compact Framework.

Introducing the .NET Framework Collection Classes

The *System.Collections* and *System.Collections.Specialized* namespaces contain a number of invaluable classes that allow developers to work with collections of objects. Table 7-1 describes the collection classes for the *System* namespace. Table 7-2 describes the collection classes for the *System.Collections* namespace, and Table 7-3 describes the collection classes for the *System.Collections.Specialized* namespace.

Table 7-1 Collection Classes in the *System* Namespace

Class	Description
Array	Provides methods for creating, manipulating, searching and sorting arrays, and is the base class for all arrays in the common language runtime. An array you create using native language features (such as *int[n]* in C#) is in fact an instance of this class. Developers should use array constructs provided by the programming language and not try to create arrays by directly instantiating this class.

Table 7-2 Collection Classes in the *System.Collections* Namespace

Class	Description
ArrayList	An array of objects whose size is dynamically increased as required.
BitArray	Manages a fixed-length compact array of bits, which are represented as Boolean values.
CaseInsensitiveComparer	Compares two objects for equivalence, ignoring the case of any strings.
CaseInsensitiveHashCodeProvider	Supplies a hash code for an object, using an algorithm that ignores the case of strings.
CollectionBase	This is an abstract class (meaning you must inherit from this class to use it) that provides the base class for a strongly typed collection. It is provided to make it easier for implementers to create a strongly typed custom collection.
Comparer	Compares two objects for equivalence, taking account of the case of any strings.
DictionaryEntry (structure)	Defines a dictionary key-and-value pair, which is the item stored in dictionary collections, such as the *Hashtable* and *ListDictionary*.
Hashtable	A collection of key-and-value pairs that are organized based on the hash value of the key.
Stack	A simple last in, first out collection of objects.

Table 7-3 Collection Classes in the *System.Collections.Specialized* Namespace

Class	Description
HybridDictionary	This is an efficient dictionary-structured collection that uses a *ListDictionary* while the size of the collection is small but then switches to a *Hashtable* when the collection size increases.
ListDictionary	A dictionary class suitable for small numbers of objects, typically containing 10 items or less.
NameObjectCollectionBase	An abstract base class for a collection of associate *String* keys and object values that can be accessed either by the key value or by numeric index.
NameValueCollection	A sorted collection of associated *String* keys and *String* values. This class inherits from *NameObjectCollectionBase*.

All the collection classes support the same basic methods found in the *System.Array* class, such as *Add*, *Clear*, and *Remove*, with the addition of extra methods that support the specific functionality of each particular collection class.

Classes Not Available in the .NET Compact Framework

The following classes from the full .NET Framework are not available in the .NET Compact Framework:

- *System.Collections.Queue*
- *System.Collections.SortedList*
- *System.Collections.ReadOnlyCollectionBase*
- *System.Collections.Specialized.CollectionsUtil*
- *System.Collections.Specialized.StringCollection*
- *System.Collections.Specialized.StringDictionary*
- *System.Collections.Specialized.StringEnumerator*

Using Simple Arrays

The *System.Array* class represents a simple collection of objects. In fact, you never instantiate this class directly. Instead, you use the built-in language features. The following C# example illustrates the use of the *Array* class:

```
int[] myIntArray = new int[10];
```

You code the same thing in Visual Basic .NET in one of two ways:

```
Dim myIntArray() As Integer = New Integer(9) {}
Dim myIntArray(9) As Integer    'implies New Integer(9)
```

In C#, you must use the *new* language keyword to initialize an array. If you leave it out, the array variable is uninitialized and points to *nothing*.

You must include the initialization braces {} when declaring an array in Visual Basic using the *New* keyword, even if you do not supply any initialization values; they are optional in C#. You can initialize the array by placing values into the braces, as in the following C# example:

```
int[] myIntArray = new int[10] {3, 6, 44, 1, 667, 0, 0, 0, 0, 1};
```

> **Important** One thing that often confuses developers moving between a C-based language and Visual Basic is that the former declares the number of elements in the array, while Visual Basic declares the upper bound of the array.
>
> In C#,
>
> ```
> int[] myIntArray = new int[10];
> ```
>
> creates 10 elements, indexed from 0 through 9. On the other hand, the Visual Basic statement
>
> ```
> Dim myIntArray() As Integer = New Integer(10) {}
> ```
>
> creates 11 elements, indexed 0 through 10.

In fact, in C# if you supply initialization values, you can omit *new int[10]* from the previous code so that the code looks like this:

```
int[] myIntArray = {3, 6, 44, 1, 667, 0, 0, 0, 0, 1};
```

The abbreviated code works because the compiler can deduce the bounds of the array from the initialization values. You code this in Visual Basic in the following way:

```
Dim myIntArray() As Integer = {3, 6, 44, 1, 667, 0, 0, 0, 0, 1}
```

The fact that language arrays derive from the *System.Array* class gives them functions not normally associated with simple arrays. You can access the *Length* property of any array or call the following static (*Shared* in Visual Basic) methods of *System.Array*: *Sort*, *Reverse*, *IndexOf*, *LastIndexOf*, and *BinarySearch*. The following example sorts and returns the index of one of the elements of the array created in the previous example:

```
int numOfElements = myIntArray.Length;
System.Array.Sort(myIntArray);
// Find the index of the '44' entry in the array
int position = System.Array.IndexOf(myIntArray, 44, 0, numOfElements);
// Position is set to 8 in this example (zero-based indexing)
```

These methods work with arrays of the .NET built-in types, but for user-defined structures and types, you must implement the *IComparable* interface in your type, as described in the section "Sorting with *IComparable*" later in this chapter.

Initializing Arrays of Reference Types

If you do not specify initialization values, arrays of value types initialize to default values for the type. For example, all elements of *int* arrays initialize to zero. Reference types are different—for performance reasons, they initialize to *null* rather than the element type. For example, if you create a simple class that has one field, such as this one:

```
class Animal
{
    public string Name;
}
```

and create an array of objects of that class, then try to set the *Name* field, you'll get an exception of type *NullReferenceException* at run time, as the following code demonstrates:

```
Animal[] myAnimalArray = new Animal[3];
myAnimalArray[0].Name = "Giraffe"; // <- Exception thrown here
```

You must initialize each element first for this to work.

```
Animal[] myAnimalArray = new Animal[3];
for (int idx = 0; idx < myAnimalArray.Length; idx++)
{
    myAnimalArray[idx] = new Animal();
}
myAnimalArray[0].Name = "Giraffe"; // <- OK now
```

Working with Multidimensional Arrays

Arrays can have more than one dimension. When you need to create a multidimensional array, you have the option of creating a standard multidimensional array (also called a rectangular array) or creating an array of arrays (also called a jagged array).

Rectangular Arrays

Rectangular arrays are multidimensional arrays that are rectangular in shape. The rectangular shape of the array is evident from the length of each dimension in the array.

In C#, you can declare an array that has three rows and two columns as follows:

```
int[,] myMultiIntArray = new int[3,2];
```

And in Visual Basic .NET, you use this code:

```
Dim myMultiIntArray () As Integer
myMultiIntArray = New Integer(2,1) {}
```

As with single-dimension arrays, you can initialize multidimensional arrays in the same statement that you declare them, and again, you can leave out the new statement in C#:

```
int[,] myMultiIntArray = {{11, 2}, {5, 4}, {14, 1}};
```

In Visual Basic .NET, you would use the following code:

```
Dim myMultiIntArray (,) As Integer = _
    New Integer(,) {{11, 2}, {5, 4}, {14, 1}}
```

Arrays of Arrays

Arrays of arrays are also called jagged arrays. Each element in the array is itself an array, and each of these arrays can be of different dimensions—hence the term *jagged*, referring to the fact that the elements do not have to be symmetrical.

You declare these by specifying the upper limit of the first dimension and then go on to initialize each element. In the following C# example, the top-level array consists of 4 elements, each of which is an array of short integers. The first element contains an array of 6 elements of type short, and the second element contains an array of 3 elements. The third and fourth elements are currently uninitialized.

```
short[][] myJaggedArray = new short[4][];
myJaggedArray[0] = new short[] {16, 45, 3, 2, 1, 6};
myJaggedArray[1] = new short[3];
myJaggedArray[1][0] = 42;
```

Here's the same code in Visual Basic .NET:

```
Dim myJaggedArray()() As Short = New Short(3)() {}   ' Assign top-level
myJaggedArray(0) = New Short(5) {16, 45, 3, 2, 1, 6}
myJaggedArray(1) = New Short(2) {}
myJaggedArray(1)(0) = 42
```

You can also declare a top-level array of type object and store arrays of different object types within it. However, the runtime does not allow you to cast an array of value types into any other type, so to store an array of integers or similar value types in an object array requires a little more coding, as discussed in the next section.

Converting Array Types

In general, conversions between arrays are allowed as long as both arrays are reference types, they have the same number of dimensions, and the elements of the source array have an implicit conversion to the types of the destination array.

```
string[] myStrings = { "A", "string", "array" };
object[] anObjectArray;
anObjectArray = myStrings;
```

This conversion works because each string array element can be converted to an object.

If you create a multidimensional or jagged array for reference types and try to use it to store an array of value types, as the following C# code shows,

```
object[][] myjaggedarray = new object[3][];
myjaggedarray[0] = new short[3]; // <- compile time error
myjaggedarray[1] = new System.Collections.BitArray[5];
myjaggedarray[2] = new string[2];
```

you get the following compile-time error:

```
Cannot implicitly convert type 'short[]' to 'object[]'
```

The solution here is to resort to the useful static method *Array.Copy*, which copies elements from one array to another, performing type casting or boxing, as required. For parameters, one definition of the *Array.Copy* method accepts a source array, an index to the source array, a destination array, an index into the destination array, and a parameter that specifies the number of elements to copy. The following code demonstrates the use of the *Array.Copy* method:

```
object[][] myjaggedarray = new object[3][];
short[] myShortArray = new short[3];

// Array.Copy copies array elements, performing type casting or
// boxing as required.
// This code creates an array of references to boxed shorts
object[] boxedShortArray = new object[myShortArray.Length];
Array.Copy(myShortArray, 0, boxedShortArray, 0, myShortArray.Length);

myjaggedarray[0] = boxedShortArray; // <- OK now
myjaggedarray[1] = new System.Collections.BitArray[5];
myjaggedarray[2] = new string[2];
```

> **Note** You do not have to resort to the *Array.Copy* method to store an array of value types in a jagged array of objects when programming in Visual Basic .NET because the compiler does this boxing for you implicitly. Just initialize an element of an object array with an array of value types and the code compiles correctly.

Using the .NET Compact Framework Collections

The .NET Framework offers a number of special-purpose collection classes that offer additional capabilities over simple arrays.

Creating an *ArrayList* Collection

The *ArrayList* collection dynamically resizes at run time as you add new members. You can create an *ArrayList* collection using the default *ArrayList* constructor, in which case the default initial capacity of 16 is used, or you can specify the initial capacity using the following constructor:

```
ArrayList(int initialcapacity)
```

If you add an item to the collection so that the number of items exceeds the capacity, the capacity is doubled. If you can estimate the maximum size of the collection at construction, you can avoid resize operations at run time.

ArrayList supports these principal methods: *Add*, *AddRange*, *Capacity*, *Contains*, *IndexOf*, *Insert*, *InsertRange*, *Item*, *Remove*, *RemoveAt*, *RemoveRange*, *Reverse*, *Sort*, *ToArray*, and *TrimToSize*. See the *ArrayList* class reference documentation in Visual Studio .NET for a full list of the methods supported. Note that *Sort* is a nonstatic member function of the *ArrayList* class, not a static member as implemented in the *System.Array* class.

The following example initializes an *ArrayList* object using the default capacity and adds items to it:

```
using System.Collections;
⋮
ArrayList myArrayList = new ArrayList();
myArrayList.Add("Fiona");
myArrayList.Add("Billy");
myArrayList.Add("Linda");
myArrayList.Sort();

int count = myArrayList.Count; // Returns 3
```

Storing Key-and-Value Pairs Using a *Hashtable* Collection

A *Hashtable* collection stores key-and-value pairs with lookups optimized through the use of hash codes. When you add an item to a *Hashtable* collection, the collection calls the *GetHashCode* method of the key item, which returns the numeric hash code. The entry is placed into a bucket based on its hash code. When you do a lookup, the hash code of the lookup key is used to identify the bucket where the target item will be if it exists, thus reducing the number of lookups that must be performed to find a particular item. The object used as the key value must implement or inherit the *Object.GetHashCode* and *Object.Equals* methods. The base class implementation of these methods compares based on object reference, but the basic built-in types such as *int*, *string*, and so on override the *GetHashCode* method to return a suitable hash code and override the *Equals* method to test equality based on value.

In the following example, the key object is a string and the value is an integer:

```
using System.Collections;
⋮
Hashtable myHashTable = new Hashtable();
myHashTable.Add("Billy", 42);
myHashTable.Add("Fiona", 18);
myHashTable.Add("Linda", 26);
```

If you try to use the *Add* method for an item that already exists, an exception of type *ArgumentException* is thrown. You can also add items by specifying the key as the indexer, as shown here:

```
myHashTable["Peter"] = 27;
```

In this case, if the item does not exist, it is created. If it already exists, no exception is thrown but the new value replaces the original. Note that when using the *foreach* statement to iterate through a *Hashtable* collection, the type of each item in the collection is *DictionaryEntry*.

```
foreach(DictionaryEntry anEntry in myHashTable)
{
    Console.WriteLine("Key: {0}, Value: {1}",
        anEntry.Key, anEntry.Value);
}
```

Items in a *Hashtable* collection are ordered in the sequence they were added; you cannot sort the sequence. The class has a number of methods and properties to assist in searches and lookups: *Add*, *Clear*, *Contains*, *ContainsKey*, *ContainsValue*, *Item*, *KeyEquals*, *Keys*, *Remove*, and *Values*.

Using the *Stack* Class

The *Stack* class represents a simple last in, first out collection. You can create *Stack* instances only with the default initial capacity of 10, although the collection expands if necessary should you add more items. The .NET Compact Framework does not support the overloaded *Stack* constructor that allows you to specify the initial capacity, as the full .NET Framework does.

The *Push* method inserts an object at the top of the stack, and the *Pull* method retrieves and removes the object at the top of the stack. *Peek* views the first item on the stack but does not remove it. When you push an object onto the stack so that the initial capacity is exceeded, the size of the stack increases to accommodate it.

The most important methods of this class include *Count*, *Peek*, *Pop*, *Push*, and *ToArray*.

Storing Elements with a *ListDictionary* Collection

The *ListDictionary* collection is a simple dictionary structured list, which is smaller and faster than a *Hashtable* collection if the number of elements is less than 10. Usage of a *ListDictionary* collection is the same as the usage of a *Hashtable* collection. Methods and properties of *ListDictionary* include *Add*, *Clear*, *Contains*, *Count*, *Keys*, *Remove*, and *Values*.

Using the *HybridDictionary* Collection

The useful *HybridDictionary* collection is recommended when the size of the collection is not known. When you initialize a *HybridDictionary* object, it is empty. While the number of items is small, it is implemented internally as a *ListDictionary* collection. Then, if the number of items grows above 10, it switches to a *Hashtable* implementation of the list to take advantage of the improved performance of that collection with larger numbers of items. Usage of the *HybridDictionary* class is the same as the usage of the *Hashtable* class.

Storing String Key-and-Value Pairs with *NameValueCollection*

The *NameValueCollection* class implements a sorted list of string keys and string values. You can refer to any item by its string key, or integer index number. Keys must be unique, although more than one string value can be stored under a single key. When you use the *Add* method, if the key value already exists, the new value is added to the existing values as a comma-separated list, as shown here:

```
NameValueCollection nvc = new NameValueCollection(10);
nvc["firstkey"] = "firstVal";        // contains "firstVal"
nvc.Add("firstkey", "secondVal");  // now contains "firstVal,SecondVal"
```

Internally, a *NameValueCollection* is a *Hashtable*, and usage of both classes is very similar.

Sorting Objects in Collections

When you have selected the appropriate collection class for your application, you might still need to add functionality to the objects in the collection to achieve the desired results. For example, the *Array* and *ArrayList* classes give you the *Sort* method to sort objects into some order. However, when you call the *Sort* method, a run-time exception is thrown if the class of the elements in the collection does not support the *IComparable* interface.

Sorting with *IComparable*

If you want to support only a single sort order for your objects, you can implement the *IComparable* interface, which consists of a single method, *CompareTo*. When sorting, the system calls this method for a particular object in the collection to compare it to an adjacent object. The method must return +1 if the object is greater than the comparative object, –1 if it is less than, and 0 if it is equal.

Take the example of a simple class used to describe animals. You can set the name and number of legs of each animal. You want to be able to sort alphabetically on the animal name, so the *CompareTo* method does a string comparison, as the following code (included with this book's sample files) shows.

SortingIComparable.cs

```
using System;

namespace NETCFDevelopersReference
{
    class SortingIComparable
    {
        static void Main(string[] args)
        {
            // Create an array of animals
            Animal[] myAnimals = {new Animal("Lion", 4),
                                  new Animal("Giraffe", 4),
```

(continued)

SortingIComparables.cs *(continued)*

```
                                    new Animal("Tarantula", 8),
                                    new Animal("Millipede", 1000000000)
                                   };
            Array.Sort(myAnimals);
            foreach(Animal anml in myAnimals)
            {
                Console.WriteLine(anml.Name);
            }
            Console.ReadLine();
        }
    }

    class Animal : IComparable
    {
        public Animal(string name, int numberOfLegs)
        {
            Name = name;
            NumberOfLegs = numberOfLegs;
        }

        public string Name;
        public int NumberOfLegs;

        int IComparable.CompareTo(object obj)
        {
            // This method must return:
            //   +1 if this object sorts after 'obj'
            //   -1 if this object sorts before 'obj'
            //    0 if this object is the same as 'obj'
            // In this case, we sort on a string property,
            // so call the String.CompareTo method
            return this.Name.CompareTo(((Animal)obj).Name);
        }
    }
}
```

Using the Windows CE .NET emulator, the preceding code produces the following output, sorted by name:

```
Giraffe
Lion
Millipede
Tarantula
```

Implementing Multiple Sort Orders with *IComparer*

The preceding approach is fine for collections where you require only a single sort order. If you want more flexibility, you can implement the *IComparer* interface. The *Array.Sort* method used in the preceding example took no parameters, but an overloaded version is of the form shown here:

```
public static void Sort(System.Array array, int index, int length,
    System.Collections.IComparer comparer)
```

You supply the implementation of *IComparer* as the fourth parameter. To take the previous *Animals* example further, we will implement the option to sort the collection alphabetically by name or numerically by the number of legs.

The implementation of *IComparer* consists of a single method, as shown here:

```
Compare(object obj1, object obj2)
```

You could implement this method directly in the *Animal* class, but that would defeat the object of the exercise. A class can implement an interface only once, so we would not be able to implement two alternative sort orders. Instead, we implement a nested class within *Animal* for each *IComparer* implementation, one for *SortByName* and another for *SortByLegs*.

> **Note** In actual fact, you could retain the *IComparable* implementation in the class to provide sorting by name using the parameterless *Sort* method. You could also implement *IComparer* in the class to give sorting by number of legs, which the client program might use by calling the *Sort(array, int, int, IComparer)* method call. However, it is much better to provide a consistent programming interface for whichever method of sorting is used, so we implement *IComparer* interfaces for both sorting by name and by number of legs, while retaining the default sorting by name through the *IComparable* interface implementation.

The SortingIComparer example project, which you'll find with this book's sample files, includes Animal.cs and SortingForm.cs. Animal.cs, which follows, is a new implementation of the *Animal* class.

Animal.cs

```
using System;
using System.Collections;

namespace NETCFDevelopersReference
{
   class Animal : IComparable
    {
        public Animal(string name, int numberOfLegs)
        {
            Name = name;
            NumberOfLegs = numberOfLegs;
        }

        public string Name;
        public int NumberOfLegs;

        /// <summary>
        /// Default comparison method
        /// </summary>
        int IComparable.CompareTo(object obj)
        {
            return this.Name.CompareTo(((Animal)obj).Name);
        }

        public static IComparer SortByName
        {
            get
            {
                return ((IComparer) new SortByNameClass());
            }
        }

        public static IComparer SortByLegs
        {
            get
            {
                return ((IComparer) new SortByLegsClass());
            }
        }

        public class SortByNameClass : IComparer
        {
            public int Compare(object obj1, object obj2)
            {
                // SortByName can use the default IComparable interface
                // so call the CompareTo method
```

(continued)

Animal.cs *(continued)*

```
                return (((IComparable) obj1).CompareTo((Animal) obj2));
            }
        }

        public class SortByLegsClass : IComparer
        {
            public int Compare(object obj1, object obj2)
            {
                // SortByLegs compares the integer property
                Animal animal1 = (Animal) obj1;
                return (animal1.NumberOfLegs.CompareTo(
                    ((Animal) obj2).NumberOfLegs));
            }
        }
    }
}
```

Notice that the default sorting functionality (the *IComparable.CompareTo* method) is still there, but in addition, there are two nested classes, *SortByNameClass* and *SortByLegsClass*. These two classes each implement *IComparer*, but they implement it for different properties.

There are two static properties in the class called *SortByName* and *SortByLegs*. These are not necessary but greatly help the usability of your application. Without these properties, a client program invokes the *SortByLegs* functionality by instantiating the appropriate nested class and passing the instance to the *Sort* method, as the following code shows:

```
System.Array.Sort(myAnimals, 0, myAnimals.Length,
    new Animal.SortByLegsClass());
```

Using the static property, however, the usage becomes much cleaner, as shown here:

```
System.Array.Sort(myAnimals, 0, myAnimals.Length, Animal.SortByLegs);
```

The SortingForm.cs listing that follows, available within the book's sample code in the SortingIComparer sample, demonstrates this functionality. The listing is from a Windows Forms application that lists animals and the number of legs for each in a ListView control. When the user clicks on the Name column header, the list sorts by animal name. When the user clicks the Name column again, the program reverses the order, behaving in a manner similar to Windows Explorer. When the Legs column is clicked, the program sorts the list of animals by number of legs. When the user clicks the Legs column again, the list is sorted in reverse order.

SortingForm.cs

```
using System;
using System.Drawing;
using System.Collections;
using System.Windows.Forms;
using System.Data;

namespace NETCFDevelopersReference
{
    public class SortingForm : System.Windows.Forms.Form
    {
        private System.Windows.Forms.ListView listView1;

        public SortingForm()
        {
            InitializeComponent();

            this.MinimizeBox = false;
            // Create an array of animals
            myAnimals = new Animal[] {new Animal("Lion", 4),
                                      new Animal("Giraffe", 4),
                                      new Animal("Tarantula", 8),
                                      new Animal("Millipede", 1000000)
                                     };
            currentSortOrder = SortOrder.NameDown;
            BindListView(currentSortOrder);
        }
        protected override void Dispose( bool disposing )
        {
            base.Dispose( disposing );
        }
        #region Windows Form Designer generated code
        /// <summary>
        /// Required method for Designer support - do not modify
        /// the contents of this method with the code editor.
        /// </summary>
        private void InitializeComponent()
        {
            this.listView1 = new System.Windows.Forms.ListView();
            //
            // listView1
            //
            this.listView1.Location = new System.Drawing.Point(8, 56);
            this.listView1.Size = new System.Drawing.Size(224, 200);
            this.listView1.ColumnClick += new System.Windows.Forms.
                ColumnClickEventHandler(this.listView1_ColumnClick);
            //
```

(continued)

SortingForm.cs *(continued)*

```
        // SortingForm
        //
        this.Controls.Add(this.listView1);
        this.Text = "Sorting with IComparer";

    }
    #endregion

    static void Main()
    {
        Application.Run(new SortingForm());
    }

    private Animal[] myAnimals;
    private enum SortOrder { NameDown, NameUp, LegsDown, LegsUp };
    private SortOrder currentSortOrder;

    private void BindListView(SortOrder order)
    {
        switch (order)
        {
            case SortOrder.LegsDown:
                // Use the SortByLegs IComparer interface
                Array.Sort(myAnimals, 0, myAnimals.Length,
                    Animal.SortByLegs);
                break;
            case SortOrder.LegsUp:
                // Use SortByLegs, then reverse it
                Array.Sort(myAnimals, 0, myAnimals.Length,
                    Animal.SortByLegs);
                Array.Reverse(myAnimals, 0, myAnimals.Length);
                break;
            case SortOrder.NameUp:
                // Use SortByName, then reverse it
                Array.Sort(myAnimals, 0, myAnimals.Length,
                    Animal.SortByName);
                Array.Reverse(myAnimals, 0, myAnimals.Length);
                break;
            case SortOrder.NameDown:
            default:
                // Use the SortByName IComparer interface
                Array.Sort(myAnimals, 0, myAnimals.Length,
                    Animal.SortByName);
                break;
        }
```

(continued)

SortingComparables.cs *(continued)*

```
            listView1.Columns.Clear();
            listView1.Columns.Add("Name", 100, HorizontalAlignment.Left);
            listView1.Columns.Add("# Legs", listView1.Width - 100,
                HorizontalAlignment.Center);
            listView1.HeaderStyle = ColumnHeaderStyle.Clickable;
            listView1.View = View.Details;
            // Add the list items
            listView1.Items.Clear();
            foreach(Animal anml in myAnimals)
            {
                listView1.Items.Add(new ListViewItem( new String[]
                    { anml.Name, anml.NumberOfLegs.ToString() }));
            }
        }

        private void listView1_ColumnClick(object sender,
            System.Windows.Forms.ColumnClickEventArgs e)
        {
            if (e.Column == 0)
            {
                if (currentSortOrder == SortOrder.NameUp)
                    currentSortOrder = SortOrder.NameDown;
                else
                    currentSortOrder = SortOrder.NameUp;
            }
            else
            {
                // Sort by number of legs
                if (currentSortOrder == SortOrder.LegsUp)
                    currentSortOrder = SortOrder.LegsDown;
                else
                    currentSortOrder = SortOrder.LegsUp;
            }
            BindListView(currentSortOrder);
        }
    }
}
```

When the application starts up, the *SortingForm* constructor calls *InitializeComponent* and then builds the collection of four *Animal* objects. The constructor then sets the initial sort ordering to *SortOrder.NameDown*, and calls the *BindListView* method to transfer the data to the ListView control. Thereafter, whenever the user clicks or taps on a column header, the event handler *listView1_ColumnClick* executes to reset the sort order as appropriate and rebind the ListView control. The output, shown in Figure 7-1, shows the user tapping on the Name column header, which orders the list in reverse alphabetical order, and then tapping on the Legs column header to order the list by increasing number of legs.

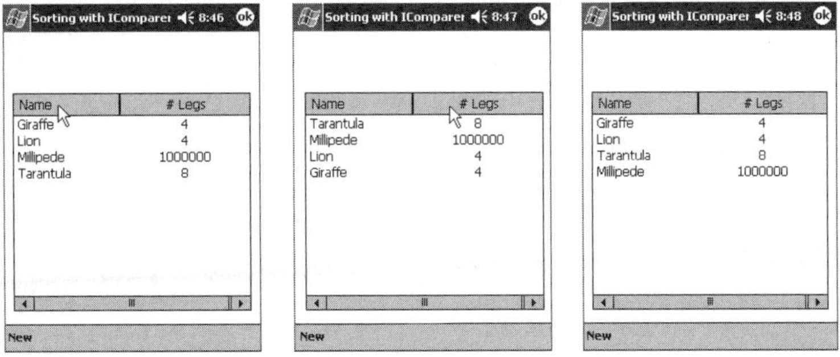

Figure 7-1 An application that supports four different sort orders for a collection of *Animal* objects.

Creating Your Own Collections

The supplied collections will satisfy most application requirements, but if you want to create your own collection class, it's quite easy to do so. With your own collection classes, you can expose the members as strongly typed items rather than as generic objects, and you can add whatever methods you need to suit the operation of that collection.

You can implement a collection from scratch, and then all you have to do to allow iteration through the collection is implement the *IEnumerable* interface. This consists of a single method, *GetEnumerator*, which returns an *IEnumerator* interface. *IEnumerator* contains the following methods and properties:

- ***bool MoveNext*** This method returns the next item in the list and returns *true* if there are more items, *false* if not.
- ***object Current*** This read-only property returns the current item.
- ***void Reset*** This method resets the iteration.

A much simpler technique is to inherit from *CollectionBase*. This abstract class has a protected property called *List*, which exposes the internal list and implements the *Clear* and *Count* methods. It also implements *IEnumerable* so that users can iterate through your collection. All you have to do is implement the *Add* and *Remove* methods, the *Item* property, as well as any additional functionality you wish your collection to have. AnimalCollection.cs, which follows and is included in this book's sample files as part of the CustomCollection project, defines a custom collection class called *AnimalCollection* that inherits from *CollectionBase*.

AnimalCollection.cs

```
using System;
using System.Collections;

namespace NETCFDevelopersReference
{
    /// <summary>
    /// A Collection of Animals.
    /// </summary>
    public class AnimalCollection : CollectionBase
    {
        public AnimalCollection() :base()
        {
        }

        // Throws exception if the animal already existed.
        public virtual void Add(string name, int numberOfLegs)
        {
            // Ensure the element does not already exist.
            if (List.Count > 0)
            {
                if (this.Item(name) != null)
                {
                    // Indicate the animal already existed.
                    throw new ArgumentException(
                        "An Animal of that name already exists");
                }
            }

            Animal anm = new Animal(name, numberOfLegs);
            List.Add(anm);
        }

        // Throws exception if the animal already existed.
        public void Add(Animal animal)
        {
            // Ensure the element does not already exist.
            if (List.Count > 0)
            {
                if (this.Item(animal.Name) != null)
                {
                    // Indicate the animal already existed.
                    throw new ArgumentException(
                        "An Animal of that name already exists");
                }
            }
```

(continued)

AnimalCollection.cs *(continued)*

```
            List.Add(animal);
        }

        public Animal Item(string name)
        {
            if (List.Count == 0)
                throw new InvalidOperationException(
                    "You cannot get an Animal "
                     + "when the collection is empty.");

            foreach (Animal anml in List)
            {
                if ( name == anml.Name)
                {
                    // This is the one...
                    return anml;
                }
            }
            return null;
        }

        public Animal Item(int i)
        {
            if (List.Count == 0)
                throw new InvalidOperationException(
                "You cannot get an Animal "
                + "when the collection is empty.");

            return (Animal) List[i];
        }

        public bool SetNumberOfLegs(string name, int numberOfLegs)
        {
            foreach (Animal anml in List)
            {
                if ( name == anml.Name)
                {
                    // Update this one!
                    anml.NumberOfLegs = numberOfLegs;
                    return true;
                }
            }
            return false;
        }
    }
}
```

The CustomCollection application has a *CustomCollectionForm* class (an extension of the *Form* class) that exercises the *AnimalCollection* class. You'll find the CustomCollection application files included with this book's sample files.

Summary

This chapter examined the different ways of supporting collections of objects in the .NET Compact Framework. We started with *System.Array*, which you use by means of the C# and Visual Basic .NET language features for supporting arrays, rather than by instantiating a *System.Array* object directly. Then we briefly described the most important collection classes in the *System.Collections* and *System.Collections.Specialized* namespaces.

Finally, we looked at implementing *IComparable* and *IComparer* in a class to support sorting and how you create your own custom collections.

8

Working with Dates and Strings

The .NET Compact Framework includes powerful features for manipulating strings and dates. In addition to the string creation and modification features of the *String* class, this chapter will examine the use of regular expressions to perform sophisticated search and replace operations on strings. The sections on formatting and parsing show how to convert other types of data to or from strings, taking into account formatting requirements and national settings.

Understanding the *String* Class

As in the full .NET Framework, strings represent sequences of Unicode characters and are immutable. Immutability in this case means that you can assign a new value to a *string* object, but this creates an entirely new *string* object, with performance implications due to the destruction of the old *string* and the creation of a new one.

```
string myString = "Curious foreboding";
// Next line destroys old instance and creates another
myString = "Change of diet";
MessageBox.Show("The string is " + myString);
```

As in the full .NET Framework, if you want to avoid these performance issues, the *StringBuilder* class, discussed in the section "Using the *StringBuilder* Class" later in this chapter, is available, and it provides mutable strings.

> **Note** The C# language interprets some escape sequences such as "\n" meaning a newline. If you don't want that to happen, precede your string literal with the @ character to switch off interpretation of escape sequences, as in the following example:
>
> ```
> myString = @"Literally \n";
> ```

Using Strings

This section deals with operations you commonly perform on strings. Note that we will defer discussion of the *String.Format* function to the section "Using Format Specifications and the *String.Format* Method" later in this chapter.

The *String* class is defined in the *System* namespace. The *string* keyword in C# is an alias for the *String* class, defined in the *System* namespace of the .NET Compact Framework.

Creating and Comparing Strings

Although the *String* class is a reference type in the .NET Compact Framework, in many ways it behaves like a value type, as shown here:

```
string myString = "Hello";
myString += " world"; // '+' is the concatenation operator
if (myString == "Hello world")
    MessageBox.Show("Greeting");
```

The == operator compares the *values* of the two strings. The *Compare* method compares two strings, returning a negative, zero, or positive integer to indicate that the first string is less than, equal to, or greater than the second string, respectively. *Compare* performs a dictionary comparison, taking into account national settings. The *CompareOrdinal* method performs the same operation but uses underlying character codes and ignores national settings. The *Equal* method tests two strings for equality. The *CompareTo* method compares this instance with an object.

Creating Strings from Other Strings

In the following fragment

```
    string s1 = "Hello";
    string s2 = s1;
```

the objects s1 and s2 are not only *equal*, holding the same string value, but also *identical*; they are the same object. You can test for identical objects by casting the strings to *Object*, which causes .NET to make a reference comparison.

```
if ((object)s1 == (object) s2) // Returns a true result
```

To create a new independent copy of a string, use the *Copy* method, as shown here:

```
s2 = string.Copy(s1); // s1, s2 are now equal but not identical
```

The *Substring* method extracts substrings.

```
// greeting becomes "Hello"
string greeting = ("Hello world").Substring(0,5);
```

The *Join* method produces a single string from an array of strings, separated by a specified separator string.

```
string[] menu = new string[] {"Salad", "Soup", "Steak", "Nuts"};
string meal = string.Join(", then ", menu);
MessageBox.Show(meal); // Salad, then Soup, then Steak, then Nuts
```

The *Split* method is the converse of *Join*. The *Split* method takes an array of *char* values and splits the string at any point where it finds one of the *char* values in the array.

```
string sentence = "Spring, Summer and Fall";
// Split at comma or space
string[] words = sentence.Split(new char[] {',', ' '});
string result = string.Join(": ", words);
```

Note that result becomes "Spring: : Summer: and: Fall". The two colons after *Spring* are caused by the fact that two splits occur after the word *Spring*, one on the comma and another on the space. You can work around this by testing your resulting array of strings to see if you have any null strings. Alternatively, the *Regex* class, discussed in the section "Using Regular Expressions" later in this chapter, has a much more powerful *Split* method that uses regular expressions.

The *Concat* method concatenates two or more strings.

Searching Strings

The *String* class provides several methods that allow you to search a string for substrings or characters.

- ***IndexOf*** returns the zero-based position of a substring, one or more *char* values within a string, or –1 if the search element is not found.
- ***IndexOfAny*** performs the same operation as *IndexOf* but searches for any element in a *char* array.
- ***LastIndexOf* and *LastIndexOfAny*** perform the same operations as IndexOf and IndexOfAny but start from the end of the string.
- ***StartsWith* and *EndsWith*** look for a substring at the start or end of a string and return a *bool* value to indicate success or failure.

Modifying Strings

The .NET Compact Framework provides a variety of methods that perform modification functions on strings.

- ***Insert*** inserts another instance of a string into a string at a specified position and returns the new string.
- ***Remove*** removes a specified number of characters from a specified position in a string.
- ***Replace*** replaces a substring with another substring. An overload exists that replaces all occurrences of a Unicode character with another Unicode character.

Using String Utility Methods

This section lists methods that perform miscellaneous operations on strings for case conversions, comparisons, and inserting or removing space characters.

- ***Equals*** compares a string to another string or to an object, which must also be a string. The *Equals* method returns *true* if both strings have the same value.
- ***Clone*** returns a reference to this instance of a string.
- ***ToLower* and *ToUpper*** are useful for case conversions.
- ***Trim*, *TrimStart*, and *TrimEnd*** remove unwanted whitespace characters, or characters that you specify in an array, from a string.
- ***PadLeft* and *PadRight*** allow you to insert spaces to the left or the right of a string, padding the string to left-align or right-align the string's characters.

Differences from the Full .NET Framework *String* Class

This section discusses differences between the implementation of the *String* class in the .NET Compact Framework and in the full .NET Framework.

Using the *CharEnumerator* Class

The *CharEnumerator* class is absent in the .NET Compact Framework; therefore, the *String* class does not possess a *GetEnumerator* method. You use the *GetEnumerator* method in the full .NET Framework to return an object, which will then iterate over the characters in the string, as shown in the following code:

```
string myString = "Hello";
CharEnumerator myCE = myString.GetEnumerator();
while (myCE.MoveNext())
{
    Console.WriteLine("Next character is " +
        myCE.Current.ToString());
}
```

Instead of this, in the .NET Compact Framework, you must use the *Chars* property in Visual Basic or the *[]* operator in C#.

```
for (int i = 0; i < myString.Length; i++)
{
    char myChar = myString[i];
    // etc
}
```

Using the *StringBuilder* Class

The purpose of the *StringBuilder* class is to provide a mutable implementation for strings that doesn't suffer the same performance penalties as the string class when you assign new values. The *StringBuilder* class provides methods and properties for setting the size of its internal buffers. In this way, you can keep the internal re-sizing operations to a minimum, if not eliminate them altogether.

The *StringBuilder* class is defined in the *System.Text* namespace, so the examples in this section require the *System* and *System.Text* namespaces.

Using *StringBuilder* Methods and Properties

The following list summarizes the *StringBuilder* methods:

- ***Constructor*** **6** overloads, which take combinations of strings, starting positions, and maximum capacities.
- ***Append*** **18** overloads to append strings, or other value types converted to strings.
- ***AppendFormat*** appends values formatted according to a *Format Specifier* and a *Format Provider*. See the section "Formatting Strings for Output" later in this chapter for a discussion of these topics.
- ***Equals*** tests for equality with another object. The *Equals* method returns *true* if the two objects have the same *string*, *Capacity*, and *MaxCapacity* values.
- ***Insert*** **and** ***Remove*** perform modifications on the *StringBuilder* instance.

The following example creates a *StringBuilder* object with the initial value "Hello" and a maximum capacity of 20 characters. We call *Append* and *Insert* to obtain "Hello again world!" and then call *Remove* to remove the final exclamation point.

```
StringBuilder mySB = new StringBuilder("Hello", 20);
mySB.Append(" world!");
mySB.Insert(6, "again ");
mySB.Remove(mySB.Length - 1, 1); // mySB is now "Hello again world"
```

Differences from the Full .NET Framework *StringBuilder* Class

This section discusses the differences in the implementation of the *StringBuilder* class in the full .NET Framework and the .NET Compact Framework.

Using the *EnsureCapacity* Method

This method is absent in the .NET Compact Framework. In the full .NET Framework, you use this method to ensure that *StringBuilder* possesses at least a certain minimum capacity for storing strings. In the .NET Compact Framework, you must use the *Capacity* property, but there are the following important differences in the way that these two methods operate:

- The *EnsureCapacity* method takes a *size* parameter. If *size* is greater than or equal to the current string size, it sets the capacity to one greater than *size*. *If this size is less than the current size of the string, the EnsureCapacity method does nothing.*

- The *Capacity* property also takes a *size* parameter. Setting this property with a size value greater than or equal to the existing capacity sets the internal buffer capacity to exactly the new size specified. *If this size is less than the current size of the string, an exception of type System.ArgumentOutOfRangeException is thrown.*

Using the *Replace* Method

This method is absent in the .NET Compact Framework. The *Replace* method replaces all occurrences of a given string in an instance with another string. The workaround for the .NET Compact Framework is to convert your *StringBuilder* object to a *string*, which possesses a *Replace* method, and then convert back. Here you are losing performance advantages, which are the main reason for using *StringBuilder* in the first place.

Using Dates

The *DateTime* structure in the .NET Compact Framework implements dates. A *DateTime* structure holds date values accurate to one *tick* (100 nanoseconds). Dates are held relative to a start date of 12:00 midnight, January 1, 1 A.D. (also known as C.E. or Common Era). Dates are immutable, which means that any operations to modify a date will actually return a new instance of a date. This has performance implications when performing many date operations.

DateTime objects hold absolute date and time values. A *TimeSpan* object, frequently used with dates, holds a relative time or a time interval. The date arithmetic code examples in the following subsections examine the use of *TimeSpan* objects. The *DateTime* and *TimeSpan* structures are defined in the *System* namespace.

Constructing Dates

There are seven overloads for the *DateTime* constructor. The following combinations of date parts account for three of the overloads:

- Year, month, day
- Year, month, day, hour, minute, second
- Year, month, day, hour, minute, second, millisecond

Three more *DateTime* constructors parallel these but allow you to specify a calendar different from the default Gregorian calendar.

The seventh overload accepts a *long* ticks parameter to build a date from a number of ticks. Note that no constructor takes a string. To convert a string to a date, use the *DateTime.Parse* static method discussed in the section "Parsing Dates" later in this chapter.

Using *DateTime* Properties

The following properties allow you to obtain dates or date parts from a *DateTime* object:

- *Date*, *Day*, *DayOfWeek*, and *DayOfYear*
- *Hour*, *Minute*, *Second*, and *Millisecond*
- *Ticks*
- *TimeOfDay*

The following properties are static properties of the *DateTime* structure:

- ***Now*** returns the local date and time on this computer.
- ***Today*** returns the current date.
- ***UTCNow*** returns the current date and time converted to Universal Standard Time (UTC).
- ***MaxValue* and *MinValue*** are the maximum and minimum allowable values for dates.

Using *DateTime* Arithmetic Methods

The *DateTime* structure has methods to add a number of any time units, from ticks to years, to a date. These methods range from *AddTicks* and *AddMilliseconds*, up through all the units to *AddYears*. There is also an *Add* method that accepts a *TimeSpan* object.

```
DateTime myDate = new DateTime(2012, 11, 10, 9, 8, 7);
    // Year, month, day, hour, minute, second
TimeSpan myTS = new TimeSpan(19, 30, 5);
    // Hours, minutes, seconds
myDate = myDate.Add(myTS);
MessageBox.Show(myDate.ToString("F"));
    // Displays "Sunday November 11, 2012 4:38:12 AM"
```

The *DateTime* structure also has a *Subtract* method with two overloads. One overload subtracts a *DateTime* value from a *DateTime* value and returns a *TimeSpan* value. The other overload subtracts a *TimeSpan* value from a *DateTime* value and returns a *DateTime* value.

Using *DateTime* Utility Methods

You'll find the following methods useful when working with the *DateTime* structure:

- ***DaysInMonth* (static)** returns days in specified month for specified year.
- ***FromFileTime* (static)** takes a system file stamp and returns an equivalent *DateTime*. *ToFileTime* performs the reverse operation.
- ***GetDateTimeFormats*** returns an array of strings with the date in all available formats (over 100 on most computers).
- ***IsLeapYear* (static)** returns *true* if the specified year is a leap year.

- ***Parse* and *ParseExact* (static)** parse a string to a date. Please refer to the section "Parsing Dates" later in this chapter for details of these methods.
- ***ToLocalTime* and *ToUniversalTime*** convert *DateTime* values to or from UTC.
- ***ToLongDateString* and *ToShortDateString*** (and other similarly named methods) perform string conversions using the format implied in the method name.

Using *DateTime* Operators

The following operators can be used on *DateTime* objects:

- Addition (+) and subtraction (–) operators. These allow you to perform the following operations only:
    - Add a *DateTime* value and a *TimeSpan* value (in that order) to produce a *DateTime* value.
    - Subtract a *DateTime* value from a *DateTime* value to produce a *TimeSpan* value.
    - Subtract a *TimeSpan* value from a *DateTime* value to produce a *DateTime* value.
- Logical operators: <, >, <=, >=, ==, and !=.

Differences from the Full .NET Framework

The *FromFileTimeUTC* and *ToFileTimeUTC* methods are absent in the .NET Compact Framework. Simply use the *FromFileTime* and *ToFileTime* methods and convert using the *ToLocalTime* and *ToUniversalTime* methods.

The *ToOADate* and *FromOADate* methods are absent in the .NET Compact Framework. These convert *DateTime* objects to and from OLE Automation dates, which as COM objects cannot be used directly in the .NET Compact Framework. It is therefore highly unlikely that you will require this functionality.

Using Regular Expressions

Regular expressions are a major topic in their own right and a full discussion of them is beyond the scope of this book. In this section, we will focus on introducing the major concepts of regular expressions and the use of the *Regex* class and associated classes in the .NET Compact Framework. The reader is referred to *Mastering Regular Expressions, Second Edition* (by Jeffrey Friedl, ISBN 05960002890, published by O'Reilly & Associates, 2002) for a full discussion of regular expressions. The *Regex* class and supporting classes are defined in the *System.Text.RegularExpressions* namespace.

> **Note** The .NET Compact Framework requires that you add a reference to *System.Text.RegularExpressions.dll* in your project in addition to the required *using* directive.

Understanding Regular Expressions

You use regular expressions to find and possibly replace text patterns within strings. Regular expressions describe text *patterns* and are used to test if a piece of text contains (or matches) that pattern; for example:

- Does a piece of text contain the letters *abc*?
- Does a piece of text contain *Visual* followed by some white space followed by either *Basic* or *C#*?
- Does the text contain a sequence of three letters or two digits, followed by the / character, then one or two digits, a / and then two or four digits? If so, what values were found at the three positions that matched digits and letters?
- Does the text contain a sequence of three letters in brackets, followed by either the word *Microsoft* or the text *MSPress*, followed by three letters in brackets, but not the same three letters as were found in the first match?

Using Simple Regular Expression Matches and the *Match* Object

This section shows you how to make some simple matches. It introduces two .NET Compact Framework classes: the *Regex* class and the *Match* class. These classes allow you to use a regular expression to examine a string, detect if a portion of the string matches a regular expression, and discover what text actually matched. The first example assumes that you want or expect a single match, which will be the first set of characters in the string that matches the regular expression, and that you want to see the text that matched.

To do this, create a *Regex* object using the pattern you want to find as the constructor parameter. (An overload for the *Regex* constructor also takes a *RegexOptions* enumeration parameter to allow you to customize your match to make it multiline, case-insensitive, and so on.) Then use the *Match* method on the *Regex* object, passing the string you want to search as the parameter. This returns a *Match* object, which has a *Success* property to tell you if a match was found and a *ToString* method to give you the text that was matched.

> **Note** Because some regular expression metacharacters clash with C# string escape sequences, you should make a habit of always using C# @-quoted strings to construct *Regex* objects to turn off interpretation of C# string escape sequences.

```
Regex myRegex = new Regex(@"[a-z]*ent\b",
    RegexOptions.IgnoreCase);
// Finds a word ending in "ent" (\b is 'word boundary')
Match myMatch = myRegex.Match("Frequently absent friends");
if (myMatch.Success) // If it matched...
{
    // ...what did it match?
    MessageBox.Show("We matched " + myMatch.ToString());
        // Outputs "We matched absent"
}
```

Processing Multiple Matches with the *MatchCollection* Object

What happens if your regular expression matches at multiple places in the target string? You can use the *NextMatch* method to return the next match, until no more matches are found. Alternatively, in the following example, more than one match is possible, so you use the *Matches* method on your *Regex* object to return a *MatchCollection*, which you then iterate through:

```
Regex myRegex = new Regex(@"[a-z]*ent\b",
    RegexOptions.IgnoreCase);
string myString = "Enlightenment of a transient nature";
MatchCollection myMatches = myRegex.Matches(myString);
MessageBox.Show("Number of matches: " + myMatches.Count);
foreach (Match myMatch in myMatches)
{
    MessageBox.Show("We matched " + myMatch.ToString());
}  // 2 matches: "Enlightenment" and "transient"
```

Using Groups and Captures

When matching, you might want to know not only what part of the string matched, but also which subsections matched. For example, if you find a date in the form *mmm/dd/yyyy*, you might want to know not just the overall date that matched, but also the month, day, and year parts that matched. You can capture parts of the match using *capture groups*. Look at the following regular expression string:

```
@"([a-z]{3})/(\d{2})/(\d{4})"
    // three lower-case letters / two digits / four digits
```

Each left parenthesis introduces a new capture group. There is always a default "Group 0" for the entire pattern that is matched, so you can imagine an invisible extra pair of parentheses around the entire expression above. The three pairs of parentheses therefore introduce groups 1, 2, and 3. These will capture the month, day, and year parts, respectively. If you apply the preceding regular expression to the string "We arrive Oct/14/2002 at 3," one match is found because there is one date. The *Match* object has 4 *Group* objects, and each *Group* object has a *CaptureCollection* object containing one *Capture* object. Applying the *ToString* method to the *Capture* object gives the captured text. The following code performs this match and outputs the various levels of capture:

```
string myOutput = "";
string myString = "We arrive Oct/14/2002 at 3";
   Regex myRegex =
        new Regex(@"([a-z]{3})/(\d{1,2})/(\d{4})",
                  RegexOptions.IgnoreCase);
   Match myMatch = myRegex.Match(myString);
   int groupCount, captureCount;
   GroupCollection myGC = myMatch.Groups;
   groupCount = 0;
   foreach (Group myGroup in myGC)
   {
       myOutput +=  ("Group: " + groupCount++  + "\n");
       CaptureCollection myCC = myGroup.Captures;
       captureCount=0;
       foreach (Capture myCapture in myCC)
       {
           myOutput += ("  Capture " + captureCount++ + ": "
                + myCapture.ToString() + "\n");
       }
   }
   MessageBox.Show(myOutput, "Groups and Captures");
```

Replacing Text Patterns

The *Replace* method of the *Regex* class replaces the matched text with fixed or dynamic replacement text. To perform a simple replacement of one piece of text with another piece of text that is fixed, use the *Replace* method, passing the original string and the replacement string. By default, the method replaces all occurrences in the pattern. Overloads of *Replace* allow you to specify a count for the number of replacements. The following example replaces one piece of text with another piece of text that is fixed:

```
string myString = "The Lion in Winter";
Regex myRegex = new Regex("Winter");
string newString = myRegex.Replace(myString, "Purple");
MessageBox.Show(newString); // The Lion in Purple
```

The next example performs a replacement of a pattern with dynamic text. To perform this replacement, pass a *MatchEvaluater* delegate, not a replacement string, to the *Replace* method as its second parameter. The *MatchEvaluator* delegate returns a *string*. This delegate is a function that you write, which must take a *Match* object parameter and return a *string*. In this example, the delegate translates the matched value to uppercase:

```
private void cmdReplace_Click(object sender, System.EventArgs e)
{
    string myDate = "Date is Jun/23/2002";
    Regex myRE = new Regex(@"[a-z]{3}/", RegexOptions.IgnoreCase);
    string newDate = myRE.Replace(myDate,
        changeString(myRE.Match(myDate)));
   MessageBox.Show (newDate); // Outputs "Date is JUN/23/2002"
}

string changeString (Match theMatch)
{
    return theMatch.ToString().ToUpper();
}
```

Using the *Split* Method

The *Regex* class has a very powerful *Split* method, which splits strings into string arrays using complex separator patterns defined by regular expressions. The *Split* method looks for occurrences of the *Regex* string in a target string and splits the string at those points. It returns an array of strings, minus the separators. The following example splits sentences into their component words. The first sentence is simple because the words are separated by a single space each time. The regular expression is constructed using just a space character. In the second sentence, the words can be separated by punctuation of one or more characters and possibly spaces. In this case, the required regular expression is constructed using *@"[^a-zA-Z]+"*, meaning "any sequence of one or more nonletters." The method splits the sentence at those points, removing the matched regular expression. It then returns a string array containing just the words in the sentence.

```
string myString = "A list of words";
string[] words = (new Regex(" ")).Split(myString);
string myOutput = string.Join(", ", words);
MessageBox.Show(myOutput);  // A, list, of, words

myString = "Words, with    separators:-spaces: (or not)";
Regex myRegex =new Regex(@"[^a-zA-Z]+");
words = myRegex.Split(myString);
myOutput = string.Join(" ",words);
MessageBox.Show(myOutput); // Words with separators spaces or not
```

Formatting Strings for Output

The .NET Compact Framework provides you with comprehensive facilities to format strings for output. In this section, you'll see how to format various data types, including numeric types, date/time types, and enumerated types. You'll also see how to provide culture-specific formatting.

Understanding Concepts and Terminology

This first section contains a brief introduction to concepts in .NET Compact Framework formatting, which involves *format specifiers*, *format specifications*, and *format providers*. In the following code fragment

```
double amount = 10.0/3.0;
string myString = amount.ToString("F4");
```

the string "F4" is a format specifier and specifies that the value amount is to be formatted as fixed-point (F) with 4 digits (the precision specifier) after the point.

In the following code fragment

```
string myFormatSp =
    "Today it is {0:F2} Fahrenheit or {1:F4} Celsius";
string myOutput = string.Format(myFormatSP, 32, 0);
```

the substrings {0:F2} and {1:F4} are format specifications, which you will notice include the format specifiers F2 and F4. The numbers 0 and 1 refer to the position in the list of values (in this case, 32 and 0) that are to be output.

Format providers are objects that provide cultural settings such as the currency symbol for use by a currency format specifier. You should bear in mind that a format provider can be used to modify much of the numerical formatting behavior described in the remainder of this section, by specifying culture-specific features such as currency symbol or decimal point characters. The section "Understanding Format Providers" later in this chapter discusses format providers in more detail.

Working with Format Specifiers

Format specifiers, also known as *format strings*, are simply short strings consisting of a character (or characters) to specify the type of output (for example, currency or fixed-point) and also optionally consisting of a precision specifier, which is one or two digits to specify precision, width, and so on. There are both standard and custom format specifiers. An example of a standard format specifier is F4, specifying fixed-point output with 4 digits after the point. An example of a custom format specifier is #.##, specifying output in digits with only 2 digits after the point.

Using Format Specifiers

The *ToString* methods of the .NET Compact Framework data types can use format specifiers, as shown in this example:

```
myOutput = loan.ToString("C4");  // Currency, 4 places after the point
myOutput = distance.ToString("#.##");
// #.## is a custom numeric format specifier for fixed-point conversion
// with 2 digits after the point
```

Classifying Format Specifiers

The .NET Compact Framework provides the following three types of format specifiers:

- Numeric format specifiers for use with numeric types
- Date format specifiers for use with *DateTime* types
- Time format specifiers for use with *DateTime* types

> **Note** The full .NET Framework enumeration format specifiers and the function that uses them, *Enum.Format*, are absent in the .NET Compact Framework.

Using Standard Numeric Format Specifiers

A string that consists of one letter with no surrounding white space, followed by zero to two digits (for example, *F4*) is interpreted as a *standard numeric format specifier*. This means that the letter, in this case *F*, must be one of the standard format specifiers shown in Table 8-1. The number *4* is the *precision specifier*, whose meaning varies depending on the type of conversion. If no precision is supplied, default values from the current *NumberFormatInfo* object are used. (See the section "Understanding Format Providers" later in this chapter.) If a string of one letter followed by zero to two digits is specified but the letter is *not* a recognized standard numeric format specifier (for example, *K9*), an exception of type *FormatException* is thrown when the string is used as a format specifier. Any other sequence of characters (for example, *##.###*) is taken to be a *custom numeric format specifier*, which we will discuss in the section "Using Custom Numeric Format Specifiers" later in this chapter.

Table 8-1 Standard Numeric Format Specifiers

Format Specifier	Name	Description
C or c	Currency	Converts to a currency with the number of digits after the point indicated by the precision specifier, and with the currency symbol defined in *NumberFormatInfo* in the current cultural settings.
D or d	Decimal	Converts an integral type to a string of decimal digits, with a minus sign if negative. The string is zero-padded to the minimum number of digits indicated by the precision specifier.
E or e	Scientific (exponential)	Converts a number to scientific format, for example, 2.34E-008 or –4.121e005. There is one digit before the point, and the precision specifier indicates the number of digits to add after the point. Six digits are added if no precision is specified. The exponent is zero-padded if necessary to three digits.
F or f	Fixed-point	Converts a number to fixed-point number (for example, –12.345), with the number digits after the point indicated by the precision specifier.

Table 8-1 Standard Numeric Format Specifiers *(continued)*

Format Specifier	Name	Description
G or g	General	The number is converted to fixed or scientific notation, whichever is the more compact. The resulting string contains the number of digits indicated by the precision specifier or, if no precision is specified, a number of digits determined by the type of number being converted, as shown here: ■ *Int16* or *UInt16*: 5 digits ■ *Int32* or *UInt32*: 10 digits ■ *Int64* or *UInt64*: 19 digits ■ *Single*: 7 digits ■ *Double*: 15 digits ■ *Decimal*: 29 digits
N or n	Number	Converts a number to the form *–d,ddd,ddd.ddd…*, where each *d* indicates a digit (0-9). The precision specifier indicates the desired number of decimal places.
P or p	Percent	Multiplies the number by 100 and then converts to a percentage. The precision specifier indicates the desired number of decimal places.
R or r	Round-trip	Used to guarantee that a floating-point value converted to a string will be parsed back to an identical value. Up to 17 digits for a *Double* and 9 digits for a *Single* are used if necessary to guarantee exact reconversion. The precision specifier is ignored.
X or x	Hexadecimal	Converts integral types only to strings in hexadecimal format using uppercase or lowercase letters as indicated by the case of the specifier and zero-padded if necessary to the minimum number of digits indicated by the precision specifier.

Using Custom Numeric Format Specifiers

Any string used where a format specifier is expected and which does not correspond to one of the standard numeric format specifiers listed earlier is taken as a *custom numeric format specifier*. These will be familiar to users of the

Format function in Visual Basic. The custom numeric format specifiers are described in Table 8-2.

Table 8-2 Custom Numeric Format Specifiers

Format Character	Name	Description
0	Zero placeholder	Reserves a place for a digit in the output string, filling any leading spaces with zeros. The number of zeros before the point expresses the required minimum number of digits, and the number after expresses the required precision.
#	Digit placeholder	As for 0 above, but leading spaces are left blank.
.	Decimal point	The first dot (.) character in the format string determines the location of the decimal separator in the formatted value; any additional dot characters are ignored.
,	Thousand separator and number scaling	Thousands separator: when a comma appears between two placeholders (0 or #), the output will contain thousands separators as defined by the current cultural settings. Number scaling: if one or more commas appear to the left of the point, each comma introduces a scaling divisor of 1000, which will be applied to the value before conversion. So, two commas before the point scale by 1,000,000.
%	Percentage placeholder	Causes a number to be multiplied by 100 before formatting and a percent character (in the current locale) to be output at the place indicated by the position of the percent placeholder in the format string.
E0 E+0 E-0 e0 e+0 e-0	Scientific notation	E<*sign*><*value*> or e<*sign*><*value*> request scientific output using an uppercase or lowercase *E*, as indicated. If <*sign*> = +, always output a sign. If <*sign*> = – or is absent, only output a sign for negative numbers. <*value*> is a list of *0*s, the number of zeros specifying the minimum number of digits to use in the exponent.

Table 8-2 Custom Numeric Format Specifiers *(continued)*

Format Character	Name	Description
\	Escape character	Used to insert escape sequences such as \n in C# and C++. In C#, to insert a backslash, use \\ or an @-quoted string. Note that this escape character is not supported in Visual Basic; however, the *ControlChars* constants provide the same functionality.
'ABC' "ABC"	Literal string	Copied literally to the output string.
;	Section separator	Used to separate negative, zero, and positive format sections.
Other	All other characters	All other characters are copied to the output string as literals in the position they appear.

Formatting Dates and Times

Dates can be output in many ways, and options available here are too numerous to detail individually. Dates can be long or short, and months can be output as numbers, abbreviations, or in full. Cultural settings introduce a further dimension of choices. This section will examine what options are available and refer the reader to the help files for details of all possibilities.

As is the case for numeric output, you can output dates using either standard or custom format specifiers. If a string consists of a single character, it is taken as being a *standard DateTime format specifier* and the single character must be a recognized standard *DateTime* format specifier (from Table 8-3), or an exception will be thrown. Any other sequence will be interpreted as a *custom DateTime format specifier*. Table 8-4 describes the custom *DateTime* format specifiers.

The *DateTime* format specifiers can be used in calls to the *ToString* method. The following example uses a standard and a custom *DateTime* format specifier:

```
DateTime myDate = new DateTime(1987, 6, 4); // year, month, day
string myOutput = myDate.ToString("D"); // "D" = Full date
    // myOutput becomes "Thursday, June 04, 1987"
myOutput = myDate.ToString("ddd MMMM/dd/yyyy");
    // myOutput becomes "Thu June/04/1987"
```

Table 8-3 Examples of Standard *DateTime* Format Specifiers

Format Specifier	Description
d	Short date, for example, 9/8/2004 in current locale
D	Long date, for example, Tuesday, May 05, 1987
t	Short time, for example, 12:00 AM
T	Long time, for example, 10:45:52 PM
f	Full date and time with short time
F	Full date and time with long time

Table 8-4 Examples of Custom *DateTime* Format Specifiers

Format Specifier	Description
d	Day of month, for example, 23 or 5.
dd	Day of month as two digits, for example, 23 or 05.
ddd	Abbreviated weekday, for example, Wed.
dddd	Full weekday, for example, Wednesday.
M	Month.
MM	Month as two digits.
MMM	Abbreviated month, for example, Oct.
MMMM	Full month, for example, October.
y	Year as 2 digits maximum.
yy	Year as 2 digits.
yyyy	Year as 4 digits.
hh, mm, ss	Hours, minutes, seconds as 2 digits. Use h, m, s to suppress leading zeroes on single digit values.

The *DateTime* class also has methods such as *ToLongDateString* that provide a convenient shortcut for common date formats. For example, using U.S. cultural settings,

```
myOutput = myDate.ToLongDateString();
```

is equivalent to

```
myOutput = myDate.ToString("dddd, MMMM dd, yyyy");
```

See also the section "Understanding Format Providers" later in this chapter for an example of how cultural settings can change the output produced by the previous examples.

Using Enumerated Type Formatting

In the full .NET Framework, you could use the *Enum.Format* method with a format specifier to output an enumerated type either as its text equivalent or as a numeric value. In addition, if the enumerated type has the attribute *FlagsAttribute* set so that its enumerated values can be combined in flag words, the *Enum.Format* method is able to separate the flag bits and output their text equivalents. The *Enum.Format* method is absent in the .NET Compact Framework.

In the .NET Compact Framework, for nonflag enumerations, use the *ToString* method of an enumerated type to convert the enumerated type's value into its text equivalents or numeric value. This performs the equivalent of a call to *Enum.Format* with the format specifier G or g.

```
enum lights = { Red, Green, Amber };
lights myLight = lights.Green;
string myOutput = myLight.ToString();
    // Sets myOutput to "Green"
```

For enumerations with the *FlagsAttribute* set, the *ToString* method will not separate the individual bit values. It is up to the programmer to perform a bitwise AND operation with each bit and then use the *ToString* method on the resulting values to output each component of the flag, as shown in the following code:

```
[FlagsAttribute] // This allows you to OR enumerated values
                 // into flag words
enum FileFlags { Read = 1, Write = 2, Delete = 4 };
⋮
FileFlags myFlags = FileFlags.Write | FileFlags.Delete;
FileFlags[] FlagValues = new FileFlags[]
    {FileFlags.Delete, FileFlags.Read, FileFlags.Write};
string myOutput = "Flags are ";
for (int i = 0; i < FlagValues.Length; i++)
{
    if ((myFlags & FlagValues[i]) != 0)
    {
        myOutput += FlagValues[i].ToString() + " ";
    }
}
MessageBox.Show(myOutput); // Outputs "Flags are Delete Write"
```

Using Format Specifications and the *String.Format* Method

Format specifications (distinct from format specifiers) can be embedded in strings and act as placeholders for substituting formatted values in a similar way as the *printf* functions of C programming days. The *String.Format* function can use these placeholders to take a string containing one or more format specifications and produce another string with the substituted, formatted values. Format specifications consist of a number and a format specifier, all inside braces, for example, {1:F3}. The number *1* refers to the position, in a list of values, of the value to which this format specification applies. This is best illustrated by an example such as the following one:

```
string myFormatSp = "Today it is {0:f2} Fahrenheit which is {1:f4} Celsius";
string myOutput = string.Format(myFormatSp, 32, 0);
// 32 (value 0), will be output with 2 digits after the point
// 0  (value 1) will be output with 4 digits after the point
```

Understanding Format Providers

A *format provider* is any class implementing the *IFormatProvider* interface. Format providers provide information for use by format specifiers, such as the decimal separation symbol used when outputting floating-point numbers or the currency symbol to use. See also the section "Resolving Parsing Issues" later in this chapter for the use of format providers when parsing.

The following objects implement the *IFormatProvider* interface:

- *NumberFormatInfo*
- *DateTimeFormatInfo*
- *CultureInfo* This object defines culture-specific aspects of formatting and contains *NumberFormatInfo* and *DateTimeFormatInfo* objects. If no *IFormatProvider* is specified when a formatting operation is requested, use the current culture, available through the *CultureInfo.CurrentCulture* static property.

Conversion functions use *NumberFormatInfo* and *DateTimeFormatInfo* objects to supply default values for formatting entities such as currency symbol and number of decimal places when these entities are not specified explicitly in the conversion. You can use *NumberFormatInfo* and *DateTimeFormatInfo* objects either by creating them independently or by using a *CultureInfo* object that contains instances of both *NumberFormatInfo* and *DateTimeFormatInfo*. Both *NumberFormatInfo* and *DateTimeFormatInfo* are defined in the *System.Globalization* namespace.

It's possible to create an independent *NumberFormatInfo* or *DateTimeFormatInfo* object, populate its properties, and use it in a call to *String.Format*, as the following example illustrates:

```
NumberFormatInfo myNFI = new NumberFormatInfo();
myNFI.CurrencySymbol= "£";
// Other members are set for CurrencyDigits, etc.
string myOutput = string.Format(myNFI, "You owe me {0:C}", 23.45);
    // gives £23.45
```

However, it is more typical to use *CultureInfo* objects, which, as mentioned earlier in this section, contain *NumberFormatInfo* and *DateTimeFormatInfo* objects. You can create *CultureInfo* objects in the following ways:

- Create a new, blank *CultureInfo* object, and populate it. This would involve a lot of code because there are many properties.
- Create a new *CultureInfo* object using a *predefined CultureInfo name*, such as *en-US* for English-U.S. or *fr-CH* for French-Switzerland. See the topic "*CultureInfo* class" in the online help for a list of predefined *CultureInfo* names.
- Find out the name of your current culture using the *CultureInfo.CurrentCulture.Name* property, and produce a new copy using that name. Then make any modifications you want.

The following example changes the currency symbol used for currency output to *USD*. First the code finds out the *Name* property of the current culture and then uses it to create a new *CultureInfo* object. The sample code then changes the *CurrencySymbol* in the *NumberFormatInfo* property and uses the new *CultureInfo* object to format currency.

```
double myValue = 23.45;
string myCultureName = CultureInfo.CurrentCulture.Name;
CultureInfo myCI = new CultureInfo(myCultureName);
myCI.NumberFormat.CurrencySymbol = "USD ";
string myOutput = string.Format(myCI, "You owe me {0:C}",
    myValue);
MessageBox.Show(myOutput); // Outputs "You owe me USD 23.45"
```

Using Cultural Settings with Date Formats

The next example shows the effect of cultural settings on date output. The example outputs the date May 4, 1987, in standard U.S. cultural settings, and then using a French-Swiss setting:

```
DateTime myDate = new DateTime(1987,5,4); // Year, month, day
string myOutput = myDate.ToString("D");
MessageBox.Show(myOutput);  // Outputs "Monday, May 04, 1987"
```

(continued)

```
CultureInfo mySwissCI = new CultureInfo("fr-CH");
myOutput = myDate.ToString("D", mySwissCI);
MessageBox.Show(myOutput); // Outputs "lundi 4. mai, 1987"
```

Parsing

Parsing is the reverse of formatting, in that it consists of producing numeric or date values from strings such as *23.456*. As a result, the concepts of format specifier and format provider discussed in the section "Formatting Strings for Output" earlier in this chapter also apply to parsing. All the .NET Compact Framework numeric types have a static *Parse* method that will parse strings to .NET Compact Framework types. You can parse any string to a numeric value, provided that it was produced or could have been produced by a format specifier. The following is a simple example of parsing:

```
string myString = "23.456";
double myDouble = double.Parse(myString);
    // myDouble will take the value 23.456
```

Resolving Parsing Issues

When parsing a numeric value, you must take account of the following items:

- Currency symbols
- Thousands separators
- Decimal separators

Normally, the default format provider for your application will be used. For example, for a U.S. locale, the currency symbol *$*, the comma thousands separator, and the dot decimal separator will be used. However, overloads for the *Parse* method allow you to specify *CultureInfo* objects to indicate a different locale. *CultureInfo* objects are discussed in the section "Understanding Format Providers" earlier in this chapter. The following is an example of parsing using standard and custom locales:

```
string number = "3.141";
double pi = double.Parse(number); // pi becomes 3.141
number = "3,141";
// Create a French CultureInfo: decimal separator is comma
pi = double.Parse(number, new CultureInfo("fr-FR"));
MessageBox.Show(pi.ToString()); // Outputs 3.141
```

Overloads for the *Parse* method take *NumberStyles* enumeration values as parameters. These allow you to specify further information about allowable characters in the string to be parsed—for example, whether you wish to allow decimal points, currency symbols, hexadecimal values, and a range of other options. The following is an example of parsing a currency using a British *CultureInfo* object:

```
string number = "£23.45";
double cost = double.Parse(number,
    NumberStyles.Currency, new CultureInfo("en-GB"));
```

Parsing Dates

The *Datetime.Parse* method accepts a string, and overloads exist that also take a *FormatProvider* parameter and a *DateTimeStyles* enumeration parameter to customize the parsing operation. The *DateTimeStyles* enumeration permits leading or trailing whitespace and can also specify to convert the resulting value to UTC if required. Note that unlike numeric parsing, no format specifier is supplied. The string parameter must therefore conform to standard formats. These are listed in the online help, under the topic "*DateTimeFormatInfo* class." The following example parses a U.S. date and then creates a German *CultureInfo* object to correctly parse the same date in German:

```
string myString = "Tuesday 14 May 2002 10:46:35";
DateTime myDate = DateTime.Parse(myString);
myString= "Dienstag 14.Mai.2002 10:46:35";
myDate = DateTime.Parse(myString, new CultureInfo("de-DE"));
```

Notice that in this example, if the string were changed to "May 14 2002 10:46:35", the parsing operation would still succeed. If you want to enforce strings submitted for parsing to conform to a certain date format or range of formats, use the *DateTime.ParseExact* method instead.

Summary

In this chapter, you've seen how to use the .NET Compact Framework to create and modify strings and dates. You've seen how to convert other types of data to or from strings and dates using the formatting facilities and the cultural support provided by the .NET Compact Framework. In the section "Using Regular Expressions," you saw how to apply sophisticated pattern matching techniques to perform powerful search and replace operations on strings.

9

Working with XML

Extensible Markup Language, or XML, provides a platform-independent way to describe complex data using hierarchical documents composed of *elements* and *attributes*. XML documents can be used to exchange data between components in the same distributed application, different applications in the same organization, or even different organizations. Because XML is a standard, text-based way to represent data, the differences between hardware platforms, operating systems, and programming languages can be overcome relatively easily, making it possible to build closely integrated solutions with components running on dissimilar systems.

For example, suppose you need to develop a distributed solution in which a product catalog for a beverage wholesaler is retrieved by a Web service from a back-end Enterprise Resource Planning (ERP) system. Client applications could use the Web service to download the product data and then operate on it locally. A sales representative with a Pocket PC might need to retrieve the product data from the Web service while in the office (and connected to the corporate network) and then persist the data locally on the Pocket PC so that it is available when meeting customers. Using XML to represent the catalog, the data can easily be exchanged between the ERP system, the Web server hosting the Web service, and the Pocket PC. Here's an example of what an XML representation of a product catalog might look like:

```
<?xml version="1.0"?>
<catalog>
  <category categoryid="1" categoryname="soft drinks">
    <product productid="1000">
      <name>Cola Flavored Drink</name>
      <salesunit>Crate of 12 x 400ml bottle</salesunit>
      <price>25.99</price>
```

(continued)

```
    </product>
    <product productid="1001">
      <name>Traditional Lemonade</name>
      <salesunit>Crate of 12 x 400ml bottle</salesunit>
      <price>22.99</price>
    </product>
    <product productid="1002">
      <name>Cherry Flavored Soda</name>
      <salesunit>Crate of 12 x 300ml can</salesunit>
      <price>19.99</price>
    </product>
  </category>
  <category categoryid="2" categoryname="alcoholic drinks">
    <product productid="2000">
      <name>French White Wine</name>
      <salesunit>Crate of 6 bottles</salesunit>
      <price>148.99</price>
    </product>
    <product productid="2001">
      <name>Californian Red Wine</name>
      <salesunit>Crate of 6 bottles</salesunit>
      <price>98.99</price>
    </product>
    <product productid="2002">
      <name>German Beer</name>
      <salesunit>Crate of 24 x 300ml can</salesunit>
      <price>29.99</price>
    </product>
  </category>
</catalog>
```

Notice that the XML document uses a combination of elements and attributes to represent the product data. Each category is represented by a *category* element, which contains *categoryid* and *categoryname* attributes, and by a *product* element for each product in the category. Each product element contains a *productid* attribute and *name*, *salesunit*, and *price* elements containing information about the product. Using XML, the catalog information can be represented in a logical, hierarchical format that can be read and processed on multiple platforms.

> **Note** For more information about using XML to represent data, see the XML 1 specification at *http://www.w3.org/XML*.

Using XML in the .NET Compact Framework

The .NET Compact Framework provides XML support in two main ways: the ability to read and write XML using the *XmlReader* and *XmlWriter* classes, and an implementation of the Document Object Model (DOM) in the *XmlDocument* class. The *XmlDocument* class builds a treelike model of a document in memory, thereby permitting navigation of the document in all directions and modification of the XML data. The cost of this flexibility is that the *XmlDocument* class requires substantial amounts of memory for large documents because the *XmlDocument* class reads the entire document into memory. The *XmlReader* and *XmlWriter* classes provide much faster, more memory-efficient features, but they allow you to navigate through the document in a forward direction only. The disadvantage of these classes is that you must write code if you want to provide more sophisticated navigation or editing facilities.

To use any of the XML-related classes, you must import the *System.Xml* namespace to your class by using an *Imports System.Xml* statement in Visual Basic .NET or a *using System.Xml* declaration in C#.

Differences from the Full .NET Framework

Certain XML features can consume a lot of resources on a compact device, and in many cases, these features can be better utilized on the server side of an application. In line with this, the following features are not supported in the .NET Compact Framework:

- Validation using Document Type Definitions (DTDs) or XML Schemas
- Extensible Stylesheet Language Transformations (XSLT) and XML Path Language (XPath)
- The *XmlDataDocument* class

Reading XML with the *XmlReader* Class

The *XmlReader* class is an abstract class defined in the *System.Xml* namespace. It provides functionality that allows you to read an XML document as a sequence of nodes, each node representing an element, attribute, text value, or other component of the XML document. The *XmlReader* class supports forward-only reading of an XML document and is therefore best suited to applications that do not require navigation through the document in any other direction, such as backwards to previous sibling nodes, or to find the parent or other ancestor of the current node. If your application requires such navigation (for example, to find a *<price>* node with a value greater than $50 and then to find its parent *<product>* node to get the product ID), using the *XmlDocument* class, discussed later in this chapter, is a more suitable approach. You can use *XmlReader* for such purposes, but only at the expense of having to implement at least some of the DOM functionality provided in the *XmlDocument* class yourself.

XmlReader is an abstract class, with methods and properties implemented by two concrete classes: *XmlTextReader* and *XmlNodeReader*. Note that the *XmlValidatingReader* class of the full .NET Framework is absent in the .NET Compact Framework because validation is not supported. The *XmlNodeReader* constructor takes an *XmlNode* object as its parameter and reads the data in that node. In other respects, it behaves as the *XmlTextReader* class. In the remainder of this chapter, I'll concentrate on showing you how to use the *XmlTextReader* class.

Understanding the *XmlTextReader* Class

You use an *XmlTextReader* class to navigate forward through the nodes of an XML document or fragment thereof that is persisted as a stream (either in memory or in a file loaded from the local file system or from a URL) or contained in a string variable. The *Read* method of the *XmlTextReader* class reads through the document in a forward-only direction, one node at a time, returning a Boolean value indicating whether the end of the XML stream has been reached. When a node has been read, you can use properties and methods of the *XmlTextReader* object to obtain information about that node, such as the type of node, its name, or its text value.

Constructing an *XmlTextReader* Object

The various overloads for the *XmlTextReader* constructor can accept parameters that are URLs, strings containing XML, or *Stream* objects. No constructor accepts a simple file name directly, so if you want to read an XML document from a file, you must load the document into a *Stream* object and use the *XmlTextReader* class to read the stream. For example, suppose you created the Pocket PC application described at the beginning of this chapter and had already implemented the code to download the catalog data from a Web service and persist it as an XML file on the local device. You could use the following code to load the XML catalog data into an *XmlTextReader* object:

```
StreamReader catRdr = new StreamReader("catalog.xml");
XmlTextReader catXML = new XmlTextReader(catRdr);
// Read the XML data
⋮
```

```
catXML.Close();
catRdr.Close();
```

You can also pass a *NameTable* object to certain *XmlTextReader* constructor overloads. A *NameTable* object is a storage area that the .NET Compact Framework uses to store string values associated with the use of *XmlTextReader*. In the event that you are processing multiple documents containing similar content, passing the same *NameTable* object to each constructor allows the .NET Compact Framework to economize on storage space for strings.

Reading an XML Document with the *XmlTextReader* Class

To read the document, you use the *Read* method of the *XmlTextReader* class. Each call to the *Read* method reads one node into memory. A node can be any component of an XML document including the opening tag of an element, a text value, the closing tag of an element, a processing instruction, or white space. When the node is read, the *NodeType* property of the *XmlTextReader* object gives the type of node as an *XmlNodeType* enumeration value. The full list of *XmlNodeType* enumeration values is shown in Table 9-1, in the section "Accessing Other Types of *XmlNode*" later in this chapter. You can use the *Name* property of the *XmlTextReader* object to retrieve the name of the current node, and you can use the *Value* property to retrieve a node's value. You should note, however, that not all nodes have names or values. For example, a node of type *XmlNodeType.Element* will have a name (the name specified in the element tag) but not a value. (The value of an element is represented by the *XmlNodeType.Text* node contained by the *XmlNodeType.Element* node.)

Suppose you want to use *XmlTextReader* to read the following simplified catalog document:

```
<?xml version="1.0"?>
<catalog>
  <category categoryid="1" categoryname="soft drinks">
    <product productid="1000">
      <name>Cola Flavored Drink</name>
      <salesunit>Crate of 12 x 400ml bottle</salesunit>
      <price>25.99</price>
    </product>
  </category>
</catalog>
```

You could use the following code to read the document and report the type, name, and value of each node. In the code, *catXML* is an *XmlTextReader* object.

```
while (catXML.Read())
{
    MessageBox.Show("NodeType:" + catXML.NodeType.ToString() +
                    " Name:" + catXML.Name +
                    " Value:" + catXML.Value);
}
```

Executing this code would produce the following sequence of messages:

```
NodeType:XmlDeclaration Name:xml Value:version="1.0"
NodeType:Whitespace Name: Value:
NodeType:Element Name:catalog Value:
NodeType:Whitespace Name: Value:
NodeType:Element Name:category Value:
NodeType:Whitespace Name: Value:
NodeType:Element Name:product Value:
NodeType:Whitespace Name: Value:
NodeType:Element Name:name Value:
NodeType:Text Name: Value:Cola Flavored Drink
NodeType:EndElement Name:name Value:
NodeType:Whitespace Name: Value:
NodeType:Element Name:salesunit Value:
NodeType:Text Name: Value:Crate of 12 x 400ml bottle
NodeType:EndElement Name:salesunit Value:
NodeType:Whitespace Name: Value:
NodeType:Element Name:price Value:
NodeType:Text Name: Value:25.99
NodeType:EndElement Name:price Value:
NodeType:Whitespace Name: Value:
NodeType:EndElement Name:product Value:
NodeType:Whitespace Name: Value:
NodeType:EndElement Name:category Value:
NodeType:Whitespace Name: Value:
NodeType:EndElement Name:catalog Value:
```

There are two interesting things to note about the output from this code. First, the *Read* method treats the XML declaration at the beginning of the document, the opening and closing tags of each element, the value of each element, and the white space (spaces or carriage returns) between the elements as nodes. This means that in most scenarios, the default behavior of the *Read* method produces a great deal of "noise" nodes that are irrelevant to the code processing the XML data. Second, the *Read* method does not read XML attributes, so if your XML document includes important values as attributes, you must write additional code to retrieve them.

Nodes have a parent/child relationship, which in most cases is exactly what you would expect, and the sequence in which the *Element* and *EndElement* nodes appear reflects the nested nature of an XML document. The reader reports the start of each element and then reports its child elements in order, reporting their *EndElement* nodes in reverse order. Thus, the *name*, *salesunit*, and *price* element nodes are children of the *product* element node, and they end before the product ends. An *EndElement* node tells you when the end element tag has been read, except in the case of empty elements (such as *<discount/>*), where only an *Element* node would be read. You can use the *IsEmptyElement* property to detect empty elements programmatically.

Disregarding Unnecessary Nodes

In most cases, you will want to read the data in the XML document without having to handle nodes such as the *XmlDeclaration* and *Whitespace* nodes. You can use the *WhitespaceHandling* property to control whether the *Read* method includes all *Whitespace* nodes, *SignificantWhitespace* nodes, or no whitespace nodes. This can significantly reduce the number of nodes that have to be processed. For example, the following code shows how to configure an *XmlTextReader* to disregard all whitespace nodes:

```
catXML.WhitespaceHandling = WhitespaceHandling.None;
```

To move to the next node that contains XML content (such as an XML element), you can use the *MoveToContent* method. This method is commonly used to bypass prolog information, such as the XML declaration and processing instructions, and move directly to the root element, as shown in this example:

```
StreamReader catRdr = new StreamReader("catalog.xml");
XmlTextReader catXML = new XmlTextReader(catRdr);
catXML.MoveToContent();
// read the XML data
catXML.Close();
catRdr.Close();
```

Reading Attribute Nodes

As mentioned, attributes are not read by the *Read* method; they are not considered children of their parent element node. To process attribute nodes, the reader must be *moved* to the attributes and then back to the element. You can use the *AttributeCount* property to determine how many attributes an element node has and then use the *MoveToAttribute* method to move to an attribute by specifying its index, its qualified name, or its local name and namespace Uniform Resource Identifier (URI). After you have finished processing the attributes, you can move the reader back to the element using the *MoveToElement* method, as shown in the following example:

```
if(catXML.AttributeCount > 0)
{
    for(int i=0; i < catXML.AttributeCount; i++)
    {
        catXML.MoveToAttribute(i);
        MessageBox.Show("Name:" + catXML.Name +
                        " Value:" + catXML.Value);
    }
    catXML.MoveToElement();
}
```

When reading the attributes of the *category* node in the simplified catalog XML document described earlier, this code produces the following messages:

```
Name:categoryid Value:1
Name:categoryname Value:soft drinks
```

Note that when reading an attribute, the value of the attribute is retrieved directly from the node representing the attribute rather than from a child node representing its value, as is the case when reading an element.

An alternative way to retrieve an attribute value is to use the *GetAttribute* method when positioned on the *Element* node that contains the required attribute. The *GetAttribute* method returns the value of the attribute without moving the position of the reader, and it allows you to specify the attribute by index, qualified name, or local name and namespace URI. The following example shows how the value of the *productid* attribute could be retrieved when reading the *product* element and then used to populate a ListView control named *productsList* with product data from the catalog document:

```
// Prepare the ListView
productsList.Clear();
productsList.Columns.Add("ID", -2, HorizontalAlignment.Left);
productsList.Columns.Add("Name", -2, HorizontalAlignment.Left);
productsList.Columns.Add("Price", -2, HorizontalAlignment.Left);
productsList.View = View.Details;

// Load the catalog document
StreamReader catRdr = new StreamReader("catalog.xml");
XmlTextReader catXML = new XmlTextReader(catRdr);
catXML.WhitespaceHandling = WhitespaceHandling.None;
catXML.MoveToContent();
```

```
// Create an array to hold the info for each product
string[] productItem = new string[3];

string prevNodeName = "";
while(catXML.Read())
{
    // The name and price are element values
    // so they'll be found in Text nodes
    if (catXML.NodeType == XmlNodeType.Text)
    {
        // Check the name of the element containing this
        // value
        switch (prevNodeName)
        {
        case "name":
            productItem[1] = catXML.Value;
            break;
        case "price":
            productItem[2] = catXML.Value;
            // This is the last value, so the item can
            // be added to the list
            productsList.Items.Add(new ListViewItem(productItem));
            break;
        }
    }
    if(catXML.NodeType == XmlNodeType.Element)
    {
        // Set prevNodeName to this element's name
        prevNodeName = catXML.Name;

        // if this is the product element, get the
        // productid attribute value
        if (prevNodeName == "product")
        {
            productItem[0] = catXML.GetAttribute("productid");
        }
    }
    else
    {
        prevNodeName = "";
    }
}
catXML.Close();
catRdr.Close();
```

Notice in this example how the attribute value can be read directly from the *Attribute* node, but to read the values of the *name* and *price* elements, the code needs to keep track of each element node name in the *prevNodeName* variable when reading the *Text* nodes inside an element. This example's listing is from the DrinksClient application, included with this book's sample files.

Handling Namespaces with *XmlTextReader*

When using *XmlTextReader* to read a document that makes use of namespaces, the *Name* property of the *Element* or *Atttribute* nodes is the fully qualified name of the node, which also has *LocalName*, *Prefix*, and *NamespaceURI* properties. When reading the namespace declaration, it is reported as an attribute. For example, suppose the catalog data included namespace declarations, as shown in the following code:

```
<?xml version="1.0"?>
<catalog xmlns:p="http://www.myuri.com/product">
  <category categoryid="1" categoryname="soft drinks">
    <p:product productid="1000">
      <p:name>Cola Flavored Drink</p:name>
      <p:salesunit>Crate of 12 x 400ml bottle</p:salesunit>
      <p:price>25.99</p:price>
    </p:product>
  </category>
</catalog>
```

The *catalog* node is read with an attribute whose name is *xmlns:p* and whose value is the URI pointed to. The reader recognizes this as a namespace declaration. When the *p:product*, *p:name*, *p:salesunit*, and *p:price* nodes are read, the *Prefix* and *NamespaceURI* properties are set to *p* and *http://www.myuri.com/product*, respectively.

Dealing with Validation, DTDs, and Entities

The XML implementation in the .NET Compact Framework does not support validation. This results in a more compact implementation because support for DTDs, XML schemas, and resolution of *Entity* nodes is not provided. Because XML applications on a portable device are normally targeted at a known XML site, developed by the same team or organization, they can get around this issue by ensuring that validation is performed on the server. If the XML document contains a *<!DOCTYPE …>* declaration, an attempt to call the *Read* method on that node will result in an exception of type *NotSupportedException* being thrown. A further consequence of this is that entities other than the standard five character entities of XML, which are: *<*, *>*, *"*, *&*, and

', are not resolved. An entity reference in your XML such as *¤cy;* will simply be reported as an *EntityReference* node with the name *currency* and no value. Standard entities such as *<* are simply translated without producing an *EntityReference* node. For example, consider the following XML fragment:

```
<name>French &beer;</name>
<salesunit>&gt; 10 bottles per box</salesunit>
```

Reading this XML produces the following sequence of nodes:

```
NodeType:Element Name:"name" Value:
NodeType:Text Name: Value:"French "
NodeType:EntityReference Name:"beer" Value:
NodeType:EndElement Name:"name" Value:
NodeType:Element Name:"salesunit" Value:
NodeType:Text Name: Value:"> 10 bottles per box"
NodeType:EndElement Name:"salesunit" Value:
```

Handling Comment Nodes

XML documents often contain comments. For example, the following catalog document contains a comment indicating where additional products should be added:

```
<?xml version="1.0"?>
<catalog>
  <category categoryid="1" categoryname="soft drinks">
    <product productid="1000">
      <name>Cola Flavored Drink</name>
      <salesunit>Crate of 12 x 400ml bottle</salesunit>
      <price>25.99</price>
    </product>
    <!-- insert additional products here -->
  </category>
</catalog>
```

Comment nodes have a *NodeType* of *XmlNodeType.Comment*. The node has no name and a value that is the text of the comment minus the <!-- and --> markup, so the *Comment* node for the comment in the catalog example would contain the value *insert additional products here.*

Handling *CDATA* Nodes

CDATA nodes result in a *NodeType* of *XmlNodeType.CDATA*. The node has no name and a value that is the text contained in the *CDATA* section. For example, for a *CDATA* section such as this

```
<![CDATA[A price < $10]]>
```

the *Value* property is set to *A price < $10*. Note that if an element has a mixture of text and *CDATA* nodes, it will be easier to read the entire text and *CDATA* content using the *ReadElementString* method of *XmlTextReader* than to write code to concatenate all the *Text* and *CDATA* nodes that could appear.

Writing XML with the *XmlWriter* Class

The *XmlWriter* class is an abstract class that provides fast, forward-only, non-cached output of XML to a file or a stream. You can use the *XmlTextWriter* class, which derives from *XmlWriter*, to create and persist XML documents. The advantages of using an *XmlTextWriter* object over performing output manually using *Stream.Write* calls or similar are threefold. First, *XmlTextWriter* will write syntactically correct XML output. Second, *XmlTextWriter* has powerful support for namespaces, avoiding the need for the user to maintain namespace stacks in a complex document. Third, *XmlTextWriter* will automatically translate any special characters in text to entities, for example, transforming *x < y* to *x < y*.

In this section, I'll describe the principal methods and properties of the *XmlTextWriter* class.

Writing an XML Document with the *XmlTextWriter* Class

Suppose you needed to extend the Pocket PC application described earlier in this chapter to allow sales representatives to take orders when visiting customers. The order details could be entered into controls on a form and saved as XML using the *XmlTextWriter* class. The XML orders could be submitted to a Web service at a later date when the sales representative returns to the office. The following XML could be used to represent a customer order:

```
<?xml version="1.0" encoding="us-ascii"?>
<order CustomerNo="1234">
  <items>
    <item>
      <productid>1001</productid>
      <quantity>20</quantity>
    </item>
    <item>
      <productid>2002</productid>
      <quantity>10</quantity>
    </item>
  </items>
</order>
```

The *XmlTextWriter* class provides a number of methods that can be used to create this XML document.

Constructing an *XmlTextWriter*

The constructor for an *XmlTextWriter* class allows you to specify where the XML should be written to. You can specify a file path, a *Stream* object, or a *TextWriter* object. If you specify a file path or a stream, you must also specify the encoding to be used when writing the XML. When a *TextWriter* object is specified, it is assumed that the appropriate encoding has already been set for the *TextWriter* object.

The following code shows how to create an *XmlTextWriter* object that will be used to write XML data to a file named Order.xml. The data will be encoded as ASCII text. (I've assumed that a *using System.Text* declaration has been added to the class.)

```
XmlTextWriter orderWriter =
  new XmlTextWriter("Order.xml", Encoding.ASCII);
```

Writing XML Data

After you have created the *XmlTextWriter* object, you can use it to write XML data. By default, the data is written as a sequential stream of XML, but you can use the *Formatting* property to specify that you want the elements to be indented, as shown here:

```
orderWriter.Formatting = Formatting.Indented;
```

Adding indentation to your XML document can make it easier to read for humans, but it makes no difference to programs that load and parse the XML. You can use the *Indentation* property to specify the number of characters you want to use to indent elements (the default is 2), and you can use the *IndentChar* property to specify which character you want to use for indentation (the default is a space).

You begin writing an XML document by calling the *WriteStartDocument* method of the *XmlTextWriter* class. This method writes an XML declaration with a *version* attribute of *1.0* and an *encoding* attribute that reflects the encoding specified for the *XmlTextWriter*. Optionally, you can specify a stand-alone Boolean value, which causes a *standalone* attribute with a value of *yes* or *no* to be added to the declaration.

For each element you want to write, you can use the *WriteStartElement* method to write the element's opening tag, specifying the element name.

Elements are closed using the *WriteEndElement* method, which does not require a parameter because it simply closes the most recently opened element. If you need to write an element that has a text value, you can open it with *WriteStartElement*, use the *WriteString* method to write the element text, and close it with *WriteEndElement*. Alternatively, you can use the *WriteElementString* method, specifying the element name and the text value as parameters, to write the entire element in one operation.

Writing an attribute is similar to writing an element. You can use the *WriteStartAttribute* method to create the attribute, call *WriteString* to write the attribute value, and call the *WriteEndAttribute* method. Alternatively, you can use the *WriteAttributeString* method to write the name and value of the attribute in a single call.

To finish a document, call the *WriteEndDocument* method. This method closes all outstanding attributes and elements and writes the closing tag for the document's root element. After you have finished with the *XmlTextWriter* object, you should call its *Close* method. The following code shows how *XmlTextWriter* could be used to create the XML order document described earlier. It assumes that the file name for the XML file has been entered into a text box named *filename*, that the customer number for the customer placing the order has been entered into a text box named *customerNo*, and that the product ID and quantity of each item required have been added to a ListView control called *orderlist*.

```
XmlTextWriter orderWriter =
    new XmlTextWriter(filename.Text, System.Text.Encoding.ASCII);
orderWriter.Formatting = Formatting.Indented;
orderWriter.WriteStartDocument();
orderWriter.WriteStartElement("order");
orderWriter.WriteAttributeString("customerno",
    customerNo.Text);
orderWriter.WriteStartElement("items");
foreach(ListViewItem orderItem in orderlist.Items)
{
    orderWriter.WriteStartElement("item");
    orderWriter.WriteElementString("productid",
        orderItem.SubItems[0].Text);
    orderWriter.WriteElementString("quantity",
        orderItem.SubItems[1].Text);
    orderWriter.WriteEndElement();
}
orderWriter.WriteEndDocument();
orderWriter.Close();
MessageBox.Show("Order Saved");
```

Handling Namespaces with *XmlTextWriter*

Namespace support is a powerful feature of the *XmlTextWriter* class. In particular, *XmlTextWriter* maintains a namespace stack for complex documents. For example, suppose you wanted to include a namespace in a simplified order document, similar to the document produced by the code in the previous section, as shown here:

```
<?xml version="1.0" encoding="us-ascii"?>
<order customerno="1234" xmlns="www.myuri.com/order">
  <items>
    <item>
      <productid>1001</productid>
      <quantity>20</quantity>
    </item>
  </items>
</order>
```

The *WriteStartElement*, *WriteElementString*, *WriteStartAttribute*, and *WriteAttributeString* methods allow you to specify a namespace and optionally a prefix (to declare a nondefault namespace). To create the order document shown previously, you would simply need to specify the namespace in the *WriteStartElement* method used to write the *order* element, as shown here:

```
XmlTextWriter orderWriter =
    new XmlTextWriter("OrderNS.xml",
                      System.Text.Encoding.ASCII);
orderWriter.Formatting = Formatting.Indented;
orderWriter.WriteStartDocument();

// Declare default namespace
orderWriter.WriteStartElement("order", "www.myuri.com/order");

orderWriter.WriteAttributeString("customerno", "1234");
orderWriter.WriteStartElement("items");
orderWriter.WriteStartElement("item");
orderWriter.WriteElementString("productid", "1001");
orderWriter.WriteElementString("quantity", "20");
orderWriter.WriteEndElement();
orderWriter.WriteEndDocument();
orderWriter.Close();
```

In cases where some elements and attributes in the document belong to a different namespace than others, you might need to use a prefix for the namespace, as shown here:

```
<?xml version="1.0" encoding="us-ascii"?>
<order customerno="1234" xmlns="www.myuri.com/order">
```

(continued)

```
  <items>
    <p:item xmlns:p="www.myuri.com/orderedproduct">
      <p:productid>1001</p:productid>
      <p:quantity>20</p:quantity>
    </p:item>
  </items>
</order>
```

The prefix can be specified in a *WriteStartElement*, *WriteElementString*, *WriteStartAttribute*, or *WriteAttributeString* method call. If a namespace that has already been prefixed in the current scope is specified without a prefix, the most recently declared prefix is used, as shown in this code:

```
XmlTextWriter orderWriter =
    new XmlTextWriter("OrderNS.xml",
                      System.Text.Encoding.ASCII);
orderWriter.Formatting = Formatting.Indented;
orderWriter.WriteStartDocument();
orderWriter.WriteStartElement("order", "www.myuri.com/order");
orderWriter.WriteAttributeString("customerno", "1234");
orderWriter.WriteStartElement("items");

// Declare "p" as the prefix for the "orderedproduct" namespace
orderWriter.WriteStartElement("p", "item",
                              "www.myuri.com/orderedproduct");

// The most recently declared prefix for the namespace is "p"
orderWriter.WriteElementString("productid",
                "www.myuri.com/orderedproduct", "1001");
orderWriter.WriteElementString("quantity",
                "www.myuri.com/orderedproduct", "20");

orderWriter.WriteEndElement();
orderWriter.WriteEndDocument();
orderWriter.Close();
```

Of course, in a real order document, there might be multiple *item* elements, so you might want to simply declare the second namespace in the root element along with the default namespace, as shown here:

```
 <?xml version="1.0" encoding="us-ascii"?>
<order customerno="1234"
               xmlns:p="www.myuri.com/orderedproduct"
               xmlns="www.myuri.com/order">
  <items>
```

```
    <p:item>
      <p:productid>1001</p:productid>
      <p:quantity>20</p:quantity>
    </p:item>
  </items>
</order>
```

Because the various methods used to declare a namespace allow you to specify only one namespace, you must write code to manually create the second namespace declaration by writing an *xmlns* attribute. You can accomplish this using the *WriteAttributeString* method, although the parameters used might at first seem a little unintuitive as you must declare *xmlns* as the prefix for this attribute, the prefix you want to apply to the namespace as the attribute name, *null* as the namespace for this attribute, and the namespace URI you want to declare as the attribute value. This is shown in the following code:

```
XmlTextWriter orderWriter =
    new XmlTextWriter("OrderNS.xml",
                      System.Text.Encoding.ASCII);
orderWriter.Formatting = Formatting.Indented;
orderWriter.WriteStartDocument();
orderWriter.WriteStartElement("order", "www.myuri.com/order");
orderWriter.WriteAttributeString("customerno", "1234");

// Declare the second namespace with a prefix of "p"
orderWriter.WriteAttributeString("xmlns", "p", null,
                          "www.myuri.com/orderedproduct");

orderWriter.WriteStartElement("items");

// The most recently declared prefix for the namespace is "p"
orderWriter.WriteStartElement("item",
                              "www.myuri.com/orderedproduct");
orderWriter.WriteElementString("productid",
                "www.myuri.com/orderedproduct", "1001");
orderWriter.WriteElementString("quantity",
                "www.myuri.com/orderedproduct", "20");

orderWriter.WriteEndElement();
orderWriter.WriteEndDocument();
orderWriter.Close();
```

The ability to declare multiple namespaces when using the *XmlTextWriter* class makes it possible to create highly complex XML documents relatively easily.

Processing XML with the *XmlDocument* Class

This section will discuss the use of the *XmlDocument* class, which is the implementation of the DOM provided in the .NET Compact Framework. The DOM is a standard specification for an object-oriented representation of an XML document. For more information about the DOM specification, visit *www.w3c.org/dom*.

Understanding the *XmlDocument* Class

Using the *XmlDocument* class differs from using the *XmlReader* and *XmlWriter* classes described in previous sections in two major ways. First, the *XmlReader* and *XmlWriter* classes provide forward-only, noncached access to an XML document, while the *XmlDocument* class builds an in-memory tree view of the XML document that can be navigated in any direction. Second, the *XmlDocument* class can be used to both read and write XML, making it possible to read, create, or modify an XML document using the same object.

The *XmlDocument* tree is composed of nodes, with each type of node (element, attribute, and so on) being represented by an implementation of the *XmlNode* abstract class. Classes derived from *XmlNode* include *XmlElement*, *XmlAttribute*, and other node-type specific classes. The tree is hierarchical, implementing mostly a parent/child relationship between nodes, with an *XmlDocument* node at the top of the tree. The *XmlDocument* node has a child *Element* node representing the root element of the document, and it also has child nodes for any XML declarations or processing instructions that the document prolog might contain. The root element can have children that are other element nodes, text nodes, comments, processing instructions, or *CDATA* sections. The *XmlDocument* and *XmlNode* classes have navigational functions for navigating through child, parent, or sibling nodes and functions for modifying the document.

Because the document is held in memory, use of the *XmlDocument* class can consume much more memory than use of the *XmlReader* or *XmlWriter* classes, especially in the case of large documents. The benefit of using the *XmlDocument* class is that because the entire document is present in memory at one time, you can exploit any type of relationship between the nodes in an application program without resorting to implementing infrastructure facilities such as navigation in the program. Note that because validation is not supported in the .NET Compact Framework, element-to-element references using the *ID*, *IDREF*, and *IDREFS* attributes are not possible.

The *XmlDocument* class is particularly useful when you need to allow the users of your application to search for specific data or select a subset of data from the XML document. For example, the beverage ordering application described earlier in this chapter could load the entire product catalog into an *XmlDocument* object. Then the application could allow users to select a category node and view the products in the specified category, or allow users to search for products that match a specific criterion. Another use of the *XmlDocument* class would be to allow an existing XML document to be loaded, read, and modified. For example, the sales representative could load previously saved orders and add or remove items.

Differences from the Full .NET Framework

The XML implementation in the .NET Compact Framework does not support validation or DTDs. This has the following impact:

- The only entities that are resolved are the five standard XML entities: *<*, *>*, *&*, *"*, and *'*. Other entities will cause an exception of type *XmlException* to be thrown during the *XmlDocument.Load* call. The workaround for this is to ensure that entities are resolved on the server.
- Documents that contain DTDs cannot be processed using the .NET Compact Framework *XmlDocument* class.

Reading XML with the *XmlDocument* Class

The first step in reading an XML document with the *XmlDocument* class is to load the XML. You can use the *XmlDocument* class's *Load* method to load an XML document from a *Stream*, *TextReader*, or *XmlReader* object, or you can use the *LoadXML* method to load an XML string. For example, suppose the product catalog document is saved as a file named Catalog.xml. After creating an *XmlDocument* object such as this

```
XmlDocument xmlDoc = new XmlDocument();
```

you could load the file into an *XmlDocument* object using the following code:

```
// Load document from a Stream object
// (FileStream derives from Stream)
xmlDoc.Load(new FileStream("catalog.xml", FileMode.Open));
```

Or you could load the document from a *TextReader* object, as follows:

```
// Load document from TextReader object
// (StreamReader derives from TextReader)
xmlDoc.Load(new StreamReader("catalog.xml"));
```

Finally you could load the document from an *XmlReader* object, like this:

```
// Load document from XmlReader object
// (XmlTextReader derives from XmlReader)
xmlDoc.Load(new XmlTextReader("catalog.xml"));
```

If the XML data is stored in a string variable, you can load it into the *XmlDocument* object using the *ReadXML* method, as shown in this example:

```
XmlDocument xmlDoc = new XmlDocument();

// Load document from string containing XML
xmlDoc.LoadXML(xmlString);
```

Navigating an XML Document

Once the document has been loaded, you can navigate through its nodes. To retrieve the root element of the document, you can simply use the *DocumentElement* property of the *XmlDocument* class, as shown in this example:

```
XmlNode rootElement = xmlDoc.DocumentElement
```

All nodes in the XML document tree (including the *XmlDocument* class itself) are extensions of the *XmlNode* abstract class. You can use a variable of type *XmlNode* to navigate through all the nodes in the document and use the *NodeType* property to ascertain which nodes are elements, comments, and so on. In the parent/child hierarchy of the tree, nodes have children, parents (except for the document node), and siblings. The *XmlNode* class has methods and properties to support navigation in all directions. The *HasChildNodes* property returns a Boolean value to indicate if child nodes are present. The *ChildNodes* property returns an *XmlNodeList* object with the child nodes of the node on which it is invoked. You can then iterate through the *ChildNodes* collection using the *Item* property (specifying the index of the required node) or the *[]* indexer in C# to obtain a reference to each node.

There are also *FirstChild* and *LastChild* properties. The *FirstChild* property is useful when you have a text-only element where you know that all you wish to do is access the value of the one text child node. The *ParentNode* property returns the node's parent. Note that the parent of the root element node is the *XmlDocument* object, whose own parent is null. You can navigate a document by starting at the *DocumentElement* node and recursively processing child nodes. For example, consider the following simplified catalog document:

```
<?xml version="1.0"?>
<catalog>
  <category categoryid="1" categoryname="soft drinks">
    <product productid="1000">
      <name>Cola Flavored Drink</name>
      <salesunit>Crate of 12 x 400ml bottle</salesunit>
```

```
      <price>25.99</price>
    </product>
  </category>
</catalog>
```

This document could be navigated using the following code:

```
XmlNode xNode = xmlDoc.FirstChild; // XML Declaration
MessageBox.Show(xNode.Name);

xNode = xmlDoc.DocumentElement; // Root element (catalog)
MessageBox.Show(xNode.Name);

xNode = xNode.FirstChild; // Category element
MessageBox.Show(xNode.Name);

xNode = xNode.FirstChild; // Product element
MessageBox.Show(xNode.Name);

// Name, salesunit, and price elements
XmlNodeList xNodes = xNode.ChildNodes;
foreach(XmlNode childNode in xNodes)
{
    MessageBox.Show(childNode.Name);
}
```

Additional navigation properties include *NextSibling* and *PreviousSibling*, which return a reference to the *XmlNode* object that immediately follows or precedes the current node (or null if no such node exists), and *OwnerDocument*, which returns the *XmlDocument* object to which the current node belongs.

Handling Namespaces

The *Name* property of *XmlNode* returns the fully qualified name of the node, including the namespace prefix. You can separate a name into prefix and local name using the *Prefix* and *LocalName* properties. The *NamespaceURI* property returns the URI that the prefix maps to.

Accessing Element Values

The *Value* property returns the text value of a node. As with the *XmlReader* class, the value of an element node is retrieved by inspecting the *Value* property of the element node's child text node. You can easily retrieve an element's text node from its *FirstChild* property, as shown in the following example. In the code that follows, *xNodes* is an *XmlNodeList* object containing the child nodes of a *product* element in the catalog XML document described earlier.

```
foreach(XmlNode childNode in xNodes)
{
    XmlNode valueNode = childNode.FirstChild;
    MessageBox.Show(childNode.Name + ": " + valueNode.Value);
}
```

You can also use the *InnerText* property to retrieve data from XML nodes. The *InnerText* property returns all the text values in the current node's child nodes. If called on a node that contains only a value, *InnerText* will return the value. For example, the *InnerText* property of the node representing the *name* element in the catalog example will return *Cola Flavored Drink*. However, the *InnerText* property of nodes that contain a hierarchy of elements will concatenate all the text values in the hierarchy. For example, the *InnerText* property of the node representing the *product* element in the catalog example will return *Cola Flavored DrinkCrate of 12 x 400ml bottles25.99*.

Accessing Attributes

As when using the *XmlReader* class, you cannot access attributes simply by navigating from parent to child. The *XmlNode* class provides an *Attributes* property that makes it possible to access an element's attributes. However, the *XmlElement* class, which derives from *XmlNode*, has a number of additional properties and methods that make it easier to access attribute data. If you have already located the node using an *XmlNode* class, you can cast the object to an *XmlElement* class and use the additional properties and methods.

You can use the *HasAttributes* property of the *XmlElement* class to find out if the current node has any attributes, or you can use the *HasAttribute* method to find out if the element has an attribute with a particular name (and optionally, a namespace), as shown in the following code:

```
// Cast an XmlNode to XmlElement
XmlElement currentElement = (XmlElement)xNode;

// Check for attributes
if (currentElement.HasAttributes);
{
    MessageBox.Show("This element has attributes");
}

// Check for a categoryname attribute
if (currentElement.HasAttribute("categoryname"));
{
    MessageBox.Show("This element has a categoryname attribute");
}
```

The *Attributes* property of both the *XmlNode* and *XmlElement* classes returns an *AttributeCollection* of all attributes for this element, including any namespace declarations. You then iterate through this collection to access each *XmlAttribute* node, as shown in the following code:

```
foreach(XmlAttribute a in currentElement.Attributes)
{
    MessageBox.Show(a.Name + ": " + a.Value);
}
```

Note that, as with the *XmlReader* class, you can return the value of an attribute using its *Value* property. Unlike an element, you do not need to access a text node under the attribute. You can also use the *Attributes* collection to access a particular attribute by specifying its name (and optionally, its namespace) or index, as shown here:

```
XmlAttribute a = currentElement.Attributes["categoryname"];
```

The *XmlElement* class also provides two methods for accessing attributes: the *GetAttribute* method, which returns the specified attribute value, and *GetAttributeNode*, which returns an *XmlAttribute* object for the specified attribute. These methods are shown in the following example:

```
// Get the value of the categoryid attribute
MessageBox.Show(currentElement.GetAttribute("categoryid"));

// Get the categoryname attribute
XmlAttribute a = currentElement.GetAttributeNode("categoryname");
MessageBox.Show(a.Value);
```

Accessing Other Types of *XmlNode*

The examples so far process only document, element, attribute, and text nodes. Once you have accessed a node, use the *NodeType* property to return an *XmlNodeType* enumeration value, which indicates the type of node in question. Then you can check the node type using the enumerated values of *XmlNodeType*.

```
XmlNodeType myNodeType = xNode.NodeType;
if (myNodeType == XmlNodeType.Element)
{
    ⋮
}
```

Table 9-1 describes the characteristics of an *XmlNode* object when its *NodeType* property is set to the various members of the *XmlNodeType* enumeration. The table also provides information on how to access some types of nodes.

Table 9-1 *XmlNode* Characteristics for Each Possible *NodeType* Setting

***NodeType* Property Setting**	***Name* Property Returns**	***Value* Property Returns**	**Comments**
Attribute	Attribute name	Attribute value	Use the *Attributes* property of an *XmlNode* object of type *Element* to return an *XmlAttributeCollection* object.
CDATA	N/A	Content of the *CDATA* section	A *CDATA* node can't have any child nodes.
Comment	#comment	Content of the comment minus the <!-- and --> markup	N/A
Document	#document	N/A	Child node types are *XmlDeclaration*, *Element* (exactly one), and *ProcessingInstruction*. The *DocumentType* child, supported in the full .NET Framework, is absent in the .NET Compact Framework.
DocumentFragment	#document-fragment	N/A	N/A
DocumentType	N/A	N/A	Not supported in the .NET Compact Framework because validation is not supported.
Element	Fully qualified element name with the namespace prefix, if applicable	N/A	Navigate to the *Text* child element to obtain text value. For mixed-content elements, you can use the *InnerText* property to retrieve concatenated string content, including multiple text children, child elements, *CDATA* sections, and so on.
EndElement	Element name	N/A	Empty elements do not cause an *EndElement* value to be reported.
EndEntity	N/A	N/A	Not supported in the .NET Compact Framework.

Table 9-1 *XmlNode* Characteristics for Each Possible *NodeType*

NodeType Property Setting	*Name* Property Returns	*Value* Property Returns	Comments
Entity	N/A	N/A	Not supported in the .NET Compact Framework.
EntityReference	N/A	N/A	Not supported in the .NET Compact Framework.
None	N/A	N/A	This *XmlNodeType* value is returned if an *XmlReader* object hasn't performed a read operation.
Notation	N/A	N/A	Not supported in the .NET Compact Framework.
Processing-Instruction	#processing-instruction	Processing instruction text	N/A
Significant-Whitespace	N/A	The whitespace between the markup	N/A
XmlDeclaration	xml	The version number and decoding string	N/A

Reading XML from an *XmlNode*

The *XmlNode* class provides two properties that can be used to retrieve XML from the node: *OuterXml* and *InnerXml*. *OuterXml* returns XML with the current node as the root element, while *InnerXml* returns an XML fragment containing the children of the current node. For example, the following code could be used to return XML from the simplified catalog document described earlier in this chapter:

```
XmlDocument xmlDoc = new XmlDocument();
StreamReader xmlFile = new StreamReader("catalog.xml");
xmlDoc.Load(xmlFile);
xmlFile.Close();
XmlNode category = xmlDoc.DocumentElement.FirstChild;
XmlNode product = category.FirstChild;
MessageBox.Show(product.OuterXml);
MessageBox.Show(product.InnerXml);
```

When the preceding code is executed, the *OuterXml* property returns the following XML:

```
<product productid="1000">
  <name>Cola Flavored Drink</name>
```

(continued)

```
  <salesunit>Crate of 12 x 400ml bottle</salesunit>
  <price>25.99</price>
</product>
```

The *InnerXml* property returns only the child elements of the *product* element, as shown here:

```
<name>Cola Flavored Drink</name>
<salesunit>Crate of 12 x 400ml bottle</salesunit>
<price>25.99</price>
```

Searching an XML Document with *GetElementsByTagName*

The full .NET Framework provides the following methods for searching a document for nodes by name or ID: *GetElementsByTagName*, *GetElementById*, *SelectNodes*, and *SelectSingleNode*. The *SelectNodes* and *SelectSingleNode* methods require XPath, which is not supported in the .NET Compact Framework, so these two methods are absent. The *GetElementById* method is also not supported because it requires validation, which is absent in the .NET Compact Framework. The ethos of compact device development should in any case encourage functions such as selecting nodes for delivery to be performed on the server, thus minimizing the amount of memory used on the device.

GetElementsByTagName is a method of the *XmlDocument* and *XmlElement* classes. It returns an *XmlNodeList* object containing the *XmlElement* objects that have the specified name (and optionally, the specified namespace). As its name suggests, *GetElementsByTagName* returns elements found at any depth, so it is not an efficient method for searching large documents. The following example shows how to use *GetElementsByTagName* to return the *product* nodes from the catalog document described earlier in this chapter. It also shows how to add the nodes' data to a ListView control named *productsList*.

```
// Prepare the ListView control
productsList.Clear();
productsList.Columns.Add("ID", -2,HorizontalAlignment.Left);
productsList.Columns.Add("Name", -2,HorizontalAlignment.Left);
productsList.Columns.Add("Unit", -2, HorizontalAlignment.Left);
productsList.Columns.Add("Price", -2,HorizontalAlignment.Left);
productsList.View = View.Details;

// Load the XML document
XmlDocument xmlDoc = new XmlDocument();
StreamReader xmlFile = new StreamReader("catalog.xml");
xmlDoc.Load(xmlFile);
xmlFile.Close();
```

```
// Get the product nodes
XmlNodeList productNodes = xmlDoc.GetElementsByTagName("product");
foreach(XmlElement p in productNodes)
{
    // Get the productid attribute
    string[] productInfo = new string[4];
    productInfo[0] = p.GetAttribute("productid");

    // Get the name element
    XmlNode n = p.FirstChild;
    productInfo[1] = n.FirstChild.Value;

    // Get the salesunit element
    n = n.NextSibling;
    productInfo[2] = n.FirstChild.Value;

    // Get the price element
    n = n.NextSibling;
    productInfo[3] = n.FirstChild.Value;

    // Add the product to the list
    productsList.Items.Add(new ListViewItem(productInfo));
}
```

Modifying an XML Document

Much of the power of using the *XmlDocument* class lies in the ability to modify or create XML document trees. For example, you could use an *XmlDocument* class to allow the sales representative to load an existing order and modify it by adding or removing items, or by adjusting the quantity of an ordered item. In this section, you will see how to edit existing nodes, create new nodes and add them to the tree, and remove or replace nodes.

Modifying Values

You can modify element values by setting the *Value* property of the text node containing the element's value. For example, you might need to change the quantity of product 1001 being ordered in the following order document:

```
<?xml version="1.0" encoding="us-ascii"?>
<order CustomerNo="1234">
  <items>
    <item>
      <productid>1001</productid>
      <quantity>20</quantity>
    </item>
    <item>
```

(continued)

```
            <productid>2002</productid>
            <quantity>10</quantity>
        </item>
    </items>
</order>
```

The following code shows how the quantity value for product 1001 could be changed:

```
// Load the XML document
XmlDocument xmlDoc = new XmlDocument();
StreamReader xmlFile = new StreamReader("order.xml");
xmlDoc.Load(xmlFile);
xmlFile.Close();

foreach(XmlNode itemNode in xmlDoc.GetElementsByTagName("item"))
{
    XmlNode iNode = itemNode.FirstChild;

    // If this is product 1001, change the quantity
    if (iNode.FirstChild.Value == "1001")
    {
        iNode = iNode.NextSibling;
        iNode.FirstChild.Value = "25";
    }
}
```

Attribute values can be modified in a similar fashion, but the *XmlElement* class provides a *SetAttribute* method that makes operations on attributes much easier. The *SetAttribute* method allows you to specify the attribute name (and optionally, its namespace) and a new value for the attribute. If the attribute exists, its value is updated. If the attribute does not exist, it is created and assigned the specified value. The following code shows how to use *SetAttribute* to modify the *customerno* attribute of the *order* element:

```
XmlElement orderElement = (XmlElement)xmlDoc.DocumentElement;
orderElement.SetAttribute("customerno", "1324");
```

Adding an Element

You can add an element to an existing document or create a brand-new XML document by instantiating an *XmlDocument* object and adding elements to it. The methods used to add elements (and attributes) provide overloads in which a namespace URI and a prefix can be specified, making it possible to create or modify XML documents that contain namespaces.

Adding an element involves several steps: First create the element using the *CreateElement* method of the *XmlDocument* class. Next create a node of type *XmlNodeType.Text* for the element's value (if any) using the *CreateTextNode* method of the *XmlDocument* class. Then append the text node to the element you are adding by calling its *AppendChild* method. Finally append the element to the node in the tree by calling the *AppendChild* method of the node you want to add it to. This approach could be used to add an item to the order document. The following code creates a new *item* element, adds *productid* and *quantity* elements to it, and appends those elements to the *item* element in the document:

```
// Load the XML document
XmlDocument xmlDoc = new XmlDocument();
StreamReader xmlFile = new StreamReader("order.xml");
xmlDoc.Load(xmlFile);
xmlFile.Close();

// Get the items node
XmlNode itemsNode = xmlDoc.DocumentElement.FirstChild;

// Create a new item element
XmlElement newItem = xmlDoc.CreateElement("item");

// Create the productid element and append it to the new item
XmlElement productID = xmlDoc.CreateElement("productid");
XmlText productIDValue = xmlDoc.CreateTextNode("1000");
productID.AppendChild(productIDValue);
newItem.AppendChild(productID);

// Create the quantity element and append it to the new item
XmlElement quantity = xmlDoc.CreateElement("quantity");
XmlText quantityValue = xmlDoc.CreateTextNode("10");
quantity.AppendChild(quantityValue);
newItem.AppendChild(quantity);

// Append the new item to the items node
itemsNode.AppendChild(newItem);
```

You can also add a new instance of an element that already exists in the document by copying the existing element using the *Clone* method or the *CloneNode* method with a parameter of *true* (to force all child nodes to be included in the copy). After you have cloned the element, you can modify the values as necessary and then append the cloned element to the appropriate node in the document. This approach is shown in the following example:

```
// Load the XML document
XmlDocument xmlDoc = new XmlDocument();
StreamReader xmlFile = new StreamReader("order.xml");
xmlDoc.Load(xmlFile);
xmlFile.Close();

// Get the items node
XmlNode itemsNode = xmlDoc.DocumentElement.FirstChild;

// Copy the first item element
XmlNode newItem = itemsNode.FirstChild.Clone();

// Set the productid and quantity values
XmlNode n = newItem.FirstChild;
n.FirstChild.Value = "1000";

n = n.NextSibling;
n.FirstChild.Value = "10";

// Append the new item to the items node
itemsNode.AppendChild(newItem);
```

Adding an Attribute

As already discussed, attributes can be added to elements using the *SetAttribute* method of the *XmlElement* class. You can also create a new *XmlAttribute* node using the *CreateAttribute* method of the *XmlDocument* class, set its *Value* property, and add it to an *XmlElement* node using the *SetAttributeNode* method, as shown here:

```
XmlAttribute custNo = xmlDoc.CreateAttribute("customerno");
custNo.Value = "4321";
XmlElement orderElement = (XmlElement)xmlDoc.DocumentElement;
orderElement.SetAttributeNode(custNo);
```

Removing Elements and Attributes

You might need to provide functionality that allows the user to remove elements or attributes from an XML document. For example, the sales representative in our beverages application example might want to remove items from an order. You can easily remove a node from the XML hierarchy using the *RemoveChild* method of the *XmlNode* class, as shown in this example, which deletes item 2002 from an order:

```
XmlNode items = xmlDoc.DocumentElement.FirstChild;
foreach(XmlNode itemNode in items.ChildNodes)
{
    // Find the item for product 2002
```

```
    XmlNode productID = itemNode.FirstChild;
    if (productID.FirstChild.Value == "2002")
    {
        // Delete the item node
        items.RemoveChild(itemNode);
    }
}
```

If you need to remove multiple sibling nodes, you can use the *RemoveAll* method of the *XmlNode* class. This method removes all child nodes and any existing attributes from the node on which it is called. For example, the following code could be used to remove all items from the *order* element:

```
XmlNode items = xmlDoc.DocumentElement.FirstChild;
Items.RemoveAll();
```

To remove a single attribute from a node, you can use the *Remove* method of the *XmlAttributeCollection* class, passing the *XmlAttribute* object to be removed. The following code uses the *Remove* method to delete the *customerno* attribute in the *order* element:

```
XmlNode order = xmlDoc.DocumentElement;
order.Attributes.Remove(order.Attributes("customerno"));
```

You can accomplish the same task by calling the *RemoveAttribute* method of the *XmlElement* class, specifying the name of the attribute to be removed, as shown here:

```
XmlElement order = (XmlElement)xmlDoc.DocumentElement;
order.RemoveAttribute("customerno");
```

The *XmlElement* class also provides a *RemoveAttributeNode* method, which removes an attribute specified by the *XmlAttribute* object passed to it; a *RemoveAttributeAt* method, which removes the attribute at the specified index location; and a *RemoveAllAttributes* method, which removes all the attributes of the element.

Saving an XML Document

You can save an XML document by calling the *Save* method of the *XmlDocument* class. The *Save* method allows you to specify the destination as a file name, an *XmlWriter*, a *TextWriter*, or a *Stream* object. The following code shows how the *order* document could be saved as a file.

```
xmlDoc.Save("NewOrder.xml");
```

Summary

In this chapter, you have seen the XML support provided in the .NET Compact Framework. You have seen that, regarding document navigation features, document modification features, and maintaining a small memory footprint, you have a choice of how to process XML documents.

The *XmlTextReader* class reads an XML document in a forward-only manner, reporting the types of XML nodes as they appear in the document. The *XmlTextWriter* class writes an XML document also in a forward-only manner. If you require only forward-only navigation or modification features, the *XmlTextReader* and *XmlTextWriter* classes provide a solution that is highly memory-efficient.

For more sophisticated navigation or document modification features, it is possible to use the *XmlTextReader* and *XmlTextWriter*, but only by writing application code. The *XmlDocument* and related classes in the .NET Compact Framework implementation of the XML DOM build a tree structure in memory that represents the entire document. Because the entire document is held in memory, this solution uses more resources than the *XmlTextReader* and *XmlTextWriter*, but it provides sophisticated features (such as navigation in all directions) and features to add, remove, or modify document elements.

10

Input and Output

The .NET Compact Framework provides powerful features for reading and writing all types of files, from simple text files using character encodings, to pure binary files that must be read as bytes. Features exist for moving the read/write pointer through a file and for copying, moving, and deleting entire files. A *file* can be an actual file on the local device, a remote file on a network, or an object that is not a file at all, but is simply a stream of bytes either in memory or arriving at a socket or other network connection. You can read and write streams synchronously, where the call you make blocks until the file operation completes. Or, in the case of *NetworkStream* objects, you can read and write streams asynchronously, which allows you to launch the read/write operation and return later to check the status of the operation.

The .NET Compact Framework supports I/O operations at two levels: low-level *byte* access using *Stream* objects, and *character* access using *StreamReader* and *StreamWriter* objects. This chapter will first discuss the use of *Stream* objects and then the use of the interface of the *StreamReader* and *StreamWriter* objects. If your I/O requirements are simple—for example, requiring only the opening of a text file, reading some lines of text, and then closing the file—it is possible that you do not require the byte-level access provided by the *Stream* class. If this is the case, you might wish to proceed directly to the section "Using the *StreamReader* and *StreamWriter* Classes" later in this chapter.

Understanding the *Stream* Class

The *Stream* abstract class provides low-level functionality for reading or writing some source of byte data. This source of data could be a local file, a remote file, or some nonfile object that you can access in a similar way to a file, for example, a buffer of bytes in memory or a stream of bytes arriving at a network socket. The most important fact concerning the use of a stream is that it reads and writes in the form of *bytes*. Contrast this with *StreamReader* and *StreamWriter* discussed later in this chapter, which read and write *characters*. If, for example, your application processes Unicode files, one character is held in 2 bytes, hence the need for the distinction. The *Stream* class has the following methods for reading one or many bytes:

```
public virtual int ReadByte();
public abstract int Read(byte[] b, int start, int length);
```

See the section "Reading and Writing Bytes Using a *FileStream* Object" later in this chapter for code examples. The *Stream* class also has equivalent *Write* operations and the *Seek* method for moving the read/write position within the stream. The *CanRead*, *CanWrite*, and *CanSeek* properties indicate whether the desired operation is permitted on this stream.

The *Stream* abstract class is the base class for the *FileStream*, *MemoryStream*, and *NetworkStream* concrete classes. The remainder of this section will examine these in turn.

> **Note** The *BufferedStream* and *CryptoStream* classes of the full .NET Framework are not supported in the .NET Compact Framework.

Creating a *FileStream* Object

This section will show how to create instances of the *FileStream* class using the constructors for that class. Note that other ways exist to create *FileStream* objects, for example, the *File.Open* method discussed in the section "Using the *File* Class to Create a File" later in this chapter. The constructor for the *FileStream* object is heavily overloaded, but it requires at a minimum the name of the file as a string and a *FileMode* enumeration value. The purpose of the *FileMode* parameter is to indicate whether the file is to be opened or created, and what action to take if the specified file does not exist. The following list shows some of the members of this enumeration and their effects when passed to a *FileStream* constructor:

- *FileMode.Open* opens an existing file, and a *System.IO.FileNotFoundException* is thrown if the file does not exist.
- *FileMode.Create* creates a new file or overwrites the file if it does exist.

- *FileMode.OpenOrCreate* creates a new file only if the file does not exist; otherwise, it opens an existing file.
- *FileMode.Append* opens or creates a file but seeks to the end of the file before any read or write operations.

When opening an existing file for write access, only *Open*, *OpenOrCreate*, and *Append* can preserve data in existing files. Other options cause data in existing files to be overwritten. The following code creates a *FileStream* object to read the file myFile.txt. The code is in a try/catch block, in case the file is not found and an exception is thrown.

```
try
{
    FileStream myFileStream = new FileStream
        ("\\myFile.txt", FileMode.Open);
}
catch (System.IO.FileNotFoundException fnfE)
{
    ⋮
}
```

Notice that the preceding example does not specify the read/write permission or sharing permission required, so the defaults of *FileAccess.ReadWrite* and *FileShare.Read* apply. It is possible to use other overloads of the *FileStream* constructor to specify different read/write and sharing permissions.

Specifying File Access Modes for Streams

Stream constructors have overloads that accept *FileAccess* enumeration parameters to specify whether the file is to be opened for read, write, or both. The members of the *FileAccess* enumeration are *Read*, *ReadWrite*, and *Write*. The value specified for file access in the *Stream* constructor might depend on the *FileMode* values discussed in the preceding section. For example, if *FileMode.Create* was specified, *FileAccess.Read* is meaningless and causes an exception of type *ArgumentException* to be thrown. The following code creates a stream to append to a file, creating the file if it does not exist:

```
FileStream myFS = new FileStream
    ("\\myFile.txt", FileMode.Append, FileAccess.Write);
```

Specifying File Sharing for Streams

When you open or create a file, you can pass a *FileShare* enumeration member to the constructor to indicate how you will share that file with other users. For example, *FileShare.Read* specifies that other users can open the file for read access only. Any attempt by any other process to open the file for write access will fail until you close the file. You can specify *FileShare.Read*, *FileShare.Write*, *FileShare.ReadWrite*, or *FileShare.None*.

The following code attempts to open a file for read access, allowing sharing with other readers. The code opens the same file twice using two *FileStream* objects: first *otherFileStream* and then *myFileStream*. The first to open will dictate the terms for sharing of the file, so in this example, the opening of *otherFileStream* specifies sharing with readers only. No other access is permitted until *otherFileStream* is closed. The following code causes no sharing exceptions because *otherFileStream* allows *FileShare.Read* and *myFileStream* requests *FileAccess.Read*. If you change the sharing mode of *otherFileStream* to *FileShare.Write* or *FileShare.None*, the attempt to open *myFileStream* throws an exception of type *IOException* because of the sharing violation.

```
FileDialog myFileDialog = new OpenFileDialog();
myFileDialog.Filter = "Text files|*.txt";
myFileDialog.InitialDirectory = @"\";
myFileDialog.ShowDialog();
String fileName = myFileDialog.FileName;
FileStream otherFileStream;
try
{
    // Open the file for sharing with readers
    otherFileStream = new
        FileStream(fileName, FileMode.Open,
            FileAccess.Read, FileShare.Read);
    // Open the same file for read access
    FileStream myFileStream = new
        FileStream(fileName, FileMode.Open,
            FileAccess.Read, FileShare.Read);
}
catch (Exception ex)
{
    MessageBox.Show(ex.ToString());
}
```

Reading and Writing Bytes Using a *FileStream* Object

Your application might need to read a file simply as bytes. You can use the *ReadByte* method of *FileStream* to do this. The following example opens a file and reads the first 20 bytes into an array:

```
FileStream myFileStream = new FileStream(
    someFileName, FileMode.Open,
```

```
        FileAccess.Read, FileShare.None);
    int[] b = new int[20];
    for (int i = 0; i < b.Length; i++)
        b[i] = myFileStream.ReadByte();
    myFileStream.Close();
```

In a similar way, you can write bytes to files using *WriteByte*. The following code writes the ASCII codes for the letters *a* through *j* as bytes. If you view the resulting file using Pocket Word, you see the text *abcdefghij*.

```
FileStream myFileStream = new FileStream(fileName,
    FileMode.OpenOrCreate,
    FileAccess.Write,
    FileShare.None);
for (int i = 0; i < 10; i++)
    myFileStream.WriteByte((byte)('a' + i));
myFileStream.Close();
```

Using the *BinaryReader* and *BinaryWriter* Classes

The *BinaryReader* and *BinaryWriter* classes allow you to read or write primitive data types such as integers or doubles directly to or from streams without performing conversions to or from characters. For example, *BinaryWriter* writes the 32-bit integer value 300 as 4 bytes containing 0x00 0x00 0x01 0x2c, not as the series of characters *300*. The only data that undergoes conversion is character data, which is written or read using a specific encoding to translate from a character to a byte or bytes. Pure binary files are not normally human-readable but can save much space when compared to text files and also save the cost of conversion to or from characters.

The use of the *BinaryWriter* and *BinaryReader* classes is best illustrated by example. The following code creates a new file and uses a *BinaryWriter* object to insert information on an order into the file by writing the string "Order", followed by an integer number representing the item, followed by a *double* value representing the price:

```
String fileName = myFileDialog.FileName;
FileStream myFileStream = new FileStream(fileName,
    FileMode.OpenOrCreate,
    FileAccess.Write,
    FileShare.None);
BinaryWriter writer = new BinaryWriter(myFileStream, Encoding.ASCII);
writer.Write("Order");
writer.Write(42);
writer.Write(3.47);
writer.Close();
```

The *Write* method of *BinaryWriter* has 16 overloads in all, accepting all the language primitive types. To see how the data is stored, use the *ReadByte* method of a *FileStream* to fetch the first part of the file into a buffer and then display the buffer in a Watch window in the debugger, as shown in Figure 10-1. (See the section "Reading and Writing Bytes Using a *FileStream* Object"earlier in this chapter.)

Watch 1

Name	Value	Type
buffer		byte[]
[0x0]	0x5	byte
[0x1]	0x4f	byte
[0x2]	0x72	byte
[0x3]	0x64	byte
[0x4]	0x65	byte
[0x5]	0x72	byte
[0x6]	0x2a	byte
[0x7]	0x0	byte
[0x8]	0x0	byte
[0x9]	0x0	byte
[0xa]	0xc3	byte
[0xb]	0xf5	byte
[0xc]	0x28	byte
[0xd]	0x5c	byte
[0xe]	0x8f	byte
[0xf]	0xc2	byte
[0x10]	0xb	byte
[0x11]	0x40	byte
[0x12]	0x0	byte

Figure 10-1 Buffer of output from the *BinaryWriter* class example.

In the buffer, the first item is the string "Order". The *BinaryWriter* class writes strings length-preceded, so the first byte in the buffer is 0x5 (the length of the string in bytes) followed by the characters of the string in the encoding specified when constructing the *BinaryWriter*. In this case, the encoding used is ASCII, so the *BinaryWriter* object uses 1 byte per character. The 4 bytes of the integer value 42 (0x2a) follow, in the byte positions 6 through 9. Then, in byte positions 10 through 17, you'll find the 8 bytes of the *double* value 3.47. If the string is longer than 127 bytes, the most significant bit in the length byte is used as a continuation bit into the next byte. A string of length 128 would have 2 length bytes: first a byte with a value of hexadecimal 80, then a byte with a value of 1. See the section "Using Encodings with *StreamReader* and *StreamWriter* Objects" later in this chapter for more information on encodings.

The following code uses the *BinaryReader* class to read the values from the file we created in the previous example. The *BinaryReader* class has methods for reading each primitive type, for example, *ReadString*, *ReadInt32*, *ReadDouble*, and so on.

```
FileStream myFileStream = new FileStream(fileName,
    FileMode.Open,
```

```
    FileAccess.Read,
    FileShare.None);
BinaryReader reader = new BinaryReader(myFileStream, Encoding.ASCII);
String data = reader.ReadString();
if (data == "Order") // Just in case
{
    int code = reader.ReadInt32();
    double cost = reader.ReadDouble();
    MessageBox.Show("Order: " + code.ToString() +
        "\nCost: " + cost.ToString());
}
else
    MessageBox.Show("File does not contain an Order");
reader.Close();
```

The preceding example uses ASCII encoding. You can specify a different encoding when constructing the *BinaryReader* object. The following encodings are available:

- ***Encoding.ASCII*** Encodes the first 128 ASCII characters as 7-bit values.
- ***Encoding.Unicode* and *Encoding.BigEndianUnicode*** Encode characters in Unicode format using little-endian or big-endian byte order, respectively.
- ***Encoding.Default*** Fetches the system's current ANSI code page.
- ***Encoding.UTF-7* and *Encoding.UTF-8*** Encode characters using UCS Transformation Format, in 7-bit or 8-bit formats. These formats are able to represent all Unicode characters by using single-byte format for ASCII characters and 2-byte format for others.

You can use the *Encoding* class method *GetEncoding* to obtain other encodings. In particular, if using Unicode, take care if the file is to be read on a different platform with a different processor. If generating the file on a little-endian processor such as a member of the Intel family, you will need to specify *BigEndianUnicode* as the encoding if the target processor uses big-endian byte ordering. Figure 10-2 shows the results if you specify *BigEndianUnicode* for the encoding, as the following code demonstrates:

```
BinaryWriter writer = new BinaryWriter
    (myFileStream, Encoding.BigEndianUnicode);
```

The "Order" string is now 10 (0xa) bytes long, with each character held in the big end of a 16-bit word. The integer and *double* values are as before.

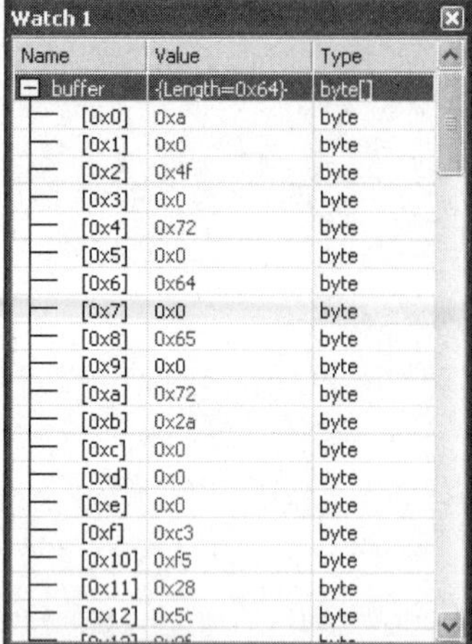

Figure 10-2 String "Order", encoded as BigEndianUnicode and displayed in a Watch window.

Seeking on Streams

The *FileStream* class supports a *Seek* method, which changes the position of the read or write pointer within the stream. The method

```
long Seek(long offset, SeekOrigin origin)
```

accepts an offset that is the number of bytes to move forward (or backward if a negative number) within the stream. The second parameter is a *SeekOrigin* enumeration member that specifies the origin to seek from, *SeekOrigin.Begin*, *.Current*, or *.End*. For example, the following line moves the pointer three bytes forward from the current position:

```
myFileStream.Seek(3, SeekOrigin.Current);
```

This line moves the pointer back to the start of the file. This could be used in error-recovery situations:

```
myFileStream.Seek(0, SeekOrigin.Begin);
```

Locking Files

You use the *Lock* and *Unlock* methods of the *FileStream* object in the full .NET Framework to lock regions within files, but these are not supported in the .NET Compact Framework. Fine-grained locking is more likely to arise as a requirement in server-side applications with major emphasis on concurrency and performance than in a client on a compact device. In the event that multiple applications require access to the same file at different times in a .NET Compact Framework application, use the file-sharing features discussed in the section "Specifying File Sharing for Streams" earlier in this chapter in order to perform locking at the file level.

Using the *NetworkStream* Class

Not all stream objects read or write files. The *NetworkStream* object is designed to provide a stream-type interface to a network connection such as a socket. The advantage of treating a network connection as a stream is that your code handles the data in the same way as other streams and can read or write data without having to know the source of the data. In addition, using a stream can hide the underlying socket so that operations on the stream do not require knowledge of how the underlying socket is established or managed.

To construct a *NetworkStream*, first create the socket that the stream will use and then pass it as a parameter into the *NetworkStream* constructor. Note that this section shows code for creating sockets without detailed explanation; the reader is referred to Chapter 11 for information on using sockets. The following code uses the constructor for the *NetworkStream* class, which takes three parameters: the socket to use, a *FileAccess* enumeration member (*Read*, *Write*, or *ReadWrite*) that specifies the required access, and a Boolean value to indicate if the caller is the owner of the socket. Only the owner of a socket can close it. This code is an example of what might be executed on the client side of a connection to create a writeable socket for sending data to a server. The code specifies write access to the socket and that the caller does not own the socket.

```
using System.Net.Sockets; // For the NetworkStream class
using System.IO;          // For other streams and readers/writers
using System.Net;         // For other network support classes
⋮
// Get a connected socket (discussed in Chapter 11)
Socket clientSocket = new Socket(
    AddressFamily.InterNetwork,
    SocketType.Stream,
    ProtocolType.Tcp);
// In the next line, use the IP address of your server
// obtained from the server application
   IPAddress theAddress = new IPAddress(ipAddressOfYourServer);
   IPEndPoint theEndPoint = new IPEndPoint(theAddress,0xff00);
   clientSocket.Connect(theEndPoint);
// Create a network stream
NetworkStream clientNetworkStream = new
    NetworkStream(clientSocket, FileAccess.Write, false);
byte[] buffer = new byte[100];
```

(continued)

```
// Fill buffer
⋮
// Write to network stream
try
{
    clientNetworkStream.Write(buffer, 0, buffer.Length);
}
catch (IOException ioe)
{
    // Important in case network connection breaks
}
```

On the server, you run the following code to create a *NetworkStream* object that communicates in the other direction:

```
// Details of socket creation discussed in Chapter 11
Socket serverSocket= new Socket(
    AddressFamily.InterNetwork,
    SocketType.Stream,
    ProtocolType.Tcp);
IPHostEntry myIPHostEntry = Dns.Resolve(Dns.GetHostName());
IPAddress myIpAddress = myIPHostEntry.AddressList[0];
IPEndPoint myEndPoint = new IPEndPoint(myIpAddress, 0xff00);
serverSocket.Bind(myEndPoint);
serverSocket.Listen(10);
Socket connectedSocket= serverSocket.Accept();
NetworkStream serverNetworkStream= new
    NetworkStream(connectedSocket, FileAccess.Read, true);
byte[] buffer= new byte[100];
// Read from network stream
try
{
    serverNetworkStream.Read(buffer, 0, buffer.Length);
}
catch (IOException ioe)
{
    // Important in case network connection breaks
}
```

Handling Network Errors When Using *NetworkStream*

To guard against network errors, such as the server closing the connection or the connection being broken in some other way, it is important to place the read or write operation in a try/catch block to catch the exception of type *IOException* that will result if the network connection is broken. For extra safety, when reading, check that data length is nonzero. If the connection breaks, both sides should close their connections and re-execute the code that establishes the connection.

Performing Asynchronous Read/Write Operations on *NetworkStream* Objects

Most operations performed on streams are synchronous—that is, the call to perform a read or write operation blocks until the operation completes. In the following code using a *NetworkStream* object, *MessageBox.Show* will not execute until the *Read* method has completed:

```
int Count = myNetworkStream.Read(buffer, 0, buffer.Length);
MessageBox.Show("Data received");
```

However, in some situations it is desirable to perform asynchronous read or write operations. In an asynchronous operation, the code makes a method call to commence the operation, but control then immediately returns to the caller, which might then continue program execution. The caller might return later to check the result of the operation, either as a result of a callback from the .NET Compact Framework code or, if no callback is specified, at a time of the caller's choosing. The advantage of an asynchronous operation is clear: while the read or write is completing, the application can execute other tasks, thus remaining more responsive to the user and making better use of processor time.

> **Note** The current release of the .NET Compact Framework supports asynchronous operations on *NetworkStream* objects only.

To perform an asynchronous read operation, use the *BeginRead* method of the *NetworkStream* object. *BeginRead* starts the operation of reading bytes from the stream and returns an *IAsyncResult* object, which must be passed to a later call to *EndRead* in order to terminate the read operation correctly. *BeginRead* takes five parameters. The first parameter is an array of bytes to receive the data, and the next two parameters are the zero-based offset and count for the bytes to be read. The fourth parameter is an *AsyncCallback* delegate. This delegate must be constructed using a void function, which accepts an *IAsyncResult* parameter. The .NET Compact Framework calls this function when the I/O operation completes, passing it an *IAsyncResult* object, which tells the function if the operation completed successfully. If it has, code in the callback function must call *EndRead*, passing the same *IAsyncResult* object. This terminates the I/O operation.

The fifth parameter is called the state parameter and is simply an object. The use of this parameter is left up to the developer; its purpose is to allow the developer to pass a user-defined object between different asynchronous method calls that could be used to save state data. You retrieve the state object in the callback method in the *IAsyncResult.State* property. You perform asynchronous write operations in a manner that is analogous to the asynchronous read operations, but you use *BeginWrite* and *EndWrite* methods.

Asynchronous operation is particularly useful when reading from a *NetworkStream* object because some time might elapse before data becomes available, and you'll probably want your application to remain responsive to the user while waiting for the data to arrive. The following example performs asynchronous read operations from a *NetworkStream* object. The *frmAsyncRead_Load* event handler performs a *BeginRead* on a *NetworkStream*, passing the *AsyncCallback* object constructed using the *getResult* function as the callback parameter. When data arrives on the stream, the runtime calls *getResult*, which then fetches the data from the buffer, performs an *EndRead* to terminate the read operation correctly, and then initiates the next read with another *BeginRead*. The example receives data encoded simply as ASCII characters.

> **Note** The example does not show the several steps required to create a *NetworkStream* object. Refer to the section "Using the *NetworkStream* Class" earlier in this chapter for detailed information on how to create a *NetworkStream* object.

```
private byte[] buffer;
private AsyncCallback myCallback;
:
private void frmAsyncRead_Load(
    object sender, System.EventArgs e)
{
    myCallback = new AsyncCallback(getResult);
    try
    {
        buffer = new byte[100];
        IAsyncResult myResult=  myNetworkStream.BeginRead
```

```
                       (buffer,              // Buffer
                        0,                   // Start
                        buffer.Length,       // Length
                        myCallback,          // Callback
                        null);               // State
    }
    catch (Exception ex)
    {
        MessageBox.Show(ex.ToString());
    }
}
void getResult(IAsyncResult myResult)
{

    if (myResult.IsCompleted)
    {
        string message = Encoding.ASCII.GetString(buffer);
        MessageBox.Show("Received " + message);
    }
    // Terminate the read operation
    myNetworkStream.EndRead(myResult);
    // Clear the buffer
    for (int i = 0; i < buffer.Length; i++)
        buffer[i] = 0;
    // Initiate the next read
    myNetworkStream.BeginRead(buffer, 0, buffer.Length,
        myCallback, null);
}
```

If the call to *EndRead* or *EndWrite* is made before the read or write operation has completed, these methods will block until the operation completes. Therefore, you can decide not to use an *IAsyncCallback* object at all. Instead, for a write operation, initiate the write with *BeginWrite*, perform some processing while the I/O operation takes its course, and call *EndWrite* later in the same method. The following code shows how you do this. Notice that the fourth parameter of *BeginWrite*, specifying the *IAsyncCallback* object, is set to null, so no callback will occur.

```
myResult = myNetworkStream.BeginWrite
(bMessage,0,bMessage.Length, null, null);
// Other processing
⋮
// End asynchronous write operation
myNetworkStream.EndWrite(myResult);
```

Using the *MemoryStream* Class

You can conceive of a *MemoryStream* object as being a stream that does not target a device but a buffer of bytes in memory. Depending on how you construct your *MemoryStream* object, it can be used to read, write, or both. A *MemoryStream* object frequently frees the developer from having to implement temporary buffers and from having to implement sizing and position-tracking features. When constructing a *MemoryStream* object, you can specify your own byte array buffer, or you can allow the .NET Compact Framework runtime to allocate and manage a buffer for you. You can request that the .NET Compact Framework allocate a buffer for you by calling the constructor with no parameters, as shown in this example:

```
MemoryStream myMS = new MemoryStream();
```

If you allow the .NET Compact Framework to allocate the buffer for you, it is readable and writeable. It is also resizable, which gives application flexibility at the expense of some performance. If, however, you provide your own byte buffer, as shown in this example,

```
byte[] buffer = new byte[someSize];
MemoryStream myMS = new MemoryStream(buffer, 0, buffer.Length);
```

the buffer is not resizable.

As with other types of stream, you can perform low-level byte reads and writes directly to the *MemoryStream* object using methods such as *Read*, *ReadByte*, *Write*, and *WriteByte*. Alternatively, you can create a *StreamReader* or *StreamWriter* object to perform string operations on the *MemoryStream* object, as in the following example:

```
MemoryStream myMS = new MemoryStream();
StreamWriter writer = new StreamWriter(myMS);
writer.Write("Hello");
writer.Write(" world");
```

You could use a *MemoryStream* object to perform a series of write operations into memory and then read back the data, either by creating another *MemoryStream* object to read the data, by seeking the existing *MemoryStream* back to the start of the buffer, or simply by accessing the buffer directly using the *GetBuffer* method.

MemoryStream methods and properties that override those of the base *Stream* class include *GetBuffer* to return the internal byte buffer, *Length* and *SetLength* to get and set the internal buffer size, and *Position* to get or set the value of the internal read/write offset within the buffer.

MemoryStream objects are frequently used when your application must retrieve byte data that arrives in packets, possibly with some end-of-message marker in the last packet. Each time you retrieve a packet, you can simply write it to the buffer, and when the end-of-message marker is read, the stream can be closed and its internal byte buffer retrieved and passed for processing. The following example reads packets from a *NetworkStream* object, writing the data to a *MemoryStream* object each time a whole packet arrives. The size of the *MemoryStream* object's buffer is 500 bytes. The reading stops when the code reads the end-of-message marker, in this case two consecutive period characters. The NetStreamReader application and a full .NET Framework application that talks to it, NetStreamWriter, are included with this book's sample files.

NetStreamReader.cs

```
using System;
using System.Data;
using System.Net;
using System.Net.Sockets;
using System.IO;
using System.Text;


namespace NETCFDevelopersReference
{
    class NetStreamReader
    {
        private int byteCount;
        private Socket mySocket;
        private NetworkStream receiveNetworkStream;
        private MemoryStream myMemoryStream;
        private AsyncCallback myCallBack;
        private byte[] buffer;

        static void Main(string[] args)
        {
            new NetStreamReader();
        }

        public NetStreamReader()
        {
            byteCount = 0;
            buffer = new byte[10];
            myMemoryStream = new MemoryStream();

            // In the following line, insert the IP address of the server
            // machine. The NetStreamWriter desktop application included
```

(continued)

NetStreamReader.cs *(continued)*

```
        // with this book's sample files will report its IP address
        // for you to copy.
        IPAddress myIPAddress = new IPAddress(<yourServerIPAddress>);

        mySocket = new Socket(AddressFamily.InterNetwork,
            SocketType.Stream, ProtocolType.Tcp);

        IPEndPoint theEndPoint = new IPEndPoint
            (myIPAddress, 0xff00); // Or your own port number
        mySocket.Connect(theEndPoint);
        receiveNetworkStream = new NetworkStream(mySocket,
            FileAccess.Read, false);

        myCallBack = new AsyncCallback(getResult);
        buffer = new byte[10];
        receiveNetworkStream.BeginRead
            (buffer, 0, buffer.Length, myCallBack, null);
        Console.ReadLine();
    }

    void getResult(IAsyncResult myResult)
    {
        byteCount += receiveNetworkStream.EndRead(myResult);
        Console.WriteLine("Packet...");
        // Write received packet to memory stream
        myMemoryStream.Write(buffer, 0, buffer.Length);
        // Check for '..' at end of message using byteCount
        if (myMemoryStream.GetBuffer()[byteCount-2] == '.'
            && myMemoryStream.GetBuffer()[byteCount-1] == '.')
        {
            string myMessage = Encoding.ASCII.GetString(
                myMemoryStream.GetBuffer(), 0, byteCount);
            Console.WriteLine("Received: " + myMessage);
        }
        else
        {
            receiveNetworkStream.BeginRead(buffer, 0, buffer.Length,
                myCallBack, null);
        }
    }

}
```

Implementing a Product Ordering Example

The example that follows shows how you use *NetworkStream* objects to transfer data from a compact client to a server where the data can be persisted. In the OrderManager application, a client (OrderClient) resides on the compact device, and a server (OrderServer), a full .NET Framework application, runs on the desktop. The application enables the user on the compact device to type in a product code and a quantity that he or she wishes to order. A Send Order button transmits the information in the form of a short XML document to the server. The server receives the order and adds it to an Access database.

Both applications use the form's *Load* event to establish the network connections. The OrderServer application creates the socket and calls the *Listen* method. When the client side calls *Connect*, the call to *Listen* on the server unblocks and a connection is established. After the connection is established, the server application uses asynchronous read operations to remain more responsive to a user.

On the OrderClient application, when the user enters a product code and quantity and then clicks the Send Order button, the code builds an order XML document using the Document Object Model (DOM). See Chapter 9 for information on the DOM. A typical XML document might look like this:

```
<order><product>ABC123</product><quantity>42</quantity></order>
```

When the server code receives this string, it creates an *XmlTextReader* object to read the information into an *XmlDocument* object. It then uses the *GetElementsByTagName* method to retrieve the *<product>* and *<quantity>* elements. Using *GetElementsByTagName* means the server should be immune to changes in the structure of the XML document. The server then uses an *OleDbCommand* object to perform a SQL *INSERT INTO* operation using the product ID and quantity values received from the client.

The user of OrderClient types a product code and quantity, and then the user clicks the Send Order button to transmit to OrderServer, which saves the order and displays the most recent order in a Label control. Figures 10-3 and 10-4 show how the application looks. You'll find the OrderServer and OrderClient applications, including the orders.mdb database file, in this book's sample files.

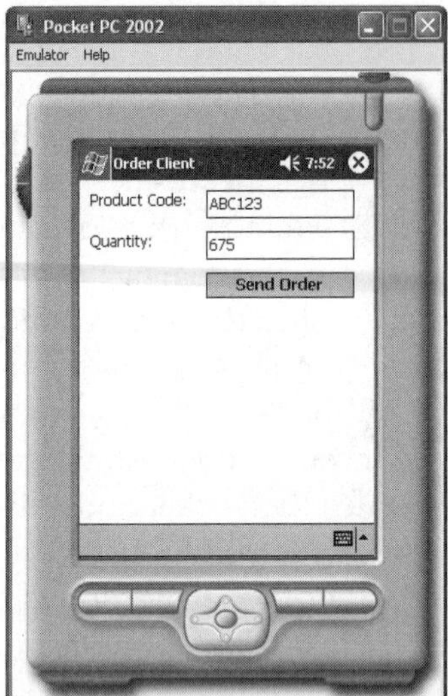

Figure 10-3 View of the OrderClient application running.

Figure 10-4 View of the OrderServer application running.

OrderClient.cs

```
using System;
using System.Drawing;
using System.Collections;
using System.Windows.Forms;
using System.Data;
using System.Net;
using System.Net.Sockets;
using System.IO;
using System.Text;
using System.Xml;

namespace NETCFDevelopersReference
{
    public class OrderClient : System.Windows.Forms.Form
    {
        private Socket mySocket;
        private NetworkStream myNetworkStream;
```

(continued)

OrderClient.cs *(continued)*

```
        private System.Windows.Forms.Label label1;
        private System.Windows.Forms.Label label2;
        private System.Windows.Forms.TextBox txtQuantity;
        private System.Windows.Forms.TextBox txtProductCode;
        private System.Windows.Forms.Button cmdSendOrder;
        private System.Windows.Forms.MainMenu mainMenu1;

        public OrderClient()
        {
            InitializeComponent();
        }

        protected override void Dispose( bool disposing )
        {
            base.Dispose( disposing );
        }

        #region Windows Form Designer generated code
        /// <summary>
        /// Required method for Designer support - do not modify
        /// the contents of this method with the code editor.
        /// </summary>
        private void InitializeComponent()
        {
            this.mainMenu1 = new System.Windows.Forms.MainMenu();
            this.label1 = new System.Windows.Forms.Label();
            this.label2 = new System.Windows.Forms.Label();
            this.cmdSendOrder = new System.Windows.Forms.Button();
            this.txtQuantity = new System.Windows.Forms.TextBox();
            this.txtProductCode = new System.Windows.Forms.TextBox();
            //
            // label1
            //
            this.label1.Location = new System.Drawing.Point(8, 8);
            this.label1.Size = new System.Drawing.Size(88, 20);
            this.label1.Text = "Product Code:";
            //
            // label2
            //
            this.label2.Location = new System.Drawing.Point(8, 40);
            this.label2.Size = new System.Drawing.Size(88, 20);
            this.label2.Text = "Quantity:";
            //
            // cmdSendOrder
            //
```

(continued)

OrderClient.cs *(continued)*

```
        this.cmdSendOrder.Location =
            new System.Drawing.Point(104, 72);
        this.cmdSendOrder.Size =
            new System.Drawing.Size(120, 20);
        this.cmdSendOrder.Text = "Send Order";
        this.cmdSendOrder.Click +=
            new System.EventHandler(this.cmdSendOrder_Click);
        //
        // txtQuantity
        //
        this.txtQuantity.Location =
            new System.Drawing.Point(104, 40);
        this.txtQuantity.Size =
            new System.Drawing.Size(120, 22);
        this.txtQuantity.Text = "";
        //
        // txtProductCode
        //
        this.txtProductCode.Location =
            new System.Drawing.Point(104, 8);
        this.txtProductCode.Size =
            new System.Drawing.Size(120, 22);
        this.txtProductCode.Text = "";
        //
        // OrderClient
        //
        this.Controls.Add(this.txtProductCode);
        this.Controls.Add(this.txtQuantity);
        this.Controls.Add(this.cmdSendOrder);
        this.Controls.Add(this.label2);
        this.Controls.Add(this.label1);
        this.Menu = this.mainMenu1;
        this.Text = "Order Client";
        this.Load += new System.EventHandler(this.OrderClient_Load);

    }
    #endregion

    static void Main()
    {
        Application.Run(new OrderClient());
    }

    private void OrderClient_Load(object sender, System.EventArgs e)
    {
```

(continued)

OrderClient.cs *(continued)*

```
        mySocket = new Socket(AddressFamily.InterNetwork,
            SocketType.Stream, ProtocolType.Tcp);
        // Substitute the address from the server application here
        IPAddress theAddress = new IPAddress(yourServersIPAddress);
        IPEndPoint theEndPoint = new IPEndPoint
            (theAddress,0xff00); // Or choose your own port number
        mySocket.Connect(theEndPoint);
        myNetworkStream = new NetworkStream
           (mySocket, FileAccess.Write, false);
    }

    private void cmdSendOrder_Click
        (object sender, System.EventArgs e)
    {
        String productID =  txtProductCode.Text;
        String quantity = txtQuantity.Text;
        XmlDocument orderDocument = new XmlDocument();
        XmlElement orderElement =
            orderDocument.CreateElement("order");

        XmlElement productElement =
            orderDocument.CreateElement("product");
        productElement.InnerText = productID;
        orderElement.AppendChild(productElement);

        XmlElement quantityElement =
            orderDocument.CreateElement("quantity");
        quantityElement.InnerText = quantity;
        orderElement.AppendChild(quantityElement);

        String message = orderElement.OuterXml;

        byte[] bMessage = Encoding.ASCII.GetBytes(message);
        try
        {
            myNetworkStream.Write(bMessage, 0, bMessage.Length);
        }
        catch (Exception ex)
        {
            MessageBox.Show(ex.ToString());
        }
    }
  }
}
```

OrderServer.cs

```
using System;
using System.Drawing;
using System.Collections;
using System.ComponentModel;
using System.Windows.Forms;
using System.Data;
using System.Data.OleDb;
using System.Net;
using System.Net.Sockets;
using System.IO;
using System.Text;
using System.Xml;

namespace OrderServer
{
    public class OrderServer : System.Windows.Forms.Form
    {
        private Socket readSocket;
        private NetworkStream receiveNetworkStream;
        private Socket mySocket;
        private AsyncCallback myCallBack;
        private byte[] buffer;

        private System.Windows.Forms.Label label1;
        private System.Windows.Forms.Label lblOrder;
        private System.Data.OleDb.OleDbConnection conOrders;

        private System.ComponentModel.Container components = null;

        public OrderServer()
        {
            InitializeComponent();
        }

        protected override void Dispose( bool disposing )
        {
            if( disposing )
            {
                if (components != null)
                {
                    components.Dispose();
                }
            }
            base.Dispose( disposing );
        }
```

(continued)

OrderServer.cs *(continued)*

```
#region Windows Form Designer generated code
/// <summary>
/// Required method for Designer support - do not modify
/// the contents of this method with the code editor.
/// </summary>
private void InitializeComponent()
{
    this.label1 = new System.Windows.Forms.Label();
    this.lblOrder = new System.Windows.Forms.Label();
    this.conOrders = new System.Data.OleDb.OleDbConnection();
    this.SuspendLayout();
    //
    // label1
    //
    this.label1.Location = new System.Drawing.Point(8, 16);
    this.label1.Name = "label1";
    this.label1.Size = new System.Drawing.Size(88, 24);
    this.label1.TabIndex = 0;
    this.label1.Text = "Received Order:";
    this.label1.TextAlign =
        System.Drawing.ContentAlignment.MiddleLeft;
    //
    // lblOrder
    //
    this.lblOrder.BorderStyle =
        System.Windows.Forms.BorderStyle.Fixed3D;
    this.lblOrder.Location = new System.Drawing.Point(104, 16);
    this.lblOrder.Name = "lblOrder";
    this.lblOrder.Size = new System.Drawing.Size(200, 23);
    this.lblOrder.TabIndex = 1;
    this.lblOrder.TextAlign =
        System.Drawing.ContentAlignment.MiddleLeft;
    //
    // conOrders
    //
    this.conOrders.ConnectionString =
        "Jet OLEDB:Global Partial Bulk Ops=2;"
        + "Jet OLEDB:Registry Path=;"
        + "Jet OLEDB:Database Locking Mode=1;"
        + "Jet OLEDB:Database Password=;"
        + "Data Source=\"..\\..\\orders.mdb\";"
        + "Password=;Jet OLEDB:Engine Type=5;"
        + "Jet OLEDB:Global Bulk Transactions=1;"
        + "Provider=\"Microsoft.Jet.OLEDB.4.0\";"
        + "Jet OLEDB:System database=;"
        + "Jet OLEDB:SFP=False;Extended Properties=;"
```

(continued)

OrderServer.cs *(continued)*

```
            + "Mode=Share Deny None;"
            + "Jet OLEDB:New Database Password=;"
            + "Jet OLEDB:Create System Database=False;"
            + "Jet OLEDB:Don't Copy Locale on Compact=False;"
            + "Jet OLEDB:Compact Without Replica Repair=False;"
            + "User ID=Admin;Jet OLEDB:Encrypt Database=False";
        //
        // OrderServer
        //
        this.AutoScaleBaseSize = new System.Drawing.Size(5, 13);
        this.ClientSize = new System.Drawing.Size(312, 54);
        this.Controls.Add(this.lblOrder);
        this.Controls.Add(this.label1);
        this.Name = "OrderServer";
        this.Text = "Order Server";
        this.Load += new System.EventHandler(this.OrderServer_Load);
        this.ResumeLayout(false);

    }
    #endregion

    /// <summary>
    /// The main entry point for the application.
    /// </summary>
    [STAThread]
    static void Main()
    {
        Application.Run(new OrderServer());
    }

    private void OrderServer_Load(object sender, System.EventArgs e)
    {
        IPHostEntry myIPHostEntry = Dns.Resolve(Dns.GetHostName());
        // Copy this IP address to the OrderClient application
        IPAddress myIpAddress = myIPHostEntry.AddressList[0];
        IPEndPoint myEndPoint = new IPEndPoint(myIpAddress, 0xff00);
        mySocket = new Socket(AddressFamily.InterNetwork,
            SocketType.Stream, ProtocolType.Tcp);
        mySocket.Blocking = true;
        mySocket.Bind(myEndPoint);

        mySocket.Listen(0);
        readSocket = mySocket.Accept();
        mySocket.Close();
        receiveNetworkStream = new NetworkStream
```

(continued)

OrderServer.cs *(continued)*

```
            (readSocket, FileAccess.Read, true);
        myCallBack = new AsyncCallback(getResult);
        buffer = new byte[100];
        this.Refresh();
        Application.DoEvents();
        receiveNetworkStream.BeginRead(buffer, 0,
            buffer.Length, myCallBack, null);
    }

    void getResult(IAsyncResult myResult)
    {
        String orderString = Encoding.ASCII.GetString(buffer);
        StringReader sr = new StringReader(orderString);
        XmlTextReader reader = new XmlTextReader(sr);
        XmlDocument orderDocument = new XmlDocument();
            orderDocument.Load(reader);
        XmlElement orderElement = orderDocument.DocumentElement;

        // Navigate to Product and Quantity values
        String productID = orderElement.GetElementsByTagName
            ("product")[0].InnerText;
        String quantity = orderElement.GetElementsByTagName
            ("quantity")[0].InnerText;
        // Report order to form
        lblOrder.Text = quantity + " of " + productID;
        try
        {
            // conOrders OleDBConnection is set up at design time
            // to point to the orders.mdb database.
            conOrders.Open();
            OleDbCommand myCommand = new OleDbCommand
                ("insert into Orders (ProductID, Quantity)"
                + " VALUES ('"
                + productID + "', " + quantity + ")");
            myCommand.Connection = conOrders;
            myCommand.ExecuteNonQuery();
            conOrders.Close();
        }
        catch (Exception ex)
        {
            MessageBox.Show(ex.ToString());
        }
        receiveNetworkStream.EndRead(myResult);
        // Zero the buffer for the next read
        for (int bi = 0; bi < buffer.Length; bi++)
            buffer[bi] = 0;
```

(continued)

OrderServer.cs *(continued)*

```
            // Initiate the next read operation
            receiveNetworkStream.BeginRead
                (buffer, 0, buffer.Length,myCallBack,null);
        }

    }
}
```

Using the *StreamReader* and *StreamWriter* Classes

The StreamReader and StreamWriter classes derive from the TextReader and TextWriter abstract classes. These classes perform input and output of characters with a stream using a particular encoding to translate the characters into bytes and bytes into characters so that the underlying stream can be read from or written to. These classes offer a simpler, higher level interface than the underlying Stream object, and they can read or write strings.

Creating *StreamReader* and *StreamWriter* Objects

The constructors for the *StreamReader* and *StreamWriter* classes allow you to create your own *Stream* object and create a *StreamReader* or *StreamWriter* class by passing the stream as a parameter. Both classes also allow you to call a constructor that will create a stream for you. If you have a stream object that refers to the file or resource you have created, you can construct a *StreamReader* or *StreamWriter* object based on that stream, which will enable you to perform your reading and writing operations at character level. The various constructors for the *StreamReader* and *StreamWriter* classes accept *Stream* objects of any type: *FileStream*, *MemoryStream*, and *NetworkStream*. They can also accept pure file names and create the relevant *FileStream* object by default. The following code creates a *FileStream* object and then a *StreamReader* object based on the *FileStream* object:

```
FileStream myFileStream = new FileStream
    ("\\myFile.txt", FileMode.Open);
StreamReader myReader = new StreamReader(myFileStream);
```

Alternatively, you can allow the *StreamReader* constructor to create a *FileStream* object implicitly, as shown here:

```
StreamReader myReader = new StreamReader("\\myFile.txt");
```

Reading a File Stream with a *StreamReader* Object

You can use a *StreamReader* object to perform character read operations on a *FileStream* object, using one of the overloads of the *Read* method of the *StreamReader* class to retrieve single characters or groups of characters from the stream. The *Read* method that doesn't take any arguments returns an integer that is the numeric encoded value of the character that was read, or -1 for the end of the file. The method

```
int Read (char[] array, int start, int length)
```

reads a maximum of *length* characters into *array* starting at *start*. The following example reads one character at a time from a file, adding the characters to a string. When it finds a period character, it stops.

```
StreamReader reader = new StreamReader
    (@"\My Documents\Personal\myFile.txt");
int myChar;
String result = "";
while ((myChar = reader.Read()) != -1)
{
    result += System.Convert.ToChar(myChar);
    if (myChar == (int)'.')
        break;
}
MessageBox.Show(result);
reader.Close();
```

Using Encodings with *StreamReader* and *StreamWriter* Objects

StreamReader and *StreamWriter* objects read and write files using encodings. The purpose of an encoding is to tell the reader or writer how to perform the translation between characters and bytes, for example, whether a file is to be written as Unicode, using 16-bit characters, or as plain ASCII with 8-bit characters. To construct a *StreamReader* or *StreamWriter* object that uses a specific encoding, use an overload, which accepts a *System.Text.Encoding* property to specify encodings such as ASCII, Unicode, or UTF-8. You can also call the *Encoding.GetEncoding* method to return an *Encoding* object for less common encodings. The following code creates a *StreamWriter* with a Unicode encoding and then writes some text to the file:

```
FileStream myFileStream = new FileStream
    (@"\myFile.txt", FileMode.OpenOrCreate);
StreamWriter writer = new StreamWriter
    (myFileStream, System.Text.Encoding.Unicode);
writer.Write("Hello world");
writer.Close();
```

If we apply the *ReadByte* example from the section "Reading and Writing Bytes Using a *FileStream* Object" earlier in this chapter to the file myFile.txt that the code in this section creates, we obtain the buffer of bytes shown in Figure 10-5.

Watch 1

Name	Value	Type
buffer	{Length=0x64}	byte[]
[0x0]	0xff	byte
[0x1]	0xfe	byte
[0x2]	0x48	byte
[0x3]	0x0	byte
[0x4]	0x65	byte
[0x5]	0x0	byte
[0x6]	0x6c	byte
[0x7]	0x0	byte
[0x8]	0x6c	byte
[0x9]	0x0	byte
[0xa]	0x6f	byte
[0xb]	0x0	byte
[0xc]	0x20	byte
[0xd]	0x0	byte
[0xe]	0x77	byte
[0xf]	0x0	byte
[0x10]	0x6f	byte
[0x11]	0x0	byte
[0x12]	0x72	byte

Figure 10-5 Data buffer output by *StreamWriter* example in Unicode encoding.

Notice the first two bytes. They make up the *byte order marker*, and they are followed by pairs of bytes, each pair representing one character, according to the Unicode specification. The character sequences 0x48, 0x65, and so on represent the letters of *Hello world* in order. See the section "Specifying Byte Ordering When Using Encodings" later in this chapter for information on specifying byte order in Unicode files.

If you compile the previous example using the *System.Text.Encoding.ASCII* encoding, the code will generate a myFile.txt file that can be represented with the byte buffer shown in Figure 10-6.

Watch 1

Name	Value	Type
buffer	{Length=0x64}	byte[]
[0x0]	0x48	byte
[0x1]	0x65	byte
[0x2]	0x6c	byte
[0x3]	0x6c	byte
[0x4]	0x6f	byte
[0x5]	0x20	byte
[0x6]	0x77	byte
[0x7]	0x6f	byte
[0x8]	0x72	byte
[0x9]	0x6c	byte
[0xa]	0x64	byte

Figure 10-6 Buffer of data created using ASCII encoding.

Here the file consists of pure text, one character per byte in 8-bit encoding with no marker bytes.

Specifying Byte Ordering When Using Encodings

When using Unicode encoding, characters can be stored in little-endian or big-endian byte orders. The default is little-endian, but an *Encoding.BigEndianUnicode* enumeration is available if you need to generate Unicode files for reading on a big-endian platform. The choice usually depends on the processor in use. Processors in the Intel family use little-endian byte order, but many other processors use big-endian byte order. Unicode files resolve this issue by storing a byte order mark as the first two bytes in a Unicode file. The byte order mark is the 16-bit hexadecimal value 0xFEFF, which appears as 0xFF followed by 0xFE on little-endian platforms and as 0xFE followed by 0xFF on big-endian platforms. The system code that reads files can make use of this marker to automatically detect that the file is in Unicode with a certain byte order, even if the user has not specified it.

Writing to a File Stream with *StreamWriter*

As with reading files, in order to write to a file or other resource, you need a *Stream* object, which abstracts the stream of data from the resource. You write to text files by creating a *StreamWriter* object and passing it the *FileStream* object you want to write to or the name of the file if you prefer the *StreamWriter* constructor to create the stream for you. The following example creates a *StreamWriter* object, implicitly creating a new file stream, and writes two lines of text to the file before closing:

```
// The following form of the StreamWriter constructor
// creates the underlying stream automatically
StreamWriter writer = new StreamWriter
    ("\\My Documents\\Personal\\myOutFile.txt");
writer.WriteLine("First line");
writer.WriteLine("Line 2");
// The following StreamWriter method closes the
// underlying stream also
writer.Close();
```

Processing Strings with *StringReader* and *StringWriter*

These classes allow you to read and write strings in memory. The *StringReader* and *StringWriter* classes derive from the *TextReader* and *TextWriter* abstract classes, which provide functionality for reading and writing characters rather than bytes. The *StringReader* has only one constructor, which takes a string parameter. Then you can use the *StringReader* to perform read operations on the string as if it were any other type of stream object, such as a *FileStream* object.

The following example creates a string and a *StringReader* object you use to read the string. It uses the *ReadLine* method to read the string one line at a time. The *StringReader* class also supports other read methods (*Read*, *ReadBlock*, and *ReadToEnd*).

```
String myString = "First line\nLine 2";
StringReader reader = new StringReader(myString);
String line;
while ((line = reader.ReadLine()) != null)
    MessageBox.Show("Read " + line);
reader.Close();
```

To use a *StringWriter* object, you need a *StringBuilder* object to provide the resizable storage that *StringWriter* requires. You can request that the .NET Compact Framework create one for you implicitly.

```
StringWriter writer = new StringWriter();
```

Or you can create one and hand it to the *StringWriter* constructor, as shown here:

```
StringBuilder sb = new StringBuilder();
StringWriter writer = new StringWriter(sb);
```

The *StringWriter* object then supports normal *TextWriter* write operations, as shown in this example:

```
writer.write("Hello");
writer.write (" world");
```

Using the *File*, *Path*, and *Directory* Classes

The *File* class provides static members for creating, copying, moving, and deleting files. The *FileInfo* class provides the same features but as instance members of the class.

Using the *File* Class to Create a File

The *Create* static method of the *File* class creates or overwrites a file and returns a *FileStream* object. You can then read the file at the byte level using the returned *FileStream*, or you can read the file at the character level using a *StreamReader*. The following code creates a file called myFile.txt and then creates a *StreamWriter* object based on the *FileStream* object returned by the call to *File.Create*. If an error arises, such as the file already being open, an exception is thrown.

```
try
{
    FileStream myFileStream = File.Create("\\myFile.txt");
    StreamWriter writer = new StreamWriter(myFileStream);
    writer.WriteLine("First line");
    writer.WriteLine("Line 2");
    writer.Close();
}
    catch (IOException ioe)
{
MessageBox.Show("IO Exception: " + ioe.ToString());
}
```

Alternatively, the *Open* method opens a new or existing file while allowing you to specify the required file open mode, file access, and file sharing. See the sections "Specifying File Access Modes for Streams" and "Specifying File Sharing for Streams" earlier in this chapter for a description of these topics. The following code opens a file called myFile.txt (creating it if it didn't exist) for write access and allowing sharing with readers only:

```
FileStream myFileStream = File.Open("\\myFile.txt",
    FileMode.OpenOrCreate,
    FileAccess.Write,
    FileShare.Read);
```

The *File* class has methods that check if a file exists and that delete, move, or copy a file by name. The following code writes some lines to a file whose name is held in the variable *fileName*. The code first checks if the file exists, and if it does, the code prompts the user to move the file or accept that it will be deleted.

```
if (File.Exists(fileName))
{
    DialogResult result = MessageBox.Show
        ("File exists. Move?\n" +
        "('No' deletes file)",
        "File Open",
        MessageBoxButtons.YesNoCancel,
        MessageBoxIcon.Question,
        MessageBoxDefaultButton.Button1);
    switch (result)
    {
        case DialogResult.Yes:
```

(continued)

```
                FileDialog newFileDialog = new SaveFileDialog();
                newFileDialog.InitialDirectory= "\\";
                newFileDialog.Filter = "Text files |*.txt";
                newFileDialog.ShowDialog();
                String newFileName = newFileDialog.FileName;
                File.Move(fileName, newFileName);
                break;
            case DialogResult.No:
                File.Delete(fileName);
                break;
            case DialogResult.Cancel:
                return;
                break;
        }
    }
FileStream myFileStream = File.Create(fileName);
StreamWriter writer = new StreamWriter(myFileStream);
writer.WriteLine("Line 1");
writer.WriteLine("Line 2");
writer.Close();
```

Note that the *Exists* method of the *File* class does not accept wildcards. For wildcard support, check the online documentation for the *GetFiles* and *GetDirectories* methods of the *Directory* class. *File* methods exist to get or set the time of creation, last write, and last access of a file. The following example displays the creation date of a file:

```
FileDialog myFileDialog = new OpenFileDialog();
myFileDialog.InitialDirectory = "\\";
myFileDialog.Filter = "Text files |*.txt";
myFileDialog.ShowDialog();
String fileName = myFileDialog.FileName;
DateTime creationDate = File.GetCreationTime(fileName);
MessageBox.Show("Creation date: \n" + creationDate.ToLongDateString());
```

Using the *Directory* Class

The *Directory* class allows you to perform operations on directories. As in the case of the *File* class, the members of *Directory* are static and there is a *DirectoryInfo* class that provides instance methods performing the same functions. The following static methods of the *Directory* class are important:

```
public static DirectoryInfo CreateDirectory(String path)
public static void Delete(String path)
public static void Delete(String path, Bool recursive)
public static bool Exists(string path)
public static void Move(string sourceDirName, string destDirName)
```

The *CreateDirectory* method creates the requested path, including subdirectories if required. The first *Delete* method deletes an empty directory, whereas the second version of *Delete*, which accepts a Boolean parameter, allows you to specify if subdirectories are to be deleted as well. The *Exists* method reports the existence of a path, and the *Move* method moves a directory, if possible.

Methods also exist to navigate through the directory tree. *GetCurrentDirectory* and *SetCurrentDirectory* report or change the current directory. To navigate to a particular directory, use *GetFiles* and *GetDirectories* to report the list of file and directory names listed in the specified directory. Both of these methods accept wildcards, so the following line returns an array of strings containing the full path names of the files that match "my*.txt" in the directory \myDir:

```
String[] fullNames = Directory.GetFiles(@"\myDir", "my*.txt");
```

The following example method, *searchDirectory*, performs a recursive search through a directory tree for a file. It returns a string with the full path names it finds. Note the use of the *Path.Combine* method to produce a full path from a directory and a file name, including the directory separator character.

```
private String searchDirectory
    (String theFile, String theDirectory)
{
    String result = "";
    String fullPathName = Path.Combine(theDirectory, theFile);
    if (File.Exists(fullPathName))
        result += " " + fullPathName;
    String[] directories =
        Directory.GetDirectories(theDirectory);
    foreach (String d in directories)
    {
        result += searchDirectory(theFile, d);
    }
    return result;
}
```

Differences from the Full .NET Framework

Pocket PC files do not have attributes such as *Hidden*, *Archive*, and so on, so the *GetAttributes* and *SetAttributes* methods are not supported in the .NET Compact Framework. Methods such as *GetCreationTime* have a *GetCreationTimeUtc* counterpart in the full .NET Framework, but not in the .NET Compact Framework. Simply use *GetCreationTime* and convert the time to UTC. See Chapter 8 for information on converting to UTC time.

Using the *Path* Class

The *Path* class contains methods for manipulating file paths, taking into account the directory separator character and the path separator for environment variables whose values contain multiple paths. There are methods for extracting the various parts of a path such as the file name, extension, and directory name. The following list shows the results of applying these methods to the path string \myDir\myFile.txt:

- *GetDirectoryName* returns \myDir.
- *GetExtension* returns .txt.
- *GetFileName* returns myFile.txt.
- *GetFileNameWithoutExtension* returns myFile.
- *GetFullPath* returns \myDir\myFile.txt.

The *Path* class allows you to combine paths in a platform-independent manner. If you take the paths \myDir and mySubdir\myFile.txt, the *Combine* method returns \myDir\mySubdir\myFile.txt. The *ChangeExtension* method changes the extension on a path string. *GetTempFileName* creates a new temporary file with a unique name. *GetTempPath* returns the path string for the system's current temporary directory.

Summary

In this chapter, you saw how to use classes that derive from *Stream* to perform byte-level input and output. You saw how to use various *Stream*-derived classes to read bytes from or write bytes to files, network connections, or memory. Then you saw how the *BinaryReader* and *BinaryWriter* classes allow you to view a file not just as raw bytes, but as an image of binary data, with fast read and write features that avoid the overhead of converting data to or from characters.

You also saw how to use the *StreamReader* and *StreamWriter* classes to read or write streams as characters. This requires the translation of characters to or from bytes. You saw how the *Encoding* class provides a mechanism for doing this easily.

Finally you saw how to use the *File*, *Directory*, and *Path* classes to perform operations directly on files and directories. These classes provide powerful facilities to allow you to create, move, delete, and otherwise manage files and directories.

11

Networking

Chapter 10 describes how to perform input and output using streams and the MemoryStream, FileStream, and NetworkStream classes. This chapter takes these topics a little further and also looks at classes designed to help you access network resources.

One of the best ways of accessing resources over the Internet from a smart device application is to use XML Web services. The .NET Compact Framework includes excellent support for a smart device functioning as a Web services client, and this topic is important enough to deserve its own chapter later in this book. If Web services are not an appropriate solution for your application, you can access network resources using the Hypertext Transfer Protocol (HTTP) with the *System.Net.WebRequest* and *System.Net.WebResponse* classes. But if you need to have direct control over a Transmission Control Protocol (TCP/IP) or a User Datagram Protocol (UDP/IP) connection to another system, use the *System.Net.Sockets.Socket* class.

This chapter also describes how to use the classes provided for infrared communications, in which the .NET Compact Framework offers capability not available in the full .NET Framework. Finally, we look at how to perform serial communications to a connected device, which is used for cable connection to other portable electronic devices, such as modems, bar code scanners, GPS receivers, digital cameras, or other RS-232 serial devices.

Using the *System.Net* Namespace

The *System.Net* namespace contains classes to access resources on the Internet. The architecture of this namespace is designed to support pluggable protocols. A *Uniform Resource Identifier* (URI) is the address of any point of content in

Internet space, and it consists of three parts: the protocol, or access mechanism, the host name, and the file name. You request a connection to a resource on the Internet using the static method *WebRequest.Create*. This method analyzes the URI that is passed to it and returns an instance of a protocol-specific descendant of *WebRequest*. The .NET Compact Framework includes *HttpWebResponse* and *HttpWebRequest*, which you use to access HTTP resources. But the .NET Compact Framework does not support the *FileWebRequest* and *FileWebResponse* classes found in the full .NET Framework that are used to access files specified using a URI with the *file://* scheme.

> **Note** To use the classes described in this chapter, your device requires a network connection. Depending on the capabilities of your device, you might be able to use a direct Ethernet connection, an 802.11b wireless LAN connection, or a wide area telecommunications link such as GPRS, GSM, or CDPD.
>
> You can also use a device that is connected to your desktop computer with infrared or by using ActiveSync, either through a USB port or a serial device cradle. ActiveSync allows a connected device to "tunnel through" the desktop host onto the network (to access file shares or the Internet). However, there are some restrictions when using an ActiveSync connection. See the sections "Understanding Your IP Network While Using the Emulators and ActiveSync" and "Performing DNS Lookups" later in this chapter for details.
>
> You can also test networking applications with the emulators. The emulators included in Visual Studio .NET have a simulated Ethernet card that also connects through the desktop host to the network.

> **Tip** If you are testing networking applications on one of the emulators, it might on occasion fail with an exception that reports that a device of the same name already exists on the network. This might be because someone else on your LAN is already running the emulator on a different system.

(continued)

> To fix this, change the network device name of the emulator by selecting Settings from the Start menu. In the Settings window, select the System tab, click About, and then select the Device ID tab. Change the name in the Device Name field to something unique, and then select Soft Reset from the emulator's File menu to ensure that the change takes effect. Remember to choose the Save Emulator State option when shutting down; otherwise, you will have to make this change again the next time you start the emulator.

Using the *WebRequest* and *WebResponse* Classes

The *WebRequest* and *WebResponse* classes, defined in the *System.Net* namespace, allow you to retrieve information from the Internet. For example, you can request an HTML Web page that would normally be displayed in a Web browser. You can then process the resulting page programmatically to extract information. This technique of *screen scraping* is useful, but your application will continue to work reliably only as long as the format of the page does not change excessively. The action of a *WebRequest* can go beyond simply fetching a page, however. It is possible to send data to the Web server to be processed by programs running on the Web server, such as a Common Gateway Interface (CGI) script. The response sent by the server can then be in whatever format your application expects; it can be a standard format such as XML or a custom format dictated by your application.

Understanding *WebRequest* and *WebResponse* Basics

The most important classes in the *System.Net* namespace are the *WebRequest* and *WebResponse* classes, which are abstract classes (*MustInherit* in Visual Basic .NET), so you cannot create an instance of these classes using the constructor. Instead, you call the static *WebRequest.Create* method, passing the URI of the resource you want to access. If the scheme of the URI is *http://* or *https://*, the *Create* method returns an instance of the *HttpWebRequest* class. The *GetResponse* method of this instance makes a request to the resource and returns an *HttpWebResponse* instance that contains the response.

At its simplest, the code required to fetch a Web page into an input stream consists of the following:

```
using System.Net;
using System.IO;
:
    WebRequest req = WebRequest.Create(uri);
    WebResponse res = req.GetResponse();
    // GetResponse blocks until the response arrives
    Stream ReceiveStream = res.GetResponseStream();
    // Read the stream into a string
    StreamReader sr = new StreamReader( ReceiveStream );
    string resultstring = sr.ReadToEnd();
```

Fetching a Resource Using HTTP

The following HttpGetSample code sample is the basis of a simple screen scraper application that fetches a Web page, which you can then process to extract information. However, in this sample, it simply writes the HTML to the output screen. If an error occurs, the program writes the error message to the screen; for the correct error message to display, you must add a reference to the error messages assembly System.SR.dll to your project. To use the sample, replace "target URL here" with the URL you want to fetch.

This code works fine for small Web pages, but if you fetch a large Web page, you might exceed the maximum string length that the Console writer can manage, in which case the program will throw an exception. Later samples in this chapter write the received data stream out in 256 byte blocks, avoiding this problem.

> **Warning** This code sample (and the majority of code samples in this chapter) must be built for a Windows CE .NET device or emulator because it uses *Console.WriteLine* to write output to the screen, which is not supported on Pocket PCs.

HttpGetSample.cs

```
using System;
using System.IO;
using System.Net;

namespace NETCFDevelopersReference
```

(continued)

HttpGetSample.cs *(continued)*

```
{
    class HttpGetSample
    {
        /// <summary>
        /// The main entry point for the application.
        /// </summary>
        static void Main(string[] args)
        {
            HttpGetSample thisclass = new HttpGetSample();
            thisclass.getPage("target URL here"); // <-- EDIT THIS!
        }

        public void getPage(String url)
        {
            WebResponse result = null;

            try
            {
                WebRequest req = WebRequest.Create(url);
                result = req.GetResponse();
                Stream ReceiveStream = result.GetResponseStream();

                //read the stream into a string
                StreamReader sr = new StreamReader( ReceiveStream );
                string resultstring = sr.ReadToEnd();

                Console.WriteLine("\r\nResponse stream received");
                Console.WriteLine(resultstring);
            }
            catch(Exception exp)
            {
                Console.Write("\r\nRequest failed. Reason:");
                Console.WriteLine(exp.Message);
            }
            finally
            {
                if ( result != null )
                {
                    result.Close();
                }
            }

            Console.WriteLine("\r\nPress Enter to exit....");
            Console.ReadLine();
        }
    }
}
```

An example of the output from this program is shown in Figure 11-1.

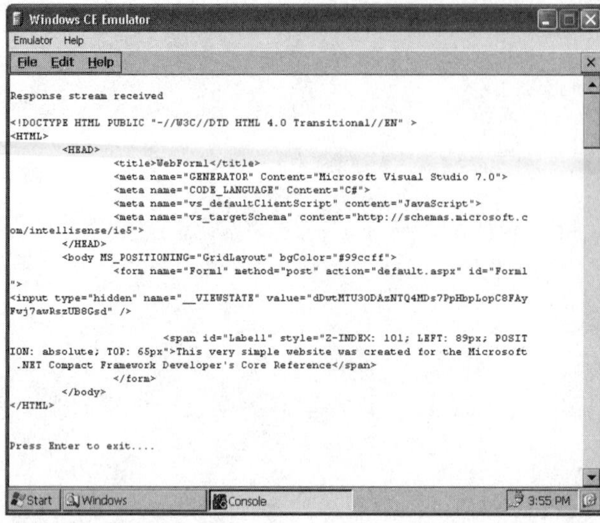

Figure 11-1 The output of a simple console program that displays the contents of a Web page.

Handling Errors

The HttpGetSample code example presented in the last section illustrates one technique that you should be careful to adopt when working with network applications. The *Finally* block ensures that the *WebResponse* object is closed, regardless of the success or failure of the program. This is important to ensure that network resources are not wasted.

However, the sample contains only rudimentary error trapping, catching errors as generic exceptions of type *System.Exception*. If you catch an exception of type *WebException* or *UriFormatException*, you get much more specific information about the nature of the error. You get an exception of type *UriFormatException* when the URI cannot be parsed or an exception of type *WebException* for other errors. The *Status* property of *WebException* returns a value from the *WebExceptionStatus* enumeration. If *Status* is *WebExceptionStatus.ProtocolError,* the exception is a result of an HTTP protocol error. You can then access the *WebException.Response* property, which returns an *HttpWebResponse* object containing the response from the server. Use the *HttpWebResponse.StatusCode* property to find out the HTTP status code the server sent back, and use *HttpWebResponse.StatusDescription* to obtain the description string that corresponds to that status code.

The error handler in the previous example could be rewritten as follows:

```
try
{
    HttpWebRequest req = (HttpWebRequest) WebRequest.Create(url);
    ⋮
}
catch (WebException WebExcp)
{
    Console.WriteLine("A WebException has been caught!");
    // Write out the Exception message
    Console.WriteLine(WebExcp.ToString());

    // Get the WebException status code
    if (WebExcp.Status == WebExceptionStatus.ProtocolError)
    {
        // Write out the WebResponse protocol status
        Console.WriteLine("Status Code : {0}",
            ((HttpWebResponse) WebExcp.Response).StatusCode);
        Console.WriteLine("Status Description : {0}",
            ((HttpWebResponse)WebExcp.Response).StatusDescription);
    }
}
catch (UriFormatException UriExcp)
{
    Console.WriteLine("A UriFormatException has been caught!");
    Console.WriteLine(UriExcp.ToString());
}
catch (Exception exc)
{
    Console.WriteLine(exc.ToString());
}
finally
{
    if ( result != null )
    {
        result.Close();
    }
}
```

Working with HTTP Headers

The HTTP protocol defines a number of headers, which are values that pass additional information about the request or the response. These headers tell the client and the server how to interpret the data they receive. For a definition of the HTTP 1.1 protocol, including the meaning of the HTTP headers, consult *http://www.w3.org/Protocols/rfc2616/rfc2616.html*.

The *HttpWebRequest* class allows you to control the HTTP headers sent with your request, which you do by setting properties or by executing methods of the class, as shown in Table 11-1.

Table 11-1 HTTP Headers Sent

HTTP Header	Set By
Accept	*HttpWebRequest.Accept* property
Connection	*HttpWebRequest.Connection* and *HttpWebRequest.KeepAlive* properties
Content-Length	*HttpWebRequest.ContentLength* property
Expect	*HttpWebRequest.Expect* property
Date	Set to the current system date
Host	Not set
If-Modified-Since	*HttpWebRequest.IfModifiedSince* property
Range	*HttpWebRequest.AddRange* method
Referer	*HttpWebRequest.Referer* property
Transfer-Encoding	*HttpWebRequest.TransferEncoding* property (the *HttpWebRequest.SendChunked* property must be *true*)
User-Agent	*HttpWebRequest.UserAgent* property

The *HttpWebResponse* instance exposes HTTP headers as properties in a similar way, as shown in Table 11-2.

Table 11-2 HTTP Headers Received

HTTP Header	Read By
Content-Encoding	*HttpWebResponse.ContentEncoding* property
Content-Length	*HttpWebResponse.ContentLength* property
Content-Type	*HttpWebResponse.ContentType* property
Length	*HttpWebResponse.Length* property
Server	*HttpWebResponse.Server* property

Both classes also have a *Headers* property that exposes HTTP headers as a *System.Net.WebHeaderCollection* instance. For example, instead of using the *UserAgent* property, you can add the User-Agent header using the following code:

```
HttpWebRequest req = (HttpWebRequest) WebRequest.Create(uri);
req.Headers.Add("User-Agent", "dotNETCF Test Program");
```

Similarly, you can retrieve the Server header, which is the name of the server, with this code:

```
HttpWebResponse res = (HttpWebResponse) req.GetResponse();
String server = res.Headers["Server"];
```

Network Transfer Encoding

All data transferred over the network is encoded. The Windows CE operating system uses Unicode to represent characters, but this requires at least 2 bytes to represent any character, which is not as efficient as the U.S. ASCII character set, which requires only one byte per character. But ASCII represents only commonly used characters in Western alphabets, so it is unusable in languages requiring other characters, such as European languages, Chinese, Japanese, or Arabic.

The compromise solution is to use character encodings. The most common of these is UTF-8, which is a variable-length multibyte encoding requiring a single byte for 7-bit characters that are in the U.S. ASCII character set and 2 bytes for characters outside it. This results in efficient encodings for Western alphabets and the flexibility to handle non-Latin characters.

Data that transfers between two systems using HTTP protocols must use a character encoding, and the sender uses the Content-Type HTTP header to communicate to the recipient which encoding has been used for the data the recipient is receiving. The default encoding assumed by the *HttpWebRequest* and *HttpWebResponse* classes is UTF-8. If you ran the samples shown earlier in this chapter, they almost certainly worked correctly on your system because both your Windows CE device and the Web server used UTF-8. However, if the Web server uses a different encoding, the result in your .NET Compact Framework application will be garbled.

For example, if you write a simple ASP.NET Web site (or use the one included in this book's sample files), edit the Web.Config file for that application to change the *responseEncoding* attribute of the *globalization* tag to utf-7, as shown here:

```
<globalization
        requestEncoding="utf-8"
        responseEncoding="utf-7"
/>
```

and then update the HttpGetSample application to fetch your Web site's page, the response that it displays will be unreadable:

```
Response stream received

+ADwAIQ-DOCTYPE HTML PUBLIC +ACI--//W3C//DTD HTML 4.0 Transitional//EN+
ACI- +AD4
-
+ADw-HTML+AD4-
        +ADw-HEAD+AD4-
                +ADw-title+AD4-WebFormn1+ADw-/title+AD4-
⋮
```

This is because the response the Web server sends uses the UTF-7 encoding, but your application has decoded it using the default encoding, UTF-8.

You can determine the character set encoding of a response by getting the *HttpWebResponse.CharacterSet* property. However, beware, there is a trick to this! You must set the *MediaType* property on the *request*; otherwise, the *CharacterSet* property on the *HttpWebResponse* will be blank. Even then, *CharacterSet* will only return the character set encoding used if the first part of the Content-Type header returned with the response (which is the media type) matches the value you set in the *MediaType* property of the request. For example, if you set *HttpWebRequest.MediaType* to "text/html" before calling *HttpWebRequest.GetResponse*, and the Content-Type header returned with the response is "text/html; charset=utf-8", the *HttpWebResponse.CharacterSet* property will contain the name of the character set encoding ("utf-8") because the "text/html" media type sent in the first part of the Content-Type header matches the value set in *HttpWebRequest.MediaType*. If the media types differ, *HttpWebResponse.CharacterSet* is a null string.

Once you determine the encoding, you can decode the server's response using the *System.Text.Encoding* class, as shown in this code sample:

```
HttpWebRequest req = (HttpWebRequest) WebRequest.Create(url);
// You MUST set the MediaType property on the request, otherwise
// the CharacterSet property on the HttpWebResponse object will be
// blank.
req.MediaType = "text/html";

HttpWebResponse result = (HttpWebResponse) req.GetResponse();

// Note that the HttpWebResponse.ContentType property always
// returns the Content-Type header, which will be something like
// "text/html; charset=utf-8"
string contenttype = result.ContentType;

// Character set encoding may be something like ISO-10646-UCS-2,
// or UTF-8, us-ascii etc
string charsetencoding = result.CharacterSet;

//read the stream using the decoder
Stream ReceiveStream = result.GetResponseStream();
Encoding encode = System.Text.Encoding.GetEncoding(charsetencoding);
StreamReader sr = new StreamReader( ReceiveStream, encode );
⋮
```

When you send data to a server, you must also encode it and tell the server which encoding you use, as demonstrated in the next section.

Sending Data to the Server with HTTP GET and HTTP POST

If you need to send data to the server application, you can append it to an HTTP GET request in the form of a query string, in which case you append the data to the request URI after a *?* character. An alternative is to use HTTP POST, which is similar to GET except the data is sent in the body of the message instead of appended to the URI.

Using HTTP GET Query String

The convention for HTTP query strings is to use *key=value* pairs, delimited by an ampersand (&). So to transfer an item called FirstName with the value Andy, and another item called LastName with the value Wigley, you would use the query string

```
?FirstName=Andy&LastName=Wigley
```

The data you send in a query string must not include characters that have significance in URLs, such as *:* or */*, so you must encode the string first, replacing these characters with the characters representing their hexadecimal equivalents, a process called *URL encoding*. For example, the *?* character translates as %3f, and the slash as %2f. In standard URL encoding, spaces translate to + characters.

For example, the query string

```
FirstName=Andy; LastName=Wigley; site=/anywhere.com
```

after URL encoding becomes

```
FirstName%3dAndy%3b+LastName%3dWigley%3b+site%3d%2fanywhere.com
```

In the full .NET Framework, the *System.Web.HttpUtility* class provides methods to encode and decode URL-encoded data, but this class is not supported in the .NET Compact Framework. You must write your own code to handle URL encoding, such as the example code shown here:

UrlEncode.cs

```
using System;
using System.IO;

namespace NETCFDevelopersReference
{
    /// <summary>
    /// Replacement for HttpUtility.UrlEncode
    /// </summary>
    public class HttpUtility
    {
        public static string UrlEncode(string instring)
```

(continued)

UrlEncode.cs *(continued)*

```
            {
                StringReader strRdr = new StringReader(instring);
                StringWriter strWtr = new StringWriter();
                int charValue = strRdr.Read();
                while (charValue != -1)
                {
                    if (((charValue >= 48) && (charValue <= 57)) // 0-9
                        ||((charValue >= 65) && (charValue <= 90)) // A-Z
                        ||((charValue >= 97) && (charValue <= 122))) // a-z
                        strWtr.Write((char) charValue);
                    else if (charValue == 32)    // Space
                        strWtr.Write('+');
                    else
                        strWtr.Write("%{0:x2}", charValue);

                    charValue = strRdr.Read();
                }

                return strWtr.ToString();
            }
        }
    }
```

Using HTTP POST

To use POST, just set the *HttpWebRequest.Method* property to "POST" and then proceed as for GET. A typical HTML page shown in a Web browser posts data as *key=value* pairs, with the data URL-encoded, so your application must format the data in that way if that is what the Web server application expects. If you are simply posting application content or XML, just post it as is.

When posting data, you must encode it to be posted and convert it to a byte array. You should also set the *ContentLength* property to the length of the encoded data, call the *GetRequestStream* method to return the request stream, and write the encoded data to that stream. Finally, you should set the *Content-Type* property to the media type of the data, for example, text/plain, text/xml, or application/x-www-form-urlencoded, to indicate to the server the nature of the content (the MIME type), and append the character set used for encoding, for example, ;charset=utf-8. The following code sample illustrates these techniques:

```
public void doPost(String url, String payload)
{
    WebRequest req = WebRequest.Create(url);
    req.Method = "POST";
    req.ContentType = "text/plain; charset=utf-8";
```

```
        // Encode the data
        byte[] encodedBytes = Encoding.UTF8.GetBytes(payload);
        req.ContentLength = encodedBytes.Length;

        // Write encoded data into request stream
        Stream requestStream = req.GetRequestStream();
        requestStream.Write(encodedBytes, 0, encodedBytes.Length);
        requestStream.Close();

        WebResponse result = req.GetResponse();
        ⋮
    }
```

Alternatives to Cookies for Session State Support

The .NET Compact Framework implementation of the *HttpWebResponse* class does not support the *Cookies* property found in the full .NET Framework implementation. Consequently, you cannot save cookies sent by the server and return them with subsequent requests as a way of identifying your client application to the server.

If you are using an ASP.NET application on the server, you can utilize the ASP.NET support for cookieless clients to track your smart device applications session. You enable this by setting *cookieless* to "true" in the *sessionState* configuration in the ASP.NET application's Web.Config file, as follows:

```
<sessionState
        mode="InProc"
        stateConnectionString="tcpip=127.0.0.1:42424"
        sqlConnectionString="data source=127.0.0.1;user id=sa;password="
        cookieless="true"
        timeout="20"
/>
```

ASP.NET uses a munged URL to track sessions for cookieless clients, meaning it embeds a session ID into the response URI. For example, if your application makes a request to *http://myserver/myserverapp.aspx*, the response URI that returns to the client is actually something like *http://myserver/(1en4l345qq203lr2f0h4xt45)/myserverapp.aspx*. To the client, it looks like a server-side redirect. In the client application, this response URI is in the *HttpWebResponse.ResponseUri* property, so the client application need only use this URI for subsequent requests for the server application to be able to identify those requests as coming from that particular client.

You can see how this works with a simple example of an ASP.NET Web site, which returns a text message to the client the first time it calls and a different message on subsequent requests. In Visual Studio .NET, create a new Visual

C# ASP.NET application. Edit the Web.Config file to set *cookieless* to "true," as described earlier. In WebForm1.aspx, click the HTML button at the bottom of the Designer View to switch to the HTML view. Delete everything on that page and replace it with the following code:

```
<%@ Page language="c#" Inherits="System.Web.UI.Page" %>
<script language="C#" runat="server">
    private void Page_Load(object sender, System.EventArgs e)
    {
        // Return one message the first time for this client
        if (Session["message"] == null)
        {
            Response.Write("Hello, newcomer!");
            Session["message"] = "So, you're back again!";
        }
        else
        {
            //and another subsequently
            Response.Write((string) Session["message"]);
        }
    }
</script>
```

This application makes use of the ASP.NET *Session* object, which is a dictionary-structured object that you access using the syntax *Session["string-key"]* and that persists across requests belonging to the same session. The first time the client accesses this application, *Session["message"]* does not exist, so the server returns the string "Hello, newcomer!", but it also creates *Session["message"]*, storing in it the string "So, you're back again!" The next time the same client calls this program, the ASP.NET runtime extracts the session ID from the munged URL used to make the request, thereby restoring the *Session* object for that client. Now *Session["message"]* exists, so the program returns that value to the caller.

The smart device client for this example is similar to those already shown, except it now makes a second request to the same resource, this time using the value in the *HttpWebResponse.ResponseUri* property, which contains the munged URL returned from the server, as shown in the following code:

```
HttpWebResponse result = null;

try
{
    Console.WriteLine("Making first request...");
    WebRequest req = WebRequest.Create(url);
    result = (HttpWebResponse) req.GetResponse();
    Stream ReceiveStream = result.GetResponseStream();
    ShowResponse(ReceiveStream);
```

```
        // Now make a subsequent request, using the response URI
        // returned from the first
        Console.WriteLine("Response URI from first request: {0}",
            result.ResponseUri);
        Console.WriteLine("Making second request...");
        req = WebRequest.Create(result.ResponseUri);
        result = (HttpWebResponse) req.GetResponse();
        ReceiveStream = result.GetResponseStream();
        ShowResponse(ReceiveStream);
}
⋮
```

The complete HttpSessionStateSample application is available with this book's sample files. On the Windows CE .NET emulator, the output from this application is as shown in Figure 11-2.

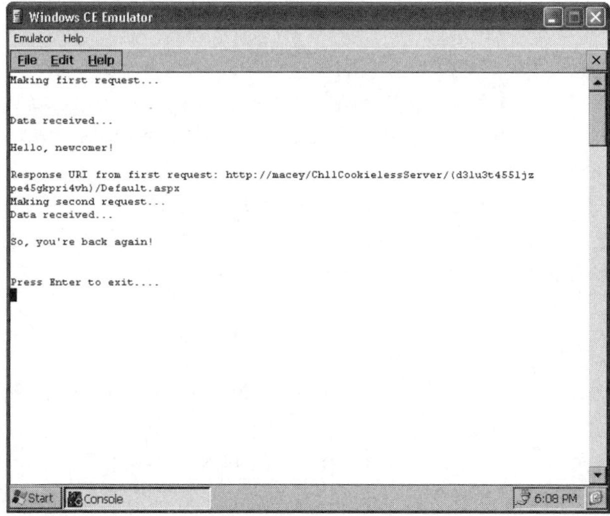

Figure 11-2 Console output from HttpSessionStateSample application.

Securing Network Transfers with SSL

Secure Sockets Layer (SSL) is the de facto standard for encrypting data transfers between a server and a client. Used in combination with HTTP Basic Authentication (discussed in the next section,) it is an effective way of securing data transfers and authenticating the client.

To use SSL with the *WebRequest* class is simplicity itself. If the scheme used in the target URI is https://, *WebRequest* automatically sets up an SSL-encrypted channel with the server. If the target Web server has a server certificate that has expired or cannot be authenticated against root certificates on the smart device, *WebRequest.Create* throws an exception of type *System.WebException*, with a *Status* property of *WebExceptionStatus.TrustFailure*.

Authenticating Requests with the *NetworkCredential* Class

Encryption without authentication is useless. If your server application does not positively identify client requests, setting up encryption to hide the contents of network data transfers makes no sense at all. You provide authentication details—a user name, a password and, for authentication schemes such as Windows NT Challenge/Response (NTLM) that require it, a domain name—by creating an instance of the *System.Net.NetworkCredential* class and attaching it to the *WebRequest* object's *Credentials* property.

> **Note** There is no support for *System.Net.CredentialCache* in the .NET Compact Framework. In the full .NET Framework, you use the *CredentialCache* class to create a cache of credentials, rather than supplying them with every request.
>
> In the .NET Compact Framework, you must create an instance of the *System.Net.NetworkCredential* class and associate it with each request that requires authentication.

You can use HTTP Basic, Digest, or NTLM authentication. In Windows CE .NET, you also have the option of using Kerberos authentication. If you use HTTP Basic Authentication, the client application sends the user name and the password to the server in clear text, so they are visible to any snoopers equipped with a network packet sniffer. However, if you use HTTP Basic in conjunction with SSL encryption, the user name and the password transfer over the SSL-encrypted channel, safe from observation.

The details of how you set up these different authentication schemes on the server are outside the scope of this chapter, but to learn how to supply login credentials from your client application, you can easily create a simple example ASP.NET Web site on your development computer by carrying out the following steps.

1. Create a simple Web site in Visual Studio .NET. It doesn't matter what you put on the Web form—a simple label control with a message will suffice. Alternatively, you can use an application site as opposed to an HTML site, such as that used for the HttpSessionStateSample described earlier. Build the application.

2. Select Control Panel from the Start menu, and then, if using the Windows XP Category View, select Performance and Maintenance. Open the Administrative Tools category and double-click the Internet Information Services icon. Expand the Web Sites node to locate the Web site you just created. Right-click it and select Properties from the shortcut menu.

3. In the Properties dialog box, select the Directory Security tab and click the Edit button in the Anonymous Access And Authentication group.

4. Clear the Anonymous Access check box and select the Basic Authentication check box. Clear the Integrated Windows Authentication check box.

This Web site now requires you to enter a valid logon user name and password to access the site. You can confirm this if you try to access the site using Internet Explorer.

If you try to access this Web resource without supplying logon credentials, such as the simple HttpGetSample application earlier in this chapter does, *WebRequest.Create* throws an exception of type *WebException* with a *Status* property of *WebExceptionStatus.ProtocolError*, indicating an HTTP error. Interrogation of the *Response* property of the exception (as described earlier in this chapter in the section "Handling Errors") reveals it to be an HTTP 401 error—Unauthorized. You can modify that application to create a *NetworkCredential* object and attach it to the *WebRequest* to supply logon credentials. You will need to edit the application to supply appropriate logon details for a user on your system, as shown in the following code:

```
WebRequest req = WebRequest.Create(url);
NetworkCredential creds =
    new NetworkCredential("andy", "pA55w0rd", "");
req.Credentials = creds;
WebResponse result = req.GetResponse();
⋮
```

Asynchronous Web Requests

Network data transfers can be fairly lengthy operations. The examples so far in this chapter use the *WebRequest.GetResponse* method to return the *WebResponse* object that contains the data from the server as a synchronous operation, but this causes a lengthy delay in the application even for quite a small amount of Web content. Instead, call the *BeginGetResponse* method, passing the address of a callback method, and the main thread continues while the Web data transfer continues on another thread in the background. The second argument to the *BeginGetResponse* method is an *object* value called *state*. When the response from the server has been completed, the callback method executes, but it executes on a different thread from the one that made the call to *BeginGetResponse*. The state object is used to make a logical connection between the initial request and the callback method executing on a different thread. You must define and instantiate your own class for the *BeginGetResponse* method's state argument. The class should suit the requirements of your application, but it must contain a reference to the *HttpWebRequest* object as shown in the following code:

```
// The RequestState class is used to pass data
// across async calls
public class RequestState
{
    public HttpWebRequest Request;

    public RequestState()
    {
        Request = null;
    }
}

/// <summary>
/// Class makes asynchronous HTTP Get to remote URL
/// </summary>
public class GetHttpAsync
{
    public void getPage(String url)
    {
        HttpWebRequest req = (HttpWebRequest) WebRequest.Create(url);
        // Create the state object
        RequestState rs = new RequestState();
        // Add the request into the state so it can be passed around
        rs.Request = req;

        // Issue the async request
        req.BeginGetResponse(
            new AsyncCallback(this.ResponseCallback), rs);
    }
⋮
```

In the callback method, get the *AsyncResult* property of the supplied parameter to retrieve the state object, and retrieve the *HttpWebRequest* object from that. Then call the *EndGetResponse* method to retrieve the *HttpWebResponse* object. Thereafter, processing continues as normal:

```
private void ResponseCallback(IAsyncResult ar)
{
    // Get the RequestState object from the async result
    RequestState rs = (RequestState) ar.AsyncState;

    // Get the HttpWebRequest from RequestState
    HttpWebRequest req = rs.Request;

    // Get the HttpWebResponse object
    HttpWebResponse resp = (HttpWebResponse) req.EndGetResponse(ar);

    // Read data from the response stream
    Stream responseStream = resp.GetResponseStream();
    StreamReader sr =
        new StreamReader( responseStream, Encoding.UTF8);
    string strContent = sr.ReadToEnd();

    // Close down the response stream
    responseStream.Close();
}
```

The following example is a simple test program that issues an asynchronous request for the page at *http://www.gotdotnet/team/netcf* and then writes a dot (.) to the screen every half second while the fetch operation continues in the background. The worker class *HttpGetAsync* raises an event to notify the main class when the operation completes, and it also writes the first 512 characters from the response to the console. Figure 11-3 shows the output from this program.

HttpGetAsyncSample\Main.cs

```
using System;
using System.IO;
using System.Threading;

namespace NETCFDevelopersReference
{
    class HttpGetAsyncSample
    {
        public static void Main(string[] args)
        {
            HttpGetAsyncSample thisclass = new HttpGetAsyncSample();
            thisclass.Run();
        }

        private bool isComplete;
```

(continued)

HttpGetAsyncSample\Main.cs *(continued)*

```
        public void Run()
        {
            Console.WriteLine();
            Console.WriteLine("Test Program makes HTTP AsyncGet"
                + " to http://www.gotdotnet.com/team/netcf");
            Console.WriteLine("Press Enter to continue...");
            Console.ReadLine();

            GetHttpAsync callit = new GetHttpAsync();
            // Wire up to handle the complete event
            callit.GetComplete += new
                GetHttpAsync.GetCompleteHandler(this.GetCompleteHandler);
            // Set the flag we will check for completion
            isComplete = false;

            Console.WriteLine("Making async call");
            callit.getPage("http://www.gotdotnet.com/team/netcf");

            Console.WriteLine("Main thread writes these dots, "
                + "while async fetch proceeds");
            Console.WriteLine("in secondary thread");
            int count = 0;
            while (!isComplete)
            {
                Console.Write(".");
                if (++count == 80) Console.WriteLine();
                Thread.Sleep(500); // Sleep for half a second
            }
            Console.WriteLine("\r\nResponse Received");
            Console.WriteLine("Press Enter to exit...");
            Console.ReadLine();

            return;
        }

        protected void GetCompleteHandler()
        {
            // Event handler for get complete
            isComplete = true;
        }
    }
}
```

HttpGetAsyncSample\GetHttpAsync.cs

```
using System;
using System.Net;
using System.IO;
using System.Text;

namespace NETCFDevelopersReference
{
    // The RequestState class is used to pass data
    // across async calls
    public class RequestState
    {
        public HttpWebRequest Request;

        public RequestState()
        {
            Request = null;
        }
    }

    /// <summary>
    /// Class makes asynchronous HTTP Get to remote URL
    /// </summary>
    public class GetHttpAsync
    {
        public delegate void GetCompleteHandler();
        public event GetCompleteHandler GetComplete;

        public void getPage(String url)
        {
            try
            {
                HttpWebRequest req =
                    (HttpWebRequest) WebRequest.Create(url);
                // Create the state object
                RequestState rs = new RequestState();

                // Add the request into the state
                // so it can be passed around
                rs.Request = req;
```

(continued)

HttpGetAsyncSample\GetHttpAsync.cs *(continued)*

```
                // Issue the async request
                req.BeginGetResponse(
                    new AsyncCallback(this.ResponseCallback), rs);
            }
            catch(Exception exp)
            {
                Console.WriteLine("\r\nRequest failed. Reason:");
                while (exp != null)
                {
                    Console.WriteLine(exp.Message);
                    exp = exp.InnerException;
                }
            }
        }

        private void ResponseCallback(IAsyncResult ar)
        {
            // Get the RequestState object from the async result
            RequestState rs = (RequestState) ar.AsyncState;

            // Get the HttpWebRequest from RequestState
            HttpWebRequest req = rs.Request;

            // Get the HttpWebResponse object
            HttpWebResponse resp =
                (HttpWebResponse) req.EndGetResponse(ar);

            // Read data from the response stream
            Stream responseStream = resp.GetResponseStream();
            StreamReader sr =
                new StreamReader( responseStream, Encoding.UTF8);
            string strContent = sr.ReadToEnd();

            // Write out the first 512 characters
            Console.WriteLine("Length: {0}", strContent.Length);
            Console.WriteLine(strContent.Substring(0,
                strContent.Length < 512 ? strContent.Length : 512));

            // Raise the completion event
            GetComplete();

            // Close down the response stream
            responseStream.Close();
        }
    }
}
```

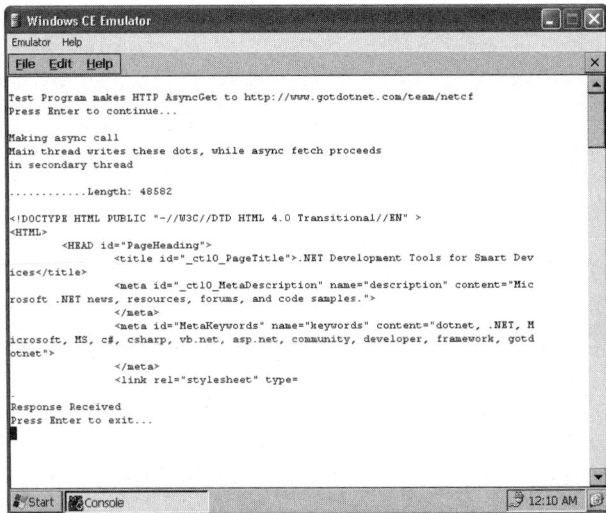

Figure 11-3 Output of HttpGetAsyncSample, which writes dots to the screen during asynchronous Web request.

Making Network Requests via a Proxy Server

Many client applications will need to access Web resources via a proxy server. This is easy to set up with the *WebRequest* class. Create an instance of *System.Net.Proxy*, passing the host name of the proxy server and the port number into the constructor, and set *WebRequest.Proxy* to point to it. Overloads of the constructor allow you to identify the proxy server by its address or by the URI.

Set the *BypassProxyOnLocal* property to *true* if you do not want requests to local Internet resources to use the proxy server. A local request is defined as one where the URI does not contain a period (.), such as *http://myserver*. You can also set this property through some overloads of the *WebProxy* constructor.

To configure a proxy, you can use code such as the following:

```
//  Pass Proxy string and bypass local machine
WebProxy myProxy = new WebProxy(
  "http://myproxyserver.mine.com:8080", true);

// ** This proxy requires authentication
myProxy.Credentials =
   new NetworkCredential("loginname","password");

Request.Proxy = myProxy;
```

Most proxy servers do not require a user name and a password, which means you don't need to provide the credentials.

The .NET Compact Framework implementation of *WebProxy* does not support a bypass list, as found in the full .NET Framework implementation.

Determining Whether the Device Is Connected

Most network applications need to know whether the device is currently connected to the network. A well-designed mobile application allows the user to make use of it even if the device isn't connected. For example, if the device has lost wireless connectivity, it should be able to operate using data cached on the device, and then possibly re-sync with a server when network connectivity is regained.

There is no class in the .NET Compact Framework that raises events to inform an application when connection to the network is lost and regained. Instead, you must code with this eventuality in mind and make sure your application is tolerant of network outages. You might need to write code that polls for a network resource to determine when the device has network connectivity.

For example, if your application uses XML Web services, you might need to connect to the service to upload data changes and download data to the device when a network connection is available. In your application, you should write a method that uses the *WebResponse* class to send an HTTP GET request to a valid URL on the server where the XML Web service is located. If the *HttpWebResponse.StatusCode* property in the response equals *HttpStatusCode.OK*, connectivity to the server is confirmed. You should call this method from a *TimerEvent* of a *System.Threading.Timer* instance to poll the server at intervals; when the method succeeds, the application knows that it can make a successful HTTP connection to the server, so the interaction with the XML Web service or access to other network resources can proceed.

Working with Sockets

The Windows operating system has long included a Windows Sockets (Winsock) interface for developers to make network connections using TCP/IP or UDP/IP. The *System.Net.Sockets* namespace provides a managed implementation of Winsock for the .NET Framework.

TCP is a connection-oriented protocol, so to make a connection there must be a socket listening for incoming TCP requests on the target system. On the client system, you then create a socket to make an outgoing request. The *System.Net.Sockets* namespace includes the *TcpListener* and the *TcpClient* classes, which contain simple methods to perform this kind of transaction.

These classes send and receive data in a blocking synchronous mode. To perform asynchronous communications, you will need to use the *Socket* class, which implements the Berkeley Sockets API and is a more capable but less user-friendly network class than *TcpListener* and *TcpClient*.

UDP is a broadcast protocol that a client uses to send datagrams out to one or more recipients, but delivery is not guaranteed. The *UdpClient* class allows simple access to connectionless network operations over UDP/IP.

> **Tip** Using any of the *System.Net.Sockets* classes, you can identify the remote system by its name or by its IP address. If you want to connect from a smart device to a process running on your desktop host while the device and the host are connected with ActiveSync, you can use the name "PPP_PEER" to identify the ActiveSync host.

Understanding Your IP Network While Using the Emulators and ActiveSync

The sample code presented in the rest of this chapter might not always work if you use either of the Pocket PC or Windows CE .NET emulators or a real device connected to your development computer using ActiveSync. For example, if you run the TcpListenerSample application on the Pocket PC emulator and try to connect to it using the TcpClientSample application running on your desktop computer, the applications cannot connect. However, if you reverse this so that the listener runs on the desktop and the client runs on the Pocket PC emulator, the application works fine. Yet all these devices are able to connect to a Web site on the Internet using Internet Explorer. Why isn't it possible to connect to a listening socket running on an emulator or an ActiveSync-connected device?

The explanation lies in the sub-networks where each of these devices resides and the network routing that is possible. The emulator is equipped with a virtual Ethernet card, so it appears that it is connected to a wired or a wireless LAN. However, when the emulator boots, it is assigned an IP address that places it in a different subnet from your development machine. The development machine acts as a network router for the emulator and can route connections out, but it does not allow connections into the emulator. In other words, applications running on the emulator can make outgoing TCP/IP connections, as in the TcpClientSample application here, but no applications can make incoming calls to a program, such as the TcpListenerSample application, running on the emulator. The network configuration that results is similar to that shown in Figure 11-4.

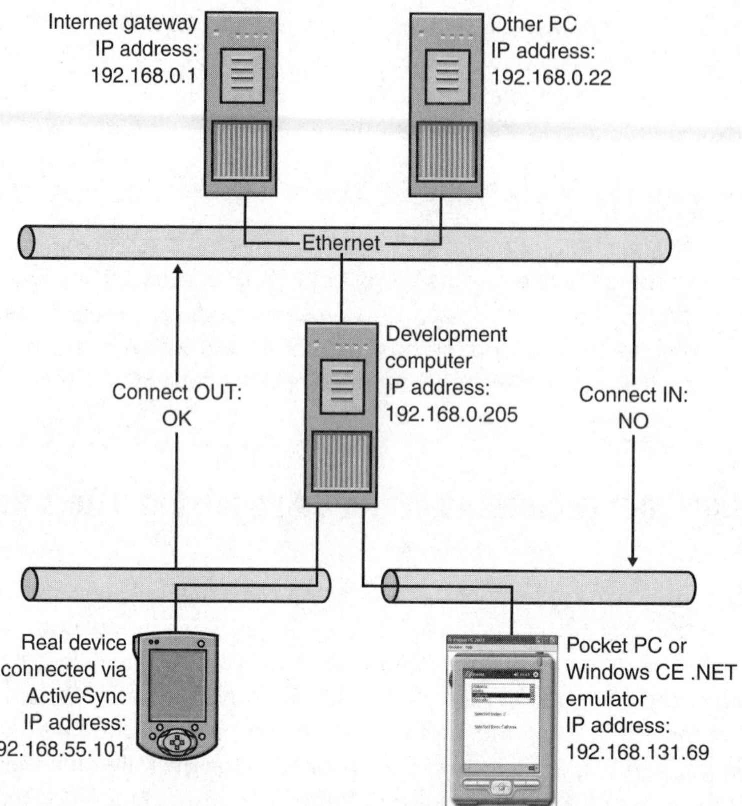

Figure 11-4 Emulators and cradled devices connecting to the network via the development machine, with the restrictions that the network imposes on the connections that can be made.

A similar situation occurs when you make a network connection from a real device that is connected to your development machine through ActiveSync. ActiveSync allows a cradled device to connect to the network. At these times, the device appears as though it has an Ethernet adapter, but as with the case of the emulator, your development machine acts as the network router. The device is assigned an IP address on a different subnet from the development machine, and as with the emulator, your development machine allows connections out from the device but will not route them into the device.

To run the samples in this chapter using an emulator or a cradled device, you must run the TcpListenerSample application on your desktop system and the TcpClientSample application on the emulator or the device.

Performing DNS Lookups

You identify hosts by their IP address or alternatively you can use their friendly names. The *System.Net.Dns* class allows you to perform Domain Name Service (DNS) lookups. One or more computers on your network provide a DNS lookup service, which maps host names to IP addresses so that you can refer to computers by their names rather than by the IP address, which is more difficult to remember. All members of this class are static methods, which allow you to send lookup queries to a DNS server. Principal static methods are:

- ***GetHostByAddress*** returns the host name for a particular IP address that you specify in as a string in dotted-quad notation ("192.168.0.1") or by passing an instance of *IPHostEntry*.
- ***GetHostByName*** returns an *IPHostEntry* instance for a particular DNS-style host name, such as "www.contentmaster.com".
- ***GetHostName*** gets the host name of the local computer.
- ***Resolve*** resolves a host name or an IP address in dotted-quad notation to an *IPHostEntry* instance.

There are also asynchronous versions in the form of *BeginGetHostByName*, *EndGetHostByName*, *BeginResolve,* and *EndResolve*.

The restrictions that apply to DNS lookups are similar to those that apply to IP connections when you're using the emulator or an ActiveSync-connected device. For example, if you have a real device and its name is POCKET_PC, you can run code on that device that uses *System.Dns* to determine the IP address of your development machine from its name. However, the reverse is not possible—code running on your development computer cannot determine the IP address of a device or an emulator from its name.

Using *System.Net.Sockets.TcpListener*

You use the *TcpListener* class to wait for and handle incoming TCP requests. A *TcpListener* instance listens on a specific IP address and port number. There are three ways you can specify the IP address and the port number:

- Listen on a particular port, using the IP address of the default interface of the host system, as illustrated here:

```
// Listen on port 695
TcpListener tcpServer = new TcpListener(695);
```

- Allow the system to assign an unused port number, by specifying the port number for the new *TcpListener* object as *0*. The system assigns the port after you call the *Start* method. You can then determine which port the *TcpListener* is listening on by getting the *LocalEndPoint* property, as illustrated in this code sample:

```
// System assigned port number
TcpListener tcpServer = new TcpListener(0);
// Start listening
tcpServer.Start();
// Find the assigned port
System.Net.IPEndPoint assignedEndpoint =
    (System.Net.IPEndPoint) tcpServer.LocalEndPoint;
int localport = assignedEndPoint.Port;
```

- Create an *IPEndPoint* object defining the port the *TcpListener* object should listen on, and pass this into the *TcpListener* constructor. For example:

```
IPEndPoint endPt = new IPEndPoint(IPAddress.Parse("192.168.0.1"), 69
5);
TcpListener tcpServer = new TcpListener(endPt);
```

With devices that have more than one network adapter, you create an *IPEndPoint* object defining the IP address of a network adapter on the system and a port number, although if you don't care which adapter is used, you can specify the IP address as *IPAddress.Any,* which is a static read-only field that is equivalent to 0.0.0.0 in dotted-quad notation and indicates that the server should listen for client activity on all network interfaces.

Use the *Start* method to begin listening for incoming network requests. The *Stop* method turns off listening. *TcpListener* can listen for more than one incoming connection. Each time a request comes in it's placed on an internal queue.

To accept a connection off the queue, use the *AcceptSocket* method (which returns a *Socket* instance) or the simpler *AcceptTcpClient* method (which returns a *TcpClient* instance). Use *Socket.Send* and *Socket.Receive* to communicate with the remote system in the former case, or use the *TcpClient.GetStream* method to return a stream in the latter case. After finishing communication with the remote client, you must remember to close the *Socket* or *TcpClient* yourself because *TcpListener* does not do this for you. When you call the *AcceptSocket* or the *AcceptTcpClient* method, program execution blocks until the *TcpListener* object receives an incoming request. If you do not want to block your main thread, call the *Pending* method to see whether there are any queued requests. This returns *true* if connections are pending in the queue.

The following program is a simple server application that waits for a connection and then sends a time-stamped message back to the caller.

TcpListener.cs

```
using System;
using System.Net;
using System.Net.Sockets;
using System.Text;

namespace NETCFDevelopersReference
{
    class TcpListenerSample
    {
        public static void Main()
        {
            String response;

            try
            {
                // listen on port 695
                TcpListener tcpServer = new TcpListener(695);
                tcpServer.Start();

                // Report where we are
                IPHostEntry thisHost = Dns.Resolve(Dns.GetHostName());
                Console.WriteLine("Host {0} listening on {1}, port {2}",
                    thisHost.HostName,
                    thisHost.AddressList[0].ToString(), 695);

                Console.WriteLine("Waiting for connection...");
                // Accept will block until someone connects
                TcpClient clientConn = tcpServer.AcceptTcpClient();

                // Send back a message including the time
                response = "Server response sent at "
                    + DateTime.Now.ToLongTimeString();

                // Convert the string to a Byte Array and send it
                Byte[] byteResponse =
                    Encoding.ASCII.GetBytes(response.ToCharArray());
```

(continued)

TcpListener.cs *(continued)*

```
                clientConn.GetStream()
                    .Write(byteResponse, 0, byteResponse.Length);
                clientConn.Close();
            }
            catch (SocketException socketError)
            {
                if (socketError.ErrorCode == 10048)
                {
                    Console.WriteLine("Error, port in use");
                }
            }
        }
    }
}
```

Notice the *catch* block in this sample. *TcpListener* returns a *SocketException* instance if it cannot initialize, for example, if the requested port is in use. See the section "Handling Errors with Sockets" later in this chapter for additional information.

Using *System.Net.Sockets.TcpClient*

A suitable client for the TcpListenerSample application shown previously uses the *TcpClient* class. *TcpClient* offers easy-to-use methods to send and receive data over a TCP connection. Use the *Connect* method to make a connection to a TCP server or pass the DNS name of the remote host and the port number in the *TcpClient* constructor, in which case the *TcpClient* object will attempt a connection as part of its initialization. Use the *GetStream* method to return the network stream that you use to send and receive messages.

The following code is from a Pocket PC Windows Forms application called TcpClientSample. TcpClientSample has a user interface consisting of a TextBox control in which you enter the IP address of the server, a multiline read-only TextBox control that displays the response, and a Button control. When the button is pressed, the application connects to the listener running on the server, receives the message, and displays it in the TextBox control. The output from this application is shown in Figure 11-5. You'll find the TcpClient-Sample application included with this book's sample files.

TcpClientForm.cs

```
using System;
using System.Text;
using System.Drawing;
```

(continued)

TcpClientForm.cs *(continued)*

```
using System.Collections;
using System.Windows.Forms;
using System.IO;
using System.Net;
using System.Net.Sockets;

namespace TcpClientSample
{
    public class TcpClientForm : System.Windows.Forms.Form
    {
        private System.Windows.Forms.Button button1;
        private System.Windows.Forms.TextBox ResponseTextBox;
        private System.Windows.Forms.TextBox ServerTextBox;
        private System.Windows.Forms.Label label1;

        public TcpClientForm()
        {
            //
            // Required for Windows Form Designer support
            //
            InitializeComponent();
        }

        protected override void Dispose( bool disposing )
        {
            base.Dispose( disposing );
        }

        #region Windows Form Designer generated code
        /// <summary>
        /// Required method for Designer support - do not modify
        /// the contents of this method with the code editor.
        /// </summary>
        private void InitializeComponent()
        {
            this.button1 = new System.Windows.Forms.Button();
            this.ResponseTextBox = new System.Windows.Forms.TextBox();
            this.label1 = new System.Windows.Forms.Label();
            this.ServerTextBox = new System.Windows.Forms.TextBox();
            //
            // button1
            //
            this.button1.Location = new System.Drawing.Point(84, 232);
            this.button1.Text = "Connect";
            this.button1.Click +=
                new System.EventHandler(this.button1_Click);
```

(continued)

TcpClientForm.cs *(continued)*

```
            //
            // ResponseTextBox
            //
            this.ResponseTextBox.Location =
                new System.Drawing.Point(28, 48);
            this.ResponseTextBox.Multiline = true;
            this.ResponseTextBox.Size = new System.Drawing.Size(184, 168);
            this.ResponseTextBox.Text = "";
            //
            // label1
            //
            this.label1.Location = new System.Drawing.Point(6, 16);
            this.label1.Size = new System.Drawing.Size(112, 16);
            this.label1.Text = "Server IP Address:";
            //
            // ServerTextBox
            //
            this.ServerTextBox.Location = new System.Drawing.Point(126, 14);
            this.ServerTextBox.Text = "0.0.0.0";
            //
            // TcpClientForm
            //
            this.Controls.Add(this.ServerTextBox);
            this.Controls.Add(this.label1);
            this.Controls.Add(this.button1);
            this.Controls.Add(this.ResponseTextBox);
            this.MinimizeBox = false;
            this.Text = "TcpClientForm";

        }
        #endregion

        static void Main()
        {
            Application.Run(new TcpClientForm());
        }

        private void button1_Click(object sender, System.EventArgs e)
        {
            IPAddress serverIP;
            try
            {
                serverIP = IPAddress.Parse(ServerTextBox.Text);
            }
            catch (FormatException fexp)
```

(continued)

TcpClientForm.cs *(continued)*

```
{
    this.ResponseTextBox.Text =
        "Invalid IP address entered - needs n.n.n.n," +
        " for example 192.168.0.103";
    return;
}

// Verify that the server exists
IPHostEntry remoteHost;
try
{
    remoteHost = Dns.Resolve(ServerTextBox.Text);
}
catch (SocketException sexp)
{
    if (sexp.ErrorCode == 11001) // No such host is known
        ResponseTextBox.Text =
            String.Format("Server {0} not known",
            ServerTextBox.Text);
    else
        ResponseTextBox.Text =
            String.Format("DNS lookup of {0} error: {1}",
            ServerTextBox.Text, sexp.Message);
    return;
}

// Try to connect to the server on port 695
TcpClient client = new TcpClient();
client.Connect(new IPEndPoint(serverIP, 695));

// Get the stream
Stream strm;
try
{
    strm = client.GetStream();
}
catch (InvalidOperationException)
{
    ResponseTextBox.Text =
        String.Format("Cannot connect to server: {0}",
        ServerTextBox.Text);
    return;
}
catch (SocketException exc)
{
    StringBuilder strB = new StringBuilder("");
```

(continued)

TopClientForm.cs *(continued)*

```
                strB.Append(
                    String.Format("Can't connect to server: {0}\r\n",
                    ServerTextBox.Text));
                strB.Append(exc.Message + "\r\n");
                strB.Append("Socket Error Code: "
                    + exc.ErrorCode.ToString());
                ResponseTextBox.Text = strB.ToString();
                return;
            }

            // Read the stream and convert it to ASCII
            Byte[] inputBuffer = new Byte[128];
            int bytes = strm.Read(inputBuffer, 0, inputBuffer.Length);
            string response =
                Encoding.ASCII.GetString(inputBuffer, 0, bytes);

            // Display the data
            ResponseTextBox.Text =
                String.Format("Received {0} bytes\r\n\r\n", bytes);
            ResponseTextBox.Text +=
                String.Format("Message received: {0}", response);

            client.Close();
        }
    }
}
```

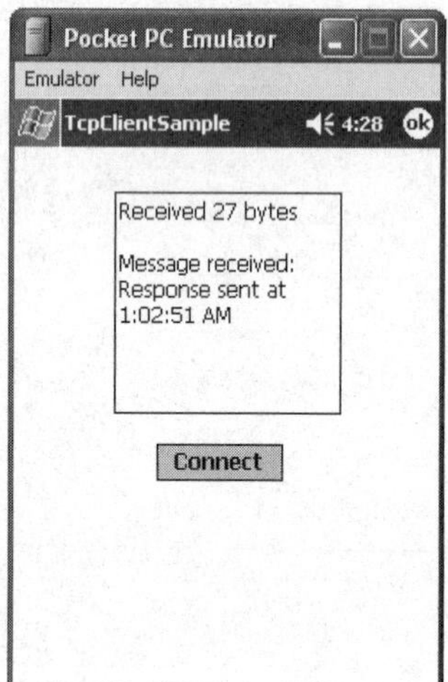

Figure 11-5 TcpClientSample application displaying a message after connecting to the server.

Using *System.Net.Sockets.UdpClient*

The *UdpClient* class allows you to send and receive UDP datagrams. As with the *TcpClient* and *TcpListener* classes, it operates in a blocking synchronous mode, so when you call the *Receive* method to wait for the receipt of a datagram, execution of the current thread blocks until a datagram is received.

UDP is a connectionless protocol, so you do not need to connect to a remote host before sending datagrams. Simply create an instance of *UdpClient*, and then call the *Send* method, passing the host name and the port number (as an *IPEndPoint* instance or as a host-name string and a port-number integer) of the remote host, as shown here:

```
UdpClient udpClient = new UdpClient();
byte[] msgBytes = System.Text.Encoding.ASCII.GetBytes("Message To Send");
udpClient.Send(msgBytes, msgBytes.Length, "TargetHostServer", 6950);
```

If you want to send a sequence of messages to the same remote target, you can establish a default remote host in one of the following two ways:

- Create an instance of *UdpClient* using either of the two forms of the constructor that takes a host name and a port number as parameters, *UdpClient(IPEndPoint)* or *UdpClient(string, int)*.
- Create an instance of *UdpClient* using the default constructor, and then call the *Connect* method passing the remote host name and the port number.

Once you've established a default remote host, calling *Send* to specify a remote host name and a port or an *IPEndPoint* parameter results in an exception being thrown.

Use the *Receive* method to receive datagrams from a remote host. The *Receive* method blocks execution until a datagram is received. When you create a *UdpClient* instance using the default constructor, the system assigns a local port number arbitrarily, and *Receive* listens on that port number. To listen on a specific port, use the *UdpClient(int)* constructor.

You can also send and receive multicast datagrams with *UdpClient*. Use the *JoinMulticastGroup* method to subscribe to a multicast group. Use the *DropMulticastGroup* method to unsubscribe to a multicast group.

Using the Socket Class

When *TcpListener*, *TcpClient*, or *UdpClient* doesn't provide you with the level of control over network operations that your application requires, or when you need to use asynchronous communications, you must use the *System.Net.Sockets.Socket* class.

The *Socket* constructor is of the form

```
Socket(AddressFamily addressFamily,
    SocketType socketType,
    ProtocolType protocolType)
```

- **The *AddressFamily*** enumeration specifies the addressing scheme that a *Socket* instance will use to resolve an address and includes options such as *AddressFamily.DecNet*, *.Osi*, *.NetBios,* and the most likely to be used, *AddressFamily.InterNetwork*, which specifies an IP version 4 address.
- **The *SocketType*** enumeration specifies the type of socket. Options include *SocketType.Dgram*, which you would use for UDP communications, *.Raw* for direct access to the underlying transport protocol, and *.Stream* to support reliable, two-way connection-based byte streams that are required for TCP communications.
- **The *ProtocolType*** enumeration specifies the required protocol. Options include *ProtocolType.Ipx*, *.IP*, *.Tcp*, *.Udp,* and *.Raw*. The low-level driver for the requested protocol must be present on the device for the *Socket* creation to be successful.

You create a Socket for TCP communications as shown here:

```
using System.Net.Sockets;
:
Socket sckt = new Socket(AddressFamily.InterNetwork,
                    SocketType.Stream, ProtocolType.Tcp);
```

After you have finished with your *Socket* instance, you must call the *Shutdown* method to disable the *Socket* instance, and then call *Close* to release all resources, as shown here:

```
sckt.Shutdown();
sckt.Close();
```

Using Sockets for Synchronous Operations

If you are using a connection-oriented protocol such as TCP and you want your application to act as a server and wait for incoming connections, you must first call the *Bind* method to bind your socket to a local IP address and port and then call the *Listen* method, as the following code illustrates:

```
// Create an IpEndPoint instance using system IP address
// and system-assigned port
IPEndPoint localEndPt = new IPEndPoint(IPAddress.Any, 0);
```

```
sckt.Bind(localEndPt);
// Allow a queue of 10 incoming connections
sckt.Listen(10);
```

This example uses 0 for the local port number, which means that the system assigns an unused port. Specify a non-zero port number to request a specific port. *Listen* throws an exception if there are already more pending connections than the number you specify in the call.

Listen blocks until it receives a connection. After a connection is received, you call the *Accept* method, which handles the incoming connection and returns another *Socket* instance that you use to communicate with the remote system. Use the *RemoteEndPoint* property of the returned *Socket* instance to identify the sending host and use the *Socket.Send* and *.Receive* methods of the returned *Socket* instance to exchange data. The following code illustrates how to accept a connection and receive data using the *Socket* class:

```
// Accept a connection
Socket connectedSckt = sckt.Accept();
byte[] recvBuf = new byte[1024];
connectedSckt.Receive(recvBuf, SocketFlags.None);

// In this example, data is a string
string data = Encoding.ASCII.GetString(recvBuf);

// Clean Up
connectedSckt.Shutdown();
connectedSckt.Close();
```

If you want your application to act as a client application over a connection-oriented protocol such as TCP, create the *Socket* object and then call the *Connect* method, passing an *IPEndPoint* instance that identifies the target system and the port number. Then call the *Send* and *Receive* methods to exchange data.

If you are using a connectionless protocol such as UDP, usage of the *Socket* class is simple. To listen for incoming datagrams, call the *ReceiveFrom* method to accept any incoming datagrams, and call the *SendTo* method to send datagrams to a remote host.

Using Sockets for Asynchronous Operations

The *Socket* class supports asynchronous operations as well. Methods *BeginConnect* and *EndConnect*, *BeginSend* and *EndSend*, and *BeginReceive* and *EndReceive* handle operations asynchronously with a client using connection-oriented protocols such as TCP. *BeginSendTo* and *EndSendTo* and *BeginReceiveFrom* and *EndReceiveFrom* handle asynchronous operations over connectionless protocols such as UDP.

The way you use these methods is consistent with the way asynchronous operations are handled elsewhere in the .NET Framework. See the section "Asynchronous Web Requests" earlier in this chapter for an example of how you achieve asynchronous operation with the *WebRequest* and *WebResponse* classes. You code asynchronous operations with the *Socket* class in much the same way.

For a complete sample using asynchronous sockets, see the section "Performing Asynchronous Read/Write Operations on *NetworkStream* Objects" in Chapter 10.

Handling Errors with Sockets

All the *System.Net.Sockets* classes can return an exception of type *SocketException* when an error is reported by the underlying Winsock application programming interface. The *ErrorCode* property of *SocketException* returns the Windows Sockets Version 2 API error code. You can find details of Winsock error codes in the Windows Sockets documentation on MSDN.

Infrared Communications

The *IrDAListener* and *IrDAClient* classes perform the same function for infrared communications that the *TcpListener* and *TcpClient* classes perform for TCP communications. The way that you use these classes is similar to the way you use their TCP counterparts. The IrDA classes are found in System.Net.IrDA.dll; to use them, you must add a reference to this dynamic link library (DLL) in your Visual Studio .NET project.

IrDA is a standard defined by the Infrared Data Association that specifies how to wirelessly transfer data via infrared radiation over distances up to 1.0 m. IrDA supports reliable stream-based connection-oriented communications similar to TCP and does not support connectionless datagram communications. However, IrDA communications call for a model that is slightly different from the TCP/IP model.

The network of IrDA devices is dynamic. Devices frequently move into and out of an infrared network. There are no IP addresses and no DNS servers to perform name-to-address mappings. Instead, every IrDA device identifies itself by its device name and a unique numeric device ID. Once a device is participating in an infrared network, a particular infrared service offered by a device in the network is identified by its *service name*. In your applications, you create an IrDA service for a particular service name using the *IrDAListener* class, and you make a connection to an IrDA service of a particular service name using the *IrDAClient* class.

Discovering InfraRed Devices with *IrDAClient.DiscoverDevices*

You can find out which devices are in the infrared network by calling the *IrDAClient.DiscoverDevices* method. This returns an array of *IrDADeviceInfo* objects. *IrDADeviceInfo* has four properties:

- ***Charset*** gets the character set used by the server as an *IrDACharset* enumerated value, one of *IrDACharset.ASCII*, *.ISO_8859_1* through *.ISO_8859_9*, and *.Unicode*.
- ***DeviceID*** gets a 4-byte value, the device identifier, as a byte array.
- ***DeviceName*** gets the device name as a string.
- ***Hints*** gets the type of the device as a value of the *IrDAHint* enumeration. Some of the possible values of *IrDAHint* are *Computer*, *LANAccess*, *PDA_ Palmtop* (includes Windows CE and Pocket PC devices), and *Telephony* (a mobile phone).

You can get this information by using *DiscoverDevices*, specifying the maximum number of devices to look for, as shown in the following code example:

```
IrDAClient irClient = new irClient();
IrDADeviceInfo[] irDevices = irClient.DiscoverDevices(10);
StringBuilder devicelist = new StringBuilder("");
Foreach (IrDADeviceInfo irDevice in irDevices)
{
    devicelist.Append(irDevice.DeviceID);
    devicelist.Append(" ");
    devicelist.Append(irDevice.DeviceName);
    devicelist.Append("\r\n");
}
textBox1.Text = devicelist.ToString();
```

Notice that these properties return information about each device, such as its name and unique numeric ID, but they don't return information on the service names of any infrared servers running on those devices.

Listening for Infrared Connections with *IrDAListener*

Create an *IrDAListener* object to listen for incoming connections for a specific service name in one of two ways:

- To advertise a service and listen for connection requests from any device requesting that service, use the *IrDAListener(string)* form of the constructor, passing the required service name:

```
// Listen for any connect request to our service
IrDAListener irListen = new IrDAListener("MyIrDASvc");
```

- To listen for a connection from one particular device in the network, create an instance of *System.Net.IrDAEndPoint*, specifying the device's ID and the service name string, and pass this instance into the *IrDAListener* constructor. See the section "Discovering InfraRed Devices with IrDAClient.DiscoverDevices" for information on how to obtain the device's ID. The following code will listen for connections from a device in the network.

```
// Discover up to 10 devices
IrDAClient irClient = new IrDAClient();
IrDADeviceInfo[] inRange = irClient.DiscoverDevices(10);
if (inRange.Length > 0)
{
    // Listen for connections from first device
    IrDAEndPoint endPt = new IrDAEndPoint(
        inRange[0].DeviceID, "MyIrDASvc");
    IrDAListener irListen = new IrDAListener(endPt);
```

The *IrDAListener* class works very much like the *TcpListener* class. Use the *Start* method to begin listening for incoming network requests. The *Stop* method turns off listening. *IrDAListener* can listen for more than one incoming connection. Each time a request comes in it's placed on an internal queue.

To accept a connection off the queue, use the *AcceptSocket* method (which returns a *Socket* instance) or the simpler *AcceptIrDAClient* method (which returns an *IrDAClient* instance). Use *Socket.Send* and *Socket.Receive* to communicate with the remote system in the former case, or use the *IrDAClient.GetStream* method to return a stream in the latter case. After finishing communication with the remote client, you must remember to call *Socket.Close* or *IrDAClient.Close* yourself because *IrDAListener* does not do this for you.

Both *AcceptSocket* and *AcceptIrDAClient* are blocking methods, so execution of the thread making the call blocks until the *IrDAListener* instance receives an incoming request. If you do not want to block your main thread, call the *Pending* method to see whether there are any queued requests. The *Pending* method returns *true* if connections are pending.

The following code example shows how to wait for an incoming connection and read the data sent by the client:

```
using System.Net;
using System.Net.Sockets;
⋮
// Listen for any connect request to our service
IrDAListener irListen = new IrDAListener("MyIrDASvc");
IrDAClient client = null;
System.IO.Stream stream = null;
int bytesRead = 0;
byte[] buffer = new byte[128];

try
{
    irListen.Start();
    client = listener.AcceptIrDAClient(); //This call blocks
    stream = client.GetStream();

    bytesRead = stream.Read(buffer, 0, buffer.Length);
}
finally
{
    if (!(stream == null))
        stream.Close();
    if (!(client == null))
        client.Close();
}
```

Making Infrared Connections with *IrDAClient*

To make a connection to an infrared service, you call the *IrDAClient.Connect* method, using one of the two overloads that give you the choice of connecting using a particular service-name string or to call *Connect* passing an instance of *IrDAEndPoint* specifying the Device ID of a particular device and the service name. Then call *GetStream* to get the underlying *Stream* object, which you can use to read and write messages.

The following IrDAClient sample uses *IrDAClient.DiscoverDevices* to list nearby infrared devices, then uses *IrDAClient.Connect* to connect to a service with the name "basic_irda_server", next sends it a short message, and finally receives a response. The output of this application is shown in Figure 11-6. The server program is a Visual C++ program that runs on a desktop computer. Both the IrDAClient application and the server are included with this book's sample files. I am grateful to Michael Scott Heydt for providing this code; you can contact Michael at michael.heydt.wt01@wharton.upenn.edu.

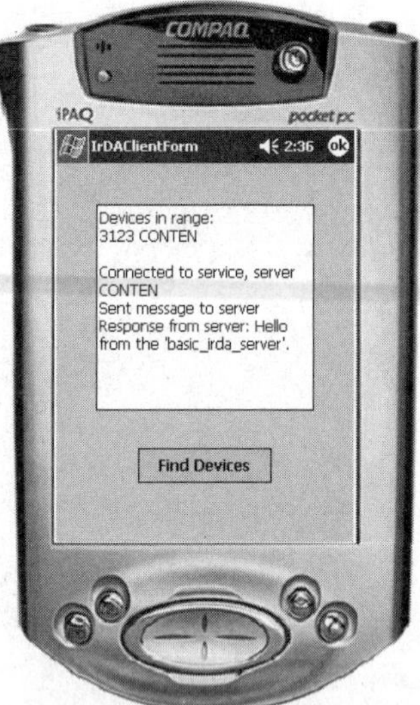

Figure 11-6 Pocket PC application that exchanges messages with a server running on an IrDA-equipped PC.

IrDAClientForm.cs

```
using System;
using System.Drawing;
using System.Collections;
using System.ComponentModel;
using System.IO;
using System.Net.Sockets;
using System.Text;
using System.Windows.Forms;

namespace IrDAClientSample
{
    /// <summary>
    /// Connects to Server on Windows desktop using IrDA
    /// </summary>
    public class IrDAClientForm : System.Windows.Forms.Form
    {
        private System.Windows.Forms.Button button1;
        private System.Windows.Forms.TextBox textBox1;

        public IrDAClientForm()
        {
            //
```

(continued)

IrDAClientForm.cs *(continued)*

```
            // Required for Windows Form Designer support
            //
            InitializeComponent();

        }

        protected override void Dispose( bool disposing )
        {
            base.Dispose( disposing );
        }

        #region Windows Form Designer generated code
        /// <summary>
        /// Required method for Designer support - do not modify
        /// the contents of this method with the code editor.
        /// </summary>
        private void InitializeComponent()
        {
            this.button1 = new System.Windows.Forms.Button();
            this.textBox1 = new System.Windows.Forms.TextBox();
            //
            // button1
            //
            this.button1.Location = new System.Drawing.Point(66, 221);
            this.button1.Size = new System.Drawing.Size(108, 27);
            this.button1.Text = "Find Devices";
            this.button1.Click +=
                new System.EventHandler(this.button1_Click);
            //
            // textBox1
            //
            this.textBox1.Location = new System.Drawing.Point(32, 32);
            this.textBox1.Multiline = true;
            this.textBox1.Size = new System.Drawing.Size(176, 160);
            this.textBox1.Text = "";
            //
            // IrDAClientForm
            //
            this.Controls.Add(this.button1);
            this.Controls.Add(this.textBox1);
            this.MinimizeBox = false;
            this.Text = "IrDAClientForm";
        }
        #endregion
```

(continued)

IrDAClientForm.cs *(continued)*

```
        /// <summary>
        /// The main entry point for the application.
        /// </summary>
        static void Main()
        {
            Application.Run(new IrDAClientForm());
        }

        private void button1_Click(object sender, System.EventArgs e)
        {
            IrDAClient irc = null;
            StringBuilder displaytext =
                new StringBuilder("Devices in range:\r\n");
            StreamWriter writer = null;
            StreamReader reader = null;

            try
            {
                irc = new IrDAClient();
                IrDADeviceInfo[] irDevices = irc.DiscoverDevices(10);
                foreach(IrDADeviceInfo irDevice in irDevices)
                {
                    // Display DeviceID as an int (is array of 4 bytes)
                    displaytext.Append(
                        BitConverter.ToInt32(irDevice.DeviceID, 0));
                    displaytext.Append(" ");
                    displaytext.Append(irDevice.DeviceName);
                    displaytext.Append("\r\n");
                }
                textBox1.Text = displaytext.ToString();

                // Connect to service
                irc.Connect("basic_irda_server");
                displaytext.Append("\r\nConnected to service, server ");
                displaytext.Append(irc.RemoteMachineName);
                textBox1.Text = displaytext.ToString();

                // Send message to server
                writer = new StreamWriter(irc.GetStream(), Encoding.ASCII);
                writer.WriteLine("Message sent by InfraRed");
                writer.Close();
                displaytext.Append("\r\nSent message to server");
                textBox1.Text = displaytext.ToString();

                // Receive response
                reader = new StreamReader(irc.GetStream(), Encoding.ASCII);
```

(continued)

IrDAClientForm.cs *(continued)*

```
                char[] buffer = new char[128];
                int charcount = reader.Read(buffer, 0, buffer.Length);
                reader.Close();
                displaytext.Append("\r\nResponse from server: ");
                displaytext.Append(buffer, 0, charcount);
                textBox1.Text = displaytext.ToString();

            }
            catch (Exception exp)
            {
                textBox1.Text = exp.Message;
            }
            finally
            {
                // Tidy up
                if (!(writer == null))
                    writer.Close();
                if (!(reader == null))
                    reader.Close();
                if (!(irc == null))
                    irc.Close();
            }
            displaytext.Append("\r\nDisconnected!!");
            textBox1.Text = displaytext.ToString();
        }
    }
}
```

Serial Communications

Many recent handheld devices support IrDA or Bluetooth wireless technology to connect to another device, but for many devices, such as modems, bar code scanners, and GPS receivers or printers, RS-232 serial communication over a cable remains the only option. Unfortunately, there are no managed classes to access the serial port on the device, so to do this you must use the native API in the underlying Windows CE operating system. Use P/Invoke to call out to the methods in the native DLLs. Chapter 22, "Interoperating with Native Code,"covers how to use P/Invoke, so we won't explain it here but we will show you the structure definitions and external function call declarations that you need. For a detailed description of how to perform serial communications in the Windows CE API, see *http://msdn.microsoft.com/library/default.asp?url=/library/en-us/wceseril/htm/cmconProgrammingSerialConnections.asp*.

More Info I am grateful to Michael Wittenburg for help with the information in this section. He developed the original Visual Basic .NET version of the serial communications library, which is included with this book's sample files. You are free to use the code in your own projects, but it is offered with no warranty or guarantee of any kind. He has written a number of applications using it, including the wonderful Pocket GPS.

Michael is happy for you to contact him with questions at michael@wittenburg.co.uk. His Web site is *http://www.wittenburg.co.uk*.

The following code samples are taken from the serial communications class library, which is included with this book's sample files. If you don't want to use this library and prefer to write your own code to perform serial communications functions, you must create a class library that encapsulates the calls to the Windows CE API. You need the following structures and external function declarations:

```
using System;
using System.Runtime.InteropServices;

namespace NETCFDevelopersReference
{
    public class SerialComms
    {
        # region Structures and Classes
        public class OVERLAPPED
        {
            public int Internal;
            public int InternalHigh;
            public int Offset;
            public int OffsetHigh;
            public int hEvent;
        }

        public struct DCB
        {
            public int DCBlength;
            public int BaudRate;
            public int fBinary;      ///* Binary Mode (skip EOF check)
            public int fParity;      // Enable parity checking
            public int fOutxCtsFlow; // CTS handshaking on output
            public int fOutxDsrFlow; // DSR handshaking on output
            public int fDtrControl;  // DTR Flow control
```

```
        public int fDsrSensitivity; // DSR Sensitivity
        public int fTXContinueOnXoff; //Continue TX when Xoff sent
        public int fOutX;         //Enable output X-ON/X-OFF
        public int fInX;          //Enable input X-ON/X-OFF
        public int fErrorChar;    //Enable Err Replacement
        public int fNull;         //Enable Null stripping
        public int fRtsControl;    //Rts Flow control
        public int fAbortOnError;  //Abort all reads and writes
        public int fDummy;        //Reserved
        public Int16 wReserved;         //Not currently used
        public Int16 XonLim;            //Transmit X-ON threshold
        public Int16 XoffLim;           //Transmit X-OFF threshold
        public byte ByteSize;          //Number of bits/byte, 4-8
        public byte Parity;            //0-4=None,Odd,Even,Mark,Space
        public byte StopBits;          //0,1,2 = 1, 1.5, 2
        public char XonChar;           //Tx and Rx X-ON character
        public char XoffChar;          //Tx and Rx X-OFF character
        public char ErrorChar;         //Error replacement char
        public char EofChar;           //End of Input character
        public char EvtChar;           //Received Event character
        public Int16 wReserved1;        //Fill for now.

    } // end DCB Struct

    #endregion

    #region Constants
    private const int GENERIC_READ  = unchecked((int)0x80000000);
    private const int GENERIC_WRITE  = 0x40000000;
    private const int OPEN_EXISTING  = 3;
    #endregion

    #region DllImports
    [DllImport("coredll.dll")]
    private static extern int
         SetCommState(int hCommDev, ref DCB lpDCB);

    [DllImport("coredll.dll")]
    private static extern int
         GetCommState(int hCommDev, ref DCB lpDCB) ;

    [DllImport("coredll.dll")]
    private static extern int
         SetupComm(int hCommDev, int dwInQueue, int dwOutQueue) ;

    [DllImport("coredll.dll")]
    private static extern int
         PurgeComm(int hCommDev, int dwFlags) ;
```

(continued)

```
[DllImport("coredll.dll")]
static extern int ReadFile(
    int hFile, Byte[] Buffer, int nNumberOfBytesToRead,
    ref int lpNumberOfBytesRead, ref OVERLAPPED lpOverlapped ) ;

[DllImport("coredll.dll")]
static extern int CreateFile(
    string lpFileName, int dwDesiredAccess, int dwShareMode,
    int lpSecurityAttributes, int dwCreationDisposition,
    int dwFlagsAndAttributes, int hTemplateFile) ;

[DllImport("coredll.dll")]
static extern int CloseHandle(int hObject);

[DllImport("coredll.dll")]
static extern int GetLastError();
#endregion
⋮
```

To open a connection to a serial port, use code similar to the following. In the next three code samples, the variable *handleSerialPort* is a *private int* data member defined in the class that contains the methods in these code samples.

```
private int Open(int port, int baudrate, byte parity,
    byte databits, byte stopbits, int txbufsize,
    int rxbufsize, int timeout )
{
    int intResult;
    int intHandle = -1;
    COMMTIMEOUTS lpCommTimeouts;
    DCB lpDCB;

    if (port > 0)
    {
        //----- open comm port and get handle to device
        intHandle = CreateFile("COM" + port.ToString() + ":",
            GENERIC_READ | GENERIC_WRITE, 0, 0,
            OPEN_EXISTING, 0, 0);
        if (intHandle != -1)
        {
            //----- Clear comm port rx and tx buffer
            intResult = PurgeComm(intHandle,
            PURGE_RXCLEAR | PURGE_TXCLEAR);

            //----- Get existing comm port configuration
            intResult = GetCommState(intHandle, out lpDCB);
```

```
            //----- Set required comm port configuration
            lpDCB.fBinary = 1;           // Binary, no EOF check
            lpDCB.fParity = 1;           // Enable parity check
            lpDCB.fOutxCtsFlow = 0;      // No CTS flow control
            lpDCB.fOutxDsrFlow = 0;      // No DSR flow control
            lpDCB.fDtrControl = 1;       // DTR flow control
            lpDCB.fDsrSensitivity = 0;   // DSR sensitivity
            lpDCB.fTXContinueOnXoff = 1; // XOFF continues Tx
            lpDCB.fOutX = 0;             // No XON/XOFF out flow ctrl
            lpDCB.fInX = 0;              // No XON/XOFF in flow ctrl
            lpDCB.fErrorChar = 0;        // Disable error replacement
            lpDCB.fNull = 0;             // Disable null stripping
            lpDCB.fRtsControl = 1;       // RTS flow control
            lpDCB.fAbortOnError = 0;     // Dont abort read/write on err
            lpDCB.StopBits = stopbits;   // 0, 1, 2 = 1, 1.5, 2
            lpDCB.ByteSize = databits;   // Number of bits/byte, 4-8
            lpDCB.Parity = parity;       // 0-4 = no,odd,even,mark,space
            lpDCB.BaudRate = baudrate;   // Baud rate (port speed)

            // XonChar may not equal XoffChar to prevent SetCommState
            // from failing. Pick a random character.
            lpDCB.XonChar = '1';

            intResult = SetCommState(intHandle, ref lpDCB);

            //----- set comm port buffer size in number of bytes
            intResult = SetupComm(intHandle, rxbufsize, txbufsize);

            //----- set comm port timeouts in milliseconds
            lpCommTimeouts.ReadIntervalTimeout = 0;
            lpCommTimeouts.ReadTotalTimeoutMultiplier = 0;
            lpCommTimeouts.ReadTotalTimeoutconstant = timeout;
            lpCommTimeouts.WriteTotalTimeoutMultiplier = 10;
            lpCommTimeouts.WriteTotalTimeoutconstant = 100;

            intResult = SetCommTimeouts(intHandle, lpCommTimeouts);
        }
    }
    else        // port <= 0
    {
        intHandle = -1;
    }

    return intHandle;    }
```

To read from the serial port, use the Windows CE *ReadFile* function. This method performs a synchronous blocking read, as shown here:

```
public string Input(int BytesToRead)
{
    string result = "";
    int intResult;
    ASCIIEncoding objEncoder = new ASCIIEncoding();
    int lpNumberOfBytesRead = 0;
    OVERLAPPED lpOverlapped;

    if (BytesToRead == 0)
        BytesToRead = 512;
    if (handleSerialPort != -1)
    {
        mbytRxBuffer = new byte[BytesToRead];
        lpOverlapped = new OVERLAPPED();
        intResult = ReadFile(handleSerialPort, mbytRxBuffer,
            BytesToRead, ref lpNumberOfBytesRead,
            ref lpOverlapped);
        if (intResult == 0)
        {
            handleSerialPort = -1;
            throw new Exception("Error reading COM1:");
        }
        else
        {
            result = objEncoder.GetString(mbytRxBuffer, 0,
                BytesToRead);
        }
    }

    return result;
}
```

To write data to the serial port, use the *WriteFile* function, as illustrated here:

```
public void Output(String Value)
{
    int lpNumberOfBytesWritten = 0;
    OVERLAPPED lpOverlapped;
    ASCIIEncoding objEncoder = new ASCIIEncoding();

    if (handleSerialPort != -1)
    {
        // Convert the string to ASCII characters
        mbytTxBuffer = new byte[Value.Length];
        mbytTxBuffer = objEncoder.GetBytes(Value);
        // Write to the port
        WriteFile(handleSerialPort, mbytTxBuffer,
            mbytTxBuffer.Length, ref lpNumberOfBytesWritten,
            ref lpOverlapped);
    }
}
```

These code samples give you an introduction to how you work with serial communications in a .NET Compact Framework application. The code for this chapter is available with the book's sample code and includes Visual Basic .NET and C# versions of a serial communications library as well as a sample application that reads from a device connected to the serial port, such as a GPS receiver. Figure 11-7 shows a Compaq iPaq connected to a GPS receiver with a version of Michael Wittenburg's GPS software running on the device.

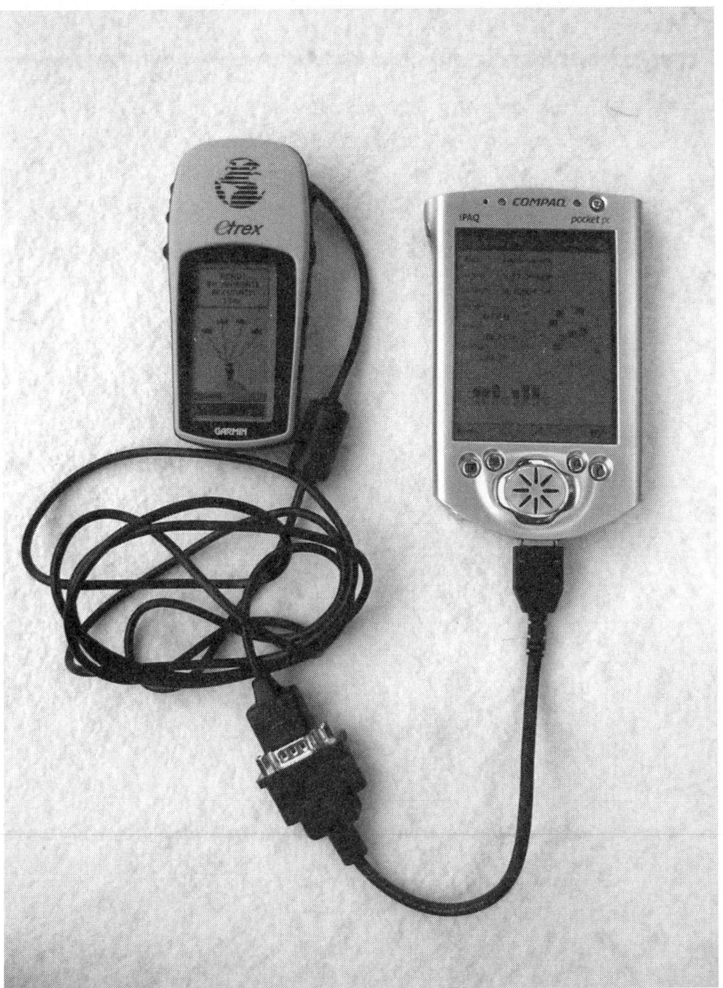

Figure 11-7 Compaq iPaq device connected by serial port and RS-232 data cable to a Garmin GPS receiver.

Summary

In this chapter, you learned about the classes in the *System.Net* and *System.Net.Sockets* namespaces. These include *WebRequest* and *WebResponse* and their descendants *HttpWebRequest* and *HttpWebResponse*, which make it easy to access Web resources using HTTP. The *System.Net.Sockets* namespace contains the *Socket* class, which you use when you want close control over network communications, and the less flexible but easier to use classes descending from *Socket*. These include *TcpClient* and *TcpListener* for TCP communications, *UdpClient* for UDP, and *IrDAClient* and *IrDAListener* for infrared communications.

The .NET Compact Framework does not include classes that provide managed access to the serial port on a smart device. This chapter provided you with an introduction to using P/Invoke to call functions in the Windows CE native API to allow you to use the serial port from a .NET Compact Framework application.

12

.NET Compact Framework Application Security

This book is a developer's reference book for the .NET Compact Framework. As such, it is full of explanations and code examples of how to write code using the framework, and you might expect that this chapter is only about secure coding techniques. However, writing secure code is only one part of implementing a secure solution. The security of your application is only as good as the weakest link, so there's no point in writing clever code in an application on the device, only to transfer data to a server over a network without using encryption or to keep the data on a server that is not secured adequately, where hackers can gain access to it.

Security must be considered right from the beginning of a project and designed in from the start. I expect that a number of readers will come to this chapter to "add some security" to an existing project—we've all done it! If you're lucky, you can add security to your application, but in many cases, ignoring security concerns during the design of a project can result in a major rewrite when you try to add security later.

Security is the number one concern for any enterprise considering deploying applications to mobile devices, with good reason. By their very nature, devices get taken away from the office, operate over wireless networks outside corporate firewalls, and, being small, are easily lost. Application designers who go to their managers with a proposal for a mobile application will not get very far if they do not have quick answers for these obvious questions:

- How do you protect our corporate data stored on this device so that if it falls into the wrong hands, a third party cannot read it?
- When a mobile device connects to our servers to download data, how do we know that our employee is the user and that the device hasn't been stolen and is being used by someone else?
- Are the wireless networks we use secure from hackers?

This chapter looks at security issues affecting applications you write and deploy using the .NET Compact Framework to help you to prepare the answers to these questions.

Considering the Basics of Handheld Device Security

Even before you start to think about the security requirements of a specific application, you should consider a number of steps to secure the device. First of all, any enterprise that wishes to deploy mobile applications should devise a security policy so that all users are clear about their responsibilities. This is particularly important because handheld devices were traditionally used only as electronic organizers, and in many cases, security concerns were not high on the agenda, which is surprising when you consider that devices often contain personal e-mail and contacts that could be valuable information to a competitor. The modern generation of Pocket PC and Windows CE .NET devices, coupled with software such as SQL Server CE and the .NET Compact Framework, provide powerful solutions for connecting mobile professionals with the enterprise. Users need to have a high regard for the security of the data stored on the device, and they need to ensure that the device doesn't become a route for access to the enterprise network, should it fall into the wrong hands.

Contemplating User Authentication

It is essential to secure devices with a strong sign-on password or some other means of user authentication so that only the intended user can use the device. Pocket PC 2002 and later versions come with a built-in power-on password facility that you can configure to require either a 4-digit PIN or a strong password, which must be at least 7 digits and must contain a combination of uppercase and lowercase characters and numerals or punctuation, as shown in Figure 12-1. The user must reenter the password after the device has been unused for a configurable interval, which defaults to 1 hour.

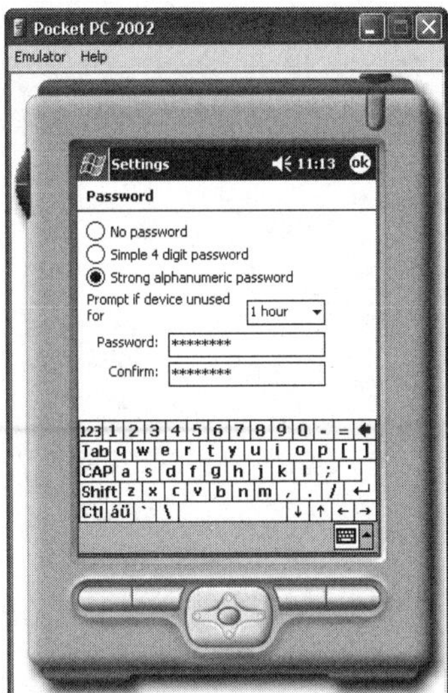

Figure 12-1 Built-in power-on password facility in Pocket PC 2002.

For companies that require stronger user-authentication measures, a number of third-party vendors offer user-authentication products, including:

- Signature recognition
- Fingerprint recognition
- Smart card security certificate authentication
- RSA SecurID cards

For a fuller description of the options available, see the whitepaper "Pocket PC Security" by Douglas Dedo of Microsoft Corporation, at *http://www.microsoft.com/mobile/enterprise/papers/security.asp.*

Using Antivirus Software

There have been no recorded viruses targeting the desktop .NET Framework at the time of this writing, but you can be sure that virus authors will turn their attention to this and the .NET Compact Framework before long. A virus can find its way onto a device as an e-mail attachment or hidden in some apparently benign application downloaded from the Internet. Once on the device, a virus can cause irritation or damage, or it might be able to wait until the device connects to the enterprise network, whereupon it makes its way into the corporate network.

Many of the big names in antivirus software, such as Computer Associates, F-Secure, McAfee, and SOFTWIN, have products available for Windows CE to prevent virus infection.

Employing Firewalls

Many handheld devices now have the capability to maintain an always-on connection to the Internet over packet-switched wireless communications technologies such as General Packet Radio Service (GPRS) or CDMA2000, a code-division multiple access version of the IMT-2000 standard developed by the International Telecommunication Union (ITU). Although constant Internet connectivity brings benefits to users, it also leaves the device more open to attack from hackers. A personal firewall, such as the one incorporated into the VPN-1 SecureClient for Microsoft Pocket PC 2002 and Handheld PC 2002 product from Check Point, protects against attacks that exploit always-on connections.

Securing Wireless Data Transmission

You can connect a handheld device to the corporate network using wired or wireless connections. For a few applications, you can equip your device with an Ethernet card and use a permanent connection to a LAN, but in the majority of cases, your device connects to the network wirelessly.

Many devices connect to the LAN using 802.11b protocols. Researchers at the University of California, Berkeley have demonstrated that the static shared-key Wired Equivalent Privacy (WEP) algorithm used to secure wireless LAN connectivity is easily defeated. Researchers are working on WEP2, which will plug the gaps in 802.11 security, and commercial companies have released interim solutions, such as RSA Security (*www.rsasecurity.com*), which has a patch based on a technology called fast-packet keying that eliminates the key vulnerability of standard 802.11b. If you're using first-generation 802.11b and your application requires secure data transmission, you must use additional encryption, such as a virtual private networking (VPN) protocol, or Secure Sockets Layer (SSL). Chapter 11 shows you how to use the *WebRequest* and *WebResponse* classes to access a resource using a URL beginning with https://, which encrypts data transfers using SSL. You can also access XML Web services over SSL.

Devices that are taken away from base connect to the Internet over a dial-up connection or an always-on wireless connection such as TCP/IP over GPRS or CDMA2000. You can use VPN and SSL to secure a data channel if your device connects to the corporate network via the Internet.

Using Virtual Private Networking

VPNs use encryption and tunneling to connect users from either within or outside a private network. Examples of such connectivity include:

- Connecting users to corporate networks from outside their private network through a public network (remote access)
- Connecting users inside a corporate network
- Connecting branch offices with the corporate headquarters' network or networks
- Connecting corporate networks to partners' networks (extranet)

Figure 12-2 shows VPN being used to connect in a secure fashion to the enterprise LAN by tunneling through the public Internet.

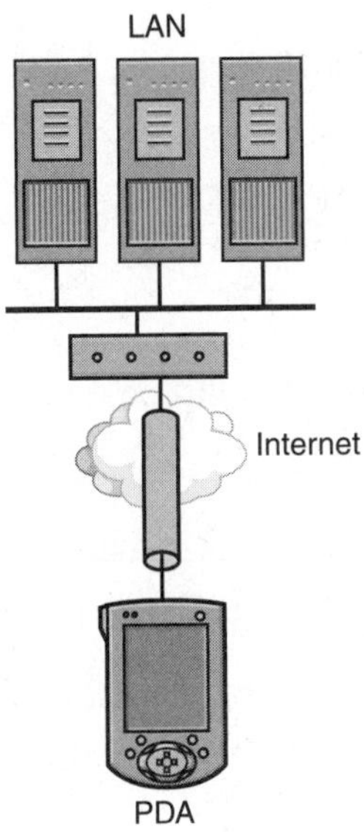

Figure 12-2 VPN used to make a secure connection to the LAN via the Internet.

Pocket PC and Windows CE .NET devices come equipped with Point-to-Point Tunneling Protocol (PPTP) for VPN connections. The device user must set up a connection to the Internet (or to the wireless LAN) and then set up a VPN connection to a VPN gateway in the corporate network. All VPN products require the client to be authenticated in some way, usually by a user name and password.

On a Pocket PC, you set up a VPN connection by tapping Start, Settings, the Connections tab, and then the Connections icon to display the Connections Settings dialog box. Tap the Modify button under Work Settings, and enter the host name or IP address of the VPN server, as shown in Figure 12-3. Now whenever you need to connect to a resource on the Internet, you can access the Connections Settings page, tap the Connect button under Work Settings, and then enter your user name, password, and domain name to make the VPN connection.

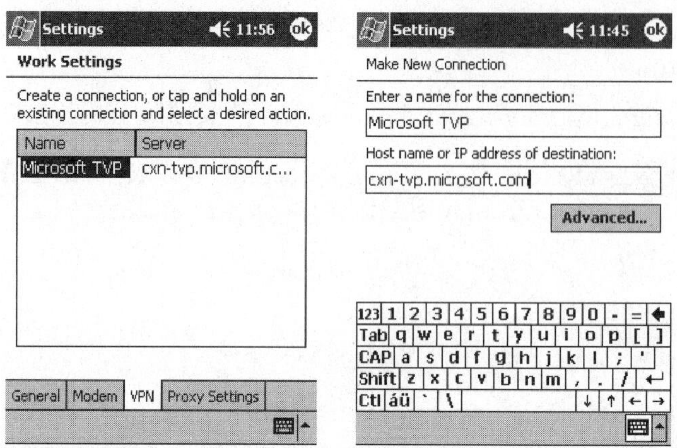

Figure 12-3 Setting up a VPN connection on Pocket PC 2002.

A number of companies offer alternative VPN solutions for Windows CE devices, some of which use IP Security (IPSec), which is an alternative protocol to PPTP.

Once a VPN connection to the private network is established, its use is transparent to a .NET Compact Framework application. You can use the *System.Net.Sockets.Socket* class to communicate with a server with TCP or UDP protocols, use *System.Net.WebRequest* and *WebResponse* to communicate using HTTP protocols, or simply work with files on a network shared folder. All data transfers are protected by the VPN encryption.

Using SSL

Windows CE .NET and Pocket PC 2002 and later support the use of SSL using 128-bit encryption keys. Support for 40-bit SSL is built into Pocket PC 2000 devices. SSL with 40-bit encryption keys give a high level of security but could be cracked by a determined attacker armed with a great deal of computing power and time. For higher security on Pocket PC 2000, you can install support for 128-bit SSL by downloading the High Encryption Pack for Pocket PC from *http://www.microsoft.com/mobile/pocketpc/downloads/ssl128.asp*.

In a .NET Compact Framework application, you take advantage of SSL encryption by accessing an https:// URL using the *System.Net.WebRequest* and *WebResponse* classes, as explained in Chapter 11. Unlike a VPN connection, SSL merely encrypts the data transfers and does not authenticate the client. Be sure to implement some form of authentication on your server, as described in the section "Authenticating and Authorizing Mobile Clients" later in this chapter. Your .NET Compact Framework application supplies logon credentials by using an instance of *System.Net.NetworkCredential* along with the *WebRequest* object, as explained in Chapter 11.

Preventing Spoofing

Spoofing is a technique that criminals use to defeat secure communications on the Web. The attacker sets up a server or a Web site that appears to be a bona fide site and that probably looks identical to the real site that it's spoofing. Clients believe they are dealing with the correct site, while in fact they are passing information to the attacker's site.

This technique is easily defeated using SSL by equipping your server with a valid server security certificate that is used to positively identify a server to a client. These are usually issued by a Certificate Authority (CA), which is a trustworthy, third-party organization, such as Entrust or Verisign, who issues a security certificate only after you have given positive evidence of your identity. If your server is dedicated to your application, you can issue a server certificate yourself using your own stand-alone CA, using facilities in Windows 2000 Server or Windows .NET Server. To find out how to install a server certificate on your Internet Information Services (IIS) server, log on to a server running IIS. Access IIS online help at *http://localhost/iishelp/iis/misc/default.asp*, and use the Index tab to locate "server certificates."

The server presents its server certificate to the client as part of the initial cryptographic exchanges, and the client checks that it has been issued by a valid CA, has not expired, and has not been tampered with. If these checks fail, a .NET Compact Framework application throws an exception. Windows CE maintains a database of trusted CAs. When a secure connection is attempted, Windows CE extracts the root certificate from the server certificate that the server presents and checks it against the CA database. If you issue an IIS server certificate using your own stand-alone CA, your root certificate is not present in the Windows CE CA database. As a result, Windows CE does not trust your IIS server certificate and an exception is thrown in your application. If you want to use server certificates that you issue yourself, you must either certify your stand-alone CA through one of the trusted certificate authorities or add your standalone CA root certificate to the Windows CE CA database. Microsoft SQL Server Windows CE Edition includes a utility (called Rootcert.exe) that can be used to easily add certificates to a Windows CE device. See the Microsoft Knowledge Base article at *http://support.microsoft.com/default.aspx?scid=kb;EN-US;Q290288* for details on how to edit the registry to configure a new root certificate.

SSL also allows the use of client certificates, which a client can present to the server to positively identify the client. The .NET Compact Framework does not support the use of client certificates.

Authenticating and Authorizing Mobile Clients

In any client-server application, the authentication and authorization mechanisms you implement on the server to verify the identity of the client application are crucial to security. Authentication is the process of identifying the client that makes the request. Once the client is identified, authorization is the process of determining what that client is allowed to do. Authorization is controlled by mechanisms such as NTFS file permissions and SQL Server permissions.

In most cases, the server is an IIS server, so you use the authentication mechanisms built into IIS. The following connectivity solutions all work through IIS:

- Connecting to an XML Web service on a Windows server
- Using SQL Server CE Remote Data Access (RDA)
- Using SQL Server CE merge replication
- Using SQL XML Support to access SQL Server using XML over HTTP
- Connecting to an IIS Web site with the *System.Net.WebRequest* and *WebResponse* classes

Digest Authentication, Kerberos Authentication, and Client Certificate Authentication are not supported on Windows CE devices. This leaves the following three forms of IIS authentication that you can use:

- **Anonymous Authentication** This actually means no authentication at all, at least as far as IIS is concerned. IIS allows all connections and logs in the user under the IIS anonymous Windows account, which is named IUSR_*computername* by default.

- **Basic Authentication** The client must supply a valid Windows user name and password. IIS attempts a user logon using the supplied user name and password, and if successful, subsequent operations are authorized based on that Windows user identity.

> **Warning** In Basic Authentication, the user name and password pass over the network in base64 encoding. This poses a security risk because it is easily decoded if intercepted by an eavesdropper.
>
> If you are using Basic Authentication, you should always use SSL encryption as well because it protects the user name and password exchange. Basic Authentication plus SSL is the most widely used method for secure, authenticated data transmissions over the Internet.

- **Integrated Windows Authentication** This method also requires a valid user name and password from the client and operates in the same way as Basic Authentication. However, the user name and password exchange are encrypted, so they are safe from eavesdroppers. However, this authentication method cannot operate through firewalls or over a proxy server, so it is only appropriate for intranet applications and should not be implemented for users connecting over the Internet (apart from those connecting over a VPN through the Internet).

You select the required form of authentication in IIS by opening the Windows Control Panel, selecting the Performance and Maintenance category (Windows XP only), clicking Administrative Tools, and then clicking Internet Information Services. This opens the IIS Microsoft Management Console (MMC) plug-in. In the left pane of that window, navigate to the Web site or Web service you want to configure, right-click it, and select Properties. In the Properties window, click the Directory Security tab and then click the Edit button in the Anonymous Access And Authentication Control section, as shown in Figure 12-4. If the Anonymous Access check box is selected, any settings in the lower half of the Authentication Method window are overridden. For Basic or Integrated Authentication, clear the Anonymous Access check box and check either Basic Authentication or Integrated Windows Authentication.

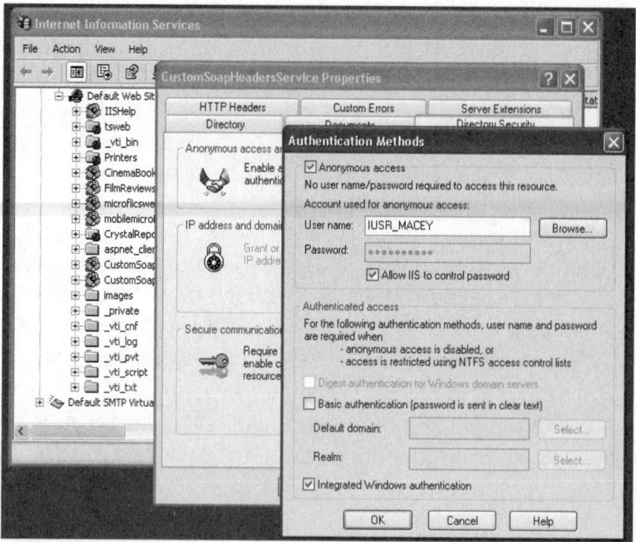

Figure 12-4 Configuring authentication in the IIS MMC.

Supplying Logon Credentials in .NET Compact Framework Applications

As explained in Chapter 11, when using the *System.Net.WebRequest* class, you supply logon credentials in a *NetworkCredential* instance and attach it to the *WebRequest* object to supply logon credentials.

```
WebRequest req = WebRequest.Create(url);
NetworkCredential creds =
    new NetworkCredential("andy", "pA55w0rd", "");
req.Credentials = creds;
WebResponse result = req.GetResponse();
⋮
```

When logging on to a resource that requires Basic Authentication, you need only supply a user name and password. If logging on to a site configured for Integrated Windows Authentication and your machine is in a network domain, you also supply the domain name in the third parameter of the *NetworkCredential* constructor.

The preceding piece of sample code uses string literals for the user name and password to keep the example simple. In practice, you should read this data from an external source and not store this kind of data inside your program code. See "Storing User Names and Passwords in Code" later in this chapter for recommendations on good practice.

Depending on the requirements of your application, you can choose to have a single sign-on account for all mobile users of the applications, or you might need to identify each mobile user uniquely, in which case each mobile user must sign on to their own Windows user account. If you set up a single sign-on account for all mobile users, the user name and password to be used with the *NetworkCredential* object can be written into the code, as in the preceding code fragment. If you choose to identify each mobile user uniquely, the user name and password must be set for each device and stored securely. As long as the device is secured with a strong power-on password or some other means of user authentication, you can store the user name and password in clear text in a file. For additional safeguards, you might want to store this data in an encrypted form on the device, as explained in the section "Securing Data on the Device" later in this chapter.

Giving Mobile Users Appropriate Authorization

Once mobile applications making network requests are authenticated, they must be authorized to carry out the requested task. As described already, an authenticated user logs on to your Windows server with a particular Windows user identity. You can configure that user account to be in different Windows logon groups associated with different levels of privilege. Do not put your mobile users in the Administrators group because that group grants more privilege than mobile users probably require to perform the function required for your application. You should always strive to give all users the minimum level of authorization required to carry out their functions.

For example, if the mobile user calls an XML Web service, the user logs on to the IIS server as a particular Windows user. If a Web method of the Web service accesses a SQL Server database, you must implement SQL access controls to allow the logged-on user to access the database. Do not put the Windows accounts used for your mobile application logons into the db_Admin group so that they have unfettered access to all data in the database. Instead, configure specific access controls so that users have access only to the particular tables (and even columns) that they need in order for your application to work. Configure read access by default, and allow modify access only if it's really required.

Securing XML Web Services

Applications you write with the .NET Compact Framework that access XML Web services do so over HTTP protocols. The mechanisms used for Basic

Authentication are actually a part of HTTP and not vendor-specific, so you can authenticate Web service clients using Basic Authentication whether the server is a Windows server running IIS or a server running other Web server software, such as Apache. You should use SSL to encrypt data in transit and ensure that it cannot be intercepted. If your application operates over an intranet and it accesses a Web service on a Windows server with IIS, you also have the option of using Integrated Windows Authentication to identify the client device.

When you add a Web reference to your Visual Studio .NET project for a Web service that requires authentication, the system will prompt you for your credentials, as shown in Figure 12-5.

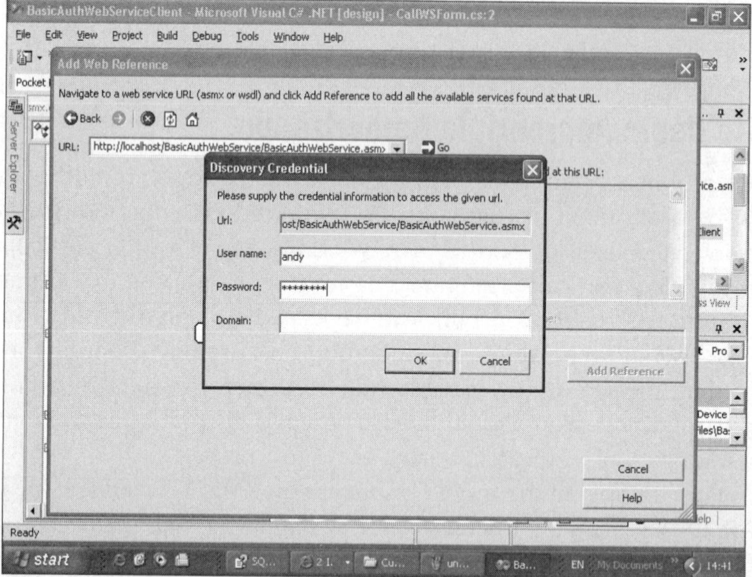

Figure 12-5 Visual Studio .NET asks for logon credentials during Web service discovery.

Visual Studio .NET uses the credentials you enter to download the Web Services Description Language (WSDL) file that defines the Web service, but it does not save these credentials in the client code it adds to your project to access the Web service. You must still create a *System.Net.NetworkCredential* object and set the *Credentials* property of your Web service proxy object, in much the same way as you do with the *System.Net.WebRequest* class.

For example, the following Windows Forms application contains two text box controls to accept a user name and password, a button that invokes a Web service when pressed, and a label to display the string sent by the Web method or to display an error message. The project has a Web reference to a Web service that has been set up to require Basic Authentication. The Web service contains a single Web method, which has the following code:

```
[WebMethod]
public string HelloWorld()
{
    return "Hello authenticated user! Your username: "
        + System.Threading.Thread.CurrentPrincipal.Identity.Name;
}
```

The code for the *button1_Click* event is:

```
private void button1_Click(object sender, System.EventArgs e)
{
    BasicAuthWebService ws = new BasicAuthWebService();
    // Create a NetworkCredential object with the username
    // and password as entered in the Textbox controls
    NetworkCredential creds = new NetworkCredential(
        UsernameTextBox.Text, PasswordTextBox.Text);
    // Use this NetworkCredential object with the Web service proxy
    ws.Credentials = creds;

    try
    {
        ResponseLabel.Text = ws.HelloWorld();
    }
    catch (Exception exp)
    {
        ResponseLabel.Text = exp.Message;
    }
}
```

The *button1_Click* method creates a new instance of the Web service proxy class, *BasicAuthWebService*. It then creates a *NetworkCredential* object and sets the *Credentials* property of the Web service proxy class instance to that object. When the user enters an incorrect user name and/or password, the call to the Web method throws an exception, with the message "The remote server returned an error: (401) Unauthorized," as shown in Figure 12-6. If valid credentials are entered, the Web service returns a string that identifies the Windows user account that the user has logged on with, as shown in Figure 12-7.

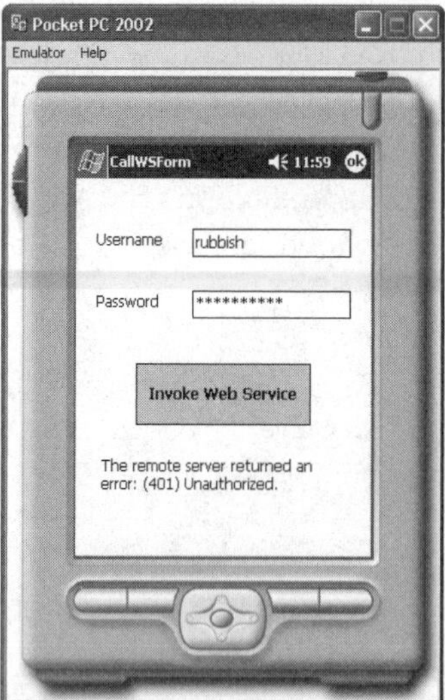

Figure 12-6 Pocket PC 2002 showing the error that the server returns if invalid logon credentials are passed.

Figure 12-7 Pocket PC 2002 showing the string that the *HelloWorld* Web method of *BasicAuthWebService* returns.

Using Custom Authentication with SOAP Headers

Another option is to pass data in the SOAP headers along with your XML Web services request. If you use this process, you do not implement authentication and authorization using the facilities of the IIS server, but instead you pass this information in code in your Web method. Consequently, this approach works with servers from any vendor. If you are using an IIS server, you should set the IIS authentication to Anonymous Authentication.

To write a Web service using ASP.NET that requires a SOAP header to be present, you first define a class that derives from *System.Web.Services.Protocols.SoapHeader*, which defines the object to be passed in the SOAP header. Then you declare a public field of that type inside your Web service class.

```
using System;
using System.ComponentModel;
using System.Web;
using System.Web.Services;
using System.Web.Services.Protocols;

namespace NETCFDevelopersReference
{

    // AuthHeader class extends from SoapHeader
    public class AuthHeader : SoapHeader
    {
        public string Username;
        public string Password;
    }

    /// <summary>
    /// SOAPheaderService will contain a Web method that requires that an
    /// AuthHeader object be passed in the SOAP headers.
    /// </summary>
    public class SOAPheaderService : System.Web.Services.WebService
    {
        // Declare a public field of type AuthHeader, which becomes
        // part of the Web service contract
        public AuthHeader AuthToken;
        ⋮
    }
}
```

Then, for any Web method where you require the client to pass an *AuthHeader* object in the SOAP headers, decorate the method with a *SoapHeader* attribute. The first parameter is the name of the public field in the class that defines the type of the header.

```
[WebMethod(Description=
    "This method requires a custom soap header set by the caller")]
[SoapHeader("AuthToken", Direction=SoapHeaderDirection.In)]
public bool Authenticate()
{
    // Check for header
    if (AuthToken == null)
    {
        throw new Exception("AuthHeader not passed in SOAP headers");
    }

    // Code to authenticate a user using the AuthToken object.
    // In this simple example, we just look for hard coded values
    // but a real application might look users up in a database or
    // use some other form of authentication.
    if (AuthToken.Username == "andy" & AuthToken.Password == "P455w0rd")
        return true;
    else
        return false;
}
```

In this example, the second parameter sets the *Direction* property of the *SoapHeaderAttribute* object, which takes a *SoapHeaderDirection* enumeration, which has the values shown in Table 12-1.

Table 12-1 *SoapHeaderDirection* Enumeration

***SoapHeaderDirection* Member**	**Description**
In	The header is sent from client to server.
InOut	The header is sent to both the server and to the client.
Out	The header is sent from server to client only.
Fault	The header is sent to the client only when the XML Web service method throws an exception.

SoapHeaderAttribute can be used to decorate methods in an XML Web service, as shown in the last code example, and it can also be used to decorate methods in the proxy class used on the client side. In this case, *SoapHeaderDirection.Fault* is not supported—if the client-side method throws an exception, it is not propagated back to the server as a SOAP exception.

On the client side, the public field *AuthHeader* is exposed in the WSDL for the Web service. When you add to your project a Web reference to the Web service, the code that is generated includes the definition of the *AuthHeader* class, and the proxy class that is generated for the Web service contains the *AuthHeaderValue* property, which the client-side code uses to set the value in the SOAP headers. The client creates an instance of *AuthHeader* and then sets the *AuthHeaderValue* property to that instance. For example, the following method creates an instance of the Web service proxy and calls the *Authenticate* method of the Web service, passing an instance of *AuthHeader* in the SOAP headers:

```
private void invokeIt()
{
    // Create a proxy for the Web service
    SOAPheaderService ws = new SOAPheaderService();
    // Create the AuthHeader object for the SOAP header
    AuthHeader hdr = new AuthHeader();
    hdr.Username = "andy";
    hdr.Password = "P455w0rd";
    // Set the AuthHeader SOAP header to our AuthHeader object instance
    ws.AuthHeaderValue = hdr;

    // Call the web method
    bool response = ws.Authenticate();
}
```

This piece of sample code uses string literals for the user name and password to keep the example simple. In practice, you should read this data from an external source and not store this kind of data inside your program code. See "Storing User Names and Passwords in Code" later in this chapter for recommendations on good practice.

You can find a full working sample of this application in the *CustomSoapHeaders* project in the code samples for this book.

Securing SQL Server CE Connectivity

If you are using RDA or replication to transfer data from a back-end SQL Server to SQL Server CE on the device (as described in Chapter 17), connectivity is managed by IIS. Data that transfers between the client and the server are compressed for efficiency, but are not encrypted. If you use these techniques from devices that connect via the Internet, you should consider setting up IIS to use SSL, as described in the section "Using SSL" earlier in this chapter.

RDA and replication do not require the use of SSL, but you should use it in the following circumstances:

- If you configure IIS to use Basic Authentication. As explained previously, the user name and password used for Basic Authentication transfer across the network in a readable format, so you should use SSL to ensure that they are not visible to anyone eavesdropping on the password exchange.
- If you're using replication and either the SQL Server Publisher or Distributor relies on SQL Server Authentication. SQL Server Distributor is using SQL Server Authentication if the *DistributorSecurityMode* property specifies *DB_AUTHENTICATION*. SQL Server Publisher is using SQL Server Authentication if the *PublisherSecurityMode* property specifies *DB_AUTHENTICATION*. When SQL Server Authentication is used, the *DistributorPassword* and *PublisherPassword* are passed across the network in clear text form. This can pose a security risk if anyone eavesdrops on the password exchange.
- If you're using RDA and your application specifies an object of type *OLEDBConnectionString* containing a password. The RDA *Pull*, *Push*, and *SubmitSQL* methods require an *OLEDBConnectionString* parameter, which is passed across the network in clear text form. This can pose a security risk if anyone eavesdrops on the password exchange.

Securing Data on the Device

What about data stored on the device? You might think that as long as a strong power-on password is in use on the device, an intruder cannot read the contents of that device if the device is lost or stolen. However, passwords are notoriously unreliable as a means of securing resources because users have a nasty habit of writing them down on pieces of paper, turning them off, or setting them to something easily guessed, such as the first name of their spouse. Stronger user authentication measures such as signature recognition or smart card authentication (or other means mentioned in the section "Contemplating User Authentication" earlier in this chapter) can lessen the risk of data stored on the device falling into the wrong hands.

Using Cryptography on a Handheld Device

There are times when you want to encrypt a relatively small amount of data, such as a file, or even a piece of data stored in a file. The full .NET Framework includes the *System.Security.Cryptography* namespace, which contains classes that provide a managed interface to the underlying Windows CryptoAPI, allowing you to encrypt and decrypt files and data streams and to perform other operations, such as hashing, random number generation, and message authentication. This namespace includes a number of *CryptoServiceProvider* classes that allow you to use DES, DSA, MD5, RC2, RSA, SHA1, or TripleDES encryption algorithms.

These classes are not supported in version 1 of the .NET Compact Framework. However, Windows CE does support an implementation of the CryptoAPI, so if you need fine-grained encryption, you can use P/Invoke to call out to it and perform cryptographic operations that way. You can find out how to use P/Invoke to call out to native APIs in Chapter 22.

Another way of encrypting data on the device is to use a third-party security solution. Many solutions are available that provide options, such as CompactFlash storage cards with hardware encryption built in or software products that often combine strong sign-on authentication with encryption of data on storage cards, in RAM memory, or in e-mail. See the white paper "Pocket PC Security" at *http://www.microsoft.com/mobile/enterprise/papers/security.asp* for a description of some of the products available. The encryption of data is transparent to your .NET Compact Framework applications, but it ensures that if your device or a storage card falls into the wrong hands, the data stored on it will be unreadable.

Securing SQL Server CE Databases

SQL Server CE offers the following two options to protect data stored in a SQL Server CE database on the device:

- You can require that a password be supplied when accessing a local database. One password is created for the database being secured, not for each user of a database.
- Data stored in a database file can be protected using 128-bit encryption, which is fully supported on Pocket PC 2002 or later and on Windows CE .NET. To take advantage of this functionality on a Pocket PC 2000 device, you must download the High Encryption Pack for Pocket PC from *http://www.microsoft.com/mobile/pocketpc/downloads/ssl128.asp*.

To create a password-protected database, use the *password* property in the connection string. To create an encrypted database, use the *encrypt database* property in the connection string. Note that you can have a password-protected database that is not encrypted, but if you choose to have an encrypted database that is not password-protected, you must still supply a database password. The following code tests whether a database already exists, and if not, it uses the *SqlCeEngine* object to create an encrypted, password-protected database:

```
if (! System.IO.File.Exists(@"\My Documents\Traffic.sdf"))
{
    System.Data.SqlServerCE.SqlCeEngine eng =
        new System.Data.SqlServerCE.SqlCeEngine();
    eng.CreateDatabase(
        @"Data Source=\My Documents\Traffic.sdf;" +
        "password=mydbpassword;encrypt database=TRUE");
}
```

This piece of sample code uses a string literal for the database password to keep the example simple. In practice, you should read this data from an external source and not store this kind of data inside your program code. See "Storing User Names and Passwords in Code" later in this chapter for recommendations on good practice.

To access an encrypted and/or password-protected database, use the *password* property in the connection string you use with the *SqlCeConnection.Open* method. The following sample creates a *SqlCeConnection* object, opens it, executes a query, and then closes the connection:

```
using System.Data.SqlServerCe;
⋮
public void InsertRow(string Reg, string Location)
{
    // Create connection string with a password
    string myConnString = @"Data Source = \My Documents\Traffic.sdf;"
        + "password=mydbpassword";

    SqlCeConnection myConnection = new SqlCeConnection(myConnString);

    string myInsertQuery   = "INSERT INTO Cars(Reg, Location) Values('"
        + Reg + "','" + Location + "')";
    SqlCeCommand myCommand = new SqlCeCommand(myInsertQuery);
    myCommand.Connection   = myConnection;

    myConnection.Open();
    myCommand.ExecuteNonQuery();
    myCommand.Connection.Close();
}
```

After an encryption setting and a password have been assigned to a database, they cannot be changed until the database is compacted. To change the encryption and password settings, use the *password* and *encrypt database* properties of the connection string you supply to the *Compact* method of *System.Data.SqlServerCe.SqlCeEngine*.

Programming .NET Compact Framework Security

So far, this chapter has looked at how you safeguard a handheld device so that only the authorized user can use it, how you authenticate mobile applications that connect to your back-end servers, and how you protect data stored on the device. What about programming for security? The full .NET Framework has a robust security architecture built upon the following key mechanisms for protecting resources and code from unauthorized code and users:

- **Code access security** uses *permissions* to control the access that a piece of code has to protected resources, such as the local file system or other sensitive resources. Permissions are objects that the runtime grants to a piece of code. They represent access to a protected resource or the ability to perform a protected operation. The runtime looks at information about the code, such as the identity of the publisher, its source of origin, or whether it is mobile code that came from a remote Web domain, and then grants permissions according to the security policies set on the machine. You can add attributes to your code so that it requests a specific set of permissions, which should be only those permissions that the code really needs to carry out its function and which have to be less than the permissions the runtime would grant according to the machine's security policy. Requesting specific permissions protects your code from being misused by malicious code, such as a virus, to perform actions that you never intended. Administrators use configuration tools to manage security policy, for example, to state that code downloaded from a particular domain is trusted. Code access security, together with the policies that govern it, are referred to as *evidence-based security*.

- **Role-based security** uses credentials supplied by a user to manage access to protected resources based on the role or identity of a user. On the desktop, the common language runtime provides support for role-based authorization based on a Windows account or a custom identity.

The .NET Compact Framework has a security architecture that is similar to that of the desktop .NET Framework. However, the *System.Security* namespace in version 1 of the .NET Compact Framework contains only the *SecurityPermissionAttribute* class (and its parent classes), which is for use with code access security, and there are no classes for role-based security. The lack of additional security features in the .NET Compact Framework is due to the fact that Windows CE does not have the same concept of a specific logon user that a desktop Windows machine does.

In version 1 of the .NET Compact Framework, there is actually nothing developers can do to manage application security. A future version will implement more fine-grained support for security programming, but in this version the fixed security policy dictates that all code run effectively with a full set of permissions.

Understanding the .NET Compact Framework Security Policy

There are no security configuration files in version 1 of the .NET Compact Framework, nor are there any tools that allow you to create or administer security policy. In effect, there is a fixed security policy that states that all .NET Compact Framework assemblies belong to the All_Code code group and are granted Full Trust. (See the following sidebar for an explanation of code groups and trust settings.)

This does not mean that there is no security architecture in the .NET Compact Framework, just that code always runs with full permissions in version 1. Future versions of the .NET Compact Framework and/or implementations on different platforms will implement a stricter security policy, but since policy is necessarily platform-specific and domain-specific, it is not possible to predict which security requirements will be placed on code in future releases or on all platforms. For example, in the future, a telecommunications network operator or an enterprise could release a device running the Microsoft Smartphone operating system with a security policy that grants full trust to applications downloaded from its own Web sites but limited trust to those downloaded from elsewhere, in order to reduce the risk of malicious code being able to run with permissions on the device.

A Brief Introduction to .NET Framework Security Policy

An assembly receives permissions to access protected resources based on evidence about the code (such as its URL of origin or its publisher certificate). In the full .NET Framework, an administrator uses tools such as the .NET Framework Configuration Tool (Mscorcfg.msc) to administer security policy at any of three policy levels: enterprise policy, machine policy, and user policy. Each policy level consists of a tree of code groups. Each code group consists of a membership condition and an associated permission set. Permission sets are named groups of permissions. For example, *FullTrust* is the named permission set that includes all the individual permissions. An assembly is granted the permission set associated with a code group if it meets the membership condition.

The following list describes the four most common code groups:

- ***All_Code*** is the root code group in every policy level.
- ***My_Computer_Zone*** is the code group that applies to code on the local computer.
- ***Internet_Zone*** is the code group that applies to code from the Internet.
- ***LocalIntranet_Zone*** is the code group that applies to code from the intranet.

The full .NET Framework installs with a default security policy in place, and administrators are free to modify it using the supplied configuration tools. Those tools include the graphical Mscorcfg.msc, accessed through the Computer Administration applet in the Control Panel, and the command-line tool, Code Access Security Policy Tool (Caspol.exe).

In version 1 of the .NET Compact Framework, there is no way to configure security policy. All code belongs to the All_Code code group, which grants full trust (all permissions) to that code.

Employing Secure Coding Practices

Although you cannot programmatically manage code access security in version 1 of the .NET Compact Framework, there are still many things that the security-minded developer should keep in mind. Virus writers exploit weaknesses in widely deployed bona fide applications or use them in ways that were not anticipated by the designer. There are a number of things you should consider to avoid your own applications being used as an unintended vehicle for destructive and malicious actions.

- Be wary of user input. Any way that you allow user input into your application could be misused. Take the example of a database-driven application that accepts the name of an item in a text box and then constructs a SQL string of the following form:
  ```
  "SELECT * FROM cars WHERE Reg = '" + Textbox1.Text + "'"
  ```
  This works fine if the user puts in a real car registration number. But if the user types in **any' DROP TABLE cars** --, a more destructive result happens. This results in the following SQL statement
  ```
  "SELECT * FROM cars WHERE Reg = 'any' DROP TABLE cars --"
  ```
  which results in the deletion of the cars table from your database. You should use the *MaxLength* property of input controls to limit the maximum length of input a user can enter, and then use regular expressions to check that the input conforms to the expected format.
- If you allow users to save data in files, write code that restricts the allowable locations and file names. You don't want to allow someone to overwrite an important file or a part of the operating system. Note that the OpenFileDialog and SaveFileDialog controls limit users to working with files in the My Documents folder.
- If your application is highly sensitive and requires user authentication, consider asking the user to reauthenticate after a period of time or after a certain number of operations to safeguard against the device being snatched while it is in use.

If you develop libraries or applications that access protected resources, you should keep in mind that future versions of the .NET Compact Framework will have a security policy that is much more restrictive than the policy in force in version 1. If you plan for that more-restrictive environment today, you will need to make fewer changes to get your code to work when moving to a later version.

- Encapsulate code that requires high trust in its own assembly. For example, code that uses P/Invoke to call out to unmanaged code will require high trust. In a future version, you can use code access security to request the elevated permissions needed just in that assembly. Then the other code in your library or application can run with only the permissions it needs, rather than all your code having to run with the elevated permissions required by the code using P/Invoke.
- Utilize only the lowest-trust APIs appropriate to each particular problem. Although all code runs with full trust today, this practice will result in applications that require the least permission to run later on in a secure domain. It is always good security practice to run with the least privilege.

Storing User Names and Passwords in Code

The code samples in this chapter usually represent user names and passwords as string literals to keep the samples simple. This is not a good idea in practice for the following reasons:

- *Compiled code does not hide its secrets!* If the executable file for your application falls into the wrong hands, it's an easy matter for attackers to use the ILDASM utility supplied with the .NET Framework SDK to find out what classes, fields, and properties you have defined. They can then write a simple program to create an instance of your class and retrieve the values of any public fields and properties. Even if you store user names and passwords in fields and properties that are private to your class, they can use classes in the *System.Reflection* namespace to find out the values.
- *It's a configuration nightmare!* What happens when you change the user name or password, or when you want to have different user names and passwords for different clients? Do you compile a new version and reissue it?

Clearly, using static values for authentication data makes no sense, both from a security point of view and from a practical one. Instead, use one of the following solutions:

- Store authentication data in an external configuration file and read it in when required. If you store it in clear text, be sure that the device uses strong user authentication measures such as those described in the section "Contemplating User Authentication" at the beginning of this chapter. Alternatively, you can provide an additional layer of security by writing some native code to encrypt the user name and password when they are written to a file and to decrypt the user name and password when they are read from a file. Then your .NET Compact Framework application can use P/Invoke to call your native code module and retrieve the unencrypted data when required.

  If you use a clear text configuration file and rely on security measures at the device level to ensure that it doesn't fall into the wrong hands, be sure to distribute pre-configured configuration files to users in a secure manner.

- Store the data in a file on a storage card or a smart card, which the user must insert when he or she uses your application. For additional security, use a card that has built-in hardware encryption, or write some native code to encrypt and decrypt the data when writing to and reading from the file on the storage card.

- Store the data in the Windows CE registry. This has the advantage of making the data difficult for an attacker to discover. Its disadvantage is that the .NET Compact Framework base class libraries don't include an API to access the registry, so you will have to write native code modules called from managed code using P/Invoke to achieve this.

- Ask the user to enter the data at runtime. Beware, though—this can get irritating for users if they have to enter a user name and password frequently, so you must balance the security requirements of your application with usability considerations.

Avoiding Malicious Downloads

Code access security provides an effective barrier against malicious mobile code in the full .NET Framework. Under the default security policy, code that a user downloads onto his or her machine from the Internet does not have privileges to perform actions such as writing to the file system. No such barrier exists in version 1 of the .NET Compact Framework because all code operates with full trust. This means that your users could navigate to a Web site in Pocket Internet Explorer and click on a link to a CAB file, and the application in the CAB file will install onto the device. This has always been a risk with native code applications, and it remains a risk with applications that run in version 1 of the .NET Compact Framework.

Future releases of the .NET Compact Framework will implement a more restrictive security policy, but for now, the only action that an enterprise can take to avoid unauthorized applications being installed onto handheld devices is to install a centralized security management product. These products allow an organization to enforce how, when, and what a mobile device can access on the network and provide centralized management functions to automate the enforcement of an organization's security policies. Other products available provide centralized configuration management of an organization's PDAs, including automated software asset inventory that allows you to monitor which software has been installed on a device.

Summary

Many mobile applications are distributed in nature and involve software running on the device, data transmission over a network, authentication and authorization mechanisms at the server, and software running on a back-end server. Security is only as good as the weakest link, so you must examine the security of all components in a distributed application.

This chapter has explained how to use authentication mechanisms to control who is allowed to use a handheld device, how to secure data that is stored on the device, how to encrypt data in transit over a network, and how to authenticate logons in an IIS server. This chapter has looked at the authentication mechanisms you can use with XML Web services, including the use of custom SOAP headers.

The chapter finished with a look at secure coding techniques. However, version 1 of the .NET Compact Framework does not provide the fine-grained code access security available in the full .NET Framework.

Part IV

Connecting with Data

13

Accessing Data

The advent of mobile devices has enabled developers to create truly distributed enterprise applications. Mobile devices can execute programs that allow a user to input, save, and query data. If you connect a device to the enterprise over a wired or wireless network, you can transfer data to or from enterprise data stores, where critical line-of-business applications running on the enterprise's host computers can process it. For devices that operate in a mostly disconnected manner, you can upload data to the enterprise servers when a network connection is available and download new or modified data onto the device at the same time. When you disconnect the device from the network, applications running on that device can access the locally cached data.

As mobile devices have evolved rapidly over the past few years, so too have the application development tools available for developers targeting them. A variety of solutions are on hand for developers to use when designing and building distributed mobile applications. At one end of the spectrum of solutions, developers can elect to make use of simple file-transfer schemes using Microsoft ActiveSync. At the other end of the spectrum, developers can employ full database access to enterprise servers over the Internet using Microsoft SQL Server CE on the device. The Microsoft .NET Compact Framework gives you the means to implement a data access strategy in a manner that most suits your organization.

The different tools and application programming interfaces that are currently available represent a broad selection of strategies for transferring data between the computers holding enterprise data and the mobile devices running applications that consume and produce that data. This chapter examines some common strategies, outlining the technical advantages and disadvantages of each approach. The following chapters in this part of the book describe how to use the technologies that underpin these strategies in more detail.

Caching, Replicating, and Resolving Conflicts

In an ideal world, all mobile devices participating in a distributed solution would have guaranteed instant access to the most up-to-date data. However, network connections cannot be 100 percent guaranteed, particularly in the wireless environment, so applications executing on remote mobile devices transmitting and receiving data must be sufficiently robust to be able to handle abrupt and unexpected disconnections. The potential unreliability of wireless connections is due to many circumstances: bandwidth availability, geography, and possibly even the prevailing weather conditions, to name but three. In general, the more an organization is willing to spend on building (or renting) a wireless infrastructure, the higher availability it will have. Nevertheless, even with a reliable wireless network, it is still good practice to design applications that can cope with operating in a disconnected manner.

How and when data transfers occur between a mobile device and the enterprise's data stores becomes the critical part of many mobile applications. In general, most disconnected solutions employ a strategy of caching data, replicating any changes when a network connection is reestablished, and then resolving any conflicts that occur as a result. These three aspects of distributed data management–caching, change replication, and conflict resolution—are the major challenges that you should consider when designing a distributed system. They are fundamentally related, and the choices made when designing a system can have a major bearing on the scalability, security, hardware costs, and implementation of the solution. Let's consider each in turn.

Caching

The more data that is cached on a mobile device, the more memory it requires (many mobile devices provide the option of additional storage cards) and the more bandwidth it needs to download that data from the enterprise. For significant quantities of data, it might be feasible to download (and upload) data only when the mobile device is physically connected to the enterprise's local area network (LAN), although this situation might change with the next generation of mobile networks. (3G networks promise peak download speeds in excess of 100 Kbps.)

Data can be held in a variety of formats, depending on how the data is to be used and shared between applications. For securing data held on a mobile device, you might want to consider using SQL Server CE. If you are holding data in a different format, such as XML, you might need to encrypt that data to ensure its security both in transit to and from the mobile device and once it is located on the device. Chapter 12 describes how to secure data on Windows CE devices.

Employing Change Replication

Caching data can provide good local performance on the mobile device because the data is available immediately. Using a data caching strategy can also allow a mobile application to continue operating even if a network connection is unavailable. However, depending on the nature of the application, data can quite quickly become stale. Periodic updates of the cached data will be necessary at a frequency determined by the application and the type of data involved. For example, in a warehouse system, pricing information for items held in a database on a mobile device might need updating only on a weekly or even monthly basis. Information about product availability and quantities in stock would need to be updated much more often.

Database management systems such as SQL Server CE include good support for transferring data through the tools provided with these packages. Data from a SQL Server database residing on an enterprise server machine can be copied to a SQL Server CE database running on a mobile device using the managed version of the Remote Data Access (RDA) API available in the *System.Data.SqlServerCE.SqlCeRemoteDataAccess* class of the .NET Compact Framework. Alternatively, a SQL Server CE database can subscribe to publications made available by a SQL Server system located elsewhere in the enterprise and exploit merge replication for coalescing changes made by a mobile application back into a replicated Microsoft SQL Server 2000 database. The *SqlCeReplication* class is provided to support this functionality.

Ordinary file transfers can also be achieved using ActiveSync, although this form of exchange is very coarse-grained, operating at the file level rather than copying individual records or fields.

Dealing with Conflict Resolution

Conflict resolution is arguably the most technically challenging problem that occurs when replicating updateable data to multiple sites. As a general rule, the simpler the replication mechanism used to disperse data to mobile devices, the more work required in resolving multiple updates to the same replicated item. In the case of a SQL Server CE database, conflict resolution is performed at the record level. Automatic resolvers are available that use simple heuristics to determine how to handle multiple updates to the same records in a replicated database. SQL Server 2000 also enables a developer to customize the resolution process if the standard mechanisms do not meet the application's requirements.

When using ActiveSync to perform file replication, conflict resolution operates at the file level. If multiple devices replicate the same file, conflict is almost inevitable unless mobile applications access the file in a read-only manner on each device. You can perform the resolution process manually or by writing code to analyze the conflicting data and resolve the changes.

Avoiding Replication

For certain applications, where a device connects to a wireless LAN or to a wireless network operating in a benign locality where the wireless signal is rarely interrupted, the device is connected to a network most of the time. In this case, where the device has reliable access to the back-end server systems in the enterprise, you might be able to avoid caching and replicating data. For example, if a connection is available, an application can use direct access to SQL Server 2000. Direct access has the advantage of allowing the application to see the entire database held by the host computer in the enterprise rather than a local subset, and the data will be live (except for changes made by other mobile devices that haven't yet synchronized). There are, however, issues of licensing and scalability. An intelligent application that employs direct access should be designed to also cache updates made to records locally if the network connection fails. When the connection is reestablished, the changes can be replicated silently back to the host server, although this opens the door to potential conflicts, as described earlier.

An alternative solution is to make use of Microsoft Message Queue (MSMQ). Applications can post changes in the form of messages to a message queue. A receiving application executing on the enterprise host computer can read messages from the queue and perform any appropriate actions. MSMQ has the advantage of being able to operate connected or disconnected from the enterprise network. The underlying software arranges for messages to be transferred from the mobile device to the destination queue automatically once a connection is established. MSMQ works best for applications designed to operate in an asynchronous manner. The major drawback of MSMQ is that it is not fully integrated into the .NET Compact Framework. You can download and install the Windows CE Message Queuing SDK from *http://www.microsoft.com/msmq/*, but you will need to use the P/Invoke services to program it from the .NET Compact Framework. MSMQ will not be considered any further in this chapter.

You should not forget the potential of Web services for accessing remote servers over wide area networks (WAN) such as an intranet or extranet. Although Web services are inherently synchronous in nature, the .NET Compact Framework also allows you to build applications that can invoke Web services asynchronously. This is useful for maintaining the responsiveness of an application. Web service interactions can be slow, and a transaction with a Web service can execute on a background thread, allowing the user interface to continue handling user input in the foreground.

A further option is to implement your solution as a Web application, using a browser such as Pocket Internet Explorer to access an enterprise Web server. Visual Studio .NET provides the ASP.NET Mobile Web Application template for building Web server applications designed to be accessed from browsers on mobile devices that can operate over the Internet or an intranet. However, Web applications are dependent on a live network connection, so they are less amenable to network failure than an application built using Web services. Web services and Web applications developed using Microsoft Internet Information Services (IIS) as the host server can make use of the integrated security features available to the Microsoft Windows operating system family.

Synchronizing Data in Mostly Disconnected Solutions

Mobile applications can be classified as those that are designed to operate in a mostly disconnected mode and those that expect to function in a mostly connected environment. The following sections will examine the issues surrounding some common mostly disconnected solutions.

Synchronizing with ActiveSync File Replication

File replication using the ActiveSync software supplied with a mobile device is arguably the simplest way to transfer data to and from the device. Regular updates to this software are freely available on the Microsoft Web site at *http://www.microsoft.com/mobile/pocketpc/downloads/default.asp*. ActiveSync supports wired connections through the serial port or an Ethernet card, and wireless connections exploiting the infrared port available on many handheld devices.

Many Pocket PC users place their devices in the cradle connected to their desktop computer at least once a day in order to synchronize the Personal Information Management (PIM) data held on the device with that on their desktop computer. In addition to e-mail, contacts, and calendar items, ActiveSync software can synchronize Notes, cached Web pages for offline viewing, and other files. ActiveSync automatically converts files and documents created by Microsoft Word, Excel, and Access to a format suitable for the Pocket PC versions of these programs.

ActiveSync creates a new folder in the My Documents folder on the desktop computer, as shown in Figure 13-1. This folder takes a name of the form *Pocket_PC My Documents*, where *Pocket_PC* is the name by which the mobile device is known on that desktop computer. You can drag files into and out of this folder using Windows Explorer on the desktop computer. ActiveSync will synchronize the contents of this folder with the mobile device.

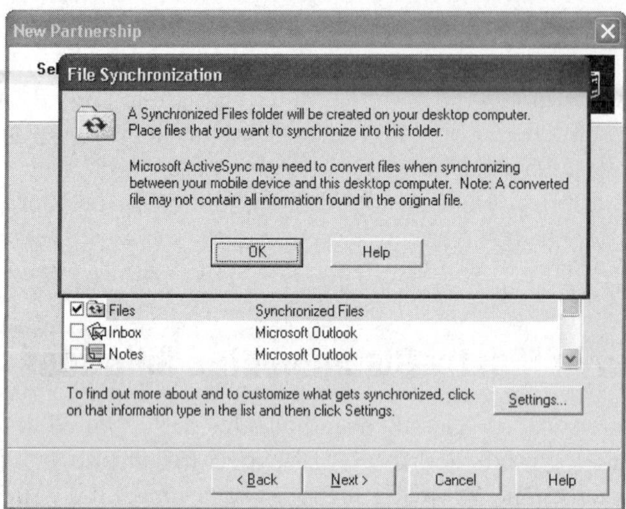

Figure 13-1 ActiveSync creating the Synchronized Files folder.

An application developer can use ActiveSync to transfer application data files; for example, XML files or files that use a custom format specific to a particular application. Applications running on the device can read or modify the data in these files. Although simple to set up, the primary disadvantage of ActiveSync is that once the data is transferred to the device and the device is disconnected from its desktop synchronization host, the data on the device cannot be updated with new enterprise data until the device is connected again.

> **Note** By default, a Pocket PC can synchronize with only a single desktop computer, so the mobile device is bound to a specific desktop host for any new data updates. However, you can transfer e-mail and other PIM data to devices using Microsoft Mobile Information Server (MIS). MIS works in conjunction with Microsoft Exchange Server. In this configuration, mobile devices synchronize with MIS rather than with a specific desktop host. You can place data files in custom Exchange folders and download them to a mobile device.

Where a mobile application simply reads data from files transferred to the device, such as reference lookup tables, this technique presents a satisfactory solution. If an application or a user updates the copy of the file (under the *Pocket_PC My Documents* folder) on the desktop host, ActiveSync will transfer the updated version to the mobile device at the next synchronization, overwriting the existing file.

The application on the mobile device can also make changes to the data in the file, and this requires special care. If the file changes on the mobile device but not on the host, ActiveSync will overwrite the copy on the host (under the *Pocket_PC My Documents* folder) with the copy from the mobile device at next synchronization. It is the responsibility of the application developer to write a program that executes on the host to ensure that the changes in the file are identified and processed to update any related information located elsewhere in the enterprise.

If ActiveSync detects that the copies on the host and on the mobile device have both been changed since the previous synchronization, it will not overwrite one with the other. Instead, it will report an "Unresolved Item" conflict. (The user can change this default behavior by modifying the synchronization rules in ActiveSync, but such modification is not recommended.) The user must manually resolve this situation. The Resolve Conflict wizard supplied with ActiveSync can help the user decide which version of the file should be retained, as shown in Figure 13-2.

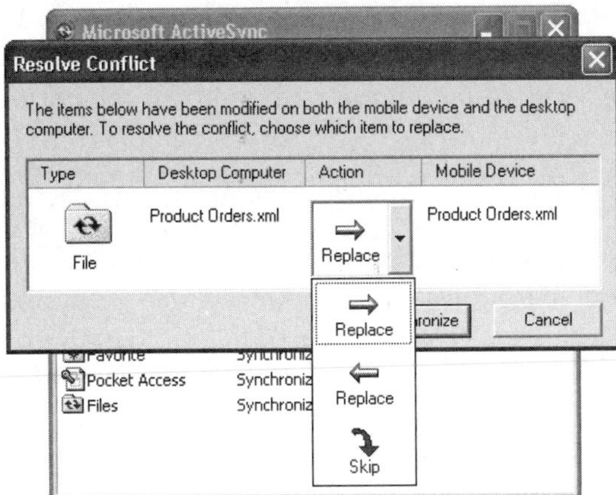

Figure 13-2 The Resolve Conflict Wizard in ActiveSync.

ActiveSync is most appropriate for data that does not require frequent refreshes or updates in the field, such as static reference information or lookup tables. For maximum portability, data can be transferred in XML format using this technique. You already saw in Chapter 9 that the .NET Compact Framework contains classes that allow developers coding in C# and Microsoft Visual Basic .NET to parse and create XML documents.

Much of the functionality of ActiveSync is made available through the interactive user interface. You can also control ActiveSync programmatically. However, the ActiveSync API is not available as a managed library with the .NET Compact Framework, so you must resort to programming in unmanaged C++.

Synchronizing with SQL Server CE RDA

SQL Server CE is a separately licensed product that provides SQL Server functionality and connectivity on mobile devices. (Each mobile device will require its own Client Access License.) SQL Server CE RDA provides a simple yet powerful way for a mobile application to update a remote SQL Server 2000 database or to transfer data back and forth between a remote SQL Server 2000 database and a SQL Server CE database stored on a mobile device.

RDA is Internet based. SQL Server CE communicates with SQL Server 2000 using IIS. By connecting through IIS, RDA takes advantage of IIS authentication and authorization services. SQL Server 2000 can be located behind a firewall or accessed through Microsoft Proxy Server. You can use RDA over LANs and WANs.

Applications built using the .NET Compact Framework use methods of the SQL Server CE ADO.NET managed provider in the *System.Data.SqlServerCe* namespace to control RDA programmatically. SQL Server CE comprises a small, but perfectly formed, database engine that runs on the CE device. The managed provider interacts with this database engine. The SQL Server CE database engine itself uses the services of another component, the SQL Server CE Client Agent, to communicate with enterprise SQL Server databases through IIS. IIS converses with the enterprise SQL server using the SQL Server CE Server Agent, as shown in Figure 13-3.

RDA supplies the functionality necessary for pulling data from an enterprise SQL Server 2000 database and loading it into tables held in a SQL Server CE database on the device. To save network bandwidth, data is compressed as it is transferred. An option of the *Pull* method of the *SqlCeRemoteDataAccess* class allows you to track changes made to data by applications running on the mobile device. You can use the *Push* method of the *SqlCeRemoteDataAccess* class to send updates back to the server for merging into the back-end data store. The details of programming RDA are covered in Chapter 17.

RDA also provides a way to execute SQL Data Manipulation Language (DML) statements that act directly on data in the SQL Server 2000 database located in the enterprise. (You can use RDA to execute any non-row-returning

Transact-SQL statement). RDA is most appropriate for performing data download from an enterprise database, as well as data capture on a mobile device and upload. (An application on the device gathers data and periodically sends the data to storage on a remote SQL Server 2000 database.)

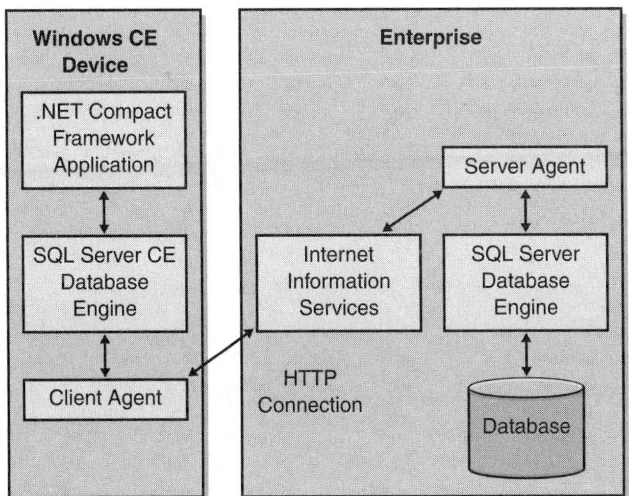

Figure 13-3 The architecture of SQL Server CE with RDA on a mobile device.

Configuring RDA is quite straightforward but requires access to IIS to create a virtual folder to host the RDA ISAPI library; a wizard is available with SQL Server CE version 2 that automates much of this process. Once configured, RDA requires a connection only when downloading and uploading data. At other times, the SQL Server CE database operates autonomously. Communication between the SQL Server CE Client Agent and the SQL Server 2000 database is performed over HTTP, so transmission through corporate firewalls presents no special challenges. As clients connect through IIS, one or more Web servers can be used to provide RDA services for mobile devices, so this solution scales very effectively. Note, however, that the SQL Server CE data engine requires around 0.8 to 1.3 MB of device RAM, depending on the CPU type used on the device, and you then need additional storage for database files. Additionally, if you use Per Seat licensing, each device connecting to SQL Server 2000 running in the enterprise through IIS requires a Client Access License (CAL).

RDA is simple to set up and to use, but its primary disadvantage is that there is no conflict resolution. A developer must implement additional logic on the server to avoid overwriting updates from one client with those from another.

Synchronizing with SQL Server 2000 Merge Replication

SQL Server CE merge replication is based on SQL Server 2000 replication; an instance of SQL Server 2000 executing in the enterprise can publish data that a SQL Server CE client can subscribe to. The replication process tracks information about subscribing clients and the data they have subscribed to. Data can be updated independently in the enterprise SQL Server 2000 database and on any subscribing client. Whenever a client resynchronizes, any updates made by the client are merged back into the master copy held in the enterprise SQL Server 2000 database. Any changes made to the master copy since the data was last replicated are similarly merged into the SQL Server CE database on the mobile device, ensuring that the client copy remains up to date.

SQL Server CE replication offers good support for wireless clients. As with RDA, replication compresses data transfers to conserve bandwidth on the wireless network connection. If a connection is lost, the transfer resumes at the point at which it was cut off once the connection is reestablished.

Replication uses a similar architecture to RDA. A replication agent on the mobile device communicates over an Internet connection with a server agent running on the IIS Web server. SQL Server CE synchronization will operate anywhere the device can obtain a connection to the Web server. IIS handles client authentication and authorization, and the data can additionally be encrypted using Secure Sockets Layer (SSL), if required. A SQL Server CE replication provider works with the SQL Server reconciler to manage replication and synchronization and to perform conflict resolution for SQL Server CE clients. When applications push updates back to the host server, standard or custom conflict resolvers determine how to handle conflicting updates. The replication process can also be controlled programmatically using the *SqlCeReplication* class.

As is the case with RDA, each mobile device acting as a replication client will require a CAL if you configure the SQL Server 2000 database engine executing in the enterprise to use Per Seat licensing.

Synchronizing Data in Mostly Connected Solutions

Mostly connected solutions expect to have a network connection available for a majority of the time. However, a well-designed, robust mobile application intended to function in a mostly connected environment should still be able to operate when disconnected, albeit with reduced functionality. The following sections will examine some of the options available for integrating data into mostly connected solutions.

Accessing SQL Server 2000 Directly

Direct access to SQL Server 2000 provides fast access to the entire enterprise database without requiring the use of SQL Server CE. Queries can be very direct and focused to the needs of the application; the application accesses data only when absolutely required (as opposed to cached solutions, which often retrieve data because it *might* be needed). The reduced need to cache data on a mobile device coupled with the absence of SQL Server CE can reduce the memory requirements of the mobile device quite considerably, although this is becoming less of an issue with higher capacity devices and storage cards (64 MB and upwards) becoming more readily available.

Direct access is particularly appropriate where the application operates in an environment where there is reliable network connectivity. If an application deploys handheld devices onto the factory floor or into other large facilities such as hospitals, for example, the devices might be permanently connected to a private wireless LAN. Direct access can be achieved using the classes provided in the *System.Data.SqlClient* namespace in the .NET Compact Framework.

A mobile application can also access SQL Server 2000 directly from remote locations over the Internet using a wireless carrier's network. To connect this way, you must configure IIS with SQL XML support in the enterprise. Applications make an HTTP request to the enterprise Web server, passing the Transact-SQL statement to execute. The Web server returns the results to the caller as XML. Applications concerned with securing the data transmitted between a mobile device and IIS should make use of SSL to encrypt the communications channel.

The primary disadvantage of this technique is scalability. This is a classic two-tier design, potentially presenting problems with scaling up if traffic volumes and the number of mobile clients increase. SQL Server 2000 executing in the enterprise should be configured with an appropriate number of worker threads to handle the anticipated traffic. Network bandwidth will also be at a premium due to the inherent nature of the exchanges between the enterprise SQL Server 2000 database and the various mobile devices.

One way of reducing network utilization is to make use of *DataSet* objects when programming with the .NET Compact Framework. A *DataSet* object acts as an in-memory buffer, located on the mobile device, of records from one or more tables in the enterprise SQL Server 2000 database. A mobile application can update the data in a *DataSet* object and post multiple changes back to the SQL Server 2000 database in a single network request. However, this solution requires additional logic to handle the possible conflicts that can occur if two mobile devices generate and modify *DataSet* objects containing the same data at the same time. Applications can also store uploaded data as a local file on the device, to be used if the device becomes disconnected, but this increases the complexity of the solution. For more information on how to use *DataSet* objects, see Chapter 14. As before, if you configure SQL Server 2000 using Per Seat licensing, each mobile device accessing the database either directly or through IIS will require a CAL.

Implementing Mobile Web Applications

In many ways, mobile Web applications are the antitheses of applications that cache data locally and execute on a mobile device. In a mobile Web application, the mobile device supplies a means of displaying and inputting data, but the application itself executes remotely, hosted by IIS executing on a Web server. Very little data or application logic is required on the mobile device; all that is needed is a means of rendering the information supplied by the Web server, typically implemented using a Web browser. Issues such as data replication and conflict resolution are greatly minimized because the Web application can be designed to access live data held in the enterprise. IIS can handle security. Licensing costs are also reduced because each mobile device no longer requires a CAL, as in the case of data being held in a SQL Server 2000 database.

The disadvantage of this approach is availability. If the mobile device cannot access the Web server for any reason, the application will not function. Furthermore, during peak times, performance might become sluggish because the network has to cope with the volume of traffic. Mobile Web applications are best deployed in environments where bandwidth and connectivity can be guaranteed.

Many mobile devices provide display facilities of varying form factors and input mechanisms that can be equally variable depending on the type of the device. The markup language used by different types of mobile devices can also vary. The full .NET Framework provides the ASP .NET Mobile Controls for building Web applications that run on an IIS server and work with browsers on a wide range of mobile devices. Use the ASP.NET Mobile Web Application project template in Visual Studio .NET to build Web applications that automatically generate the appropriate markup for the requesting client device, whether it is HTML, Wireless Markup Language (WML), Compact HTML (CHTML), or Extensible HTML (XHTML).

Using Web Services

XML Web services are distributed software components accessible using standard Web protocols. A Web service comprises one or more Web methods, which a client can invoke to perform some application-defined function. Data returned from a Web method is transferred as an XML stream over HTTP, and any platform that can parse XML can consume a Web service.

Web services can be hosted by an IIS server configured to use the .NET Framework and ASP.NET, or by suitably configured Web servers from other suppliers. As a result, Web services are accessible to any HTTP-connected client. IIS client authentication and data encryption techniques can be used to safeguard the security of the Web service and to ensure that enterprise data is available only to authenticated clients. Windows CE devices support SSL encryption to protect data as it is transmitted between the client and server.

The .NET Compact Framework includes classes required to invoke Web services and to parse the resulting XML data. Visual Studio .NET provides tools that automatically generate client-side code to access Web services in a .NET Compact Framework application on the client device. These automatically-generated proxy classes hide the underlying details of HTTP and XML, and they make a Web method appear like a regular, local method call to the mobile client.

Web services have many useful advantages over other forms of data access. XML Web services use industry-standard protocols, so no additional infrastructure is required, other than support of a regular Web site. Web methods exposed by Web services through client proxies are similar to remote procedure calls; they can retrieve or modify data located in the enterprise. The Web services model also allows the developer to offload computationally intensive tasks to the application running on a server inside the enterprise, rather than perform these tasks on the mobile device.

There are several disadvantages that need to be balanced against the advantages offered by Web services. Access to Web services requires an active network connection on the client. The format used when transmitting data is not as compact as other formats, such as the binary format used when accessing SQL Server 2000 directly. Bandwidth can become an issue if Web methods take or return large amounts of data, such as *DataSet* objects containing hundreds of rows. A Web method might take a long time to complete. To offset this, the Web service proxy classes generated by the .NET Compact Framework expose methods allowing Web services to be invoked asynchronously on a separate thread, while the main program thread carries on performing other application tasks. Chapter 16 describes how to create and consume Web services using the .NET Compact Framework.

Employing Other Network Solutions

Apart from the options listed in the preceding sections, developers and designers can also employ a variety of lower-level technologies to match varying circumstances, some of which are described in the following sections. For full details on these technologies, consult Chapter 11.

Working with Sockets

Sockets are a common network paradigm implemented not only by Microsoft, but also by most other operating system vendors. Therefore, sockets provide good cross-platform connectivity.

Other than a network connection, sockets require no additional system services to function. The primary cost is the development effort required; developers must build not only the software that executes on the mobile device, but also the low-level services that the mobile software communicates with in the enterprise.

The .NET Compact Framework can ease part of the development burden because it supplies classes in the *System.Net.Sockets* namespace that can hide some of the more obscure details of programming sockets. Similar toolkits to perform the same function are available for most enterprise and desktop platforms (including the full .NET Framework). However, the developer is still left with the task of designing and implementing the protocol to ensure that messages are exchanged between the mobile device and the enterprise in a manner and format that both understand.

Sockets provide very limited error-trapping facilities, so a reliable network connection is essential. The asynchronous capabilities of the *Socket* class implemented in the .NET Compact Framework make it relatively easy to design and build multithreaded applications that can send data or process data appearing on a socket while managing user input at the same time, leading to responsive systems.

Exploiting Infrared Light

Many mobile devices provide an infrared port that can be used to transmit and receive data over short distances (a matter of a few meters) at speeds between 2.4 Kbps and 16 Mbps, depending on the capabilities of the device. Devices and computers from many vendors support the Infrared Data Association (IrDA) standards, so this technique is useful for communication between Windows and non-Windows platforms. The .NET Compact Framework contains extensions to the *Sockets* library exclusively for sending and reading data through the infrared port. These classes can be used to facilitate the exchange of data between mobile devices. The code below shows part of an IrDA client application that connects to an IrDA service named *Greetings* and sends the message *Hello, World* to an IrDA server listening to the same service. The server sends a reply, which the client receives.

```
using System.IO;
using System.Net;
using System.Net.Sockets;
⋮
IrDAClient client = new IrDAClient();
client.Connect("Greetings");
StreamWriter output = new StreamWriter(client.GetStream());
output.WriteLine("Hello, World");
output.Flush();
StreamReader input = new StreamReader(client.GetStream());
string reply = input.ReadLine();
client.Close();
```

The following code fragment shows the complementary code for the server. The program listens for a client request, reads the message sent by the client, and sends a response.

```
IrDAListener listener = new IrDAListener("Greetings");
listener.Start();
client = listener.AcceptIrDAClient();
StreamReader input = new StreamReader(client.GetStream());
string message = input.ReadLine();
⋮
StreamWriter output = new StreamWriter(client.GetStream());
output.WriteLine("Message received");
output.Flush();
client.Close();
```

You'll find the full listings for this code in the IrDA Sender and IrDA Receiver projects in this book's sample files.

The *IrDAClient* and *IrDAListener* classes are located in the *System.Net.Sockets* namespace of the .NET Compact Framework, but they are not available in other implementations of the .NET Framework. Developers building software executing on desktop and server computers should instead write native applications using the IrDA extensions to Windows Sockets provided in the Microsoft Windows Platform SDK.

> **Note** To use the IrDA extensions supplied with the .NET Compact Framework, you must add a reference to the System.Net.IrDA assembly to your project.

Summary

In this chapter, we examined the various options available for accessing, storing, and manipulating data used by mobile applications developed with the .NET Compact Framework. We looked at the different techniques available for caching and replicating data, and how conflicting changes can be resolved. We also considered mechanisms for accessing data directly, avoiding the need for replication and conflict resolution, but noting the bandwidth and reliability requirements of such a scheme.

In the following chapters, we will expand on these ideas and look in more detail at using ADO .NET and XML Web services. We will also discuss integrating data with SQL Server.

14

ADO.NET Data Objects

A major part of most applications you develop is storing, retrieving, and updating data. The .NET Compact Framework provides data access by implementing ADO.NET classes with connections available to a central or an enterprise SQL Server database, to a SQL Server Compact Edition (CE) database running on the smart device, and to XML Web services.

First this chapter examines in detail how to use some of the basic ADO.NET classes. You'll see how these classes provide a simple and convenient way of representing, creating, and manipulating the data that an application needs. Next you'll see how some of the ADO.NET objects can be used to provide a locally persisted data store through their ability to read and write XML files. Finally this chapter examines support for data binding and for updating, sorting, and filtering data rows. Data binding is a powerful mechanism for displaying data from a local store in controls and for collecting the changes from the controls to update the local store, perhaps prior to updating a data source. This chapter also highlights differences between the way in which the full .NET Framework and the .NET Compact Framework implement the ADO.NET classes.

Recognizing the Advantages of ADO.NET

ADO.NET has been designed to support sophisticated multitier applications, which can use the Internet to connect together. ADO.NET is connectionless, is centered on XML, and enables data binding. Thus, ADO.NET is an improvement on previous data access programming libraries. The following sections discuss the advantages of ADO.NET in detail.

ADO.NET Is Connectionless

Connectionless behaviour in a database application is useful for mobile devices, where connection time is premium and where connections can sometimes be unavailable or cut off at any time. The objects in ADO.NET do not depend on live connections to a data source being held open continuously, as traditional client-server objects do. They can be created independently of a data source such as SQL Server. You can then connect to a data source for as long as it takes to obtain necessary data before cutting the connection and manipulating the data offline. When local processing and updating is complete, a connection can be re-established and the new data can be merged back to the data source. You will see later how the ADO.NET objects manage the detail of data version and status to ensure that the update process completes successfully. ADO.NET objects hold details of the update status and the different versions of the data to allow very fine control over the merging process.

Imagine an application for a travelling technician. In the morning, the technician would need to connect to a central database to collect the day's schedule of jobs. During the working day, the technician would need to record reports and observations using a smart device. However, due to the nature of the work, a connection to the central database wouldn't be available for these updates. At the end of the day, the central database would need to be updated so that clients could be billed and the schedule for the next day could be calculated. The disconnected nature of ADO.NET classes would allow you to program this application.

ADO.NET Is Centered on XML

XML is an internationally recognized language of data exchange. XML is also a text format, so it contains no binary information. As such, it can pass through firewalls, which generally block binary information such as executables and COM objects, enabling ADO.NET objects to communicate using HTTP over the Internet.

Another major advantage of holding data in XML format is the ease of data exchange it provides with applications installed on other machines and even applications written in different languages. ADO.NET objects are able to write their contents as XML to a text file or to a data transmission mechanism (for example, a *Stream* object used to send text to a Web page). ADO.NET objects can also write a description of the data they hold (known as a *schema*). The schema itself is written in XML and can be stored and transmitted. For example, a schema could be read back into a different ADO.NET object to re-create a data structure for input of new data.

ADO.NET Enables Data Binding

ADO.NET objects can be used to provide data to bound controls in the user interface (UI) tier of an application. They can also receive changes to the data from the bound controls, which means a developer does not have to program the mechanics of data display and local storage, and can concentrate on the application instead. Data binding allows very fast development of a UI that manipulates data.

Introducing the ADO.NET Objects

Central to the way that ADO.NET supports data-rich applications is the concept of independent but cooperating objects. You will see how many of the objects in ADO.NET can be created standalone and then added to a structure in which they can cooperate. This structure can be a hierarchy or one of the many collections in ADO.NET. Figure 14-1 shows a few ADO.NET objects cooperating with each other in a structure.

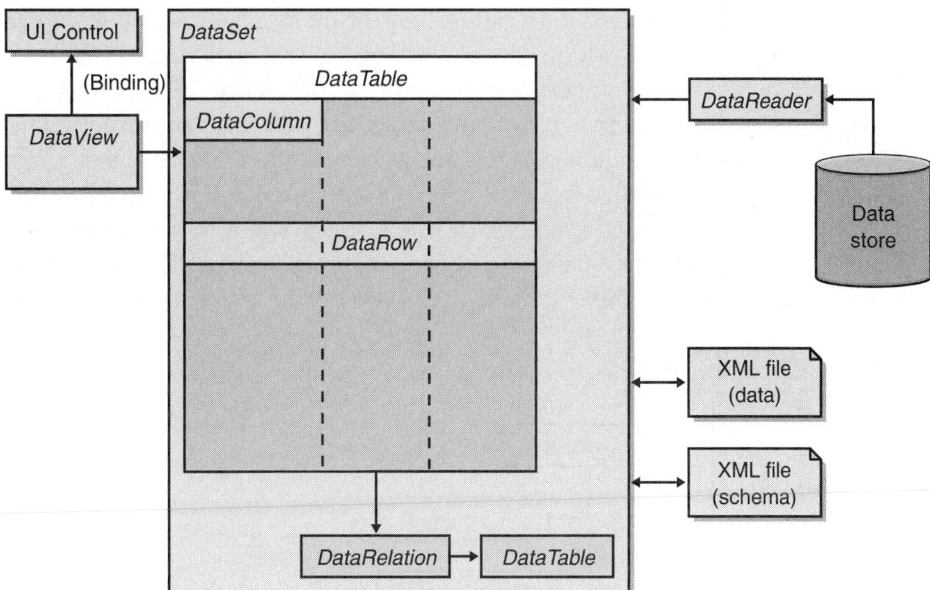

Figure 14-1 Some of the ADO.NET objects in cooperation.

The following ADO.NET objects are discussed in this chapter in detail, leaving the others for later chapters in Part IV:

- *DataSet*
- *DataTable*
- *DataColumn*
- *DataRow*
- *DataRelation*
- *DataView*

The following sections examine each object in turn, showing the role the object plays in ADO.NET and describing why the object is useful to the developer.

Understanding the *DataSet* Object

The *DataSet* object is the most important object in the hierarchy, and it is fundamental to the connectionless nature of ADO.NET. Basically, a *DataSet* object is a container for data being held in memory. This is crucial for a database application in a connectionless environment because it allows data to be cached and changed locally while a connection to a persistent data source (such as SQL Server) is not available. In addition to representing the data to the programmer in tables, rows, and columns, the *DataSet* object is capable of representing multiple tables of data in a structured and relational way that is familiar to database programmers. In this respect, it resembles the *RecordSet* or *Table* objects of other database programming libraries. The internal structure of a *DataSet* object uses collections of dependent objects, as Figure 14-2 shows.

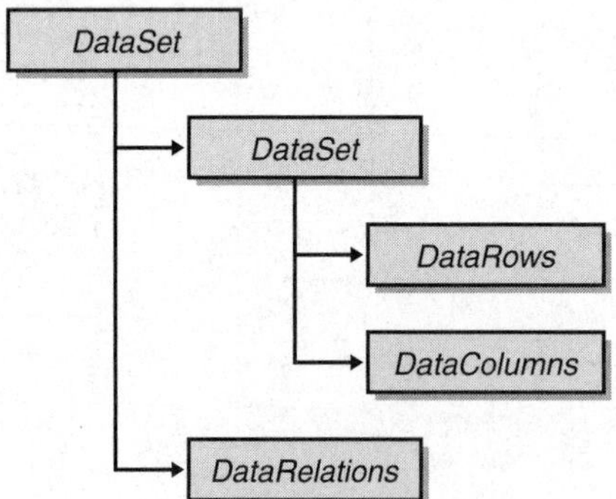

Figure 14-2 Some of the collections in a *DataSet* object.

When a connection to persistent storage becomes available, the local data in a *DataSet* object can be read from or written to a data source such as SQL Server using other ADO.NET objects that will be covered in more detail in Chapter 15. In addition, the *DataSet* object is capable of reading data from an XML source, and it can output its contents to XML. In the section "Saving a *DataSet* Object Locally" later in this chapter, you'll see how a *DataSet* object can also read and write its structure in XML format, which can be important when you need to create a new but empty copy of a *DataSet* object or when you need to verify whether some existing data is compatible with the *DataSet* object.

In practice, you'll use *DataSet* objects for containing and handling data in both the UI and business tiers of a distributed application. In their XML representation, *DataSet* objects can be passed between parts of an application, between applications, and even between organizations. We will see that *DataSet* objects can be created in code at run time and in various ways at design time.

Representing Data Tables

A *DataSet* object can comprise one or more *DataTable* objects. (See Figure 14-2.) A *DataTable* object represents rows and columns of data held in memory inside the *DataSet* object. It works like a database table, except it is all available at once and there is no concept of a "current row." The format of each column (data type, length, and so on) is represented by a collection of *DataColumn* objects belonging to the *DataTable* object. A *DataTable* object has a collection of *DataRow* objects, which you use to access the data itself and to control updates to the data.

Defining Relations with the *DataRelation* Object

If your *DataSet* object contains two tables, it is possible to define a relationship between them in code using a *DataRelation* object. For example, you might have a parent/children or assembly/components relationship to model in your application, such as a project that contains a number of tasks, as Figure 14-3 depicts.

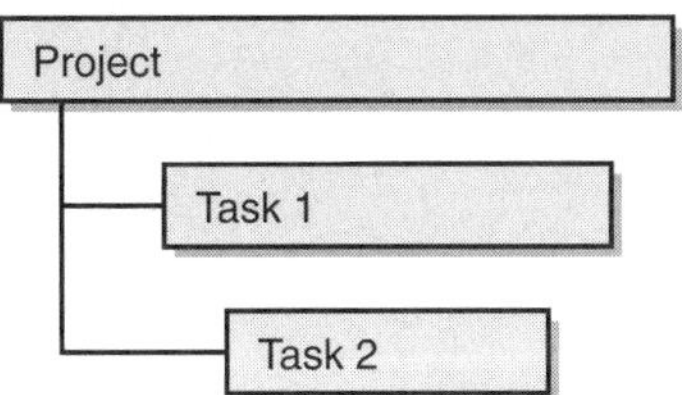

Figure 14-3 Example relationship—project and tasks.

The *DataRelation* object is set up in way similar to the way a foreign key relationship is set up in a database. It can maintain the integrity of the relationship by using constraints to force you to fill in the data correctly. So, for example, it can provide cascading deletes of all task rows when a project row is deleted, and it can help navigate the relationship to provide all the task rows for a given project row.

Understanding the *DataView* Object

The *DataView* object acts as a layer on top of a *DataTable* object. It can provide sorting, filtering, and most importantly, data binding. Sorting and filtering are achieved without changing the underlying data, and you can have multiple *DataView* objects providing views on a single table of data. Filtering can use criteria based on the data values and on the data row update status.

Building a *DataSet* Object from Scratch

The *DataSet* object is the core of data handling in ADO.NET, so the following sample will start with an in-depth look at the basic parts of a *DataSet* object. You'll find the sample application, called SimpleDataSetSample, with this book's sample files. The application starts out as a list of suitcases you have to remember to pack in the car to take on vacation. Figure 14-4 shows the main screen of the application on a Pocket PC device.

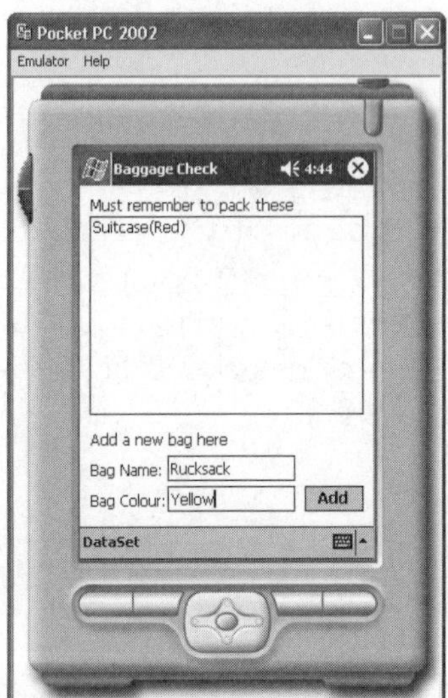

Figure 14-4 The SimpleDataSetSample application.

The SimpleDataSetSample application uses a *DataSet* object, which contains a *DataTable* object that represents a table called *dtMyBags*, which is structured as shown in Figure 14-5.

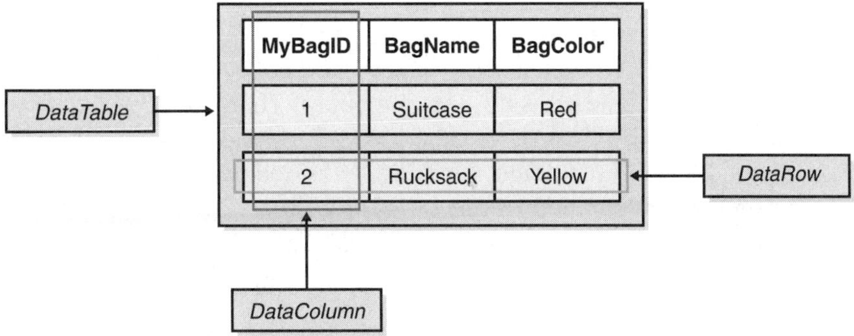

Figure 14-5 Representation of the dtMyBags *DataTable* object.

To create the SimpleDataSetSample application yourself, create a new project in Visual Studio .NET, using a C# Smart Device Application template, and choose the Pocket PC as a target platform. Copy the form layout shown in Figure 14-4, using four Label controls, one ListBox control, two TextBox controls, and one Button control. Name the Button control *buttonAdd*, the first TextBox control *textBoxBagName*, and the second TextBox control *textBoxBagColor*. The following sections will guide you through the creation of the rest of the application.

Adding the *DataSet*, *DataTable*, and *DataColumn* Objects

You need to create a new *DataSet* object with a single table called MyBags to record the different suitcases you might take on vacation. The table will record the name, ID number, and color of the bag. You will use the form to add bags to the luggage list. Add a declaration for a *DataSet* member at form level, as shown here:

```
private System.Data.DataSet dsBagCheck;
```

Now add code to populate the *DataSet* object in the form's *Load* event handler.

```
private void Form1_Load(object sender, System.EventArgs e)
{
    dsBagCheck = new DataSet();
    // Add some structure to the dataset
    DataTable dtMyBags = new DataTable("MyBags");
    dtMyBags.Columns.Add("BagID",
        System.Type.GetType("System.Int32"));
```

(continued)

```
    dtMyBags.Columns.Add("BagName",
        System.Type.GetType("System.String"));
    dtMyBags.Columns.Add("BagColor",
        System.Type.GetType("System.String"));
    dsBagCheck.Tables.Add(dtMyBags);
}
```

Now look in detail at the objects and collections in the preceding sample. First the code initializes the *DataSet* object. Then the code declares a new local variable of type *DataTable* called *dtMyBags* and initializes the variable with a new table called MyBags. Next the code defines the structure of the table by using the *Add* method of the *DataTable* object's *Columns* collection. The *Columns* property exposes a collection of class *DataColumnCollection*, and the *Add* method allows columns to be added directly, as shown in the sample.

Adding *DataRow* Objects

Now you'll program the sample application to add rows to the MyBags table when the user clicks the Add button. Here is some sample code for the *buttonAdd_Click* event:

```
private void buttonAdd_Click(object sender, System.EventArgs e)
{
    int i;
    DataRow drNewBag;
    DataTableCollection tablesCol = dsBagCheck.Tables;
    DataTable dtMyBags = tablesCol["MyBags"];
    i = dtMyBags.Rows.Count + 1;
    drNewBag = dtMyBags.NewRow();
    drNewBag["BagID"] = i;
    drNewBag["BagName"] = textBoxBagName.Text;
    drNewBag["BagColor"] = textBoxBagColor.Text;
    dtMyBags.Rows.Add(drNewBag);
    listBoxBags.Items.Add(textBoxName.Text +
        "(" + textBoxColor.Text + ")");
}
```

This sample code declares the *DataRow* object *drNewBag* and then initializes it by using the *DataTable* object's *NewRow* method, which ensures that the new row has the correct columns. Next, the integer *i* and the data from the *Text* property of each TextBox control are used to populate the columns of the *DataRow* object. The last step is to add the new row to the *DataTable* object's *Rows* collection.

Reading, Updating, or Deleting a *DataRow Object*

Notice in the previous sample how the *Items* property of the new *DataRow* object is accessed using the string key of the column. There is also a numerical index. You could read or update the value using this kind of syntax. To remove a row, call its *Delete* method, but take care not to try to access columns in *DataRow* objects that have been deleted, or you will get an exception. In the section "Tracking *DataSet* Updates," later in this chapter, you'll see that you can test a *DataRow* property called *RowState* to see if the *DataRow* object has been deleted. Here is a sample using the *Delete* method:

```
string strColor = drThisBag ["BagColor"];
drThisBag ["BagColor"] = "Red";
drThisBag [3] = "Red"; // Risky!
drThisBag.Delete();
```

We'll see again later, in the section "Tracking *DataSet* Updates," that there's a further step to commit (that is, to confirm) the changes in the *DataSet* object.

> **Tip** Note that no type checking is carried out by the compiler if you use the index to access an item in a collection (see the line marked `// Risky!` in the previous code sample), so it is important to ensure that the correct data type is assigned or you will get a run-time exception.

Finding a *DataRow* Object

The *DataTable* object has a *Select* method to help you find specific *DataRow* objects. You need to give the criteria as if it were part of a SQL *WHERE* clause but without the word *WHERE*. Here is a sample using the *Select* method:

```
string strCriteria = "BagColor = Red";
DataRow[] foundRows;
foundRows = dsBagCheck.Tables["MyBags"].Select(strCriteria);
```

The *Select* method returns an array of *DataRow* objects because you might get one or more matches for the given criteria. You must also remember to code for the possibility that no matches are found.

Viewing the XML Representation of a *DataSet* Object

Now take a few moments to delve under the hood of the *DataSet* object that you created in the previous sample. You want to see the XML representation of the ADO.NET objects that you have just created in memory. To do this in the sample, add a menu and a new TextBox control to the form. Cover the whole form with the new TextBox control (as shown in Figure 14-6), but set the control's *Visible* property to *false* so that the control isn't visible when the application starts. In the sample code, the TextBox control is named *textBoxXML*. Set the menu's text to *DataSet*, and add submenu items for View XML and View Schema.

You will use the *GetXml* and *GetXmlSchema* methods of the *DataSet* object to examine the object's data and structure in XML format. Selecting View XML or View Schema from the DataSet menu will write the XML data to the TextBox control and make the TextBox control visible.

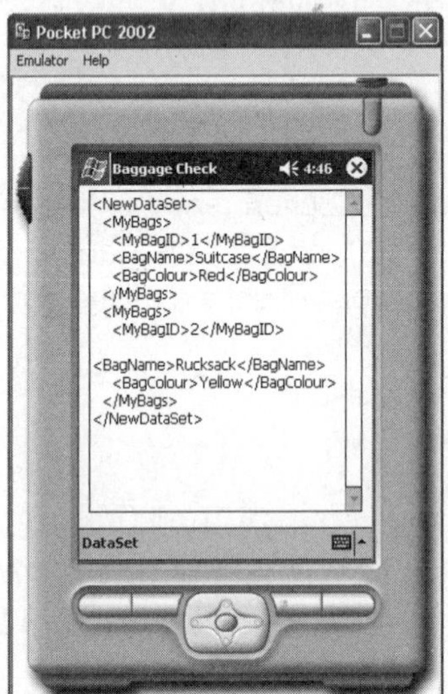

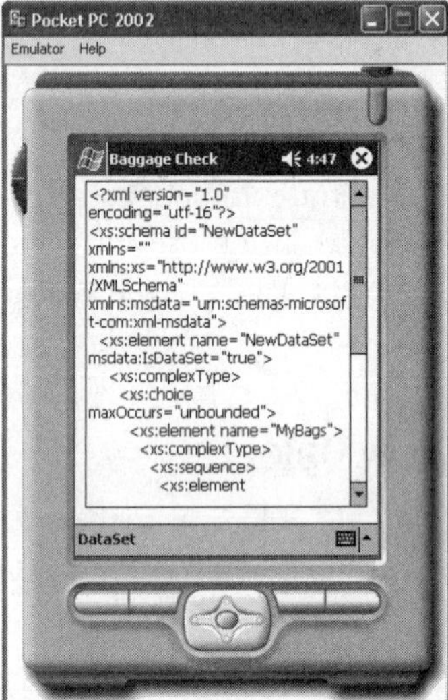

Figure 14-6 Viewing the XML and the XML Schema representations of the *DataSet* object.

Here is some sample code for displaying the XML and making the TextBox visible:

```
textBoxXML.Text = dsBagCheck.GetXml();
textBoxXML.Visible = true;
```

See this book's sample files for the rest of the code for the View XML or View Schema menu items.

Using Typed *DataSet* Objects

So far you have worked with an untyped *DataSet* object. An untyped *DataSet* object can be built dynamically at run time in the way shown in the previous sections. This might be useful when no schema is available or when the schema is very simple, as in the previous sample. But, as mentioned, filling an untyped *DataSet* object might result in run-time data-type conversion errors and errors caused by the key being invalid.

When using the full .NET Framework, Visual Studio .NET provides you with the ability to create typed *DataSet* objects. This allows you to define a *DataSet* object at design time that is stored as a schema file (.xsd). The availability of type information in the schema file allows Visual Studio .NET to generate a subclass of the original *DataSet* class that has type checking and direct-access properties for *DataTable* objects and *DataColumn* objects. So, syntax such as this becomes possible:

```
NewBagRow.BagName = txtBagName.Text;
MyDataSet.BagsTable.Rows.Add(NewBagRow);
```

If you have declared a typed *DataSet*, these direct-access properties (in the above sample, *BagName* and *BagsTable*) appear on the IntelliSense pop-up list when you're typing your code. However, you can't generate a typed *DataSet* object for applications targeting the .NET Compact Framework because, among other reasons, the code generator that creates the typed *DataSet* object creates code that needs classes from the *System.Runtime.Serialization* namespace, which is not available in the .NET Compact Framework.

> **Note** The lack of support for typed *DataSet* objects is an important difference between the desktop .NET Framework and the .NET Compact Framework because it will change the way you program, especially with a persistent data source such SQL Server or with an XML Web service. For details, refer to Chapter 15 and Chapter 16 of this book.

Creating a *DataSet* Object with the DataSet Designer

Now let's revisit the previous sample, but let's use the DataSet Designer to draw out the MyBags *DataTable* object and its *DataColumn* objects. You'll find the sample application, called DesignedDataSetSample, with this book's sample files.

> **Note** The XML Schema template is not available for Smart Device Application projects, but that need not stop you from using one as a *Content* file in a Smart Device Application project.

This sample is based on the solution from the previous sample. To create the DesignedDataSetSample yourself, copy the previous sample and load it into Visual Studio. Add a new empty project to the solution, and then add a new item to the project (choose the XML Schema template); name the new file BagCheck.xsd. Visual Studio displays the designer for the new XML Schema. Figure 14-7 shows the DataSet view of the MyBags table.

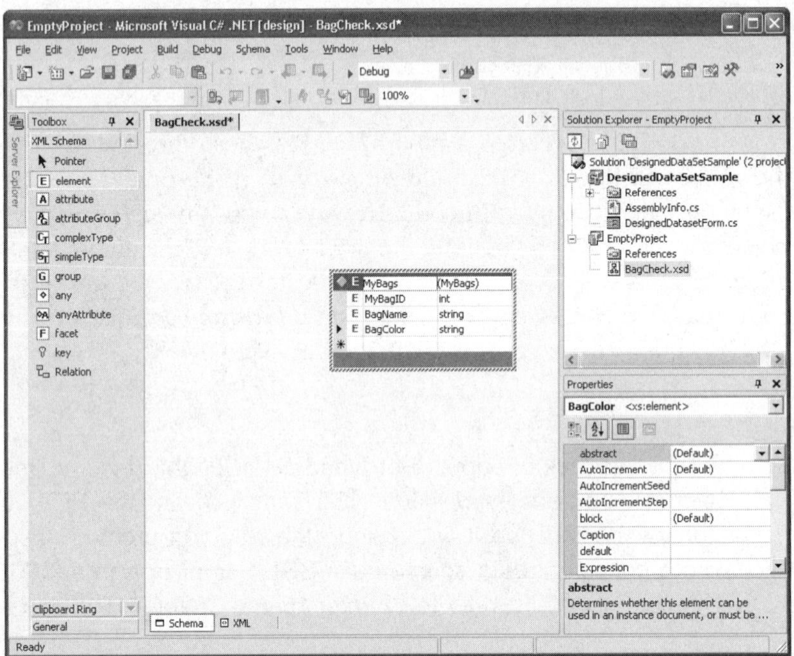

Figure 14-7 The XML Schema Designer.

From the toolbox, drag an XML element and name it as the required table, in this case, MyBags. Then add the rows to the element to define the columns of the table: MyBagID, BagName, and BagColor. Notice that by default, the designer shows the blue *E* for *element* in the rows of the "table" element. This will define the "columns" as sub-elements. You could define the columns as attributes of the table element, which works as long as you have standard data types for your columns (and generally you do). Data types in XML are either standard or complex. You're not allowed to use complex data types in the attributes of an element. You can view the XML schema source by clicking the XML tab. When you have finished creating the XML schema, save the new project and then remove it from the solution. Now right-click your Designed-DataSetSample project, select Add and then Existing Item from the shortcut menu, and browse to locate the BagCheck.xsd file.

Loading a Saved Schema

Visual Studio .NET deploys .NET Compact Framework projects to a location (a folder) that you can specify in the Device section of the project's Property Pages dialog box. Figure 14-8 shows the project's Property Pages dialog box.

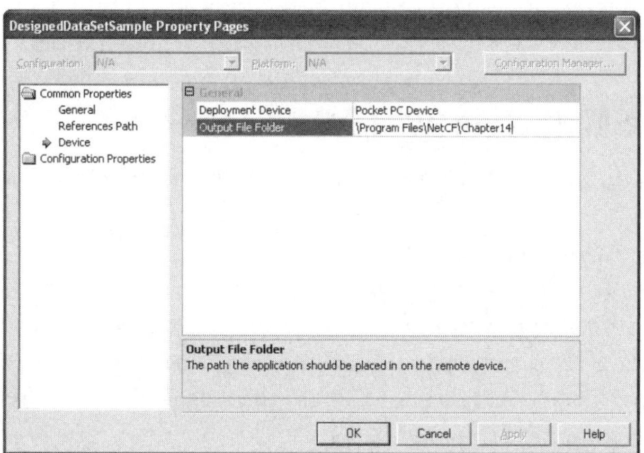

Figure 14-8 Project Property Pages dialog box—Output File Folder.

When you add a dataset schema file (.xsd) to a project, Visual Studio .NET sets the file's Build Action property to Content by default, which means that the dataset schema file will be copied to the output file folder you specify for the target device in the project's Property Pages dialog box. So, your code can open the dataset schema file at run time and read it to create the internal structure of a *DataSet* object. The following code replaces the code in the form's *Load* event:

```
string fileName = @"\Program Files\NetCF\Chapter14\DataSet2.xsd";
dsBagCheck = new DataSet();
if (File.Exists(fileName))
FileStream fs = new FileStream(fileName, FileMode.Open, FileAccess.Read);
XmlTextReader xtr = new XmlTextReader(fs);
dsBagCheck.ReadXmlSchema(xtr);
xtr.Close();    // The DataSet object is now loaded with the schema
```

This code uses the *File* class to check that the file exists and uses an *XmlTextReader* class to read the schema. The *File* class is part of the *System.IO* namespace, and the *XmlTextReader* class is part of the *System.Xml* namespace, so you'll need to include the following lines at the beginning of your class definition:

```
using System.IO;
using System.Xml;
```

The rest of the sample can remain exactly the same as before.

Using Multitable *DataSet* Objects

Few practical applications have just one data table, and often the data in multiple tables is related in some way. The following sections look at the support for relations between multiple tables in ADO.NET using the .NET Compact Framework.

Defining Relations in a Multitable *DataSet* Object

You can express the data requirements for the packing check list sample application as follows:

"I have more than one suitcase."

"A suitcase can contain one or more items."

"An item cannot be in more than one suitcase at any one time!"

The preceding requirements suggest a one-to-many parent-child relationship between the tables MyBags and PackedItems. This relationship can be expressed in database modeling terms as:

"MyBags contains one or more PackedItems."

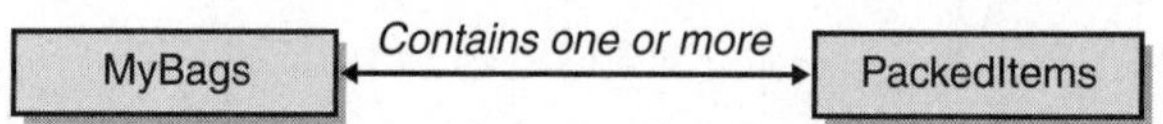

Adding a Relation with XML Schema Designer

To create this relationship in the XML Schema Designer, find the XML schema file you added before, which already has the definition of the *MyBags* element. Table 14-1 describes the elements of the PackedItems table.

Table 14-1 Elements of the PackedItems Table

Element Name	Type	Comment
PackedItemID	*int*	Primary key of this table.
MyBagID	*int*	Foreign key will relate to the MyBags table.
ItemName	*string*	

To create the second table, drag a new element from the toolbox to a clear space in the XML Schema Designer. Rename the new element *PackedItems*, and add subelements to represent the columns in the previous table. Now that you have two table elements, you are ready to add a relation. The relation will use key elements of the two table elements. You could set up the keys before adding the Relation item, but the XML Schema Designer will allow you to add the necessary keys while adding the relation. To add the relation, drag the Relation item from the toolbox and drop it onto the MyBags element. The Edit Relation dialog box will appear. Start by changing the Relation item's name to *MyBagContents*. Use the drop-down list boxes to select MyBags for Parent Element and PackedItems for Child Element. Figure 14-9 shows the Edit Relation dialog box as it should look after you make these changes.

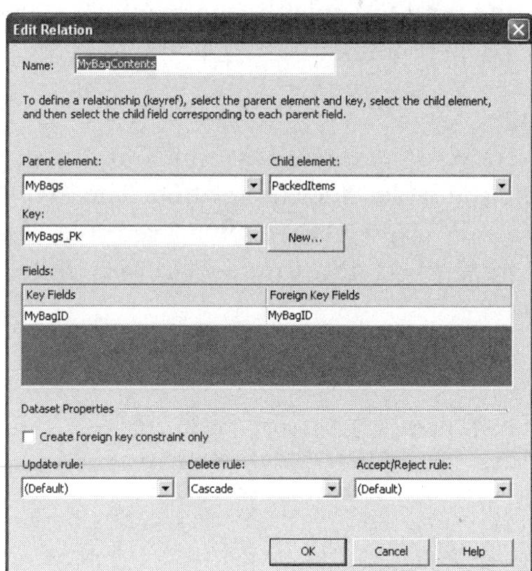

Figure 14-9 Edit Relation dialog box.

Relations can be established only if one of the tables has a primary key defined. If there are no primary keys defined, the OK button remains faded. The New button next to the Key text box displays the Edit Key dialog box, which will allow you to define a new key. Call the new key *MyBags_PK*.

This enables the Fields table, and you can now define the two related fields: MyBagID in MyBags and MyBagID in PackedItems. You'll also want to implement a cascading delete rule. To do so, select Cascade from the Delete Rule drop-down list. When you're finished, the XML Schema Designer will show that the relation has been added, as Figure 14-10 illustrates.

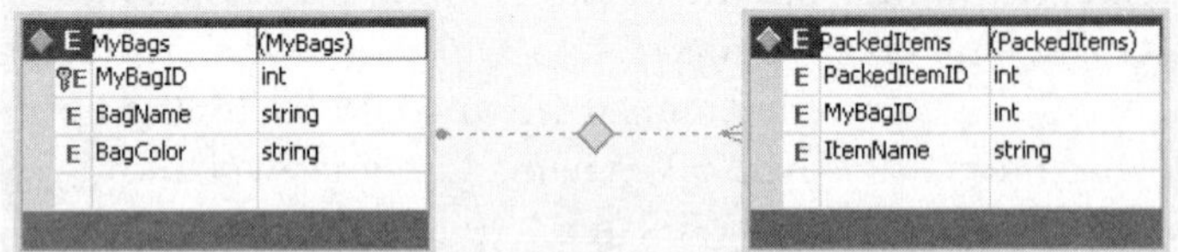

Figure 14-10 Relation in the XML Schema Designer.

The diamond represents the relation and can be right-clicked to return to the Edit Relation dialog box. Notice the line connecting the two tables has a dot at one end and is splayed at the other. The ends represent the one-to-many relationship: the dot is the one, and the splay is the many. The line is saying, "one bag can contain many packed items."

Adding the Relation in Code

You can add a relation in code, or you can save an XML Schema and then reload it at run time to create the tables and the relation. The *ReadXmlSchema* method will load relations from a saved XML Schema (.xsd) file. If you need to add a new relation to a *DataSet*, you add to the *Relations* collection of the *DataSet* object, as follows:

```
DataColumn columnParent;
DataColumn columnChild;
columnParent = MyDataSet.Tables["MyBags"].Columns["MyBagID"];
columnChild = MyDataSet.Tables["PackedItems"].Columns["MyBagID"];
DataRelation relationNew = new DataRelation("MyBagContents",
    columnParent, columnChild);
MyDataSet.Relations.Add(relationNew);
```

The constructor for the *DataRelation* class is overloaded in many ways. (See the online .NET Framework help.) The previous sample shows one of the easier ways to use the constructor: just reference the columns that you want to link together, and give the relation a name.

> **Tip** Don't forget to add the new relation to the *DataSet* object's *Relations* collection.

Navigating the Relation in Code

Once the relation is loaded into the *DataSet* object, you can navigate the parent-child relation by using the *DataRow.GetChildRows* method to return an array of *DataRows* from the child table.

```
DataRow parentRow = myDataSet.Tables["MyBags"].Rows[0];
DataRow[] childRows;
DataRelation relBagContents = myDataSet.Relations["MyBagContents"];
childRows = parentRow.GetChildRows(relBagContents);
foreach (DataRow row in childRows)
{
    listBoxItems.Items.Add(row["ItemName"]);
}
```

There are a few overloads of *GetChildRows*. The previous code shows the one that uses a *DataRelation* object. You'll find the preceding sample code for relationships in the sample application, called RelationDataSetSample, with the book's sample files.

Setting Constraints in a *DataRelation* Object

A useful feature of a *DataRelation* object is its ability to keep relational data correct. This behavior of a *DataRelation* object is governed by a number of *constraints*. ADO.NET has the following two types of constraint:

- Foreign key constraint
- Unique constraint

The reference to a parent row, held on a child row, is known as a *foreign key*. A foreign key constraint ensures that only child rows referencing an existing parent row can be added to the child table.

A unique constraint guarantees that values in a column can be uniquely identified. For example, it is essential that values in a column in the parent table of a relation are unique. Otherwise, it would not be possible, from a given child row, to find a single related parent row.

The *DataRelation* constructor adds a foreign key constraint and a unique constraint for you. You can access the foreign key constraint via the *DataRelation* class's *ChildKeyConstraint* property, and you can access the unique constraint through the *ParentKeyConstraint* property. It's worth considering the various data-tidying options, which include a cascading delete setting. The *ChildKeyConstraint* property of the *DataRelation* class returns a *ForeignKeyConstraint* object, which has two properties (*DeleteRule* and *UpdateRule*) that you can set to aid in data tidying. Both of these properties accept values from the *System.Data.Rule* enumeration, described in Table 14-2.

Table 14-2 *System.Data.Rule* Enumeration

Value	Description
Cascade	Deleting a parent row removes all the related child rows. This is a useful setting, and it is the default.
SetNull	When a parent row is deleted, child rows are not deleted but their foreign key is set to null. This might be useful when you want to allow orphan child rows (which you might want to reattach to a different parent later).
SetDefault	When a parent row is deleted, the foreign key of the child rows is set to its default value. This is likely to result in invalid relation data.
None	The child rows are left as they are. This is guaranteed to result in invalid relation data.

In the sample application that you've been building, you'll want to ensure that when you delete a bag from the MyBags table, all the items the bag contains also get removed from the dataset. This sample shows how you can set up this relation:

```
DataColumn columnParent;
DataColumn columnChild;
columnParent = MyDataSet.Tables["MyBags"].Columns["MyBagID"];
columnChild = MyDataSet.Tables["PackedItems"].Columns["MyBagID"];
DataRelation relationNew = new DataRelation("MyBagContents",
    columnParent, columnChild, true);
relationNew.ChildKeyConstraint.DeleteRule = Rule.Cascade;
MyDataSet.Relations.Add(relationNew);
```

The preceding sample adds a cascading delete rule to the relation between the tables MyBags and PackedItems, which means that you can implement a simple remove function for the bag, which also clears out all its contents.

Saving a *DataSet* Object Locally

Chapter 15 and Chapter 17 will describe storing data in a database, but this chapter will now continue by looking at how you can save a partially filled DataSet object to the local file storage of the smart device and then retrieve it again. To do so, you will use the WriteXml and ReadXml methods of the DataSet class.

Due to the limited quantity of local storage available on a smart device, persisting local data in this way has the disadvantage of being suitable only for small volumes of data. However, the advantage of storing data locally using XML is that doing so requires no connection to a network, no further components on the device or elsewhere, and no database on the device or elsewhere. So there is no "footprint" of other software on the device to consider.

Writing the Data

General considerations for reading and writing files were discussed in Chapter 10, and detail of working with XML files is covered in Chapter 9. So, the following sample excludes code to check for enough space for our *DataSet* object's XML file, and this chapter will not provide a detailed discussion of XML. The following code saves the data in a *DataSet* object to a file:

```
string fileName = @"\Program Files\NetCF\Chapter14\BagsDataSet.xml";
FileStream fs = new FileStream(filename,
    FileMode.OpenOrCreate, FileAccess.Write);
XmlTextWriter myWriter = new XmlTextWriter(fs,
    System.Text.Encoding.Unicode);
MyDataSet.WriteXml(myWriter,
    System.Data.XmlWriteMode.WriteSchema);
myWriter.Close();
```

The sample always saves to the same file. It shows the overload of *WriteXml* that uses an *XmlTextWriter* object because that overload provides a fast way to write well-formed XML. The sample specifies the value *System.Data.XmlWriteMode.WriteSchema* as the second parameter of *WriteXml* so that the reference to the schema is written into the XML file. You can use the File Explorer and Internet Explorer on the device to examine the written file, as shown in Figure 14-11.

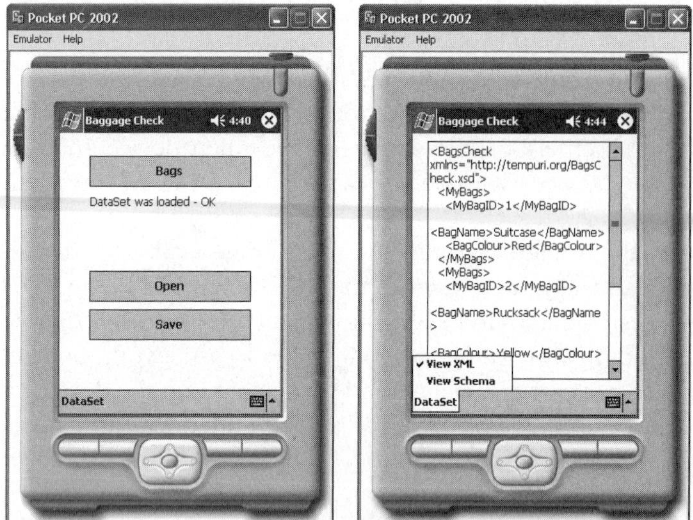

Figure 14-11 *DataSet* object saved to local storage as XML.

Reading the Data

You can also read an existing XML file into a *DataSet* object using the *ReadXML* method. There are a number of overloads of this method available. The sample below uses the overload that takes an *XmlTextReader* object. This overload provides fast, non-cached, forward-only access to XML data, but it doesn't validate against the schema, which is adequate in this case.

```
FileStream fs = new FileStream(fileName,
    FileMode.Open, FileAccess.Read);
XmlTextReader myReader = new XmlTextReader(fs);
MyDataSet.Reset();
MyDataSet.ReadXml(myReader, System.Data.XmlReadMode.ReadSchema);
myReader.Close();
```

If the XML file does not contain an inline schema and the *DataSet* object does not have a schema, then it is possible to *infer* a schema from the XML data with the *ReadXml* method. The code to read an XML file and infer the XML data's schema looks exactly like the previous sample code, except for the call to *ReadXml*. To infer the schema, you call *ReadXml* specifying the *XmlReadMode* value *InferSchema* as the second parameter.

Putting It All Together

You can now put all the techniques discussed so far in this chapter together into the SavedDataSetSample application. Figure 14-12 shows two views of the application's home screen, which is the first screen that appears when the application starts.

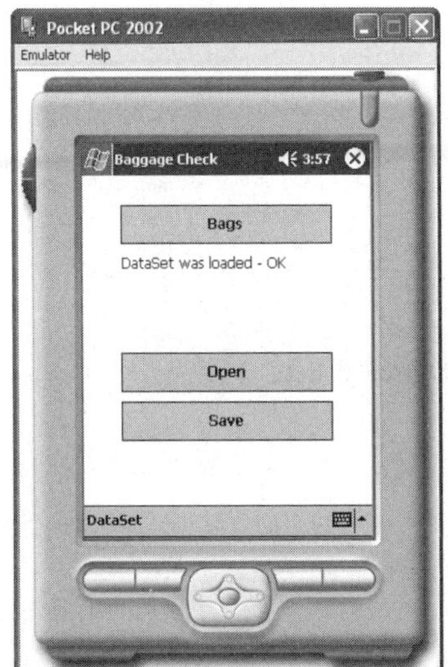

Figure 14-12 Home screen of the SavedDataSetSample application.

The first screen loads the XML schema from the local file \Program Files\NetCF\Chapter14\BagsCheck.xsd and shows buttons to access the Bags screen and to open and save the dataset. A simple menu allows the user a peek at the XML "under the hood." Figure 14-13 shows the Bags screen. The Bags screen takes the *DataSet* object created by the home screen as a parameter in its constructor. It then uses a *DataRow* object to add rows to the MyBags table.

The Packed Items screen takes the *DataSet* object from the Bags screen and the name and ID of the chosen bag. It uses the *Select* method on the MyBags table in the *DataSet* object to reference the chosen bag, and it uses a *DataRelation* object to list all the packed items related to the given bag. The Packed Items screen also allows packed items to be added.

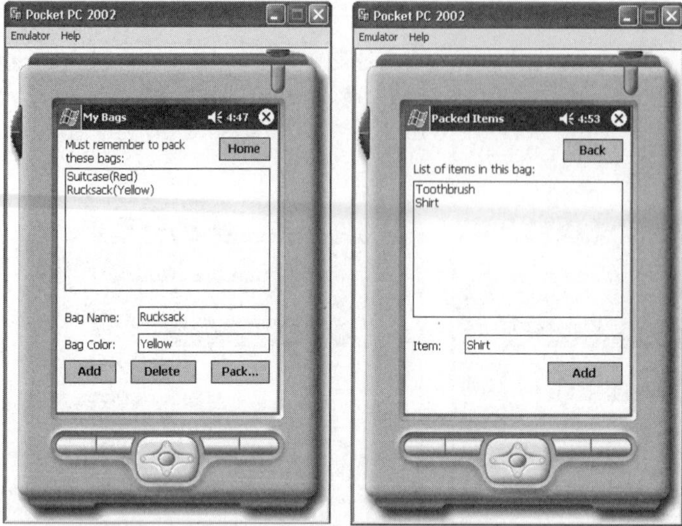

Figure 14-13 Adding bags and packed items.

Back on the Bags screen, a Delete button allows the user to remove a selected bag from the dataset. Because of the active cascading delete constraint on the relation between bags and their packed items (parent-child), removing a bag causes all related packed items to be deleted as well. Table 14-3 summarizes the use this application makes of the various ADO.NET objects and their properties, methods, and values.

Table 14-3 Objects, Properties, Methods, and Values Used by SavedDataSetSample

Screen	Object	Property, Method, Value	Notes
Home	*File*	*Exists* method	Used to check that the .xsd schema file exists.
Home	*FileStream*	Constructor	Used to create a new *FileStream* object for opening the file for reading.
Home	*XmlTextReader*	Constructor	Creates an *XmlTextReader* object using a *FileStream* object.

Table 14-3 Objects, Properties, Methods, and Values Used by SavedDataSetSample *(continued)*

Screen	Object	Property, Method, Value	Notes
Home	*DataSet*	*ReadSchema* method	Used to read the schema for a multitable *DataSet* object from the .xds schema file. *ReadSchema* fails to load the data relation between the two tables.
Home	*DataColumn*	Reference	Used to reference the parent and child columns for the *DataRelation* object, and accessed via the *Tables* collection of the *DataSet* object.
Home	*DataRelation*	Constructor	Used to create a parent-child relation between bags and their packed items.
Home	*DataSet*	*Relations* collection, *Add* method	Used to add the new relation to the *DataSet* object.
Home	*DataSet*	*ReadXml* method	Used to populate the *DataSet* object from a previously stored local file.
Home	*DataSet*	*XmlReadMode*, *.ReadSchema* value	Used to read the XML data and schema from the stored file.
Home	*XmlDataWriter*	Constructor	Used to create an *XmlDataWriter* object using a *FileStream* object for opening (or creating) an XML file with write access.
Home	*DataSet*	*WriteXml* method	Used to write the *DataSet* object to a local XML file.
Home	*DataSet*	*XmlWriteMode*, *.WriteSchema* value	Used to write the inline schema reference in the XML file.
Home	*DataSet*	*GetXml* method	Used to provide a "peek" at the XML structure of the *DataSet* object's data.
Home	*DataSet*	*GetXmlSchema* method	Used to provide a "peek" at the XML schema of the *DataSet* object.

(continued)

Table 14-3 Objects, Properties, Methods, and Values Used by SavedDataSetSample *(continued)*

Screen	Object	Property, Method, Value	Notes
Bags	*DataSet*	*Tables* collection	Used to reference one of the tables in the *DataSet* object.
Bags	*DataTable*	*NewRow* method	Used to create a new *DataRow* object for adding new data to the MyBags table.
Bags	*DataRow*	*DataColumns* collection	Used to set the new column values in the new row of data.
Bags	*DataTable*	*Rows* collection, *Add* method	Used to add the new row of data to the table in the *DataSet* object.
Bags	*DataTable*	*Rows* collection, *Remove* method	Used to delete a row from the MyBags table in the *DataSet* object.
Packed Items	*DataTable*	*Select* method	Used to locate a particular record in the MyBags table.
Packed Items	*DataSet*	*Relations* collection	Used to reference the parent-child relation between bags and their packed items.
Packed Items	*DataRow*	*GetChildRows* method	Used to list all the child rows for the given parent row.

Working with Updates, Data Views, and Data Binding

Data binding automatically retrieves data from a dataset, places it into controls, and updates the dataset when the values in the controls are changed. There a two types of data binding. *Simple* data binding displays a single row at a time, with its column values in controls such as TextBox controls or Label controls. *Complex* data binding uses controls such as the ListBox control to display multiple rows.

Tracking *DataSet* Updates

Data binding automatically retrieves data from a dataset and updates rows in a dataset. So this chapter will introduce how a *DataSet* object handles updates to its locally held cache of *DataRow* objects. (This book continues this topic in Chapters 15, 16 and 17 and examines how the locally held data can be reconciled with a remote data source.) To track what has been changed and when, the *DataSet* object maintains a flag that indicates how a row has been changed. The *DataSet* object also keeps multiple versions of the row.

Understanding Row States

The *RowState* property of a *DataRow* object indicates how the *DataRow* object has been changed. There are five possible states, encapsulated in the *DataRowState* enumeration. Table 14-4 describes the possible states.

Table 14-4 *DataRowState* Enumeration

Value	Description
Added	The row has recently been added. There is no original version of the row. The row did not exist when *AcceptChanges* was last called.
Deleted	The row has been deleted.
Detached	The row has been created but not yet added to the *Rows* collection.
Modified	One of the columns in the row has been changed in some way.
Unchanged	The row has not changed since *AcceptChanges* was last called.

Understanding Row Versions

When using the *Item* property or the *GetChildRows* method of a *DataRow* object, you can specify a *DataRowVersion* value so that a particular version of the *DataRow* object is retrieved. Table 14-5 lists the members of the *DataRowVersion* enumeration.

Table 14-5 *DataRowVersion* Enumeration

Value	Description
Current	The current version of the row shows all modifications made since the last time *AcceptChanges* was called. Note that there is no current row for rows that have been deleted. The current row for an added row shows the data from the point at which it was added to the *Rows* collection.
Default	The row with all its data defaults applied. These defaults can be defined in the dataset's schema.
Original	The original version of the record at the time it was read from a data source. There is no original for an added row, but it does exist for a deleted row.
Proposed	This version of the row is available only between the start and end of an update. For example, in code, it is possible to use the *BeginEdit* and *EndEdit* methods and then handle validation before the change is committed.

Working with the *DataView* Object

DataView objects play a crucial part in data binding. A data view can

- Present a sorted view of the underlying data to the bound control.
- Present a filtered view by including only rows that match criteria based on the values in one or more columns.
- Present a filtered view by including only rows with a particular set of row states.

> **Note** In the section "Working with Default Data Views" later in this chapter, you'll see that even when a *DataTable* object is specified as the data source of a binding, a *DataView* object *is* in use, and this is the default view that every *DataTable* object has.

Using the *Sort* Property

The *Sort* property of a *DataView* class accepts a string with one or more columns, separated by commas. In the string, each column name can be followed by *ASC* or *DESC* to specify the sort order for the column. The syntax is like the SQL *ORDER BY* clause but without the *ORDER BY* keywords.

```
MyDataView.Sort = "Date DESC, Surname ASC";
```

Using the *RowFilter* Property

The *RowFilter* property of the *DataView* class can provide criteria based on one or more columns. The syntax is like the syntax of the SQL *WHERE* clause.

```
MyDataView.RowFilter = "Date <= '1 Jan 2002'";
```

Using the *RowStateFilter* Property

Using the *RowStateFilter* property of a *DataView* object, it is possible to list only rows with a certain *RowState* and to retrieve the different row version values, by using one or a combination of the *DataViewRowState* enumeration values listed in Table 14-6.

Table 14-6 *DataViewRowState* Enumeration

Value	Description
Added	Show added rows (has to be the current version).
CurrentRows	Include added, modified, and unchanged rows. Retrieve their current version.
Deleted	Show deleted rows (has to be the original version).
ModifiedCurrent	Show modified rows and retrieve their current version.
ModifiedOriginal	Show modified rows, and retrieve their original version.
OriginalRows	Include unchanged and deleted rows, and retrieve their original version.
Unchanged	Show unchanged rows, and retrieve their original version.
None	Include no rows.

Combinations are added together using the logical OR to perform a bitwise operation. For example, to get added and modified rows, use the following code:

```
myView.RowStateFilter = DataViewRowState.Added |
    DataViewRowState.ModifiedCurrent;
```

Commiting Changes

The *AcceptChanges* method commits changes made to the rows of a *DataSet* object and alters the rows' state and the versions that are kept of the rows. The method exists at three levels, as described in Table 14-7.

Table 14-7 Objects with the *AcceptChanges* Method

Object and Method	Description
DataRow.AcceptChanges	Commits changes for only the row
DataTable.AcceptChanges	Commits changes for all rows in the table
DataSet.AcceptChanges	Commits changes for all rows in all tables

AcceptChanges has the following effects on row state and row versions: In modified rows, the original version of the row is overwritten using values from the current version and the row's *RowState* property is set to unchanged. Any rows with a *RowState* property value of *DataRowState.Deleted* are removed from the *DataSet* object.

Examining Data Binding

As you have seen, the .NET Compact Framework does not support typed *DataSet* objects, which means that you cannot set up data binding at design time by using the Generate DataSet function as you can in the full .NET Framework. Also remember that references to the data objects in a *DataSet* object have to be made via members of a collection; there are no direct-access properties.

Understanding Simple Data Binding

Simple data binding can be added in code. Simple data binding uses a data source, a data member, and the name of the control property being bound (usually the *Text* property). The data source can be a *DataTable* object or a *DataView* object. Figure 14-14 shows the simple data binding relationship between a bound control and the data view the control is bound to.

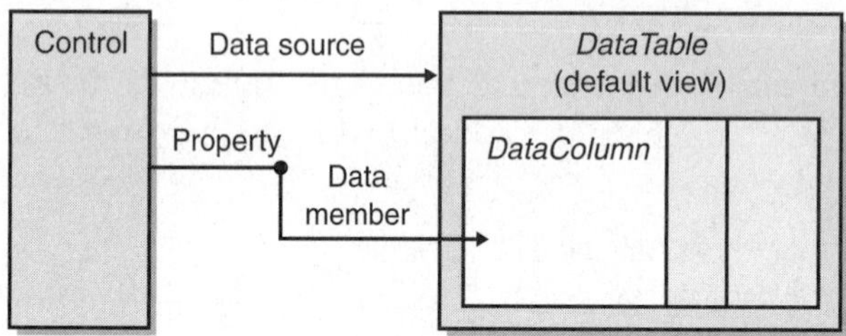

Figure 14-14 Simple data biding.

Understanding Complex Data Binding

Complex data binding can also be added in code. Complex data binding uses a data source object and, depending on the control being bound, sometimes also the names of *DataColumn* objects. Again, the data source can be a *DataTable* object or a *DataView* object. For example, to bind a DataGrid control, you use the *DataSource* property alone, but to bind a ListBox control, there are two additional properties: the *DisplayMember* property, which specifies the *DataColumn* object to display in the list, and the *ValueMember* property, which gives a *DataColumn* to use as a hidden value list. Figure 14-15 shows a ListBox control using complex data binding to connect to a data source.

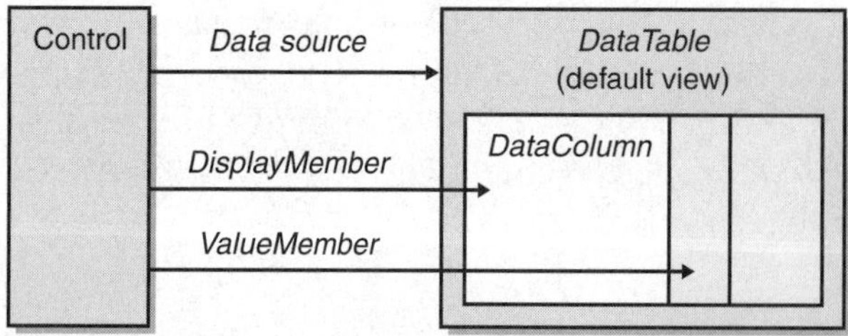

Figure 14-15 Complex data binding for a ListBox control.

Creating Data Bindings in Code

You have seen that data binding must be set up in code in the .NET Compact Framework. Here is some sample code for setting up both simple and complex binding:

```
DataTable dtMyBags = dsBagCheck.Tables["MyBags"];
// ListBox control - Complex Binding:
listBoxBags.DataSource = dtMyBags;
listBoxBags.DisplayMember = "BagName";

// TextBox controls - Simple Binding:
textBoxBagName.DataBindings.Add("Text", dtMyBags, "BagName");
textBoxColor.DataBindings.Add("Text", dtMyBags, "BagColor");
```

Working with Default Data Views

But where are the data views? To explore this issue, stop the code with a breakpoint after the first line. In the command window, enter the following command:

```
?dtMyBags.DefaultView
```

Visual Studio .NET will display information about the default view for *dtMyBags*, as Figure 14-16 shows.

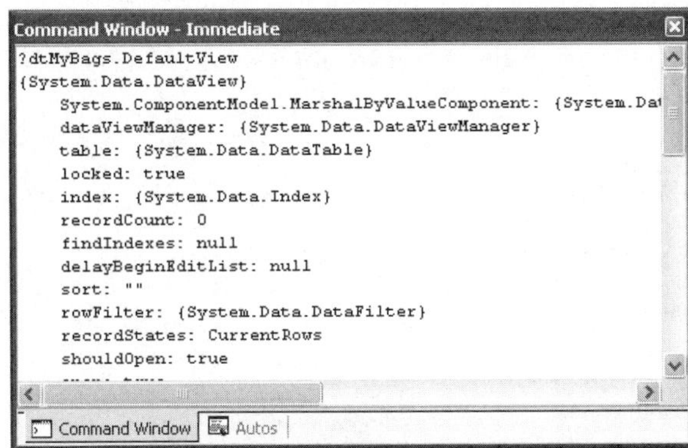

Figure 14-16 Command window—investigating the default view.

The binding we created in the previous code will use the default *DataView* object. The default *DataView* object is not sorted, and the row state filter is set to *CurrentRows*. With this knowledge, you can refine the binding to sort the ListBox control in alphabetical order using the BagName column.

```
dtMyBags.DefaultView.Sort = "BagName ASC";
```

And to make a new row or changes to an existing row appear in the view, we will need to call *AcceptChanges*.

```
dtMyBags.AcceptChanges();
```

Tracking the Current Row in a DataGrid

Frequently, you will need to access the *DataRow* object that corresponds to the row in the grid on the screen that the user has selected. The DataGrid control has a *CurrentRowIndex* property that returns the index of the *DataRow* object in the *Rows* collection in the bound *DataTable* object that corresponds to the row in the grid on the screen that the user has selected. For example, to delete the row that the user has selected on the screen, you could write code such as this:

```
int iRow = dataGridBags.CurrentRowIndex;
try
{
    DataRow drBag = dsBagCheck.Tables["MyBags"].Rows[iRow];
    drBag.Delete();
}
```

Implementing a Data Binding Sample

This is the final version of the Baggage Check application, called Bound-DataSetSample. It uses both a DataGrid control and a ListBox control that are data bound to the two tables in the *DataSet* object. Figure 14-17 shows the data binding sample.

Figure 14-17 Data binding sample.

In this sample, the data binding for the DataGrid control simply uses the *DataSource* property and omits any code that could format the presentation of the data; the code to format the presentation of data has already been covered in more detail in Chapter 3 of this book. The data binding for the ListBox control includes *DataValue* as well as *DataMember* properties. This simplifies the calculation of what the user has selected in the list by allowing use of the ListBox control's *SelectedValue* property.

A *DataRelation* object is used as shown earlier to set up a cascading delete on the parent-child relation between bags and their packed items. But this time, because the lists are data bound, the *SelectedIndexChanged* event of the bags list contains code to filter the packed items list, using the underlying table's default *DataView* object. Table 14-8 lists the objects, properties, and methods that the BoundDataSetSample application uses.

Table 14-8 Objects, Properties, Methods, and Values Used by BoundDataSetSample

Object	Property, Method, Value	Notes
DataTable	*DefaultView* property	Used to access the default *DataView* object for the table
DataView	*Sort* property	Used to view the data sorted
DataView	*RowStateFilter* property	Used to filter the view based on a row state
DataView	*DataViewRowState* enumeration	Used to specify the filter based on row state
DataGrid	*DataSource* property	Used to bind the DataGrid control to a *DataTable* object via its default *DataView* object
ListBox	*DataSource* property	Used to bind the ListBox control to a *DataTable* object via its default *DataView* object
ListBox	*DisplayMember* property	Used to specify a *DataColumn* object to display in the bound ListBox control
ListBox	*ValueMember* property	Used to specify the *DataColumn* object, which provides the hidden value column of the ListBox control
TextBox	*DataBindings* collection, *Add* method	Used to add simple data binding to the *TextBox* control
DataTable	*AcceptChanges* method	Used to commit changes on all rows in a table after adding or deleting a row

Table 14-8 Objects, Properties, Methods, and Values Used by BoundDataSetSample *(continued)*

Object	Property, Method, Value	Notes
DataRow	*AcceptChanges* method	Used to commit changes in a row after changes were made in a bound control
DataSet	*AcceptChanges* method	Used to commit changes throughout all rows in the *DataSet* object, after the deletion of a parent record causes a cascading deletion of child records

Summary

This chapter has shown you how to use some of the ADO.NET objects that form the basis of data handling in the .NET Compact Framework. The most important object is the *DataSet* object, which forms a local data store in memory that allows data to be manipulated offline without a connection to a remote persistent data source. You have seen how the *DataSet* object can represent data in a relational way, how the *DataSet* object can persist its data and structure to a local XML file, and how it can use data binding to display data values and retrieve changes from UI controls. This chapter has shown that the *DataSet* object stores changed and original versions of data rows and tracks their status to enable a merging back into a remote data source.

The details of connecting to remote data sources are covered in later chapters, which expand the use of ADO.NET objects by looking at retrieving data from a SQL Server (Chapter 15) and from an XML Web service (Chapter 16). We will also be looking at using SQL Server CE on a smart device (Chapter 17).

15

Integrating Data with SQL Server

The .NET Compact Framework includes the ability to access data in Microsoft SQL Server databases on a remote computer. One of the great strengths of the data access objects available in the .NET Compact Framework is their ability to work disconnected from their data source.

This chapter will first examine the retrieval and update of data from a SQL Server database. The chapter will discuss getting the data into an application on a smart device so that the data can be edited on the device while the application is disconnected from the data source. It will also examine in detail the process of reconnecting to the data source and sending updated data back into the database. Then this chapter will examine the use of SQL Server stored procedures and their parameters. Finally this chapter will briefly introduce the ability of SQL Server 2000 to provide and update data in XML format using a new set of features called XML for SQL (SQLXML).

The .NET Compact Framework also includes the ability to access a SQL Server database located on the smart device using SQL Server CE. This subject is covered in Chapter 17 of this book.

Examining Data Access Architecture

In the previous chapter, you looked in some detail at the *DataSet*, *DataTable*, *DataRow*, *DataColumn*, and *DataView* objects, which allow manipulation of a local data store in a smart device application. In this chapter, you will examine how to get data from a SQL Server database and how to update the database with changes.

> **Note** The smart device must have a direct network connection to SQL Server, either an 802.11 or an Ethernet connection. Retrieving data from SQL Server with a smart device in the way this chapter describes won't work over an Internet connection.

Using the SQL Server 2000 Managed Provider

A managed provider is the part of the data access architecture that allows you to connect your application to a data source such as SQL Server. A managed provider is supplied as a separate class library. The full .NET Framework gives you a choice of managed providers: the OLE DB managed provider and the SQL Server managed provider. The .NET Compact Framework allows you to use only the SQL Server 2000 managed provider. Figure 15-1 shows a diagram of the SQL Server managed provider.

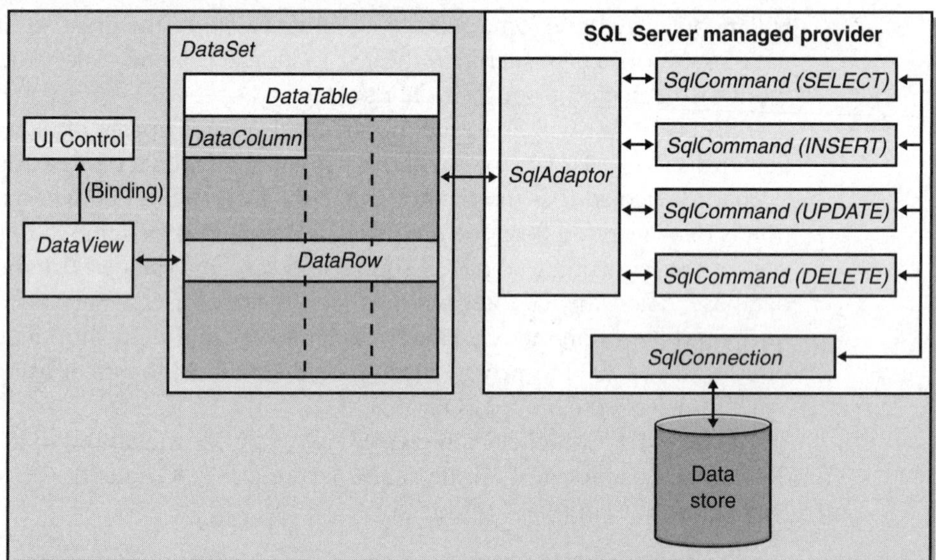

Figure 15-1 The SQL Server managed provider in context.

Before you can connect to SQL Server from an application, you must add a reference in the Visual Studio .NET project to the SQL Server managed provider, which is listed in the Add Reference dialog box as *System.Data.SqlClient*. You'll also need to add a reference to the *System.Data.Common* class library.

Figure 15-2 shows both of these components being selected in the Visual Studio .NET Add Reference dialog box.

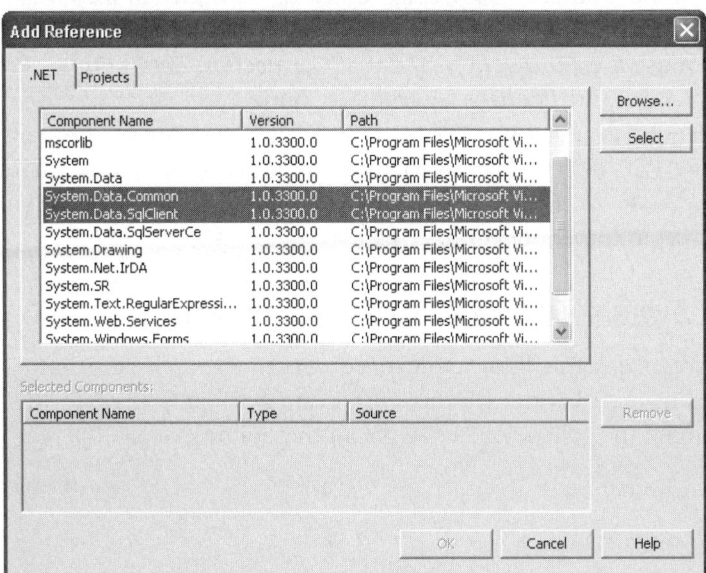

Figure 15-2 Adding references to the SQL Server managed provider and the *System.Data.Common* class library.

Understanding Differences from the Desktop .NET Framework

Before we examine the *System.Data.SqlClient* namespace in detail, this section will mention some of its differences between the .NET Compact Framework and the desktop .NET Framework.

Using Forms Designer

In a Smart Device Application project, you can't drag and drop items from the toolbar into Forms Designer to create managed provider and dataset objects. You must create any such objects that you need in code. Visual Studio .NET will display a No Entry cursor if you try to use drag and drop to create a managed provider or a dataset object.

Implementing Transactions

The .NET Compact Framework doesn't support distributed transactions across databases or servers like SQL Server Distributed Transaction Coordinator (DTC), Microsoft Transaction Services (MTS), and COM+ components do. You can use transactions on a single database on one server.

Establishing Connections

The .NET Compact Framework doesn't support connection pooling. You can't use any of the connection-pooling keywords or values in the connection string. (You'll get an error if you try it!) Specifically, the connection string values that are not in use are *Connection Lifetime*, *Connection Reset*, *Enlist*, *Max Pool Size*, *Min Pool Size*, and *Pooling*. Encrypted connections are not supported either. You'll also get an error if use *Encrypt=true* in the connection string.

Only TCP/IP connections to SQL Server are supported. You'll get an error if use the *Network Library* keyword with any network library name (other than the default) in the connection string.

Introducing the *System.Data.SqlClient* Namespace

The *System.Data.SqlClient* namespace contains the classes that form the SQL Server managed provider for the .NET Compact Framework. In this section, we will examine the following classes from that namespace:

- *SqlConnection*
- *SqlCommand*
- *SqlParameter*
- *SqlDataReader*
- *SqlDataAdapter*
- *SqlCommandBuilder*
- *SqlException* and *SqlError*

The following sections will introduce each class, describe what the class represents, and broadly discuss what you would use the class for.

Introducing the *SqlConnection* Object

An object created from the *SqlConnection* class represents a unique session connected to a SQL Server data source. It has properties to allow you to specify how to locate and access the data source, and it has methods to explicitly open and close the connection. Although you will use a *SqlConnection* object almost every time you access SQL Server data or perform an operation on SQL Server data, it is rarely used on its own in a .NET Compact Framework application. Mostly, you will use a connection object as a convenient way of specifying the connection for objects of one of the other *System.Data.SqlClient* classes.

Introducing the *SqlCommand* Object

An object created from the *SqlCommand* class can represent a Transact-SQL statement or a stored procedure for use on a SQL Server database. You will use a *SqlCommand* object with a *SqlConnection* object to specify the access, the database, and the server with which the command is to be executed. The *SqlCommand* object has properties that allow you to specify a Transact-SQL or a stored procedure, methods to execute the command, and further properties and events to monitor the progress and state of the command's execution.

It is worth noting that a well-structured application will rarely embed SQL in the user interface tier, which is your smart device application. To promote maintainability and performance of your application, you should encapsulate all SQL in well-defined commands. In many practical circumstances, you'll use a *SqlCommand* object, possibly in association with one or more *SqlParameter* objects, to represent a stored procedure.

Introducing the *SqlParameter* Object

An object of class *SqlParameter* represents a parameter to be used when calling a SQL Server stored procedure, represented by a *SqlCommand* object. Parameters can be used for input, for supplying criteria for the command, or for output of information from a command. Stored procedures optionally return final values, and we shall see how these are also handled using a *SqlParameter* object.

Introducing the *SqlDataReader* Object

You can use a *SqlDataReader* object to provide a fast, forward-only stream of data rows from a SQL Server database. You use a *SqlConnection* object to specify the data source from which the data will be read, and you use a *SqlCommand* object to supply the Transact-SQL or stored procedure that specifies the data for the *SqlDataReader* to select.

If you use a *SqlDataReader* object, you must process the data in the sequence in which it is provided. You cannot go backward or start again. An example of the use of a *SqlDataReader* object is if you are filling a list box from which your user can pick values.

Introducing the *SqlDataAdapter* Object

If you need to keep a copy of data retrieved from a SQL Server database for presenting in multiple ways or for processing locally, you can create an object from the *SqlDataAdapter* class as an alternative to an object of class *SqlDataReader*. A *SqlDataAdapter* object can be used to fill a local *DataSet* object with data, after which the data is available for offline processing and ultimately for updating the SQL Server data source.

The *SqlDataAdapter* object provides the following properties for the four *SqlCommand* objects that it needs to function fully:

- *SelectCommand*
- *UpdateCommand*
- *InsertCommand*
- *DeleteCommand*

We'll refer to the *SqlCommand* objects that we create for these properties as the select command, the update command, the insert command, and the delete command. We'll see in the section "Using the *SqlCommand* Object" later in this chapter how you create each command, using parameters where appropriate.

Introducing the *SqlCommandBuilder* Object

An object created from the *SqlCommandBuilder* class can help reduce the programming work that you have to do to setup a *SqlDataAdapter* object. The *SqlCommandBuilder* object takes a *SqlDataAdapter* object containing a select command and generates the corresponding update, insert, and delete commands, including the necessary parameters, to give you a fully functioning *SqlDataAdapter* object. However, the *SqlCommandBuilder* object works only when the *SqlDataAdapter* object's select command is issued against a single data table.

Introducing the *SqlException* and *SqlError* Objects

When SQL Server returns a warning or an error, an exception is thrown into your application. This exception is represented by the properties of a *SqlException* object. Detailed information about the problem is represented by one or more *SqlError* objects contained in the *Errors* collection of the *SqlException* object, as Figure 15-3 depicts.

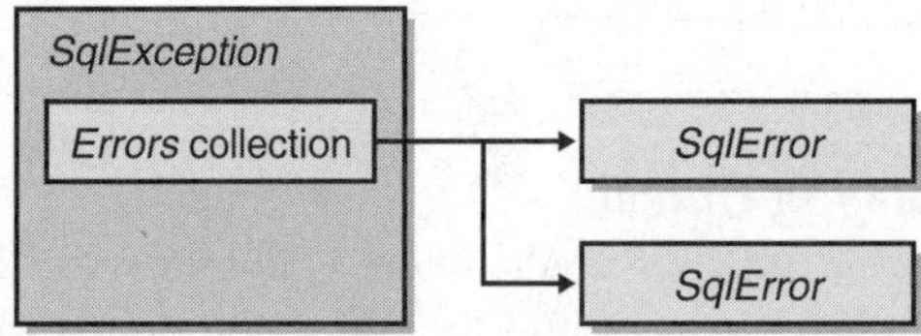

Figure 15-3 *SqlException Errors* collection.

To get the full information regarding any exception thrown during an operation using a SQL database, you will need to write a loop around the *Errors* collection. The section "Using the *SqlException* Object" later in this chapter shows code that loops through the *Errors* collection.

Retrieving Data

A detailed look at accessing data in a SQL Server database, with a sample application, follows. The sample application, GettingSQLDataSample, is available with this book's sample files. The application's code retrieves some data that is to be read-only in the application and that can be collected all in one go. The sample application includes the Transact-SQL that's required for selecting the data, but before you try the sample, you'll need to set up the DotNetCF database that this sample accesses. (See the Readme file included with this chapter's sample files.)

GettingSQLDataSample uses the following *System.Data.SqlClient* objects (in the order that you'll meet them):

- *SqlConnection*
- *SqlCommand*
- *SqlDataReader*
- *SqlException* and *SqlError*

To create the GettingSQLDataSample application yourself, create a new project in Visual Studio .NET using a C# Smart Device Application template. Specify Pocket PC for the target platform and Windows Application for the project type. Copy the form layout as shown in Figure 15-4, and then name the ListBox control *listBoxResults*, the Button control *buttonGetData*, and the Label control *labelStatus*. Remember to add a reference to the System.Data.Common and System.Data.SqlClient assemblies, and add the following code to the top of the form class:

```
using System.Data;
using System.Data.SqlClient;
```

The sample application retrieves the data into the ListBox control when the user clicks the button. (In practice, however, this sort of code might be found in the form's *Load* event handler, rather than in a button's *Click* event handler.)

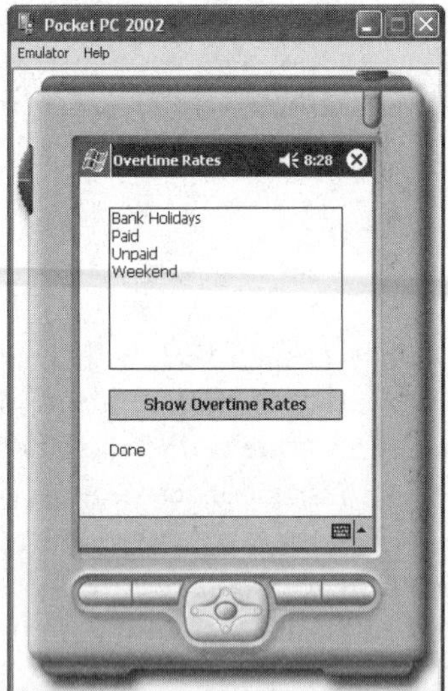

Figure 15-4 GettingSQLDataSample application.

Creating a *SqlConnection* Object

To prepare a *SqlConnection* object, you can set the properties of the object to specify location and access to a SQL Server database, or you can provide this information all at once using the *ConnectionString* property. The *ConnectionString* property allows you to provide the sort of connection string that you might have encountered previously when using ODBC connections. Note that some of the settings available in the connection string do not have an equivalent property.

> **Tip** You'll notice that the GettingSQLDataSample application can take some time to establish a connection to SQL Server. Connection pooling is not an option in the .NET Compact Framework, so the GettingSQLDataSample application will experience this delay every time it connects to the database. To prevent this delay, the application should create a form-level reference to a connection, open it in the form's *Load* event, keep it open, and then close it when the application closes.

Table 15-1 gives the connection-string keywords and their equivalent *SqlConnection* properties.

Table 15-1 Connection-String Keywords and Equivalent *SqlConnection* Properties

Keyword	Property	Description
Application Name	(Not available)	The name of your application. This helps a database administrator identify which applications are using a database. The default is *Microsoft Visual Studio .NET*.
AttachDBFilename	(Not available)	The name and full path of the primary file of an attachable database. Note that you must also specify the name of the database using the *Database* keyword.
Connect Timeout or *Connection Timeout*	*ConnectionTimeout*	The time in seconds to wait for a connection to be successfully established with the given server before generating an error.
Data Source or *Server* or *Address* or *Addr* or *Network Address*	*DataSource*	The name or network address of the instance of SQL Server to connect to.
Database or *Initial Catalog*	*Database*	The name of the database.
Integrated Security or *Trusted_Connection*	(Not available)	Whether the connection is secured. Values can be *true*, *false* and *SSPI* (same as *true*).
Packet Size	*PacketSize*	The size in bytes of the network packets used to communicate with SQL Server.
Password or *Pwd*	(Not available)	The user password to use if you're not using integrated security.
Persist Security Info	(Not available)	When set to *false* (the default), the password is never returned as part of the connection.
User ID or*UID*	(Not available)	The user logon account if you're not using integrated security.
WorkStation ID	*WorkStationId*	A name to identify your local computer. This helps the database administrator identify your workstation. Omit this keyword or leave the property to default to the network name of the computer.

The following code passes a connection string to the constructor of a new *SqlConnection* object:

```
SqlConnection conSql2000 = new SqlConnection(
    "Integrated Security=SSPI;"
    + @"Data Source=G62000\SQL2000; Database=DotNetCF");
```

In the GettingSQLDataSample application you started to create in the previous section, you can add this code to *buttonGetData*'s *Click* event handler. There are two points of interest in the preceding code:

- Connecting to an instance of SQL Server
- Security Options

Connecting to an Instance of SQL Server

SQL Server 2000 and later allow the presence of more than one instance of SQL Server on a single physical server. You must specify both the server name and the instance name when connecting to a SQL Server that has been set up with a second instance. In the previous sample, you would use

```
Data Source=G62000\SQL2000;
```

if you are connecting to a SQL Server 2000 instance called *SQL2000* that is on the network server called *G62000*.

Specifying Security Options

An important role of the *SqlConnection* object is to specify the security access to the SQL Server database from your client application. Although the data itself cannot be encrypted in the .NET Compact Framework, access to the database can be authenticated using Windows integrated security. It is strongly recommended that data connections use integrated security set to Security Support Provider Interface (SSPI) rather than a SQL Server logon account name and password.

> **Note** To get the emulator to connect to SQL Server, you'll need to enable the Windows Guest account (or get your network administrator to do this). Next, using SQL Server, create a *Login Name* for the account. Then you'll need to create the new *Login Name* as a *User* on the DotNetCF database and give the user permission to read and write to the tables in the database.

Using the *SqlCommand* Object

In the following sample, the *SqlCommand* object will contain the Transact-SQL required to retrieve all the overtime-rate ID numbers and descriptions in alphabetical order. The *SqlCommand* object will use a *SqlConnection* object, *conSql2000*, to access the SQL Server database. The *SqlDataReader* object will use the *SqlCommand* object to provide the rows of data to fill the list box.

```
SqlCommand sqlGetOvertimeRates = new SqlCommand(
    "SELECT OvertimeRateID, Description "
    + "FROM OvertimeRates "
    + "ORDER BY Description",
    conSql2000);
```

This code uses the overload of the *SqlCommand* constructor that takes some SQL in a string and a *SqlConnection* object. Again, in the GettingSQL-DataSample application, you can add this code to the button's *Click* event.

Using the *SqlDataReader* Object

The GettingSQLDataSample application uses a *SqlDataReader* object to get the data rows. The *SqlDataReader* object can be created only by calling the *ExecuteReader* method of the *SqlCommand* object. Once *ExecuteReader* has been called, you can access a sequence of rows of data using the *SqlDataReader.Read* method. This method returns *true* while there are still rows to be read and *false* when the last row is reached. Columns in each retrieved row can be accessed by index. In the following example, the second column (the Description column, with an index of 1) is loaded into the list box for each row returned by the *SqlDataReader*:

```
SqlDataReader rdrOvertimeRates;
conSql2000.Open();
rdrOvertimeRates = sqlGetOvertimeRates.ExecuteReader();
while (rdrOvertimeRates.Read())
{
    listBoxResults.Items.Add(rdrOvertimeRates.GetString(1));
}
rdrOvertimeRates.Close();
conSql2000.Close();
```

The preceding sample uses the *Open* method of the *SqlConnection* object to explicitly open the connection. You do not have many connections to use with the .NET Compact Framework, so it is important to remember to use the *Close* method of the *SqlConnection* object after use. The sample also explicitly calls the *SqlDataReader* object's *Close* method. In the GetSQLDataSample application, you can add the preceding code to the button's *Click* event handler.

> **Note** You must explicitly call the *SqlConnection* object's *Open* method before you attempt to use the *ExecuteReader* method of the *SqlCommand* object or any of the methods of the *SqlDataReader* object.

Figure 15-5 shows the relationship among the objects this sample code uses.

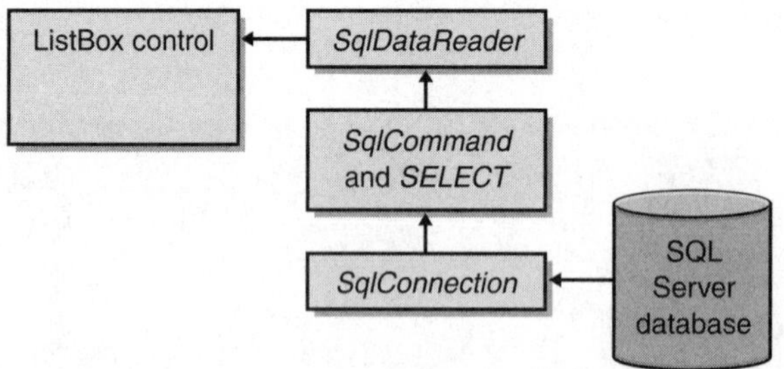

Figure 15-5 Getting data using the *SqlDataReader* object.

Using the *SqlException* Object

Many things can go wrong with data access! For example, the server could be offline or your user might not have security access for the data he or she is trying to get or change. So some form of error handling is essential.

You might find it practical to trap errors from the managed provider separately from others. To do this, the *System.Data.SqlClient* namespace provides a special object you can use when you expect a data access error: *SqlException*. I have added exception handlers to the data access code in my samples like this:

```
try
{
    // Do something with SQL Server
}

catch(SqlException errSqlException)
{
    DisplaySqlErrors(errSqlException);
}
```

The preceding sample uses the function *DisplaySqlErrors* to show the errors in message boxes. The *DisplaySqlErrors* function shown in the next listing might not be the right approach for a production application because of its use of message boxes, but it certainly helps when debugging.

The thing to remember about errors in data access is that often more than one database error is explaining the same exception raised in your application. For example, a failure to add a row to a table might be the result of an attempt to insert a duplicate into a column with a unique constraint. In this case, the main error message will report the overall failure to insert, while a second message will give the detail of which constraint has been enforced. The *SqlException* object accommodates for errors with multiple messages by containing an *Errors* property, which returns a collection of one or more *SqlError* objects. To read all the information available when your program stops, you must look at each item in the *Errors* collection, as shown here:

```
private void DisplaySqlErrors(SqlException errSqlException)
{
    for (int i = 0; i < errSqlException.Errors.Count; i++)
    {
        MessageBox.Show("Index #" + i + "\n"
            + "Error: " + errSqlException.Errors[i].ToString()
            + "\n");
    }
}
```

Binding Data

You can achieve fast development of a user interface that manipulates data by taking advantage of data binding. Data binding allows a control to automatically display data from a *DataSet* object and transfer changes back into the *DataSet* object. The next sample looks in detail at retrieving data from a single table in a SQL Server data source into a *DataTable* object inside a *DataSet* object, and then it binds the table to some controls for display. We will discuss how to update data in the section "Updating Data" later in this chapter.

Figure 15-6 shows the application running. You'll find the code for this application, BindingSQLDataSample, included with this book's sample files. BindingSQLDataSample displays three columns from the Jobs table in a DataGrid control and, when the user selects a row from the DataGrid control, updates the Job ID and Job Number Label controls that are visible in Figure 15-6.

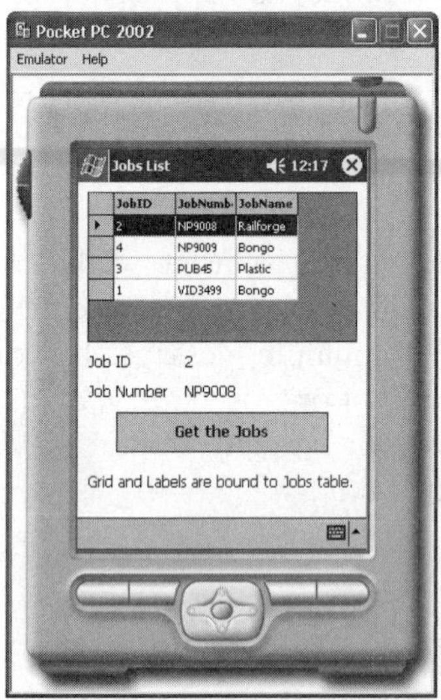

Figure 15-6 BindingSQLDataSample sample application using data binding to update its controls with data from a SQL Server database.

Using the *DataSet* and *SqlDataAdapter* Objects

Data binding links *DataRow* objects and *DataColumn* objects of a *DataTable* object (held within a *DataSet* object) to controls on a form. The schema of the *DataTable*, and the retrieval of the data itself into the *DataRow* objects, is done by a *SqlDataAdapter* object. The *SqlDataAdapter* object uses a *SqlCommand* object, a select command, which defines the SQL *SELECT* command (or stored procedure) to be used. The *SqlCommand* object, in turn, uses a *SqlConnection* object to access a SQL Server database. Figure 15-7 shows all these objects at work with three read-only, data-bound controls.

> **Note** You do not have to explicitly open and close a connection represented by a *SqlConnection* object. The *SqlDataAdapter* object will open a closed connection automatically and then close it again when the *SqlDataAdapter* object no longer needs the connection.

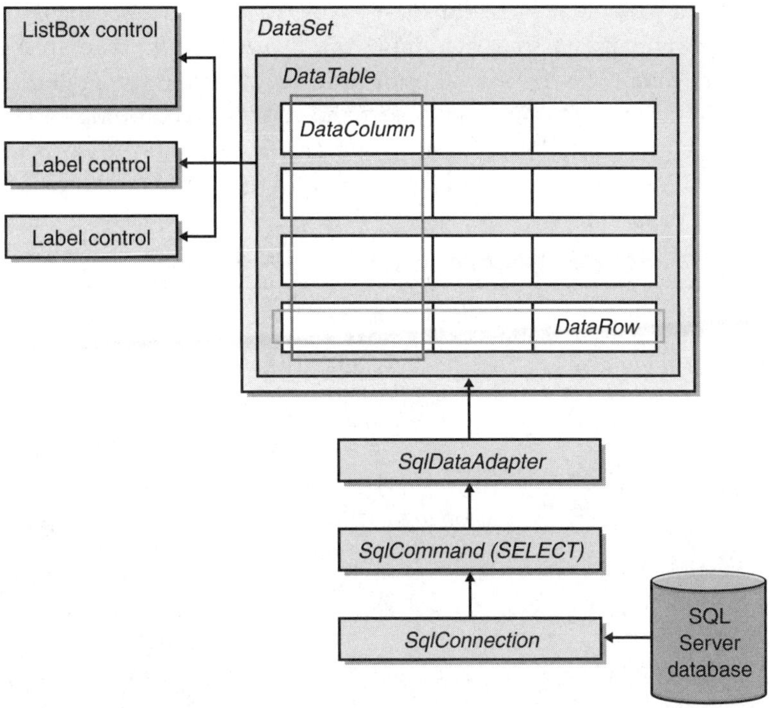

Figure 15-7 Data Bound Controls—Read Only.

When building an application such as BindingSQLDataSample, use the *Select-Command* property of the *SqlDataAdapter* object to attach a new *SqlCommand* object containing a SQL *SELECT* command, as the following code illustrates:

```
daJobs = new SqlDataAdapter();
daJobs.SelectCommand = new SqlCommand (
    "SELECT JobID, JobNumber, JobName " +
    "FROM Jobs ORDER BY JobNumber" ,
    conSql2000);
```

The preceding code, taken from the BindingSQLDataSample sample application, assumes a *SqlConnection* object called *conSql2000* was set up as the section "Creating a *SqlConnection* Object" earlier in this chapter shows. After the *SelectCommand* property has been set, the application can fill a *DataSet* object with the schema and data of the Jobs table. However, before doing that, let's consider the fill process and look at some property settings and an event that might help control the fill process.

Before the fill starts, the *DataSet* object is empty and the data source (in this case, the Jobs table in the SQL Server database) has both a schema and some data rows. Matching the source table to a *DataTable* object in the dataset and matching a data source column to a *DataColumn* object in the *DataTable* object is called a *mapping*. The fill process will have to create the *DataTable* object in the specified *DataSet* object and create the mapping before it can load the data rows. Table 15-2 describes two properties of the *SqlDataAdapter* object that you'll need to be aware of when mapping data from the data source.

Table 15-2 *SqlDataAdapter* Properties (Partial List)

Property	Description	Values
MissingMappingAction	Determines what happens if incoming data does not have a table or column mapping	*Error* *Ignore* *Passthrough* (Default)
MissingSchemaAction	Determines what happens if incoming data does not match an existing *DataSet* schema	*Add* (Default) *AddWithKey* *Error* *Ignore*

By default, the fill process will use the names of the columns as they are in the data source (the *MissingMappingAction* property defaults to *Passthrough*) and will automatically add new columns as they are encountered (the *MissingSchemaAction* property defaults to *Add*).

The following code, from the BindingSQLDataSample sample, explicitly sets the *MissingSchemaAction* property to its default value as an example (which is not necessary in practice) and then calls the *Fill* method. Exception handling code has been omitted.

```
daJobs.MissingSchemaAction = MissingSchemaAction.Add;
⋮
daJobs.Fill(dsJobs, "Jobs");
```

The *Fill* method will first load the necessary schema. It will create a *DataTable* object called Jobs, as specified, and then *DataColumn* objects to match the incoming data but using the names of the columns as they appear in the data source (*Passthrough*).

You'll also need to be aware of the *FillError* event of the *SqlDataAdapter* class, raised when an error occurs during the fill process. The event handler receives a *FillErrorEventArgs* object containing data relating to the event. The *FillErrorEventArgs* object has properties that provide details of the error that raised the event and the values in the row that caused the error, allowing you to decide if you want to continue processing. Table 15-3 describes those *FillErrorEventArgs* properties.

Table 15-3 ***FillErrorEventArgs* Properties (Partial List)**

Property	Description
Continue	Gets or sets a value indicating whether to continue the fill operation despite the error
DataTable	Returns a reference to the *DataTable* object being updated when the error occurred
Errors	The collection of error messages for the error being handled
Values	Returns the values for the row being updated when the error occurred

Let's investigate the fill process in a little more detail. Remember that a *DataSet* object is capable of showing you both its data in XML format (via the *GetXml* method) and its schema in XML format (via the *GetXmlSchema* method). If you stop the BindingSQLDataSample program just after using the *Fill* method (with a break point, for example) and use the Visual Studio .NET Immediate window to explore the XML, you'll see something like Figure 15-8.

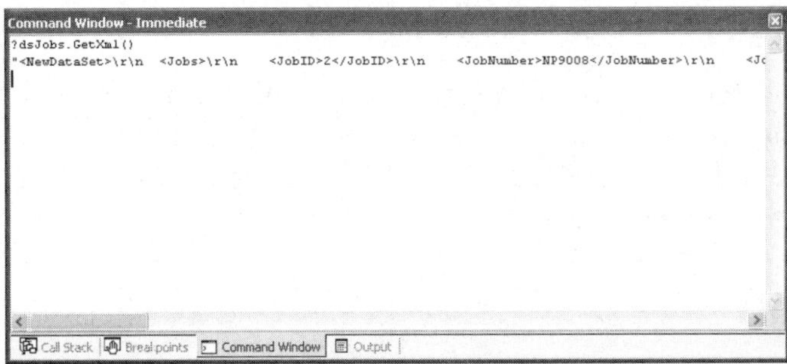

Figure 15-8 XML representation of data from SQL Server in a dataset.

You could also try something similar with the *GetXmlSchema* method.

Once the data is in the dataset, binding to controls can be set up in the usual way. (Data binding is covered in more detail in Chapter 14.) For example, for complex binding of all the rows to a ListBox control, use the *DataSource* property to specify a *DataTable* object and provide column names for the *DisplayMember* and *ValueMember* properties.

```
listBoxJobs.DataSource = dtJobs;
listBoxJobs.DisplayMember = "JobName";
listBoxJobs.ValueMember = "JobID";
```

Similarly, for complex binding to a DataGrid control, use the *DataSource* property to specify a *DataTable* object.

```
dataGridJobs.DataSource = dtJobs;
```

For simple binding to a label, add a binding to the *DataBindings* collection, giving the name of the property being bound, the data source, and the data column name.

```
labelJobID.DataBindings.Add("Text", dtJobs, "JobID");
```

Both these examples, taken from the BindingSQLDataSample application, assume that *dtJobs* is a reference to the Jobs table in an existing *DataSet* object.

Updating Data

So far, this chapter has concentrated on getting data from SQL Server onto the smart device using some of the objects in the *System.Data.SqlClient* namespace. Once data is retrieved, the .NET Compact Framework application can make changes to the data and then update the data source. This chapter will look at two different update techniques:

- Updating bound data
- Updating by executing a stored procedure

You will see how to use a stored procedure to update SQL Server data directly in the section "Using SQL Server Stored Procedures" later in this chapter; let's start now by looking at how to update the database with changes made in a *DataTable* by bound controls.

Updating Bound Data

When a *DataTable* object is bound to controls that allow editing (such as the TextBox control), the values in the table's *DataRow* objects are updated as necessary by the data binding mechanism. You can make new rows appear in the bound controls by adding *DataRow* objects to the *DataTable* object. Similarly, you can remove rows by deleting their corresponding *DataRow* objects. (All this is covered in Chapter 14.)

However, these changes are all made to the data held locally in the *DataSet* object, and they are not reflected immediately in the SQL Server database. This is fine because you will want your smart device application to operate without a continuous connection to SQL Server, but a point will come when you want to update the SQL Server database with your changes.

You can use the *SqlDataAdapter* object to help update the data source with changes you have made to the locally held dataset. This requires you to specify three additional *SqlCommand* objects for the *SqlDataAdapter* object's *UpdateCommand*, *InsertCommand*, and *DeleteCommand* properties, to handle update, insert, and delete operations. These *SqlCommand* objects will require *SqlParameter* objects to take new values for update and insert operations, and to identify records for all three operations. Figure 15-9 shows the relationship among the various objects you'll need to update the data source with your local changes.

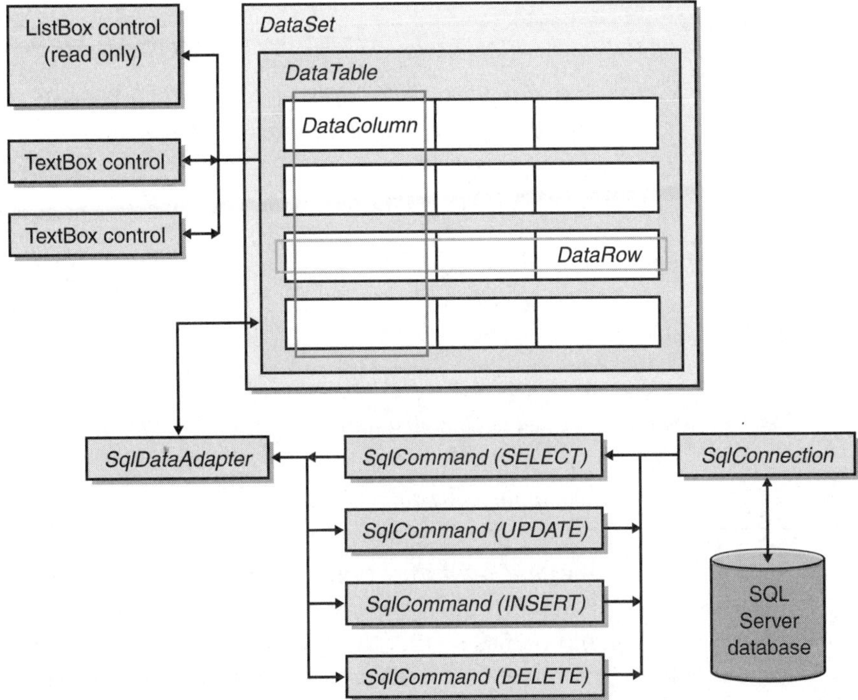

Figure 15-9 Updating bound data using a *SqlDataAdapter* object.

The UpdatingSQLDataSample sample application, available with this book's sample files, illustrates how to update bound data using a *SqlDataAdaptor* object. Table 15-4 describes the *SqlCommand* objects that UpdatingSQL-DataSample specifies for its *SqlDataAdapter* object's *UpdateCommand*, *InsertCommand*, and *DeleteCommand* properties.

Table 15-4 *SqlCommand* Objects That UpdatingSQLDataSample Defines for Updating Its Data Source

SqlDataAdapter Property	SQL	Parameters
UpdateCommand	*UPDATE Jobs SET*	*@JobName varchar(50)*
	JobName = @JobName,	*@JobNumber varchar(15)*
	JobNumber = @JobNumber	*@JobID int*
	WHERE	
	JobID = @JobID	
InsertCommand	*INSERT INTO Jobs*	*@JobName varchar(50)*
	(JobName, JobNumber)	*@JobNumber varchar(15)*
	VALUES(	
	@JobName, @JobNumber)	
DeleteCommand	*DELETE FROM Jobs*	*@JobID int*
	WHERE	
	JobID = @JobID	

When creating *SqlCommand* objects for a *SqlDataAdapter* object, you must specify the parameters in the correct order and you must map the *DataTable* object's column names so that the *SqlDataAdapter* object knows where to get the values. Parameters are added to the *Parameters* collection of the *SqlCommand* objects. You will need to provide a name, data type, length, and mapping column name for each parameter. The following code, from the UpdatingSQLDataSample sample application, creates the three commands listed in Table 15-4 and adds their parameters:

```
// Update command
string sUpdateSQL = "UPDATE Jobs " +
    "SET JobName = @JobName, " +
        "JobNumber = @JobNumber " +
    "WHERE JobID = @JobID";
daJobs.UpdateCommand = new SqlCommand (sUpdateSQL, conSql2000);
daJobs.UpdateCommand.Parameters.Add("@JobID", SqlDbType.Int);
daJobs.UpdateCommand.Parameters.Add(
    "@JobName", SqlDbType.VarChar, 50);
daJobs.UpdateCommand.Parameters.Add(
    "@JobNumber", SqlDbType.VarChar, 15);
// Delete command
string sDeleteSQL = "DELETE FROM Jobs " +
    "WHERE JobID = @JobID";
daJobs.DeleteCommand = new SqlCommand(sDeleteSQL, conSql2000);
daJobs.DeleteCommand.Parameters.Add(
```

```
    "@JobID", SqlDbType.Int, 4, "JobID");
// Add command
string sInsertSQL = "INSERT INTO Jobs(JobNumber, JobName) " +
    "VALUES(@JobNumber, @JobName)";
daJobs.InsertCommand = new SqlCommand(sInsertSQL, conSql2000);
daJobs.InsertCommand.Parameters.Add(
    "@JobNumber", SqlDbType.VarChar, 15, "JobNumber");
daJobs.InsertCommand.Parameters.Add(
    "@JobName", SqlDbType.VarChar, 50, "JobName");
```

> **Note** The *SqlDataAdapter* class expects to reference parameters in sequence. This means that you must add the parameters for new values to the insert and update commands in the same order as the columns appear in the select command's SQL, or you will get an exception.

With a *SqlDataAdapter* object set up and the user having made some changes to the data held locally in the *DataSet* object, we are ready to send the changes back to the data source. To do so, you simply call the *Update* method on the *SqlDataAdapter* object. The *Update* method has several useful overloads, described in Table 15-5, to provide different levels of update.

Table 15-5 *SqlDataAdapter.Update* Method Overloads

Arguments	Description of Update
Array of *DataRow* objects	Calls the relevant command for each row in the array with changes
DataSet object	Calls the relevant command for each changed row in all the *DataTable* objects in the *DataSet* object
DataTable object	Calls the relevant command for each changed row in the given *DataTable* object
DataSet object, *DataTable* name	Calls the relevant command for each changed row in the *DataTable* object with the given name, in the given *DataSet* object

The following code chooses the fourth overload, passing it a reference to the *DataSet* object and a string with the name of the source table to be updated:

```
daJobs.Update(dsJobs, "Jobs");
```

The section "Handling Update Events" later in this chapter describes in more detail exactly what happens to the *DataRow* objects during the update and what happens if an error occurs.

Using *SqlCommandBuilder*

A lot of code is needed to set up the update, insert, and delete commands for the *SqlDataAdapter* object. Luckily, if your *DataTable* object is built against a single source table, you can use a *SqlCommandBuilder* object to generate the update, insert, and delete commands for you. You still need to create and add the select command yourself. I've assumed that command has already been created in the following sample code:

```
SqlCommandBuilder cbrJobs;
cbrJobs = new SqlCommandBuilder(daJobs);
```

The UpdatingSQLDataSample sample application provides some menu items to show the SQL of the generated commands in a message box. The View menu contains a Command menu item with Update, Insert, and Delete submenu items. These submenu items are programmed to show the SQL generated by using the *GetUpdateCommand*, *GetInsertCommand*, or *GetDeleteCommand* methods of the *SqlCommandBuilder* object, as the following code shows:

```
MessageBox.Show(cbrJobs.GetInsertCommand().CommandText);
```

Figure 15-10 shows the UpdatingSQLDataSample application displaying the SQL from the insert command generated by *SqlCommandBuilder*.

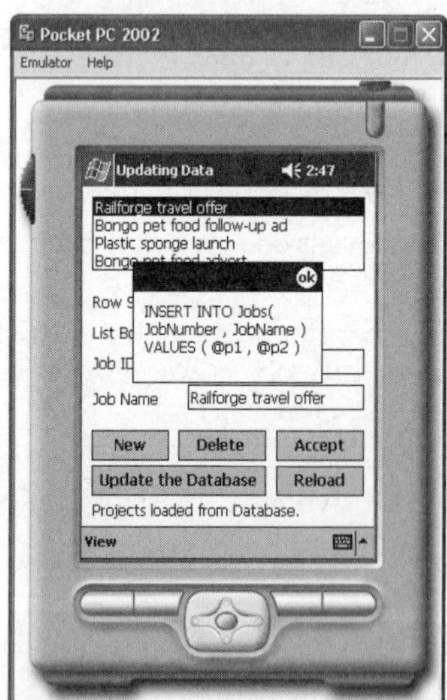

Figure 15-10 Insert command generated by the *SQLCommandBuilder* object.

> **Note** As often happens, you don't get something for nothing: using the *SqlCommandBuilder* object results in a decline in performance because more round-trips are required to the server to discover metadata required to build the extra commands for you.

Handling the Update Process

The following sections look in more detail at controlling and monitoring the update process after a call to the *SqlDataAdapter* object's *Update* method.

Handling Update Events

When you call the *Update* method specifying a *DataSet* object, a *DataTable* object, or an array of *DataRow* objects, *SqlDataAdapter* processes each row in turn as follows:

1. The values in the *DataRow* object are moved into the relevant command parameters.
2. The *RowUpdating* event is raised.
3. The command is executed against the data source.
4. The *RowUpdated* event is raised.
5. *AcceptChanges* is called to reset the *RowState* property to *Unchanged*.

The event handlers for the *RowUpdating* and *RowUpdated* events receive arguments that provide useful properties that allow you to monitor and control the update process. Table 15-6 lists these properties.

Table 15-6 Properties of *RowUpdatingEventArgs* and *RowUpdatedEventArgs*

Property	Object/When Used	Description
Command	Both	Reference to the command that will be used or that was used.
Errors	Both; has a value after the command has been executed.	Shows the errors that occurred (if any). This is a usual application exception class (not a *SqlException*).

(continued)

Table 15-6 Properties of *RowUpdatingEventArgs* and *RowUpdatedEventArgs* *(continued)*

Property	Object/When Used	Description
Row	Both	Gets the *DataRow* object that is being sent for update or that was sent for update.
RecordsAffected	*UpdatedEventArgs* only	Returns the count of rows affected by the command.
StatementType	Both	Gets the type of SQL statement that will be executed or that was executed.
Status	Both, used to control the rest of the update.	Values are members of the *UpdateStatus* enumeration. (See Table 15-7.)
TableMapping	Both	Gets the *DataTableMapping* object used in the update.

As a result of processing the events, you can decide whether an update is to be allowed to continue by setting the value of the *Status* property to one of the members of the *UpdateStatus* enumeration, described in Table 15-7.

Table 15-7 *UpdateStatus* Enumeration Values

Value	Description
Continue	No error has occurred, and the *SqlDataAdapter* will continue to process the update.
ErrorsOccurred	An error has occurred; you should examine the details before deciding whether to continue.
SkipAllRemainingRows	Set this value to abort all remaining rows in the update.
SkipCurrentRow	Set this value to abandon the update of the current row but continue with the remaining rows.

Handling Update Exceptions

Update exceptions are raised even if you are processing the *RowUpdating* and *RowUpdated* events. You'll need to handle them in the way we have already discussed. Some of these exceptions can be raised by using the *SqlException* object.

Using SQL Server Stored Procedures

Many system architects choose to use SQL Server stored procedures as part of their application designs, especially when a SQL Server is already being considered for data storage, because stored procedures provide centralized management of the SQL code, encapsulate all access to the data for performance tuning, and allow detailed security control. Stored procedures can be used for data retrieval, selection (to a given criteria), and manipulation.

Here are a few of the many advantages of using SQL Server stored procedures:

- Central control of SQL code
- Optimal speed for data operations
- Transactional control
- Data security
- Data access control
- Data selection and manipulation procedures common to all client applications

Some of the preceding advantages are amplified when you're using the .NET Compact Framework on a smart device. For example, because of the lack of local storage space and processing power, it is advantageous to do as much data processing on the server as possible and retrieve as little information as possible onto the smart device. Stored procedures provide an excellent way of offloading much of your application's processing onto a server.

With the data on SQL Server, and the SQL that selects and manipulates the data, you can make use of SQL Server query-optimization techniques. These techniques are beyond the scope of this book; you'll find a good discussion of the subject in *Microsoft SQL Server 2000 Performance Tuning Technical Reference* by Edward Whalen, Marcilina Garcia, Steve Adrien DeLuca, and Dean Thompson, published by Microsoft Press, 2001. Also, you can use the SQL Server object-level security to control access to the data and the stored procedures for your application and for any other applications that might have to share the database.

Using Transactions in the .NET Compact Framework

Transactions are used to ensure that data remains in a consistent state. They can ensure that all updates (even across different servers and organizations) are successful, and if a failure is detected, that all operations are rolled back to their original state.

One of the limitations of the .NET Compact Framework is that no support is provided for managing a transaction spanning databases or servers. However, the *SqlConnection* object does have a *BeginTransaction* method, which returns a *SqlTransaction* object that you can use to implement a transaction that is not distributed but is based on one SQL Server database.

> **Tip** You could leverage SQL Server's ability to coordinate transactions that span servers by writing a stored procedure that uses a transaction with a database on a *Linked Server*. See SQL Server 2000 Books Online for more detail on using Linked Servers.

Overall, it is not recommended to use transactions from the user interface tier of a smart device application. You can only perform transactions that are not distributed across databases anyway, and database performance can be *severely* affected if you allow a client application to leave transactions uncommitted for any length of time. (For example, if you allowed the application to start a transaction or begin an edit, and then permitted users to go for lunch and not commit the changes until their return.) The SQL Server host is the place to begin and commit transactions, and if you use stored procedures, you can use Transact-SQL code to perform the transactions. The following is an example of Transact-SQL structure for using a transaction:

```
CREATE PROC qUserTransaction
AS
BEGIN TRANSACTION
-- rest of the SQL here
IF @@ERROR=0 BEGIN
    COMMIT TRANSACTION
    RETURN 0 - success
END
ELSE BEGIN
    ROLLBACK TRANSACTION
    RETURN @@ERROR
END
```

Using Stored Procedures That Get Data

Stored procedures that get data can be used in place of embedded SQL *SELECT* statements in your application. Two kinds of data can be returned directly from a stored procedure:

- A result set
- A scalar

Figure 15-11 depicts the UsingSQLSPsSample application using a stored procedure to retrieve the jobs assigned to Ed Smith.

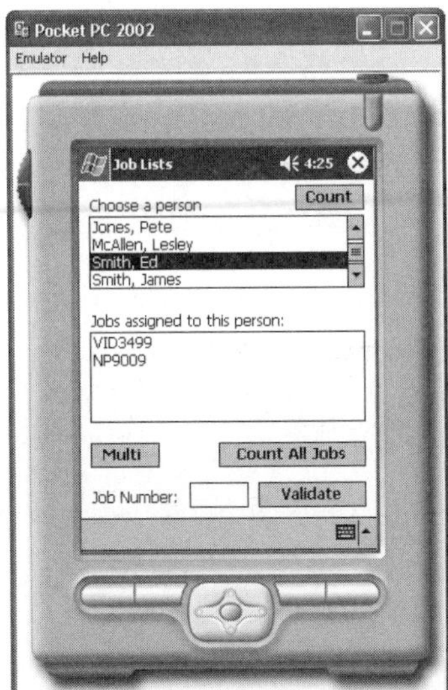

Figure 15-11 UsingSQLSPsSample application using stored procedures.

The UsingSQLSPsSample application, available with this book's sample files, uses stored procedures to access data in the example DotNetCF database. To create the UsingSQLSPsSample application yourself, create a new project in Visual Studio .NET, using a C# Smart Device Application template, and choose the Pocket PC as a target platform. Copy the form layout shown in Figure 15-11, using two ListBox controls, three Button controls, a TextBox control, and two Label controls. Table 15-8 lists the stored procedures that are available in the DotNetCF database. These stored procedures are used in the code samples that follow.

Table 15-8 Stored Procedures in the DotNetCF Database

Stored Procedure	Parameters	Returns
qPeopleList	None	Result set and return value
qCountPeople	None	Scalar
qPersonalJobList	*@PersonID int*	Result set
qValidateJobNumber	*@JobNumber varchar(15), @JobID int OUTPUT, @JobName varchar(50) OUTPUT*	None, but has output parameters

Returning Result Sets

The following code will use a simple stored procedure to fill a *DataSet* object. The stored procedure has no parameters. All you are doing here is moving the SQL code out of the client application. Place the following code in the *Load* event handler of your new form:

```
SqlConnection conG62000 = new SqlConnection(
    @"Data Source=YourServer;"
    + "Database=DotNetCF;Integrated Security=SSPI");
SqlCommand sqlGetPeople = new SqlCommand("qPeopleList", conG62000);
sqlGetPeople.CommandType = CommandType.StoredProcedure;
try
{
    // Fill the dataset
    dsPeople = new DataSet();
    SqlDataAdapter daPeople = new SqlDataAdapter(sqlGetPeople);
    daPeople.Fill(dsPeople, "People");
    DataTable dtPeople = dsPeople.Tables["People"];
    // Bind to a list box
    listBoxPeople.DataSource = dtPeople;
    listBoxPeople.DisplayMember = "PersonName";
    listBoxPeople.ValueMember = "PersonID";
}
catch (SqlException errSql)
{
    DisplaySqlErrors(errSql);
}
```

First the sample creates a *SqlConnection* object in exactly the same way the code from previous sections did. Next it prepares a *SqlCommand* object to use as the select command of the *SqlDataAdapter* object. The sample uses the overload of the *SqlDataAdapter* constructor that takes the *SqlCommand* object as an argument. The remaining code uses the *Fill* method and then binds the resulting table to a list box control, as we've done before.

Returning Scalars

Some stored procedures return a single value (known as a *scalar*) using the SQL *SELECT* statement. For example, a count of rows or a maximum value can be returned in this way. The sample stored procedure *qCountPeople* uses the following SQL:

```
SELECT COUNT(*) FROM People
```

In fact, a scalar is returned in a *DataSet* with just one row and one column, so it can be handled in exactly the way we have just covered.

Returning Multiple Result Sets

Some stored procedures return more than one result set. If you use the *Fill* method with such a stored procedure, multiple *DataTable* objects will be added to the *DataSet* object. For example, this SQL will return two result sets:

```
SELECT COUNT(*) FROM People
SELECT Firstname, Lastname FROM People
```

If you specify a table name, it is used for the first *DataTable* created. Subsequent tables are numbered. For example, if you specify *MyTable* for the table name, multiple tables are created with the names *MyTable*, *MyTable1*, *MyTable2*, and so on.

Using Stored Procedures with Parameters

Most stored procedures that you'll meet in practice will use parameters of some sort. Parameters can be classified into three types, as Table 15-9 shows.

Table 15-9 Stored Procedure Parameter Types

Parameter Type	How to Recognize It from the SQL
Input	The parameter is declared in the header of the stored procedure (before the *AS* keyword) and given a data type. You do not need to specify a direction because input is the default.
Output	The parameter is declared in the header of the stored procedure, given a data type, and given the *output* keyword.
Return value	Although treated as a parameter by the *SqlCommand* object, this type is not declared as a parameter in SQL. Look for the *return* keyword together with a value in the SQL.

Creating Input Parameters

You already met input parameters when we prepared the update, insert, and delete commands for the *SQLDataAdapter* object. At minimum, you'll need to provide a name and data type for each parameter. For data types with a specific length (such as *char* and *varchar*), you must also supply the length, which you can do in one of the overloads of the *SqlParameter* constructor. You don't need to specify the direction of an input parameter because the input direction is the default.

> **Note** The SQL Server data types can be found as values in the *SqlDbType* enumeration.

Once you have created the *SqlParameter* object, you can supply a value to the parameter using the *Value* property, or you can do it all in the same line.

```
SqlCommand sqlGetPersonJobs = new
   SqlCommand("qPersonalJobList", conG62000);
sqlGetPersonJobs.CommandType = CommandType.StoredProcedure;
sqlGetPersonJobs.Parameters.Add(
   "@PersonID", SqlDbType.Int).Value = PersonID;
```

Creating Output Parameters

Output parameters are created in a similar way, but with the additional step of specifying a direction using the *Direction* property and the *ParameterDirection* enumeration, as the following code illustrates.

```
SqlParameter p;
p = sqlValidateJob.Parameters.Add("@JobID", SqlDbType.Int);
p.Direction = ParameterDirection.Output;
```

> **Note** It is important to remember that you'll get an error if you assign a value to an output parameter or attempt to read the value before the command has been executed.

You can get the value of the output parameter (after the command has been executed) using the *Value* property.

Accessing Return Values

Although return values come from a different part of the SQL syntax of a stored procedure, they are treated as output parameters by the *SqlCommand* object. The following fragment of SQL demonstrates a return value being used in Transact-SQL:

```
CREATE PROC qReturnValue
AS
--some other SQL which does something here
RETURN -1006
```

You can access a return value by creating a special output parameter with the special *Direction* property value of *ParameterDirection.ReturnValue*, as shown here:

```
sqlGetPeople.Parameters.Add("returnval", SqlDbType.Int);
sqlGetPeople.Parameters["returnval"].Direction =
   ParameterDirection.ReturnValue;
```

You can then retrieve the value (after the command has been executed) using the *Value* property.

Executing Stored Procedures That Do Not Return Data

Some stored procedures are designed purely for updating data. These might use input parameters and might have a return value or output parameters, but they don't return either a result set or a scalar. If you're not getting a result set or if you don't require the result set or scalar returned by a stored procedure, you don't need a *SqlDataAdapter* object and you won't be using the *Fill* method. You can execute a *SqlCommand* object alone, using its *ExecuteNonQuery* method, as shown in the following code:

```
sqlGetPeople.ExecuteNonQuery();
iReturn = (int)(sqlGetPeople.Parameters["returnval"].Value);
```

This sample shows that after calling the *ExecuteNonQuery* method, the values of the output parameters are available.

SQLXML

So far, this chapter has looked in detail at how to extract and update relational data from a SQL Server data source using the *System.Data.SqlClient* objects. You've seen how the data can be read into a *DataSet* (from where it can be represented) or saved locally as XML. At this stage, you should be aware that an alternative route called SQLXML exists for XML data when using SQL Server as the data source. SQLXML enables developers to bridge the gap between XML and relational data.

Using SQLXML, you can

- Create XML views of existing relational data, and work with them as if they were XML files.
- Query SQL Server relational data using XPath, via a URL on the Web browser, or from a Web application.
- Query relational data with SQL, and return results in XML.
- Update relational data as if it were XML.
- Load XML files into an existing SQL Server database, converting the XML data to relational data.

SQLXML can be programmed from the .NET environment. SQLXML could, in theory, be used to retrieve and update XML data on a SQL Server database in applications for smart devices written with the .NET Compact Framework. In practice, however, programming SQLXML is more likely to occur in the business tier of a multitier application, where it is not subject to the restrictions of the smart device platform.

In a typical architecture, the smart device application can get and update XML produced by SQLXML via XML Web services, which are the subject of the next chapter of this book. Figure 15-12 shows a typical architecture for SQLXML.

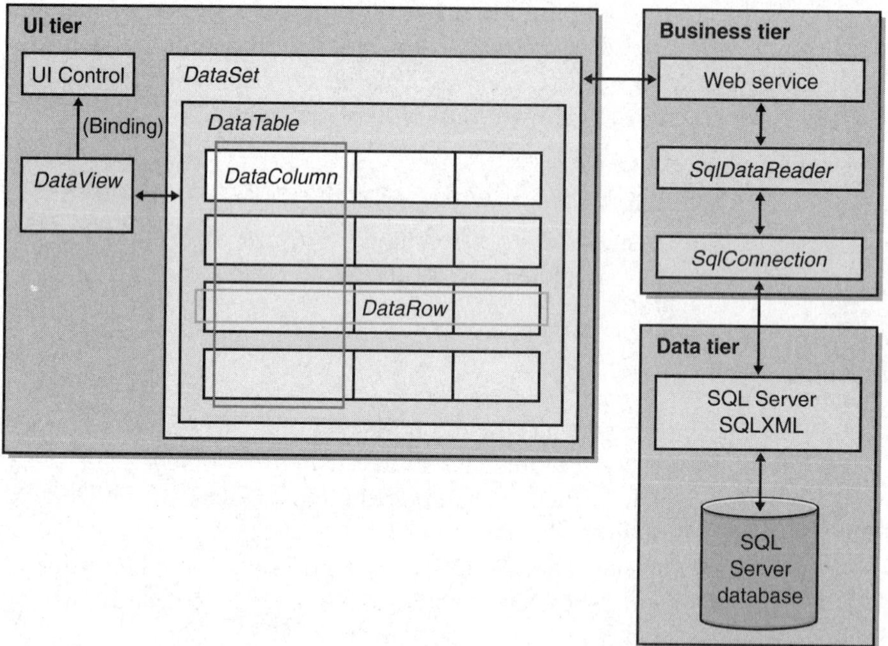

Figure 15-12 Example SQLXML architecture.

Using SQLXML in an Application

The UsingSQLXMLSample application is a brief introduction to the SQL Server XML abilities. You'll find the UsingSQLXMLSample application with this book's sample files. Figure 15-13 shows the UsingSQLXMLSample application retrieving some XML directly from SQL Server.

The UsingSQLXMLSample application uses a *SqlDataReader* object to get the single row and column that is generated by SQL Server as the result of using its XML keywords. It uses the following SQL to generate XML in SQL Server:

```
SELECT * FROM Jobs for xml auto
```

> **Note** Notice the important difference here to what we have seen before: this XML was generated not by the *DataSet* object, but by SQL Server itself.

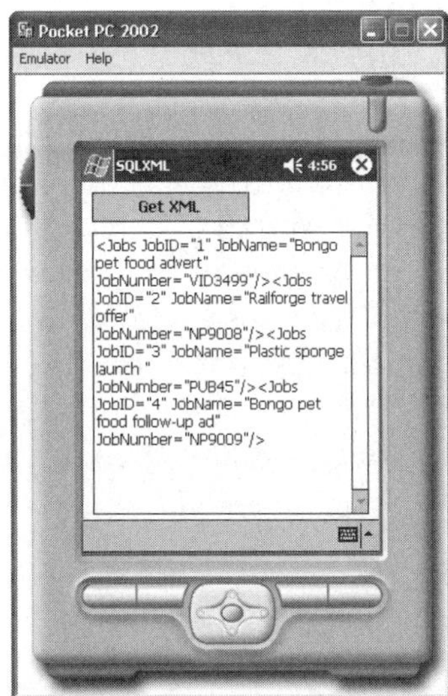

Figure 15-13 UsingSQLXMLSample application.

Further Reading

It is beyond the scope of this chapter to go further into how to use or program SQLXML. For a detailed introduction to the subject, refer to this book's companion volume, *Programming Microsoft SQL Server 2000 with XML, Second Edition* by Graeme Malcolm, published by Microsoft Press, 2002.

Summary

In this chapter, you have seen how to use the objects in the *System.Data.SqlClient* namespace to retrieve and update data. You have used the *SqlConnection* object to make a connection to a remote SQL Server from a smart device application, and you have used the *SqlDataReader* and *SqlDataAdapter* objects to retrieve data. You have seen how a *SqlDataAdapter* object can be used to retrieve data for a *DataSet* object, which can then use data binding to display values and retrieve changes in user interface controls. For both data retrieval and update, this chapter covered using SQL text and a stored procedure in a *SqlCommand* object, with its parameters represented by *SqlParameter* objects.

This chapter has also discussed the use of transactions with objects from the *System.Data.SqlClient* namespace, and it has introduced the native XML capabilities of SQL Server, known as SQLXML. Chapter 16 looks at a different use of XML for the retrieval and update of data: the XML Web service.

16

Working with XML Web Services

XML Web services enable access to remote and enterprise-level functions and data on a mobile device. They use Web standards to access functions via Hypertext Transmission Protocol (HTTP) on an Intranet or across the Internet. A connection with the server providing the XML Web service is required only while a function is being called and the reply is being returned to the smart device. XML Web service access can be configured easily through a firewall, and access to an XML Web service can be integrated with Windows security, secured with a plain text user name and password, or configured for anonymous use. Also, a smart device application can use XML Web services without installing additional software.

For example, an XML Web service could be used to connect waiters who are taking orders in a restaurant with an ordering system over a wireless network. The application could retrieve a menu, showing stock levels and the chef's special dishes, and then transmit an order. The system would reduce the stock levels, transmit the order to the kitchen, and prepare the customer's bill, which the waiter could retrieve later for payment at the table.

This chapter describes how you can connect to XML Web services from a smart device. It starts with an outline of the XML Web services system architecture. It then looks at how to create XML Web services and how to use the .NET Compact Framework to build smart device client applications for them. The samples for this chapter will start with a simple Web service that provides a single return value. Then a Web service will be shown that can provide more complex data in the form of an XML dataset populated with data that has been retrieved from a SQL Server database. Finally this chapter will look at a Web service capable of receiving a dataset that has been modified locally and updating a database with the changes. This chapter will also examine the possibilities for asynchronous processing of Web service operations.

> **Note** The samples presented in this chapter use the same database as Chapter 15. You will need to set up the sample database before trying the samples for this chapter.

XML Web Services Architecture

XML Web services allow you to publish business logic that can be accessed programmatically over a network (in particular, over the Internet). The data is described and represented in XML and is transmitted using standard HTTP, which allows it to pass through firewalls that are configured to prevent the passage of binary data. The operations supported by an XML Web service describe themselves in a standard format, also using XML. Because of the standard and neutral way in which a Web service connects two applications, it is ideal for

- Connecting applications on different operating systems.
- Leveraging legacy systems.
- Providing processing services on the Internet.

For example, a growing number of mapping services exist on the Internet, including Microsoft's MapPoint .NET Web service. MapPoint .NET is exposed as an XML Web service, allowing geographical information to be accessed programmatically over the Internet and incorporated into your own applications.

As a start, the following sections will describe where an XML Web service can fit into system architecture before looking in more detail at how the XML Web service works. Take a database application as an example. In Chapter 15, we covered how to connect a smart device application to a SQL Server database over your local network. We accomplished this connection using the *SqlClient* objects, and you needed to know what the server is called, the name of the database, and how to logon.

In contrast, a Web service gets the data to the smart device application while hiding the details of how the database connection is made and how the database objects are used from the client application. From the point of view of developing using the .NET Compact Framework, using a Web service has great advantages. An XML Web service is built to run on the server, with the full .NET

Framework and all the resources of a large machine. An XML Web service uses ASP.NET and runs under Microsoft Internet Information Services (IIS). All your smart device application has to do is create a proxy object capable of connecting to the Web service and invoking its methods. Figure 16-1 shows the context within which a Web service might be used to connect a smart device application with a SQL Server database.

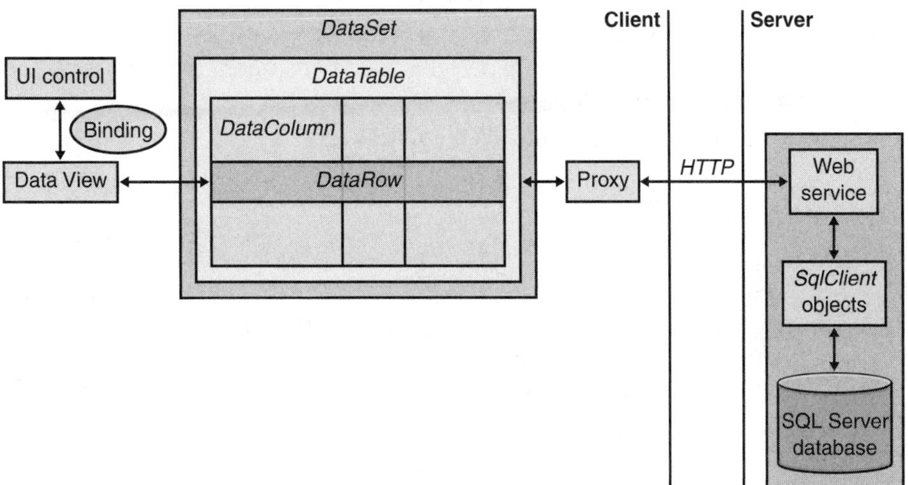

Figure 16-1 Web services and SQL Server data.

XML Web Services Infrastructure

This chapter now looks in a bit more detail at the infrastructure that provides a standard basis for locating services, describing how to use the services, and formatting of communications for XML Web services. The XML Web services infrastructure comprises the following services:

- XML Web services directories
- XML Web services discovery
- XML Web services description
- XML Web services wire formats

XML Web Services Directories

If you wanted to include an externally provided Web service in your application, it would be very difficult to locate it on the Internet without a way to search for it. *XML Web services directories* provide a central, Internet-based location for descriptions of Web services provided by other organizations.

> **Note** If you are using XML Web services simply as a mechanism to connect your smart device application to your enterprise servers on an Intranet, Web services directories and discovery documents (.disco files, discussed in the "XML Web Services Discovery" section later in this chapter) are not part of your development process. Skip straight to the section "XML Web Services Description." If you are using an externally provided XML Web service, read on.

An example of an Internet-based Web services directory is the Universal Discovery, Description, and Integration (UDDI) registry maintained by Microsoft at *http://uddi.microsoft.com*. A Web services directory, such as UDDI, defines a standard way to publish and discover information about XML Web services. It is searchable programmatically to allow potential XML Web service clients to query the information held in its registry.

The information held in an XML Web services directory falls into four categories:

- Business information
- Service information
- Binding information
- Documentation and specifications

This information is held in *discovery documents*, which are written in XML. During the process of adding a Web reference (which we will look at in the "Web Reference" section later in this chapter), Visual Studio .NET presents two example UDDI sites hosted by Microsoft.

XML Web Services Discovery

XML Web services discovery is the process of learning of the existence of a particular Web service and finding the location of the documents that describe it. The discovery process is assisted by reading a discovery document normally stored as a .disco file that is written in XML and contains the locations of description documents for Web services. DISCO is a Microsoft-sponsored discovery mechanism that uses the Internet and that can be programmatic. Here is the discovery document for one of the example Web services you will build later in the chapter, in the section "The TimesheetService Web Service":

```
<?xml version="1.0" encoding="utf-8"?>
<discovery xmlns:xsd="http://www.w3.org/2001/XMLSchema"
    xmlns:xsi="http://www.w3.org/2001/XMLSchema-instance"
    xmlns="http://schemas.xmlsoap.org/disco/">
  <contractRef
      ref="http://192.168.0.6/ProjectWebService/
          TimeSheetService.asmx?wsdl"
      docRef=http://192.168.0.6/ProjectWebService/
          TimeSheetService.asmx
      xmlns="http://schemas.xmlsoap.org/disco/scl/" />
  <soap address=
      http://192.168.0.6/ProjectWebService/TimeSheetService.asmx
      xmlns:q1=http://tempuri.org/
      binding="q1:TimeSheetServiceSoap"
      xmlns="http://schemas.xmlsoap.org/disco/soap/"/>
</discovery>
```

This chapter will not cover the full format of the DISCO file. (See the Microsoft DISCO Web site at *http://uddi.microsoft.com* for more details.) Notice, however, the link to the TimesheetService.asmx?wsdl description file in the preceding example. The next section discusses description files.

> **Note** The link to the Web service uses the IP address 192.168.0.6 instead of the machine name. We will cover the reason for this later in this chapter, in the section "Web Reference."

XML Web Services Description

A formal description of an XML Web service is written in XML using the Web Services Description Language (WSDL) and stored in a .wsdl file. If you use Visual Studio .NET to write the XML Web service, it automatically generates the WSDL file for you. This file defines the programming interface of the functions provided by the XML Web service, together with the formats of the messages that the XML Web service understands. You could click the URL given in the *<contractRef>* tag of the discovery file listed earlier to view the WSDL for the Web service in Internet Explorer. Figure 16-2 shows Internet Explorer displaying the contents of a WSDL file.

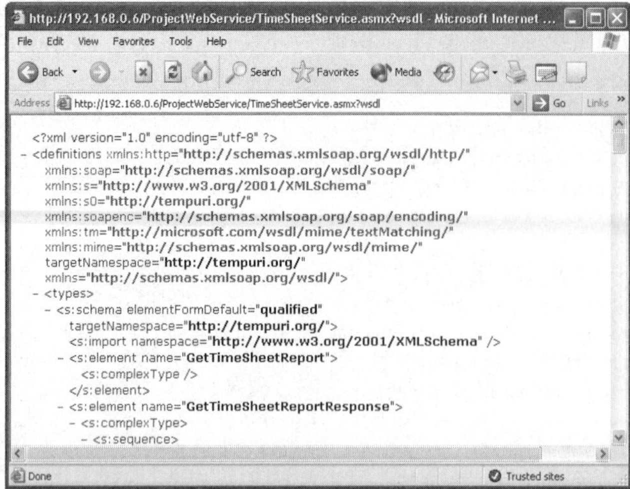

Figure 16-2 XML Web Services Description.

A detailed discussion of the contents of the WSDL file is beyond the scope of this chapter. The WSDL specification is maintained by the World Wide Web Consortium (W3C), so for more details, you can refer to their Web site at *http://www.w3c.org/TR/wsdl*. When you write a .NET Compact Framework application that consumes an XML Web service, you make a Web reference to a WSDL file, and Visual Studio .NET retrieves the WSDL and analyzes it to find out what functions are in the programming interface of the XML Web service.

XML Web Services Wire Formats

In theory, you can construct XML Web services to work with any protocol, but in practice, it is easier to stick to the three open protocols that are commonly used: HTTP-GET, HTTP-POST, and Simple Object Access Protocol (SOAP). If you build an XML Web service with Visual Studio .NET, it automatically supports these protocols.

HTTP is one of the standard Web protocols, and the GET and POST verbs are used for encoding and passing parameters in the header of a request. GET passes parameters in name-value pairs that are appended to the URL of the Web page being requested. GET parameters are URL-encoded to prevent confusion between the structure and the data of the request, and to allow non-text characters to be passed. POST also passes name-value pairs, but POST hides them inside the actual HTTP request message. XML Web services created using Visual Studio .NET support both HTTP-GET and HTTP-POST.

The SOAP specification defines how to use XML to represent data and how to use XML to describe encoding rules, message exchange patterns, and transport protocols. The result is that you can send more complex data across HTTP on the Web, and you can represent it in your client application as an object with properties and methods.

If you refer back to the listing of the WSDL file again, you can also see the *<message>*, *<portype>*, and *<binding>* tags for the SOAP protocol.

The SOAP specification itself is very flexible and can be implemented in many ways. A more detailed discussion of the internal mechanisms of SOAP is beyond the scope of this book; in any case, the details of the SOAP messages are abstracted by a proxy object generated by Visual Studio .NET. The .NET Compact Framework provides classes that represent a SOAP implementation, and Visual Studio .NET provides tools that generate code to enable an XML Web service to use SOAP to communicate across HTTP.

Outline of an XML Web Service at Work

This chapter has just discussed the *infrastructure* that is in place for an XML Web service to use. We will now look in overview at how a Web service is developed and at how it works at run time.

The XML Web Service Client

As discussed earlier, an XML Web service is developed using ASP.NET, with the full .NET Framework, and it runs in an IIS application on a Web server. Visual Studio .NET automatically writes WSDL files and DISCO files for Web services that you develop.

> **Note** Visual Studio .NET writes discovery files with the file extension .vsdisco.

To write the client application for a Web service, you need to go through some stages that mirror the infrastructure that we described earlier. These stages are described in Table 16-1.

Table 16-1 Stages in Writing an XML Web Service Client Application

Stage	Description
Directory	You might need to discover the Web service that you are to use. This stage will return a link to a discovery document. This process could be programmatic; for example, you might use the tools provided by a directory Web site. However, if you are using a Web service that you developed yourself, you can skip this stage because you should already know where to find the description documents.
Discovery	Using a discovery document, you (or the tool you're using) can find a link to a description document for the Web service that you want to use. Again, if you are using a Web service that you developed yourself, you can skip this stage because you already know where to find the description documents! This stage returns a link to a description document written in WSDL.
Description	You use a link to a WSDL document called a Web reference to obtain the WSDL document itself.
Development	You pass the information in the WSDL document to a tool that builds a Web service proxy class for you. The proxy class will represent the Web service on the client, and it allows you to develop and build the client application. (See Figure 16-3.) This stage delivers the XML Web service client application.
Run time	The client application calls the methods of the XML Web service, and the service's response is returned.

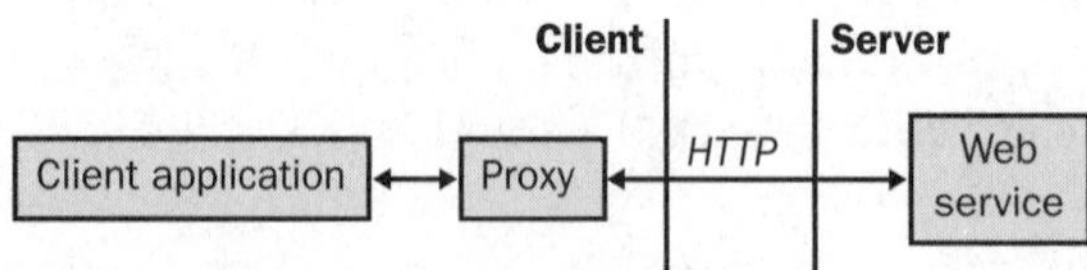

Figure 16-3 A Web service proxy.

The Web Service at Run Time

Figure 16-4 illustrates what is happening at run time in the life of a client application using a Web service.

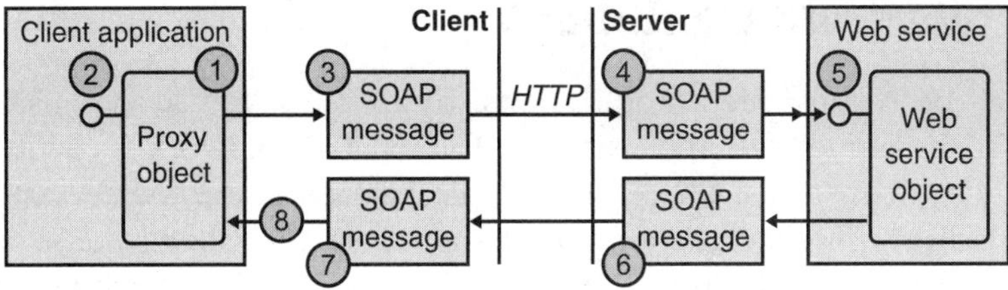

Figure 16-4 Web service client and Web service at run time.

Figure 16-4 depicts the following events, numbered in the order in which they occur:

1. The client application creates an instance of the Web service proxy.
2. The client application calls one of the methods of the Web service proxy.
3. The Web services infrastructure on the client serializes the arguments of the method into a new SOAP message and sends the message over the network to the Web service.
4. The Web services infrastructure on the server receives the SOAP message and creates an instance of the class implementing the Web service. It re-creates the arguments of the method from the SOAP message.
5. The method is called on the instance of the class implementing the Web service using the re-created arguments; the method executes, creating any output parameters and a return value.
6. The Web services infrastructure on the server creates a SOAP message and saves the output parameters and return value in it. The infrastructure then sends the message over the network to the client.
7. The Web services infrastructure on the client receives the SOAP message and retrieves the output parameters and return value.
8. The client receives the values of the output parameters and the return value.

Compact Framework Limitations

You'll be writing client applications for an XML Web service using the .NET Compact Framework and using the full .NET Framework for writing the Web services themselves. Therefore, any limitations of the .NET Compact Framework affect only the client applications. Table 16-2 shows some of the limitations of the .NET Compact Framework with respect to writing an XML Web service client application. You have already met some of these limitations in previous chapters.

Table 16-2 .NET Compact Framework Limitations for Writing XML Web Service Client Applications

Limitation	Description
Typed dataset	There is no support for typed datasets. You cannot consume a Web service that uses a typed dataset in its methods because you cannot successfully compile the Web service proxy for it.
Serialization (the ability of an object to write its own current state—usually indicated by the value of its member variables—to persistent storage)	There is no support for binary serialization using *BinaryFormatter* or for SOAP serialization using *SoapFormatter*. However, the XML Web services infrastructure does provide serialization support for transmitting object data using SOAP.
Deserialization (An object can be re-created by reading, or deserializing, the object's state from the storage.)	See Serialization description.

A Simple XML Web Service

This chapter uses a time sheet example of an XML Web service. A central database contains data on the jobs that are being worked on by the users of the sample application. Jobs are allocated to the users in another part of the enterprise, and they have a reference job number and a name. Your application will eventually allow a user to fill in the hours in a day that have been worked against each job allocated. The data is kept in a SQL Server database called DotNetCF. The database file and the sample application are included with this book's sample files. You'll need to set up this database before starting the samples for this chapter. (See the accompanying Readme file.)

The first sample simply provides a validation service for a job number. You can call a method with a trial job number, and if it is found in the database, the full name of the job is returned. This first sample is in two parts: creating a simple XML Web service, and creating a client for the simple XML Web service.

To create the simple XML Web service, start a new project in Visual Studio .NET, choose the ASP.NET Web Service Template, and call your project *JobWebServicesSample*. (See Figure 16-5.) This creates a Web service with a default class named *Service1*. Rename the class *JobsService*, rename the class's file JobsService.asmx, and open the designer. The DotNetCF database contains the stored procedure *qValidateJobNumber*. View the Server Explorer window, and locate the DotNetCF database. Drag the *qValidateJobNumber* stored procedure onto the *JobsService* designer. Visual Studio .NET will create an *SqlConnection* object and an *SqlCommand* object. You can see the stored procedure's parameters by selecting the *SqlCommand* object and clicking the ellipsis (...) button next to the *Parameters* property in the Properties window. The ellipsis button opens the SqlParameter Collection Editor shown in Figure 16-6.

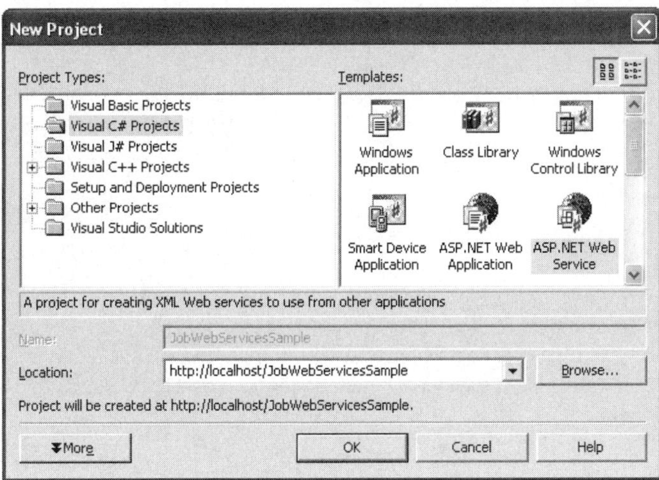

Figure 16-5 ASP.NET Web Service Template.

> **Tip** Remember that the Web service is created using the full .NET Framework, not the .NET Compact Framework. So you benefit from all the designer and code-generating features of the full .NET Framework, including the advantage of using named parameters for the *SqlCommand* object.

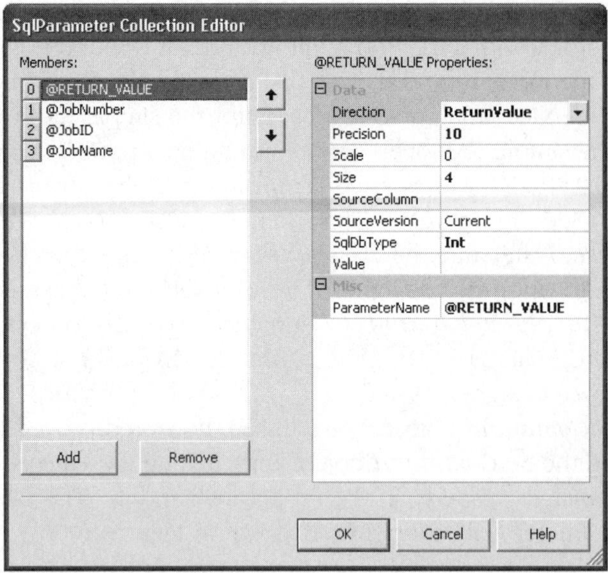

Figure 16-6 SqlParameter Collection Editor dialog box.

Now view the code in the *JobsService* class, and you can modify the example Web method called *HelloWorld*, which is commented out, to create the new method *ValidateJobNumber*. The sample Web method code is as follows:

```
[WebMethod]
public string ValidateJobNumber(string TryNumber)
{
    sqlCommand1.Parameters["@JobNumber"].Value = TryNumber;
    sqlCommand1.Connection.Open();
    sqlCommand1.ExecuteNonQuery();
    int JobID = (int)(sqlCommand1.Parameters["@JobID"].Value);
    string JobName;

    if (JobID > 0)
    {
        JobName = sqlCommand1.Parameters["@JobName"].Value.ToString();
    }
    else
    {
        JobName = "Not Found";
    }

    return JobName;
}
```

When you attach the *WebMethod* attribute to a public method, it is exposed as an operation of the Web service, which can be invoked by an XML Web service client application.

Locate the declaration of the *JobsService* class, and insert a *WebService* attribute, as shown here:

```
[WebService (Namespace="http://servername/xmlwebservices/",
   Description="Some descriptive text could go here.")]
```

Notice the *Namespace* value of the *WebService* attribute. This value changes the namespace for the Web service from the built-in default (*http://tempuri.org*). You should replace *servername* with the name of your XML Web services server. You could also add some general description of your Web service using the *Description* value.

> **Important** It is good practice to change the *namespace* attribute even for a simple example such as this one.

Compile and run the Web service, and you'll see the discovery screen for the *JobsService*, as shown in Figure 16-7.

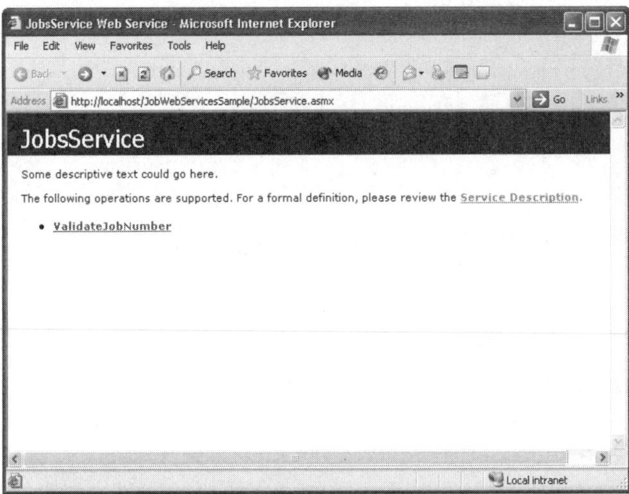

Figure 16-7 Discovering the *JobsService* XML Web service.

The Service Description link shows the formal WSDL file for the service. You can even test the Web service's operations from here. This is a useful "Test

Me" capability for ASP.NET XML Web services provided by IIS. Click *ValidateJobNumber* to invoke the operation. The test screen collects the parameters for the operation, as shown in Figure 16-8.

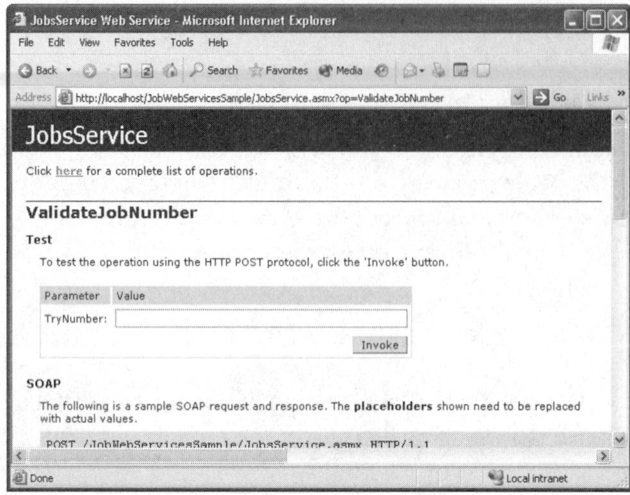

Figure 16-8 Testing the *ValidateJobNumber* Web method.

You will see the return value from the operation displayed in Internet Explorer. For example, the job number NP9008 does exist, and it returns the following job name:

```
<?xml version="1.0" encoding="utf-8" ?>
<string xmlns="http://mynamespace.org/">Bongo pet food follow-up ad
</string>
```

A Client for the Simple XML Web Service

Now you will extend the sample by writing a client for the simple Web service, using the .NET Compact Framework. Create a new Smart Device Application to be the client for the *JobsService* Web service. The next step is to add a Web reference to the project. This will provide the information that Visual Studio .NET will need to generate a Web service proxy class for you.

Web Reference

Use the Project menu or the Solution Explorer window to add a Web reference. Visual Studio .NET shows the Add Web Reference dialog box. (See Figure 16-9.) The first page shows two Microsoft Web services directory sites that are currently available on the Internet.

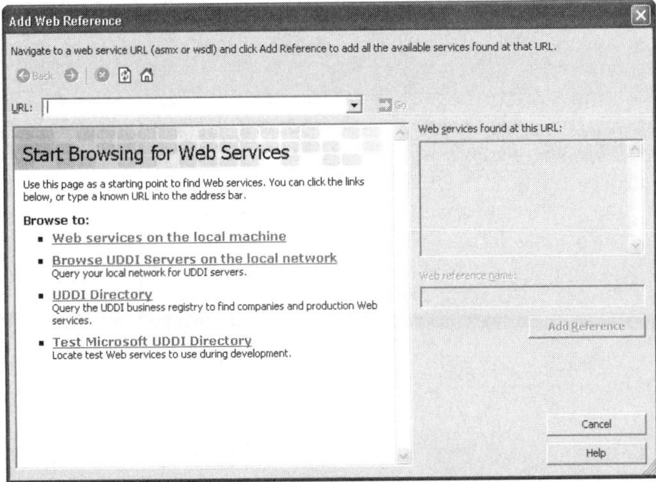

Figure 16-9 Web services UDDI directories.

However, you will not be registering every one of your test Web services on the Internet, so you can go straight for the description of your new *JobsService* Web service by typing the URL to its .asmx file, with the following code:

```
http://localhost/JobWebServicesSample/JobsService.asmx
```

The dialog box downloads the WSDL file for the service, analyzes it, and then displays the description of *JobsService*, which you last saw when testing the Web service project. (Compare Figure 16-7 with Figure 16-10.) When the download finishes, you can click the Add Reference button to add a Web reference to your project.

> **Warning** The emulator (or smart device) is not the same host as your development machine, so *http://localhost* will not be as recognized as a Web server. If you have difficulty resolving the network name of the Web services server, you can use the IP address of the Web services server in the reference at this stage, such as
>
> http://192.168.0.6/JobWebServicesSample/JobsService.asmx

It is a good practice to change the name of the Web reference. You do so by clicking on the name of the Web reference in the Solution Explorer window and changing the Folder Name property in the Properties window.

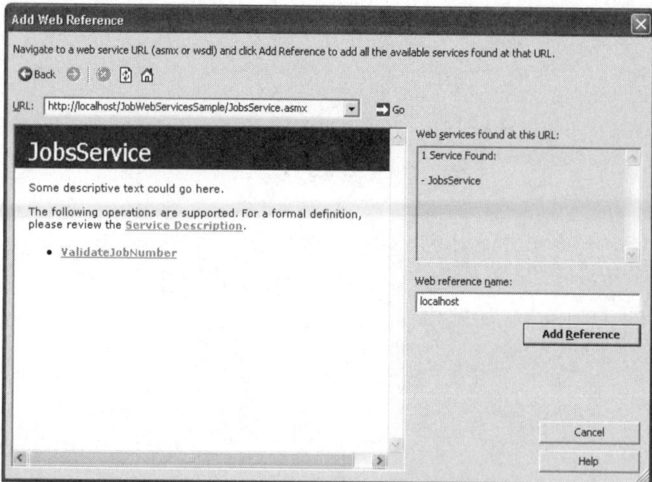

Figure 16-10 Add Web Reference dialog box.

Proxy Generation

When you click the Add Reference button, Visual Studio .NET generates proxy classes to interface between your application and the Web service. You cannot immediately see these classes in the Solution Explorer window because the window hides all the code-behind objects by default. If you want to look at the generated class, click the Show All Files button in the Solution Explorer window and expand the Reference.map node to show the hidden Reference.cs file. (See Figure 16-11.)

Figure 16-11 The Reference.cs proxy class source file.

Proxy Class Allows Dynamic Web Service URL

Look at the Reference.cs class, and you'll see that the proxy class generated by Visual Studio .NET provides a *URL* property. This property allows the path to the XML Web service to be determined at run time.

XML Web Service Consumption

Next you will write the client application code that uses (*consumes*) the functions in the XML Web service. (See Figure 16-12 for the layout of the form.) Most of the program code is in the *Click* event handler for the Test button. First you should import the Web reference that you made earlier.

```
using WebServiceClient.JobsWebReference;
```

Now the main task is to create an object from the XML Web service proxy class and invoke its *ValidateJobNumber* method, taking the *TryNumber* parameter from the first text box and populating the other text box with the results. If the *TryNumber* parameter contains a valid job number, the *ValidateJobNumber* method returns the full job name.

```
private void buttonTest_Click(object sender, System.EventArgs e)
{
    string sTry = textBoxTry.Text;
    string sJobName;
    JobsService ws = new JobsService ();
    sJobName = ws.ValidateJobNumber(sTry);
    textBoxJobName.Text = sJobName;
}
```

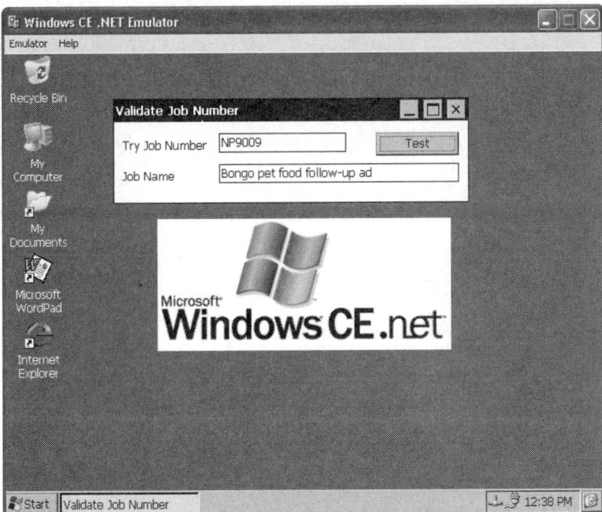

Figure 16-12 Client for the JobsService Web service.

A Web Service That Returns a Dataset

The previous sample returned a single piece of information. In practice, you might want to return more complex and structured data. Visual Studio .NET provides support for XML Web services that pass data in a dataset.

Although the .NET Compact Framework does not support typed datasets and also lacks support for the *Merge*, *Clone*, and some other methods of the *DataSet* class, workarounds are available for consuming an XML Web service that uses a typed dataset as a return type or as a parameter type.

> **Tip** If you are writing an XML Web service specifically to connect a smart device application to the enterprise, it is helpful to provide methods that do not use typed datasets as a return type or as a parameter type.

The .NET Compact Framework has sufficient infrastructure to be able to pass datasets as the parameters of Web service methods. The next sample returns a dataset containing a small report from the DotNetCF database.

The TimesheetService Web Service

In this sample, you will extend the existing Web service project with a new Web service class named *TimesheetService*. Add a new Web service file to the *JobWebServicesSample* project, and rename it to *TimesheetService*. From the Server Explorer window, drag the stored procedure *qTimesheetReport*. Now drag a *SqlDataAdaptor* from the toolbox and connect the *SqlCommand* object to its *SelectCommand* property. You can leave the *DeleteCommand*, *InsertCommand*, and *UpdateCommand* properties alone because this report will be read-only. Now use the Generate Dataset item on the Data menu. I have called the new *DataSet* object *dsTimeSheetReport*.

Your next task is to create the Web method that will provide the *DataSet* to a client application. For the purposes of this example, make a deliberate mistake here: forget (temporarily) that the .NET Compact Framework does not support typed datasets.

```
[WebMethod]
public dsTimeSheetReport GetTimeSheetReport()
{
    dsTimeSheetReport ds = new dsTimeSheetReport();
    sqlDataAdapter1.Fill(ds);
    return ds;
}
```

Compile and test this Web service in the same way as before; you can use the URL *http://localhost/JobWebService/TimeSheetService.asmx?* to test the new *TimesheetService* Web service. If you test the *GetTimeSheetReport* method with the Invoke button, you should get results similar to the following XML:

```
<?xml version="1.0" encoding="utf-8" ?>
<dsTimeSheetReport xmlns="http://tempuri.org/">
  <xs:schema id="dsTimeSheetReport"
      targetNamespace="http://www.tempuri.org/dsTimeSheetReport.xsd"
      xmlns:mstns="http://www.tempuri.org/dsTimeSheetReport.xsd"
      xmlns="http://www.tempuri.org/dsTimeSheetReport.xsd"
      xmlns:xs="http://www.w3.org/2001/XMLSchema"
      xmlns:msdata="urn:schemas-microsoft-com:xml-msdata"
      attributeFormDefault="qualified"
      elementFormDefault="qualified">
    <xs:element name="dsTimeSheetReport"
        msdata:IsDataSet="true"
        msdata:Locale="en-GB">
      <xs:complexType>
        <xs:choice maxOccurs="unbounded">
          <xs:element name="Table">
            <xs:complexType>
              <xs:sequence>
                <xs:element name="Surname"
                    type="xs:string" />
                <xs:element name="Firstname"
                    type="xs:string"
                    minOccurs="0" />
                <xs:element name="ProjectName"
                    type="xs:string" />
                <xs:element name="TotalHours"
                    msdata:ReadOnly="true"
                    type="xs:double"
                    minOccurs="0" />
              </xs:sequence>
            </xs:complexType>
          </xs:element>
        </xs:choice>
      </xs:complexType>
    </xs:element>
  </xs:schema>
  <diffgr:diffgram
      xmlns:msdata="urn:schemas-microsoft-com:xml-msdata"
      xmlns:diffgr="urn:schemas-microsoft-com:xml-diffgram-v1">
    <dsTimeSheetReport
        xmlns="http://www.tempuri.org/dsTimeSheetReport.xsd">
      <Table diffgr:id="Table1" msdata:rowOrder="0">
        <Surname>Smith</Surname>
        <Firstname>Ed</Firstname>
```

(continued)

```
        <ProjectName>Bongo pet food advert</ProjectName>
        <TotalHours>20</TotalHours>
      </Table>
      <Table diffgr:id="Table2" msdata:rowOrder="1">
        <Surname>Smith</Surname>
        <Firstname>Ed</Firstname>
        <ProjectName>Railforge travel offer</ProjectName>
        <TotalHours>12</TotalHours>
      </Table>
    </dsTimeSheetReport>
  </diffgr:diffgram>
</dsTimeSheetReport>
```

You can see that the report contains a single *<xs:elementname="Table">* tag followed by the rows of data. This sample continues by seeing what happens if you try to build a .NET Compact Framework client application for this Web service.

An XML Web Service Client with a Typed Dataset

To show the problems that you'll encounter if you try using the typed dataset Web service we have just written, create a new smart device Windows application. Add a new project, and choose the Smart Device Application template. Add a Web reference to the *TimesheetService* Web service, and attempt to build the new project. You should get build errors such as those shown in Figure 16-13. You can see some hints in the messages about serialization, and if you follow the links, you'll find the errors are all in the (hidden) Mappings.cs class that Visual Studio .NET has built to support the *dsTimeSheetReport* typed dataset.

> **Note** Remember that the .NET Compact Framework does not include support for serialization using the *BinaryFormatter* class or support for SOAP serialization using the *SoapFormatter* class.

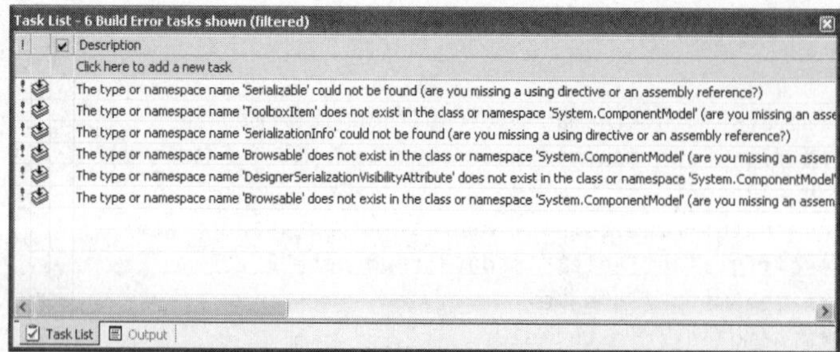

Figure 16-13 Build errors when using a typed *DataSet*.

Techniques for Changing a Web Service to Use Standard Datasets

Here are some suggestions for techniques for using typed datasets with a .NET Compact Framework client application:

- Change the XML Web service so that it uses only standard datasets.
- Change the XML Web service so that it adds functions that use standard datasets.
- Create a new XML Web service that consumes the original typed datasets and converts them to standard datasets.

You might choose the first option if the sole reason for creating the XML Web service is to connect a smart device application to the enterprise, and you might choose the second option if you need to add support for full .NET Framework applications as well as for .NET Compact Framework applications. However, both of these first two options assume that you're in control of the XML Web service. If your client application is consuming an external XML Web service, you might have to consider the third option of creating a new XML Web service of your own to convert the typed dataset to a standard dataset. This choice will be at the expense of some performance overhead.

You can change the Web service so that it doesn't use a typed dataset as the return type of its method. To do this, simply declare the return type as *DataSet* and copy the results from the typed dataset into a standard dataset, as shown here:

```
[WebMethod]
public DataSet GetTimeSheetReport()
{
    dsTimeSheetReport ds = new dsTimeSheetReport();
    sqlDataAdapter1.Fill(ds);
    DataSet ds2 = ds;
    return ds2;
}
```

You can test this revised Web service by using the same URL reference to the *TimesheetService* Web service as before.

Web Service Client with a Standard Dataset

To correct the client application, refresh the Web reference by using the Update Web Reference menu item. This re-creates the Mappings.cs file that was causing the build errors. Now try another build—you should be successful this time!

Now you will add some code to use the Web service. You can see the form that the application uses to call the Web service and display the data returned in Figure 16-14. The form contains a command button control and a text box control. The idea is to retrieve the report dataset and then use its *DataTable* object to write a report into the text box.

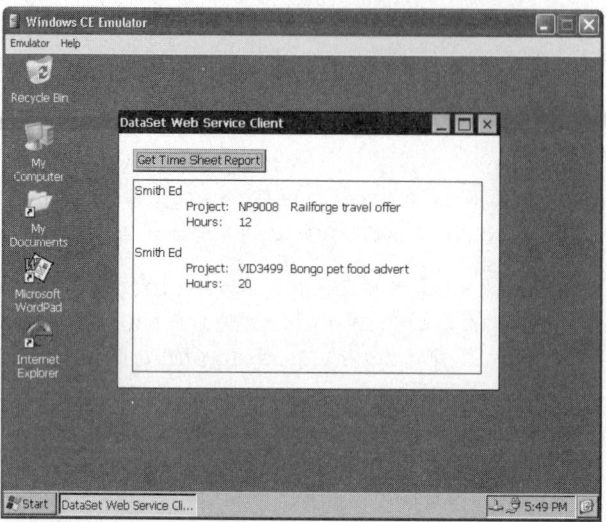

Figure 16-14 XML Web service client using a *DataSet* object.

The following sample shows the code for the Get Time Sheet Report button. (We covered the details of how to use the *DataSet* object and its *DataTable* and *DataRow* objects in Chapter 14.)

```
using System.Xml;
using NETCFDevelopersReference.TimesheetWebReference;
:

private void buttonGo_Click(object sender, System.EventArgs e)
{
    TimeSheetService ws = new TimeSheetService();
    DataSet ds = ws.GetTimeSheetReport();
    DataTable dt = ds.Tables[0];
    string sReport = "";
    foreach (DataRow row in dt.Rows)
    {
        sReport = sReport + row[0].ToString() + " "
            + row[1].ToString() + "\r\n "
            + "\tProject:\t" + row[2].ToString() + "\t"
            + row[3].ToString() + "\r\n"
            + "\tHours:\t" + row[4].ToString() + "\r\n\r\n";
    }
    textBoxReport.Text = sReport;
}
```

If you have tried this example, you will have noticed that it takes over 15 seconds to run the report. This delay occurs because there is a deliberate delay of 15 seconds in the stored procedure to simulate a much longer running report. The delay will help you understand the asynchronous operation of the Web service methods.

Asynchronous Operation

As mentioned in the beginning of this chapter, calls to Web service methods can be made asynchronously, and you don't have to write any extra support for these calls in the Web service—the Web service proxy in the client application and the XML Web services infrastructure provide all the functionality for asynchronous operations. For example, if your Web service method is named *GetTimeSheetReport*, Visual Studio .NET creates two methods for asynchronous operation, *BeginGetTimeSheetReport* and *EndGetTimeSheetReport*. The *Begin* method has the same parameters as *GetTimeSheetReport* plus two additional optional parameters for *AsyncCallback* and *asyncState* objects. The *End* method takes an *IAsyncResult* object as its parameter and returns the same return type as your original method.

The first part of creating a Web service client for asynchronous operation follows the steps for the other clients you have already written, right up to the point where you call the method on the Web service proxy. When you're using a Web service method asynchronously, you can choose to use a callback function or you can use a synchronization object to wait for processing to finish. The following examples look at both of those options in turn.

The first example looks at the callback function. To use a callback, you need to write a *public static* function that will be called when processing is complete.

```
public static void ReportCallBack(IAsyncResult ar)
{
    MessageBox.Show("Done!");
}
```

Next, in the function that calls the Web service method, create a callback object that references the new callback function. Then call the *Begin* version of your method, passing in any of the original parameters (in this example, there are none) plus the callback object and the reference to the Web service object (which supports the *IAsyncResult* interface).

```
AsyncCallback cb = new AsyncCallback(
    AsyncWebServiceClient.Form1.ReportCallBack);
IAsyncResult ar= ws.BeginGetTimeSheetReport(cb, ws);
```

In this code, *ws* is the reference to the Web service. (The declaration and instantiation of *ws* are not shown.)

You can call the *End* version of the method in the callback to retrieve the results of the Web service operation. The reference to the Web service was passed in the call to the *Begin* version of the method, and it is then available as part of the *IAsyncResult* object, which forms the only argument of the callback function. So, code such as this should work:

```
public static void ReportCallBack(IAsyncResult ar)
{
    TimeSheetService ws = (TimeSheetService) ar.AsyncState;
    DataSet ds = ws.EndGetTimeSheetReport(ar);
}
```

The second example looks at using the asynchronous methods provided by the Web service proxy class. In this sample, you won't use a callback but will instead wait for the process to be signaled as complete by using the *AsyncWaitHandle.WaitOne* method of the *IAsyncResult* object, as shown in the following code:

```
TimeSheetService ws = new TimeSheetService();
IAsyncResult ar = ws.BeginGetTimeSheetReport(null,null);
ar.AsyncWaitHandle.WaitOne(); // Wait
// Get results
DataSet ds = ws.EndGetTimeSheetReport(ar);
// Output the results as before...
```

Procedure for Returning a Dataset for Update

Now we'll look at creating a Web service capable of receiving a *DataSet* object and passing changes all the way back to a SQL Server database for update. To do so, you can add a new Web method to the Web service class that takes a *DataSet* object as one of its arguments. Inside the method, you call the *Update* method of an *SqlDataAdapter* object that has been given suitable *SqlCommand* objects for the *InsertCommand*, *DeleteCommand*, and *UpdateCommand* properties. The sample code for the XML Web service looks like this:

```
[WebMethod]
public DataSet UpdateTimeSheet(DataSet dsUpdate)
{
    sqlDataAdapter2.Update(dsUpdate);
    return dsUpdate;
}
```

Refer to Chapter 15 for details of how the *Update* method of the *SqlDataAdapter* works. Notice that the *UpdateTimeSheet* method returns the *DataSet* object back to the client application, so the results of the update can be processed.

Inside the XML Web service client application, changes are made locally to a *DataSet* object retrieved using the *GetTimeSheetReport* method. Changes can be made either programmatically or by using data binding. (Refer to Chapter 14 for more details of data binding with datasets in a smart device application.) The modified *DataSet* object is then sent for update using the *UpdateTimeSheet* method, as shown here:

```
private void buttonUpdate_Click(object sender, System.EventArgs e)
{
    TimeSheetService ws = new TimeSheetService();
    dsTimesheets = ws.UpdateTimeSheet(dsTimesheets);
}
```

In this code, *dsTimesheets* is the *DataSet* object that was originally retrieved.

> **Note** Remember not to call *AcceptChanges* on the *DataSet* object in the client application because doing so will set the *RowState* property of the changed rows to *Unchanged*. When the *Update* method on the *SqlDataAdapter* object in the Web service class is called, the *Update* command is not run for data rows having the *Unchanged* status, so your changes will not reach the database.

Design Considerations for XML Web Services

This chapter on XML Web services finishes by bringing together some of the design considerations that have been mentioned and some more general points that are especially relevant if you are designing a Web service for consumption by a smart device application written using the .NET Compact Framework. Table 16-3 describes these considerations.

Table 16-3 Design Considerations for XML Web Services

Consideration	Description
Typed *DataSets*	Do not design a Web service that uses only typed *DataSets* in the arguments and return type of its methods. Provide alternatives that use the plain *DataSet*.
DataSet size	Keep the restrictions of the smart device in mind when returning data from a Web service method. Use highly selective criteria, and send a small number of rows to the client at any one time. Allow the client to return one batch before requiring it to load another.
Web references	Remember that the Web server is not on the smart device, so the Web reference cannot be made using the *localhost* name (which you would never do in a real application anyway).
Asynchronous operation	Where possible, call XML Web services asynchronously. Provide a wait cursor or progress bar to inform users that a lengthy operation is in progress, or enable other functions of the application to operate while the asynchronous call is in progress.

Summary

This chapter has shown you how to write some simple XML Web services that can connect a smart device application to the enterprise (and therefore to the central or enterprise databases). It has shown how the support in Visual Studio .NET for the XML Web service infrastructure helps programming of a client application using the .NET Compact Framework. This chapter has covered techniques for using both simple return values and datasets with XML Web services, and also for using the support available for asynchronous processing.

17

Using SQL Server CE

This chapter describes how to program a smart device application to work with a local SQL Server 2000 Windows CE Edition (SQL Server CE) database, and it discusses methods of creating the database and synchronizing it with a central or an enterprise SQL Server database. For example, a delivery service driver could download the day's delivery schedule at a central depot at the start of a day into a local SQL Server CE database. During the day, the driver could use a smart device application to check the loading of goods and record the deliveries into the local SQL Server CE database. On returning to the depot after completing the day's rounds, the driver could reconnect to the central database to coordinate stock control and permanently record the deliveries' status. Reconciliation of the local and central data could also occur over a wireless connection at any point during the day from the cab of the delivery vehicle to provide up-to-the-minute tracking information for the customers.

SQL Server CE provides an ideal local storage mechanism for this sort of application because its connectivity solutions can be encrypted for security of data and are optimized for occasional connection and for wireless communication. Using SQL Server CE also provides the smart application developer with a familiar SQL Server environment (SQL Server CE supports a subset of Transact-SQL), which can be programmed using the .NET Compact Framework with techniques similar to those used to program a desktop .NET Framework application against a SQL Server 2000 database.

This chapter starts by looking in overview at SQL Server CE and how it fits into system architecture with a smart device application. It continues with a detailed look at how to create and program a SQL Server CE database on the smart device using the objects in the data provider for SQL Server CE, which forms part of the Smart Device Extensions. Finally it describes two of the available approaches for synchronizing local SQL Server CE data with a central or enterprise database: remote data access (RDA) and merge replication. The relative merits of these approaches are discussed, and samples of both are presented.

Using SQL Server on a Smart Device

SQL Server CE is a remarkably small implementation of a SQL database suitable for installation on a smart device. SQL Server CE can be installed independently on a smart device or as part of the deployment of a .NET Compact Framework application.

> **Note** To develop applications using SQL Server CE, you need to purchase a SQL Server 2000 developer license, which permits you to download and install SQL Server CE.

Some server-side components enable connection between a local SQL Server CE database and a central or an enterprise SQL Server database. The installation and configuration of these components will be covered in detail later in this chapter.

SQL Server CE comprises a database engine, a client agent program (for connecting to enterprise databases, discussed later, in the section "Getting Data to and from SQL Server), and a tiny version of the Query Analyzer program (Isqlw.exe). The Query Analyzer program allows you to graphically create and structure a database with a tree-view of the database objects, as shown in the Objects tab in Figure 17-1. (Graphical functions such as this are available only in the Enterprise Manager in SQL Server 2000.) Query Analyzer also includes a SQL query tab and a results Grid tab, shown in Figure 17-2. You can use these tabs to perform selections, updates, inserts, and deletions against the local database. You can also run Data Definition Language (DDL) SQL statements to alter or build objects in the local database.

SQL Server CE supports databases up to 2 GB, with support for Binary Large Objects (BLOBS) up to 1 GB. In practice, the maximum size of the database will be limited by the available local storage on your target smart device. Table 17-1 summarizes the capabilities of SQL Server CE.

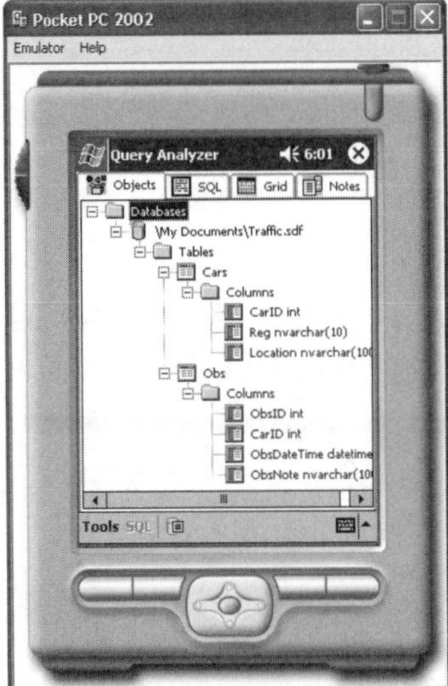

Figure 17-1 Query Analyzer Objects tab.

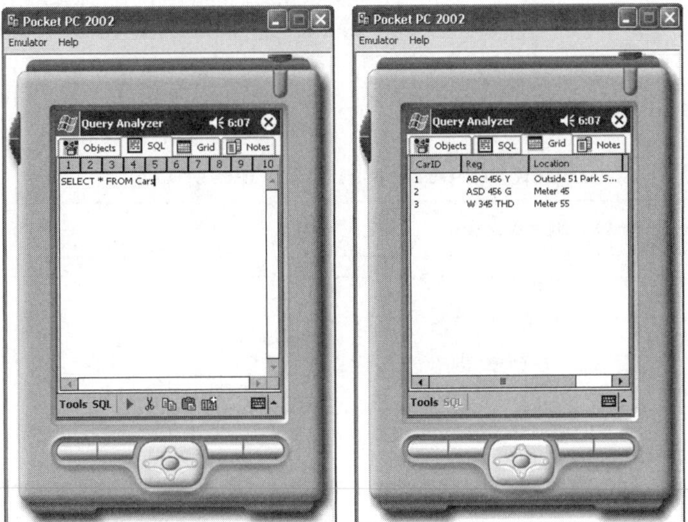

Figure 17-2 Query Analyzer SQL and Grid tabs.

Table 17-1 Supported Features of SQL Server CE

Feature	Supported
Data Definition Language (DDL)	*CREATE DATABASE*, *CREATE TABLE*, *ALTER TABLE*, create for primary key, unique and foreign key constraints, and defaults. Also *CREATE INDEX*, *DROP INDEX*, and *DROP TABLE*.
Data Manipulation Language (DML)	*SELECT*, *DELETE*, *UPDATE*, and *INSERT*. *SELECT* supports aggregate functions (*INNER JOIN* and *OUTER JOIN*, subqueries, *ORDER BY*, *GROUP BY*, and *HAVING*).
Indexes, constraints, and defaults	Single and multiple column indexes. The primary key column of a table can be identified and constrained. Column defaults are supported.
Transactions	Nested transactions are supported.
Cursors	Scrollable and forward-only cursors are supported.
Encryption and security	Data can be encrypted at 128-bit file level. Databases can be password protected.

SQL Server CE supports a subset of data types, as described in Table 17-2.

Table 17-2 Data Types Supported in SQL Server CE

Data Type Family	Supported
Integer	*tinyint*, *smallint*, *integer*, and *bigint*
Numeric	*real*, *numeric*, and *float*
Binary	*bit*, *binary*, *varbinary*, and *image*
Unicode	*national character* (*nchar*), *national character varying* (*nvarchar*), and *ntext*
Others	*money*, *datetime*, and *uniqueidentifier*

Data type *int* can form an identity column, and data type *uniqueidentifier* can form a globally unique identifier (*rowguidcol*) column.

Getting Data to and from SQL Server

This chapter continues by describing how to create a SQL Server CE database locally on the smart device with a sample application. However, in practice, many applications will require you to transfer data to and from a central or an enterprise database such as SQL Server 2000. (We'll call this the *central SQL*

Server database.) Later this chapter will explain in detail how to use two different techniques for transferring data between SQL Server CE and a central SQL server: RDA and merge application.

Programming a SQL Server CE Application

There are three distinct phases to programming with SQL Server CE: creating the local SQL Server CE database, updating the local data, and merging the locally changed data back to a central database. This section examines the creation of a local SQL Server CE database in code and updating the database from a smart device application programmed using the .NET Compact Framework.

The sample application is designed to help several car-parking attendants record the position and length of stay of vehicles using a smart device application. In this first part, the sample simply records the registration plate and description of the position of a vehicle, as shown in Figure 17-3.

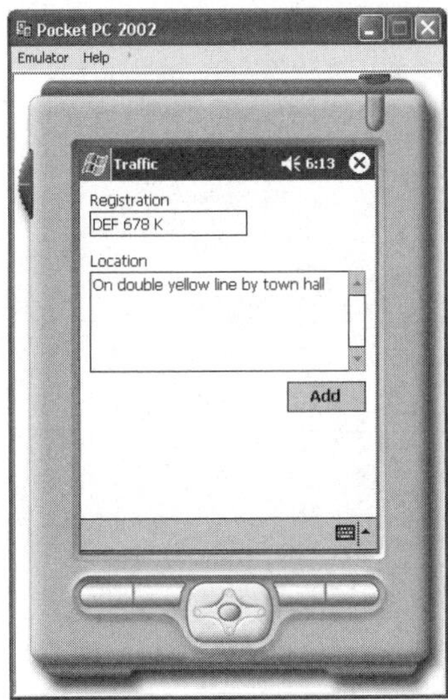

Figure 17-3 UsingSQLCESample application—Add Vehicle form.

You'll find the sample application, UsingSQLCESample, with this book's sample files. To follow this sample, create a new project called UsingSQLCESample in Visual Studio .NET, using a C# Smart Device Application template, and choose the Pocket PC as a target platform. Change the caption of the form, call the form *FormTraffic*, and add controls to match the layout shown in Figure 17-3.

Figure 17-4 shows that you use both the SQL Server CE Data Provider and ADO.NET to connect to a SQL Server CE database. This means that you need to make references in your project to both the System.Data.SqlServerCe and System.Data.Common components. (See Figure 17-5.) The SQL Server CE Data Provider data programming objects exist in the *System.Data.SqlServerCe* namespace, so you should also add the following *using* directives:

```
using System.Data.Common;
using System.Data.SqlServerCe;
```

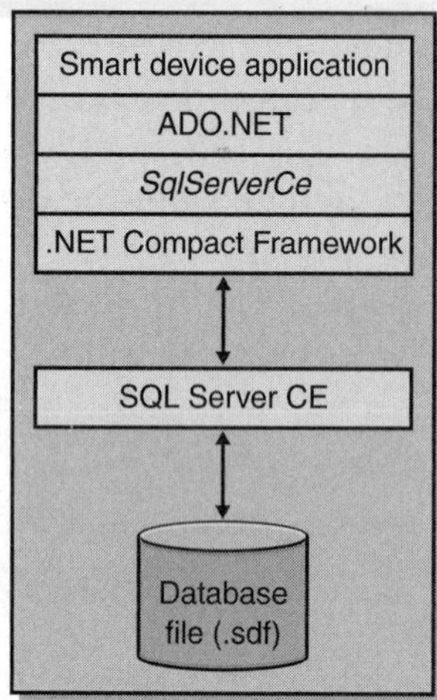

Figure 17-4 Programming SQL Server CE.

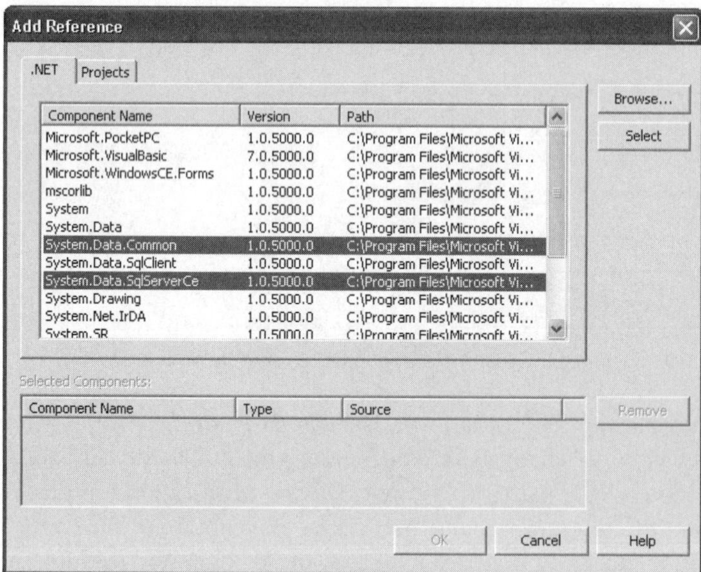

Figure 17-5 References for SQL Server CE.

Introducing *SqlServerCe* Data Programming Objects

Because the SQL Server CE Data Provider's classes are defined in the *System.Data.SqlServerCe* namespace, we'll use the terms SQL Server CE Data Provider and *SqlServerCe* interchangeably throughout the rest of this chapter. You'll meet all the *SqlServerCe* classes by the end of the chapter, but these are the *SqlServerCe* objects that you'll use first:

- *SqlCeEngine*
- *SqlCeConnection*
- *SqlCeCommand*
- *SqlCeException* and *SqlCeError*
- *SqlCeDataReader*
- *SqlCeDataAdapter*
- *SqlCeCommandBuilder*
- *SqlCeParameter*

> **Tip** You'll notice that the capabilities of the SQL Server CE Data Provider are similar to those in the SQL Server 2000 Data Provider. (The SQL Server Data Provider is covered in detail in Chapter 15 of this book.)

Creating a Local Database in Code

Your first step is to create the local SQL Server CE database file. To do so, you create a *SqlCeEngine* object. The sample below shows the overload of the *SqlCeEngine* constructor, which takes the name of the database file as its argument. Once you have created the *SqlCeEngine* object, you simply call the *CreateDatabase* method, as shown here:

```
if (! System.IO.File.Exists(@"\My Documents\Traffic.sdf"))
{
    SqlCeEngine eng = new SqlCeEngine(
        @"Data Source=\My Documents\Traffic.sdf");
    eng.CreateDatabase();
}
```

You could put this code in the *FormTraffic_Load* event handler. This sample also uses a test to see whether the database already exists.

Your next step is to add some data tables to the database by making a connection to the new database and then executing some SQL DDL statements. You make the connection using the *SqlCeConnection* object. The connection requires a *ConnectionString* provided either as an argument to its constructor or as the value of the *ConnectionString* property. The connection string for a *SqlCeConnection* object is simpler than its full SQL Server 2000 Data Provider equivalent. Table 17-3 lists the *ConnectionString* properties supported by SQL Server CE.

Table 17-3 *ConnectionString* Properties Supported by SQL Server CE

Property	Description of Use
Data Source	The name of the SQL Server CE database file to connect to, for example, My Documents\Traffic.sdf.
Password	If the database is to be password protected, a password of up to 40 characters in length can be used.
Persist Security Info	Values True or False.
Encrypt Database	For security, the data file itself can be encrypted using 128-bit encryption.
Max Buffer Size	In-memory buffer size (in kilobytes).
Locale Identifier	Locale ID (LCID) of preference.

> **Note** In practice, you don't need to provide more than just the *Data Source* property in the *ConnectionString*.

Having connected to the database, you use a *SqlCeCommand* object to issue the DDL that creates the database table. The *SqlCeCommand* constructor takes the SQL command and the reference to the connection as arguments. Once you have created the *SqlCeCommand* object, use its *ExecuteNonQuery* method to run the DDL to create the table. The sample code repeats this process to create two tables, as shown in Table 17-4.

Table 17-4 Data Structure of the Sample Database

Table	Column	Type	Size/Use
Cars	CarID	*int*	*IDENTITY(1, 1) PRIMARY KEY*
	Reg	*nvarchar*	10
	Location	*nvarchar*	100
Obs	ObsID	*int*	*IDENTITY(1, 1) PRIMARY KEY*

Table 17-4 Data Structure of the Sample Database *(continued)*

Table	Column	Type	Size/Use
	CarID	*int*	*FOREIGN KEY*
	ObsDateTime	*datetime*	-
	ObsNote	*nvarchar*	100

Here's the code to connect to the database and create the two tables:

```
SqlCeConnection cn = new SqlCeConnection(
    @"Data Source=\My Documents\Traffic.sdf");
cn.Open();
string DDL1 = "CREATE TABLE Cars(CarID int not null identity(1,1),"
    + " Reg nvarchar(10) not null,"
    + " Location nvarchar(100) null)";
SqlCeCommand cmdDDL1 = new SqlCeCommand(DDL1, cn);
cmdDDL1.CommandType = CommandType.Text;
cmdDDL1.ExecuteNonQuery();
string DDL2 = "CREATE TABLE Obs("
    + " ObsID int not null identity(1,1),"
    + " CarID int not null,"
    + " ObsDateTime datetime not null,"
    + " ObsNote nvarchar(100) null)";
SqlCeCommand cmdDDL2 = new SqlCeCommand(DDL2, cn);
cmdDDL2.CommandType = CommandType.Text;
cmdDDL2.ExecuteNonQuery();
cn.Close();
```

> **Note** The sample closes the connection after it's finished. It's important to conserve resources by explicitly closing or disposing of *SqlServerCe* objects.

After running the preceding code, you can check that the database had been created correctly by using the Query Analyzer to display the database objects (as shown in Figure 17-1).

Adding Data Using SQL

You can use the *SqlCeCommand* object to run a SQL Data Manipulation Language (DML) statement against the local database. The sample provides inputs and a button to allow the user to add records to the Cars table; the user records the registration plate and the location where a vehicle is parked. The following sample uses the *SqlCeCommand* object to add new vehicles to the Cars table:

```
private void buttonAdd_Click(object sender, System.EventArgs e)
{
    SqlCeConnection cn = new SqlCeConnection(
        @"Data Source=\My Documents\Traffic.sdf");
    cn.Open();

    string DML = "INSERT INTO Cars(Reg , Location) "
        + "VALUES ( '" + textBoxReg.Text + "','"
        + textBoxLocation.Text + "')";
    SqlCeCommand cmdDML = new SqlCeCommand(DML,cn);
    cmdDML.CommandType = CommandType.Text;
    try
    {
        cmdDML.ExecuteNonQuery();
        MessageBox.Show("Added");
        textBoxReg.Text = "";
        textBoxLocation.Text = "";
    }
    catch (SqlCeException ex)
    {
        DisplaySQLCEErrors(ex);
    }
    cn.Close();
}
```

This sample also introduces some exception handling. You can catch the *SqlCeException* object, which contains an *Errors* collection. Each item of the *Errors* collection is a *SqlCeError* object that gives details of the SQL Server CE error that has occurred. A simple function such as the following could display any errors that occur in my *SqlServerCe* code:

```
private void DisplaySQLCEErrors(SqlCeException ex)
{
    for (int i=0; i < ex.Errors.Count; i++)
    {
        MessageBox.Show("Index #" + i + "\n"
            + "Error: " + ex.Errors[i].ToString()
            + "\n");
    }
}
```

> **Note** Again, you can test that your sample application is correctly inserting records into the Cars table by using the Query Analyzer. You could run the statement *SELECT * FROM Cars* in the SQL tab and view the results on the Grid tab. (See Figure 17-2.)

Retrieving Data Rows

The SQL Server CE Data Provider gives you the following two ways of retrieving data rows from a local SQL Server CE database into your smart device application:

- Data reader
- Data adapter and the *DataSet* class

The data reader is implemented by the *SqlCeDataReader* object and provides a fast, sequential, forward-only way of accessing data rows. The *SqlCeDataAdapter* object implements the data adapter. The data adapter provides a *Fill* method for filling a *DataSet* object with data, and this means you are able to use data binding.

Using the *SqlCeDataReader* Class

To demonstrate the use of the *SqlCeDataReader* class, add a TabControl control to the sample form and create three tabs with the captions *Cars*, *Add Car*, and *Observe*. Move the controls you added previously onto the Add Car tab, and then add a ListView control and a button named Refresh to the Cars tab. You'll also need to add three columns to the ListView control with the captions *ID*, *Reg*, and *Location*. See Figure 17-6 for the layout of the Cars tab.

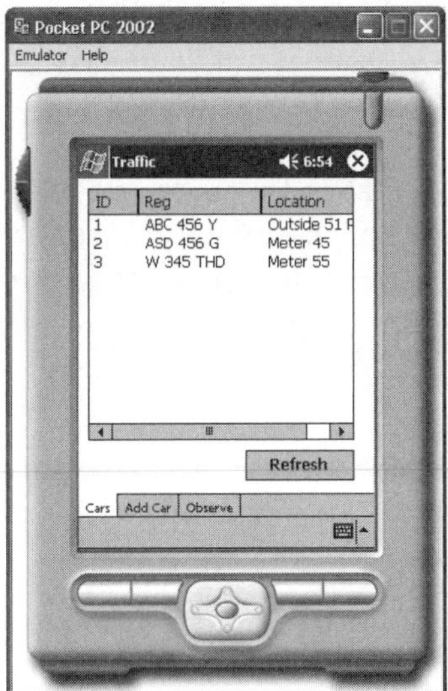

Figure 17-6 ListView control loaded using *SqlCeDataReader*.

The *SqlCeDataReader* object requires a *SqlCeCommand* object with some SQL that selects rows together with a *SqlCeConnection* object that connects to the SQL Server CE database (in the same way as you have already seen in the *FormTraffic_Load* event handler). You then call the *ExecuteReader* method on the *SqlCeCommand* object to create the *SqlCeDataReader* object.

```
SqlCeDataReader dtr = cmd.ExecuteReader(CommandBehavior.Default);
```

You can specify a *CommandBehavior* value for the read operation (although there is also an overload in which the parameter can be omitted). Table 17-5 lists the choices expressed by the *CommandBehavior* enumeration.

Table 17-5 Values of *CommandBehavior*

Value	Description
CloseConnection	Closes the connection when the data reader is closed.
Default	The query can return multiple result sets.
KeyInfo	The query returns column and primary key information.
SchemaOnly	The query returns only column information.
SequentialAccess	Provides a way for the data reader to handle rows containing columns with large binary values.
SingleResult	The query is expected to return a single result set.
SingleRow	The query is expected to return a single row. If multiple result sets are returned, each has a single row. If your query is expected to return a single row, this setting can improve performance.

With the *SqlCeDataReader* object initialized, you call its *Read* method to retrieve each row and use its *Get* family of methods to access the columns within the row. The *Read* method returns *true* until the end of the result set is reached. The following sample code uses a loop to load the result set into the *ListView* control:

```
SqlCeConnection cn = new SqlCeConnection(
    @"Data Source=\My Documents\Traffic.sdf");
string sSQL = "SELECT CarID, Reg, Location  FROM Cars ";
SqlCeCommand cmdSelect = new SqlCeCommand(sSQL,cn);
cmdSelect.CommandType = CommandType.Text;
SqlCeDataReader dtr = cmd.ExecuteReader(CommandBehavior.Default);
while (dtr.Read())
{
    ListViewItem item = new ListViewItem(dtr.GetInt32(0).ToString());
    item.SubItems.Add(dtr.GetString(1));
    item.SubItems.Add(dtr.GetString(2));
    listViewCars.Items.Add(item);
}
```

You can put all this code in a function and call the function from the *Click* event handler for the Refresh button. You also need to call the function in the *FormTraffic_Load* event handler.

Using a Dataset and Data Binding

This section expands the previous sample to add observation records with a date and time. This will allow the parking attendants to tell when a vehicle has overstayed its permitted time.

The sample now retrieves records into a *DataTable* object inside a *DataSet* object. Once a *DataSet* has been filled with data this way, you'll be able to use data binding to display and update data in controls. The *SqlCeDataAdapter* object is capable of filling a *DataSet* object and then updating the underlying database with any changes. The *SqlCeDataAdapter* class has the following four properties that you can use to specify SQL for database operations:

- *SelectCommand*
- *InsertCommand*
- *UpdateCommand*
- *DeleteCommand*

These properties accept references to *SqlCeCommand* objects that we'll call the select command, insert command, update command, and delete command. As with its *SqlClient* cousin (discussed in Chapter 15), you have several options for the creation of the commands needed for a *SqlCeDataAdapter*. Table 17-6 shows various scenarios for creating *SqlCeCommand* objects for a *SqlCeDataAdapter* object.

The following code uses the *SqlCeCommandBuilder* object to generate the update, delete, and insert commands. First, though, we need to prepare the select command. You need to track the current CarID by using the *listViewCars_SelectedIndexChanged* event handler, and you need to dig into the ListView control's *Items* and *SubItems* collections to find the value in the first column of the selected row.

```
private void listViewCars_SelectedIndexChanged(object sender,
    System.EventArgs e)
{
    ListView.SelectedIndexCollection sel;
    sel = listViewCars.SelectedIndices;
    int iIndex;
    int newCarID;
    if (sel.Count > 0)
```

(continued)

```
    {
        iIndex = sel[0];
        newCarID = Convert.ToInt32(
            listViewCars.Items[iIndex].SubItems[0].Text);
```

Table 17-6 Scenarios for Creating Data Adapter Commands

Scenario	Outline of Task
Read-only dataset	You need only supply the select command.
Updatable dataset; you do all the programming	You supply all four command objects; each property uses a different *SqlCeCommand* object. The disadvantage of this approach is the increased quantity of code. The advantage is that you have full control of the SQL that will be executed against your database.
Updatable dataset with generated commands	You supply the select command for the *SelectCommand* property and then use a *SqlCeCommandBuilder* object to generate the remaining update, delete, and insert commands. The advantage of this approach is convenience, and unless your update requirements are complex, the *SqlCeCommandBuilder* object can cope with writing the required SQL.

Now you need to select the observation data related to the selected car. You build up some SQL to fetch the information in the formats that you'll need. The required SQL looks like this:

```
SELECT ObsID,
    convert(nvarchar(11),ObsDateTime,106) AS Date,
    convert(nvarchar(8),ObsDateTime,108) AS Time,
    ObsNote AS Note
    FROM Obs
WHERE CarID = <CarId>
```

The *<CarId>* at the end will be replaced by the selected CarID. The SQL needs to be assembled into a string, and then the *SqlCeDataAdapter* object can be created. You need to keep in mind what the final SQL should look like while you write code like this.

```
string SQL = "SELECT ObsID, "
    + "    convert(nvarchar(11),ObsDateTime,106) AS Date, "
    + "    convert(nvarchar(8),ObsDateTime,108) AS Time, "
    + "    ObsNote AS Note "
    + "    FROM Obs WHERE CarID = " + m_CurrentCarID.ToString();

SqlCeDataAdapter da = new SqlCeDataAdapter(SQL, cn);
SqlCeCommandBuilder cb = new SqlCeCommandBuilder(da);
```

This code creates the *SqlCeDataAdapter* using the overload of its constructor that takes the SQL of the select command and a connection. Then it passes the reference to the data adapter as an argument of the constructor of a *SqlCeCommandBuilder* object. This generates the update, delete, and insert commands for you.

Now you're ready to fill the *DataSet* object and bind the data controls to it. The bound controls will be a DataGrid and three TextBox controls. First call the *Fill* method on the *SqlCeDataAdapter* object to populate the *DataSet* object. Optionally, you can also give a name for the resulting *DataTable* object as the second argument. Next you create the data bindings for the controls. Note that because this procedure might be called multiple times, you need to clear any old data bindings before creating new ones.

For binding the DataGrid control, you reference its *DataSource* property to the *DataTable* object in the *DataSet* object. For binding the three TextBox controls, you append items to their *Bindings* collections. Here is the sample code:

```
da.Fill(dsObs, "Obs");
DataTable dt = dsObs.Tables["Obs"];
DataGridObs.DataSource = dt;
textBoxObsDate.DataBindings.Clear();
textBoxObsDate.DataBindings.Add("Text", dt, "Date");
textBoxObsTime.DataBindings.Clear();
textBoxObsTime.DataBindings.Add("Text", dt, "Time");
textBoxObsNote.DataBindings.Clear();
textBoxObsNote.DataBindings.Add("Text", dt, "Note");
```

Figure 17-7 shows the resulting data display.

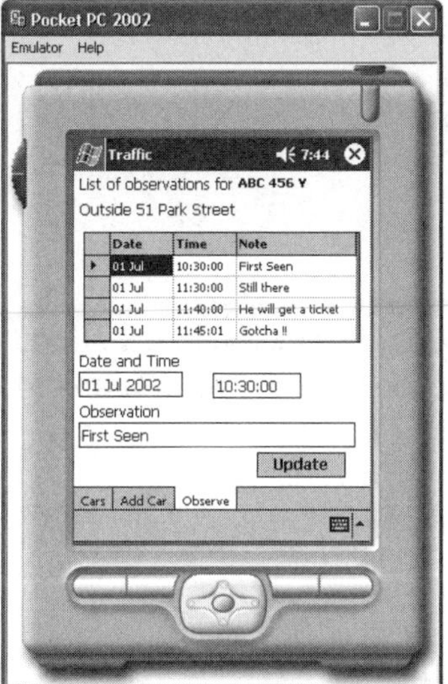

Figure 17-7 Bound controls.

Using the *SqlCeCommand* Object with Parameters

This section looks at the use of parameters in SQL Server CE. For example, you could have written the SQL for the select command in the previous example using a format such as this:

```
SELECT * FROM Cars WHERE CarID = ?
```

In this format, the query has a parameter, so you can prepare the command once and call it many times, each time supplying a different number in place of the question mark (*?*). This technique can then be extended to create a *prepared statement* by calling the *Prepare* method on the *SqlCeCommand* object after setting the object's *CommandText* property and the parameters. This compiles the statement on the data source, giving faster subsequent executions and a performance advantage if the *SqlCeCommand* object is to be used more than once (as is the case in this sample application).

A *SqlCeCommand* object created using the example SQL shown earlier would take a single parameter. You can create the parameter using a *SqlCeParameter* object and then add it to the *SqlCeCommand* object's *Parameters* collection, as shown in this example:

```
SqlCeConnection cn = new SqlCeConnection(
    @"Data Source=\My Documents\Traffic.sdf");
cn.Open();
string SQL = "SELECT ObsID, "
    + "    convert(nvarchar(11),ObsDateTime,106) AS Date, "
    + "    convert(nvarchar(8),ObsDateTime,108) AS Time, "
    + "    ObsNote AS Note "
    + "    FROM Obs WHERE CarID = ?";
SqlCeCommand cmdObs = new SqlCeCommand(SQL, cn);
SqlCeParameter p = new SqlCeParameter("CarID", SqlDbType.Int);
cmdObs.Parameters.Add(p);
cmdObs.Prepare;
daObs = new SqlCeDataAdapter(cmdObs);
cn.Close();
```

> **Note** SQL Server CE does not support the creation of stored procedures on the local database, so the use of the *SqlCeParameter* object is limited to that described here.

If you need to use more than one parameter, you indicate the positions of the parameters in the SQL with multiple question marks. In this case, you must ensure that you add *SqlCeParameter* objects to the *Parameters* collection of the *SqlCeCommand* object in the correct order (reading left to right) of the question marks. In the previous example, you gave the *SqlCeParameter* object a name in its constructor, but parameters cannot be referenced by name, only by index within the *Parameters* collection. Any code that you write that uses the *SqlCe-Command* object will rely entirely on you having added the parameters in the correct order.

Each time you use the *SqlCeCommand* object that has been prepared, you need to first set the value of any parameters. The following sample sets the value of a single parameter (type *Int32*) from the contents of a *TextBox* by accessing the parameter through the *SelectCommand.Parameters* collection on the *SqlCeDataAdapter* object.

```
daObs.SelectCommand.Parameters[0].Value =
    Convert.ToInt32(textBoxCarID.Text);
```

Updating with Data Binding

So far you have seen how to update the local SQL Server CE database using the *ExecuteNonQuery* method of a *SqlCeCommand* object to execute a DML SQL statement. In the scenario implemented by the sample application, individual parking attendants will want to share and coordinate their observations. So the following code will show how to update the database when controls are bound to a *DataSet* object using data binding. (Refer to Chapter 15 for a detailed examination of how a data adapter operates when changes made in a *DataSet* object are sent back to the underlying database.) The principle is that you call the *Update* method on the *SqlCeDataAdapter*, and the relevant commands (update, delete, or insert) are executed to change the database.

```
daObs.Update(dsObs, "Obs");
```

> **Note** Remember that the *SqlCeCommandBuilder* object will be unable to generate update, insert, and delete commands for complex updates involving more than one table or where the primary key of the table is not retrieved by the select command.

Programming Remote Data Access

In the preceding sample, you saw how to create a local SQL Server CE database in code, and then used it with some of the *SqlServerCe* objects. However, in practice many applications will require you to load data from a central database, make changes or additions locally, and then send your changes back to the central SQL Server database so that other users can see them. RDA is the first of two techniques this chapter covers for loading and updating a central SQL Server database (the second is covered later, in the section "Using Merge Replication"). Table 17-7 lists the platforms for SQL Server CE devices that support RDA.

Table 17-7 SQL Server CE Devices That Support RDA

Platform	Version
Handheld PC Pro	2.11 or later
Palm-size PC	2.11 or later
Pocket PC	3 or later
Handheld PC 2000	3 or later

Introducing RDA Architecture

RDA makes use of the SQL Server CE Database Engine and the SQL Server CE Client Agent on the smart device client. (See Figure 17-8.)

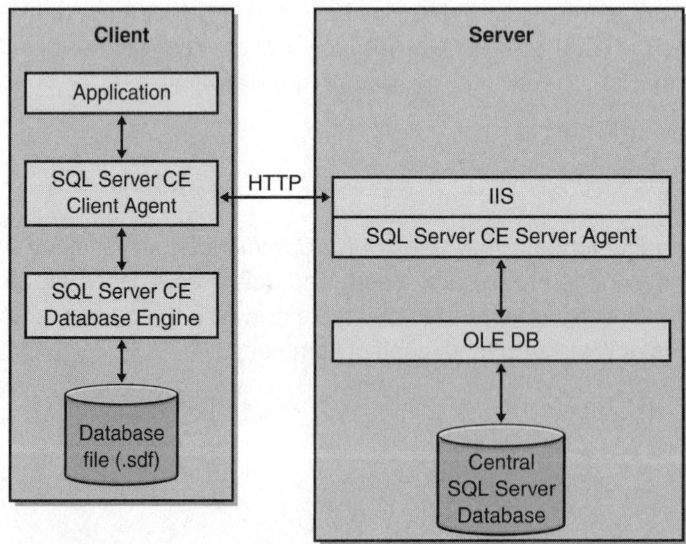

Figure 17-8 RDA architecture.

When data is required from the central SQL Server database, SQL Server CE Client Agent makes a request to SQL Server CE Server Agent over HTTP. The server agent runs as an ISAPI extension under Internet Information Services (IIS). It is implemented in the Sscesa20.dll file, which is located in a designated RDA Web site.

> **Note** You'll need to install SQL Server CE Server Agent on the Web server where IIS is located by running the Server.exe setup program, which comes with the SQL Server CE 2 setup files.

Data is retrieved from the SQL Server Database using OLE DB and then transmitted back to the client by SQL Server CE Server Agent. On the client, it is received by SQL Server CE Client Agent and stored in a table in a local SQL Server CE database file (using the .sdf file extension normally). Once data is in the local SQL Server CE database, it can be manipulated by the client smart device application. This data retrieval is called the RDA *pull*.

You can return a table from a local SQL Server CE database to update the central SQL Server database. RDA calls this data update the *push*. The SQL Server CE Client Agent sends the data across HTTP to the SQL Server CE Server Agent. The SQL Server CE Server Agent updates the SQL Server database using OLE DB and returns any errors that occur to the client. As you'll see later, in the section "Running Commands on the Remote Database," in addition to the push and pull of data, RDA provides a way of executing SQL statements directly on the server.

You can use RDA with SQL Server 6.5 and later, and it's relatively simple to set up. The RDA communication protocol is suited to wireless transports. The data is compressed and can be encrypted during transmission. However, the process by which RDA merges data back into the central database is also simple, but it is not suitable for complex data structures or multiuser applications where many users are trying to update the same data.

> **Note** Note that you can't use RDA with a case-sensitive SQL Server database.

Installing RDA Server

The following sections show you how to set up RDA for the sample application. Here is an outline of the tasks:

- Install the SQL Server CE Server Agent on your Web server.
- Use the SQL Server Connectivity Management tool to create a virtual directory containing the SQL Server CE Server Agent DLL (Sscesa20.dll). (See Figure 17-9.)
- Choose an authentication method for the new site. (See the section "Configuring RDA Security" later in this chapter.)
- Check that the identity authorized by IIS has a corresponding logon to SQL Server and has permission to use the relevant database and permissions to access and make any required changes to the database objects.

> **Note** Create a new database using SQL Server Enterprise Manager, and run the MakeDatabase.sql script to create the tables used in these samples. You'll find the MakeDatabase.sql script included with this book's sample files.

Installing the SQL Server CE Server Agent

Locate and run the SQL Server CE Server.exe setup program on the server that you'll use as the Web server for RDA. This file will then extract files before presenting the Microsoft SQL Server CE 2.0 Server Tools Setup Wizard. Follow the wizard through the license agreement and location of program files to the Confirm Installation screen. Click Install, and the wizard copies the server tools and the Microsoft Data Access Components (MDAC) 2.6 data access components onto the server. When installation is complete, the wizard offers you the option to run the SQL Server CE Virtual Directory Creation Wizard. Leave this option checked, and click Close. The SQL Server CE Virtual Directory Creation Wizard displays, as shown in Figure 17-9.

Click Next to start the wizard. The next screen, shown in Figure 17-10, allows you set up a virtual directory name. Enter **TrafficRDA**, and click Next. The wizard now displays the authentication choices for RDA.

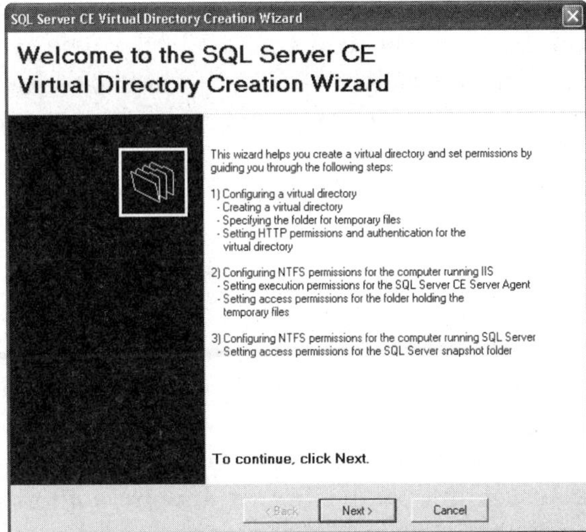

Figure 17-9 Virtual Directory Creation Wizard.

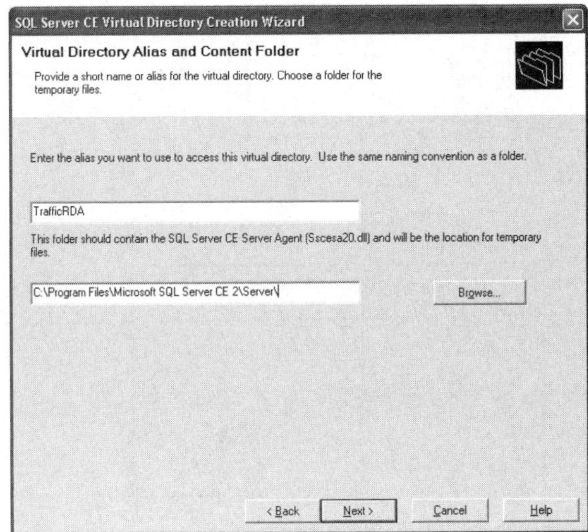

Figure 17-10 Virtual Directory Creation Wizard prompting for a name for the RDA virtual directory.

Configuring RDA Security

Many of the problems that you might encounter in practice when you use RDA will be caused by the security mechanisms in the chain of applications that participate in RDA operations. You must pass through the following four checkpoints between your smart device application and the data that you want out of the central SQL Server database:

- IIS Authentication
- SQL Server Authentication
- SQL Server database access
- SQL Server object permissions

Refer to Figure 17-11, which shows these checkpoints as gates which will open only if you are successfully authenticated and are authorized to have access. As well as the gates, you can see three computers, which represent the three identities that you might be assuming as you pass each control.

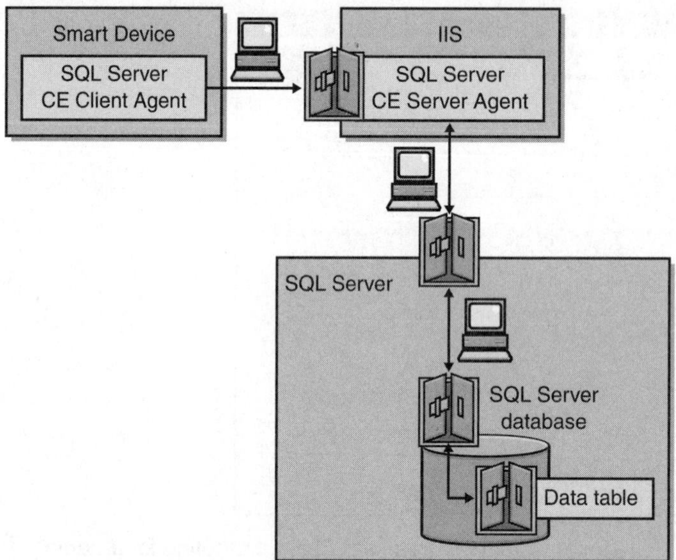

Figure 17-11 RDA security checkpoints.

At this point in the setup of a virtual directory for RDA, you'll be asked to choose the authentication that IIS is to use (at the first gate). Figure 17-12 shows the dialog box from the SQL Server CE Virtual Directory Creation Wizard.

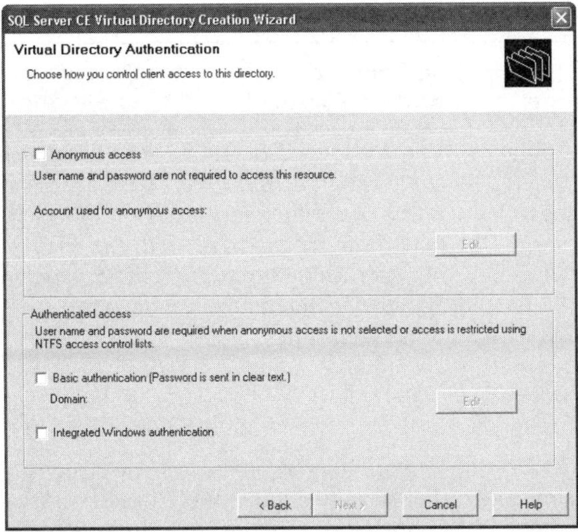

Figure 17-12 IIS RDA Virtual Directory Authentication security options.

The sample application will use the Integrated Windows Authentication mechanism, so you should select the bottom check box and then click Next to proceed to the next stage of the security setup.

This set of three Virtual Directory Authentication choices, along with the option to specify a SQL Server logon in the OLE DB connection string used by the RDA methods (more details on these methods later, in the sections "Using RDA Pull" and "Pushing Changes Back to the Remote Database"), give you four possible authentication schemes for the RDA security setup. Table 17-8 details the identities and authentication checks that will be made for each of these schemes. It should help you check your security setup if you have problems connecting using one of the RDA methods.

The next step in the security setup for the sample application is to secure NTFS access permissions to the virtual directory. The screen for this step is shown in Figure 17-13. Because the sample application will use Integrated Windows Authentication, you should enter the domain and user name of a test user or the domain and Windows NT group name of a test user.

Click Next to show the next screen. Leave the Applications Requiring SQL Server Merge Replication option unchecked, and click Next again. On the last screen, click Finish to complete this part of the security setup.

Table 17-8 Identities and Authentication Checks in RDA

Authentication Scheme	IIS Authentication	SQL Server Authentication	SQL Server Permissions
Anonymous	You do not provide a user name or password. Instead, you're logged on to the Windows server using the credentials specified for anonymous access. (By default, the IUSR_*machinename* local account is used.)	You are logged on as *computer*\IUSR_*machine name* or another specified anonymous Internet user account using SQL Server Integrated Authentication.	You need to grant database access and relevant object permissions to the *computer* \IUSR_*machinename* account.
Basic	You must provide a Windows user name and password. The credentials are passed to the IIS server in plain text. You should use Secure Sockets Layer (SSL) to create an HTTPS connection when using basic authentication.	You are logged on as the user specified in the connection string, using SQL Server Integrated Authentication.	You need to grant database access and relevant object permissions to the Internet logon or to a Windows NT group to which the Internet logon belongs.
Integrated Windows	Your current Windows credentials are passed in an encrypted form to IIS. Note that you cannot use this form of authentication through a proxy server.	You are logged on as your current Windows user logon using SQL Server Integrated Authentication.	You need to grant database access and relevant object permissions to the Internet logon or to a Windows NT group to which the Internet logon belongs.
Anonymous, Basic, or Integrated Windows, with SQL Server User ID/Password specified in the OLE DB connection string parameter of an RDA method		You are logged on using the user ID and password specified in the OLE DB connection string.	You need to grant database access and relevant object permissions to the SQL Server user specified in the OLE DB connection string.

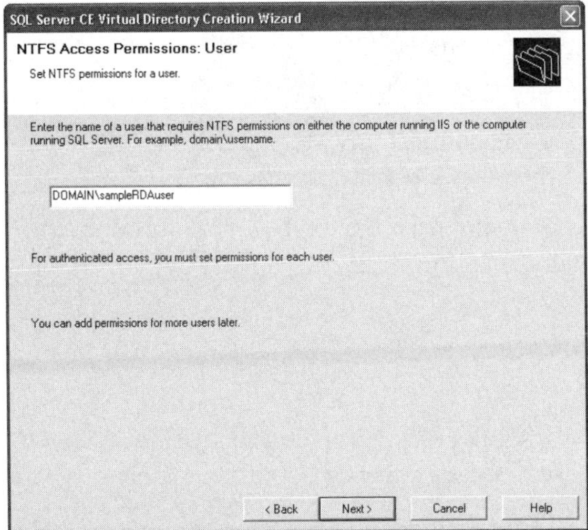

Figure 17-13 NTFS access permissions.

> **Note** You do not have to use the Virtual Directory Creation Wizard to make these Web site and NTFS security settings. You can use the Internet Services Manager (from Administrative Tools) for the Web site setup, and the Security tab on the Properties dialog box of the Windows File Explorer for the NTFS settings. If you use these tools, you must copy the DLL (Sscesa20.dll) to the Web site's local path yourself.

To complete the security setup in the database, run the SQL Server Enterprise Manager and locate the sample database called Traffic. Make sure that your domain user or NT group are added as a logon to the server and have permission to access the Traffic sample database. Check that it also has permission to read and update the Cars and Obs tables in the Traffic database.

Pulling Data into a Local Database

This section extends the sample application started previously of a parking management system. However, this time you'll see how to load the initial data from a central SQL Server database using RDA.

Using RDA Pull

You use the following steps to use RDA to pull data from a SQL Server database onto a smart device:

- Use the SQL Server CE Connectivity Management tool to create a SQL Server CE virtual directory on your Web server.
- Check the security path from the Web server through to the SQL Server 2000 database logon. (See the earlier section "Configuring RDA Security".)
- Create the target SQL Server CE database on the device using the *SqlCeEngine* object.
- If the target database already exists, connect using a *SqlCeConnection* object and use a *SqlCeCommand* object to delete any tables that are part of the pull.
- Transfer the data using the *Pull* method of a *SqlCeRemoteDataAccess* object.

You have already done the first two steps in the section "Installing RDA Server." So now you need to do the housekeeping tasks of creating a local database and deleting any existing tables. The section "Introducing *SqlServerCe* Data Programming Objects" included sample code that showed you how to create the local database using the *SqlCeEngine*, *SqlCeConnection*, and *SqlCeCommand* objects. You'll need to use DDL SQL to remove any existing tables, as shown here:

```
DROP TABLE Cars
```

Finally you achieve the last step, transferring the data, by creating a *SqlCeRemoteDataAccess* object and setting some properties before calling the object's *Pull* method. Table 17-9 examines the specific properties you need to set. You might find it helpful to trace some of these through on the architecture diagram in Figure 17-8.

Table 17-9 Properties of the *SqlCeRemoteDataAccess* Object

Property	Description	Comment
InternetUrl	The URL string to the SQL CE Server Agent DLL	You must include the name of the DLL (Sscesa20.dll).
InternetLogin	The IIS logon name	The default is no logon string. You don't need to give a value if you are using Anonymous or Integrated Windows Authentication.

Table 17-9 Properties of the *SqlCeRemoteDataAccess* Object *(continued)*

Property	Description	Comment
InternetPassword	The IIS password string	As above, you don't need to give a password for Anonymous or Integrated Windows Authentication.
InternetProxyServer	Proxy server name and port	Both the server name (or IP address) and port must be given using the format *ProxyServerName:Port*. You don't set this property if you are not using a proxy server.
InternetProxyLogin	Logon for the proxy server	You need to set this property if you are using Basic or Integrated Windows Authentication on the proxy server. You don't set this property if you aren't using a proxy server.
InternetProxyPassword	Password for the proxy server	You need to set this property if you are using Basic or Integrated Windows Authentication on the proxy server. You don't set this property if you aren't using a proxy server.
LocalConnectionString	The OLE DB connection string for SQL Server CE.	The OLE DB connection string for logging on to SQL Server CE on the smart device.

The remaining details of the route from the central SQL Server database to the SQL Server CE database are provided by the arguments of the *Pull* method itself. Table 17-10 gives guidance on their use.

Table 17-10 Arguments of the *Pull* Method

Argument	Description	Comment
LocalTableName	The name of a SQL Server CE table that will receive the extracted SQL Server records	You need to drop the table if it already exists.
SqlSelectString	SQL that specifies which columns and rows of SQL Server data to transfer	This can contain any valid Transact-SQL statement or function. This SQL is executed against the SQL Server database; you must check that you have all the permissions needed.

(continued)

Table 17-10 Arguments of the *Pull* Method *(continued)*

Argument	Description	Comment
OLEDBConnectionString	The OLE DB connection string for the SQL Server database	This is the OLE DB connection string for the SQL Server CE Server Agent to use when it connects to the central SQL Server database.
RDATrackingOption	Indicates whether SQL Server CE should track changes made to the pulled table (to allow you to send them back to the SQL Server)	Options are: *TrackingOn*, *TrackingOff*, *TrackingOnWithIndexes*, and *TrackingOffWithIndexes*. See the following section, "Tracking Options."
ErrorTableName	Name of a table in the local SQL Server CE database to be used for errors	Each local table you create must use a separate local error table. If you try to reuse an error table name, the pull will fail.

The following code, similar to the code in the UsingSQLCERDASample application included with this book's sample files, shows how to achieve an RDA pull.

```
private void RDAPull()
{
    // Create the database
    if (! System.IO.File.Exists(@"\My Documents\TrafficRDA.sdf"))
    {
        SqlCeEngine eng = new SqlCeEngine(
            @"Data Source=\My Documents\TrafficRDA.sdf");
        eng.CreateDatabase();
    }
    // Clear out old table
    SqlCeConnection cn = new SqlCeConnection(
        @"Data Source=\My Documents\TrafficRDA.sdf");
    SqlCeCommand cmd = new SqlCeCommand("DROP TABLE Cars", cn);
    SqlCeCommand cmd2 = new SqlCeCommand("DROP TABLE Obs", cn);
    cn.Open();
    try
    {
        cmd.ExecuteNonQuery();
        cmd2.ExecuteNonQuery();
    }
    catch (SqlCeException sqlCeEx)
    {
        DisplaySQLCEErrors(sqlCeEx);
    }
```

```
    cn.Close();
    cn.Dispose();
    SqlCeRemoteDataAccess rda = new SqlCeRemoteDataAccess();
    string sCon = @"Provider=SQLOLEDB;Data Source=MySvr;"
        + @"Initial Catalog=Traffic;integrated security=SSPI;"
        + @"Persist Security Info=False";

    rda.InternetUrl = @"http://MySvr/TrafficRDA/sscesa20.dll";
    rda.LocalConnectionString =
        @"Data Source=\My Documents\TrafficRDA.sdf";
    try
    {
        rda.Pull("Cars", "SELECT * FROM Cars",
            sCon, RdaTrackOption.TrackingOn, "rdaCarErrors");
        rda.Pull("Obs", "SELECT * FROM Obs",
            sCon, RdaTrackOption.TrackingOn, "rdaObsErrors");
    }
    catch (SqlCeException sqlCeEx)
    {
        DisplaySQLCEErrors(sqlCeEx);
    }
    rda.Dispose();
}
```

Once again, you could test your code by using the Query Analyzer tool on the smart device. By connecting to the new database after executing the RDA pull and examining the Objects tab, you can see both the pulled tables and their error tables, as shown in Figure 17-14.

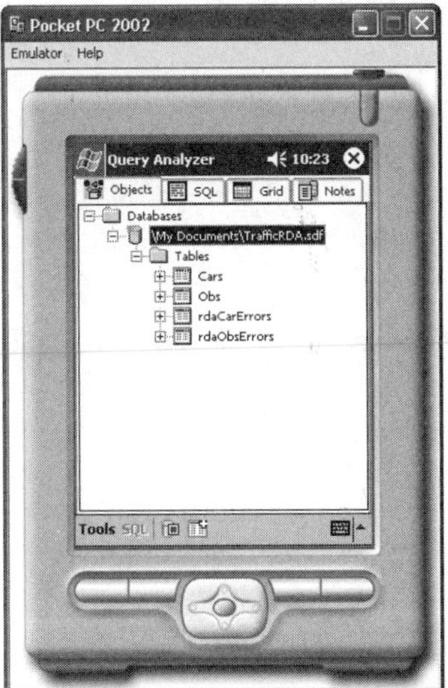

Figure 17-14 RDA pulled tables and error tables.

Tracking Options

There are four *RdaTrackOption* values to choose from for the *RDATrackingOption* parameter of the *Pull* method of the *SqlCeRemoteDataAccess* object. Your choice is important because it affects whether you can subsequently call the *Push* method and the behavior of the pulled table. Table 17-11 lists the effects of each value.

Table 17-11 *RdaTrackOption* Values

Value	Description
TrackingOn	SQL Server CE will keep track of every record that is inserted, updated, or deleted. You'll be able to push these changes back to the central SQL Server. You must select an updatable record set containing the primary key of the source table. In practice, the selection is restricted to a single table or a SQL Server updatable view. If you specify the name of an errors table, push errors will be logged.
TrackingOff	No tracking of changes is done, and you won't be able to call the *Push* method.
TrackingOnWithIndexes	As *TrackingOn*, but additionally copies the indexes during the pull. This might be useful if you have unique constraints on the table that are implemented by an index, for example.
TrackingOffWithIndexes	As *TrackingOff*, but the indexes are copied during the pull.

Understanding RDA Pull Data Type Conversions

SQL Server CE uses a subset of the data types used by SQL Server. Some of the data types supported by SQL Server are directly comparable with their SQL Server CE equivalents, and can be converted directly. Other SQL Server data types are compatible with SQL Server CE within certain size limits. These data types are converted by the RDA *Pull* method. The remaining SQL Server data types cannot be used with SQL Server CE.

Table 17-12 gives a guide to the mappings between SQL Server and SQL Server CE data types and to the conversions that are performed during an RDA pull.

Table 17-12 SQL Server and SQL Server CE Data Type Mappings

SQL Server	SQL Server CE	Comment
BIGINT	*bigint*	
BINARY(n)	*binary(n)* or *image*	510 bytes or less maps to *binary(n)*; otherwise, *image* is used. Watch the length of an *image* column; it might get too big for the SQL Server *BINARY* column, and you won't be able to push the data back to SQL Server. Remember there is an overall 1GB limit for the column and a 2 GB limit for the whole database.
BIT	*bit*	
CHAR	*nvarchar* or *ntext*	255 or fewer characters maps to *nvarchar*; otherwise, *ntext* is used. Again, watch the length; it might get too big to push back to SQL Server.
VARCHAR	*nvarchar* or *ntext*	As above.
COMPUTED COLUMNS	Not supported	
DATETIME	*datetime*	
DECIMAL	*numeric*	
DOUBLE PRECISION	*double precision*	
FLOAT	*float*	
IMAGE	*image*	
INT	*int*	
MONEY	*money*	
NCHAR	*nchar* or *ntext*	255 or fewer characters maps to *nchar*; otherwise, *ntext* is used. Watch the length; it might get too big to push back to SQL Server.
NTEXT	*ntext*	
NUMERIC	*numeric*	

Table 17-12 SQL Server and SQL Server CE Data Type Mappings *(continued)*

SQL Server	SQL Server CE	Comment
NVARCHAR	*nvarchar* or *ntext*	255 or fewer characters maps to *nvarchar*; otherwise, *ntext* is used. Watch the length; it might get too big to push back to SQL Server.
REAL	*real*	
SMALLDATETIME	*smalldatetime*	
SMALLINT	*smallint*	
SMALLMONEY	*smallmoney*	
SQL_VARIANT	Not supported	
TEXT	*ntext*	Watch for the 1GB limit.
TIMESTAMP	*timestamp*	
TINYINT	*tinyint*	
UNIQUEIDENTIFIER	*uniqueidentifier*	
VARBINARY	*varbinary* or *image*	510 or fewer bytes maps to *varbinary*; otherwise, *image* is used. Watch the length; it might get too big to push back to SQL Server, or it might exceed the 1GB limit.

Making Changes to a Pulled Table

Although a *SqlCeCommand* object will generally give you a wide range of DDL SQL commands, keep in mind some restrictions if you are trying to change a local table that has been pulled using RDA. Table 17-13 lists what you can and can't do.

Table 17-13 *SqlCeCommand* Restrictions in the Use of DDL SQL

Permitted	Not Permitted
Drop the table.	Rename the table.
Add or drop indexes.	Drop the primary key.
Add or drop default values.	Add, drop, or rename columns.
Change the seed or increment of the identity column.	Alter the data type of a column.
Add or drop foreign key restraints.	

Pushing Changes Back to the Remote Database

You can write commands to update the local database once it has been pulled from SQL Server using *SqlServerCe* objects the way we studied in the first part of this chapter. When you're ready to update the central SQL Server database with additions, changes, and deletions that you've made, you call the *Push* method of the *SqlCeRemoteDataAccess* object.

Using Optimistic Concurrency

RDA uses optimistic concurrency control on the central SQL Server database. When records are pulled, they are not locked on the central SQL Server database, and when you push changes back, the SQL Server CE Server Agent will overwrite any changes that might have been made by another user. The RDA *Push* method is suited to applications where this kind of "lost update" is acceptable.

Using the *Push* method

You use the same set of properties on the *SqlCeRemoteDataAccess* object as for the *Pull*, so they are not repeated here. The *Push* method can take two or optionally three arguments, as described in Table 17-14.

As with the *Pull* method, you must check that the authentication method you're using has access to the table on the SQL Server database and that it also has authorization to change the data. Here is a sample function to perform an RDA push:

```
private void RDAPushCars()
{
    SqlCeRemoteDataAccess rda = new SqlCeRemoteDataAccess();
    string sCon = @"Provider=SQLOLEDB;Data Source=MySvr;"
        + @"Initial Catalog=Traffic;Integrated Security=SSPI;"
        + @"Persist Security Info=False";

    rda.InternetUrl = @"http://MySvr/TrafficRDA/sscesa20.dll";
    rda.LocalConnectionString =
        @"Data Source=\My Documents\TrafficRDA.sdf";
    try
    {
        rda.Push("Cars", sCon);
    }
    catch (SqlCeException sqlCeEx)
    {
        DisplaySQLCEErrors(sqlCeEx);
    }
    rda.Dispose();
}
```

Table 17-14 Arguments of the *Push* Method

Argument	Description	Comment
LocalTableName	The SQL Server CE table that will be the source of the changes	This argument can contain any valid Transact-SQL statement or function. This SQL is executed against the SQL Server database; you must check that you have all the permissions needed.
OLEDBConnectionString	The OLE DB connection string for the SQL Server database	This argument is the OLE DB connection string for the SQL Server CE Server Agent to use when it connects to the SQL Server database.
BatchOption	Optional third argument giving the *RdaBatchOption* enumeration setting (*RdaBatchingOn* or *RdaBatchingOff*).	This argument specifies whether SQL Server CE should batch changes being sent to the SQL Server as a single transaction. The default is *RdaBatchingOff*, which means that the success or failure of each change has no effect on other changes.

The UsingSQLCERDASample application calls this function from a Button control called *buttonPushCars* on its Cars tab.

Examining the RDA Errors Table

If an *ErrorTableName* argument was given during the *Pull* of the *LocalTableName* that is being pushed, any errors detected during the push will be logged in the *ErrorTableName* table in the SQL Server CE database. You can examine this table by retrieving its records using one of the *SqlServerCe* techniques covered earlier in this chapter in the section "Retrieving Data Rows."

Running Commands on the Remote Database

In addition to *Push* and *Pull*, the *SqlCeRemoteDataAccess* object has a *SubmitSql* method that allows you to run SQL statements on the central SQL Server database. The *SubmitSql* method requires you to set up the same properties as for the *Pull* method, and you must have the correct authorization to run the SQL on the central SQL Server database. Table 17-15 describes the two arguments of the *SubmitSql* method.

Table 17-15 Arguments of the *SubmitSql* Method

Argument	Description	Comment
SQLString	The SQL string to execute	This argument can contain any valid Transact-SQL statement or function, and it must not return any rows.
OLEDBConnectionString	The OLE DB connection string for the SQL Server database	This argument is the OLE DB connection string for the SQL Server CE Server Agent to use when it connects to the SQL Server database.

The following sample code sets an archive flag on all the cars in the central database, which is used at the end of the day to close off all observations:

```
private void RDASubmitSQL()
{
    SqlCeRemoteDataAccess rda = new SqlCeRemoteDataAccess();
    string sCon = @"Provider=SQLOLEDB;Data Source=MySvr;"
        + @"Initial Catalog=Traffic;integrated security=SSPI;"
        + @"Persist Security Info=False";
    rda.InternetUrl = @"http://MySvr/TestSQLCE/sscesa20.dll";
    rda.LocalConnectionString = @"Data Source=\My Documents\TrafficRDA.sdf";
    try
    {
        rda.SubmitSql("UPDATE Cars SET Archive = 1",sCon);
    }
    catch (SqlCeException ex)
    {
        DisplaySQLCEErrors(ex);
    }
    rda.Dispose();
}
```

Troubleshooting RDA

As you saw in the section "Introducing RDA Architecture," there are a number of layers making up the RDA architecture. When you are developing a system using RDA, a problem might occur in any one of the layers. Table 17-16 lists some of the problems that you might encounter if you are developing using RDA and helps you track down their sources and reach resolutions.

Table 17-16 Potential Problems and Resolutions with RDA

Problem	Reason	Resolution
Cannot pull table (native error reports 0 or 4060)	You will get a pull error if you have not set up the security access correctly.	Check your security setup.
Cannot push table with no primary key (native error reports 29010)	You cannot update a central SQL Server table that has no primary key (although you will be able to pull it successfully).	Alter the table on the central SQL Server database to have a primary key.
Duplicate key values (native error reports 25016)	If you pull a table that has an identity column, you'll get this error if you attempt to run an insert against it locally.	Alter the identity seed to be the next key value after the table has been pulled and before you attempt any inserts. For example: `ALTER TABLE Cars ALTER COLUMN CarID IDENTITY(3,1)`
Cannot push table with identity column (native error reports 28537)	The SQL Server CE Client Agent receives the error that it is unable to establish an identity range for any new records you add to a table that contains an identity column.	You'll need to consider using merge replication if your application has to push identity columns back to the central SQL Server database. Consider a workaround if you want to stick to RDA.

For a full list of SQL Server CE error messages and numbers, search the SQL Server CE Books Online for "SQL Server CE Errors."

Using Merge Replication

This section looks in detail at the alternative to RDA: SQL Server CE merge replication (referred to as *merge replication* from here). Although merge replication is more powerful and simpler to program than RDA, you'll find that merge replication is more complex to set up, especially the security configuration. This section will start by taking you through the main points.

> **Note** Remember that merge replication is available only for SQL Server 2000.

Introducing Merge Replication Architecture

Although SQL Server CE merge replication has similarities with SQL Server 2000 merge replication, it is not identical. As with all forms of SQL Server replication, three databases are involved, as follows:

- Publisher
- Distributor
- Subscriber

The *publisher* is a database that makes data available for replication, the *distributor* is a database that contains the data and metadata required to manage the replication, and the *subscriber* is a database that receives the replicated data. In the simplest replication configuration, the publisher and the distributor reside on the same server. It is beyond the scope of this chapter to consider multiple server physical architecture for SQL Server replication. Refer to SQL Server Books Online. The main difference between full SQL Server 2000 merge replication and SQL Server CE merge replication is that IIS sits between the client (and the subscriber database) and the other databases, which allows the replication data and communications to be sent over HTTP, as shown in Figure 17-15.

Like RDA, SQL Server CE merge replication makes use of the SQL Server CE Database Engine and the SQL Server CE Client Agent on the smart device client. When data is first required (called *initialization*), the application calls a method that invokes the SQL Server CE Client Agent, which in turn calls the SQL Server CE Server Agent over HTTP. (The same server agent is used for RDA.) The server agent invokes the SQL Server CE replication provider, and an initial record set (called a *snapshot*) is selected from the central SQL Server database and returned via HTTP to the client agent. The client agent is then able to build the local SQL Server CE database (called the *subscription database*) on the smart device.

Once the subscription database has been built, you can use the *SqlServerCe* objects to manipulate its structure and data locally. The SQL Server CE Database Engine tracks all the changes that you make using a small amount of tracking information for each record.

Periodically, your application will need to send its changes to the central SQL Server database and to receive any changes made centrally or by other remote users. This is the process of *synchronization*, and you will see later, in the section "Synchronizing Data," that it can be initiated from the client application using the *SqlServerCe* merge replication object. The client agent calls the server agent over HTTP, sending details of the changes tracked since the last synchronization (or since initialization if this is the first synchronization). The server agent then writes an input message (.in) file, which is passed to the SQL Server CE Replication Provider for loading into the central SQL Server database. The SQL Server reconciler merges the new input data into the central database and then informs the SQL Server CE replication provider about changes made at the publisher that must be applied to the subscription database. The SQL Server CE replication provider writes an output message (.out) file, which is passed back to the server agent and then on to the client agent. The client agent is finally able to apply the changes to the subscription database on the smart device. It's interesting to note that the output message file is written to the client and processed in blocks to avoid overloading the smart device with large quantities of changes all at once.

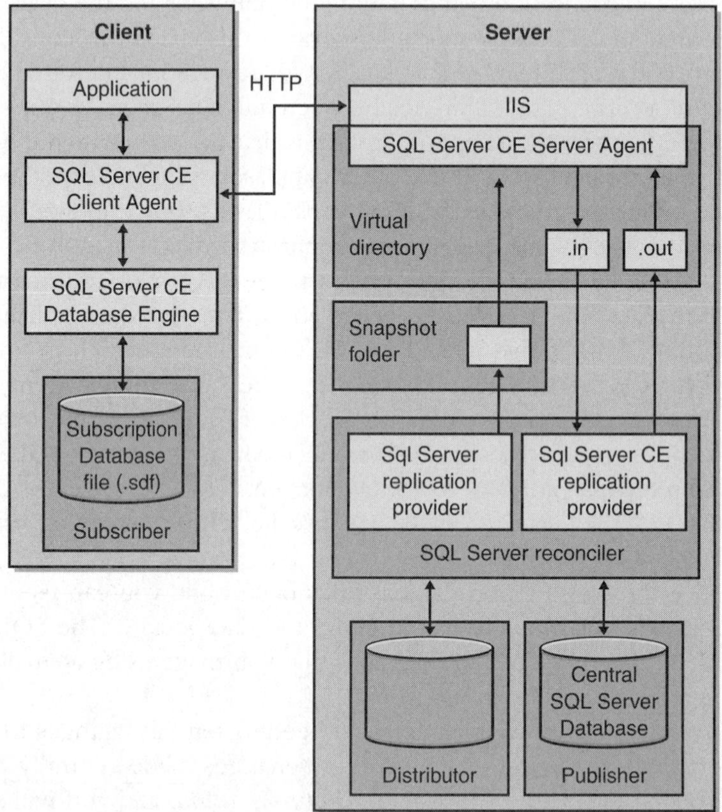

Figure 17-15 SQL Server CE merge replication architecture.

Setting Up Merge Replication

You should start by installing the following service packs (at minimum) for SQL Server and the SQL Server CE Server Agent: SQL Server 2000 Service Pack 2 and SQL Server CE Server Agent Service Pack 2. Some of the steps of the merge replication setup follow those for the RDA setup. However, there are extra steps both in SQL Server and in the creation and securing of the replication *snapshot folder*. The snapshot folder is a folder used to contain the merge replication files used to pass data from the SQL Server replication provider and the SQL Server CE Server Agent. (You can see the snapshot folder in Figure 17-15.) The main steps for setting up merge replication are as follows:

- Make sure that SQL Server and the SQL Server Agent services are running under an account other than *localsystem*.
- Set up a default replication snapshot folder for SQL Server.
- Create a publication of a SQL Server 2000 database.
- Install the SQL Server CE Server Agent on your Web server.
- Use the SQL Server Connectivity Management tool to create a virtual directory containing the SQL Server CE Server Agent DLL (Sscesa20.dll).
- Choose an authentication method for the new site.
- Secure the virtual directory using NTFS.
- Share and secure the snapshot folder using NTFS.
- Check that the identity that IIS authorizes has a corresponding logon to SQL Server and that the identity has permission to subscribe to the publication.

Setting Up the Publication

You'll need an administrator's logon to SQL Server for this setup. If you have not already used SQL Server for replication, you will first need to run the Configure Publishing and Distribution Wizard. (Skip this paragraph if you have already used this SQL Server for replication.) Access the Configure Publishing and Distribution Wizard by selecting Wizards from the Tools menu option and then expanding the Replication item in the outline list. Run the Configure Publishing and Distribution Wizard. On the first screen, leave the SQL Server as its own distribution database and then click Next. The next screen, shown in Figure 17-16, shows the location of the snapshot folder. You can accept the default here, but make a note of its location—you'll need the location when you set up the merge replication Web server. Click Next twice, and then click Finish to complete the setup.

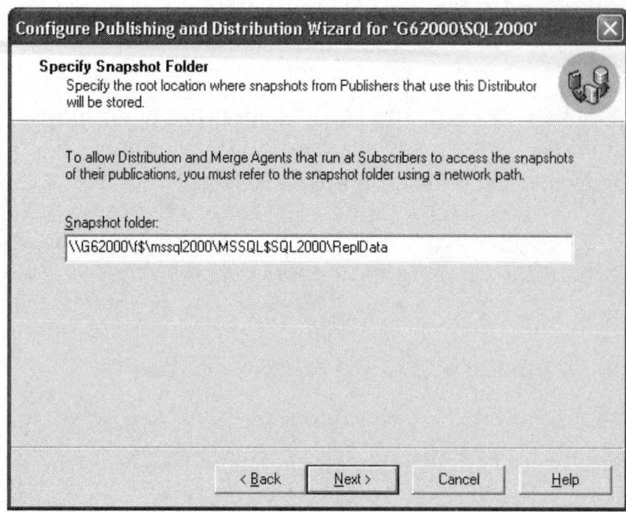

Figure 17-16 SQL Server Configure Publishing and Distribution Wizard.

Run SQL Server Enterprise Manager, and select Replication, then Publications. Select New Publication from the Action menu to run the Create Publication Wizard. (Alternatively, you can find the Create Publication Wizard by selecting Wizards from the Tools menu.) Click Next, select the traffic database for replication, and click Next again. On the Select Publication Type screen, click the bottom option for Merge Replication and then click Next. On the Specify Subscriber Types step, check both the SQL Server 2000 and SQL Server CE options and then click Next.

On the Specify Articles step, shown in Figure 17-17, check both the Cars and the Obs tables, and then click Next. Give the publication a name (this sample uses TrafficCE), and click Next. There is no need to further customize the replication for the sample. Leave the No option selected, click Next, and then click Finish to complete the setup.

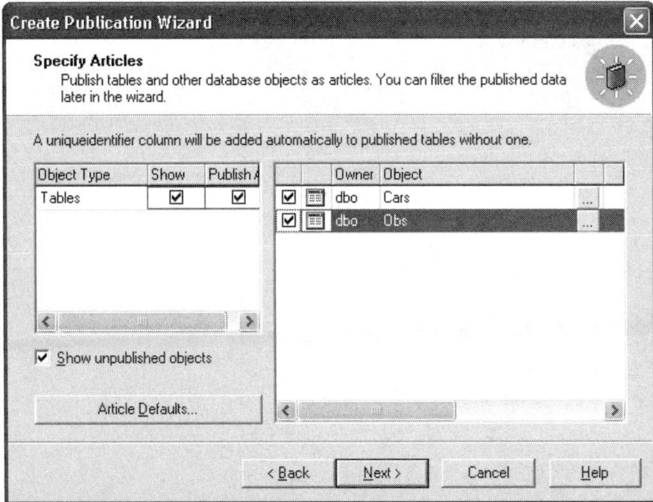

Figure 17-17 SQL Server Create Publication Wizard.

Setting Up the Web Server

Start the setup for the merge replication sample by running the SQL Server CE Connectivity Management tool that was installed on your Web server when you set up RDA for the previous sample. You should see the TrafficRDA virtual directory that you created earlier, in the section "Installing the SQL Server CE Server Agent." Double-click the Create A Virtual Directory item in the list to run the SQL Server CE Virtual Directory Creation Wizard for a second time. Create a new virtual directory named TrafficMR, and click Next. Again, the sample will use Integrated Windows Authentication, so select the bottom option on the Virtual Directory Authentication screen and then click Next. Add the domain and user name or the domain and Windows NT group for NTFS access to the virtual directory, and click Next. On the next screen, select the check box for merge replication and click Next.

The final step is to secure the merge replication user for access to the snapshot folder. Enter the network location of the snapshot folder, as shown in Figure 17-18, click Next, and then click Finish to complete the setup. The Web server portion of the setup for Merge Replication is now complete.

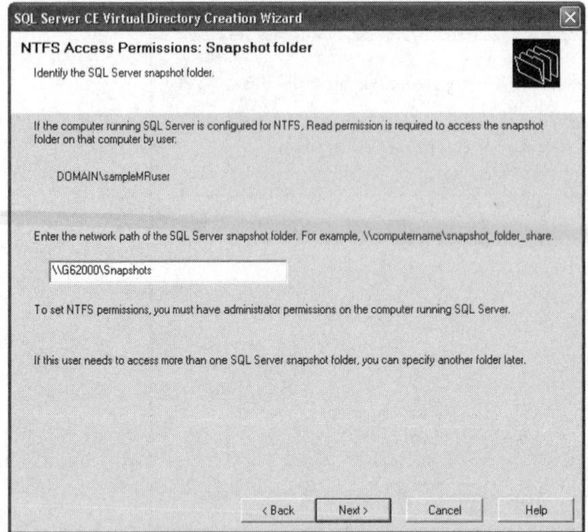

Figure 17-18 Merge replication snapshot folder NTFS security.

Understanding Merge Replication Security

Merge replication can use NTFS file security to provide control over the two folders that it uses: the virtual directory and the snapshot folder. This is in addition to the user authentication provided by IIS and SQL Server. SQL Server also controls access at a database level, and it controls access to the publication via the publication access list (PAL). There is an additional optional level of security in SQL Server called *Check Permissions*. Check Permissions provides an enhanced level of control by ensuring that the SQL Server CE Server Agent logon has permissions to perform insert, update, and delete operations on the data.

Figure 17-19 shows the general security scheme, using the gates to represent security checks and using computer terminals to represent the identities that you might assume at the various stages.

As with RDA security configuration, you have a choice of four authentication schemes. You'll make the choice when you configure the virtual directory using the SQL Server CE Virtual Directory Creation Wizard (discussed in the section "Installing the SQL Server CE Server Agent") by choosing a specific combination of the *InternetLogin*, *InternetPassword*, and OLE DB connection string. Table 17-17 shows each of the four schemes and the identities and authentication checks involved.

For merge replication, in addition to the IIS and SQL Server setup, you'll need to set up the following NTFS permissions:

- Allow SQL Server and its agents full control to create the initial snapshot files and folder structure in the snapshot folder.
- Allow the SQL Server CE Agent to read the snapshot files in the snapshot folder.
- Allow the SQL Server CE Agent to read and write the message files in the virtual directory.
- Allow SQL Server and its agents full control over the message files in the virtual directory.
- Allow the user to execute the SQL Server CE Agent (Sscesa.dll).

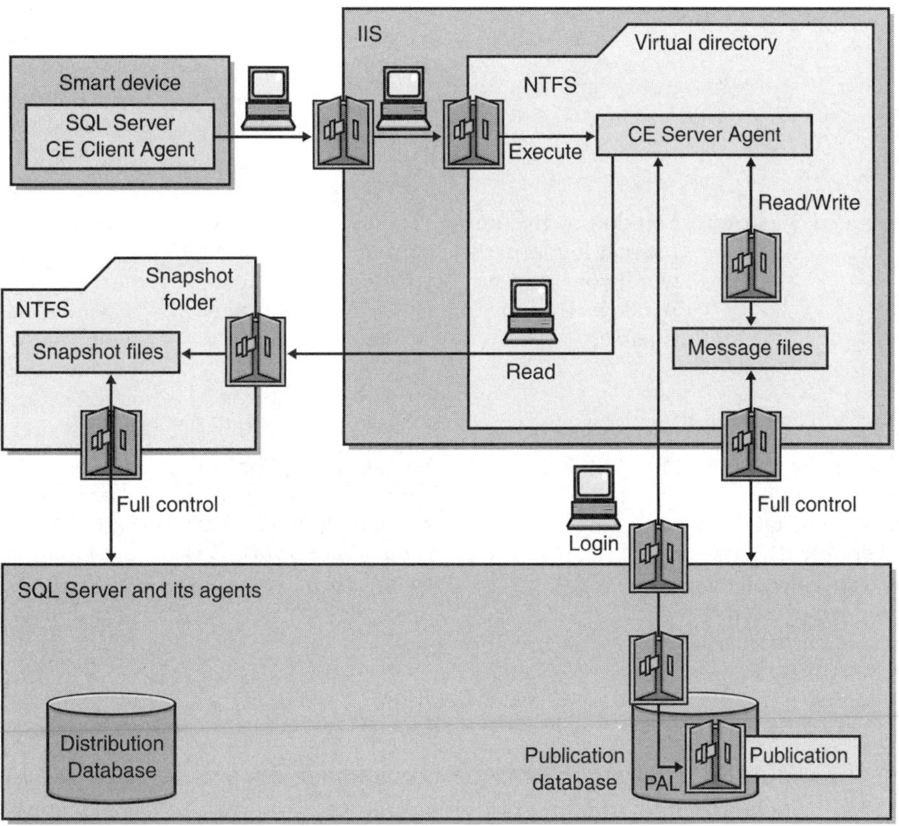

Figure 17-19 Merge replication security.

Table 17-17 Authentication Schemes in Merge Replication

Authentication Scheme	IIS Authentication	SQL Server Authentication	SQL Server Permissions
Anonymous	You do not give an Internet logon/password.	You are logged on as *computer*\IUSR_*machine-name* or another specified anonymous Internet user account using SQL Server Integrated Authentication.	You need to grant database access to the *computer*\IUSR_*machine name* logon and add it to the PAL.
Basic	You must give an Internet logon/password.	You are logged on as the user specified in the Internet logon using SQL Server Integrated Authentication.	You need to grant database access to the logon specified by the Internet logon or to a Windows NT group to which the Internet logon belongs, and add the logon or group to the PAL.
Integrated Windows	You do not give an Internet logon/password; your current Windows user logon is passed.	You are logged on as your current Windows user with SQL Server Integrated Authentication.	You need to grant database access to the Windows user account or to a Windows NT group to which the Windows user belongs, and add the logon or group to the PAL.
Anonymous, Basic, or Integrated Windows, with SQL Server user ID/password specified in the *PublisherLogin/Password* or *DistributerLogin/Password* properties.		You are logged on using the user ID/password specified in the *PublisherLogin/Password* or *DistributerLogin/Password* properties.	You need to grant database access to the SQL Server user specified in the *PublisherLogin* or *DistributerLogin* property, and add it to the *PAL*.

Table 17-18 expands on the previous list for each of the four authentication schemes and adds the additional file security requirements to give a full list of the NTFS permissions you need to set up.

Table 17-18 Required NTFS Permissions

Authentication Scheme	IIS Authentication	NTFS Permissions
Anonymous	You do not give an Internet logon/password.	For the *computer*\IUSR_*machinename* logon, you need to grant read and write access to the virtual directory and read access to the snapshot folder.
Basic	You must give an Internet logon/password.	For the Internet logon or for a Windows NT group to which the Internet logon belongs, you need to grant read and write access to the virtual directory and read access to the snapshot folder.
Integrated Windows	You do not give an Internet logon/password; your current Windows user logon is passed.	For the Windows user account or for a Windows NT group to which the Windows user belongs, you need to grant read and write access to the virtual directory and read access to the snapshot folder.
Anonymous, Basic, or Integrated Windows, with SQL Server user ID/password specified in the *PublisherLogin/Password* or *DistributerLogin/Password* properties.		Apply NTFS permissions as per the scenario above, which matches the IIS authentication mode chosen.
Any		The user, in which SQL Server and its agents are started, must be given full control to the virtual directory and to the snapshot folder.

Programming Merge Replication

With the server setup completed, you're ready to see how to program SQL Server CE Merge Replication. You'll find the UsingSQLCEMRSample application with this book's sample files. The UsingSQLCEMRSample application contains the code shown in the rest of this section, and you can follow the sample by opening the UsingSQLCEMRSample project in Visual Studio .NET. The Using-SQLCEMRSample application uses the *TrafficMR* virtual directory that is described earlier, in the sections "Setting Up the Publication" and "Setting Up the Web Server."

If you're following the sample, locate the *Merge* function in the code for the form called *FormMR*. You can see that the first step for programming merge replication is to create an instance of the *SqlCeReplication* object, which is part of *SqlServerCe*. Table 17-19 lists the methods available on the *SqlCeReplication* object and describes their uses.

Table 17-19 Methods of the *SqlCeReplication* Object

Method	Description
SqlCeReplication (constructor)	The UsingSQLCEMRSample application uses the second overload of the constructor in the merge replication example. This constructor takes arguments for all the properties that are required for synchronization. (See Table 17-20.)
AddSubscription	Used to create a new subscription to the published database and, optionally, to create the local SQL Server CE database. You must call the *Synchronize* method to actually retrieve the data.
DropSubscription	Used to drop the subscription to the published database and, optionally, to delete the local SQL Server CE database file.
ReinitializeSubscription	Used to mark a subscription for reinitialization. (SQL Server re-creates the snapshot of data.) You must call the *Synchronize* method (which reloads the snapshot) to see data based on the reinitialization.
Synchronize	Call this to invoke the merge replication.

> **Note** SQL Server CE merge replication supports the same set of data types as RDA and uses the same mappings from SQL Server data types.

Adding a Subscription

For the first stage of the merge replication, you need to create the subscription database on the smart device and create the subscription to the published database on the server. The UsingSQLCEMRSample application does this by creating a *SqlCeReplication* object, passing certain required arguments to its constructor, and then calling its *AddSubscription* method. Table 17-20 lists the required properties (passed as arguments).

Table 17-20 Properties of the *SqlCeReplication* Object

Property	Description
InternetURL	The URL to the Sscesa20.dll.
InternetLogin	Required only if not using Anonymous authentication mode.
InternetPassword	Required only if not using Anonymous authentication mode.
Publisher	Name of the publishing server. If this is an instance of SQL Server 2000, it will be in the format *ServerName/InstanceName*.
PublisherDatabase	The name of the published database.
Publication	The name of the publication on the published database.
Subscriber	The name of your subscription.
SubscriberConnectionString	The local connection string for the SQL Server CE database file (*.sdf).

After calling the *AddSubscription* method, your local SQL Server CE database file will have been created, but the tables and their initial snapshot of data will not yet be present. (You could confirm this by using the Query Analyzer tool to look at the local database objects.) You must call the *Synchronize* method to transfer the initial snapshot of data to the new SQL Server CE database.

Synchronizing Data

The *Synchronize* method of the *SqlCeReplication* object will get the initial snapshot of data for your local SQL Server CE database if this is the first time you call it (or the first time after the publication has been marked for resynchronization). Once the initialization of data has taken place, subsequent calls you make to the *Synchronize* method will invoke the merge replication and only changes to the data will be sent and received.

The following sample code, from the UsingSQLCEMRSample application, shows a subscription being set up only if the local database file does not already exist. Notice how the code disposes of the *SqlCeReplication* object at the end but doesn't drop the subscription. The next time it runs the code, there is no initialization of data.

```
SqlCeReplication rep = new SqlCeReplication(
    @"http://MySvr/TrafficMR/sscesa20.dll",
    @"CETest","cetest",
    @"G62000\SQL2000",
    "Traffic",
    "TrafficCE",
    "Testing",
    @"Data Source=\My Documents\TrafficMR.sdf");
try
{
    if (!System.IO.File.Exists(@"\My Documents\TrafficMR.sdf"))
    {
        rep.AddSubscription(AddOption.CreateDatabase);
    }
    rep.Synchronize();
}
catch (SqlCeException ex)
{
    DisplaySQLCEErrors(ex);
}
finally
{
    rep.Dispose();
}
```

Once you have created a subscription and the initial transfer of snapshot data has been used to create the local database, you can use the *SqlServerCe* objects to update, insert, and delete data. Any changes you make will be merged into the published database the next time you call the *Synchronize* method. The UsingSQLCEMRSample application then continues by retrieving the data into a bound DataGrid control. The details of this technique were covered earlier, in the section "Using a Dataset and Data Binding."

Troubleshooting Merge Replication

As with RDA, most of the problems you'll get with merge replication can be traced back to the security setup. The following gives a sequence of checks that you can use to locate and resolve problems with merge replication:

- Check the users and permissions at each stage of the sequence from the specification for *InternetLogin* to the published database.
- Check that you're using the recommended service packs for SQL Server and the SQL Server CE Server Agent (Service Pack 2, at minimum, for both).

- Check that you're not attempting to use a snapshot folder other than the default one specified in SQL Server. SQL Server CE merge replication will work only with the default folder.
- Check that you're running SQL Server and the SQL Server Agent services under an account other than the *localsystem* account, and check that the account has full control over the snapshot folder in NTFS.
- If you're using an identity column, you need to find the next available number and reseed before an insert can be successful. You'll also have to set up ranged identity columns on the published database to prevent errors when the new data is merged.

Choosing Between RDA and Merge Replication

This chapter has looked at both RDA and merge replication used with SQL Server CE. When designing an application that is to use both SQL Server CE and SQL Server, you have to choose between RDA and merge replication as ways of sharing data between the central database and the smart device application. To help you make this choice, Table 17-21 compares some of the features of each.

Table 17-21 Comparison of RDA and Merge Replication

RDA	Merge Replication
SQL Server 6.5 (Service Pack 5) or later.	SQL Server 2000 (Service Pack 2) or later.
Relatively simple to set up and secure.	More complex to set up, and security can be quite difficult because there are more components of the architecture.
Uses optimistic locking; can lose updates.	Uses merge conflict resolution; can lose updates like optimistic locking, but also can be configured and programmed for much finer control.
Works well on a simple table. You'll be involved in extensive programming if you need to relate tables or split data between users.	Can publish relationship information and partition tables as part of the replication system on SQL Server 2000.
SQL Server CE device controls the data flow.	The central databases control the flow of data, security, and the merge process.

You might think (correctly) that the fastest way to get up and running with sharing central SQL Server data to smart device applications is by using RDA. However, unless you have a specific requirement to support pre–SQL Server 2000 databases, it's recommended that you invest the extra initial effort (in the setup) to use merge replication. The considerable extra server-side functionality provided by merge replication will enable you to deal with any future increase in the complexity of your application, and ultimately, to support larger numbers of users through your ability to improve the SQL Server replication configuration by partitioning data and using more physical servers.

Summary

This chapter has shown you how to use the SQL Server CE Data Provider on a smart device to create and modify a database and how to update the data held in the local SQL Server CE database. It has also shown how to use RDA and merge replication to fetch data from a central SQL Server database and how changes made locally can be returned to the central database.

Part V

Advanced Mobile Application Development

18

Custom Controls

The controls in the .NET Compact Framework contain a useful subset of the control functionality found in the full .NET Framework. One facility shared by both Frameworks is the ability to create customized versions of a control to promote code reuse. Controls that can be reused within the confines of a single application can reduce the file sizes and memory requirements of an application in much the same way that gathering common code into a method can. Modularizing the code in this way also helps to ensure consistency in design because the same user interface component can be reused. As an additional benefit, a custom control can be packaged in a separate assembly to get binary reuse.

Inheriting from a Toolbox Control

The .NET Framework's strong support for inheritance makes customization of controls fairly straightforward. If you want to build a custom control that is closely related to an existing control, especially if it is a refinement of the behavior of an existing control, the most appropriate technique is usually inheritance.

As an example, consider a text control that allows only numeric characters to be entered. In the following example, the custom control is defined in a class called *NumericTextBox*, which inherits from the *TextBox* class. Within this class, a new version of the *OnKeyPress* method is provided to catch keyboard input.

The *OnKeyPress* event handler is called whenever a keystroke is processed by the control. Overriding this method in a derived class allows the developer to customize the control's behavior. The *KeyPressEventArgs* parameter holds information about the keystroke, and the code that follows accepts only digits and the control characters for backspace by setting the *Handled* flag for any other characters. When overriding *OnKeyPress* in a derived class, the derived class should call the *OnKeyPress* method of the base class so that registered delegates receive the event.

NumericTextBox.cs

```
using System;
using System.Windows.Forms;

namespace a
{
   public class NumericTextBox: System.Windows.Forms.TextBox
   {
        protected override void OnKeyPress(KeyPressEventArgs e)
        {
            if (!(Char.IsDigit(e.KeyChar) ||
                e.KeyChar=='\b' || e.KeyChar==13))
            {
                e.Handled=true;
            }
            base.OnKeyPress(e);
        }
   }
}
```

All other behavior of the control is derived from the .NET Compact Framework's *TextBox* class from which *NumericTextBox* inherits.

To use this control, it must be instantiated inside a container. The most commonly used container is a form. At this stage, the derived control has no designer support and cannot be placed in the toolbox or edited visually, so all instantiation has to be done through manual coding.

The container form that follows contains a private class variable *numText* that holds an instance of the *NumericTextBox* class. The constructor of the form initializes this variable after the call to *InitializeComponent*.

NumericTextBoxDemo.cs

```
using System;
using System.Drawing;
using System.Collections;
using System.ComponentModel;
using System.Windows.Forms;
```

(continued)

NumericTextBoxDemo.cs *(continued)*

```
namespace CustomControlDemo
{
    public class NumericTextBoxDemo : System.Windows.Forms.Form
    {
        private NumericTextBox numText;

        public NumericTextBoxDemo()
        {
            InitializeComponent();

            numText = new NumericTextBox();
            numText.Location = new System.Drawing.Point(8, 108);
            numText.Size = new Size(92, 16);

            this.Controls.Add(numText);

        }

        /// <summary>
        /// Clean up any resources being used.
        /// </summary>
        protected override void Dispose( bool disposing )
        {
            base.Dispose( disposing );
        }

        #region Windows Form Designer generated code
        /// <summary>
        /// Required method for Designer support - do not modify
        /// the contents of this method with the code editor.
        /// </summary>
        private void InitializeComponent()
        {
            //
            // NumericTextBoxDemo
            //
            this.ClientSize = new System.Drawing.Size(240, 295);
            this.MinimizeBox = false;
            this.Text = "NumericTextBoxDemo";
        }
        #endregion

    }
}
```

> **Important** The code that instantiates the custom control is very similar to that generated inside *InitializeComponent* when controls are added from the Visual Studio .NET toolbox. However, note that this code is placed *after* the call to *InitializeComponent*, not *inside* it. When using Visual Studio .NET, you should not change the body of *InitializeComponent* in the code editor. The Windows Forms Designer relies on a particular layout of code, and if you edit it manually, it might fail to recognize your form in the designer, or it might possibly ignore some of the changes you make. However, it is often convenient to examine the code for *InitializeComponent* to see examples of how a built-in control is instantiated.

When the application is run, the control will be created inside the form. Only numeric characters can be typed into the control. It is, however, still possible to enter non-numeric data using the clipboard. To see this for yourself, use Pocket Word to copy some text to the clipboard, return to the application, and press Shift+Insert while the numeric edit field has focus. To resolve this problem, you can add an additional event handler for *OnKeyDown* that ignores the Insert key if Shift is pressed.

```
protected override void OnKeyDown(KeyEventArgs e)
{
    if (e.Shift && e.KeyCode==Keys.Insert)
    {
        e.Handled=true;
    }
    base.OnKeyDown(e);
}
```

The *OnKeyPress* method operates at a higher level of abstraction than do the *OnKeyUp* and *OnKeyDown* methods. The latter methods are called whenever any key, or simulated key in the case of the Pocket PC soft input panel (SIP), is pressed or released, and the event parameter includes information about key codes. *OnKeyPress*, in contrast, is invoked only when the combination of key presses and releases has generated a Unicode character. For a further discussion of these methods, refer to the .NET documentation.

> **Tip** Programmers who are familiar with the full .NET Framework might wonder why the previous example does not use the *OnValidating* or *OnValidated* methods of the full .NET Framework. The reason is that they are not supported in the .NET Compact Framework's TextBox control.

As a further enhancement to the custom control, you can override the *OnGotFocus* and *OnLostFocus* events to change the appearance of the control when the user enters that control. In the following example code fragment, the control will have a background of yellow whenever it is selected, and when it is deselected, it will revert to the background color of the parent form:

```
protected override void OnGotFocus(EventArgs e)
{
    this.BackColor = Color.Yellow;
    base.OnGotFocus(e);
}
protected override void OnLostFocus(EventArgs e)
{
    this.BackColor = this.Parent.BackColor;
    base.OnLostFocus(e);
}
```

> **Tip** When writing a custom control, remember that *this* (*Me* in Visual Basic .NET) refers to the current instance to the control, which is in contrast to a typical forms-based class, where *this* refers to the current form instance.

Inheriting from the Control Class

Inheriting from an existing control is a useful technique if the control you want to build can be described and implemented conveniently using the inheritance relationship "is a." In the previous sample, a text box with numeric-only input "is a" special kind of text box. This is not always the case, especially if the custom control is not closely related to any existing controls or if the custom control is a collection of existing controls.

If the new control is not related to an existing control, you must inherit from a more generic class. The .NET Compact Framework allows the developer to inherit from the *Windows.System.Forms.Control* class. Figure 18-1 shows a portion of the .NET Framework class hierarchy in which you can appreciate how the *TextBox* class inherits from the *Control* class.

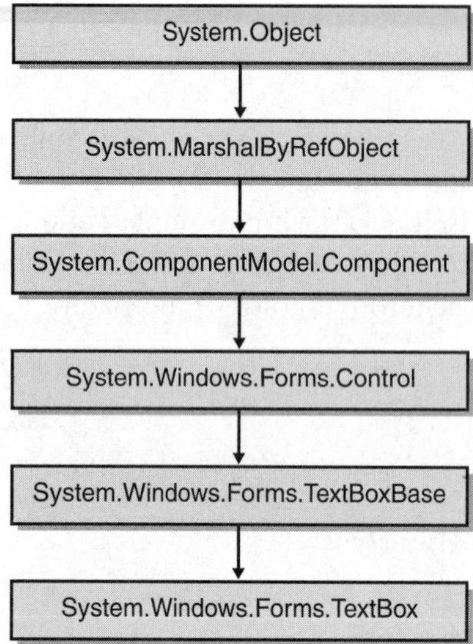

Figure 18-1 Extract from the .NET Framework class hierarchy showing the *TextBox* class.

The *Windows.System.Forms.Control* class is at the root of the hierarchy of user interface components and therefore contains common behavior for all controls and forms. You need to inherit from this class to get the basic behavior common to all controls but without inheriting any specific class functionality from other user interface classes in the .NET Compact Framework.

The *Control* class handles user input through the keyboard and mouse, defines the bounds and size of the control, and handles basic interfacing to the underlying operating system. However, it does not incorporate any rendering of the graphical interface of the control, or anything else for that matter. As the control author, you must provide all of these aspects through custom code.

> **Tip** The full .NET Framework provides a *UserControl* class that simplifies the process of creating custom controls. This class is not present in the .NET Compact Framework, so more work is required on the part of the control author in some cases.

Creating a Clickable Label Control

One of the features of the Label control class in the .NET Compact Framework is that it raises no events based on mouse or keyboard input. The following sample shows how a custom label control named ClickableLabel can be created by inheriting from *Windows.System.Forms.Control*. One advantage of this approach is that the *Control* class raises *Click* events, unlike the *Label* class. The code that follows will not seek to duplicate all the features of the built-in *Label* class.

The following code, from the ClickableLabel project included with this book's sample files, shows how the *ClickableLabel* class derives directly from *System.Windows.Forms.Control*:

```
public class ClickableLabel : System.Windows.Forms.Control
{
    ⋮
}
```

Because *ClickableLabel* inherits all the public properties of *Control* automatically, it already has a number of useful properties.

- The *Text* property is a string that holds the text to be displayed in the label.
- The *Font* property describes the output font to use.
- The *ForeColor* property specifies the foreground color.

As the control author, you must provide a mechanism for displaying the text on the display. To allow the application developer to specify the alignment of the text within the label, two enumerated types are defined outside the *ClickableLabel* class; one represents the vertical alignment, and one represents the horizontal alignment.

```
// Vertical alignment
public enum VAlign { Top, Middle, Bottom }

// Horizontal alignment
public enum HAlign { Left, Middle, Right }
```

The *ClickableLabel* class declares private variables to hold the current alignment settings for each instance.

```
private VAlign vrtAlign = VAlign.Middle;
private HAlign hrzAlign = HAlign.Middle;
```

The class also creates a private variable to define the border style. The .NET Compact Framework already has a suitable enumerated type, *BorderStyle*.

```
private BorderStyle bdrStyle = BorderStyle.None;
```

Each of these variables is then encapsulated by public properties that can be used to read and write the property values. This encapsulation serves the following two purposes:

- It is a sound, although not essential, programming technique that allows encapsulation and, where relevant, data validation on assignment.
- It allows the control to take action whenever the property value changes. In this case, if the alignment or border style properties are changed at run time, the clickable label control should be redrawn.

```
// VAlign property
public VAlign VAlign
{
    get { return VAlign; }
    set
    {
        vrtAlign = value;
        Invalidate();
    }
}

// HAlign property
public HAlign HAlign
{
    get { return HAlign; }
    set
    {
        hrzAlign = value;
        Invalidate();
    }
}

// BorderStyle Property
public BorderStyle BorderStyle
{
    get { return bdrStyle; }
    set
    {
        bdrStyle = value;
        Invalidate();
    }
}
```

The *ClickableLabel* class also overrides the *Text* property's *set* method so that the *Invalidate* method can be called when the *Text* property is changed.

Only the *set* method is overridden, and in doing so, the base class *set* method is invoked. The *Text* property's *get* method, inherited from *Control*, is not affected.

```
public override string Text
{
    set
    {
        base.Text = value;
        Invalidate();
    }
}
```

The *ClickableLabel* class overrides the *OnPaint* method of the *Control* class to draw the text in the appropriate location. The implementation of *OnPaint* for the *Control* class does nothing except raise a *Paint* event that can be used in the containing form. Note that the *OnPaint* method is not called directly by the control. Instead, the *Invalidate* method marks the control as needing a refresh. The underlying operating system waits until the principal thread of the application is not busy and then refreshes all the parts of the screen that need updating. If you require immediate updating, use the *Refresh* method, which calls *OnPaint* directly without waiting.

```
protected override void OnPaint(PaintEventArgs pe)
{
    int borderSpace = 0;
    Graphics gr = pe.Graphics;

    using (Pen penDraw = new Pen(Color.Black))
    {
        switch(BorderStyle)
        {
            case BorderStyle.FixedSingle:
                gr.DrawRectangle(penDraw, 0, 0, Width - 1, Height - 1);
                borderSpace = 2;
                break;
            case BorderStyle.Fixed3D:
                gr.DrawRectangle(penDraw, ClientRectangle);
                borderSpace = 2;
                break;
            case BorderStyle.None:
                // No border to draw
                borderSpace = 0;
                break;
        }

        SizeF sizeText = gr.MeasureString(Text, Font);
```

(continued)

```
        float posX=0.0F;
        float posY=0.0F;

        switch (hrzAlign)
        {
            case HAlign.Left:
                posX = borderSpace;
                break;
            case HAlign.Middle:
                posX = (Width-sizeText.Width)/2;
                break;
            case HAlign.Right:
                posX = Width - sizeText.Width - borderSpace;
                break;
        }

        switch (vrtAlign)
        {
            case VAlign.Top:
                posY = borderSpace;
                break;
            case VAlign.Middle:
                posY = (Height - sizeText.Height)/2;
                break;
            case VAlign.Bottom:
                posY = Height - sizeText.Height - borderSpace;
                break;
        }

        SolidBrush b  = new SolidBrush(ForeColor);
        gr.DrawString(Text, Font, b, posX, posY);
        b.Dispose();
    }

    base.OnPaint(pe);
}
```

The final statement of the *OnPaint* method should be a call to the base class implementation of *OnPaint* to ensure that the *Paint* event is fired correctly for any users of the control.

This control can be instantiated inside a form, as shown earlier for the NumericTextBox control. The ClickableLabel control has a *Click* event, inherited from the *Control* class, for which an event handler can be created in the usual way. The following code, from the ClickableLabelDemo.cs file that's available with this book's sample files, demonstrates how to instantiate a ClickableLabel control and handle its *Click* event:

```
public class ClickableLabelDemo : System.Windows.Forms.Form
{
    ⋮
    private ClickableLabel clickLabel;
    ⋮
    public ClickableLabelDemo()
    {
        InitializeComponent();
        ⋮
        clickLabel = new ClickableLabel();
        clickLabel.Location = new System.Drawing.Point(8, 108);
        clickLabel.Size = new Size(92, 92);

        this.Controls.Add(clickLabel);

        clickLabel.Click += new EventHandler(clickLabel_Click);

        clickLabel.Text = "Hello, world!";
        clickLabel.BorderStyle = BorderStyle.FixedSingle;
        ⋮
    }
    ⋮
    private void clickLabel_Click(object sender, EventArgs e)
    {
        MessageBox.Show("The label was clicked");
    }
    ⋮
}
```

Adding Custom Events: SlideShow

The following example is a "slide show" component into which a number of images can be loaded and then displayed in sequence. The control is called SlideShow. It contains two private variables: *pics* to hold an *ArrayList* object containing *Image* references, and *pos* to hold the current position in the slide show.

```
public class SlideShow : System.Windows.Forms.Control
{
    private ArrayList              pics;
    private int                    pos;
    ⋮
}
```

These variables are given suitable initial values in the control's constructor.

```
public SlideShow()
{
    pics = new ArrayList();
    pos  = 0;
    ⋮
}
```

The public method *AddImage* allows the user of the control to add an image reference, which is added to the list held in *pics*.

```
public void AddImage(Image img)
{
    pics.Add(img);
}
```

To display the current image on the screen, you must override the *OnPaint* method. The implementation of *OnPaint* for the *SlideShow* class needs to display the current image from the *pics* list and draw a frame around the edge of the control. The *OnPaint* method accepts a single parameter, *pe*, of type *PaintEventArgs* that holds information about the part of the display that is to be redrawn. The *Graphics* property of *PaintEventArgs* provides methods for drawing objects on the display device. If no images are loaded into the control, nothing needs to be done. Otherwise, the *Image* to be drawn is selected from the *pics* list by indexing with the *pos* member variable. Then the *DrawImage* method displays the image at the upper left of the drawing area, offset by one pixel to avoid drawing over the control's border.

To draw the frame around the edge of the screen, a *Pen* object is created using blue as the initial color. Because the *Pen* object uses the *Dispose* method to return scarce system resources to the operating system, the code that draws the frame is enclosed within a *using* statement. The *DrawRectangle* method is used to draw a rectangle, using the *ClientRectangle* method to determine the boundaries of the client area. Finally the method calls the base class implementation of *OnPaint* to ensure that the *Paint* event is fired correctly for any users of the control.

```
protected override void OnPaint(PaintEventArgs pe)
{
    Graphics gr = pe.Graphics;
    if (pics.Count != 0)
    {
        // Retrieve image
        Image img = (Image)pics[pos];
        // Draw image
        gr.DrawImage(img, 1, 1);
```

```
            // Draw frame
            using (Pen borderPen = new Pen(Color.Blue))
            {
                Rectangle rClient = ClientRectangle;
                gr.DrawRectangle(borderPen,
                    rClient.X, rClient.Y,
                    rClient.Right-1, rClient.Bottom-1);
            }
        }
        base.OnPaint(pe);
    }
```

The *SlideShow* class's public property *Position* holds the position. The *get* accessor returns the current value of *pos*. The *set* accessor changes the value of *pos*, but first it checks that the value is in the range of values permitted by the size of the *pics* list. If the new value of *pos* differs from the old one, the *set* accessor's code calls *Invalidate*.

```
public int Position
{
    get { return pos; }
    set
    {
        // Must be zero, or less than pics.Count
        if (value < 0 || value >= pics.Count)
        {
            throw new IndexOutOfRangeException();
        }
        if (pos != value)
        {
            pos = value;
            this.Invalidate();
        }
    }
}
```

The *Step* method is provided to move the current position forward and backward, taking care that the position remains within the range established by the *pics* list.

```
public void Step(bool isForward)
{
    int newPos;
    int increment = isForward ? 1 : -1;
    if (pics.Count != 0)
    {
```

(continued)

```
            // Calculate next image number
            newPos = pos + increment;
            if (newPos >= pics.Count)
                newPos=0;
            else if (newPos < 0)
                newPos = 0;

            // Set new position
            Position = newPos;
        }
    }
```

For convenience of users of the control, the *SlideShow* class includes another overloaded version of *Step* with no parameters that advances the position by one.

```
public void Step()
{
Step(true);
}
```

> **Tip** When designing a control (or any class, in fact), take time to consider ways that the control can be made easier to use by its clients. Supplying different overloaded versions of the same method is one technique that you can use. It's particularly useful, as with the *Step* method example just given, to provide a version of a method with a different parameter list. You should always ensure that the general intent of all the overloaded methods is the same and reasonably consistent with other methods that differ from it only by signature. It would not, for example, be sensible to define a *Step* method with a different parameter list if that method were to, for example, invert all the images in the control.

The *SlideShow* class provides a *Clear* method to empty the images from the list.

```
public void Clear()
{
    pics.Clear();
    pos = 0;
    Invalidate();
}
```

Having created the code for the *SlideShow* class, it must be instantiated in a form, as demonstrated earlier with *NumericTextBox*. A private form variable is created to hold an instance of the *SlideShow* class, and the variable is initialized after the call to *InitializeComponent*. The following code, from the SlideShow-Demo.cs file available with this book's sample files, illustrates how this is done:

```
public class SlideShowDemo : System.Windows.Forms.Form
{
    private SlideShow slideShow;
    ⋮
    public SlideShowDemo()
    {
        InitializeComponent();

        slideShow = new SlideShow();
        slideShow.Location = new System.Drawing.Point(8, 92);
        slideShow.Size = new Size(92, 92);
        this.Controls.Add(slideShow);
        ⋮
    }
    ⋮
}
```

The images are loaded in the form's constructor, using the *SlideShow.Add* method.

```
        Image imgTemp;
        imgTemp = new Bitmap(AppDir() + "pic1.bmp");
        slideShow.AddImage(imgTemp);
        imgTemp = new Bitmap(AppDir() + "pic2.bmp");
        slideShow.AddImage(imgTemp);
        imgTemp = new Bitmap(AppDir() + "pic3.bmp");
        slideShow.AddImage(imgTemp);
```

The files pic1.bmp, pic2.bmp, and pic3.bmp must be added to the project to ensure that they are deployed into the target environment along with the executables. To do so, select Add Existing Item from the Project menu.

Within the container form, two buttons named *cmdNext* and *cmdPrevious* are used to move to the next and previous image. The following code shows you how to handle the *Click* event for these buttons:

```
private void cmdNext_Click(object sender, System.EventArgs e)
{
    slideShow.Step(true);
}

private void cmdPrevious_Click(object sender, System.EventArgs e)
{
    slideShow.Step(false);
}
```

Adding a Custom Event to the Control

The convention adopted in the .NET Framework is that each event is raised by a protected method having the same name as the method but prefixed with *On*. For example, the *KeyPress* event is raised by the protected method *OnKeyPress*. The methods are protected to ensure that they're not accessible to users of the class but are accessible in derived objects. The convention is also that descendant classes that override one of these methods should call the same method in the base class to ensure that any event handlers attached to the event are correctly triggered. The .NET Compact Framework does not force you to design controls in this way, but it makes sense to follow the conventions to reduce confusion.

In this sample, you'll augment the *SlideShow* class with a new event named *PositionChanged*. This event is triggered after the value of the *Position* property changes. Following the convention just outlined, the control will raise this event in a protected method called *OnPositionChanged*.

The *SlideShow* class inherits from *Control*; therefore, it inherits all the standard events that *Control* raises. You might want to raise additional events from a control, which can be done by defining and raising your own events.

Within the namespace declaration, but outside the *SlideShow* class, add a definition for the delegate that defines the signature of the event handler. In this case, for simplicity, it is a delegate that has no parameters and returns *void*. Within the *SlideShow* class, define a public event *PositionChanged* that uses this delegate.

```
public delegate void PositionChangedDelegate();
⋮
public event PositionChangedDelegate PositionChanged;
```

Within the *SlideShow* class, create a protected method named *OnPositionChanged* that invokes delegates attached to the event handler. It's necessary to check that the event variable is not *null* before raising the event.

```
protected void OnPositionChanged()
{
if (PositionChanged != null)
PositionChanged();
}
```

Unlike the *OnPaint* and *OnKeyPress* methods discussed earlier, you don't need to invoke a base method because there isn't one in this case. Now it's necessary to ensure that the *OnPositionChanged* method is called whenever the *Position* property of the control is changed.

```
public int Position
{
    ⋮
    set
    {
        ⋮
        if (pos != value)
        {
            pos = value;
            OnPositionChanged();
            this.Invalidate();
        }
    }
}
```

Enhancing the SlideShow Control with a Timer

As a further enhancement, you can add a timer to automatically move to the next picture at a specified interval. Within the *SlideShow* class, create a private variable of type *System.Windows.Forms.Timer*, which provides the timing function, and another variable to hold the interval between slides, measured in milliseconds. The *Interval* property provides a read/write interface to the interval value.

```
⋮
private Timer tmr;
private int slideInterval;
⋮
public int Interval
{
    get
    {
        return slideInterval;
    }
    set
    {
        slideInterval = value;
    }
}
```

The *AutoMode* property is used to start and stop the timer. When *AutoMode* is *true*, *tmr* refers to a *Timer* object that calls the update event *Tick*. When *AutoMode* is *false*, the timer is set to *null* and does not operate.

```
public bool AutoMode
{
    get
    {
```

(continued)

```
            return (tmr != null);
        }
        set
        {
            if (value && tmr == null)
            {
                // Turn on the timer
                pos = 0;
                tmr = new Timer();
                tmr.Tick += new EventHandler(Tick);
                tmr.Interval = Interval;
                tmr.Enabled = true;
            }
            else if (!value && tmr != null)
            {
                // Turn off the timer
                tmr.Enabled = false;
                tmr.Dispose();
                tmr = null;
            }
        }
    }
```

When the timer is running, it invokes the *Tick* event handler, which, as the following code shows, calls the *Step* method to advance to the next slide:

```
private void Tick(object sender, EventArgs e)
{
    // Next slide
    Step();
}
```

It's necessary for *Tick* to have the signature just shown to match the *EventHandler* delegate type required by the *Timer* component. The container class, *SlideShowDemo*, has code that provides an initial value for the interval and an additional button to start and stop automatic mode.

```
⋮
public frmSlideDemo()
{
    ⋮
    // Set interval
    slideShow.Interval = 1000;
}
⋮
private void cmdAuto_Click(object sender, System.EventArgs e)
{
    if (slideShow.AutoMode)
```

```
    {
        slideShow.AutoMode        = false;
        this.cmdNext.Enabled      = true;
        this.cmdPrevious.Enabled = true;
    }
    else
    {
        slideShow.AutoMode        = true;
        this.cmdNext.Enabled      = false;
        this.cmdPrevious.Enabled = false;
}
}
```

You'll find the complete listing for the *SlideShowDemo* class in the CustomControlDemo project included with this book's sample files.

Placing a Custom Control in Its Own Assembly

All the samples of custom controls shown so far have the source code for the custom control in the same assembly as the code that uses it. It's also possible to compile the code for the custom control in its own assembly and deploy it independently from the application that uses it. This technique is particularly useful if you want to distribute a custom control without distributing its source code. It can also allow applications to share the same control, reducing deployment size.

To move an existing control from an application into its own assembly, start a new project for the .NET Compact Framework, using the template that creates a DLL, and move the class files that define the control into the new project. Because the custom control is now in its own assembly, the application developer must add a reference to the control's assembly to the main application.

> **Tip** When Visual Studio .NET creates a new project containing a class library, it does not add references to the *System.Drawing* and *System.Windows.Forms* assemblies by default. If your component interacts with the user interface, you'll need to add these project references.

Creating a Component

The controls demonstrated so far have been visual; they have a size and a position on the screen. Not all controls have position on the designer surface. Consider the *Timer* and *MainMenu* controls from the toolbox. You can create custom controls of this kind by basing your control on the *Component* class rather than on the *Control* class or a specific toolbox class such as *TextBox*. The *Component* class is simpler than *Control*: it provides an implementation of the *IComponent* interface, which works alongside the *ISite* interface provided by a container class such as a form.

The following code is a simple component called CalcComponent that adds and subtracts integers with *Add* and *Subtract* methods. Clearly, it is not sophisticated, but it demonstrates how this kind of component can be written.

CalcComponent.cs

```
public class CalcComponent : System.ComponentModel.Component
{
    public CalcComponent()
    {
        InitializeComponent();
    }
    public int Add(int a, int b)
    {
        return a+b;
    }
    public int Subtract(int a, int b)
    {
        return a-b;
    }
    #region Component Designer generated code
    /// <summary>
    /// Required method for Designer support - do not modify
    /// the contents of this method with the code editor.
    /// </summary>
    private void InitializeComponent()
    {
    }
    #endregion
}
```

This class can be instantiated in much the same way as other custom controls.

CalcComponentDemo.cs

```
using System;
using System.Drawing;
using System.Collections;
using System.ComponentModel;
using System.Windows.Forms;
```

(continued)

CalcComponentDemo.cs *(continued)*

```
namespace CustomControlDemo
{
    public class CalcComponentDemo : System.Windows.Forms.Form
    {
        private System.Windows.Forms.Button cmdCalc;
        private CalcComponent calcComponent;

        public CalcComponentDemo()
        {
            InitializeComponent();

            calcComponent = new CalcComponent();
        }

        protected override void Dispose( bool disposing )
        {
            base.Dispose( disposing );
        }

        #region Windows Form Designer generated code
        /// <summary>
        /// Required method for Designer support - do not modify
        /// the contents of this method with the code editor.
        /// </summary>
        private void InitializeComponent()
        {
            this.cmdCalc = new System.Windows.Forms.Button();
            //
            // cmdCalc
            //
            this.cmdCalc.Location = new System.Drawing.Point(80, 64);
            this.cmdCalc.Text = "Calc";
            this.cmdCalc.Click +=
                new System.EventHandler(this.cmdCalc_Click);
            //
            // CalcComponentDemo
            //
            this.ClientSize = new System.Drawing.Size(240, 295);
            this.Controls.Add(this.cmdCalc);
            this.MinimizeBox = false;
            this.Text = "CalcComponentDemo";

        }
        #endregion

        private void cmdCalc_Click(object sender, System.EventArgs e)
        {
```

(continued)

CalcComponentDemo.cs *(continued)*

```
            int result = calcComponent.Add(1,2);
            MessageBox.Show(result.ToString());
        }
    }
}
```

It would appear at first glance from this example that inheriting from *Component* does not add a great deal to the functionality of the derived class. After all, the *Add* and *Subtract* functionality would work just as well for any class, regardless of its position in an inheritance hierarchy. However, the functionality in *Component* allows a class derived from it to be placed on a design surface, such as Forms Designer. In practice, this means that with a little work, you can place the custom control or component into the toolbox and become more productive.

Creating a Design-Time Custom Control

In all the examples presented so far in this chapter, you've had to instantiate objects of the custom control or component classes by explicit programming. This technique works, as you've seen, but it is not as convenient as dragging, say, a list box from the toolbox onto your form. This section explains how to integrate your custom controls with the Forms Designer so that you can place your custom controls in the toolbox and have all the convenience that entails.

Dragging one of the built-in controls onto a form design surface makes Forms Designer perform the following actions:

- Pick a name for the instance of the control (for example, *listBox1*).
- Create a private reference variable of the appropriate type inside the form.
- Add code to *InitializeComponent* that instantiates the control at run time.
- Display the control at design time.
- Allow the developer to access properties through the Properties window.

Creating a Designer Version of a Custom Control

You can create designers for any control or component that is designed to target the .NET Compact Framework. However, graphical controls must be derived directly or indirectly from *System.Windows.Forms.Control*, and non-graphical controls must be derived directly or indirectly from *System.ComponentModel.Component*.

In the full .NET Framework, the same DLL is typically used at design time to interact with the toolbox and at run time to interact with the rest of your application. In the .NET Compact Framework, one very important consideration is that the environment in which Visual Studio .NET is running is very different from the environment in which the custom control is to be executed. If the control is to interact with Forms Designer, it must be built to use the assemblies of the full .NET Framework.

In the samples you've seen so far, the custom control has been compiled for deployment under the .NET Compact Framework. If you want your control or component to integrate with Visual Studio .NET, it must be recompiled and re-linked for execution in the full .NET Framework. You must provide two different assemblies: one for design time and one for run time.

When the design-time code for the control is running within Forms Designer, it must be aware that it can generate code that will be suitable for use in the .NET Compact Framework. For example, the *NumericTextBox* example class has no *Validating* or *Validated* events in the .NET Compact Framework. However, if you were to compile *NumericTextBox* in the full .NET Framework environment, it would inherit these event handlers from *TextBox* in the full .NET Framework by default.

This problem is resolved by linking the design-time version of the control with designer libraries that execute in the full .NET Framework but that are aware of the subset of features of the .NET environment. By default, these designer libraries are found in the folder C:\program files\Microsoft Visual Studio .NET 2003\CompactFrameworkSDK\v1.0.5000\Windows CE\Designer.

Differences Between the Full .NET Framework and the .NET Compact Framework

Because the .NET Compact Framework is a subset of the full .NET Framework, your custom control is unlikely to need extensive source code changes. Most of the code will compile in the full .NET Framework for the design-time version of the control. Note, however, the following concerns:

- If you make calls to unmanaged assemblies (DLLs) in the operating system, your code might not compile. The names of many DLLs differ between the Win32 and Windows CE APIs. You might want to use conditional compilation to encapsulate any *extern* methods.

- If any code in the control is specific to the device platform, it needs to be rewritten or removed to work in the full .NET Framework. This requirement includes use of .NET Compact Framework classes that aren't available in the full .NET Framework and the use of unmanaged code functions on the platform. For code that you want compiled only for the full .NET Framework, you can use conditional compilation.

Chapter 23 contains further details of these techniques.

Connecting the Design-Time Assembly to the .NET Compact Framework Runtime

For Visual Studio .NET to know which design-time assembly is associated with which run-time assembly, you need the assembly attribute *RuntimeAssemblyAttribute*, which is found in the *System.CF.Design* namespace. This area is one where the design-time control must differ from the run-time version; the attribute *RuntimeAssemblyAttribute* is required only in the design-time version. Accordingly, you can use conditional compilation with a symbol that evaluates to *true* only when compiling for the design-time version.

```
#if FULLFRAMEWORK_DESIGNER

[assembly: System.CF.Design.RuntimeAssembly
   ("SlideShow, Version=1.2.3.4, Culture=neutral, PublicKeyToken=null")
]
#endif
```

In this code, if *FULLFRAMEWORK_DESIGNER* is not set (the default for the run-time version of the control), the attribute is ignored.

The attribute *RuntimeAssemblyAttribute* takes one parameter: the full name of the design-time assembly. This string contains the class name, version, culture, and public key information. The name of the class alone is not sufficient; it is important that the design-time and run-time versions of the control have the same version string.

> **Note** By default, Visual Studio .NET creates a version attribute in AssemblyInfo.cs such as *[assembly: AssemblyVersion("1.0.*")]*. If you retain this default, the build number and revision will be determined by Visual Studio .NET at compile time and will automatically increment. It will be awkward to compile the design-time version because the source code will have to be updated repeatedly. It's usually easier to change the attribute to a fixed version number, such as *[assembly: AssemblyVersion("1.2.3.4")]*. Of course, if you do this, you must update the version number yourself between releases.

Specifying a Designer for the Class

By default, your control will inherit its design-time attributes from its base classes. You don't need to specify any designer attributes to have the design-time version of your control work. If you want, you can override attributes by specifying them explicitly in your class.

The design-time version of the control can be told which designer to use. The attribute *System.ComponentModel.DesignerAttribute* is added to the design-time version of the class. This attribute code is also bracketed by conditional compilation because it's not relevant to the run-time version.

```
#if FULLFRAMEWORK_DESIGNER
using System.ComponentModel;
#endif
:
#if FULLFRAMEWORK_DESIGNER
[Designer(typeof(System.Windows.Forms.Design.ControlDesigner))]
#endif
public class SlideShow : System.Windows.Forms.Control
{
:
}
```

In a similar way, you can add the attributes *DescriptionAttribute* and *DefaultValueAttribute* to methods, events, and properties. These attributes enrich the development experience by providing more information about the methods, events, and properties to the IntelliSense editor of Visual Studio .NET.

```
#if FULLFRAMEWORK_DESIGNER
[DefaultValue(0)]
[Description("Position within image list")]
#endif
public int Position
{
:
}
```

Building and Deploying the Design-Time Control

The developer must compile the control with the .NET Compact Framework designer libraries to create a design-time version of the control. After creating the run-time and design-time versions of the control, they must be deployed to be used by the development environment. The run-time version of the control must be copied into the directory C:\Program Files\Microsoft Visual Studio .NET 2003\CompactFrameworkSDK\v1.0.5000\Windows CE. The design-time version of the control must be copied to the Designer subdirectory below this directory, which can be done outside the Visual Studio .NET environment by using a batch file that invokes the command-line version of the compiler and copies the files to the correct locations.

BuildDesigner.bat

```
csc /noconfig @designer.rsp
copy bin\debug\SlideShow.* "C:\Program Files\…
 …Microsoft Visual Studio .NET 2003\CompactFrameworkSDK\v1.0.5000\…
 …Windows CE"
copy SlideShowDesigner.* "C:\Program Files\…
 …Microsoft Visual Studio .NET 2003\CompactFrameworkSDK\v1.0.5000\…
 …Windows CE\Designer"
```

The BuildDesigner.bat batch file uses the following response file for the csc invocation.

Designer.rsp

```
/define:FULLFRAMEWORK_DESIGNER
/out:SlideShowDesigner.dll
/target:library
SlideShow.cs
AssemblyInfo.cs
/r:"C:\Program Files\Microsoft Visual Studio .NET 2003\→
 …CompactFrameworkSDK\v1.0.5000\Windows CE\Designer\System.CF.Design.dll"
/r:"C:\Program Files\Microsoft Visual Studio .NET 2003\→
 …CompactFrameworkSDK\v1.0.5000\Windows CE\Designer\
 …System.CF.Windows.Forms.dll"
/r:"C:\Program Files\Microsoft Visual Studio .NET 2003\→
 …CompactFrameworkSDK\v1.0.5000\Windows CE\Designer\System.CF.Drawing.dll"
/r:System.Windows.Forms.dll
/r:System.Drawing.dll
/r:System.dll
/nowarn:1595
```

The options supplied in the response file compile the two source files that constitute the SlideShow control and then link the resultant object files with the .NET Compact Framework designer libraries. The order of linking is important—the .NET Compact Framework design libraries must be listed first, and the full .NET Framework libraries must follow. Under normal circumstances, this would result in a number of warnings from the linker because some symbols are defined in both sets of assemblies. These warnings are suppressed with the /nowarn:1595 option.

Adding the Control to the Toolbox

To add the control to the toolbox, right-click the Device Controls toolbox and select Add/Remove Items. The Customize Toolbox dialog box will appear. In this dialog box, select the .NET Framework Components tab at the top and then select the browse button. Browse to the Designer subdirectory, and select the design-time version of your control. (For the SlideShow control, this will be SlideShow.Designer.dll.) It should appear in the dialog box list with a check mark beside it. Click the OK button.

The device toolbox should now have your control included. If you drag the control onto a form, it will automatically add the run-time version as a reference.

> **Tip** If you see that Forms Designer adds a reference to the design-time version of the control, it couldn't find the run-time version of the assembly. When maintaining controls that have design-time versions, make sure you rebuild and reinstall the design-time copy of the control in sync with the run-time version.

Summary

In this chapter, you've seen how custom controls can be developed and deployed, and you've also seen how the benefits of code reuse and inheritance can be applied to the design environment.

19

Globalization and Localization

In many cases, you must develop an application that will be used internationally across multiple cultural and language boundaries. Designing an application to be adaptable to different cultures can require considerably more planning than an application that is not culturally aware, but the necessary investment of time can reap great benefits because it is much harder to retrofit culture-related refinements to an already complete application. In this chapter, we'll explore the features of the .NET Compact Framework that make it possible to build international solutions.

The title of this chapter is "Globalization and Localization," and it's worth spending some time defining these two terms. Globalization refers to an application design in which no part of the core logic of the application will prevent it from being used in multiple cultures. An application that supports globalization uses neutral data formats and separates resources that need to be translated for different cultures. An application in which date or currency formats are hard-coded, or in which user interface elements are embedded in the business logic, is much harder to use internationally. Localization consists of customizing the application for specific local cultures, mainly by translating user interface text into a target language and ensuring that local presentation formats for numbers or dates are used.

The .NET Compact Framework supports globalization and localization through the provision of culturally neutral and culture-specific functionality. For example, suppose you wanted to build a simple BillingCalculator application in which a consultant specifies an hourly rate and number of days to be worked, and the program calculates the total to be billed to the customer. The .NET

Compact Framework provides the classes you need to ensure that the application works across multiple cultures regardless of date or currency formats, different calendars, and language-specific user interface elements.

Cultures and the *CultureInfo* Class

To implement an application that adapts to the user's local culture, we need some way of identifying cultures and differentiating between them. A culture represents local conventions such as language, calendar, and presentation formats for currency, date, and numeric values. To help identify a large number of different cultures throughout the world, Request for Comment (RFC) 1766 defines a protocol for culture names. These names are used to identify cultures in the .NET Compact Framework. Each culture name consists of a *neutral* culture that defines the language used in this culture and optionally a *specific* subculture that defines a geographic location. The neutral culture portion of the name consists of two lowercase letters; for example, "en" represents English. A specific subculture is indicated by adding a hyphen (-) and two uppercase letters to the neutral culture; for example, "en-US" represents English in the United States, and "en-GB" represents English in the United Kingdom. This separation of neutral culture (language) and specific culture (geographic location) allows for the same language to be used in multiple locations (for example, French in France or Canada, represented as "fr-FR" and "fr-CA," respectively) or different languages to be used in the same location (for example, English or Afrikaans in South Africa, represented as "en-ZA" or "af-ZA," respectively).

In cases where the specific subculture is irrelevant, you can simply specify a neutral culture. For example, "fr" represents French, regardless of geographic location. Additionally, an *invariant* culture exists to represent culturally insensitive information. The invariant culture is associated with the English language but not with any specific location. It is represented by an empty string ("").

In addition to a culture name, the .NET Compact Framework also identifies each culture using a locale/culture identifier (LCID). For example, the "fr-FR" culture is identified by the hexadecimal value 0x040C (1036).

> **Note** You can find a complete list of culture names in the *CultureInfo* Class topic of the .NET Framework reference documentation.

The *CultureInfo* Class

The .NET Compact Framework provides the *CultureInfo* class, which provides a programmatic representation of a culture. This class is defined in the *System.Globalization* namespace, and it is commonly used to determine the current culture as defined in the user's system settings or to create an instance of a culture to display information in a culture-specific format. You can use the *Name* property of the *CultureInfo* class to return the culture name code, for example, "en-US." You can also obtain the full name of the culture represented by a *CultureInfo* object in English using the *EnglishName* property.

Determining the Current Culture

The *CultureInfo* class provides two static properties that can be used to determine information about the user's current culture: *CurrentCulture* and *CurrentUICulture*. *CurrentCulture* returns a *CultureInfo* object that represents the culture of the currently executing thread. This culture is used for formatting of culture-specific data such as numbers, dates, and currency values. The *CurrentUICulture* property returns the culture used by the *ResourceManager* class to load culture-specific resources at run time. On the Windows CE platform, both of these properties are initialized from the system's regional settings.

To see how you can use the *CultureInfo* class to determine the current culture, use Visual Studio .NET to create a new C# Smart Device Application project named BillingCalculator. The application should be a Windows application for the Pocket PC platform. After the project has been created, view the code behind *Form1* and add the following code to the list of *using* statements at the beginning of the class:

```
using System.Globalization;
```

View the form in Design view, double-click it to create the *Form1_Load* event handler, and then add the following code to *Form1_Load*:

```
CultureInfo current = CultureInfo.CurrentCulture;

string currentName = "Name: " + current.Name
            + "\nEnglishName: " + current.EnglishName;

MessageBox.Show(currentName, "Current Culture");
```

Start the Pocket PC Emulator (or the Pocket PC on which you plan to test the application), and access the Regional Settings application in the System tab of the Settings program. Change the current culture to English (United Kingdom).

After you've configured the Pocket PC, execute the project and deploy the application to the emulator or Pocket PC you want to test it with. When the application starts, it should display a message box containing the following text:

```
Name: en-GB
EnglishName: English (United Kingdom)
```

Close the application, stop the project, and then use the Regional Settings application on your Pocket PC or emulator to change the current culture to "Swahili (Kenya)." Run the project again. This time the message box should contain the following text:

```
Name: sw-KE
EnglishName: Swahili (Kenya)
```

Stop the project (and reset your Pocket PC regional settings if you want).

Creating a New *CultureInfo* Instance

In some cases, you might want to create an instance of the *CultureInfo* class to represent a different culture from the one selected in the system's regional settings. For example, you might want to allow the user of your application to select a specific culture regardless of the regional settings for the underlying operating system.

The *CultureInfo* class's constructor supports the following four overloads:

```
public CultureInfo(int culture);

public CultureInfo(string name);

public CultureInfo(int culture, bool useUserOverride);

public CultureInfo (string name, bool useUserOverride);
```

The *culture* parameter is an integer variable containing the LCID that represents the required culture (for example, 0x040C). The *name* parameter is a *string* variable with the name of the required culture (for example, "fr-FR"). The *useUserOverride* parameter specifies whether a user's custom settings should override the culture defaults.

As you can see from these constructor signatures, you can instantiate a *CultureInfo* using the name or the LCID of the culture you want to create an instance of. By default, if the user has modified the cultural settings for the culture in the Regional Settings application (for example, by changing the default currency or calendar), the user-specific settings will override the culture's default settings. In some cases, you might want to prevent a user's custom settings from overriding the defaults (for example, if an application requires all currency in

France to be based in euros, not francs). You can use one of the constructors that supports the Boolean *useUserOverride* parameter to control this behavior.

To see how you can create a *CultureInfo* instance representing a particular culture, modify the BillingCalculator project by adding a ComboBox control named *cultureList* and a Label named *currentCulturelabel* to the form. Then replace the existing code in the *Form1_Load* procedure with the following code:

```
cultureList.Items.Add("Default");
cultureList.Items.Add("en-US");
cultureList.Items.Add("en-GB");
cultureList.Items.Add("fr-FR");
cultureList.Items.Add("sv-SE");
cultureList.Items.Add("de-DE");
cultureList.SelectedIndex = 0;
setCulture();
```

This populates the ComboBox control with a list of five cultures that the user can choose from, as well as a "Default" choice that will be used to select the current culture setting for the system. Notice that a function named *setCulture* is then called to set the currently selected culture. The user's choice of culture will be stored in a variable named *selectedCulture*, which you should declare at class level using the following declaration:

```
private CultureInfo selectedCulture;
```

The *setCulture* function contains the code necessary to change the selected culture when the user chooses an alternative culture. The *setCulture* function is shown below:

```
private void setCulture()
{
    if(cultureList.SelectedIndex > 0)
    {
        selectedCulture = new CultureInfo(cultureList.Text);
    }
    else
    {
        selectedCulture = CultureInfo.CurrentCulture;
    }
    currentCultureLabel.Text = selectedCulture.EnglishName;
}
```

Finally we need to call the *setCulture* function whenever the user chooses an item in the ComboBox control. Double-click the ComboBox to create the *cultureList_SelectedIndexChanged* procedure, and add the following code to it:

```
setCulture();
```

When you run the project, you should see a form like the one shown in Figure 19-1. Selecting an alternative culture from the ComboBox control should result in the name of the selected culture being displayed in the Label control.

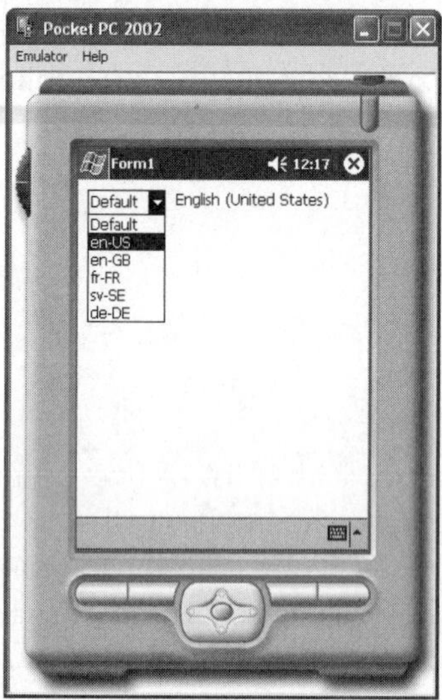

Figure 19-1 An application that allows the user to select a culture.

As you will see later in this chapter, the ability to create an instance of a culture that is different from the system-configured one can be useful if you want to allow users to select a culture for the application and display data in a format that is appropriate for that culture.

> **Note** The full implementation of the .NET Framework allows you to change the *CurrentCulture* property of the *CurrentThread* object, thus changing the default culture for your application. The .NET Compact Framework does not support this capability (because it is extremely rare that a mobile application would require different cultural settings from the device itself). To support an alternative culture in a .NET Compact Framework application, you must store the alternative culture in a *CultureInfo* object variable, as demonstrated in the BillingCalculator example.

Data for Specific Cultures

When your application will be used in multiple geographic regions, you need to be sure that variations in the way certain types of data are treated and formatted are catered to. The .NET Compact Framework provides classes that modify the way they format data based on the *CultureInfo.CurrentCulture* value, so in many cases, the localization issues are taken care of by default. However, if you want to allow users of your application to choose an alternative culture (different from the one specified in the regional settings of the operating system), you must ensure that you treat all data appropriately for the selected culture.

Numbers for Specific Cultures

Different cultures use different formats to represent numbers. For example, if you want to represent the value "ten thousand, three hundred and twenty one, and a half" in the United States, you would write "10,321.50," while in France, you would write "10 321,50." Even more obviously, you might have to represent numbers as local currency values, which requires the appropriate currency symbol to be displayed.

The *ToString* method provided by numeric types such as *int*, *decimal*, and *double* is overloaded to allow a format to be specified using a string-based code. For example, you can specify "c" to have the number assigned to a string as a currency value, "d" to have the number displayed as a decimal value, or "n" to use a numerical format that includes separators and decimal digits. The *CultureInfo* class exposes a public *NumberFormat* property, which is implemented as a *NumberFormatInfo* class that defines the way numbers are formatted for the particular culture when a formatting code is specified. By default, when you call *ToString* and specify a formatting code, the appropriate format is determined by the *NumberFormat* property of the *CultureInfo.CurrentCulture* object representing the regional settings for the operating system. For example, you could display a currency value using the following code:

```
double myVal = 10321.5;
string myNumericVal = myVal.ToString("n");
MessageBox.Show(myNumericVal);
```

Executing this code on a Pocket PC with the regional settings configured for English (United Kingdom) will produce the following output:

```
10,321.50
```

Executing the same code on a Pocket PC with a regional setting of French (France) would produce:

```
10 321,50
```

You can specify an alternative culture by passing a *CultureInfo* object to the *ToString* method, which allows you to format numbers for a culture other than the one specified in the regional settings. For example, the following code could be used to format the number 10321.5 for the English (United Kingdom) culture, regardless of the regional settings for the operating system:

```
CultureInfo uk = new CultureInfo("en-GB");
double myVal = 10321.5;
string myNumericVal = myVal.ToString("n", uk);
MessageBox.Show(myNumericVal);
```

The same automatic formatting also works for currency values when the "c" format code is specified. If no *CultureInfo* object is specified in the *ToString* method call, the value is formatted as the local currency for the culture specified in the regional settings. If a *CultureInfo* object is supplied, the value is formatted as the currency for that culture. However, there is an issue to look out for. For the English (United States) culture, the value 10321.5 will be displayed as $10,321.50 when converted to currency, as you would expect. However, in countries where the euro has been adopted, the currency symbol used will depend on the version of the operating system and whether the user has specified a symbol other than the euro (such as the F symbol for francs in France). For a system with a regional setting of French (France), the value 10321.5 could be formatted as 10 321,50 _ or 10 321.50 F.

> **Note** Cultures where the euro has been adopted are configured to use the _ symbol by default on Pocket PC 2002 devices. Pocket PC 2000, however, configures all European countries to use their national currency (for example, the F symbol is used in France).

To overcome this problem, you can create a *CultureInfo* object with the *useUserOverride* parameter set to *false*, forcing the euro symbol to be used regardless of the configuration in the operating system's regional settings. For example, the following code could be used to force all currency values to be formatted as euros:

```
CultureInfo fr = new CultureInfo("fr-FR", false);
double myVal = 10321.5;
string myNumericVal = myVal.ToString("c", fr);
MessageBox.Show(myNumericVal);
```

When this code is executed, the value 10 321,50 _ will always be displayed, even if the regional settings are configured to display French currency as francs.

To see the .NET Compact Framework's ability to format numbers into culturally appropriate strings, we can add some functionality to the BillingCalculator project described earlier in this chapter. Add the following controls to *Form1*:

- A Label control with the *Text* property set to *Hourly Rate*
- A TextBox control with the *Name* property set to *rate* and the *Text* property set to *100*
- A Label control with the *Text* property set to *Days*
- A TextBox control with the *Name* property set to *days* and the *Text* property set to *100*
- A Button control with the *Name* property set to *calculate* and the *Text* property set to *Calculate*
- A Label control with the *Name* property set to *result* and the *Text* property set to "" (the empty string)

Double-click the Calculate button to create its *Click* event handler, and add the following code:

```
double hourlyRate = double.Parse(rate.Text);
int hours = (int.Parse(days.Text)) * 8;
double finalAmount = hourlyRate * hours;
result.Text = hours.ToString("n", selectedCulture) +
  " hours = " + finalAmount.ToString("c", selectedCulture);
```

When you run the project, clicking the Calculate button should display a message in which the number of hours worked (assuming an 8-hour working day) and the final billable amount is displayed in a format appropriate to the selected culture, as shown in Figure 19-2.

Figure 19-2 Displaying culturally appropriate numeric values.

You can use the *NumberFormat* property of the *CultureInfo* class to find out how a particular culture will format numbers. The *NumberFormat* property returns a *NumberFormatInfo* object, which provides a number of properties indicating various aspects of numeric formatting. For example, the following code could be used to find out how many decimal places are used in the numeric format for the current culture:

```
MessageBox.Show
  (CultureInfo.CurrentCulture.NumberFormat.NumberDecimalDigits.ToString());
```

Culturally Aware String Comparisons

There are many occasions when you need to be able to sort string values. In cases where the system's regional settings are used to determine the correct culture, standard .NET Framework classes and methods such as the *Sort* method of the *Array* class or the *Compare* method of the *String* class can be used. Cultural variations in the way strings are sorted will be taken into account automatically. For example, suppose the user of the BillingCalculator application has two customers named Ändrë and Andrew, and a sorted list of customers is required. The following code could be used to sort the customers:

```
string[] customerList = new String[2];
customerList[0] = "Ändrë";
customerList[1] = "Andrew";
Array.Sort(customerList);
MessageBox.Show(customerList[0] + ", " + customerList[1]);
```

If the regional settings are configured for the German (Germany) culture, the resulting message box will display the text "Ändrë, Andrew." However, if the regional settings are configured for the Swedish (Sweden) culture (in which "Ä" is sorted after "A"), the message box will display "Andrew, Ändrë."

You could also compare the two customer names using the *Compare* method of the string class, as shown here:

```
string cust1 = "Ändrë";
string cust2 = "Andrew";
int sortResult = string.Compare(cust1, cust2);
string sortList;
if(sortResult > 0)
{
    sortList = cust2 + ", " + cust1;
}
else
{
    sortList = cust1 + ", " + cust2;
}
MessageBox.Show(sortList);
```

The *Compare* method returns an integer result in which a negative value indicates that the first string should be sorted before the second string, a positive value indicates that the second string should be sorted before the first string, and zero indicates that the strings are equal. If the preceding code were to be executed on a system with the regional settings configured for German (Germany), the *sortResult* variable would be set to –1 (because in the German culture, "Ändrë" is before "Andrew"), but on systems configured for Swedish (Sweden), *sortResult* would be set to 1.

If you need to compare strings in a culture other than the one specified in the regional settings, you can pass a *CultureInfo* object and a Boolean value to indicate case-insensitivity to the *Compare* method of the *string* class. The following code shows how the *string* class's *Compare* method can be used to compare two strings for a particular culture:

```
string cust1 = "Ändrë";
string cust2 = "Andrew";
int sortResult = string.Compare(cust1, cust2, true, selectedCulture);
string sortList;
if(sortResult > 0)
{
    sortList = cust2 + ", " + cust1;
}
else
{
    sortList = cust1 + ", " + cust2;
}
MessageBox.Show(sortList);
```

Notice that in this example, the *ignoreCase* parameter of the *Compare* method is set to *true*, forcing a case-insensitive sort. Notice also that a *CultureInfo* object variable named *selectedCulture* is used to specify the cultural settings to use for the comparison.

As an alternative to using the *Compare* method of the *string* class, you could use a *CompareInfo* class. The *CompareInfo* class encapsulates the sorting rules for a particular culture and exposes a *Compare* method that behaves in a way similar to the *Compare* method of the *string* class. You can instantiate a *CompareInfo* class using its *GetCompareInfo* method, which requires an integer LCID parameter identifying the culture you want to use. Alternatively, if you already have a *CultureInfo* object for the required culture, you can use its *CompareInfo* property. The following code shows how the customer comparison could be performed using a *CompareInfo* class:

```
string cust1 = "Ändrë";
string cust2 = "Andrew";
int sortResult = selectedCulture.CompareInfo.Compare(cust1, cust2);
string sortList;
if(sortResult > 0)
{
    sortList = cust2 + ", " + cust1;
}
else
{
    sortList = cust1 + ", " + cust2;
}
MessageBox.Show(sortList);
```

In this example, the *CompareInfo* class is obtained using the *CompareInfo* property of an existing *CultureInfo* object named *selectedCulture*. The *Compare* method of the *CompareInfo* class is overloaded to allow you to compare partial strings and to specify a *CompareOptions* enumeration to control case-sensitivity, kana-sensitivity, and other sorting options.

Date and Time Values for Specific Cultures

As with numbers, different cultures use different formats for dates. For example, in the United States, the date "19th of July 2002" would be represented by the short date format "07/19/2002," while in the United Kingdom, the same date would be represented as "19/07/2002."

To display a date in the appropriate format for the culture selected in the system's regional settings, you need to use one of the following methods of the *DateTime* structure:

- *ToString*
- *ToShortDateString*
- *ToShortTimeString*
- *ToLongDateString*
- *ToLongTimeString*

With the generic *ToString* method of the *DateTime* structure you can specify a date pattern such as "dd-MM-yyyy."

The following code could be used to display today's date in the appropriate short date format for the current culture:

```
DateTime today = DateTime.Now;
MessageBox.Show(today.ToShortDateString());
```

To display a date in a format for an alternative culture, you can use the *DateTimeFormat* property of the *CultureInfo* class to specify an appropriate format for the date. The *DateTimeFormat* property is an instance of the *DateTimeFormatInfo* class, which includes a number of properties that identify the appropriate date pattern for different date formats. These patterns can be passed to the *ToString* method of the *DateTime* structure to display the date appropriately. For example, the following code could be used to display today's date in an appropriate format for the culture defined by the *CultureInfo* object *selectedCulture*:

```
DateTime today = DateTime.Now;
MessageBox.Show
  (today.ToString(selectedCulture.DateTimeFormat.ShortDatePattern));
```

> **Note** Passing a *DateTimeFormatInfo* object to the *ToString* method without specifying a pattern property results in the default short date and time pattern for the appropriate culture being used.

Similarly, you can use the *DateTime* structure's *Parse* method to create a *DateTime* object from a string. By default, the *Parse* method assumes that the date string is formatted appropriately for the regional settings of the device, but you can specify a *CultureInfo* object to allow the date to be formatted for an alternative culture. For example, suppose we wanted our BillingCalculator application to be able to calculate the end date of a contract based on a given start date and the number of days for which the consultant has been contracted. We could add a TextBox control named *startDate* to allow the user to enter the start date, and we could use the *Parse* method to create a *DateTime* object from the data entered. We could then use the *AddDays* method of the *DateTime* structure, as shown in the following modification to the *calculate_Click* event handler in the BillingCalculator application:

```
double hourlyRate = double.Parse(rate.Text);
int hours = (int.Parse(days.Text)) * 8;
double finalAmount = hourlyRate * hours;
DateTime start = DateTime.Parse(startDate.Text, selectedCulture);
DateTime end = start.AddDays(int.Parse(days.Text));
result.Text = hours.ToString("n", selectedCulture) +
  " hours = " + finalAmount.ToString("c", selectedCulture) +
  ".\nCompletion Date: " +
  end.ToString(selectedCulture.DateTimeFormat.ShortDatePattern);
```

The expected result of executing this code is shown in Figure 19-3.

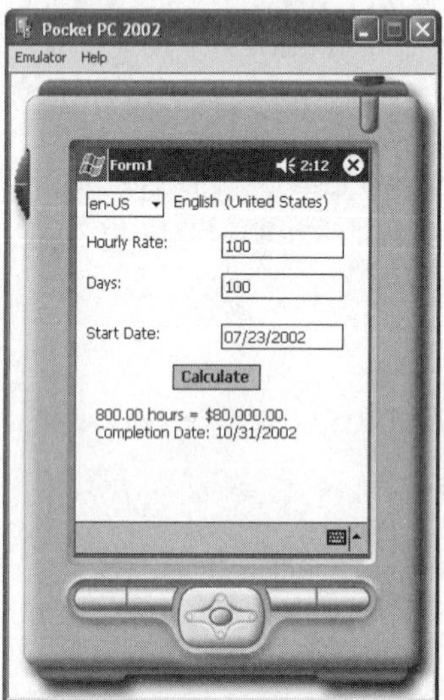

Figure 19-3 *DateTime* calculations.

> **Note** The *DateTime* structure also provides a *ParseExact* method, which is used to create a *DateTime* object based on a string with a format that matches a *DateTimeFormat* pattern exactly.

Handling Time Zones

If an application needs to store *DateTime* information, you might want to make sure that the stored value remains absolute, even when regional settings or the current time zone are changed. For example, suppose your application saved the *DateTime* value 22/07/2002 23:00:00 with the current culture set to English (United Kindgom) and the time zone set to GMT London, Dublin. If the data is reloaded with the regional settings configured for English (United States) and the time zone changed to GMT – 8 Pacific US, the loaded value should be 7/22/2002 3:00:00 PM because when the data was saved at 11:00 P.M. in the UK, it was 3:00 P.M. on the Pacific coast of the United States.

To ensure that *DateTime* values can be read, regardless of the current culture, you should use the invariant culture *DateTime* format when persisting and loading *DateTime* data. This approach results in a consistent format for all *DateTime* values, even if the regional settings are changed between persisting and reloading the data.

When you want the application to take time zones into account, you should convert all *DateTime* values to *universal time* (more commonly referred to as Greenwich Mean Time or GMT), persist the value, and then convert the result back to the local time when the data is reloaded. You can use the *ToUniversalTime* method of the *DateTime* class to convert a *DateTime* value to universal time, and you can use the *ToLocalTime* method to convert a universal time value to the appropriate *DateTime* value for the current time zone. This approach allows you to persist a *DateTime* value and ensure that the same absolute date and time is reloaded, even if a clock program has been used to change the system time since the data was persisted. The following code shows how you could implement functions to persist and reload *DateTime* values using the invariant culture and universal time.

```
// Save the current time
private void SaveCurrentTime_Click(object sender, System.EventArgs e)
{
    SaveDateTime(DateTime.Now);
}

// Load the persisted DateTime value
private void LoadSavedTime_Click(object sender, System.EventArgs e)
{
    DateTime d = LoadDateTime();
    MessageBox.Show(d.ToString());
}

// Function to save DateTime value
private void SaveDateTime(DateTime localDateTime)
```

(continued)

```
    {
        // Convert the value to universal time
        DateTime udtDate = localDateTime.ToUniversalTime();

        // Format the date string using the invariant culture
        string dataToSave = udtDate.ToString(CultureInfo.InvariantCulture);

        // Save the data
        StreamWriter f = new StreamWriter("SavedData.txt");
        f.WriteLine(dataToSave);
        f.Close();
    }

    // Function to load a saved time
    private DateTime LoadDateTime()
    {
        // Load the data
        StreamReader f = new StreamReader("SavedData.txt");
        string loadedData = f.ReadToEnd();
        f.Close();

        // Create a DateTime object based on the string value formatted for
        // the invariant culture
        DateTime udtDate =
            DateTime.Parse(loadedData, CultureInfo.InvariantCulture);

        // Convert the value to local time and return it
        return udtDate.ToLocalTime();
    }
```

> **Note** The *Parse* and *ParseExact* methods of the *DateTime* structure allow you to specify a *styles* parameter of *DateTimeStyles.AdjustToUniversal* to automatically read a date in a local time zone and adjust it to universal time. This parameter makes it easy to accept input in the local *DateTime* format and use universal time internally.

Using Alternative Calendars

Different cultures use different calendars. Although most people in the world are familiar with the Gregorian calendar used in the western world, a globalized application should support the use of other calendars in cultures where they might be appropriate. For example, in Japan, most people use a localized version of the Gregorian calendar, but many aspects of Japanese society relate to the Japanese calendar, which is based on the life of the Japanese emperor.

Each culture has a default calendar, and other calendars supported in the culture can be discovered by querying the *OptionalCalendars* property of the *CultureInfo* class, as shown in the following code:

```
StringBuilder calendarlist = new StringBuilder();
CultureInfo currentCulture = CultureInfo.CurrentCulture;

// Get the default calendar for the current culture
Calendar defaultCalendar = currentCulture.Calendar;
calendarlist.Append ("Default Calendar: ");
calendarlist.Append(defaultCalendar.ToString());

// If it's a Gregorian calendar, what type is it?
if (defaultCalendar is GregorianCalendar)
{
    GregorianCalendar g = (GregorianCalendar)defaultCalendar;
    calendarlist.Append(" (");
    calendarlist.Append(g.CalendarType);
    calendarlist.Append(")");
}

// Get the optional calendars
foreach(Calendar c in currentCulture.OptionalCalendars)
{
    calendarlist.Append("\nOptional Calendar: ");
    calendarlist.Append(c.ToString());

    // If it's a Gregorian calendar, what type is it?
    if (c is GregorianCalendar)
    {
        GregorianCalendar g = (GregorianCalendar)c;
        calendarlist.Append(" (");
        calendarlist.Append(g.CalendarType);
        calendarlist.Append(")");
    }
}
MessageBox.Show(calendarlist.ToString());
```

As you run this code, you might notice that many cultures have multiple entries for the Gregorian calendar. The multiple entries are because the Gregorian calendar supports subtypes (to allow for standard and localized implementations). You can determine the type of Gregorian calendar from the *CalendarType* property of the *GregorianCalendar* class.

You can create an instance of a specific calendar using the following classes:

- *GregorianCalendar*
- *JulianCalendar*
- *JapaneseCalendar*
- *ThaiBuddhistCalendar*
- *KoreanCalendar*
- *TaiwanCalendar*

Notice that the *HebrewCalendar* and *HijriCalendar* classes available in the full .NET Framework are not supported in the .NET Compact Framework.

All calendar classes derive from the *System.Globalization.Calendar* class, which provides methods for performing *DateTime* calculations and extracting information about a given date in that calendar. For example, the following code extracts information about the previous year in the Japanese calendar:

```
DateTime today = DateTime.Now;

// Create Japanese Calendar
JapaneseCalendar j = new JapaneseCalendar();

// Subtract 1 year
DateTime jLastYear = j.AddYears(today, -1);

// Get information about last year (in Japanese calendar)
int jYear = j.GetYear(jLastYear);
int jEra = j.GetEra(jLastYear);
int jMonthsInYear = j.GetMonthsInYear(jYear);

// Display information
StringBuilder calInfo = new StringBuilder();
calInfo.Append("Year :");
calInfo.Append(jYear.ToString());
calInfo.Append("\nEra :");
calInfo.Append(jEra.ToString());
calInfo.Append ("\nMonths in Year: ");
calInfo.Append (jMonthsInYear.ToString());
MessageBox.Show(calInfo.ToString());
```

The ability to work with alternative calendars makes it possible to build applications that can perform *DateTime* functions in multiple cultures.

Character Encoding

The .NET Compact Framework uses Unicode internally to represent character data. Unicode is a useful way to store character data because it provides a way to identify the characters used in any language in the world. You can use encoding to map Unicode characters to other character representations, which can be useful if your application must provide character data as an array of bytes specific to a *code page* such as ASCII or Windows-1252.

You can use the *GetEncoding* static method of the *Encoding* class to create an *Encoding* object for a specific code page. The *Encoding* class is defined in the *System.Text* namespace. The *Encoding* class provides the *GetBytes* method, which can be used to convert Unicode data to a code page–specific byte array. The *Encoding* class also provides the *GetChars* method, which can be used to convert a byte array to an array of Unicode characters. The following code sample shows how you can use the *Encoding* class to convert Unicode data to an array of code page–specific bytes:

```
string dataToEncode = "Important Data";

// Get an encoding for ASCII (codepage 20127)
Encoding asciiEnc = Encoding.GetEncoding(20127);

// Encode data in an array of ASCII bytes
byte[] asciiBytes = asciiEnc.GetBytes(dataToEncode);
```

You should use Unicode for all internal character storage and operations, which will make it easier to handle localization. However, you should make use of the *Encoding* class to allow data entry of international characters.

Localized Resource Files

The .NET Compact Framework supports the use of resource files for localized content, which allows you to create a single application assembly with multiple *satellite assemblies*, each containing embedded resource files for a particular culture. At run time, the application can load the appropriate resource file based on the regional settings of the operating system. You can create resource files in three formats: text, XML, and binary. Text files have the extension ".txt" and consist of name-value pairs for string resources. XML resource files have the extension .resx and contain XML elements for each string or binary resource (such as an image). Binary resource files have the extension .resource and contain binary representations of each string or binary resource. Only binary (.resource) files can be embedded in a satellite assembly.

The basic idea of using resource files in satellite assemblies is simple: you create a resource file for each localized culture you intend to support and a fallback resource file to be used when there is no specific resource file for the currently selected culture. You can choose to create resource files for language cultures only (for example, you could create a resource file for all "fr" cultures in which French is the preferred language), or you can create resource files for specific cultures (for example, you could create separate "fr-FR" and "fr-CA" resource files for France and Canada). At run time, the .NET Compact Framework will load the most specific resources it can find for the current culture.

Localized Resource Creation

Visual Studio .NET allows you to add XML (".resx") resource files to a project and automatically generates and embeds a binary version of the file when the project is compiled. You can use the resource editing window in Visual Studio .NET to add string and encoded binary resources to a resource file, as shown in Figure 19-4.

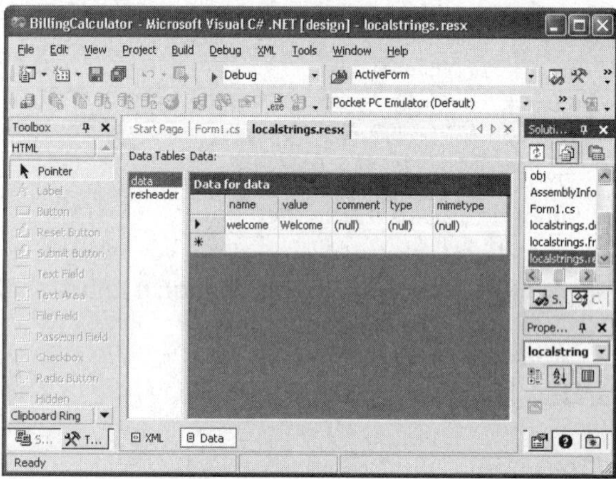

Figure 19-4 Editing a resource file in Visual Studio .NET.

If you need to include images in your resource file, you might find it easier to use the Resource Editor (ResEditor) sample application provided with the .NET Framework SDK tutorial on Resources and Localization, as shown in Figure 19-5. This utility generates the appropriate encoded binary values for the images you import into the file.

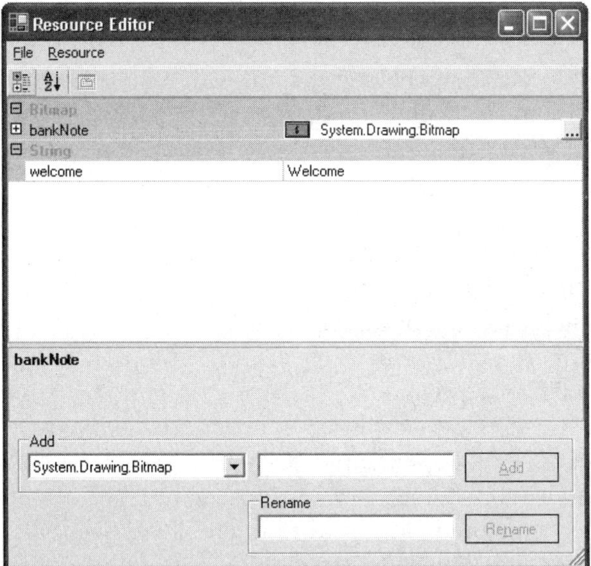

Figure 19-5 The Resource Editor sample application.

> **Note** You can also create an XML resource file from a single image file using the ResXGen sample application provided with the .NET Framework SDK. For more information about using sample tools for resource packaging, see the .NET Framework SDK documentation.

The easiest way to create a localized application that uses resource files in satellite assemblies is to use Visual Studio .NET. For example, to add localized resources to the BillingCalculator application described earlier in this chapter, we would simply need to add a resource file for each culture to be targeted, and we would need to add another resource file to act as the fallback for non-targeted cultures. To create the fallback resource file, simply add an Assembly Resource File item to the project and add the required string or binary resources to it. Name the resource file using a meaningful name with the extension ".resx". Then add an Assembly Resource File item for each targeted culture using the naming convention <*fallbackname*>.<*culturecode*>.resx, and add the localized resources to the files. For example, we could add a fallback resource file named localstrings.resx and localized resource files named localstrings.fr.resx and localstrings.de.resx to the BillingCalculator project to target French-speaking and German-speaking cultures. If a specific culture must be targeted, you can use the full culture code instead of just the character language code (for example, you could add a resource file for French-speaking Canadians named localstrings.fr-CA.resx).

After the resource files have been created, you must add the resources to the files, ensuring that each localized resource is entered with the same name in each file. For example, suppose we wanted a localized welcome message to be displayed in the BillingCalculator application. You could create an entry for a string resource named *welcome* in each resource file and assign the values "Welcome" in the fallback resource file, "Bienvenue" in the French resource file, and "Willkommen" in the German resource file. Localized binary resources can be added in the same way. For example, an appropriate image of a bank note can be added as a resource named *bankNote* in each of the resource files.

When a project containing localized resource files is compiled, Visual Studio automatically generates binary resource files and embeds them in satellite assemblies. The fallback resource file is embedded in the main application assembly, and the localized resource files are embedded in satellite assemblies that are stored in culture-specific folders under the main project output folder. For example, Figure 19-6 shows the debug mode output of the BillingCalculator project when resource files have been added. The fallback resource file is embedded in the main BillingCalculator.exe assembly, and the French and German resource files are embedded in BillingCalculator.resources.dll assemblies in folders named fr and de, respectively.

Figure 19-6 Compilation output for the localized BillingCalculator project.

Note The .NET Framework SDK also provides command-line utilities that can be used to embed resource files in satellite assemblies. You can use the Resource Generator utility (resgen.exe) to generate a binary (.resource) file from an XML (.resx) resource file, and then use the Assembly Linker tool (al.exe) to generate the satellite assemblies. For more detailed information about using these tools, consult the .NET Framework SDK documentation.

Localized Resource Retrieval

To retrieve resources from embedded resource files, you need to create an instance of the *ResourceManager* class. The *ResourceManager* class is defined in the *System.Resources* namespace and is used to load resources from the appropriate resource file for a given culture.

To instantiate a *ResourceManager* object to load resources from satellite assemblies (or the main assembly if the fallback resource file is required), use the constructor that allows you to specify *baseName* and *assembly* parameters. The *baseName* parameter should be the root name of the resource files, including the namespace. For example, the *baseName* parameter for the localstrings.resources, localstrings.fr.resources, and localstrings.de.resources resource files in the BillingCalculator application is BillingCalculator.localstrings. The assembly parameter is used to specify the main assembly for the resources. The main assembly is usually the assembly in which the code to create the *ResourceManager* object resides, and you can specify the current assembly by passing *this.GetType().Assembly* to the constructor. The following code could be used to instantiate a *ResourceManager* object for the BillingCalculator application (assuming that the *System.Resources* namespace has been imported):

```
ResourceManager resMan =
  new ResourceManager("BillingCalculator.localstrings",
                      this.GetType().Assembly);
```

Note You can use the *ResourceManager* class's *CreateFileBasedResourceManager* static method to create a *ResourceManager* object that reads resources directly from resource files you have deployed with the application, but in most cases, you should deploy resource files embedded in satellite assemblies and read them from there.

You can retrieve string resources by using the *GetString* method of the *ResourceClass* class and passing the name of the resource to be retrieved. For example, the appropriate "welcome" string resource for the current culture (as defined in the *CultureInfo.CurrentUICulture* object) can be retrieved using the following code:

```
string welcomeMessage = resMan.GetString("welcome");
```

The *GetString* method is overloaded to allow you to pass a *CultureInfo* object and therefore retrieve a resource for a culture other than the one currently selected in the regional settings. For example, the *setCulture* function in the BillingCalculator application could be updated to display an appropriate welcome message for the culture selected by the user. The message could be displayed in a label named *welcome*, as shown in the following code:

```
private void setCulture()
{
    if(cultureList.SelectedIndex > 0)
    {
        selectedCulture = new CultureInfo(cultureList.Text);
    }
    else
    {
        selectedCulture = CultureInfo.CurrentCulture;
    }
    currentCultureLabel.Text = selectedCulture.EnglishName;

    // Display the localized welcome message
    ResourceManager resMan =
    new ResourceManager("BillingCalculator.localstrings",
                         this.GetType().Assembly);
    welcome.Text = resMan.GetString("welcome", selectedCulture);
}
```

No matter which overload of the *GetString* method you use, the most specific resource available for the culture will be used. If no matching resource file is found, the fallback resource file is used.

Binary resources such as images can be retrieved using the *GetObject* method of the *ResourceManager* class. For example, a bitmap image named *bankNote* could be retrieved for the current culture using the following code:

```
picMoney.Image = (Image)resMan.GetObject("bankNote");
```

As with the *GetString* method, a *CultureInfo* object can be passed to the *GetObject* method to retrieve a binary resource for a culture other than the one selected in regional settings. For example, a PictureBox control named *picMoney* could be added to the BillingCalculator application, and the following code could be added to the *setCulture* function to display an appropriate image:

```
picMoney.Image = (Image)resMan.GetObject("bankNote", selectedCulture);
```

When the BillingCalculator application is executed, the appropriate welcome message and image for the selected culture is displayed, as shown in Figure 19-7.

Figure 19-7 An application that displays localized resources.

If your application will be deployed in multiple cultures, you should create a resource file for each culture you want to target and add entries for user interface elements you want to localize (such as captions or images on buttons, labels, and so on). You should also create a fallback resource file with default resources for non-targeted cultures. Doing so will make your application much easier for users in multiple cultures to use.

Summary

If there is any possibility that your application will be deployed in multiple international locations, you should take globalization and localization into account in its design. Most of the .NET Compact Framework classes provide culturally sensitive formatting functionality based on the regional settings of the operating system, but you must ensure that your application does not use custom formats or parsing logic that will fail if the regional settings are changed. You can use the *CultureInfo* class to retrieve information about the currently selected culture or to represent alternative cultures within your application.

You should use Unicode internally in your application for all character data. However, you should use the *Encoding* class to enable input and output of data in a specific code page where necessary.

One of the most important aspects of making an application truly global is to separate the user interface resources from the application logic. You should use resource files to store localized user interface text and images, and you should use the *ResourceManager* class to localize the user interface dynamically at run time. Make sure you always provide a fallback resource file with default user interface elements for non-targeted cultures.

20

Multithreading

The .NET Compact Framework provides powerful multithreading facilities. In this chapter, you'll see the multithreading support provided by the .NET Compact Framework and learn how you can use multithreading to make your applications more responsive and more scalable. An application is said to be responsive when it's able to respond to user input while it's performing some lengthy task such as searching a database or fetching data from the Internet. It's scalable when the developer can easily respond to some new requirement such as fetching additional data from a Web service without having to re-engineer the parts of the application that fetch data from other sources.

Multithreading can also improve the throughput of many applications. When you can divide processing into two or more separate tasks that can proceed in parallel, the processing can be completed more quickly than it can when each task must be completed serially. This faster processing can make a major difference in applications on constrained devices, because they don't enjoy the levels of processing power present in desktop machines.

> **Note** Multi-processor machines and operating systems can make multithreading easier to manage. However, the discussion of multithreading in this chapter assumes the single-processor environment supported by the .NET Compact Framework.

Understanding Multithreading

Multithreading traditionally refers to the ability of one application to appear to perform more than one task at a time. Contrast this with multiprocessing, in which one machine can run several applications, such as Microsoft Excel, Microsoft Word, and Microsoft Visual Studio .NET, at the same time. Multiprocessing allows applications to run as separate processes, with memory spaces isolated from each other by the hardware of the processor. The operating system makes them appear to run simultaneously by switching between them many times per second, using a mechanism called *scheduling*. With multithreading, multiple separate execution threads, sometimes called *tasks*, are created within a single application. The operating system is able to schedule individual threads within an application so that a single application can appear to perform multiple tasks simultaneously. Figure 20-1 compares multiprocessing with multithreading.

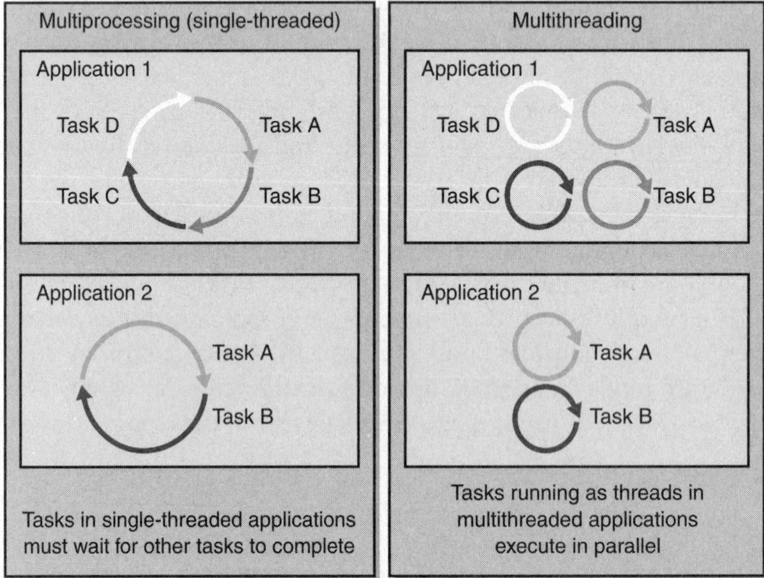

Figure 20-1 Difference between multiprocessing and multithreading.

> **Note** Multithreading is used in many .NET Compact Framework base class libraries that provide asynchronous execution. For example, the *Stream.BeginRead* and *Stream.BeginWrite* methods for input and output, respectively, make asynchronous callbacks using threading support. Other methods with names that start with *Begin* and *End* exist in .NET Compact Framework namespaces covering functions ranging from networking to supporting Web services, and those methods also use the underlying threading support of the .NET Compact Framework.

Understanding the Advantages of Multithreading

In a single-threaded application, everything must execute in a predefined order. Take the case of an application that must perform two main tasks: first, it must accept some input from the user; and second, it must use that input to perform some lengthy operation such as searching a database on a server. If this application is single-threaded, and if the user wishes to perform two or more database searches, the user is unable to enter the data for the second search until the first search is over and the application has returned to the point at which it accepts user input. This application has poor user response. Splitting this application into two threads—one thread to collect data from the user and another to perform the database search—would greatly improve it. Once the user typed in the data for the first search, the thread that handles user input would simply transmit the data to the search thread and then immediately respond to more user input while the database search progressed in its own thread. The user could then enter data for several searches without waiting for any one search to complete. Provided the developer had made good use of graphical user interface (GUI) design techniques to present the data in a clear and structured manner, splitting the application into two threads could make for a very rich and responsive user experience.

Multithreading can also improve the throughput of certain applications by making better use of processor time, as shown in Figure 20-2. Consider a StockPurchase application that must accept input from the user in the form of stock identifiers, use the stock identifiers to fetch some currency exchange rates from a Web service and some stock prices from a database server, and then, based on the three sets of data, make a recommendation for a purchase of stock. In a single-threaded design, the program accepts data from the user and then, say, retrieves the stock prices from the database. Once the program has sent the request to the server, it has to wait for the result. The program is idle when it isn't performing any useful function. Once the wait is over, the program requests the exchange rates from the Web service, and once again waits idly while the data arrives. If the database search takes 4 seconds and fetching the data from the Web service takes 3 seconds, this program will always take a total of 7 seconds to perform the two operations. If you place the database search and the Web service access in two separate threads, when the database search sends its request to the server and starts waiting, the operating system is able to schedule the Web service thread, which can initiate its request and then perform its wait in parallel with the wait for database access. In this way the total time required for the two accesses should be close to the longer of the two access times—in other words, 4 seconds, not 7.

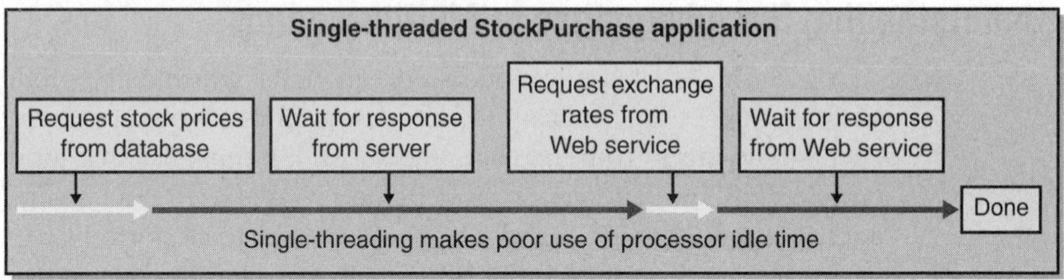

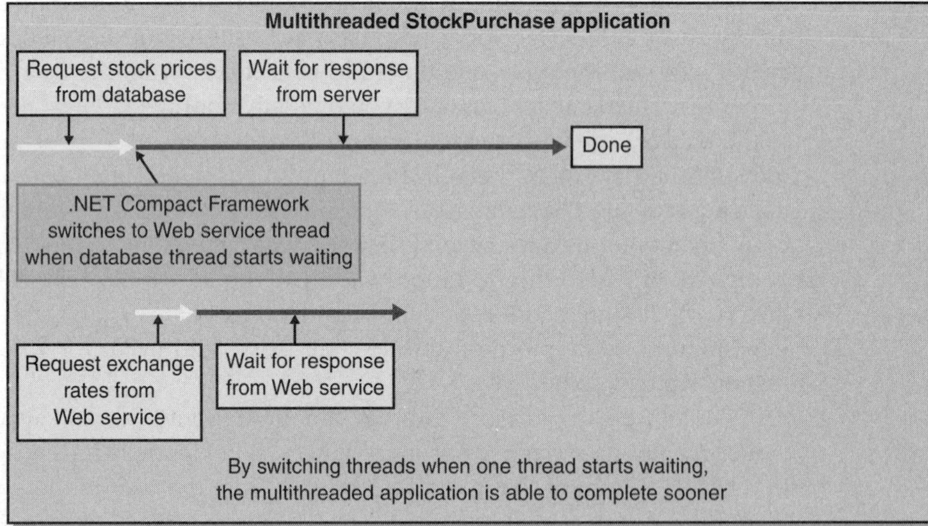

Figure 20-2 How multithreading a StockPurchase application can improve throughput.

A multithreaded application is typically more scalable than a single-threaded application. Take the stock purchase example just discussed. If a new requirement were to arise to search a second database for stock available on foreign exchanges, it's much easier to add an extra thread whose sole responsibility is to perform that single database access than it is to modify a single thread that already performs two operations in order to introduce a third. Having multiple threads, each with a single responsibility, is cleaner from the design point of view than having a single do-everything thread. Multiple threads also allow the application to automatically make better use of the processor because the operating system switches from a thread that is waiting for response to one that is ready to run.

Avoiding Pitfalls in Multithreading

Multithreading is an advanced programming technique and requires great care. It also doesn't solve every problem. For example, if your application has no idle time, as it would if it were waiting for data from a Web service or database server, it's highly unlikely that introducing multithreading will make your application any faster. You must also avoid the waiting loop syndrome in which your program simply loops around waiting for some condition to arise. The operating system is unaware that your thread isn't doing anything useful and thus won't switch to a running thread; instead it will leave your thread in a loop until its timeslice expires. You should always introduce timeouts or sleeps when you wait for conditions so that the scheduler can give the processor to another running thread and thereby improve the processor use of your application. So avoid code like this:

```
while ( someData.NotReady() )
;
```

The operating system is unable to detect that this is idle time, so it will schedule time for this thread simply to perform its tight loop. Introduce a *Sleep* or other blocking method that tells the operating system that your thread is waiting so that it can give the processor to another thread.

Multithreading can also introduce subtle programming challenges. In a multiprocessing situation, in which you have, for example, a StockPurchase process and a CurrencyViewer process running alongside each other, the operating system isolates the address space of one from the other using the hardware of the processor. It would be difficult for one application to corrupt or otherwise interfere with the data of the other. This scenario, however, doesn't apply to multithreading. A multithreaded StockPurchase application, for example, runs in a single application domain, with the threads created by the application being contained within that application domain and therefore sharing the same address space. (See the section "Using Application Domains" later in this chapter.) It's now extremely easy for one thread to interfere with the data of another. In the section "Synchronizing Threads and Thread Safety" later in this chapter, you'll see the types of subtle problems that can arise in multithreaded applications and the features provided by the .NET Compact Framework to solve these problems.

Scheduling

The term *scheduling* refers to the task undertaken by the operating system of deciding which thread will run at any one time. In your computer, there might be multiple threads but only one processor to execute them. In this way the scheduler resembles the manager of an office that has only one critical resource, such as a photocopier, which must be shared among various office personnel. The manager can decide to implement a "fair shares for all" policy, in which each person is allocated the photocopier for a fixed length of time, called a *timeslice.* In scheduling terms, this is often called *round-robin* scheduling. The manager stipulates a condition for a person being allocated a timeslice: she has to actually need to use the photocopier at that time. In scheduling terms, we would say that her thread is *running*. Also, if her timeslice is 10 minutes, and she completes what she has to do after 5 minutes, the photocopier is allocated to someone who needs it at that time. This is called *pre-emptive scheduling*: the processor can actually be taken away from someone who no longer requires it and given to someone who does. In the case of a thread, the length of a timeslice is short—of the order of milliseconds—but the amount of time depends on the operating system and the processor. The operating system varies the timeslice according to internal heuristics that are designed to maintain maximum responsiveness and throughput.

> **Note** In the full .NET Framework, each thread has a priority. This allows the developer to make a distinction between, say, threads that perform local services to the user and threads that perform server functions for client computers. Normally server functions are made higher priority than local services. In the .NET Compact Framework, each thread is of equal priority.

Creating a Multithreaded Application

Any application you write already has a single thread. For example, in a Microsoft Visual C# application, there is a thread that runs the *Main* function, known as the *primary* thread. Any extra threads within that application are created by the application code as it runs and are known as *secondary*, or *worker*, threads. After your program creates and starts an extra thread, the operating system schedules it to run in parallel to the primary thread on the basis that only running threads will be scheduled for execution. Your application now appears to be performing two tasks at once.

You can create new threads explicitly by constructing new *Thread* objects or implicitly by using the *Timer* class or the *ThreadPool* class. The following sections examine these in turn.

Constructing a new *Thread* Object

To create a new *Thread* object, first write a *void* method that takes no parameters and contains the code you want the thread to execute. Pass the address of this method to the constructor of a *ThreadStart* object, which you pass in turn to the constructor of a *Thread*. Then invoke the *Start* method on the *Thread* object. This puts the thread into the running state in which the .NET Compact Framework can schedule it to execute.

The following code, CreatingThreads.cs from the CreatingThreads Microsoft Windows CE console application, executes a primary thread and creates one worker thread using the code of the function *workerFunction*. The primary thread simply writes a message identifying itself to the screen and then waits 1 second using the *Thread.Sleep* static function. It does this three times. The worker thread is similar, but the message is different, the wait interval is 700 milliseconds, and it repeats 10 times.

CreatingThreads.cs

```
using System;
using System.Data;
using System.Threading;

namespace NETCFDevelopersReference
{
    class CreateThreads
    {
        static void Main(string[] args)
        {
            new CreateThreads().doCreate();
```

(continued)

CreatingThreads.cs *(continued)*

```
        }
        public void doCreate()
        {
            ThreadStart startWorker = new ThreadStart(workerFunction);
            Thread workerThread = new Thread(startWorker);
            workerThread.Start();
            for (int i = 0; i < 3; i++)
            {
                Console.WriteLine("This is the primary thread");
                Thread.Sleep(1000);
            }
            Console.WriteLine("Primary thread exiting");
            Console.ReadLine();
        }
        private void workerFunction()
        {
            for (int i = 0; i < 7; i++)
            {
                Console.WriteLine("Message from worker thread");
                Thread.Sleep(700);
            }
        }
    }
}
```

This program produces the following output:

```
This is the primary thread
Message from worker thread
Message from worker thread
This is the primary thread
Message from worker thread
This is the primary thread
Message from worker thread
Message from worker thread
Primary thread exiting
Message from worker thread
Message from worker thread
```

As you can see from CreatingThreads.cs, the two threads run in parallel, and the operating system schedules them once their sleep time is over. The program doesn't terminate until the final thread exits. A thread exits when it reaches its closing brace or executes a *return* statement. Note that if you run this program on the Windows CE Emulator, the wait times might be longer than those actually specified because of the performance overhead introduced by the emulator.

Putting a Thread to Sleep

You put a thread to sleep by calling the *Thread.Sleep* static method from within your thread. When your thread executes a call to the *Sleep* method, the .NET Compact Framework places the thread in a non-ready state and runs the scheduler to decide which thread should now have the processor. When the number of milliseconds specified in the call to *Sleep* has elapsed, your thread is ready to run again. Note that this doesn't automatically mean the thread will immediately get processor time. The thread is simply placed on the list of running threads, so it will get processor time when a timeslice becomes available. Calling *Thread.Sleep* with an integer argument of 0 causes your thread to allow another thread to gain the processor.

Using Timers

You can achieve the asynchronous execution of threads by using timers. The *Timer* object performs callbacks to a designated method at intervals specified during the timer's construction. You specify an interval that is to elapse before the first callback and an interval between each subsequent callback. It's important to note that when an asynchronous method executes, class fields and properties aren't accessible. Yet you might want to keep track of state from one callback to another. You can do this by passing a *state* object to the constructor of the timer. The .NET Compact Framework passes the *state* object as the single parameter of the *TimerCallback* delegate each time it's called. The UseTimers.cs code example uses the following overload of the Timer constructor to construct its timers:

```
public Timer(TimerCallback callback,
    object state,
    int dueTime,
    int period);
```

The code in UseTimers.cs creates two timers using the same callback method. The sample creates a *TimerState* class containing a single integer that is incremented by each callback. The timer *myTimer* starts with a *TimerState* object with a value of 0 and the timer *otherTimer* starts with a *TimerState* object with a value of 100, so you can see that the two timers keep track of their own states. The callback function prints its thread's hash code and the integer value of the *state* parameter.

The example stops the two timers by calling the *Timer.Change* method, which is used to alter the periodicity of a timer. To stop the timers, the code specifies *Timeout.Infinite* for the *dueTime* parameter of the *Change* method.

UseTimers.cs

```
using System;
using System.Data;
using System.Threading;
using System.Text;

namespace NETCFDevelopersReference
{
    class useTimers
    {
        static void Main(string[] args)
        {
            new useTimers();
        }
        public useTimers()
        {
            Timer myTimer = new Timer
                (new TimerCallback(CallBackFunction),
                 new TimerState(0),0,1000);
            Timer otherTimer = new Timer
                (new TimerCallback(CallBackFunction),
                new TimerState(100),0,500);
            Thread.Sleep(3000);
            myTimer.Change(Timeout.Infinite,0);
            otherTimer.Change(Timeout.Infinite,0);
            Console.ReadLine();
        }
        void CallBackFunction(object state)
        {
            int threadNumber = Thread.CurrentThread.GetHashCode();
            int n = ++((TimerState)state).Value;
            Console.WriteLine("State is " + n
                + " from thread " + threadNumber.ToString());

        }
        public class TimerState
        {
            public int Value;
            public TimerState(int v)
            {
                Value=v;
            }
        }
    }
}
```

The output from UseTimers.cs is shown next. The timer running the state starting at 1 has a period of 1 second, the timer that started at 100 has a period of half a second; Note that different thread hash codes arise from the fact that the .NET Compact Framework uses threads from the *ThreadPool* class (discussed in the next section) to service the timer callback.

```
State is 1 from thread 278172
State is 101 from thread 368784
State is 102 from thread 369532
State is 2 from thread 369576
State is 103 from thread 369620
State is 104 from thread 369664
State is 3 from thread 369708
State is 105 from thread 369752
```

Using Thread Pools

The *ThreadPool* class provides a pool of threads that you use on an ad hoc basis for posting processing that is required from time to time. The advantage of using *ThreadPool* is this: if you know you have *n* items of processing to perform, you can create *n* threads. Because these threads might spend much of their time waiting for resources and some might complete before others even begin, the actual number of threads required could be considerably less than *n*, but it would be difficult to predict or manage this number.

You can queue work items to a *ThreadPool* object using the following method of the *ThreadPool* class:

```
public static QueueUserWorkItem(WaitCallback myCallback, object state)
```

The *WaitCallBack* delegate parameter specifies the method to execute, and the *state* parameter communicates any information to the thread. If you've queued several items to a *ThreadPool* object, the object uses *one* thread to monitor the status of all the wait operations within the queued items. When a wait completes, the *ThreadPool* object designates one of its worker threads to execute the *WaitCallback* function. In this way, if *n* processing items are queued to the *ThreadPool* object, it's possible that many fewer than *n* threads will actually be required to perform the specified processing, avoiding the overhead of creating and deleting threads. The code in UseThreadPools.cs illustrates how the *ThreadPool* class works.

> **Note** In the .NET Compact Framework, the *ThreadPool* class supports only the *QueueUserWorkItem* static method and none of the other methods and properties of the full .NET Framework's *ThreadPool* class.

UseThreadPools.cs

```
using System;
using System.Data;
using System.Threading;

namespace NETCFDevelopersReference
{
    class useThreadPools
    {
        static void Main(string[] args)
        {
            new useThreadPools();
        }
        public useThreadPools()
        {
            WaitCallback wcb = new WaitCallback(theCallback);
            ThreadPool.QueueUserWorkItem(wcb,(object)"Hello");
            Thread.Sleep(1000);
            ThreadPool.QueueUserWorkItem(wcb,(object)"again");
            Thread.Sleep(1000);
            ThreadPool.QueueUserWorkItem(wcb,null);
            Console.ReadLine();
        }
        private void theCallback(object state)
        {
            if (state == null)
                state = "No data";
            int threadNumber = Thread.CurrentThread.GetHashCode();
            Console.WriteLine("State is " + state.ToString() +
                " from thread " + threadNumber);
        }
    }
}
```

Synchronizing Threads and Thread Safety

In the output of the CreatingThreads.cs example, two threads write to the screen using *Console.WriteLine*. At no point does the output from the two threads get mixed up on the screen. This is because the *Console.WriteLine* method is *thread safe*: you can safely call it from more than one thread in a process and know that the critical part in the method where the method actually performs the write operation cannot be entered by more than one thread at a time. If it could, the output of the two threads could be mixed up on the screen.

Thread safety is a very important issue in multithreaded development, and the causes of thread safety problems are often very subtle. Thread safety problems aren't always easy to spot in code, and they don't always surface easily in testing. In the example just discussed, both threads actually spend most of their time sleeping, making the likelihood of a thread switch at the wrong moment extremely low. Thus, if a thread safety problem were present, you could run your application many times and the problem might not appear. Thread safety problems can depend on subtle timing issues, and an application might run correctly on your machine but not on a different machine with a faster or slower processor. Making a thread safe involves a number of issues, including knowing exactly where and how your thread data is stored. The sections that follow examine these issues. For further information, see the article "Threading Design Guidelines," accessible from the online documentation Contents window by selecting Visual Studio .NET\.NET Framework\Reference\Design Guidelines for Class Library Developers.

Determining What Memory Is Used by Threads

The data belonging to your thread is stored in memory according to where and how it is declared.

- A variable *int localVar* declared inside the body of the thread method is stored on the stack of the thread. Because the .NET Compact Framework allocates a separate stack to each thread, each thread has its own independent instance of *localVar*.
- A variable *int instVar* that is an instance variable of the class to which the thread method belongs is stored on the stack of the instance. Because the thread is created from within one instance, there is only one instance of *instVar*.
- A static variable *static int staticVar* declared in the class is stored on the data segment. There is only one instance of *staticVar*.

The StorageClass.cs example that follows illustrates this by creating two threads based on the function *myThread*. This function has an automatic variable *int localVar*. The class has an instance variable *int instVar* and a static variable *static int staticVar*. Each thread loops three times, incrementing each of these variables and printing them. You can see from the output that there are two independent instances of *localVar* but only one instance of *instVar* and one instance of *staticVar*.

> **Important** To make this example thread safe, the *Interlocked.Increment* method has been used instead of *++staticVar*. See the previous section, "Synchronizing Threads and Thread Safety," for a discussion of thread safety. The *Interlocked* class and the reasons for using the *Interlocked* class are discussed in the section "Using the *Interlocked* Class."

StorageClass.cs

```
using System;
using System.Data;
using System.Threading;

namespace NETCFDevelopersReference
{
    class storageClass
    {
        int instVar;
        static int staticVar;
        static void Main(string[] args)
        {
            new storageClass();
        }
        public storageClass()
        {
            instVar = 0;
            new Thread(new ThreadStart(myThread)).Start();
            new Thread(new ThreadStart(myThread)).Start();
            Console.ReadLine();
        }
        void myThread()
        {
            int myNumber = Thread.CurrentThread.GetHashCode();
            for (int localVar = 0; localVar < 3; localVar++)
            {
```

```
                Console.WriteLine("localVar is {0}, from thread {1}",
                    localVar, myNumber);
                Console.WriteLine("instVar is {0}, from thread {1}",
                    Interlocked.Increment(ref instVar), myNumber);
                Console.WriteLine("staticVar is {0}, from thread {1}",
                    Interlocked.Increment(ref staticVar), myNumber);
                Thread.Sleep(500);
            }
        }
    }
}
```

The output from this example looks like this:

```
localVar is 0 from thread 303284
localVar is 0 from thread 303220
instVar is 1 from thread 303284
instVar is 2 from thread 303220
staticVar is 1 from thread 303284
staticVar is 2 from thread 303220
localVar is 1 from thread 303284
localVar is 1 from thread 303220
instVar is 3 from thread 303284
instVar is 4 from thread 303220
staticVar is 3 from thread 303220
staticVar is 4 from thread 303284
localVar is 2 from thread 303284
localVar is 2 from thread 303220
instVar is 5 from thread 303284
instVar is 6 from thread 303220
staticVar is 5 from thread 303284
staticVar is 6 from thread 303220
```

In the output, you can see that *staticVar* and *instVar* increase each time irrespective of the thread, but the value of *localVar* depends on which thread is outputting it. Thread safety issues are unlikely to arise from the use of method local variables, but using static or class instance variables requires close attention to thread safety when multiple threads must access them, especially if there is more than one thread that modifies the variable.

Understanding Thread Safety

When you use multithreading, your code might no longer run in the predictable order you were accustomed to in the single-threaded world. The scheduler now decides when to interrupt your thread and give the processor to another thread. Suppose in the StorageClass.cs code example you wrote this:

```
LocalVar = staticVar++;
```

This line of code is not thread safe: if it's interrupted at a certain point, it could produce unexpected results. The problem arises because the increment on *staticVar*, a static variable, consists of multiple steps that can be interrupted at the wrong moment. The process of evaluating the expression *staticVar++* looks like this:

1. Store the value of *staticVar* in a temporary variable.
2. Increment *staticVar*.
3. Return the temporary as the result of the operation.

In a very small percentage of cases, the scheduler could interrupt your thread after Step 1. Another thread that performed Step 1 would read the same value of *staticVar*, so both threads would report the same number. This is a classic read/modify/write operation, which usually gives rise to thread safety problems. The real world is full of such examples. For instance, imagine two threads, A and B, attempting to withdraw from a single bank account. Thread A looks at the balance and then makes a withdrawal based on the information that states $1000 is in the account. If the scheduler switches to thread B after A has read but not yet modified and written, and B is also trying to make a withdrawal, both A and B might attempt to withdraw $1000 and cause the account to go into debit. The term *critical section* is frequently used to refer to a section of code such as this: code that must execute in its entirety without allowing a switch to another thread. The term *atomic* refers to updates of this type, which consist of multiple steps that must execute uninterrupted.

Exploring Synchronization Features of the .NET Compact Framework

The .NET Compact Framework provides a number of synchronization primitives to allow your threads to coordinate their actions, including ensuring atomicity of updates. These are the *Monitor*, *Mutex*, *ManualResetEvent*, *AutoResetEvent*, and *Interlocked* classes. The following sections discuss these classes in more detail.

Using the *Monitor* Class

The *Monitor* class is a sealed class that you can use to lock and unlock critical sections of code so that while the lock is applied, the scheduler doesn't release that lock to another thread. If you ensure that all threads that must use a critical section request the lock, only one thread will enter the section at a time. The *Monitor* class works by locking an object. All .NET Compact Framework objects are lockable. To prevent two or more threads from entering the same critical section of code, these threads must use the *Monitor* class to lock the same object. The object can be any object that you decide both threads will lock before performing a certain operation. In our bank account example, the threads might lock, for example, the Account object they want to use to make a withdrawal. A thread that has locked a different object will be able to enter the critical section.

To lock an object using the *Monitor* class, use the *Monitor.Enter* method, passing as a parameter the object that needs to be locked. *Monitor.Enter* will block when necessary until the object is able to be locked. Then use the critical section (or other resource) and ensure that you call *Monitor.Exit*, passing the same object, to free it for other threads. If a thread invoked *Enter* on an object, it might re-invoke it successfully any number of times. However, the thread must make a matching number of calls to *Exit* to unlock the object.

Note also that this locking mechanism is merely a protocol and requires that all threads using a critical section request the lock first. A badly behaved thread could simply bypass the call to *Monitor.Enter* and ignore the lock. The following example, UseMonitor.cs, creates two threads based on a single function. The function prints a message that it's waiting for a lock. It then calls the *Monitor.Enter* method, passing *this* as a parameter, so that the current *useMonitor* instance is the object that gets locked. Only one thread actually gains the lock and proceeds past the *Monitor.Enter* line. The thread then loops three times, printing its own thread hash code and sleeping. Sleeping would normally cause a switch to the other thread. You will see from the output that this doesn't happen because the other thread is blocked by the call to *Monitor.Enter*.

> **Note** The .NET Compact Framework doesn't support the following *Monitor* methods from the full .NET Framework: *TryEnter*, *Wait*, *Pulse*, *PulseAll*. You must replace calls to *Wait*, *Pulse*, and *PulseAll* with the *Enter* and *Exit* methods. There is no way to replicate the non-blocking *TryEnter* method.

UseMonitor.cs

```
using System;
using System.Data;
using System.Threading;

namespace NETCFDevelopersReference
{
    class useMonitor
```

(continued)

UseMonitor.cs *(continued)*

```
    {
        static void Main(string[] args)
        {
            new useMonitor();
        }
        public useMonitor()
        {
            new Thread(new ThreadStart(myThread)).Start();
            new Thread(new ThreadStart(myThread)).Start();
            Console.ReadLine();
        }
        private void myThread()
        {
            int threadNumber = Thread.CurrentThread.GetHashCode();
            Console.WriteLine("Thread " + threadNumber +
                " waiting for lock");
            Monitor.Enter(this);
            for (int i = 0; i < 3; i++)
            {
                Thread.Sleep(500);
                Console.WriteLine(threadNumber + " has lock");
            }
            Console.WriteLine(threadNumber + " releasing lock");
            Monitor.Exit(this);
        }
    }
}
```

The output from the example is:

```
Thread 304180 waiting for lock
Thread 304244 waiting for lock
304180 has lock
304180 has lock
304180 has lock
304180 releasing lock
304244 has lock
304244 has lock
304244 has lock
304244 releasing lock
```

It's clear from the output that the first thread with the number 304180 has acquired the lock. It loops without interruption even though it sleeps on each loop, which would normally cause another thread to run. The other thread is blocked on the call to *Enter* on the same object until the first thread releases it.

All .NET Compact Framework objects are lockable. If you've implemented an *Account* class, you can solve the read/modify/write problem like this:

```
Account theAccount = new Account("A. Person", 100);
Monitor.Enter(theAccount);
if (theAccount.GetBalance >= 100)
    theAccount.Withdraw(100);
Monitor.Exit(theAccount) ;
```

> **Note** The *lock* statement in Visual C# is equivalent to the *Monitor.Enter* method.

Using the *Mutex* Class

The *Mutex* (short for mutual exclusion) object is a mechanism for granting to exactly one thread at a time exclusive access to a shared resource. A *Mutex* object can be in the owned or unowned state, but it can be owned by only one thread at any time. Mutual exclusion is achieved by two or more threads requesting ownership of the *Mutex* object before they access the shared object and then releasing ownership afterwards. The first to gain ownership will cause the other to block until ownership is released.

Use the *Mutex.WaitOne* method to request ownership of a *Mutex* object and *Mutex.ReleaseMutex* to release ownership. Once a thread has become the owning thread, it might make further calls to *WaitOne* without blocking its execution. However, it must make a matching number of calls to the *ReleaseMutex* method to release ownership of the *Mutex* object.

The following code example, UseMutexes.cs, creates a *Mutex* object that is owned by the main thread. It then creates a worker thread that tries to acquire the *Mutex* object. The worker thread blocks until the main thread calls *ReleaseMutex*. When this call is made, the thread waiting for the *Mutex* object is granted ownership. The main thread then tries to claim the *Mutex* object but is blocked until the worker thread releases it.

> **Note** The .NET Compact Framework's *Mutex* class can not be used across processes. You can use the *MessageWindow* class to perform cross-process communication and synchronization. Refer to the section "Understanding the *MessageWindow* Component," in Chapter 22.

UseMutexes.cs

```
using System;
using System.Data;
using System.Threading;

namespace NETCFDevelopersReference
{
    class useMutexes
    {
        Mutex myMutex;
        static void Main(string[] args)
        {
            new useMutexes();
        }
        public useMutexes()
        {
            myMutex = new Mutex(true); // Main thread owns the mutex
            new Thread(new ThreadStart(myFunction)).Start();
            Thread.Sleep(500);
            Console.WriteLine("Main releasing mutex");
            myMutex.ReleaseMutex();
            myMutex.WaitOne();
            Console.WriteLine("Main regains mutex");
            Console.ReadLine();
        }
        private void myFunction()
        {
            Console.WriteLine("Second thread waiting for mutex");
            myMutex.WaitOne();
            Console.WriteLine("Second thread has mutex");
            myMutex.ReleaseMutex();
            Console.WriteLine("Second thread releasing mutex");
        }
    }
}
```

The output from this code is:

```
Second thread waiting for mutex
Main releasing mutex
Second thread has mutex
Second thread releasing mutex
Main regains mutex
```

Using the *ManualResetEvent* and *AutoResetEvent* Classes

The *ManualResetEvent* and *AutoResetEvent* classes allow a thread to block waiting for some event. In the .NET Compact Framework, an event can be in the *signaled* (the event has occurred) or *non-signaled* state. If a thread executes the

WaitOne method for a *ManualResetEvent* or *AutoResetEvent* object that is non-signaled, the thread blocks until some other thread uses the *Set* method of the *ManualResetEvent* object or *AutoResetEvent* object to signal that event. The waiting thread will then unblock. The difference between the *AutoResetEvent* class and the *ManualResetEvent* class (illustrated in Figure 20-3) is that when a thread waits for an *AutoResetEvent* object and the event is set, when the waiting thread unblocks, the .NET Compact Framework automatically sets the event to non-signaled again. This ensures that *only* one thread will unblock. In the case of the *ManualResetEvent* class, no such automatic reset occurs, and the event must be reset to non-signaled by the code using the *Reset* method. This allows more than one thread to unblock as a result of the event.

The following example, UseEvents.cs, first creates an *AutoResetEvent* object and then creates two worker threads that wait for the event. The primary thread uses the *Set* method to set that event so that one of the waiting threads unblocks.

UseEvents.cs

```
using System;
using System.Data;
using System.Threading;

namespace NETCFDevelopersReference
{
    class useEvents
    {
        private AutoResetEvent theEvent;
        static void Main(string[] args)
        {
            new useEvents();
        }
        public useEvents()
        {
            theEvent = new AutoResetEvent(false);
            new Thread(new ThreadStart(waiterThread)).Start();
            new Thread(new ThreadStart(waiterThread)).Start();
            theEvent.Set();
            Console.ReadLine();
        }
        private void waiterThread()
        {
            int threadNumber = Thread.CurrentThread.GetHashCode();
            Console.WriteLine("Waiter thread " + threadNumber + " waiting");
            theEvent.WaitOne();
            Console.WriteLine("Waiter thread " +
                threadNumber + " received event");
        }
    }
}
```

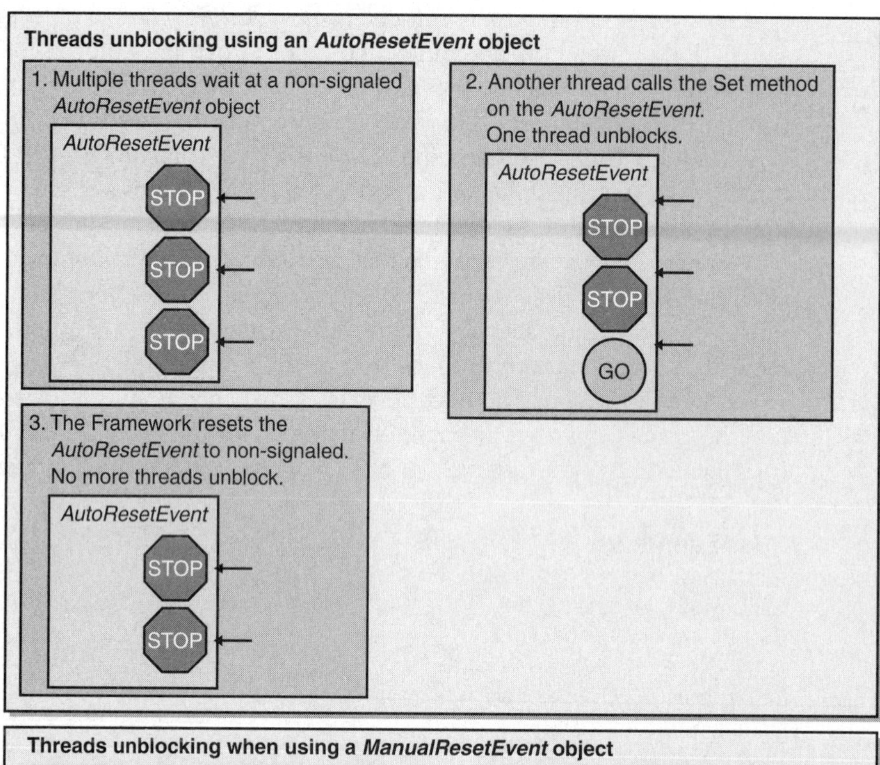

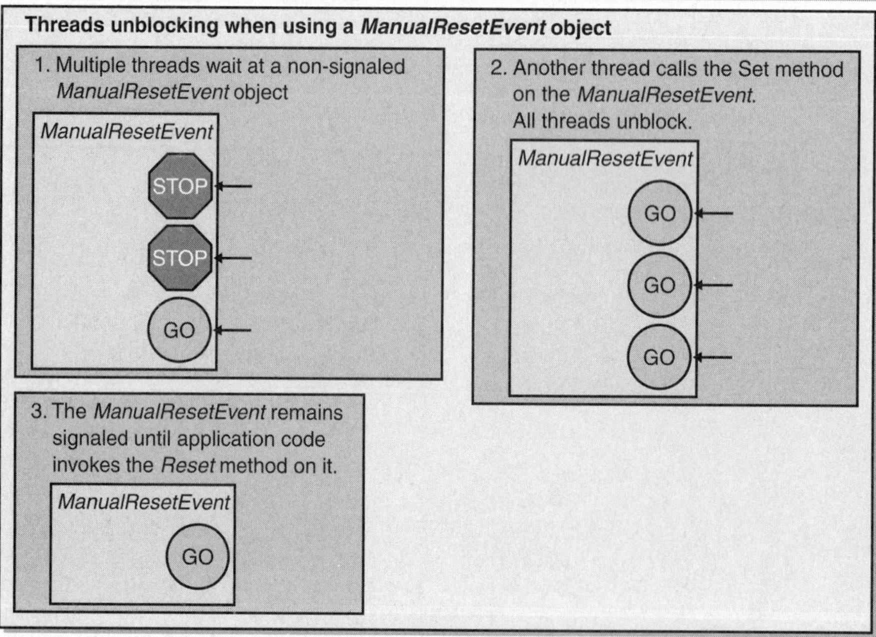

Figure 20-3 Difference between threads unblocking by using the *AutoResetEvent* class and the *ManualResetEvent* class.

The output from this example follows:

```
Thread 304180 waiting
Thread 304180 received event
Thread 314224 waiting
```

The program never terminates because the second worker thread is waiting for an event that will never happen. The single call to *Set* performed by the main thread allowed the first waiting thread to unblock, but it was immediately reset by the .NET Compact Framework. If you change the *AutoResetEvent* to *ManualResetEvent* in this example and then run the example, when the first worker thread receives the event, no automatic reset occurs, the second thread also unblocks, and the program terminates.

Using the *Interlocked* Class

The methods of the *Interlocked* class allow you to prevent errors that can arise when performing a read/modify/write operation on shared data. For example, performing a post increment such as *staticVar++* on a shared variable and exchanging a shared variable are non-atomic operations that, if interrupted by the scheduler at a certain moment, can cause unexpected results. The *Interlocked* class provides methods for performing simple operations on shared data in an atomic manner.

The static methods *Increment(ref int)* and *Decrement(ref int)* increment and decrement, respectively, integral values. Overloads of these methods accept *ref long* parameters. The safe way of incrementing *staticVar* is as follows:

```
System.Threading.Interlocked.Increment(staticVar);
```

The following method of *Interlocked* compares two variables and, based on the result of the comparison, stores a third value in one of the variables. This process is performed as an atomic operation.

```
public static int CompareExchange(ref int location,
    int value, int comparand);
```

If *location* and *comparand* are equal, *location* is set to the value of *value*. The following *Exchange* method exchanges the values of two variables as an atomic operation:

```
public static Exchange(ref int location, int value);
```

Some overloads accept *float* or *object* parameters.

Avoiding Deadlocks

It's quite possible in a multithreaded application to create a situation in which two threads are waiting for resources without realizing that each is waiting for a resource held by the other. Take the example of threads A and B, and resources R1 and R2. Thread A acquires R1. Thread B acquires R2. Thread A then requests R2 and thread B requests R1. The result is a *deadlock*, because thread A is waiting for something thread B is holding (R2), but thread B won't release R2 because thread B also is waiting for something held by thread A. Deadlocks usually arise when threads must acquire multiple resources and the sequence in which they acquire those resources is not well defined.

One easy solution is to ensure that threads in your application do not request more than one resource at a time. Alternatively, if a group of threads must acquire multiple resources, ensure that the threads request the resources in the same order. The deadlock example just described arose because the two threads requested R1 and R2 in reverse order.

Creating Thread-Safe Wrappers

When you create a new class or component, you can choose to make all its methods thread safe. This makes the component easy to use, but there is also a cost: thread safety has an impact on performance. If you wanted to use the component in a single-threaded application, you might not want to pay the price of thread safety if your application doesn't require it. You might therefore choose to provide a non-thread-safe component with the option of a thread-safe version for those who require it.

Take the case of a *widget* class with a non-thread-safe method *A* and a thread-safe method *B*. You can create a thread-safe wrapper using inheritance, overriding *A* with a thread-safe version by using a *Monitor* object or other locking mechanism:

```
public class ThreadSafeWidget : widget
{
    public void A()
    {
        Monitor.Enter(this);
        base.A();
        Monitor.Exit(this);
    }
}
```

You can also create a thread-safe wrapper using composition so that the *ThreadSafeWidget* class actually has a *widget* contained inside it. There is a major advantage to this approach for existing applications that use *widget* objects—you can now provide a constructor to create a *ThreadSafeWidget* object from a *widget* object, allowing you to make calls such as this:

```
ThreadSafeWidget tsw = new ThreadSafeWidget(oldWidget);
```

The .NET Compact Framework provides both thread-safe and non-thread-safe versions of classes. Collection classes such as *HashTable* and *ArrayList* have the static *Synchronized* factory method, which allows the developer to choose between the performance advantage of a non-thread-safe version for single-threaded applications and a thread-safe version for multithreaded applications. For example, the following creates a thread-safe *ArrayList* object:

```
ArrayList myArrayList = new ArrayList();
myArrayList.Add("One entry");
myArrayList.Add("Another entry");
ArrayList myArrayListSyncWrapper = ArrayList.Synchronized(myArrayList);
```

The variable *myArrayListSyncWrapper* is a thread-safe wrapper to the collection. The objects stored in the collection are the same, but any thread can enumerate the collection and manipulate its contents in safety using the thread-safe wrapper class.

Using Multithreading with Controls

When a thread creates a control, it "owns" that control. The .NET Compact Framework dictates that only the owner thread can make method calls to controls. If you call control methods from a non-owning thread, you risk causing your application to freeze. The .NET Compact Framework therefore provides the *Control.Invoke* method, which permits method execution on controls in a safe manner. You can't call *Control.Invoke* from the thread that owns the control, but you can safely call the method from any other thread. *Control.Invoke* has two overloads:

```
public object Control.Invoke(Delegate method)
public virtual object Control.Invoke(Delegate method, Object[] args)
```

This code causes the execution of the specified delegate on the thread that owns the control.

Note The .NET Compact Framework doesn't support a number of related methods, properties, and classes that are found in the full .NET Framework. The asynchronous forms of *Invoke*, *BeginInvoke*, and *EndInvoke* are not supported. *InvokeRequired*, which returns a Boolean value indicating whether the caller must use *Invoke* to make method calls on the control because it's on another thread, isn't supported.

The *MethodInvoker* class isn't supported. *MethodInvoker* implements a ready-to-use delegate for use with *Invoke*. You must declare your own delegate to use *Invoke* with the .NET Compact Framework.

The following code creates a thread that updates a ProgressBar control by declaring a delegate called *myDelegate*. It declares an *updateProgress* method with the same signature as *myDelegate* and passes *updateProgress* to the *Invoke* method, passing two parameters as an object array.

```
private void updateProgress(int theValue, int theMax)
{
    if (theMax != 0)
        proStatus.Maximum = theMax;
    proStatus.Value = theValue;
}
private delegate void myDelegate(int theValue, int theMax);
private void myThread()
{
    for (int i = 0; i < 10; i ++)
    {
        this.Invoke(new myDelegate(updateProgress),
            new object[] {i * 10,100});
        Thread.Sleep(500);
    }
}
private void cmdCreateThread_Click(object sender,
    System.EventArgs e)
{
    new Thread(new ThreadStart(myThread)).Start();
}
```

Comparing the Two Frameworks

The full .NET Framework must provide support for processor-intensive, high-performance server applications and services, whereas the .NET Compact Framework is used in a client environment. There are several threading features of the desktop framework that the .NET Compact Framework doesn't support, and these are discussed in the following sections.

Setting Thread Priorities

Threads in the .NET Compact Framework don't have priorities.

Using the *Join* Method

In the full .NET Framework, when a thread calls *otherThread.Join*, the calling thread blocks until *otherThread* terminates. Overloads that accept timeout parameters are available. This feature is not supported in the .NET Compact Framework. If you require notification that a thread has terminated, you must place in that thread code that sets some synchronization mechanism such as a *Mutex* before the thread exits and then, in your waiting thread, place code that performs a call to the *WaitForOne* method on the *Mutex* object.

Using the *Suspend* and *Resume* Methods

The *Suspend* and *Resume* methods allow one thread to suspend and resume, respectively, execution of another thread. However, they aren't supported in the .NET Compact Framework. Instead, signal to a thread through a *Mutex*, *AutoResetEvent*, or *ManualResetEvent* object that you want it to suspend and resume execution.

Using Application Domains

An application domain, encapsulated by the *AppDomain* class, is a .NET feature designed to provide the same kind of memory space isolation as an operating system process but without the considerable overhead that a separate process involves. The *AppDomain* class also has methods to allow threads to set and get data within the application domain. (See Chapter 2 for more information.) Although every .NET Compact Framework supports application domains in the sense that every .NET Compact Framework application runs in an application domain, the methods for creating new domains and sharing data are not supported.

Using the *Thread* Class's *Abort* and *Interrupt* Methods

The *Thread.Abort* method in the full .NET Framework raises an exception of type *ThreadAbortException* to the designated thread, which normally results in the termination of the thread. This is not supported in the .NET Compact Framework. .NET Compact Framework threads must be written so that they can terminate themselves.

Thread.Interrupt isn't supported in the .NET Compact Framework. It interrupts a thread that is in the *WaitSleepJoin* state.

A thread in the .NET Compact Framework must be written so that it can terminate itself in response to a signal from a *Mutex*, an *AutoResetEvent*, or a *ManualResetEvent* object.

Using the *ReaderWriterLock* Class

The *ReaderWriterLock* class provides locks for multiple readers and single writers and is not supported in the .NET Compact Framework. Use the *Monitor* class instead.

Employing Background Threads

A background thread does not terminate when the owning application dies. This is a feature more commonly used in server applications and isn't supported in the .NET Compact Framework.

Using the *SynchronizationAttribute* Class

When applied to a class, the *SynchronizationAttribute* attribute ensures that only one thread at a time can access an object of that class. This is not supported in the .NET Compact Framework. Use the *Monitor* class or some other means of synchronization instead.

Summary

Multithreading is an advanced programming technique. In this chapter, you've learned about the multithreading features provided by the .NET Compact Framework and how to apply them to improve the responsiveness, scalability, and throughput of your applications. You can use the .NET Compact Framework classes to solve synchronization and thread-safety issues that can arise in multithreaded applications.

This chapter also explained the issues that arise when using multithreading with Windows forms and controls and how you can use .NET Compact Framework features to call control and form methods safely.

21

Graphics Programming

This chapter describes how to display graphics on a form or custom a control, and discusses how to draw shapes, lines, text, and bitmaps using the *Graphics* object created from a form or custom control or passed as part of *PaintEventArgs* in the *OnPaint* event of a form or a custom control. This chapter also covers how to load bitmaps, icons, and fonts.

The ability to programmatically create graphics can be extremely useful in a number of scenarios. For example, suppose you need to create an application that dynamically displays a graph of sales figures over a period of time. The examples in this chapter are taken from a sample application, SalesGraphs, which produces different graphs for the sales figures over a year. You'll find the SalesGraphs application included with this book's sample files.

Classes for Graphics Programming

The .NET Compact Framework includes a number of classes that can be used for graphics-related programming. These classes are defined in the *System.Drawing* namespace and can be used to create shapes, lines, images, and text on drawing surfaces such as forms and controls.

The core class for all graphics-related programming is the *Graphics* class, which defines a drawing surface on which you can programmatically create visual effects. The methods of the *Graphics* class make use of other graphics-related classes such as the *Pen*, *Brush*, *Color*, *Rectangle*, *Point*, *Line*, *Image*, and *Region* classes.

Classes Used to Draw Shapes, Bitmaps, and Text

There are a number of other classes that the methods of the *Graphics* object use to draw shapes, bitmaps, and text to its drawing surface, and I will take some time here to briefly describe them before discussing the *Graphics* class itself.

The *Pen* Class

The *Pen* class is used to draw outline shapes and lines. Unlike the full .NET Framework, the .NET Compact Framework allows you to create a *Pen* object only by specifying the color you want the *Pen* to draw—you can't create a *Pen* object from a *Brush* object or specify the size of the *Pen*. However, you can change the color of the *Pen* after you have created it by using the *Color* property of the *Pen* object. The following sample code shows how to create the *Pen* objects that will be needed in the SalesGraphs sample application:

```
Pen whitePen = new Pen(Color.White);
Pen blackPen = new Pen(Color.Black);
Pen greyPen = new Pen(Color.LightGray);
Pen redPen = new Pen(Color.Red);
Pen yellowPen = new Pen(Color.Yellow);
```

The *SolidBrush* Class

The *Brush* class is an abstract class with methods to draw solid shapes and text to the drawing surface of the *Graphics* object. With the .NET Compact Framework, you can create an instance of the *SolidBrush* class, which derives from the *Brush* class. The *TextureBrush* and *LinearGradientBrush* classes that are available in the full .NET Framework are not supported in the .NET Compact Framework.

When you create your *SolidBrush* object, you specify the color that you want it to draw. The *Color* property of the *SolidBrush* object is used to change the color of the brush used to draw to the drawing surface.

The following sample code shows how to create the *SolidBrush* objects that are required by the SalesGraphs sample application:

```
SolidBrush whiteBrush = new SolidBrush(Color.White);
SolidBrush yellowBrush = new SolidBrush(Color.Yellow);
SolidBrush redBrush = new SolidBrush(Color.Red);
SolidBrush blackBrush = new SolidBrush(Color.Black);
SolidBrush skyBlueBrush = new SolidBrush(Color.SkyBlue);
SolidBrush darkBlueBrush = new SolidBrush(Color.DarkBlue);
```

Several colored brushes are required for the various graph elements used in the sample application.

The *Color* Class

When you create a pen or a brush, you need to specify the color the pen or brush will use to draw to the *Graphics* object. You create a *Color* object by using one of the color enumerations defined in the *System.Drawing* namespace (as shown in the examples so far in this chapter) or by specifying the alpha, red, green, and blue (ARGB) components of the color. You create a *Color* object from the ARGB components of a color using the *FromArgb* method of the *Color* class, in which you specify the ARGB components using a 32-bit ARGB value or the individual 8-bit red, green, and blue (RGB) integer values of the color. The byte order for the ARGB value is as follows: the first byte represents the alpha value and the second, third, and fourth bytes represent the red, green, and blue values, respectively. When specifying the color using the individual RGB values, the alpha value is always set as 255, which is fully opaque. The following sample code shows how to create two *Color* objects, one using the *Red* property of the *Color* class and another using red, green, and blue integer values:

```
Color Color1 = new Color.Red;
Color Color2 = new Color.FromArgb(234, 255, 0);
```

The *Font* Class

The *Font* class is used by the *Graphics* class when rendering text to the drawing surface. You create a new *Font* object by specifying the font family as a *FontFamily* enumeration or by specifying the font name as a string. You also need to specify the size of the new font and a *FontStyle* enumeration value (*Bold*, *Italic*, *Regular*, *Strikeout*, or *Underline*). The following sample code shows the creation of the three fonts used in the SalesGraphs sample application. Each of the fonts is defined using the *FontFamily* enumeration.

```
Font genericFont =
    new Font(FontFamily.GenericSansSerif, 6, FontStyle.Regular);
Font titleFont =
    new Font(FontFamily.GenericSansSerif, 8, FontStyle.Regular);
Font keyFont =
    new Font(FontFamily.GenericSansSerif, 7, FontStyle.Regular);
```

The following code shows how to define a font using the string name of the font:

```
Font MyFontTwo = new Font("GenericSerif", 12, FontStyle.Bold);
```

The *Icon* Class

The *Icon* object is used by the *DrawIcon* method to draw an icon to the drawing surface of the *Graphics* object. You initialize a new instance of an *Icon* object by specifying the data stream you want to use to load the icon and, optionally, the width and height of the icon. The following code shows how to load an icon from the embedded resource stream of the application's executable file:

```
Icon MyIcon = new Icon(Assembly.GetExecutingAssembly()
    .GetManifestResourceStream("TestApp.Icon.ico"));
```

The *Bitmap* Class

The *Bitmap* class holds the pixel data and the image attributes for a bitmap image. You can load a bitmap into a *Bitmap* object from a *Stream* object, from an existing *Bitmap* object, or by specifying a file name as a string. You can also create a new blank *Bitmap* object simply by specifying the size of the bitmap. The following code shows how to create a *Bitmap* object from a bitmap file:

```
Bitmap companyLogo = new Bitmap(
    @"/Program Files/NetCF/Chapter21/SalesGraphs/Logo.bmp");
```

You can use the *Height*, *Width*, and *Size* properties of the *Bitmap* object to find out or change the height, width, and size of the *Bitmap* object. You find the color of a pixel in the *Bitmap* object by using the *GetPixel* method of the *Bitmap* object. You specify the X and Y coordinates of the pixel within the *Bitmap* object, and the *GetPixel* method returns the color as a *System.Drawing.Color* object. To change the color of a pixel of the *Bitmap* object, you use the *SetPixel* method. You specify the X and Y coordinates of the pixel to change and the color to set that pixel to. The following code shows the use of the *GetPixel* and *SetPixel* methods. The code uses the *Bitmap* object created in the previous sample to create a new *Bitmap* object.

```
Bitmap MyBitmap = new Bitmap(companyLogo);
int x = MyBitmap.Width / 2;
int y = MyBitmap.Height / 2;
Color CenterColor = MyBitmap.GetPixel(x, y);

Bitmap MyNewBitmap = new Bitmap(13, 13);
MyNewBitmap.SetPixel(7, 7, Color.Blue);
```

The *Point* Structure

The *Point* structure represents a point on a two-dimensional drawing surface using X and Y coordinates. You can create an array of *Point* objects to define a number of points on the drawing surface. This array of points, or *graphics path*, can be used by the *DrawPolygon* method of the *Graphics* object to draw a shape with the number of sides defined by the number of points in the *Point* object array. The only constructor supported by the .NET Compact Framework for the creation of a *Point* object is to specify the X and Y coordinates of the point on the drawing surface. The following code shows how to define the points of an octagon. You would then pass the *anOctagon* object to the *DrawPolygon* or *FillPolygon* methods of the *Graphics* object to draw the octagon to the drawing surface of the *Graphics* object.

```
Point [] anOctagon =
{
    new Point(100,50),
    new Point(150,50),
    new Point(200,100),
    new Point(200,150),
    new Point(150,200),
    new Point(100,200),
    new Point(50,150),
    new Point(50,100),
    new Point(100,50)
};
```

The *Rectangle* Structure

The *Rectangle* structure defines the size and position of a rectangular region of the drawing surface. You define the rectangular area using an X coordinate, a Y coordinate, a width, and a height for the area. The X and Y coordinates define the upper-left of the rectangle relative to the drawing surface. The following code shows how to define a rectangle at position X = 10 and Y = 10, with a width of 100 pixels and a height of 200 pixels:

```
Rectangle MyRectangle = new Rectangle(10, 10, 100, 200);
```

The *Region* Class

Although the *Region* class can be instantiated only by using a *Rectangle* object, a complex region shape can be defined by using the *Exclude*, *Intersect*, *Union*, and *Xor* methods of the *Region* object. The *Exclude* method includes only areas of the *Region* object that are not intersected by the second *Region* or *Rectangle* object specified in the call to the method. The *Intersect* method includes only areas of the *Region* object that are intersected by the second *Region* or *Rectangle* object specified in the call to the method. The *Union* method includes areas from both the original *Region* object and the *Region* or *Rectangle* object specified in the call to the method. The *Xor* method includes areas from both the *Region* object and the second *Region* object or the *Rectangle* object specified in the call to the method, but it excludes areas where the two objects intersect. The following code shows how to define a complex region using these methods:

```
Region MyRegion = new Region(new Rectangle(10, 10, 200, 100));
MyRegion.Exclude(new Rectangle(20, 20, 50, 25));
MyRegion.Union(new Rectangle(10, 110, 10, 100));
MyRegion.Xor(new Rectangle(150, 50, 50, 100));
```

Graphics Class Drawing Methods

To begin using any of the graphics functions in the .NET Compact Framework, you must first obtain an instance of the *Graphics* class. You can then use its methods to render shapes, lines, text, and bitmaps to its surface. You obtain a *Graphics* object reference in one of the following ways:

- Use the *CreateGraphics* method of the form or custom control to obtain a reference to the *Graphics* object that represents the drawing surface of the control or form. This method is used to draw to a form or custom control that already exists, as shown in the following code:

  ```
  Graphics MyGraphicsObject = this.CreateGraphics();
  ```

- Use the *FromImage* method to work with an object that inherits from the *Image* class (such as a bitmap). Using this method, you can alter an existing image or create a new image that can later be used as the source for a *PictureBox* or saved as a bitmap file. The SalesGraphs sample application creates a blank bitmap and draws the graphs to the bitmap's surface using the *FromImage* method of the *Graphics* class. The application then uses a *PictureBox* control, named *graphs*, to display the modified bitmap. The following code shows this method:

```
System.Drawing.Bitmap bmp = new Bitmap(220,220);
Graphics graphicsObject = Graphics.FromImage(bmp);

// ***********************
// Graph drawing functions
⋮
// ***********************

graphs.Image = bmp;
```

- Receive a *Graphics* object reference as part of the *PaintEventArgs* object passed to the *Paint* and *OnPaint* events of the form or control.

```
Protected override void OnPaint(PaintEventArgs e)
{
    Graphics MyGraphicsObject = e.Graphics;
}
```

After you have obtained a reference to a *Graphics* object, you can use it to draw shapes, lines, text, and bitmaps using the following methods:

- ***DrawImage*** Draw an existing image such as a bitmap.
- ***DrawIcon*** Draw an existing icon.
- ***FillRegion*** Fill the interior of a *Region* object (which might be composed of multiple rectangles).
- ***DrawRectangle*** Draw the outline of a rectangle.
- ***FillRectangle*** Draw a filled rectangle.
- ***DrawLine*** Draw a line.
- ***DrawString*** Used to add text to the graphic.
- ***DrawEllipse*** Draw the outline of an ellipse.
- ***FillEllipse*** Draw a filled ellipse.
- ***DrawPolygon*** Draw the outline of a polygon.
- ***FillPolygon*** Draw a filled polygon.

Notice that not all methods of the full .NET Framework are available in the .NET Compact Framework. The following sections describe the methods supported by the .NET Compact Framework and point out any differences from the full .NET Framework.

The *DrawImage* Method

The *DrawImage* method is used to display a bitmap image on the drawing surface of the *Graphics* object. The bitmap can be any bitmap created using the *Bitmap* class. There are four overloads of the *DrawImage* method, allowing you to draw all or part of a bitmap image on the graphics object.

The simplest overload of the *DrawImage* method requires that you specify the image to be displayed and the X and Y coordinates on the drawing surface where the bitmap should be drawn. The following code shows a company logo being displayed in the upper left of the form in the SalesGraphs sample application. The code is placed inside the *OnPaint* event, which we'll cover in the section "The *OnPaint* Method" later in this chapter. Figure 21-1 shows the bitmap displayed on the form.

```
protected override void OnPaint(PaintEventArgs e)
{
    Graphics graphicsObject = e.Graphics;
    graphicsObject.DrawImage(companyLogo, 0, 0);
}
```

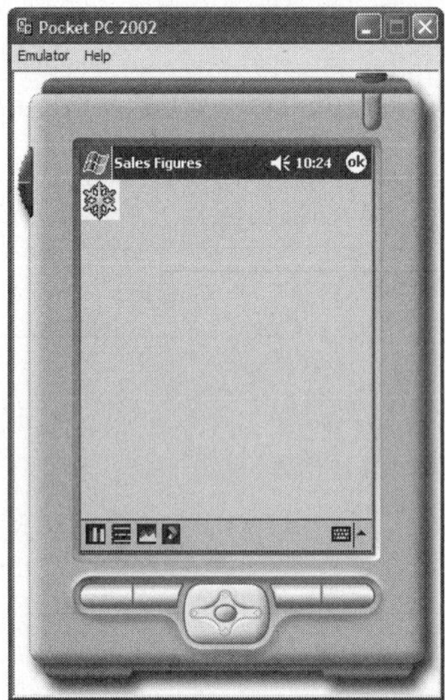

Figure 21-1 Company logo displayed on the form.

To display a portion of a bitmap, you can use an overload that allows you to specify the area of the bitmap to be displayed. For example, the following code uses an overload of the *DrawImage* method that requires you to use a *Rectangle* object to specify the portion of the bitmap to be shown. This overload also requires the unit of measurement for the image to be specified using a *GraphicsUnit* enumeration. The .NET Compact Framework supports only the *GraphicsUnit.Pixel* enumeration, which specifies that all image measurements be in pixels.

```
Bitmap myBMP = new bitmap("myPicture.bmp");
Graphics myGraphicsObject = this.CreateGraphics();
Rectangle imagePortion = new Rectangle(1, 1, 25, 25);
myGraphicsObject.DrawImage(myBMP, 1, 1,
    imagePortion, GraphicsUnit.Pixel);
```

Using a *Rectangle* object, you can also specify the location on the drawing surface where the image should be drawn. When you use this technique, the image portion is scaled to fit the rectangle on the drawing surface. This approach is demonstrated in the following code:

```
Bitmap myBMP = new bitmap("myPicture.bmp");
Graphics myGraphicsObject = this.CreateGraphics();
Rectangle imagePortion = new Rectangle(1, 1, 25, 25);
Rectangle imageToDraw = new Rectangle(1, 1, 50, 50);
myGraphicsObject.DrawImage(myBMP, imageToDraw,
    imagePortion, GraphicsUnit.Pixel);
```

Often, you'll want to change the attributes of an image so that one or more colors appear transparent. For example, you might want to load a bitmap that contains a colored background but want to make the background of the bitmap transparent so that the background color of the drawing surface is seen. Bitmap attributes that control the way the bitmap is displayed can be specified using an *ImageAttributes* object, which is defined in the *System.Drawing.Imaging* namespace. The .NET Compact Framework supports only the *SetColorKey* method of the *ImageAttributes* class, which allows you to set the low and high color values to specify transparency. Any color that is between the low and high color specified will be transparent. In the .NET Compact Framework the low and high color for the *ImageAttributes* object must be the same color because only color-keyed transparency is supported. Pixel-by-pixel blending of source and background colors is not supported in the .NET Compact Framework. If you need to make multiple colors in the image transparent, you must call the *SetColorKey* method once for each transparent color. You can use an overload of the *DrawImage* method to specify image attributes. Note that this overload requires that the location where the bitmap should be drawn be specified as a *Rectangle* object, but that the portion of the image to be drawn must be specified using X and Y coordinates and height and width dimensions. You must also import the *System.Drawing.Imaging* namespace into your code file before using the *ImageAttributes* class.

```
Bitmap myBMP = new bitmap("myPicture.bmp");
Graphics myGraphicsObject = this.CreateGraphics();
ImageAttributes att = new ImageAttributes();
Att.setColorKey(Color.White, Color.White);
Rectangle imageToDraw = new Rectangle(1, 1, 50, 50);
myGraphicsObject.DrawImage(myBMP, imageToDraw, 1, 1, 25, 25,
    GraphicsUnit.Pixel, att);
```

The *DrawIcon* Method

The *DrawIcon* method draws the supplied icon to the drawing surface of the *Graphics* object using the specified coordinates. The following code shows how to display an icon using the *DrawIcon* method of the *Graphics* object. The *Icon* object is created using an icon embedded in the executable file of the application.

```
Graphics MyGraphicsObject = this.CreateGraphics();
Icon MyIcon = new Icon(Assembly.GetExecutingAssembly()
    .GetManifestResourceStream("TestApp.Icon.ico"));

MyGraphicsObject.DrawIcon(MyIcon, 10,10);
```

The *FillRegion* Method

The *FillRegion* method fills the region of the drawing surface defined using the *Region* object. At first glance, the *FillRegion* method seems to produce the same results as the *FillRectangle* method because the *Region* object can be constructed only by using a *Rectangle* object. However, when you take a closer look at the *Region* structure and its methods for redefining the region, you should see that there is potential for creating more complex shapes.

The following code creates the background for the graphs in the SalesGraphs sample application. The code first defines a rectangle area for the whole of the bitmap, named *backgroundRegion*, and then uses the *Exclude* method of the *Region* class to exclude a smaller rectangle from the center of *backgroundRegion*. Figure 21-2 shows the output from this sample code.

```
private void drawBackground(Graphics graphicsObject)
{
    Region backgroundRegion =
        new Region(new Rectangle(0, 0, 220, 220));

    graphicsObject.FillRegion(darkBlueBrush, backgroundRegion);
    backgroundRegion.Exclude(new Rectangle(5, 5, 210, 210));
    graphicsObject.FillRegion(skyBlueBrush, backgroundRegion);
}
```

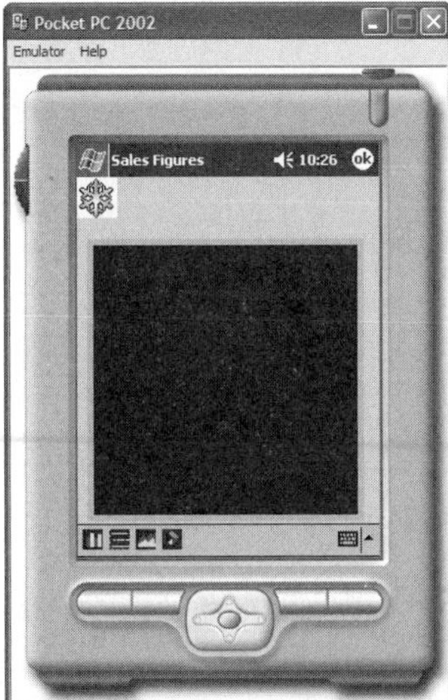

Figure 21-2 Background region for the PictureBox control.

The *DrawRectangle* and *FillRectangle* Methods

The *DrawRectangle* method is used to draw a rectangle to the drawing surface of the *Graphics* object. The *FillRectangle* method draws a filled rectangle to the drawing surface of the *Graphics* object. The only difference between the *DrawRectangle* method and the *FillRectangle* method is that a *Pen* object is specified for the *DrawRectangle* method and a *Brush* object is specified for the *FillRectangle* method. You define the rectangle to be drawn by specifying the coordinates of the upper-left and lower-right corners of the rectangle or by using a *Rectangle* object specifying a pair of coordinates, a width, and a height.

The SalesGraphs sample application uses a custom function named *drawBarGraph* to draw a bar graph of the sales figures for each quarter of the year. The function uses the *DrawRectangle* and *FillRectangle* methods to draw the bars of the bar graph. The sales figures for each quarter are converted into the height of the bar to be drawn on the graph. The *FillRectangle* method is used to draw the bar to the graph in red for the target figures and yellow for the actual figures. The *DrawRectangle* method is used to draw a black border around each bar drawn. The code on the next page shows the *drawBarGraph* function from the SalesGraphs sample application.

```
//=========================================================
// Draw Bar Graph
//
private void drawBarGraph()
{
    Bitmap bmp = new Bitmap(220, 220);
    Graphics graphicsObject = Graphics.FromImage(bmp);

    drawBackground(graphicsObject);
    drawGrid(graphicsObject);
    drawKey(graphicsObject);
    graphTitle.Text = "Bar Graph";

    foreach (DataRow row in salesFigs.Rows)
    {
        decimal salesTarget = Convert.ToDecimal(row["Target"]);
        decimal salesActual = Convert.ToDecimal(row["Actual"]);
        int x = Convert.ToInt32(row["Quarter"]) * 40;
        int y = 180;

        decimal barHeight = ((8000-salesTarget)/1000) * 20 + 40;
        graphicsObject.FillRectangle(redBrush, x,
            (int)barHeight, 20, y - (int)barHeight);

        barHeight = ((8000-salesActual) / 1000) * 20 + 40;
        graphicsObject.FillRectangle(yellowBrush, x + 20,
            (int)barHeight, 20, y - (int)barHeight);
    }

    graphs.Image = bmp;
}
```

The following code draws the grid and axes for the bar and line graphs of the SalesGraphs sample application. The *drawGrid* function uses the *DrawRectangle* method to draw the border that contains the axes for the graphs. The function also uses the *DrawLine* and *DrawString* methods to draw the grid lines for the graph and to label the axes, Q1 to Q4 across the bottom and 1000 to 7000 from bottom to top on the left of the graph. Figure 21-3 shows the output after running this sample code.

```
private void drawGrid(Graphics graphicsObject)
{
    graphicsObject.DrawRectangle(whitePen, 40, 20, 160, 160);
    graphicsObject.DrawString("Sales",
        titleFont, yellowBrush, 8, 15);
    for (int y = 40; y < 180; y += 20)
    {
```

```
            graphicsObject.DrawLine(greyPen, 40, y, 200,y);
            graphicsObject.DrawString(
                Convert.ToString(((y - 40) / 20) + 1) + "000",
                genericFont, whiteBrush, 20, 195 - y);
        }
        graphicsObject.DrawString("Quarters",
            titleFont, yellowBrush, 90, 195);
        for (int x = 80; x < 220; x += 40)
        {
            graphicsObject.DrawLine(greyPen, x, 180, x, 20);
            graphicsObject.DrawString(
                "Q" + Convert.ToString(((x - 80) / 40) + 1),
                genericFont, whiteBrush, x - 30, 185);
        }
    }
```

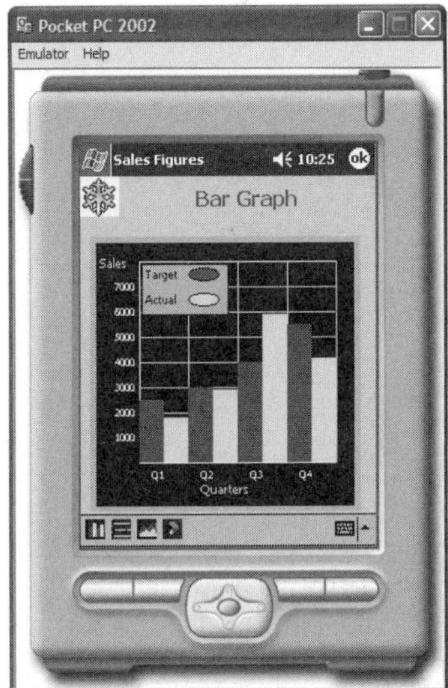

Figure 21-3 Bar graph drawn with the *drawBarGraph* and *drawGrid* functions of the SalesGraphs sample application.

The *DrawLine* Method

To draw a straight line, you use the *DrawLine* method of the *Graphics* object. The line to be drawn is defined using a starting coordinate pair and an ending coordinate pair. *DrawLine* will draw a line, using the specified *Pen* object, between these two sets of coordinates.

In the SalesGraphs sample application, we use the *DrawLine* method to plot the target and actual sales figures onto the graph. The following code listing, of the *drawLineGraph* function, shows how the points to be drawn are calculated from the sales figures for each quarter. The *DrawLine* method is then used to draw a line from the last point plotted to the calculated point for the sales figure for each quarter of the year on the graph. Figure 21-4 shows the output after running this sample code.

```
//==========================================================
// Draw Line Graph
//
private void drawLineGraph()
{
    int ty = 0;
    int ay = 0;
    int sx = 40;
    int asy = 180;
    int tsy = 180;
    int x = 0;
    Bitmap bmp = new Bitmap(220, 220);
    Graphics graphicsObject = Graphics.FromImage(bmp);

    drawBackground(graphicsObject);
    drawGrid(graphicsObject);
    drawKey(graphicsObject);
    graphTitle.Text = "Line Graph";

    foreach (DataRow row in salesFigs.Rows)
    {
        decimal salesTarget = Convert.ToDecimal(row["Target"]);
        decimal salesActual = Convert.ToDecimal(row["Actual"]);
        int quarter = Convert.ToInt32(row["Quarter"]);
        decimal y = ((8000 - salesTarget) / 1000) * 20 + 40;
        ty = (int)y;

        y = ((8000 - salesActual) / 1000) * 20 + 40;
        ay = (int)y;
        x= 20 + (quarter * 40);

        graphicsObject.DrawLine(redPen, sx, tsy, x, ty);
        graphicsObject.DrawLine(yellowPen, sx, asy, x, ay);
        sx = x;
        asy = ay;
        tsy = ty;
    }
```

```
    graphicsObject.DrawLine(redPen, sx, tsy, 200, 180);
    graphicsObject.DrawLine(yellowPen, sx, asy, 200, 180);

    graphs.Image = bmp;
}
```

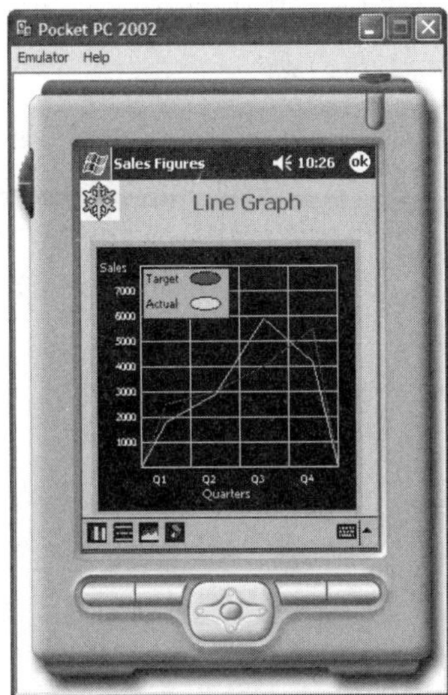

Figure 21-4 Line graph drawn with the *drawLineGraph* function of the SalesGraphs sample application.

The *DrawString* Method

To draw text to the *Graphics* object, you use the *DrawString* method. This method draws the specified string to the drawing surface of the *Graphics* object using the supplied *Font* and *Brush* objects to define the appearance of the text. The text is positioned on the drawing surface using either a pair of coordinates or a *Rectangle* structure. If a *Rectangle* structure is used to call the *DrawString* method and the text to be drawn does not fit within the defined rectangle, the text is truncated. The text will wrap around inside the rectangle if the rectangle has been defined with enough height to allow the text to fit on more than one line. The line height is defined by the size of the font used to draw the text to the drawing surface. See the *drawGrid* function example in the section "The *DrawRectangle* and *FillRectangle* Methods" earlier in this chapter for an example of using the *DrawString* method.

The *DrawEllipse* and *FillEllipse* Methods

The *DrawEllipse* method is used to draw an outline ellipse. A rectangle is used to specify the bounds of the ellipse. As with the *DrawEllipse* method, the *FillEllipse* method draws an ellipse shape to the *Graphics* object's drawing surface. The only difference is that the *FillEllipse* method uses the supplied *Brush* object to fill the interior of the shape.

You specify the rectangle that bounds the ellipse either by specifying a set of coordinates that define the upper-left and lower-right of the rectangle or by using a *Rectangle* structure that uses a pair of coordinates, a width, and a height to define the rectangle the ellipse will be drawn within. The following code shows how the *DrawEllipse* and *FillEllipse* methods are used to draw the graph key in the SalesGraphs sample application:

```
private void drawKey(Graphics graphicsObject)
{
    graphicsObject.FillRectangle(skyBlueBrush, 42, 22, 70, 40);
    graphicsObject.DrawRectangle(blackPen, 42, 22, 70, 40);
    graphicsObject.DrawString("Target", keyFont, blackBrush, 45, 25);
    graphicsObject.FillEllipse(redBrush, 80, 25, 25, 10);
    graphicsObject.DrawEllipse(blackPen, 80, 25, 25, 10);
    graphicsObject.DrawString("Actual", keyFont, blackBrush, 45, 45);
    graphicsObject.FillEllipse(yellowBrush, 80, 45, 25, 10);
    graphicsObject.DrawEllipse(blackPen, 80, 45, 25, 10);
}
```

The *DrawPolygon* and *FillPolygon* Methods

Using the *DrawPolygon* method, you are able to draw any shape that you can define using an array of *Point* objects. The *DrawPolygon* method will always close the shape when it has been drawn; if your points do not return to the original point in the set, the *DrawPolygon* method will draw a line from the last point in the array to the first point in the array. The *DrawPolygon* method can be used to draw a shaped line such as an arc, but you need to retrace your points back to the starting point in your point set. Any number of points can be used to define the polygon shape that you want to draw; the more points you use, the smoother your shape will appear. The SalesGraphs sample application uses the *DrawPolygon* and *FillPolygon* methods to draw the filled line graph and the pie chart.

The SalesGraphs application's *fillLineGraph* function calculates the points to plot on the graph in exactly the same way that the *drawLineGraph* function did, but the *fillLineGraph* function stores the graph points in a *Point* array, which it then uses to draw a polygon using the *FillPolygon* method. The following listing is the code for the *fillLineGraph* function. Figure 21-5 shows the output after running this sample code.

```
//=========================================================
// Draw filled Line Graph
//
private void fillLineGraph()
{
    int[] ty = new int[4];
    int[] ay = new int[4];
    Bitmap bmp = new Bitmap(220, 220);
    Graphics graphicsObject = Graphics.FromImage(bmp);

    drawBackground(graphicsObject);
    drawGrid(graphicsObject);
    graphTitle.Text="Filled Line Graph";

    foreach (DataRow row in salesFigs.Rows)
    {
        decimal salesTarget = Convert.ToDecimal(row["Target"]);
        decimal salesActual = Convert.ToDecimal(row["Actual"]);
        int quarter = Convert.ToInt32(row["Quarter"]);
        decimal  y = ((8000 - salesTarget) / 1000) * 20 + 40;
        ty[quarter - 1] = (int)y;

        y = ((8000 - salesActual) / 1000) * 20 + 40;
        ay[quarter - 1] = (int)y;
    }

    Point[] salesTargetPoints =
        {
            new Point(40, 180),
            new Point(60, ty[0]),
            new Point(100, ty[1]),
            new Point(140, ty[2]),
            new Point(180, ty[3]),
            new Point(200, 180)
        };

    graphicsObject.FillPolygon(redBrush,salesTargetPoints);

    Point[] salesActualPoints =
        {
            new Point(40, 180),
            new Point(60, ay[0]),
            new Point(100, ay[1]),
            new Point(140, ay[2]),
            new Point(180, ay[3]),
            new Point(200, 180)
        };
```

(continued)

```
    graphicsObject.FillPolygon(yellowBrush,salesActualPoints);
    drawKey(graphicsObject);

    graphs.Image = bmp;
}
```

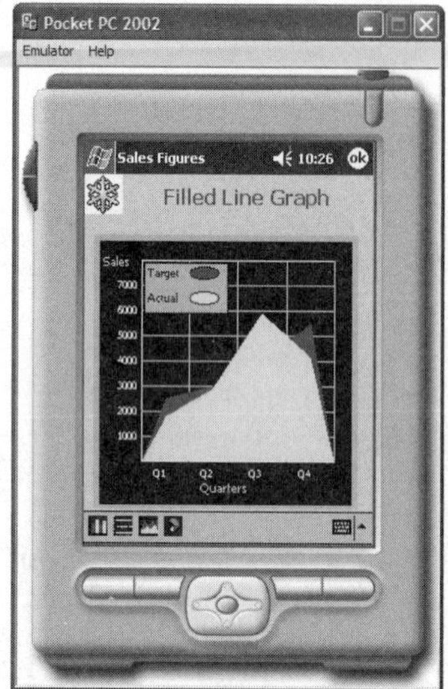

Figure 21-5 Filled line graph drawn with the *fillLineGraph* function of the SalesGraphs application.

The *drawPieChart* function draws a pie chart. Because the *DrawPie* method is not supported in the .NET Compact Framework, two functions were written to draw pie chart segments. The *fillPie* function draws a filled pie chart segment, and the *drawPie* function draws an outlined pie chart segment. These two functions are used by the *drawPieChart* function to draw each segment of the pie chart. The *fillPie* function is used to draw a pie chart segment for each quarter of the year in a different color. The *drawPie* function is used to draw a black border around each pie chart segment.

The following code shows the *drawPieChart*, *drawPie*, and *fillPie* functions. The *drawPieChart* function calls the *drawPie* and *fillPie* functions to draw a pie segment for each quarter of the year. The sales figures for each quarter are converted into a percentage of the total sales, and then they are converted into start and sweep angles to be used by the *drawPie* and *fillPie* functions. The *drawPie* and *fillPie* functions draw a polygon to represent the segment of the pie chart. The start and end points of the polygon are the center of the pie chart. The other points of the polygon are calculated from the start and sweep angles passed to the function. All the points are stored in a *Point* array, and the *Point* array is then used in the *FillPolygon* and *DrawPolygon* methods to draw the polygon for the pie segment. The calculations use both a width and a height parameter to calculate each point of the circle of the pie chart to allow for an elliptical pie chart. Figure 21-6 shows the output after running this sample code.

```
//=======================================================
//Draw Pie Chart
//
private void drawPieChart()
{
    int x = 140;
    int y = 140;
    int width = 120;
    int height = 120;
    double startAngle = 0;
    double sweepAngle = 0;
    double p = 0;
    int i = 0;
    SolidBrush[] solidBrush =
        {
            new SolidBrush(Color.Red),
            new SolidBrush(Color.Blue),
            new SolidBrush(Color.Green),
            new SolidBrush(Color.Yellow)
        };

    double totalActual = 0;

    foreach (DataRow row in salesFigs.Rows)
    {
        totalActual += Convert.ToDouble(row["Actual"]);
    }

    System.Drawing.Bitmap bmp = new Bitmap(220, 220);
    Graphics graphicsObject = Graphics.FromImage(bmp);

    drawBackground(graphicsObject);
    graphTitle.Text = "Pie Chart";

    foreach (DataRow row in salesFigs.Rows)
    {
        p = Convert.ToDouble(row["Actual"]) / totalActual * 100;
        sweepAngle = startAngle + (p * 3.6);

        fillPie(graphicsObject, solidBrush[i++],
            x, y, width, height, startAngle, sweepAngle);
```

(continued)

```
            startAngle = sweepAngle;
        }

        i = 0;
        startAngle = 0;
        foreach (DataRow row in salesFigs.Rows)
        {
            p = Convert.ToDouble(row["Actual"]) / totalActual * 100;
            sweepAngle = startAngle + (p * 3.6);

            drawPie(graphicsObject, blackPen,
                x, y, width, height, startAngle, sweepAngle);
            startAngle = sweepAngle;
        }

        graphicsObject.FillRectangle(skyBlueBrush, 20, 20, 70, 65);
        graphicsObject.DrawRectangle(blackPen, 20, 20, 70, 65);
        for (int t = 0; t < 4; t++)
        {
            graphicsObject.DrawString("Q" + Convert.ToString(t+1),
                keyFont, blackBrush, 25, 25 + (t * 15));
            graphicsObject.FillEllipse(solidBrush[t],
                60, 25 + (t * 15), 25, 10);
            graphicsObject.DrawEllipse(blackPen, 60, 25 + (t * 15), 25, 10);
        }

        graphs.Image = bmp;
    }

    //=======================================================
    //Draw Filled Pie segment
    //
    //    graphicsObject - Drawing surface for pie segment
    //    solidBrush     - Brush to use to draw pie segment
    //    x,y            - Center Coordinates of pie chart
    //    width          - width of pie chart
    //    height         - height of pie chart
    //    startAngle     - Angle of start of pie segment
    //    sweepAngle     - Angle of end of pie segment
    //
    private void fillPie(   Graphics graphicsObject,
                            SolidBrush solidBrush,
                            int x, int y,
                            int width, int height,
                            double startAngle, double sweepAngle)
    {
        double[] xAngle = new double[12];
        double[] yAngle = new double[12];
```

```
    double angleIncrement = (sweepAngle - startAngle) / 10;
    double angle = startAngle;

    for (int i = 0; i <= 10; i++)
    {
        xAngle[i] = x + (Math.Cos(angle * (Math.PI / 180))
                        * (width / 2));
        yAngle[i] = y + (Math.Sin(angle * (Math.PI / 180))
                        * (height / 2));
        angle += angleIncrement;
    }
    xAngle[11] = x + (Math.Cos(sweepAngle * (Math.PI / 180))
                    * (width / 2));
    yAngle[11] = y + (Math.Sin(sweepAngle * (Math.PI / 180))
                    * (height / 2));

    Point[] anglePoints =
        {
            new Point(x, y),
            new Point((int)xAngle[0], (int)yAngle[0]),
            new Point((int)xAngle[1], (int)yAngle[1]),
            new Point((int)xAngle[2], (int)yAngle[2]),
            new Point((int)xAngle[3], (int)yAngle[3]),
            new Point((int)xAngle[4], (int)yAngle[4]),
            new Point((int)xAngle[5], (int)yAngle[5]),
            new Point((int)xAngle[6], (int)yAngle[6]),
            new Point((int)xAngle[7], (int)yAngle[7]),
            new Point((int)xAngle[8], (int)yAngle[8]),
            new Point((int)xAngle[9], (int)yAngle[9]),
            new Point((int)xAngle[10], (int)yAngle[10]),
            new Point((int)xAngle[11], (int)yAngle[11])
        };

    graphicsObject.FillPolygon(solidBrush, anglePoints);
}

//======================================================
//Draw Pie segment
//
//    graphicsObject - Drawing surface for pie segment
//    pen            - Pen to use to draw pie segment
//    x,y            - Center Coordinates of pie chart
//    width          - width of pie chart
//    height         - height of pie chart
//    startAngle     - Angle of start of pie segment
//    sweepAngle     - Angle of end of pie segment
//
private void drawPie(   Graphics graphicsObject,
```

(continued)

```
                              Pen pen,
                              int x, int y,
                              int width, int height,
                              double startAngle, double sweepAngle)
{
    double[] xAngle = new double[12];
    double[] yAngle = new double[12];
    double angleIncrement = (sweepAngle-startAngle)/10;
    double angle = startAngle;

    for (int i=0; i<=10; i++)
    {
        xAngle[i] = x + (Math.Cos(angle*(Math.PI/180))
                    *(width/2));
        yAngle[i] = y + (Math.Sin(angle*(Math.PI/180))
                    *(height/2));
        angle += angleIncrement;
    }
    xAngle[11] = x + (Math.Cos(sweepAngle*(Math.PI/180))
                *(width/2));
    yAngle[11] = y + (Math.Sin(sweepAngle*(Math.PI/180))
                *(height/2));

    Point[] anglePoints =
        {
            new Point(x,y),
            new Point((int)xAngle[0],(int)yAngle[0]),
            new Point((int)xAngle[1],(int)yAngle[1]),
            new Point((int)xAngle[2],(int)yAngle[2]),
            new Point((int)xAngle[3],(int)yAngle[3]),
            new Point((int)xAngle[4],(int)yAngle[4]),
            new Point((int)xAngle[5],(int)yAngle[5]),
            new Point((int)xAngle[6],(int)yAngle[6]),
            new Point((int)xAngle[7],(int)yAngle[7]),
            new Point((int)xAngle[8],(int)yAngle[8]),
            new Point((int)xAngle[9],(int)yAngle[9]),
            new Point((int)xAngle[10],(int)yAngle[10]),
            new Point((int)xAngle[11],(int)yAngle[11])
        };

    graphicsObject.DrawPolygon(pen,anglePoints);
}
```

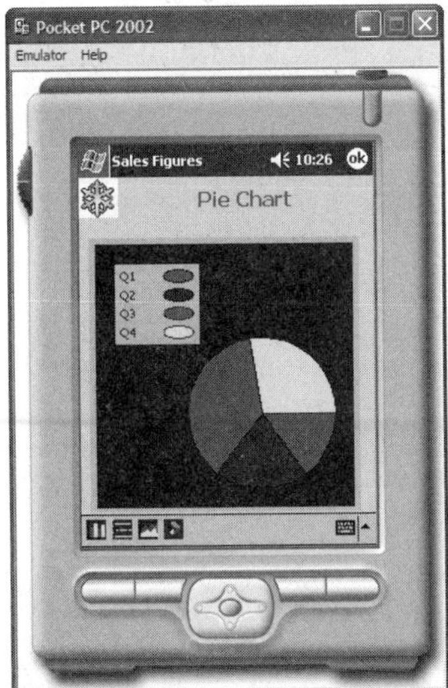

Figure 21-6 Pie chart drawn with the SalesGraphs application's *fillPie*, *drawPie*, and *drawPieChart* functions.

The *OnPaint* Method

The *OnPaint* method for a form or a control is called by the operating system whenever part or all of that form or control is obscured by another form or control and needs to be redrawn. A *Graphics* object is passed as part of the *PaintEventArgs* parameter for the *OnPaint* method. Using this *Graphics* object, you redraw the portion of the display that has been obscured. You use the *ClipRectangle* property, which defines a *Rectangle* structure that represents the area of the display that has been obscured, to test whether you need to redraw your graphics. Testing the *ClipRectangle* before redrawing your graphics reduces unnecessary processing of commands.

> **Note** Note that the *Paint* event handler for a form or a control, such as *Form1_Paint*, has two parameters: an *object* that represents the sender and a *PaintEventArgs* object that encapsulates information about the *Paint* event.

The following code shows how to use the *ClipRectangle* property to test if you need to redraw your custom graphics. This code tests only the upper-left position of the rectangle to be redrawn to see if it is within the area that you have drawn your custom graphics.

```
protected override void OnPaint(PaintEventArgs e)
{
    Graphics MyGraphicsObject = e.Graphics;

    if (e.ClipRectangle.Top < 100 && e.ClipRectangle.Left < 100)
    {
        Pen MyPen = new Pen(Color.Blue);
        MyGraphicsObject.DrawRectangle(MyPen, new Rectangle(10, 10, 50, 20));
        MyGraphicsObject.DrawEllipse(MyPen, 20, 20, 50, 70);
    }
}
```

The SalesGraphs sample application draws its graphs onto a blank bitmap and then uses a *PictureBox* control to display the results. The *PictureBox* control handles the redrawing of the bitmap image it is displaying after it is obscured by another window or menu list. Thus, the SalesGraphs application does not need to worry about redrawing any of the graphs it displays. The only graphic that the SalesGraphs application must redraw, after it has been obscured, is the company logo. The logo is redrawn by drawing the company logo's bitmap in the *OnPaint* method of the main form of the application.

Summary

In this chapter, we covered the basics for producing your own custom graphics. We introduced the *Graphics* object, as well as the objects that you need to draw shapes, text, and images. We examined the different methods for drawing outlines and solid shapes, text, icons, and bitmaps. We discussed the *Region* object and how you can create complex shapes using the *Exclude*, *Intersect*, *Xor*, and *Union* methods of the *Region* object. We discussed the *OnPaint* method and how it should be used to make sure that the graphics you have drawn onto your form or custom control redraw after they have been obscured by another form or custom control.

Throughout this chapter, we used the example of producing graphs of sales figures for a company. The SalesGraphs sample application demonstrated how this could be achieved.

22

Interoperating with Native Code

Not all programming for the .NET Compact Framework involves pure .NET coding with C#, Microsoft Visual Basic .NET, or other Common Language Infrastructure (CLI) languages. From time to time, you'll have to call code written in languages such as C or C++ in the form of Win32 DLLs or COM components. Code written for the .NET Compact Framework is called *managed code*, and code written for other environments is called *unmanaged code*. Perhaps, one day, most programming for Windows CE will use only managed code, but until that time, it's important to consider interoperability with the existing unmanaged code base. This consideration is particularly important because the Windows CE operating system itself is not written as managed code; you will have to interface to the operating system in many situations where the .NET Compact Framework is unable to provide you with certain services. You might also have existing unmanaged code libraries that you want to use without the overhead of rewriting them as managed code.

The full .NET Framework has a comprehensive interoperability layer, which divides into the following two main areas:

- The Platform Invoke (P/Invoke) layer allows managed code to call into Windows DLLs.
- The COM Interoperability layer allows managed code to interact with COM objects with a very high degree of transparency.

The .NET Compact Framework, as might be expected, supports a subset of the full .NET Framework in these areas.

- A significant subset of P/Invoke functionality is supported. Most common interfacing requirements are handled automatically, and several other situations can be handled with a little extra coding.
- A subset of COM interoperability is supported. COM Interop is a powerful feature in the full .NET Framework, but it requires significant memory and processor resources that are not available in the current generation of smart devices. In any case, there are a relatively small number of legacy COM and ActiveX components for the Windows CE environment. To use COM components in the .NET Compact Framework, a developer must write an unmanaged code wrapper using C or C++.

Understanding Managed and Unmanaged Code

As mentioned earlier, code that is designed for execution by the common language runtime (CLR) is called *managed code.* Code that is designed for execution outside the .NET environment is called *unmanaged code*. The terms *managed* and *unmanaged* relate primarily to the ways in which memory is allocated and how access to memory addresses is controlled. A comparison of the key differences between managed and unmanaged code can be found in Table 22-1.

Table 22-1 Managed and Unmanaged Code Comparison

Feature	Managed	Unmanaged
Memory Management	Memory is allocated and deallocated by the .NET runtime. Garbage collection is performed.	Program code manages memory explicitly. No garbage collection is performed unless provided by the language itself.
Processor	Executable files contain Microsoft Intermediate Language (MSIL), which is compiled to native code on demand by the just-in-time (JIT) compiler.	Executable files contain processor-specific code.
Language Interoperability	Intermediate language design gives a high degree of language interoperability.	Languages are interoperable only within limits.

Writing Custom Unmanaged DLLs

This section will give a very brief introduction to writing native code using eMbedded Visual C++ 4. These details will vary from compiler to compiler; if you are using a different C++ compiler, you might need to make changes.

Choosing an eMbedded Visual C++ 4 Project Type

When using eMbedded Visual C++ 4, the developer can use either the WCE Dynamic-Link Library or the WCE MFC AppWizard (dll) project type. The former is used for simple DLL projects, and the latter is used for DLLs that make use of the Microsoft Foundation Classes (MFC) library. For simplicity, we won't consider MFC projects in this chapter; in any case, marshaling between managed and unmanaged code is unaffected by MFC considerations. Figure 22-1 shows the dialog box for creating a Windows CE DLL in eMbedded Visual C++ 4.

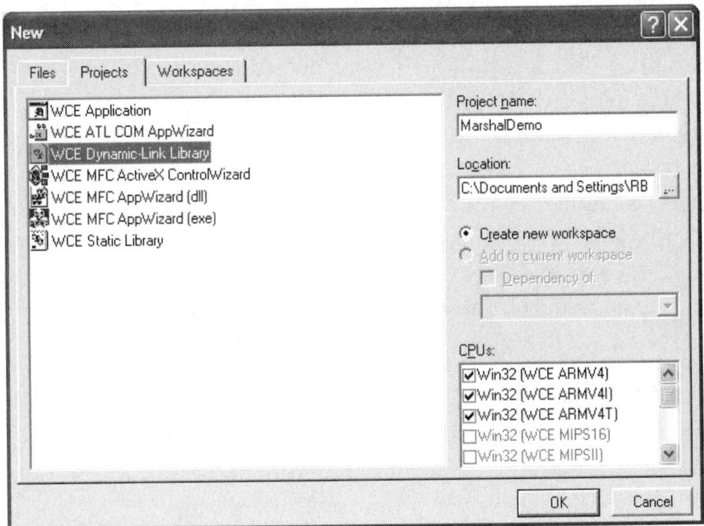

Figure 22-1 Creating a Windows CE DLL in eMbedded Visual C++ 4.

Specifying Processor-Specific Options

There is no equivalent of intermediate language or JIT compilation for the unmanaged code environment. The developer must target a DLL at a specific processor. If you want to support several different platforms, you'll have to provide separate builds of the DLL for each platform. The eMbedded C++ compiler is able to build DLLs for a variety of processors, including ARM, SH, and MIPS processors. Remember, you'll probably also want to build an Intel x86 version of every DLL to run in the emulation environment.

Dealing with C++ Name Mangling

C++ was one of the first languages for the Windows environment that popularized the use of overloaded functions—several functions having the same name but different parameter lists. The earliest object file formats did not support multiple functions having the same name. To circumvent the problem, the compiler generates special names for each C++ function based on the underlying function name and its parameter list, which helps ensure that overloaded C++ functions have distinct names for the linker. This compiler trick (no longer required for more recent languages and link file formats) is often called, rather inelegantly, *name mangling*.

Unfortunately, name mangling can be confusing when a managed code assembly wants to make a call to unmanaged code. Each compiler handles the name mangling differently, and it's awkward for the developer to know the final exported name of an entry point.

In C++, the *extern "C"* declaration can be used in front of a function to force the compiler not to name mangle and to make the name of the function identical to the name as it appears in the source code. For convenience, the Windows header files define an *EXTERN_C* macro that is equivalent to the *extern "C"* declaration when compiling for C++. When compiling for C, where *extern "C"* is not needed, the macro expands to a blank.

Exporting Entry Points

Any function that can be called from outside the DLL must be marked as exported. Each compiler marks exported functions in a different way, but the easiest way to mark an exported function in eMbedded C++ 4 is to prefix the function declaration with *__declspec(dllexport)*.

Using DUMPBIN to Determine Entry Points

The DUMPBIN utility can be used, among other things, to examine the DLL file produced by the C/C++ compiler and linker to make sure that the correct functions are exported with the expected names. To use DUMPBIN in this way, open a Visual Studio .NET command prompt (to ensure that the *PATH* environment variable includes the location of the tool) and enter **DUMPBIN /EXPORTS** followed by the name of the DLL file.

In Figure 22-2, the DUMPBIN utility has been used on the file ComWrapperDll.dll with the /EXPORTS flag. Among other pieces of information displayed in the console window, you can see a list of exported names, including *DOMDocument_CreateObject* and *TransformXml.*

```
Visual Studio .NET Command Prompt

C:\Documents and Settings\RBurbidge\My Documents\Visual Studio Projects\ComWrapp
erDemo>dumpbin /exports ComWrapperDll.dll
Microsoft (R) COFF/PE Dumper Version 7.10.2198
Copyright (C) Microsoft Corporation.  All rights reserved.


Dump of file ComWrapperDll.dll

File Type: DLL

  Section contains the following exports for ComWrapperDll.dll

    00000000 characteristics
    3D2A85B9 time date stamp Tue Jul 09 07:42:01 2002
        0.00 version
           1 ordinal base
           5 number of functions
           5 number of names

    ordinal hint RVA      name

          1    0 00001005 DOMDocument_CreateObject
          2    1 00001019 DOMDocument_LoadXML
          3    2 0000101E DOMDocument_Release
          4    3 00001014 DOMDocument_TransformNode
          5    4 0000100A TransformXml

  Summary

        1000 .data
        1000 .idata
        1000 .rdata
        1000 .reloc
        2000 .text

C:\Documents and Settings\RBurbidge\My Documents\Visual Studio Projects\ComWrapp
erDemo>_
```

Figure 22-2 Using DUMPBIN with the /EXPORTS flag.

Deploying Unmanaged DLLs

eMbedded Visual C++ supports deployment into actual devices through Platform Manager but deploys into its own emulation environment, which is not the same as that used by Visual Studio .NET. To deploy into the Visual Studio .NET emulators, the developer must create the DLL in the Visual C++ environment and manually copy the resulting DLL file into the Visual Studio .NET project.

Ensuring Compatibility with Different Windows CE Versions

By default, eMbedded C++ generates DLL files for Windows CE .NET. (In effect, Windows CE .NET is Windows CE version 4.) Such files will not load in the Pocket PC 3 or Windows CE 3 environment because of the file version. To generate DLLs that are compatible with Pocket PC 3 environments, a developer must use eMbedded Visual C++ 3, which is outside the scope of this discussion, or eMbedded Visual C++ 4 and edit the output binary file.

The command-line tool EDITBIN can be used to change the header information on a DLL to make it compatible with an earlier version of Windows CE.

```
EDITBIN /SUBSYTEM:WINDOWSCE,3.0 /VERSION:3.0 <yourdll.dll>
```

Marking an executable this way will enable it to load in the Pocket PC environment. However, if the DLL tries to invoke features of the Windows CE .NET operating system that are not present in the Pocket PC environment, the results are not defined.

Using P/Invoke

P/Invoke functions and attributes are found in the *System.Runtime.InteropServices* namespace. The .NET Compact Framework supports a useful subset of P/Invoke functions from the full .NET Framework. Most simple unmanaged code functions can be called without difficulty from managed code. Unmanaged code functions with more complex parameter passing requirements will need some additional support in the managed code caller.

Declaring an Unmanaged Code Function

To call a function in unmanaged code using P/Invoke, that function must be exported from a DLL. An exported function is one that can be called across an EXE/DLL or DLL/DLL boundary.

From the .NET point of view, unmanaged code functions are static. They do not operate on instances of objects, and they do not have a value for *this* (C#) or *Me* (Visual Basic .NET).

Declaring Unmanaged Code Functions Using C#

Unmanaged code functions are declared in C# using the *extern* keyword. For example, the following statement declares an unmanaged code function named *NoParameters* that has no parameters and no return value. It is declared as *static* because it is a class method rather than an instance method.

```
extern static void NoParameters();
```

The *extern* keyword indicates that the function's body will not be found within the current assembly. The *extern* keyword is necessary but not sufficient because the developer must also indicate the DLL in which the function can be found at run time. The *DllImport* attribute must be placed before the declaration, as shown here:

```
using System.Runtime.InteropServices;
⋮
[DllImport("MarshalDemoDll.Dll")]
extern static void NoParameters();
```

The string parameter is the name of the DLL in which the unmanaged code can be found.

Declaring Unmanaged Code Functions Using Visual Basic .NET

Visual Basic .NET users can use the *DllImport* attribute, using a similar syntax as for C#, as shown here:

```
<DllImport("MarshalDemoDll.dll")> _
Public Shared Sub NoParameters()
End Sub
```

Alternatively, the *Declare* statement inherited from previous versions of Visual Basic can also be used.

```
Declare Sub NoParameters Lib "MarshalDemoDll.dll" ()
```

Calling the Unmanaged Code Function

The syntax for calling the unmanaged code function is just the same as for calling managed code. In C#, you call the *NoParameters* function declared earlier, as follows:

```
NoParameters();
```

The .NET runtime performs the following actions:

1. It finds the DLL specified in the *DllImport* attribute. If the DLL has not previously been loaded into the current process, it is loaded and initialized. If a full path is specified in the *DllImport* attribute, the DLL is loaded from the specified location. If only a file name is specified, the current directory and path are searched.
2. It locates the entry point by name within the DLL.
3. It makes the function call.
4. When the unmanaged function completes, control is transferred back to the CLR.

Handling Run-Time Errors

Loading the DLL and looking up the entry point are both tasks that are performed at run time, not compile time. The compiler is unable to check either the existence of the DLL or the existence of the entry point within it. If problems occur loading the library or locating the entry point, an exception of type *MissingMethodException* is thrown by P/Invoke. You can handle this exception in the usual way by using a *try/catch* block. For increased robustness, it is strongly advised that you catch the *MissingMethodException* exception whenever you make calls to unmanaged code.

```
try
{
    NoParameters();
}
catch (MissingMethodException)
{
    MessageBox.Show("Error - cannot call method");
    ⋮
}
```

> **Note** The name of the exception suggests that it's thrown only when a method cannot be located within the DLL. However, this exception is also thrown if the DLL doesn't exist, cannot be located, is corrupt, or is inappropriate for the operating system.

Dealing with Special Cases: The *EntryPoint* Property

Generally, the name of the entry point in the C# or Visual Basic .NET calling code matches the function name exported by the DLL. Sometimes, this matching is inconvenient because the name in the DLL might conflict with a reserved word (consider a function named *finally*) or with another identifier in the managed code.

The *EntryPoint* property of the *DllImport* attribute can be used to specify the actual name of the entry point as it appears in the DLL, while the name that appears in the declaration is the name used by the managed code. In the following code fragment, the exported function *NoParameters* appears to the C# code as *Nope*:

```
using System.Runtime.InteropServices;
⋮
```

```
[DllImport("MarshalDemoDll.dll", EntryPoint="NoParameters")]
extern static void Nope();
⋮
Nope();
```

Unmanaged DLLs have exported entry points that are occasionally exported and documented by ordinal number rather than by name. In such cases, the *EntryPoint* property can be used to specify the entry point by means of a string beginning with a hash mark. If, for example, the *NoParameters* function was exported as ordinal 6, the declaration and call would be as follows:

```
[DllImport("MarshalDemoDll.dll", EntryPoint="#6")]
extern static void NoParameters();
⋮
NoParameters();
```

Marshaling Parameters

Because the memory management conventions and data representations of managed and unmanaged code are different, some conversions will occur when the flow of control crosses the managed/unmanaged boundary. Performing these conversions is referred to as *marshaling*. Marshaling of data types is automatic for most simple cases.

The .NET Compact Framework does not have as much support for automatic marshaling as the full .NET Framework. As a result, some situations that the full .NET Framework can handle automatically might require manual marshaling in the .NET Compact Framework environment.

Marshaling Value and Reference Types

Value types are relatively simple to marshal because, as the name suggests, they are simple types whose value can typically be held in a few bytes of storage. Reference types, such as strings, arrays, and structures, are more complex to marshal because they consist of a reference to an area of memory in the .NET Framework's garbage-collected heap.

Value types are passed to the unmanaged code on the stack. Reference types are passed by address: a pointer is passed on the stack, and the pointer contains the address of the marshaled data on the heap.

There is an internal distinction between blittable and non-blittable types. Blittable types have a common representation in managed and unmanaged code, and therefore, they can be marshaled with nothing more complex than a block memory copy. Non-blittable types, in contrast, require more complex marshaling because their managed and unmanaged representations differ.

Passing Value Parameters

Table 22-2 shows common value types in C# and Visual Basic .NET that can be automatically marshaled by value using P/Invoke, and it shows their equivalents in the native Windows CE C/C++ compilers.

Table 22-2 Common Value Types That Can Be Automatically Marshaled

C#	Visual Basic .NET	Native C/C++	Size (Bits)
int	Integer	int	32
short	*Short*	*short*	16
bool	*Boolean*	*BYTE*	8
char	*Char*	*WCHAR*	16

Parameters of these types, when passed by value, are always marshaled automatically. To take a simple example, here is a C/C++ function that takes three integers and calculates their arithmetic mean:

```
EXTERN_C
__declspec(dllexport)
int IntMean3(int a, int b, int c)
{
    return (a + b + c) / 3;
}
```

This routine can be declared and called from C#. The following C# code calculates the mean value of 1, 17, and 6 (that is, 8) and displays it:

```
using System.Runtime.InteropServices;
⋮
[DllImport("MarshalDemoDll.dll")]
extern static int IntMean3(int a, int b, int c);
⋮
int mean = IntMean3(1, 17, 6);
MessageBox.Show(
    String.Format("Mean is {0}", mean)
);
```

> **Note** In the .NET Compact Framework, *long* types (64-bit integer) and floating-point types (*float* and *double*) cannot be marshaled by value into unmanaged code. If you want to pass these values, you should pass them by reference. In the full .NET Framework, there is no such restriction.

Marshaling Alternative Types

The *MarshalAs* attribute of the full .NET Framework is not available in the .NET Compact Framework. Therefore, there is no way to make one type marshal as if it were a different type for the purpose of a particular method call. If type conversions are required before or after a call, they must be performed explicitly in managed code.

Using Directional Attributes

By default, value types are passed by value. However, C# supports the *out* and *ref* keywords that allow values to be passed for output and by reference. In a similar way, Visual Basic .NET supports the *ByRef* keyword. When parameters are passed by reference, the unmanaged code receives a pointer to the data. Because the C/C++ code receives a pointer, it is possible for the routine to modify the data held by the caller. The following example C/C++ routine takes three double parameters, passed by pointer, and returns an arithmetic mean through a fourth parameter, which is also passed as a pointer:

```
EXTERN_C
__declspec(dllexport)
void DoubleMean3(double * a, double * b, double * c, double * mean)
{
    *mean = (*a + *b + *c) / 3.0;
}
```

This routine can be declared and called from C# as follows:

```
[DllImport("MarshalDemoDll.dll")]
extern static void DoubleMean3(
    ref double val1,
    ref double val2,
    ref double val3,
    out double mean);
⋮
double val1 = 1.0;
double val2 = 17.0;
double val3 = 6.0;
double mean;
DoubleMean3(ref val1, ref val2, ref val3, out mean);
MessageBox.Show(
    String.Format("Mean is {0}", mean)
);
```

Because the three input values must have a value before the call, they are passed using *ref*. The mean parameter is output only and needs to have no value before the call, so it is passed as *out*. Note that the values of *long*, *float*, and *double* types *can* be automatically marshaled when passed by reference, unlike when passed by value.

Working with Symbolic Constants and Enumerated Types

Many methods in unmanaged code, particularly in the Windows API, use symbolic constants to define certain constants for parameters. For historical reasons, many of these values are defined as macro symbols in C/C++ using the *#define* directive. When calling these external functions from C#, you can translate the macro symbols into *const* declarations. For example, consider the C/C++ definition of values for the flags for the *sndPlaySound* API call:

```
#define SND_SYNC      0
#define SND_ASYNC     1
#define SND_NODEFAULT 2
#define SND_MEMORY    4
#define SND_LOOP      8
#define SND_NOSTOP    16
```

These could be translated into C# as constants, as shown here:

```
const int SND_SYNC      = 0;
const int SND_ASYNC     = 1;
const int SND_NODEFAULT = 2;
const int SND_MEMORY    = 4;
const int SND_LOOP      = 8;
const int SND_NOSTOP    = 16;
```

Alternatively, you can define the constant values using an enumerated type, as shown in the following code, which is more in keeping with modern programming practice:

```
[Flags]
enum SoundFlags: uint
{
    Sync      = 0x00000000,
    Async     = 0x00000001,
    NoDefault = 0x00000002,
    Memory    = 0x00000004,
    Loop      = 0x00000008,
    NoStop    = 0x00000010
}
```

By default, enumerated types are marshaled as *short* value types. If the developer wants the convenience of enumerated types but wants them to be marshaled into unmanaged code as some other integral type, base the enumeration on that other integral type. The *[Flags]* attribute is commonly used to indicate that values in the enumerated type can be combined as bit fields.

Processing Reference Types

Processing reference types is generally more complex than processing value types. There are three key issues:

- Reference types are stored as pointers into the heap. This is not a major issue because C and C++ can deal with pointer types.
- The CLR memory management system might move blocks of memory around the heap. This is generally transparent to CLR-compatible languages but is not generally the way in which C/C++ behaves.
- The CLR might store data internally in a way that is not directly compatible with C/C++ data types.

Passing Arrays

C/C++ handles array parameters as pointers to a contiguous region of memory. All array elements are addressed as offsets from this pointer, beginning with zero. The .NET marshaler ensures that this format is adhered to when calling unmanaged code. In this C/C++ example routine, an array is searched to locate the smallest value:

```
EXTERN_C
__declspec(dllexport)
void int MinArray(int * pData, int length)
{
    if (length < 1)
        return -1; // Should not happen really

    int minData = pData[0];
    int pos;

    for (pos = 1; pos < length; ++pos)
        if (pData[pos] < minData)
            minData = pData[pos];

    return minData;
}
```

The following code declares the routine and calls it from C#:

```
[DllImport("MarshalDemoDll.dll")]
extern static int MinIntArray(int[] pData, int length);
⋮
```

```
int[] sampleData = new int[] { 8, 6, 1963 };
int result = MinIntArray(sampleData, sampleData.Length);
MessageBox.Show(
    String.Format("Smallest integer is {0}", result)
);
```

Passing *String* and *StringBuilder* Variables

The CLR *String* and *StringBuilder* classes have similar marshaling behavior.

- Both kinds of string are marshaled as *Unicode* character arrays to which the address of the first character is passed. Each character appears in native C/C++ code as a *WCHAR* (wide character) value.
- To conform with generally accepted C/C++ practice, the marshaling runtime adds a null terminating word (*L'\0'*) at the end of a string so that traditional C string processing can be used.

Both the *String* and *StringBuilder* classes can be used to pass character data into unmanaged code. However, strings in the .NET environment are immutable by design and therefore cannot be changed. If a developer wants the unmanaged code to modify a string, the *StringBuilder* type should be used. Any changes made to the contents of a *StringBuilder* parameter are marshaled back into the .NET managed code framework.

The *StringBuilder* class is, therefore, particularly useful when a fixed-length character buffer must be passed into unmanaged code. When the managed code initializes a *StringBuilder* buffer to a capacity of *N* characters, the marshaler provides a buffer of size (*N* + 1) characters because the unmanaged string has a null terminator. Many unmanaged code functions require a separate parameter to denote the maximum size of the buffer in a *StringBuilder* variable—the *Capacity* property is very useful for this purpose.

> **Tip** Always let the .NET Compact Framework allocate the space for the *StringBuilder* object, to take advantage of .NET garbage collection. The unmanaged code might want to modify a string's length. The developer should ensure that the string passed into the unmanaged code is sufficiently long to hold any desired result string. In principle, you could allocate memory in the unmanaged heap by using C/C++ memory management functions such as *malloc* and *free* or *new* and *delete*. However, unmanaged code memory management is considerably more complex because there is no garbage collection, and accordingly, it is not recommended.

As an example, the following unmanaged function takes a null-terminated string as input and reverses the characters in the string, placing the result into a presupplied string buffer:

```
EXTERN_C __declspec(dllexport)
void ReverseString(WCHAR * pStr, WCHAR * pStrRev)
{
    size_t len = wcslen(pStr);
    size_t k;
    for (k = 0; k < len; ++k)
    {
        pStrRev[k] = pStr[len - 1 - k];
    }
    pStrRev[len] = '\0';
}
```

This function can be declared and used in C# as follows:

```
[DllImport("MarshalDemoDll.dll")]
extern static void ReverseString(string instr, StringBuilder outstr);
:
string sIn = "Hello, World";
StringBuilder sOut = new StringBuilder(sIn.Length);
ReverseString(sIn, sOut);
MessageBox.Show(
    String.Format("'{0}' reversed is '{1}'",
        sIn,
        sOut)
);
```

Notice that in this example, the first parameter is passed as a *String*, and the second as a *StringBuilder*. The first parameter could have been passed as either type, but the second parameter must be passed as a *StringBuilder* because it contains data that the unmanaged code will modify.

Passing Structures and Classes

Structure and class variables can be marshaled to and from managed code. The .NET Compact Framework supports automatic marshaling only for structures and classes that contain simple value types. All fields are laid out sequentially in memory in the same order as they appear in the structure or class definition, with no packing bytes (that is, all elements lie on byte boundaries and are not aligned in any way for efficiency). Both structures and classes appear in native code as pointers to a C/C++ struct, despite the internal differences within .NET regarding their memory management. Whether stored on the stack or on the heap, they still appear as pointers to unmanaged code.

Here is a C/C++ structure that defines coordinates in terms of two double-precision values, and a routine for calculating the distance between two such coordinates:

```
struct coord
{
    double x;
    double y;
};

EXTERN_C
__declspec(dllexport)
void DistanceBetween(coord * p1, coord * p2, double * pDistance)
{
    double dx = p1->x - p2->x;
    double dy = p1->y - p2->y;
    *pDistance = sqrt(dx*dx + dy*dy);
}
```

This unmanaged code can be called from C# as follows:

```
public struct Coord
{
    public double x;
    public double y;
    public Coord(double x, double y)
    {
        this.x = x;
        this.y = y;
    }
};
⋮
[DllImport("MarshalDemoDll.dll")]
extern static void DistanceBetween(
    ref Coord p1,
    ref Coord p2,
    out double result);
⋮
Coord c1 = new Coord(1.0, 1.0);
Coord c2 = new Coord(4.0, 5.0);
double resultDistance;
try
{
    DistanceBetween(ref c1, ref c2, out resultDistance);
}
catch(Exception ex)
{
    MessageBox.Show(ex.Message, "Exception calling DistanceBetween");
```

```
    resultDistance = double.NaN;
}
MessageBox.Show(
    String.Format("Distance is {0}", resultDistance)
);
```

Objects in the managed heap can be moved around in memory at any time, so their physical addresses might change without notice. P/Invoke automatically pins down managed memory passed as a reference for the lifetime of each method call, so any pointers passed to unmanaged code will be valid for that one call. Bear in mind that there is no guarantee that the object will not subsequently be moved in memory and therefore might have a different address on subsequent calls.

There is no marshaling of a class's method entry points, only data. It's not possible for unmanaged code to invoke a method of a class to which it had been passed a pointer.

The *StructLayout* attribute from the full .NET Framework is not supported, so it's not possible to control the offset of a field within the structure nor to create union types (where one member of a structure or class is forced to overlay another in memory).

Marshaling More Complex Structures

In the .NET Compact Framework, a structure can be automatically marshaled only if it contains value types and no reference types. A structure that contains members that are reference types will *not* be automatically marshaled; any attempt to do so will raise a *NotSupportedException* at the point of call.

Consider the following C# structure:

```
public struct ThreeName
{
    public string FirstName;
    public string MiddleName;
    public string LastName;
    public ThreeName(string first, string middle, string last)
    {
        FirstName  = first;
        MiddleName = middle;
        LastName   = last;
    }
};
```

This structure contains three reference types, so it cannot be automatically marshaled in the .NET Compact Framework.

Now consider the following C/C++ code, which defines a structure containing three strings and a function to display the data in that structure:

```
struct ThreeName
{
    WCHAR * FirstName;
    WCHAR * MiddleName;
    WCHAR * LastName;
};
:
EXTERN_C __declspec(dllexport)
void DisplayName(ThreeName * pName)
{
    if (pName)
    {
        if (pName->FirstName)
            ::MessageBox(NULL, pName->FirstName,  L"First name",  MB_OK);
        if (pName->MiddleName)
            ::MessageBox(NULL, pName->MiddleName, L"Middle name", MB_OK);
        if (pName->LastName)
            ::MessageBox(NULL, pName->LastName,   L"Last name",   MB_OK);
    }
}
```

The two versions of the *ThreeName* structure are not equivalent. The C# structure contains references to *String* values on the CLR heap. The C/C++ structure contains pointers to null-terminated strings in unmanaged memory. Manual marshaling is therefore needed.

A C# version of the unmanaged structure can be declared as follows:

```
unsafe public struct ThreeNameUnmanaged
{
    public char * FirstName;
    public char * MiddleName;
    public char * LastName;
};
```

C# supports pointer types (in this case, *char **) only in contexts defined with the *unsafe* keyword and only when the Allow Unsafe Code Blocks option is in force.

The entry point for *DisplayName* is declared in C# using this structure definition:

```
[DllImport("MarshalDemoDll.dll")]
extern static void DisplayName(ref ThreeNameUnmanaged name);
```

To call the function, manual marshaling must be carried out between the managed and unmanaged data structures.

```
// Managed data
ThreeName person = new ThreeName("Robert", "Andrew", "Burbidge");
// Marshal to unmanaged data representation
char [] firstBuffer  = MarshalHelper(person.FirstName);
char [] middleBuffer = MarshalHelper(person.MiddleName);
char [] lastBuffer   = MarshalHelper(person.LastName);
```

When called in contexts such as this, the *String* references are *not* converted into null-terminated strings. The *MarshalHelper* function takes the CLR string, adds a null-terminating character, and returns the new string as a character array. This conversion enables the developer to pass the address of the first element of the array to the unmanaged code.

```
// Manually marshal a CLR string
// into a null-terminated character array
private char[] MarshalHelper(string s)
{
s = s + "\0";
return s.ToCharArray();
}
```

To obtain the address of the three character arrays, the *fixed* keyword must be used. The *fixed* statement sets a pointer to a managed variable and pins that variable during the execution of statement. The C# compiler will allow setting a pointer to a managed variable only in a *fixed* statement.

The following code pins the character buffers so that they will not be moved by the CLR, obtains addresses for the start of the three character buffers, and places the addresses into the unmanaged structure. The *fixed* keyword requires an *unsafe* context.

```
ThreeNameUnmanaged unmanagedPerson = new ThreeNameUnmanaged();
unsafe
{
    fixed (char *
        pFirst  = &firstBuffer[0],
        pMiddle = &middleBuffer[0],
        pLast   = &lastBuffer[0])
    {
        unmanagedPerson.FirstName  = pFirst;
        unmanagedPerson.MiddleName = pMiddle;
        unmanagedPerson.LastName   = pLast;

        // Having set up the unmanaged structure,
        // it can now be used in the call.

        DisplayName(ref unmanagedPerson);
    }
}
```

> **Tip** In the preceding example, the *unsafe* keyword could have been added to the method declaration and omitted from the body of the function. However, since not all the code in this function is inherently *unsafe*, it makes more sense to localize the *unsafe* sections of code wherever possible to prevent the likelihood of errors.

The C# compiler will not compile *unsafe* code unless the appropriate compiler options have been set on a per-project basis. Figure 22-3 shows the Build page of the Project Property Pages dialog box, where the Allow Unsafe Code Blocks option can be set.

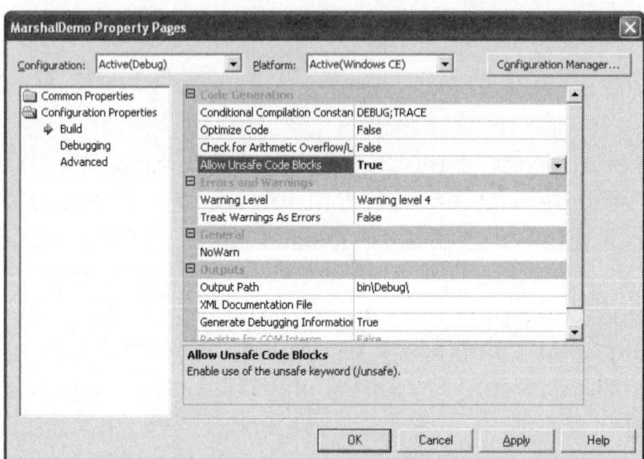

Figure 22-3 Allowing *unsafe* code.

Calling Conventions

The .NET Compact Framework supports only the *WINAPI* calling convention, which is defined to be the calling convention used by the Windows API on a particular platform. Fortunately, this calling convention, as well as being used extensively by the Windows CE API, is used in many other Windows CE DLLs. If a developer needs to call code that was written using a different calling convention, that developer will have to do so through a wrapper function written in C/C++ that itself is called using the *WINAPI* calling convention.

> **Note** In desktop versions of Windows, the *WINAPI* calling convention is the same as *stdcall*, but in Windows CE, the *WINAPI* calling convention is equivalent to *cdecl*.

Using Callbacks and Delegates

The .NET Compact Framework does not support any callbacks from unmanaged code into managed code. Certain Windows API functions that require callbacks cannot be used directly, and a developer cannot create delegates in managed code and call the delegates from unmanaged code. This problem can be worked around by using unmanaged wrapper code in C/C++ or by using the MessageWindow component, as detailed in the section "Understanding the MessageWindow Component" later in this chapter.

Marshaling *DateTime* Objects

The .NET Compact Framework has no support for marshaling of *DateTime* types. To pass dates and times between managed and unmanaged code, the developer has a number of possible techniques.

- Pass the individual date and time components as simple types (day, hour, minute, and so on).
- Create a custom structure for the purpose, and pass the components of the date and time as simple types within that structure.
- Normalize the *DateTime* value into some kind of simple value, such as elapsed seconds since a reference time.

Calling the Windows CE API

To call functions in the Windows CE API, you use the same P/Invoke mechanisms as have been discussed thus far. The key difference is that the Windows CE API is packaged in prewritten DLL files, rather than custom files created using tools such as eMbedded Visual C++.

The following example shows how a simple Windows CE API call can be made from managed code. The *MessageBeep* API function accepts a single 32-bit integer (for our purposes, this value can always be zero) and returns no value to the caller. As the name suggests, it sounds a short beep using the Windows CE sound system. This API function is found in the coredll.dll library.

> **Tip** Much of the Windows CE API is found in the coredll.dll library. Developers who are moving from desktop versions of Windows might want to note that this DLL contains broadly equivalent functionality to kernel32.dll, gdi32.dll, and user32.dll found in the desktop versions of Windows.

The API function is declared in C# as follows:

```
using System.Runtime.InteropServices;
⋮
[DllImport("coredll.dll")] extern static void MessageBeep(uint BeepType);
```

This code can be called just as if it were a managed code function, as shown here:

```
MessageBeep(0);
```

For a more complex example, consider the API function *sndPlaySound*, which plays a sampled sound file (.wav extension). This function takes two parameters, the first of which is a null-terminated string holding the file name of the sound file, and the second of which is one or more flags that control the way the sound is played. The return value of the function is a *BOOL* that is *FALSE* if problems were detected and *TRUE* if the function was successful.

The flags can be defined as an enumerated type that supports bitwise OR operations.

```
[Flags]
enum SoundFlags
{
    Sync      = 0x00000000,
    Async     = 0x00000001,
    NoDefault = 0x00000002,
    Memory    = 0x00000004,
    Loop      = 0x00000008,
    NoStop    = 0x00000010
}
```

Having declared the flags, it is possible to declare the entry point itself.

```
[DllImport("coredll.dll", EntryPoint="sndPlaySoundW")]
extern static int SndPlaySound(string soundFile, SoundFlags flags);
```

The return value for *SndPlaySound* is actually *int*, not *bool*. The *BOOL* type used in the standard Windows API is actually an integer.

> **Note** The actual entry point name for this function is *sndPlaySoundW*. The Windows API supports two versions of each API call that processes strings, one for 8-bit character sets (ANSI) and one for 16-bit character sets (Unicode). The names of functions that accept strings are appended with either an *A* (for ANSI) or a *W* (for wide) depending on the version. Windows CE inherits this convention of the Win32 API. Functions that don't process character strings have no suffix. Windows CE only supports the Unicode character set. The *W* suffix is merely a convention observed by the Windows API. When interfacing to third-party libraries, the convention might not apply; consult your documentation.
>
> When compiling for the .NET Compact Framework, Visual Basic does not support the *Ansi*, *Unicode*, or *Auto* modifiers for the *Declare* statement.

With these declarations, it is possible to call the unmanaged code function.

```
res = SndPlaySound(
   "GlassShatter.wav",
    SoundFlags.Sync | SoundFlags.NoDefault);
if(res == 0)
    MessageBox.Show("Problem playing sound");
```

Retrieving Windows Error Codes

A Windows CE API call (or other unmanaged code) might call the *SetLastError* function, which sets the "last error code" for the current thread. Windows stores this error code on a per-thread basis, and it can be retrieved by an application using *GetLastError*. This function is typically used to pass error information back to the caller.

By default, P/Invoke disregards these error codes. If you need to retrieve the Win32 error code from within managed code, do *not* make a direct call to *GetLastError*. The CLR might have made other calls to APIs that change the error value. To make P/Invoke remember the error code for a given unmanaged method, set the *SetLastError* attribute to *true* in the *DllImport* attribute for that method.

```
[DllImport("coredll.dll", SetLastError = true, EntryPoint="sndPlaySoundW")]
extern static int SndPlaySound(string soundFile, SoundFlags flags);
```

When the method call returns to the .NET Compact Framework, the error code will be recorded and can be retrieved using the *GetLastWin32Error* method of the *Marshal* class.

```
if (SndPlaySound(sound, flags) == 0)
{
    int errCode = Marshal.GetLastWin32Error();
    MessageBox.Show("Error " + errCode);
}
```

You might want to throw an exception from managed code.

```
if (SndPlaySound(sound, flags) == 0)
{
    string errMsg = String.Format(
        "SndPlaySound returned error {0}",
        Marshal.GetLastWin32Error());
    throw new ApplicationException(errMsg);
}
```

Understanding the MessageWindow Component

Many Windows API features use run-time objects found in the Windows environment, such as windows, display contexts, and tasks. Windows maintains internal data structures (in unmanaged code, of course) for these objects and dispenses run-time handles to them when they are created. The controls in the full .NET Framework provide access to some of these handles through standard properties such as *hWnd*. The .NET Compact Framework does not provide these properties. Another limitation of P/Invoke for the .NET Compact Framework is that delegate types cannot be marshaled into unmanaged code. Consequently, it is not possible for unmanaged code to call back directly to functions in managed code.

The MessageWindow component, supplied as part of the .NET Compact Framework, allows some of these limitations to be worked around. It provides access to window handles and a simple callback mechanism based on Windows messaging.

For readers who are unfamiliar with the low-level Windows API, the following review notes might be helpful:

- Forms and controls are run-time instances of window objects.
- Each window has a unique run-time instance handle of type *HWND*.

- Messages are sent to windows by the operating system (for example, in response to external events such as mouse clicks) or by other user-written code.
- Messages can be handled immediately by the window or be placed on a queue for sequential processing.
- Each window has a message processing function that handles incoming messages.
- Some messages have predefined meanings assigned by the operating system designers, and others are free for developers to use however they want.
- Developers might want to think of forms and controls as instances of classes. The Windows messages are similar in concept to virtual method calls.

> **Note** Experienced developers will recognize that the overview of Windows messaging has been slightly simplified. Those who are interested in pursuing the subject further can consult the online documentation for the platform SDK, which is part of Visual Studio .NET. Another thorough reference to Windows and Windows messaging is Charles Petzold's book *Programming Windows*, Fifth Edition, Microsoft Press, 2002.

The *MessageWindow* class is a managed code interface to a simple window and its message passing mechanism.

Using *MessageWindow* and Sending Messages

In the following example, the *MessageWindow* class will be used to send and receive a Windows message from within managed code. *MessageWindow* is in the *Microsoft.WindowsCE.Forms* namespace. The assembly containing this component is not referenced by default in a standard Smart Device Application project, so it must be added manually. Figure 22-4 shows the Microsoft.WindowsCE.Forms assembly selected in the Add Reference dialog box.

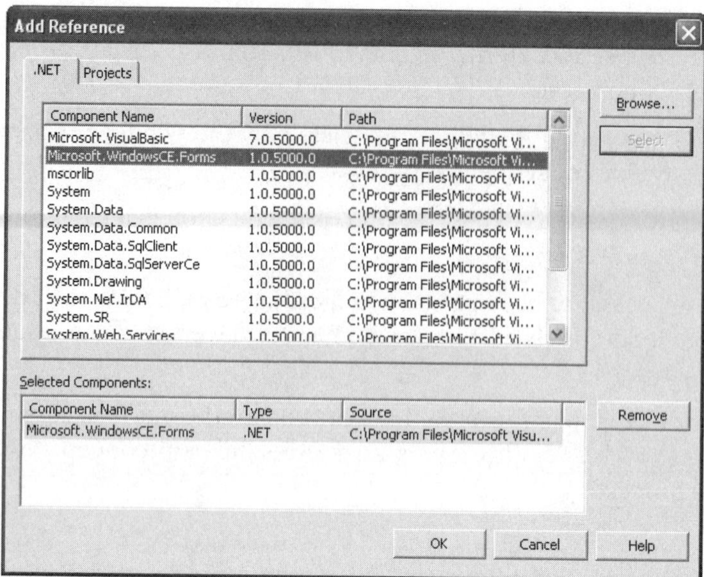

Figure 22-4 Adding a reference to the Microsoft.WindowsCE.Forms assembly.

In the following code listing, the main window is of class *MessageWindowDemoForm*, and the class derived from *MessageWindow* is *CatchCallback*. This listing is part of the MessageWindowDemo application, which you'll find included with this book's sample files.

CatchCallback.cs

```
using System;
using System.Windows.Forms;
using Microsoft.WindowsCE.Forms;

namespace MessageWindowDemo
{
    public class CatchCallback : MessageWindow
    {
        public const int WM_USER = 0x400;
        public const int WM_CALLBACK_MESSAGE = WM_USER+0;

        private MessageWindowDemoForm container;

        public CatchCallback(MessageWindowDemoForm container)
        {
            this.container = container;
        }
```

(continued)

CatchCallback.cs *(continued)*

```
        protected override void WndProc(ref Message msg)
        {
            switch(msg.Msg)
            {
                case WM_CALLBACK_MESSAGE:
                    container.Callback();
                    break;
            }
            base.WndProc(ref msg);
        }
    }
}
```

All messages in windows have an associated number, and the constant *WM_USER*, taken from the Windows SDK, is the number of the first message that is available for user-defined messages. The constant *WM_CALLBACK_MESSAGE* is defined using *WM_USER* as a base value. *WM_CALLBACK_MESSAGE* will be the number of the message used in the callback process.

When the new class is initialized, a reference to the containing form (an instance of *MessageWindowDemoForm*) is stored in the *container* private variable. This variable will be used later to action the callback into the main form instance.

The new class must override *WndProc* to handle any messages of interest. The *Message* class is a .NET Compact Framework representation of a Windows API message. Table 22-3 describes the members of the *Message* class.

Table 22-3 *Message* Class Members

Member	Type	Purpose
Hwnd	IntPtr	Handle of the window to which the message is to be sent
Msg	*Integer*	Message number
WParam	*IntPtr*	First parameter
LParam	*IntPtr*	Second parameter
Result	*IntPtr*	Result of message

In the *CatchCallback* class, only the *WM_CALLBACK_MESSAGE* is of interest, and the *case* statement simply calls the *Callback* method of the container form. Having processed any messages that are of interest to the control, the new class calls the base class version of *WndProc*, which is essential because the application might behave erratically if certain internal messages are not correctly processed.

In the following code, from the MessageWindowDemo application, the form creates an instance of the *CatchCallback* class, passing a reference to *this* as part of the constructor. The *Callback* method displays a message to indicate that it has been called.

```
using System;
⋮
using Microsoft.WindowsCE.Forms;
using System.Runtime.InteropServices;

namespace MessageWindowDemo
{
    public class MessageWindowDemoForm : System.Windows.Forms.Form
    {
        ⋮
        private CatchCallback msgWinCall;

        public MessageWindowDemoForm()
        {
            ⋮
            msgWinCall = new CatchCallback(this);
        }
        ⋮
        // Called by the message handler in CatchCallback
        public void Callback()
        {
            MessageBox.Show("Callback");
        }
        ⋮
```

The following code demonstrates how messages can be passed to the message control while still staying within managed code:

```
Message msg = Message.Create(
    msgWinCall.Hwnd,
    CatchCallback.WM_CALLBACK_MESSAGE,
    IntPtr.Zero,
    IntPtr.Zero);
MessageWindow.SendMessage(ref msg);
```

In this fragment, a new *Message* object is created using *Message.Create*. After creating the message, the *MessageWindow.SendMessage* method is used to send the message to the instance of *CatchCallback*, which will, in turn, invoke the *WndProc* method with a *msg.Msg* value of *WM_CALLBACK_MESSAGE*. Finally the main form's *Callback* method will be invoked. For simplicity, no additional parameters or return values are used, so zero values are provided for *WParam* and *LParam*. The flow of control is summarized in Figure 22-5.

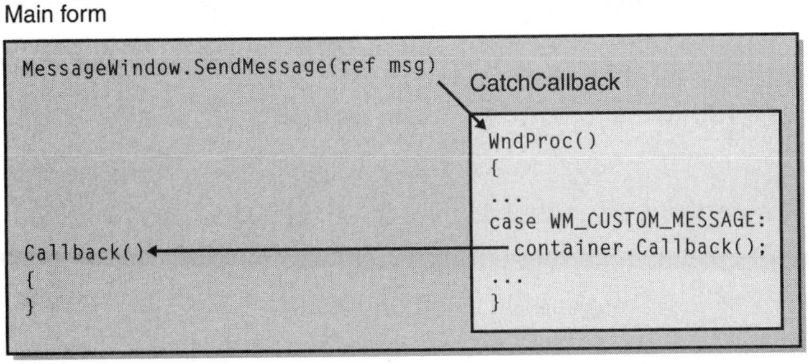

Main form

```
MessageWindow.SendMessage(ref msg)
                                   CatchCallback
                                   WndProc()
                                   {
                                   ...
                                   case WM_CUSTOM_MESSAGE:
Callback() <------------------------- container.Callback();
{                                  ...
}                                  }
```

Figure 22-5 Sending and receiving a custom message.

> **Note** *SendMessage* calls the *WndProc* of the appropriate window directly, rather like a method call. The alternative, *PostMessage*, places the message on the application queue for later processing. Most common message processing is done using *SendMessage*.

Calling from Unmanaged Code to Managed Code

So far, what we've seen is simply a complex way of calling the *Callback* method. However, the real power of this technique is that there is an exact equivalent of *SendMessage* in the Windows API. Consider the following unmanaged C++ code, from the MessageWindowDemoDll project, which you'll find included with this book's sample files.

MessageWindowDemoDll.cpp

```
#include "stdafx.h"

BOOL APIENTRY DllMain( HANDLE hModule,
                       DWORD  ul_reason_for_call,
                       LPVOID lpReserved )
{
    return TRUE;
}

const int WM_CUSTOM_MESSAGE = WM_USER+0;
```

(continued)

MessageWindowDemoDll.cpp *(continued)*

```
EXTERN_C _declspec(dllexport)
void CallbackDemo(HWND hWnd)
{
    ::MessageBox(NULL, L"In unmanaged code. Press OK to send", L"", MB_OK);
    ::SendMessage(hWnd, WM_CUSTOM_MESSAGE, 0, 0);
    ::MessageBox(NULL, L"Back in unmanaged code", L"", MB_OK);
}
```

Given this unmanaged code DLL, the following code can be added to the main .NET Compact Framework application, MessageWindowDemoForm, to invoke it:

```
[DllImport("MessageWindowDemoDll.dll")]
extern private static void CallbackDemo(IntPtr hWnd);
⋮
CallbackDemo(msgWinCall.Hwnd);
```

When the unmanaged code is executed, the *::SendMessage* API call will send a *WM_CUSTOM_MESSAGE* to the *CatchCallback* instance. Although more complex than the use of delegate types, this technique allows unmanaged code to call into managed code as required. The flow of control is summarized in Figure 22-6.

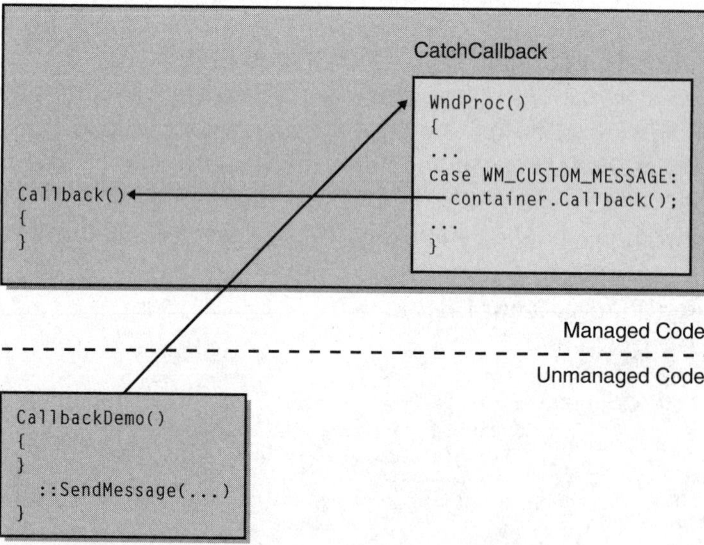

Figure 22-6 Using unmanaged code to send a message.

The technique also allows for arbitrary parameter passing through window messages. If parameter information can be placed in integers, integral values can be passed for *WParam* and *LParam*. If the parameter and result information is more complex, the *WParam* and *LParam* fields can represent pointers to unmanaged memory blocks. In general, manual marshaling techniques must be used to pass more complex parameters and results. For more information, see the appropriate sections of this chapter.

Intercepting Messages Using MessageWindow

In the ActDeact example, the MessageWindow component is used to intercept messages that are passed to the main window of an application. This technique is of particular interest to Pocket PC developers because without it, there is no way to intercept the *WM_ACTIVATE* messages that are sent from Windows to a top-level window when it moves from the background to the foreground and back again, or when the window is minimized and reactivated. Pocket PC applications should release resources, whenever possible, when they are placed in the background.

In this example, the Windows CE API function *SetWindowLong* is used to replace the standard message-processing function of the application's top-level window with a custom function. The technique is a primitive form of inheritance supported by the Windows CE API. Replacing the message-processing function allows all messages to the top-level window to be intercepted. The application traps the *WM_ACTIVATE* message. In the ActDeact sample application included with this book's sample files, the only action taken is to update the display to show that the messages have been processed.

The following C++ code implements the functions that call the Win32 CE API to trap the *WM_ACTIVATE* message. Notice that the code uses the *FindWindow* function to get the window handle of the main form of the application, so for this technique to work, the main window of your application must have a unique name from that of any other application running on the device.

ActDeact.cpp

```
// ActDeact. cpp : Defines the entry point for the DLL application.
//

#include "stdafx.h"
#include "ActDeact.h"

BOOL APIENTRY DllMain( HANDLE hModule,
```

(continued)

ActDeact.cpp *(continued)*

```
                         DWORD  ul_reason_for_call,
                         LPVOID lpReserved
                       )
{
    switch (ul_reason_for_call)
    {
        case DLL_PROCESS_ATTACH:
        case DLL_THREAD_ATTACH:
        case DLL_THREAD_DETACH:
        case DLL_PROCESS_DETACH:
            break;
    }
    return TRUE;
}


WNDPROC wpOrigFormProc;
HWND hwndForm;
HWND hwndMessageWindow;


// This exported function sub classes the Form window
// to substitute an alternative window proc. This allows
// us to discover when WM_ACTIVATE messages are sent to
// the form, so we can raise events in the .NET Compact Framework
// form class.
EXTERN_C
ACTDEACT_API int fnActDeactInit(LPCTSTR lpWindowName, HWND hwndMsgWindow)
{
    // Retrieve the handle to the application Form
    hwndForm = FindWindow( NULL, lpWindowName);
    if (hwndForm == 0) return -1;

    // Save the window handle of the MessageWindow in the managed code
    hwndMessageWindow = hwndMsgWindow;

    // Subclass the Form control
    wpOrigFormProc = (WNDPROC) SetWindowLong(hwndForm,
        GWL_WNDPROC, (LONG) FormSubclassProc);

    return 0;
}

// This exported function reverses the sub classing of the Form
EXTERN_C
ACTDEACT_API void fnActDeactDestroy(void)
```

(continued)

ActDeact.cpp *(continued)*

```
{
    // Remove the subclass from the Form control
    SetWindowLong(hwndForm, GWL_WNDPROC, (LONG) wpOrigFormProc);
}

LRESULT APIENTRY FormSubclassProc(
    HWND hwnd,
    UINT uMsg,
    WPARAM wParam,
    LPARAM lParam)
{
    LRESULT res =
        CallWindowProc(wpOrigFormProc, hwnd, uMsg, wParam, lParam);

    if (uMsg == WM_ACTIVATE)
    {
        // Send a message to the MessageWindow
        ::SendMessage(
           hwndMessageWindow, WM_CUSTOM_ACTIVATE, wParam, lParam);
    }

    return res;
}
```

The external function *fnActDeactInit* takes two parameters: the title of the main form, which the function needs so that it can use *FindWindow* to obtain the window handle of the form, and the window handle of the MessageWindow component in the managed code. In the *FormSubclassProc* function, when a *WM_ACTIVATE* message is sent to the form, a custom Windows message named *WM_CUSTOM_ACTIVATE* is sent to the MessageWindow component.

The managed code is a component named *WindowsMessages* that creates an instance of a class named *myMessageWindow*. *myMessageWindow* subclasses *MessageWindow* so that it can override the *MessageWindow.WndProc* method and process the *WM_CUSTOM_ACTIVATE* message. When *myMessageWindow* receives one of these messages, it analyzes the *WParam* member of the message to determine whether the main window is activating or deactivating. *myMessageWindow* then calls the *OnActivate* or *OnDeactivate* method of the *WindowsMessages* class, as appropriate. These methods raise the *Activate* and *Deactivate* events, respectively, which users of this component can subscribe to.

Note that the *WindowsMessages* constructor takes a parameter that is the form for which *Activate* and *Deactivate* events are to be raised. *WindowsMessages* calls the *fnActDeactInit* function when the *Load* event of that form fires, and *WindowsMessages* calls the *fnActDeactDestroy* method when the form fires the *Closed* event.

WindowsMessages.cs

```
using System;
using System.Windows.Forms;
using Microsoft.WindowsCE.Forms;
using System.Runtime.InteropServices;

namespace NETCFDevelopersReference
{
    /// <summary>
    /// This component is used to raise Activate and Deactivate events
    /// for a .NET Compact Framework Windows Form.
    /// LIMITATION - the form that creates this component must have a
    /// unique name from any other form currently running on the device,
    /// otherwise this will not work.
    /// You must create an instance of this component before the
    /// Form_Load event fires, recommended in your Form constructor.
    /// </summary>
    public class WindowsMessages
    {
        [DllImport("ActDeact.dll")]
        extern static int fnActDeactInit
            (string WindowName, IntPtr hwndMessageWindow);

        [DllImport("ActDeact.dll")]
        extern static void fnActDeactDestroy();

        myMessageWindow messageWindow;
        Form parentForm;

        // Events that users of this component may subscribe to.
        public delegate void ActDeactEventHandler(
            object sender, ActDeactEventArgs e);
        public event ActDeactEventHandler Activate;
        public event ActDeactEventHandler Deactivate;

        public WindowsMessages(Form ParentForm)
        {
            //
            // Create an instance of the MessageWindow
            // and attach to events on the Form
            //
            messageWindow = new myMessageWindow(this);
            this.parentForm = (Form)ParentForm.TopLevelControl;
            parentForm.Load +=
```

(continued)

WindowsMessages.cs *(continued)*

```
            new System.EventHandler(this.parentForm_Load);
        parentForm.Closed +=
            new System.EventHandler(this.parentForm_Closed);
    }

    /// <summary>
    /// Call the Win32 API function that subclasses the WindowProc
    /// of the parent form
    /// </summary>
    private void parentForm_Load(object sender, System.EventArgs e)
    {
        int ret = fnActDeactInit(
            this.parentForm.Text, this.messageWindow.Hwnd);
        if (ret != 0)
            throw new ApplicationException("Bad WindowsMessages init");
    }

    /// <summary>
    /// Reverse subclassing of the WindowProc of the parent form
    /// </summary>
    private void parentForm_Closed(object sender, System.EventArgs e)
    {
        fnActDeactDestroy();
    }

    // This method is called from myMessageWindow when the custom
    // window message is received.
    public void OnActivate(int activeState, bool isMinimized)
    {
        if (this.Activate != null)
            this.Activate(this, new ActDeactEventArgs(isMinimized));
    }

    // This method is called from myMessageWindow when the custom
    // window message is received.
    public void OnDeactivate(bool isMinimized)
    {
        if (this.Deactivate != null)
            this.Deactivate(this, new ActDeactEventArgs(isMinimized));
    }
}

// Subclass MessageWindow to support checking for the appropriate
// window message and for notifing someone when the appropriate
// message is received
public class myMessageWindow : MessageWindow
```

(continued)

WindowsMessages.cs *(continued)*

```
{
    // User messages start at WM_USER which is 0x400
    public const int WM_CUSTOM_ACTIVATE = 0x400;
    /*
     * WM_ACTIVATE state values
     */
    public const int WA_INACTIVE = 0;
    public const int WA_ACTIVE = 1;
    public const int WA_CLICKACTIVE = 2;

    //private reference to parent class
    WindowsMessages parent;

    // Save reference to the managed app so it can be notified
    // when the specific window message is received.
    public myMessageWindow(WindowsMessages Parent)
    {
        this.parent = Parent;
    }

    // Override the default WndProc behavior to watch for the
    // specific window message.  When the message is received,
    // call back and notify the original form that created the
    // message window.
    protected override void WndProc(ref Message msg)
    {
        switch(msg.Msg)
        {
            case WM_CUSTOM_ACTIVATE:
                int active = (int)msg.WParam & 0x00FF;
                int minimized = (int)msg.WParam & 0xFF00;
                if ((active == WA_ACTIVE) ||
                    (active == WA_CLICKACTIVE))
                {
                    this.parent.OnActivate(active, minimized != 0);
                }
                else
                {
                    this.parent.OnDeactivate(minimized != 0);
                }
                break;
        }

        // call the base class WndProc for default message handling
        base.WndProc(ref msg);
    }
}
```

(continued)

WindowsMessages.cs *(continued)*

```
    public class ActDeactEventArgs : EventArgs
    {
        private bool _minimized;

        public ActDeactEventArgs(bool Minimized)
        {
            _minimized = Minimized;
        }

        public bool IsMinimized
        {
            get
            {
                return _minimized;
            }
        }
    }
}
```

In use, a form needs only to create an instance of the *WindowsMessages* component in its own constructor and wire up event handlers for the *Activate* and *Deactivate* events, as shown in this example:

```
public class ActivateDeactivateForm : System.Windows.Forms.Form
{
    private NETCFDevelopersReference.WindowsMessages myWindowsMessages;

    public ActivateDeactivateForm()
    {
        //
        // Required for Windows Form Designer support
        //
        InitializeComponent();

        //
        // Wire up events on the Windows Messages component
        //
        myWindowsMessages = new WindowsMessages(this);
        myWindowsMessages.Activate +=
            new WindowsMessages.ActDeactEventHandler(
                myWindowsMessages_OnActivate);
        myWindowsMessages.Deactivate +=
            new WindowsMessages.ActDeactEventHandler(
                myWindowsMessages_OnDeactivate);
    }
```

```
        ⋮

        private void myWindowsMessages_OnActivate(
            object sender, ActDeactEventArgs e)
        {
            // Do something...
        }

        private void myWindowsMessages_OnDeactivate(
            object sender, ActDeactEventArgs e)
        {
           // Do something...
        }
    }
```

You can find the code for the ActDeact library and the WindowsMessages application included with this book's sample files, along with a simple example Windows Forms application, ActDeactForm, which uses this technique.

Calling COM Objects

The full .NET Framework provides a high degree of transparent calling between unmanaged code in COM components and managed .NET code. In particular, the full .NET Framework arranges for method calls between the two environments to be almost transparent, and to a large extent, legacy COM objects can be treated in the same way as .NET classes. The following section assumes a familiarity with COM development. A full discussion of COM development is outside the scope of this book. You might want to refer to a book such as David Iseminger's *COM+ Developer's Reference Library (Windows Programming Reference Series)*, Microsoft Press, 2000.

In comparison to the full .NET Framework, COM wrapper functionality in the .NET Compact Framework is very basic. COM and .NET components can coexist in the same process in the .NET Compact Framework. However, the .NET Compact Framework provides no automatic marshaling for COM components other than that provided by P/Invoke. In practice, a developer will have to write unmanaged wrapper code in C or C++ to interface between the managed and unmanaged code.

ActiveX controls that require event handling and callbacks to a container object are not supported. Unlike the desktop .NET environment, there is only a modest body of legacy ActiveX controls in existence for Windows CE. Therefore, there is not a great demand for transparent integration of ActiveX controls, especially in view of the high overhead such integration would require.

All threads created by the CLR are aware of COM at a very basic level. When a thread is created, the *CoInitializeEx* API is called automatically, and the *CoUninitialize* API is also called when the thread is terminated. All threads are marked as free-threaded, so the .NET Compact Framework developer does not have to worry about cross-thread marshaling. Apartment-model threading is not supported.

Beyond this basic support, all other COM handling must be done through P/Invoke. Marshaling of data is subject to the same rules and restrictions, and the memory management is very similar. Simple datatypes can be marshaled automatically with few limitations, but more complex data types might need some explicit support from managed code to marshal correctly. Managed code objects are never exposed as COM objects, and they cannot be instantiated using *CoCreateInstance* in unmanaged code.

Using Wrapper Functions for COM Objects

Because COM objects cannot be exposed directly to managed code, you must write wrapper functions that can be called from .NET Compact Framework languages and that create COM objects, invoke methods, and release the objects.

To illustrate how COM objects can be accessed through such a wrapper, the examples in the sections that follow will show how the MSXML COM component can be used to provide Extensible Stylesheet Language Transformations (XSLT). The .NET Compact Framework supports XML document processing but does not have any direct support for stylesheet transformations. However, the Microsoft XML COM components do have support for transformations. By creating a COM wrapper, you can get around some of the limitations of the .NET Compact Framework.

These examples assume a basic understanding of the MSXML object model as well as COM itself. For further information on MSXML, it is suggested that you refer to the online documentation or the Microsoft MSDN Web site (*http://msdn.microsoft.com*).

> **Note** The native support for MSXML on the Pocket PC 3 platform is relatively limited compared to the level of support found in Windows CE .NET. The code listed in the next section will operate on both platforms, but the XSLT capability on the first platform is not based on the final W3C recommendations and is relatively basic.

Developing a Simple COM Wrapper

The simplest approach to writing a COM wrapper is to create a function that completely encapsulates most or all COM implementation details for the caller. The wrapper will create all necessary COM objects and make all required COM method calls, wrapping up the functionality in a function-based interface.

The following example wrapper contains two functions. The first function, *BuildXml*, is a private (internal) helper function that takes a string as input and loads that string into a new MSXML COM object returning a reference to that object to the caller. The second function, *TransformXml*, performs a stylesheet transformation of one document against another using *BuildXml* internally. Here's the listing for the *BuildXml* function:

```
static IXMLDOMDocument * BuildXml(WCHAR* pXml)
{
    IXMLDOMDocument * pDoc;
    HRESULT hr;
    CLSID ClsIdDomDoc;

    // Get CLSID for Microsoft.XMLDOM
    ::CLSIDFromProgID(L"Microsoft.XMLDOM", &ClsIdDomDoc);

    // Create instance of document class
    hr = ::CoCreateInstance(
        ClsIdDomDoc,
        NULL,
        CLSCTX_INPROC_SERVER,
        IID_IXMLDOMDocument,
        (void**) &pDoc);

    if (hr==S_OK)
    {
        VARIANT_BOOL isSuccessful=0;

        // Set property: no asynchronous loading
        pDoc->put_async(VARIANT_FALSE);
        // Set property: no validation
        pDoc->put_validateOnParse(VARIANT_FALSE);

        // Load the document
        hr=pDoc->loadXML(pXml, &isSuccessful);

        // Release document if there was any kind of problem
        if (!(hr==S_OK && isSuccessful))
        {
            pDoc->Release();
            pDoc = NULL;
```

```
        }
    }
    else
    {
        // Cannot get COM object and interface
        pDoc = NULL;
    }

    // Document to caller (NULL if errors)
    return pDoc;
}
```

Calls to *CoInitializeEx* and *CoUninitialize* are not required because they are handled by the COM support in the .NET Compact Framework.

BuildXml returns a pointer to a type *IXMLDOMDocument*, which is an interface to an instance of the *MSXML.DOMDocument* class. After recovering the CLSID of the *DOMDocument* class, an instance of the object is created using *CoCreateInstance*. If that instantiation is successful, the text of the XML document is loaded into the document instance, having first set the COM properties *async* and *validateOnParse*. Care is taken to check for document loading errors at two levels: the *LoadXML* method might fail at the COM level (a non-zero *HRESULT* value), or it might succeed but have high-level XML problems such as an invalidly formed XML string (which would result in a zero for the *isSuccessful* flag).

The *TransformXml* function takes the text of two XML documents (one for source data and one for a stylesheet) and a text buffer to hold the result of the transformation. Using *BuildXml* internally, it loads up the two XML documents and then uses the *transformNode* method to generate stylesheet results. Here's the listing for the *TransformXml* function:

```
EXTERN_C
__declspec(dllexport)
HRESULT TransformXml
    (WCHAR* pXmlSrc,
     WCHAR* pXmlXslt,
     WCHAR* pXmlResult,
     INT32  maxLen,
     INT32* pResultSize)
{
    HRESULT hr;
    IXMLDOMDocument *xmlSrc;
    IXMLDOMDocument *xmlXslt;

    // Load source document
    xmlSrc  = BuildXml(pXmlSrc);

    if (xmlSrc != NULL)
```

```
    {
        // Load style sheet
        xmlXslt  = BuildXml(pXmlXslt);
        if (xmlXslt != NULL)
        {
            BSTR bstrResult;

            // Transform

            hr = xmlSrc->transformNode(xmlXslt, &bstrResult);
            if (hr == S_OK)
            {
                // Return result string
                wcsncpy(pXmlResult, bstrResult, maxLen);
                *pResultSize = ::SysStringLen(bstrResult);
                ::SysFreeString(bstrResult);
            }
            else
            {
                wcsncpy(pXmlResult, L"Transform failed", maxLen);
            }
            xmlXslt->Release();
            xmlSrc->Release();
        }
        else
        {
            xmlSrc->Release();
        }
    }

    return S_OK;
}
```

The *TransformXml* method is exported using the C/C++ *__declspec(dllexport)* declaration. To ensure that the correct name is placed into the output file, the *EXTERN_C* macro prevents name mangling.

Inside the function, the two XML documents are loaded and appropriate error checking is performed to ensure that both loaded correctly. Notice that COM objects must be explicitly garbage collected when no longer required using the *Release* method. Unlike the CLR, COM has no garbage collector.

After a successful *transformNode* method call, the result string is copied into the buffer provided. In this situation, the COM string, referenced by the *BSTR* variable *bstrResult*, is released using the *SysFreeString* function after its contents have been copied to the *pXmlResult* buffer. Using *wsncpy* ensures that the maximum buffer length is not exceeded, in case of a long string being returned as the result.

To declare the call in C#, the following declaration can be made:

```
[DllImport("ComWrapperDll.dll")]
extern static void TransformXml(
    string xmlSrc,
    string xmlXslt,
    StringBuilder xmlResult,
    int maxLength,
    out int resultLength);
```

The function can be invoked using code such as this:

```
string sourceText;
string styleSheetText;

sourceText = LoadFile(DeployDir + "Order.xml");
styleSheetText = LoadFile(DeployDir + "OrderStyle.xml");

int maxLength = 1000;
StringBuilder sb = new StringBuilder(maxLength+1);
int resultLength;

TransformXml(sourceText, styleSheetText, sb, maxLength, out resultLength);

⋮

private string LoadFile(string FileName)
{
    StreamReader sr = new System.IO.StreamReader(FileName);
    string contents = sr.ReadToEnd();
    sr.Close();
    return contents;
}
```

After the *TransformXml* call, the result of the transformation is held in the *sb* variable.

Maintaining State with a COM Wrapper

It is not always appropriate to create a COM object for each call, particularly if the instantiation time for the object is long or if you require the COM object to retain state information between calls. If you require persistence of a COM object's state between calls, you'll need a separate external method for creation, for release, and for each method call. You'll also need to retain a reference to the object instance. It's often convenient to provide two levels of wrapper. A wrapper in managed code can be created to provide a classlike interface to the code, and an unmanaged code wrapper can be created with a set of functions for each operation that is required on the COM objects. This approach is more complex, but it does allow for persistence of the COM objects in a process over time.

Here's a listing for an unmanaged code wrapper that has functions for each operation that is required on a COM object:

```
EXTERN_C
__declspec(dllexport)
HRESULT DOMDocument_CreateObject(IXMLDOMDocument ** piDOMDocument)
{
    HRESULT hr;
    CLSID ClsIdDomDoc;

    hr = ::CLSIDFromProgID(L"Microsoft.XMLDOM", &ClsIdDomDoc);

    if (hr == S_OK)
    {
        hr = ::CoCreateInstance(
            ClsIdDomDoc,
            NULL,
            CLSCTX_INPROC_SERVER,
            IID_IXMLDOMDocument,
             (void**) piDOMDocument);
    }

    return hr;
}

EXTERN_C
__declspec(dllexport)
HRESULT DOMDocument_Release(IXMLDOMDocument * iDOMDocument)
{
    return iDOMDocument->Release();
}

EXTERN_C
__declspec(dllexport)
HRESULT DOMDocument_LoadXML(
    IXMLDOMDocument * iDOMDocument,
    WCHAR *pTextXml,
    BOOL *pbSucceed)
{
    HRESULT hr;
    VARIANT_BOOL isSuccessful = VARIANT_FALSE;

    iDOMDocument->put_async(VARIANT_FALSE);
    iDOMDocument->put_validateOnParse(VARIANT_FALSE);
```

```
    hr = iDOMDocument->loadXML(pTextXml, &isSuccessful);
    *pbSucceed = isSuccessful;

    return hr;
}


EXTERN_C
__declspec(dllexport)
HRESULT DOMDocument_TransformNode(
    IXMLDOMDocument* iSource,
    IXMLDOMDocument* iStylesheet,
    WCHAR* pXmlResult,
    INT32  maxLen)
{
    HRESULT hr;
    BSTR bstrResult;

    hr = iSource->transformNode(iStylesheet, &bstrResult);

    if (hr == S_OK)
    {
        wcsncpy(pXmlResult, bstrResult, maxLen);
        ::SysFreeString(bstrResult);
    }
    else
    {
        wcsncpy(pXmlResult, L"", maxLen);
    }

    return hr;
}
```

As before, exported functions are marked with *EXTERN_C* and *__declspec(dllexport)*. In this form of the wrapper, there are many more entry points for the DLL.

Unlike the previous wrapper example, this code does have a certain amount of persistence between calls. A COM object is created, and a pointer to it is returned from *DOMDocument_CreateObject*. This object is retained in memory between calls, and the interface pointer is passed as a parameter to the other routines. The .NET Compact Framework supplies a useful type named *IntPtr* that provides opaque encapsulation of a pointer type such as *void ** or *HWND*. Managed code can store an *IntPtr* value but can perform no operations on it apart from assignment and comparison to *IntPtr.Zero* (which corresponds to the C/C++ *NULL* value).

The functions in the previous unmanaged code wrapper can be conveniently encapsulated inside a small C# class, as follows:

```
public class DomDocument : IDisposable
{
    [DllImport("ComWrapperDll.dll")]
    extern static uint DOMDocument_CreateObject(
        out IntPtr iXmlDomDocument);

    [DllImport("ComWrapperDll.dll")]
    extern static uint DOMDocument_Release(IntPtr iXmlDomDocument);

    [DllImport("ComWrapperDll.dll")]
    extern static uint DOMDocument_LoadXML(
        IntPtr iXmlDomDocument,
        string xmlText,
        out int bSucceed);

    [DllImport("ComWrapperDll.dll")]
    extern static uint DOMDocument_TransformNode(
        IntPtr iXmlDomDocument,
        IntPtr iXmlStyleSheet,
        StringBuilder resultBuffer,
        int maxLength);

    // Interface pointer
    protected IntPtr iXmlDomDocument;

    public DomDocument()
    {
        CheckHResult(DOMDocument_CreateObject(out iXmlDomDocument));
    }

    public void Dispose()
    {
        if (iXmlDomDocument != IntPtr.Zero)
        {
            CheckHResult(DOMDocument_Release(iXmlDomDocument));
            iXmlDomDocument = IntPtr.Zero;
        }
    }

    public void LoadXml(string xmlText)
    {
        int bSucceed;
        CheckHResult(DOMDocument_LoadXML(
            iXmlDomDocument, xmlText, out bSucceed));
        if (bSucceed==0)
```

```
            throw new ApplicationException("Cannot load XML");
    }

    public string TransformNode(DomDocument styleSheet)
    {
        StringBuilder resultText;
        int maxLength = 1000;
        resultText = new StringBuilder(maxLength+1);
        CheckHResult(
            DOMDocument_TransformNode(
            iXmlDomDocument,
            styleSheet.iXmlDomDocument,
            resultText,
            maxLength));
        return resultText.ToString();
    }

    private static void CheckHResult(uint hr)
    {
        if (hr != 0)
            throw new ApplicationException(
                String.Format("COM Wrapper Error:{0:x}", hr));
    }
}
```

Therefore, the *DomDocument* class presents a managed code encapsulation of the COM object. It can be called as follows:

```
DomDocument xmlSource;
DomDocument xmlStyleSheet;

string sourceText;
string styleSheetText;
string transformText;

sourceText = LoadFile(DeployDir + "Order.xml");
xmlSource = new DomDocument();
xmlSource.LoadXml(sourceText);

styleSheetText = LoadFile(DeployDir + "OrderStyle.xml");
xmlStyleSheet = new DomDocument();
xmlStyleSheet.LoadXml(styleSheetText);

transformText = xmlSource.TransformNode(xmlStyleSheet);
```

After this code, the transformed output is found in *transformText*.

Summary

The .NET Compact Framework, as we have seen, allows managed code to call unmanaged legacy code as long as that legacy code is packaged in a DLL or a COM component. The P/Invoke facility is a useful subset of the P/Invoke facilities of the full .NET framework, although it lacks some of the more complex parameter marshaling features. The MessageWindow component can be used to intercept low-level Windows messages and provides support for simple callbacks from unmanaged to managed code. Support for COM components requires support from custom unmanaged DLLs.

A developer who needs to integrate an unmanaged code base into a .NET application or library must be familiar with the C and C++ languages and must be prepared to write helper functions in these languages to support marshaling of complex types and calls to COM components.

23

Migrating eMbedded Visual Tools Applications and Cross-Framework Development

As a developer, you might be creating your smart device application without reference to any pre-existing code base for Windows CE. On the other hand, you might have to migrate an existing application written using the eMbedded Visual Tools suite. This chapter offers some suggestions for migrating applications from the older tool suites to Visual Studio .NET. In addition, this chapter also discusses some of the issues faced by a developer who wants to maintain a single managed code base for both the full .NET Framework and the .NET Compact Framework.

Migrating eMbedded Visual Tools Applications

In comparison with the older tools, Visual Studio .NET offers several major enhancements, such as the following:

- Choice of powerful, modern, object-oriented languages (C#, Visual Basic .NET)
- Full capability of Visual Studio .NET for development
- ADO.NET for data access

- Rich local applications using Web forms
- Rich XML Web service clients

For development of code in the Windows CE environment, the following key tools were available prior to the arrival of the .NET Compact Framework:

- eMbedded Visual C++ version 3
- eMbedded Visual Basic version 3
- eMbedded Visual C++ version 4

eMbedded Visual C++ version 3 generates native code from C/C++ source code. It targets the Windows CE 3, Pocket PC 2000, and Pocket PC 2002 environments, but executables are generally also compatible with Windows CE .NET. Developers can create EXE and DLL files and COM components.

eMbedded Visual Basic version 3 is an interpreted dialect of Visual Basic Scripting Edition (VBScript). It generates pseudocode (.vb) files, which are interpreted at run time by an interpreter process (Pvbload.exe). Executables are targeted at Windows CE 3 but will execute on later versions of the operating system. This tool cannot build DLLs or COM components, although it can act as a COM automation client using late binding.

eMbedded Visual C++ version 4 generates native code from C/C++ source code. It targets the Windows CE .NET environment. Executables can be adapted to work in Windows CE 3 and Pocket PC 3 environments. (See Chapter 22.) Both EXE and DLL files can be generated. Custom COM components can also be built.

Binary Compatibility

It's worth noting that applications built with previous toolsets will still run under Windows CE .NET and the .NET Compact Framework. It might be practical to keep using the older tools for some or all of your application suite, depending on your specific needs. Executables generated using eMbedded Visual C++ 3 and 4 will still run, and the eMbedded Visual Basic interpreter (Pvbload.exe) will also execute.

Language Changes

Visual Basic .NET, despite the similarity of name, is different in many ways from eMbedded Visual Basic. The former is a complete redesign of the Visual Basic language to incorporate .NET features. The latter is closest in spirit to VBScript. There is no automatic conversion tool between the two languages.

> **Tip** Visual Basic .NET has the ability to import a Visual Basic 6 project and attempt a conversion to the new framework. If you already have a desktop Windows version of the user interface of an eMbedded Visual Basic application, you might want to try converting it to a desktop implementation using full .NET Framework first and then to the .NET Compact Framework. This might be useful in some situations, although if you have no intention of providing a desktop version of your product, it's probably not a sensible use of a developer's time.

C# is a new programming language, and there will be no pre-existing code base for Windows CE. At the time of writing, development for the .NET Compact Framework using managed C++ is not supported. There is, accordingly, no automatic upgrade path for existing eMbedded Visual C++ code.

User Interface Programming Model

The Window Forms programming model is quite different from that supported by eMbedded Visual Basic, or Microsoft Foundation Classes (MFC) and C++. The underlying principles are still the same: user interfaces are based on forms that contain interacting visual components. The detailed syntax is different. Any user interface application that needs to be ported to Visual Studio .NET will require considerable rewriting. In this respect, developers for the .NET Compact Framework are in a very similar position to developers for the full .NET Framework who are porting an existing Visual Basic 6 or Visual C++ application to .NET.

ActiveX Controls

Legacy ActiveX controls are not supported in the .NET Compact Framework. If you have obtained an ActiveX control from a third party, contact that third party to see if a .NET version of the control is available. If the ActiveX control was written in-house, it must be rewritten as part of the rewrite of the user interface.

User Interface and Business Logic Decoupled

It's generally a good design principle to factor out the user interface code from the underlying business logic. This kind of decoupling is helpful in any case because it generally leads to clearer code. When moving to .NET languages, which have powerful component-building mechanisms, you should at least consider moving business logic out of the forms framework and into its own set of classes. It might also be worthwhile to deploy the business-related classes in their own DLL.

Transitional Arrangements

It might not be desirable to port an entire suite of applications at once. You might want to have some of your application moved to the .NET Compact Framework to fulfill a short-term business need, while you keep some existing legacy code generated with the older toolset.

If your existing code has already factored out components into DLLs, you might be able to rewrite the code for the user interface into C# or Visual Basic .NET and use P/Invoke to call into the legacy DLLs. Bear in mind, however, that there is no COM Interoperability in the .NET Compact Framework, and developers will have to write wrapper DLLs to handle existing COM components. See Chapter 22 for more details of P/Invoke and COM interoperability.

Databases

The CEDB database engine is not supported in the .NET Compact Framework. In general, developers should design for database development using SQL Server. A variety of techniques are supported, including local SQL Server CE access, merge replication or remote data access to an enterprise database, and SQLXML, all discussed in Chapters 15 through 17. If you have an existing code base using CEDB that cannot conveniently be rewritten, you might consider writing a wrapper DLL in C/C++ that can be called from .NET applications using P/Invoke.

The database coding techniques have also changed. In previous tool suites, the preferred technique was to use the ADOCE COM components. For .NET database applications, use the ADO.NET classes in the *System.Data.** namespaces.

COM Interoperability

As covered in detail in Chapter 22, interaction with COM in the .NET Compact Framework requires the construction of wrapper libraries to handle the marshaling requirements. If your existing application depends extensively on COM components, consider purchasing or writing .NET equivalents of those components.

Writing Cross-Framework Applications

In certain circumstances, you might want to run applications on a desktop machine that were compiled to run in the .NET Compact Framework. Version 1.1 of the full .NET Framework supports the concept of retargetable assemblies that allows you to run applications this way.

Retargetable Assemblies

Many of the .NET Compact Framework assemblies represent compatible subsets of full .NET Framework functionality. These assemblies carry a special attribute that identifies them as *retargetable*.

When a .NET Compact Framework application targets one of these assemblies, the *Retargetable* flag is copied into the resulting assembly reference. If the application is later launched on the desktop using the full version of the common language runtime (CLR), the *Retargetable* flag in the assembly reference at run time activates retargeting policy. This policy allows compatible full .NET Framework assemblies to be substituted for their corresponding .NET Compact Framework counterparts. The application then runs with the substituted assemblies rather than with the .NET Compact Framework assemblies. In effect, the .NET Compact Framework binaries run transparently on the full .NET Framework.

Although the .NET Compact Framework and the full .NET Framework have many assemblies with the same names, classes, methods, and attributes, the strong names for each set of assemblies are different. Strong-naming was introduced with .NET to avoid problems associated with multiple incompatible versions of the same DLL. The .NET Compact Framework assemblies are signed with different strong-name key pairs so that the CLR can distinguish them from their full .NET Framework counterparts.

The *AssemblyNameFlags* enumeration has a value *Retargetable*, which specifies that the assembly can be retargeted at run time to an assembly from a different publisher. The following code demonstrates the use of *AssemblyNameFlags.Retargetable*:

```
⋮
[assembly: AssemblyFlags(AssemblyNameFlags.Retargetable)]
⋮
```

The following assembles are marked as retargetable:

- mscorlib.dll
- System.dll
- System.Xml.dll
- System.Data.dll
- System.Data.Common.dll
- System.Data.SqlClient.dll
- System.Drawing.dll
- System.Web.Services.dll
- System.Windows.Forms.dll
- Microsoft.VisualBasic.dll
- System.Windows.Forms.DataGrid.dll

As the .NET Compact Framework evolves, other assemblies might also be marked as retargetable. Developers can use the Ildasm tool to inspect the manifest of any assembly to see if it carries the *retargetable* assembly flag in its metadata, as shown in Figure 23-1.

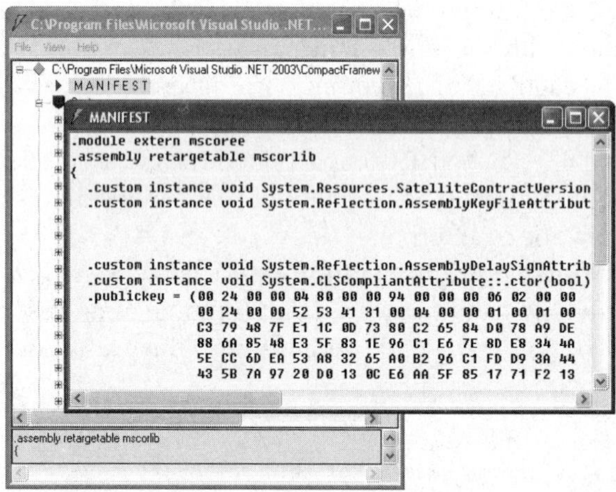

Figure 23-1 Ildasm tool showing the manifest for a retargetable assembly.

Note If you reference functionality that is unique to the .NET Compact Framework, such as Pocket PC–specific user interface controls, your program will fail to bind to the full .NET Framework. The Framework as a whole has been designed to factor out device-specific functionality into discrete namespaces and assemblies to avoid binding conflicts. It is possible that there will be some cases of incompatible factoring that can't be handled automatically. In these cases, inadvertent use of the device-specific functionality with the full .NET Framework will cause a run-time exception.

Should you use the retargetable features of the .NET Framework? The key benefit is that a developer can maintain a single code base for both the .NET Compact Framework and the full .NET Framework, with subsequent potential improvements in productivity. However, by its very nature, such an approach encourages a "lowest common denominator" approach to functionality. As can be seen from many other chapters of this book, the .NET Compact Framework is designed to have a subset of the functionality of the full .NET Framework, which implies that the most powerful code will probably be target-specific. There are some situations where the retargetable features of the .NET Framework require some additional help from the developer to be truly platform-independent.

Run-Time Determination of the Operating System

If a single assembly can execute on different platforms, it might be useful to determine at run time which environment is being used. The *System.Environment.OSVersion* variable returns an object of class *OperatingSystem*, whose property *Platform* contains a string that describes the current operating system.

```
OperatingSystem osInfo = Environment.OSVersion;
switch (osInfo.Platform)
{
    case PlatformID.WinCE:
        // Special code for Windows CE
        ⋮
        break;
    case PlatformID.Win32NT:
        // Special code for NT, 2000 or XP
```

(continued)

```
        :
        break;
    case PlatformID.Win32Windows:
        // Special code for Windows 95, 98 or Me
        :
        break;
}
```

The *Version* property can be used to determine which version of a particular platform is in use.

Conditional Compilation

There are some situations in which it is not feasible to make run-time decisions dependent on the operating system. For example, if an application makes calls to operating system DLLs, the code must take into account that the names of many DLLs differ between the Win32 and Windows CE APIs. Conditional compilation is useful in these circumstances. The following code fragment shows how to have a single code base that calls the appropriate version of *MessageBeep* in the desktop and Windows CE environments:

```
#if FULLFRAMEWORK
    [DllImport("user32.dll")]
    private static extern void MessageBeep(uint beepType);
#else
    [DllImport("coredll.dll")]
    private static extern void MessageBeep(uint beepType);
#endif
```

Developers can set up conditional compilation flags from the Visual Studio .NET environment by selecting Properties from the Project menu and then selecting Configuration Properties and Build from the tree at the left of the dialog box. The conditional compilation flags for the current build will be shown in the Conditional Compilation Constants entry. You can add additional conditional compilation flags by editing this list of items, separated by semicolons, as shown in Figure 23-2.

> **Note** The Release and Debug configurations can be adjusted independently; make sure that you make consistent changes to both when adding conditional compilation flags to a project. In this example, it would make sense to include the *FULLFRAMEWORK* constant in both configurations or exclude it in both, depending on the desired target environment.

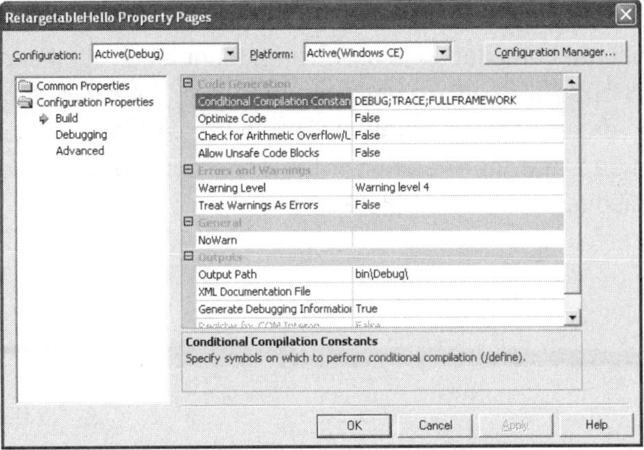

Figure 23-2 Editing conditional compilation flags.

The call to play the sound file is then the same regardless of the environment in which the application is executing. The conditional compilation flags ensure that the correct DLL is loaded.

```
try
{
    MessageBeep((uint)MessageBoxIcon.Exclamation);
}
catch(Exception ex)
{
    MessageBox.Show(
        String.Format(
            "Exception {0} occurred making DLL call.\n" +
            "Check you have compiled for the correct platform",
            ex.Message)
        );
}
```

Conditional compilation constants allow the developer to have a single source code base, but it will still be necessary to create two different Visual Studio .NET projects that use the source code. One project will be a smart device project, and the other project will target the full Windows environment. It's not possible to have a single project that can generate assemblies for both. You might want to keep both projects in the same source directories to avoid having to duplicate the source code files.

> **Tip** Conditional compilation is a powerful technique, but it can make for awkward code if used excessively. Wherever possible, factor out the platform-dependent code into separate classes and assemblies, which will mean that the majority of the code can be written cleanly, free of conditional compilation blocks.

Summary

Development of software for the Windows CE environment rarely takes place independently of other operating environments. In this chapter, we have discussed some techniques that can be used to port existing software from previous versions of Windows CE to the .NET Compact Framework. The technological jump from the older platforms to the new one is quite substantial, and therefore, porting is non-trivial. This chapter also discussed how it's possible to have the same code base execute under both the full .NET Framework and the .NET Compact Framework when developing .NET code using the retargetable assembly flag, run-time determination of the underlying environment, and conditional compilation.

Appendix

.NET Compact Framework Base Class Libraries

This appendix lists all namespaces in the full .NET Framework version 1.1. For those namespaces that are not implemented in the .NET Compact Framework version 1, no classes or structures are listed. For those namespaces that are present in both implementations, all classes and structures in the full .NET Framework version 1.1 namespace are listed. Classes and structures that are not supported in the .NET Compact Framework version 1 are noted in the tables as "not supported."

Not all the methods or method overloads found in the desktop .NET Framework implementation are supported for the same classes in the .NET Compact Framework implementation. To find out which class members are supported in the .NET Compact Framework, refer to the *Class Library Comparison Tool* in the .NET Compact Framework Classes documentation in Microsoft Visual Studio .NET online help. In addition to this tool, you can refer to the detailed online class reference documentation, which is common to both the .NET Framework and the .NET Compact Framework. However, in the Members topic of any class or structure documented in the online class reference, properties and methods supported in the .NET Compact Framework implementation are noted with the phrase "Supported by the .NET Compact Framework."

This appendix does not list any delegates, enumerations, or interfaces in the .NET Frameworks. You must consult the product documentation for this information.

Microsoft.VisualBasic Namespace

The *Microsoft.VisualBasic* namespace implements the Microsoft Visual Basic .NET runtime. Individual classes are not listed because they are used indirectly through Visual Basic .NET language keywords, rather than explicitly as with other classes in the .NET Framework.

However, it should be noted that the Visual Basic .NET runtime in the .NET Compact Framework does not support the Microsoft.VisualBasic.FileSystem module. You must use classes in the .NET Compact Framework *System.IO* namespace to work with the file system, rather than traditional Visual Basic keywords such as *FileOpen*, *MkDir*, *PrintLine*, and so on.

Microsoft.WindowsCE.Forms Namespace

The *Microsoft.WindowsCE.Forms* namespace contains classes and structures that implement components to give access to shell features that are unique to Microsoft Windows CE devices. None of these classes are available in the desktop .NET Framework. This namespace is implemented in Microsoft.WindowsCE.Forms.dll. The classes and structures in the Microsoft.WindowsCE.Forms namespace are listed in Table A-1.

Table A-1 Classes and Structures in the *Microsoft.WindowsCE.Forms* Namespace

Class or Structure	Description
InputPanel class	Implements a component that controls the soft input panel (SIP) on the Pocket PC. The SIP is the primary means for the user to enter data.
Message structure	Implements a Windows message.
MessageWindow class	This class supports communication between native Windows applications and managed applications by using Windows message constructs.

System Namespace

The *System* namespace is primarily in the assembly Mscorlib.dll. It contains fundamental classes and structures and base classes that define commonly used value and reference data types. These classes and structures are listed in Table A-2.

Table A-2 Classes and Structures in the *System* Namespace

Class or Structure	Description
Activator class	Contains methods to create types of objects locally or remotely, or to obtain references to existing remote objects.
AppDomain class	Represents an application domain, which is an isolated environment where applications execute.
AppDomainSetup class	Not supported.
AppDomainUnloadedException class	Not supported.
ApplicationException class	The exception that is thrown when a non-fatal application error occurs.
ArgIterator structure	Not supported.
ArgumentException class	The exception that is thrown when one of the arguments provided to a method is not valid.
ArgumentNullException class	The exception that is thrown when a *null* reference (*Nothing* in Visual Basic) is passed to a method that doesn't accept the reference as a valid argument.
ArgumentOutOfRangeException class	The exception that is thrown when the value of an argument is outside the allowable range of values as defined by the invoked method.
ArithmeticException class	The exception that is thrown for errors in an arithmetic, casting, or conversion operation.
Array class	Provides methods for creating, manipulating, searching, and sorting arrays, thereby serving as the base class for all arrays in the common language runtime (CLR).
ArrayTypeMismatchException class	The exception that is thrown when an attempt is made to store an element of the wrong type within an array.
AssemblyLoadEventArgs class	Not supported.
Attribute class	The base class for custom attributes.
AttributeUsageAttribute class	Specifies the usage of another attribute class.
BadImageFormatException class	Not supported.

(continued)

Table A-2 Classes and Structures in the *System* Namespace *(continued)*

Class or Structure	Description
BitConverter class	Converts base data types to an array of bytes, and an array of bytes to base data types.
Boolean structure	Represents a Boolean value.
Buffer class	Manipulates unmanaged memory represented as arrays of bytes.
Byte structure	Represents an 8-bit unsigned integer.
CannotUnloadAppDomainException class	Not supported.
Char structure	Represents a Unicode character.
CharEnumerator class	Supports iterating over a String and reading its individual characters.
CLSCompliantAttribute class	Indicates whether a program element is compliant with the Common Language Specification (CLS).
Console class	Represents the standard input, output, and error streams for console applications.
ContextBoundObject class	Not supported.
ContextMarshalException class	Not supported.
ContextStaticAttribute class	Not supported.
Convert class	Converts a base data type to another base data type.
DateTime structure	Represents an instant in time, typically expressed as a date and a time of day.
DBNull class	Represents a *null* value.
Decimal structure	Represents a decimal number.
Delegate class	Represents a delegate, which is a data structure that refers to a static method or to a class instance and an instance method of that class.
DivideByZeroException class	The exception that is thrown when there is an attempt to divide an integral value or a decimal value by zero.
DllNotFoundException class	The exception that is thrown when a DLL specified in a DLL import cannot be found.
Double structure	Represents a double-precision floating-point number.

Table A-2 Classes and Structures in the *System* Namespace *(continued)*

Class or Structure	Description
DuplicateWaitObjectException class	Not supported.
EntryPointNotFoundException class	The exception that is thrown when an attempt to load a class fails due to the absence of an entry method.
Enum class	Provides the base class for enumerations.
Environment class	Provides information about, and the means to manipulate, the current environment and platform.
EventArgs class	*EventArgs* is the base class for classes containing event data.
Exception class	Represents errors that occur during application execution.
ExecutionEngineException class	Not supported.
FieldAccessException class	Not supported.
FlagsAttribute class	Indicates that an enumeration can be treated as a bit field—that is, a set of flags.
FormatException class	The exception that is thrown when the format of an argument does not meet the parameter specifications of the invoked method.
GC class	Controls the system garbage collector, a service that automatically reclaims unused memory.
Guid structure	Represents a globally unique identifier (GUID).
IndexOutOfRangeException class	The exception that is thrown when an attempt is made to access an element of an array with an index that is outside the bounds of the array.
Int16 structure	Represents a 16-bit signed integer.
Int32 structure	Represents a 32-bit signed integer.
Int64 structure	Represents a 64-bit signed integer.
IntPtr structure	A platform-specific type that is used to represent a pointer or a handle.
InvalidCastException class	The exception that is thrown for invalid casting or explicit conversion.
InvalidOperationException class	The exception that is thrown when a method call is invalid for the object's current state.

(continued)

Table A-2 Classes and Structures in the *System* Namespace *(continued)*

Class or Structure	Description
InvalidProgramException class	The exception that is thrown when a program contains invalid intermediate language (IL) or metadata. Generally this indicates a bug in a compiler.
LoaderOptimizationAttribute class	Not supported.
LocalDataStoreSlot class	Encapsulates a memory slot to store local data.
MarshalByRefObject class	Enables access to objects across application domain boundaries in applications that support remoting.
Math class	Provides constants and static methods for trigonometric, logarithmic, and other common mathematical functions.
MemberAccessException class	The exception that is thrown when an attempt to access a class member fails.
MethodAccessException class	Not supported.
MissingFieldException class	The exception that is thrown when there is an attempt to dynamically access a field that does not exist.
MissingMemberException class	The exception that is thrown when there is an attempt to dynamically access a class member that does not exist.
MissingMethodException class	The exception that is thrown when there is an attempt to dynamically access a method that does not exist.
MTAThreadAttribute class	Not supported.
MulticastDelegate class	Represents a multicast delegate—that is, a delegate that can have more than one element in its invocation list.
MulticastNotSupportedException class	The exception that is thrown when there is an attempt to combine two instances of a non-combinable delegate type unless one of the operands is a *null* reference (*Nothing* in Visual Basic).
NonSerializedAttribute class	Indicates that a field of a serializable class should not be serialized.
NotFiniteNumberException class	The exception that is thrown when a floating-point value is positive infinity, negative infinity, or Not-a-Number (NaN).

Table A-2 Classes and Structures in the *System* Namespace *(continued)*

Class or Structure	Description
NotImplementedException class	Not supported.
NotSupportedException class	The exception that is thrown when an invoked method is not supported, or when there is an attempt to read, seek, or write to a stream that does not support the invoked functionality.
NullReferenceException class	The exception that is thrown when there is an attempt to dereference a *null* object reference.
Object class	Supports all classes in the .NET Framework class hierarchy and provides low-level services to derived classes. This is the ultimate super class of all classes in the .NET Framework; it is the root of the type hierarchy.
ObjectDisposedException class	The exception that is thrown when an operation is performed on a disposed object.
ObsoleteAttribute class	Marks the program elements that are no longer in use.
OperatingSystem class	Represents information about an operating system, such as the version and platform identifier.
OutOfMemoryException class	The exception that is thrown when there is not enough memory to continue the execution of a program.
OverflowException class	The exception that is thrown when an arithmetic, casting, or conversion operation in a checked context results in an overflow.
ParamArrayAttribute class	Indicates that the method will allow a variable number of arguments in its invocation.
PlatformNotSupportedException class	The exception that is thrown when a feature does not run on a particular platform.
Random class	Represents a pseudo-random number generator, a device that produces a sequence of numbers that meet certain statistical requirements for randomness.
RankException class	The exception that is thrown when an array with the wrong number of dimensions is passed to a method.
ResolveEventArgs class	Not supported.

(continued)

Table A-2 Classes and Structures in the *System* Namespace *(continued)*

Class or Structure	Description
RuntimeArgumentHandle structure	Not supported.
RuntimeFieldHandle structure	Represents a field using an internal metadata token.
RuntimeMethodHandle structure	The *RuntimeMethodHandle* is a handle to the internal metadata representation of a method.
RuntimeTypeHandle structure	Represents a type using an internal metadata token.
SByte structure	Represents an 8-bit signed integer.
SerializableAttribute class	Not supported.
Single structure	Represents a single-precision floating-point number.
StackOverflowException class	The exception that is thrown when the execution stack overflows by having too many pending method calls.
STAThreadAttribute class	Not supported.
String class	Represents an immutable series of characters.
SystemException class	Defines the base class for predefined exceptions in the *System* namespace.
ThreadStaticAttribute class	Not supported.
TimeSpan structure	Represents a time interval.
TimeZone class	Represents a time zone.
Type class	Represents type declarations: class types, interface types, array types, value types, and enumeration types.
TypedReference structure	Describes objects that contain both a managed pointer to a location and a run-time representation of the type that might be stored at that location.
TypeInitializationException class	Not supported.
TypeLoadException class	The exception that is thrown when type-loading failures occur.
TypeUnloadedException class	Not supported.
UInt16 structure	Represents a 16-bit unsigned integer.
UInt32 structure	Represents a 32-bit unsigned integer.

Table A-2 Classes and Structures in the *System* Namespace *(continued)*

Class or Structure	Description
UInt64 structure	Represents a 64-bit unsigned integer.
UIntPtr structure	A platform-specific type that is used to represent a pointer or a handle.
UnauthorizedAccessException class	The exception that is thrown when the operating system denies access because of an I/O error or a specific type of security error.
UnhandledExceptionEventArgs class	Not supported.
Uri class	Provides an object representation of a Uniform Resource Identifier (URI) and easy access to the parts of the URI.
UriBuilder class	Not supported.
UriFormatException class	The exception that is thrown when an invalid Uniform Resource Identifier (URI) is detected.
ValueType class	Provides the base class for value types.
Version class	Represents the version number for a common language runtime assembly.
Void structure	Indicates a method that does not return a value, that is, the method has the void return type.
WeakReference class	Represents a weak reference, which references an object while still allowing it to be garbage collected.

System.CodeDom Namespace

The *System.CodeDom* namespace and the *System.CodeDom.Compiler* namespace contain classes that help compilers model and compile source code. They are not supported in the .NET Compact Framework.

System.Collections Namespace

The *System.Collections* namespace contains classes and structures that allow you to handle collections of objects. It is implemented in the Mscorlib.dll assembly. The classes and structures of this namespace are listed in Table A-3.

Table A-3 Classes and Structures in the *System.Collections* Namespace

Class or Structure	Description
ArrayList class	Implements the *IList* interface using an array whose size is dynamically increased as required.
BitArray class	Manages a compact array of bit values, which are represented as Boolean values, where *true* indicates that the bit is on (1) and *false* indicates the bit is off (0).
CaseInsensitiveComparer class	Compares two objects for equivalence, ignoring the case of strings.
CaseInsensitiveHashCodeProvider class	Supplies a hashcode for an object, using a hashing algorithm that ignores the case of strings.
CollectionBase class	Provides the abstract base class (*MustInherit* in Visual Basic) for a strongly typed collection.
Comparer class	Compares two objects for equivalence, where string comparisons are case-sensitive.
DictionaryBase class	Not supported.
DictionaryEntry structure	Defines a dictionary key-and-value pair that can be set or retrieved.
Hashtable class	Represents a collection of key-and-value pairs that are organized based on the hashcode of the key.
Queue class	Not supported.
ReadOnlyCollectionBase class	Not supported.
SortedList class	Not supported.
Stack class	Represents a simple last in, first out collection of objects.

System.Collections.Specialized Namespace

The *System.Collections.Specialized* namespace contains specialized and strongly typed collections. It is implemented in the System.dll assembly. Classes and structures in this namespace are listed in Table A-4.

Table A-4 Classes and Structures in the *System.Collections.Specialized* Namespace

Class or Structure	Description
BitVector32 structure	Provides a simple structure that stores Boolean values and small integers in 32 bits of memory.
BitVector32.Section structure	Represents a section of the vector that can contain an integer number.
CollectionsUtil class	Not supported.
HybridDictionary class	Implements *IDictionary* by using a *ListDictionary* while the collection is small and then switching to a *Hashtable* when the collection gets large.
ListDictionary class	Implements *IDictionary* using a singly linked list. Recommended for collections that typically contain 10 items or fewer.
NameObjectCollectionBase class	Provides the abstract base class (*MustInherit* in Visual Basic) for a sorted collection of associated *String* keys and *Object* values that can be accessed either with the key or with the index.
NameObjectCollection-Base.KeysCollection class	Represents a collection of the *String* keys of a collection.
NameValueCollection class	Represents a sorted collection of associated *String* keys and *String* values that can be accessed either with the key or with the index.
StringCollection class	Not supported.
StringDictionary class	Not supported.
StringEnumerator class	Not supported.

System.ComponentModel Namespace

The *System.ComponentModel* namespace provides classes that implement design-time and run-time behavior of components and controls. It is implemented in the System.dll assembly. Classes in this namespace are listed in Table A-5.

Table A-5 Classes in the *System.ComponentModel* Namespace

Class	Description
AmbientValueAttribute	Not supported.
ArrayConverter	Not supported.

(continued)

Table A-5 Classes in the *System.ComponentModel* Namespace *(continued)*

Class	Description
AttributeCollection	Represents a collection of attributes.
BaseNumberConverter	Not supported.
BindableAttribute	Not supported.
BooleanConverter	Not supported.
BrowsableAttribute	Not supported.
ByteConverter	Not supported.
CancelEventArgs	Provides data for a cancelable event.
CategoryAttribute	Not supported.
CharConverter	Not supported.
CollectionChangeEventArgs	Provides data for the *CollectionChanged event*.
CollectionConverter	Not supported.
Component	Provides the base implementation for the *IComponent* interface and enables object-sharing between applications.
ComponentCollection	Not supported.
ComponentConverter	Not supported.
ComponentEditor	Not supported.
ComponentResourceManager	This class is a ResourceManager object that provides simple functionality for enumerating resources for a component or an object.
Container	Encapsulates zero or more components.
CultureInfoConverter	Not supported.
DateTimeConverter	Not supported.
DecimalConverter	Not supported.
DefaultEventAttribute	Not supported.
DefaultPropertyAttribute	Not supported.
DefaultValueAttribute	Specifies the default value for a property.
DescriptionAttribute	Not supported.
DesignerAttribute	Not supported.
DesignerCategoryAttribute	Specifies that the designer for a class belongs to a certain category.
DesignerSerializationVisibilityAttribute	Not supported.

Table A-5 Classes in the *System.ComponentModel* Namespace *(continued)*

Class	Description
DesignOnlyAttribute	Not supported.
DoubleConverter	Not supported.
EditorAttribute	Not supported.
EditorBrowsableAttribute	Specifies that a property or method is viewable in an editor.
EnumConverter	Not supported.
EventDescriptor	Provides information about an event.
EventDescriptorCollection	Represents a collection of *EventDescriptor* objects.
EventHandlerList	Provides a simple list of delegates.
ExpandableObjectConverter	Not supported.
GuidConverter	Not supported.
ImmutableObjectAttribute	Not supported.
InheritanceAttribute	Not supported.
InstallerTypeAttribute	Not supported.
Int16Converter	Not supported.
Int32Converter	Not supported.
Int64Converter	Not supported.
InvalidEnumArgumentException	Not supported.
License	Not supported.
LicenseContext	Not supported.
LicenseException	Not supported.
LicenseManager	Not supported.
LicenseProvider	Not supported.
LicenseProviderAttribute	Not supported.
LicFileLicenseProvider	Not supported.
ListBindableAttribute	Not supported.
ListChangedEventArgs	Provides data for the *ListChanged* event.
LocalizableAttribute	Not supported.
MarshalByValueComponent	Implements *IComponent* and provides the base implementation for remotable components that are marshaled by value (a copy of the serialized object is passed).

(continued)

Table A-5 Classes in the *System.ComponentModel* Namespace *(continued)*

Class	Description
MemberDescriptor	An abstract base class that represents a class member, such as a property or an event.
MergablePropertyAttribute	Not supported.
NotifyParentPropertyAttribute	Not supported.
ParenthesizePropertyNameAttribute	Not supported.
PropertyChangedEventArgs	Provides data for the *PropertyChanged* event.
PropertyDescriptor	Provides an abstraction of a property on a class.
PropertyDescriptorCollection	Represents a collection of *Property-Descriptor* objects.
PropertyTabAttribute	Not supported.
ProvidePropertyAttribute	Not supported.
ReadOnlyAttribute	Not supported.
RecommendedAsConfigurableAttribute	Not supported.
ReferenceConverter	Not supported.
RefreshEventArgs	Not supported.
RefreshPropertiesAttribute	Not supported.
RunInstallerAttribute	Not supported.
SByteConverter	Not supported.
SingleConverter	Not supported.
StringConverter	Not supported.
TimeSpanConverter	Not supported.
ToolboxItemAttribute	Not supported.
ToolboxItemFilterAttribute	Not supported.
TypeConverter	Provides a unified way of converting types of values to other types, as well as for accessing standard values and sub-properties.
TypeConverter.SimplePropertyDescriptor	Not supported.
TypeConverter.StandardValuesCollection	Not supported.
TypeConverterAttribute	Not supported.

Table A-5 Classes in the *System.ComponentModel* Namespace *(continued)*

Class	Description
TypeDescriptor	Provides information about the properties and events for a component.
TypeListConverter	Not supported.
Uint16Converter	Not supported.
Uint32Converter	Not supported.
Uint64Converter	Not supported.
WarningException	Not supported.
Win32Exception	The exception that is thrown for a Microsoft Win32 error code.

System.ComponentModel.Design Namespace

The *System.ComponentModel.Design* namespace enables developers to provide custom design-time behavior for custom controls. It is not supported in the .NET Compact Framework.

*System.Configuration.** Namespaces

The classes in the *System.Configuration*, *System.Configuration.Assemblies*, and *System.Configuration.Install* namespaces allow desktop applications to programmatically access application configuration (.config) files. Application configuration files are not supported in the .NET Compact Framework. The only objects from these namespaces implemented are the *System.Configuration.Assemblies.AssemblyHashAlgorithm* enumeration and the *System.Configuration.Assemblies.AssemblyVersionCompatibility* enumeration.

System.Data Namespace

The *System.Data* namespace contains the classes that implement the ADO.NET architecture. This namespace is implemented in System.Data.dll. The classes in this namespace are listed in Table A-6.

Table A-6 Classes in the *System.Data* Namespace

Class	Description
Constraint	Represents a constraint that can be enforced on one or more *DataColumn* objects.
ConstraintCollection	Represents a collection of constraints for a *DataTable*.
ConstraintException	Represents the exception that is thrown when attempting an action that violates a constraint.
DataColumn	Represents the schema of a column in a *DataTable*.
DataColumnChangeEventArgs	Provides data for the *ColumnChanging* event.
DataColumnCollection	Represents a collection of *DataColumn* objects for a *DataTable*.
DataException	Represents the exception that is thrown when errors are generated using ADO.NET components.
DataRelation	Represents a parent/child relationship between two *DataTable* objects.
DataRelationCollection	Represents the collection of *DataRelation* objects for this *DataSet*.
DataRow	Represents a row of data in a *DataTable*.
DataRowBuilder	The *DataRowBuilder* type supports the .NET Framework infrastructure and is not intended to be used directly from your code.
DataRowChangeEventArgs	Provides data for the *RowChanged*, *RowChanging*, *OnRowDeleting*, and *OnRowDeleted* events.
DataRowCollection	Represents a collection of rows for a *DataTable*.
DataRowView	Represents a customized view of a *DataRow* exposed as a fully featured Windows Forms control.
DataSet	Represents an in-memory cache of data.
DataSysDescriptionAttribute	Not supported.
DataTable	Represents one table of in-memory data.
DataTableCollection	Represents the collection of tables for the *DataSet*.
DataView	Represents a data-bindable, customized view of a *DataTable* for sorting, filtering, searching, editing, and navigation.

Table A-6 Classes in the *System.Data* Namespace *(continued)*

Class	Description
DataViewManager	Contains a default *DataViewSettingCollection* for each *DataTable* in a *DataSet*.
DataViewSetting	Represents the default settings for *ApplyDefaultSort*, *DataViewManager*, *RowFilter*, *RowStateFilter*, *Sort*, and *Table* for *DataViews* created from the *DataViewManager*.
DataViewSettingCollection	Contains a read-only collection of *DataViewSetting* objects for each *DataTable* in a *DataSet*.
DBConcurrencyException	The exception that is thrown by the *DataAdapter* during the update operation if the number of rows affected equals zero.
DeletedRowInaccessibleException	Represents the exception that is thrown when an action is attempted on a *DataRow* that has been deleted.
DuplicateNameException	Represents the exception that is thrown when a duplicate database object name is encountered during an add operation in a *DataSet*-related object.
EvaluateException	Represents the exception that is thrown when the *Expression* property of a *DataColumn* cannot be evaluated.
FillErrorEventArgs	Provides data for the *FillError* event of a *DbDataAdapter*.
ForeignKeyConstraint	Represents an action restriction enforced on a set of columns in a primary key/foreign key relationship when a value or row is either deleted or updated.
InRowChangingEventException	Represents the exception that is thrown when calling the *EndEdit* method within the *RowChanging* event.
InternalDataCollectionBase	Provides the base functionality for creating collections.
InvalidConstraintException	Represents the exception that is thrown when incorrectly attempting to create or access a relation.
InvalidExpressionException	Represents the exception that is thrown when attempting to add a *DataColumn* containing an invalid *Expression* to a *DataColumnCollection*.
MergeFailedEventArgs	Not supported.

(continued)

Table A-6 Classes in the *System.Data* Namespace *(continued)*

Class	Description
MissingPrimaryKeyException	Represents the exception that is thrown when attempting to access a row in a table that has no primary key.
NoNullAllowedException	Represents the exception that is thrown when attempting to insert a *null* value into a column in which *AllowDBNull* is set to *false*.
PropertyCollection	Represents a collection of properties that can be added to *DataColumn*, *DataSet*, or *DataTable*.
ReadOnlyException	Represents the exception that is thrown when attempting to change the value of a read-only column.
RowNotInTableException	Represents the exception that is thrown when trying to perform an operation on a *DataRow* that is not in a *DataTable*.
StateChangeEventArgs	Provides data for the state change event of a .NET data provider.
StrongTypingException	Not supported.
SyntaxErrorException	Represents the exception that is thrown when the *Expression* property of a *DataColumn* contains a syntax error.
TypedDataSetGenerator	Not supported.
TypedDataSetGeneratorException	Not supported.
UniqueConstraint	Represents a restriction on a set of columns in which all values must be unique.
VersionNotFoundException	Represents the exception that is thrown when attempting to return a version of a *DataRow* that has been deleted.

System.Data.Common Namespace

The *System.Data.Common* namespace contains classes common to all ADO.NET data providers. This namespace is implemented in System.Data.Common.dll. The classes in this namespace are listed in Table A-7.

Table A-7 Classes in the System.Data.Common Namespace

Class	Description
DataAdapter	Represents a set of data commands and a database connection that are used to fill the *DataSet* and update the data source.
DataColumnMapping	Contains a generic column mapping for an object that inherits from *DataAdapter*.
DataColumnMappingCollection	Contains a collection of *DataColumnMapping* objects.
DataTableMapping	Contains a description of a mapped relationship between a source table and a *DataTable* object. This class is used by a *DataAdapter* object when populating a *DataSet* object.
DataTableMappingCollection	A collection of *DataTableMapping* objects.
DbDataAdapter	Aids implementation of the *IDbDataAdapter* interface. Inheritors of *DbDataAdapter* implement a set of functions to provide strong typing but inherit most of the functionality needed to fully implement a *DataAdapter* object.
DbDataRecord	Implements *IDataRecord* and *ICustomTypeDescriptor*, and provides data binding support for *DbEnumerator*.
DBDataPermission	Not supported.
DBDataPermissionAttribute	Not supported.
DbEnumerator	Exposes the *GetEnumerator* method, which supports a simple iteration over a collection by a .NET Framework data provider.
RowUpdatedEventArg	Provides data for the *RowUpdated* event of a .NET data provider.
RowUpdatingEventArgs	Provides the data for the *RowUpdating* event of a .NET data provider.

System.Data.Odbc Namespace

The *System.Data.Odbc* namespace contains a managed data provider to an ODBC data source. It is not supported in the .NET Compact Framework.

System.Data.OleDb Namespace

The *System.Data.OleDb* namespace contains a managed data provider to an OLE DB data source. It is not supported in the .NET Compact Framework.

System.Data.SqlClient Namespace

The *System.Data.SqlClient* namespace contains a managed data provider for SQL Server. This namespace is implemented in System.Data.SqlClient.dll. You use the classes in Table A-8 to access a SQL Server database directly over a network connection.

Table A-8 Classes in the *System.Data.SqlClient* Namespace

Class	Description
SqlClientPermission	Not supported.
SqlClientPermissionAttribute	Not supported.
SqlCommand	Represents a Transact-SQL statement or a stored procedure to execute against a SQL Server database.
SqlCommandBuilder	Provides a means of automatically generating single-table commands used to reconcile changes made to a *DataSet* with the associated SQL Server database.
SqlConnection	Represents an open connection to a SQL Server database.
SqlDataAdapter	Represents a set of data commands and a database connection that are used to fill the *DataSet* and update a SQL Server database.
SqlDataReader	Provides a means of reading a forward-only stream of rows from a SQL Server database.
SqlError	Collects information relevant to a warning or an error returned by SQL Server.
SqlErrorCollection	Collects all errors generated by the SQL .NET Data Provider.
SqlException	The exception that is thrown when SQL Server returns a warning or an error.
SqlInfoMessageEventArgs	Provides data for the *InfoMessage* event.
SqlParameter	Represents a parameter to a *SqlCommand*, and optionally, its mapping to *DataSet* columns.
SqlParameterCollection	Collects all parameters relevant to a *SqlCommand* as well as their respective mappings to *DataSet* columns.

Table A-8 Classes in the *System.Data.SqlClient* Namespace *(continued)*

Class	Description
SqlRowUpdatedEventArgs	Provides data for the *RowUpdated* event.
SqlRowUpdatingEventArgs	Provides data for the *RowUpdating* event.
SqlTransaction	Represents a Transact-SQL transaction to be made in a SQL Server database.

System.Data.SqlServerCe Namespace

The *System.Data.SqlServerCe* namespace is not found in the desktop .NET Framework. It includes classes, listed in Table A-9, that manipulate a SQL Server CE database on the device and replicate data to and from an enterprise SQL Server using Remote Data Access (RDA) or merge replication. This namespace is implemented in System.Data.SqlServerCe.dll.

Table A-9 Classes in the *System.Data.SqlServerCe* Namespace

Class	Description
SqlCeCommand	Represents a Transact-SQL statement to execute against a data source.
SqlCeCommandBuilder	Provides a means of automatically generating single-table commands used to reconcile changes made to a *DataSet* with the associated SQL Server CE database.
SqlCeConnection	Represents an open connection to a SQL Server CE database.
SqlCeDataAdapter	Represents a set of data commands and a database connection that are used to fill the *DataSet* and update the data source.
SqlCeDataReader	Provides a means of reading a forward-only stream of rows from a SQL Server CE database.
SqlCeEngine	Represents the properties, methods, and other objects of the SQL Server CE Database Engine.
SqlCeError	Collects information relevant to a warning or an error returned from the data source.
SqlCeErrorCollection	Collects all errors generated by the SQL Server CE .NET Data Provider.
SqlCeException	The exception that is thrown when the underlying provider returns a warning or an error for a SQL Server CE data source.

(continued)

Table A-9 Classes in the *System.Data.SqlServerCe* Namespace *(continued)*

Class	Description
SqlCeInfoMessageEventArgs	Provides data for the *InfoMessage* event.
SqlCeParameter	Represents a parameter to *SqlCeCommand*, and optionally, its mapping to *DataSet* columns.
SqlCeParameterCollection	Collects all parameters relevant to *SqlCeCommand* as well as their respective mappings to *DataSet* columns.
SqlCeRemoteDataAccess	Initializes a new instance of the *SqlCeRemoteData-Access* object.
SqlCeReplication	Initializes a new instance of the *SqlCeReplication* object.
SqlCeRowUpdatedEventArgs	Provides data for the *RowUpdated* event.
SqlCeRowUpdatingEventArgs	Provides data for the *RowUpdating* event.
SqlCeTransaction	Represents a Transact-SQL transaction to be made at a data source.

System.Data.SqlTypes Namespace

The *System.Data.SqlTypes* namespace contains classes and structures for native types in SQL Server. It is implemented in the System.Data.Common.dll assembly. Table A-10 lists these classes and structures.

Table A-10 Classes and Structures in the *System.Data.SqlTypes* Namespace

Class or Structure	Description
SqlBinary structure	Used for *binary*, *image*, *timestamp*, and *varbinary* native SQL Server types.
SqlBoolean structure	Represents an integer value that is either 1 or 0 to be stored on or retrieved from a database.
SqlByte structure	Used for the *tinyint* native SQL Server type.
SqlDateTime structure	Used for *datetime* and *smalldatetime* native SQL Server types.
SqlDecimal structure	Used for *decimal* and *numeric* native SQL Server types.
SqlDouble structure	Used for the *float* native SQL Server type.
SqlGuid structure	Used for the *uniqueidentifier* native SQL Server type.

Table A-10 Classes and Structures in the *System.Data.SqlTypes* Namespace

Class or Structure	Description
SqlInt16 structure	Used for the *smallint* native SQL Server type.
SqlInt32 structure	Used for the *int* native SQL Server type.
SqlInt64 structure	Used for the *bigint* native SQL Server type.
SqlMoney structure	Used for *money* and *smallmoney* native SQL Server types.
SqlNullValueException class	The exception that is thrown when the *Value* property of a *SqlTypes* structure is set to *null*.
SqlSingle structure	Used for the *real* native SQL Server type.
SqlString structure	Used for *nchar, ntext, nvarchar, sysname, text*, and *varchar* native SQL Server types.
SqlTruncateException class	The exception that is thrown when setting a value into a *SqlType* structure would truncate that value.
SqlTypeException class	The base exception class for the *System.Data.SqlTypes*.

System.Diagnostics Namespace

The *System.Diagnostics* namespace contains classes that allow you to debug your application. In the desktop implementation, these classes also allow you to interact with system processes, event logs, and performance counters, but they are not implemented in the .NET Compact Framework. The namespace is implemented in the mscorlib.dll assembly. Table A-11 lists the classes in the *System.Diagnostics* namespace.

Table A-11 Classes in the *System.Diagnostics* Namespace

Class	Description
BooleanSwitch	Not supported.
ConditionalAttribute	Indicates to compilers that a method is callable if a specified preprocessing identifier is applied to the method.
*Counter** classes	Not supported.
Debug	Provides a set of methods and properties that help debug your code.

(continued)

Table A-11 Classes in the *System.Diagnostics* Namespace *(continued)*

Class	Description
DebuggableAttribute	Modifies code generation for run-time just-in-time (JIT) debugging.
Debugger	Enables communication with a debugger.
DebuggerHiddenAttribute	Not supported.
DebuggerStepThroughAttribute	Specifies the *DebuggerStepThroughAttribute*.
DefaultTraceListener	Provides the default output methods and behavior for tracing.
EntryWrittenEventArgs	Not supported.
*EventLog** classes	Not supported.
FileVersionInfo	Not supported.
*InstanceData** classes	Not supported.
MonitoringDescriptionAttribute	Not supported.
*PerformanceCounter** classes	Not supported.
*Process** classes	Not supported.
StackFrame	Not supported.
StackTrace	Not supported.
Switch	Not supported.
TextWriterTraceListener	Not supported.
Trace	Provides a set of methods and properties that help you trace the execution of your code.
TraceListener	Provides the abstract base class (*MustInherit* in Visual Basic) for the listeners who monitor trace and debug output.
TraceListenerCollection	Provides a thread-safe list of *TraceListener* objects.
TraceSwitch	Not supported.

System.DirectoryServices Namespace

The *System.DirectoryServices* namespace provides access to Active Directory from managed code. It is not supported in the .NET Compact Framework.

System.Drawing Namespace

The *System.Drawing* namespace provides access to basic graphics functionality. It is implemented in the System.Drawing.dll assembly. Its classes and structures are listed in Table A-12.

Table A-12 Classes and Structures in the *System.Drawing* Namespace

Class or Structure	Description
Bitmap class	Encapsulates a GDI+ bitmap, which consists of the pixel data for a graphics image and its attributes. A *Bitmap* object is an object used to work with images defined by pixel data.
Brush class	Classes derived from this abstract base class define objects used to fill the interiors of graphical shapes such as rectangles, ellipses, pies, polygons, and paths.
Brushes class	Not supported.
CharacterRange structure	Not supported.
Color structure	Represents an ARGB color.
ColorConverter class	Not supported.
ColorTranslator class	Not supported.
Font class	Defines a particular format for text, including font face, size, and style attributes.
FontConverter class	Not supported.
FontFamily class	Defines a group of typefaces having a similar basic design and certain variations in styles.
Graphics class	Encapsulates a GDI+ drawing surface.
Icon class	Represents a Windows icon, which is a small bitmap image used to represent an object. Icons can be thought of as transparent bitmaps, although their size is determined by the system.
IconConverter class	Not supported.
Image class	An abstract base class that provides functionality for *Bitmap*, *Icon*, and *Metafile* descended classes.
ImageAnimator class	Not supported.
ImageConverter class	Not supported.

(continued)

Table A-12 Classes and Structures in the *System.Drawing* Namespace *(continued)*

Class or Structure	Description
ImageFormatConverter class	Not supported.
Pen class	Defines an object used to draw lines and curves.
Pens class	Not supported.
Point structure	Represents an ordered pair of integer *x*- and *y*-coordinates that defines a point in a two-dimensional plane.
PointConverter class	Not supported.
PointF structure	Not supported.
Rectangle structure	Stores the location and size of a rectangular region. For more advanced region functions, use a *Region* object.
RectangleConverter class	Not supported.
RectangleF structure	Stores the location and size of a rectangular region. For more advanced region functions, use a *Region* object.
Region class	Describes the interior of a graphics shape composed of rectangles and paths.
Size structure	Represents the size of a rectangular region with an ordered pair of width and height.
SizeConverter class	Not supported.
SizeF structure	Represents the size of a rectangular region with an ordered pair of width and height.
SolidBrush class	Defines a brush of a single color. Brushes are used to fill graphics shapes, such as rectangles, ellipses, pies, polygons, and paths.
StringFormat class	Not supported.
SystemBrushes class	Not supported.
SystemColors class	Each property of the *SystemColors* class is a *Color* structure that is the color of a Windows display element.
SystemIcons class	Not supported.
SystemPens class	Not supported.
TextureBrush class	Not supported.
ToolboxBitmapAttribute class	Not supported.

System.Drawing.Design Namespace

The *System.Drawing.Design* namespace contains classes to help with drawing operations that are used with controls at design time, or to create custom toolbox items. It is not supported in the .NET Compact Framework.

System.Drawing.Drawing2D Namespace

The *System.Drawing.Drawing2D* namespace provides advanced two-dimensional and vector graphics functionality. This functionality is not supported in the .NET Compact Framework. Only the *CombineMode* enumeration, which is required by classes in other drawing namespaces, is implemented.

System.Drawing.Imaging Namespace

The *System.Drawing.Imaging* namespace provides advanced GDI+ imaging capability. This functionality is not supported in the .NET Compact Framework. However, this namespace does exist and contains only the *ImageAttributes* class. Classes in the *System.Drawing.Imaging* namespace are listed in Table A-13.

Table A-13 Classes in the *System.Drawing.Imaging* Namespace

Class	Description
ImageAttributes	Contains information about how image colors are manipulated during rendering. Supported methods are *ImageAttributes*, *ClearColorKey*, and *SetColorKey*.
All other classes	Not supported.

System.Drawing.Printing Namespace

The *System.Drawing.Printing* namespace provides printing services. It is not supported in the .NET Compact Framework.

System.Drawing.Text Namespace

The *System.Drawing.Text* namespace provides advanced GDI+ typography capability. This functionality is not supported in the .NET Compact Framework.

System.EnterpriseServices Namespaces

The *System.EnterpriseServices, System.EnterpriseServices.CompensatingResourceManager*, and *System.EnterpriseServices.Internal* namespaces provide access to COM+ functionality for a desktop application. COM+ is not supported in the .NET Compact Framework.

System.Globalization Namespace

The *System.Globalization* namespace contains classes that define culture-related information, including the language, the sort orders for strings, the calendars, and the formats for currencies and numbers. It is implemented in Mscorlib.dll. The classes for this namespace are listed in Table A-14.

Table A-14 Classes in the *System.Globalization* Namespace

Class	Description
Calendar	Represents time in divisions, such as weeks, months, and years.
CompareInfo	Implements a set of methods for culture-sensitive string comparisons.
CultureInfo	Represents information about a specific culture, including the names of the culture, the writing system, and the calendar used; as well as access to culture-specific objects that provide methods for common operations, such as formatting dates and sorting strings.
DateTimeFormatInfo	Defines how *DateTime* values are formatted and displayed, depending on the culture.
DaylightTime	Defines the period of daylight saving time.
GregorianCalendar	Represents the Gregorian calendar.
HebrewCalendar	Not supported.
HijriCalendar	Not supported.
JapaneseCalendar	Represents the Japanese calendar.
JulianCalendar	Not supported.
KoreanCalendar	Represents the Korean calendar.
NumberFormatInfo	Defines how numeric values are formatted and displayed, depending on the culture.
RegionInfo	Contains information about the country/region.
SortKey	Not supported.

Table A-14 Classes in the *System.Globalization* Namespace *(continued)*

Class	Description
StringInfo	Provides functionality to split a string into text elements and to iterate through those text elements.
TaiwanCalendar	Represents the Taiwan calendar.
TextElementEnumerator	Enumerates the text elements of a string.
TextInfo	Defines properties and behaviors, such as casing, that are specific to a writing system.
ThaiBuddhistCalendar	Represents the Thai Buddhist calendar.

System.IO Namespace

The *System.IO* namespace contains classes and structures that allow synchronous and asynchronous reading and writing on data streams and files. It is implemented in Mscorlib.dll. Note that the *System.IO.IsolatedStorage* namespace is not supported in the .NET Compact Framework. Table A-15 lists the classes and structures of the *System.IO* namespace.

Table A-15 Classes and Structures in the *System.IO* Namespace

Class or Structure	Description
BinaryReader class	Reads primitive data types as binary values in a specific encoding.
BinaryWriter class	Writes primitive types in binary to a stream and supports writing strings in a specific encoding.
BufferedStream class	Not supported.
Directory class	Exposes static methods for creating, moving, and enumerating through directories and subdirectories.
DirectoryInfo class	Exposes instance methods for creating, moving, and enumerating through directories and subdirectories.
DirectoryNotFoundException class	The exception that is thrown when part of a file or directory cannot be found.
EndOfStreamException class	The exception that is thrown when reading is attempted past the end of a stream.
ErrorEventArgs class	Not supported.

(continued)

Table A-15 Classes and Structures in the *System.IO* Namespace *(continued)*

Class or Structure	Description
File class	Provides static methods for the creation, copying, deletion, moving, and opening of files, and aids in the creation of *FileStream* objects.
FileInfo class	Provides instance methods for the creation, copying, deletion, moving, and opening of files, and aids in the creation of *FileStream* objects.
FileLoadException class	Not supported.
FileNotFoundException class	The exception that is thrown when an attempt to access a file that does not exist on disk fails.
FileStream class	Exposes a *Stream* around a file, supporting both synchronous and asynchronous read and write operations.
FileSystemEventArgs class	Not supported.
FileSystemInfo class	Provides the base class for both *FileInfo* and *DirectoryInfo* objects.
FileSystemWatcher class	Not supported.
InternalBufferOverflowException class	Not supported.
IODescriptionAttribute class	Not supported.
IOException class	The exception that is thrown when an I/O error occurs.
MemoryStream class	Creates a stream whose backing store is memory.
Path class	Performs operations on *String* instances that contain file or directory path information. These operations are performed in a cross-platform manner.
PathTooLongException class	The exception that is thrown when a pathname or filename is longer than the system-defined maximum length.
RenamedEventArgs class	Not supported.
Stream class	Provides a generic view of a sequence of bytes.
StreamReader class	Implements a *TextReader* class that reads characters from a byte stream in a particular encoding.

Table A-15 Classes and Structures in the *System.IO* Namespace *(continued)*

Class or Structure	Description
StreamWriter class	Implements a *TextWriter* class for writing characters to a stream in a particular encoding.
StringReader class	Implements a *TextReader* class that reads from a string.
StringWriter class	Writes information to a string. The information is stored in an underlying *StringBuilder* class.
TextReader class	Represents a reader that can read a sequential series of characters.
TextWriter class	Represents a writer that can write a sequential series of characters. This class is abstract.
WaitForChangedResult structure	Not supported.

System.Management Namespaces

The *System.Management* and *System.Management.Instrumentation* namespaces allow access to management information and events about the system, devices, and applications instrumented to the Windows Management Instrumentation (WMI) infrastructure. These namespaces are not supported in the .NET Compact Framework.

System.Messaging Namespace

The *System.Messaging* namespace allows desktop applications to work with messages in the Microsoft Message Queuing (MSMQ) infrastructure. This is not supported in the .NET Compact Framework.

System.Net Namespace

The *System.Net* namespace provides a simple API that allows use of many of the protocols used on the network today. It is implemented primarily in System.dll. However, the IrDA (Infrared) classes are in a separate assembly, System.Net.IrDA.dll. Table A-16 lists the classes of this namespace.

Table A-16 Classes in the *System.Net* Namespace

Class	Description
AuthenticationManager	Manages the authentication modules called during the client authentication process.
Authorization	Contains an authentication message for an Internet server.
Cookie	Not supported.
CookieCollection	Not supported.
CookieContainer	Not supported.
CookieException	Not supported.
CredentialCache	Not supported.
Dns	Provides simple domain name resolution functionality.
DnsPermission	Not supported.
DnsPermissionAttribute	Not supported.
EndPoint	Identifies a network address. This is an abstract class (*MustInherit* in Visual Basic).
EndpointPermission	Not supported.
FileWebRequest	Not supported.
FileWebResponse	Not supported.
GlobalProxySelection	Contains a global default proxy instance for all HTTP requests.
HttpVersion	Defines the HTTP version numbers supported by the *HttpWebRequest* and *HttpWebResponse* classes.
HttpWebRequest	Provides an HTTP-specific implementation of the *WebRequest* class.
HttpWebResponse	Provides an HTTP-specific implementation of the *WebResponse* class.
IPAddress	Provides an Internet Protocol (IP) address.
IPEndPoint	Represents a network endpoint as an IP address and a port number.
IPHostEntry	Provides a container class for Internet host address information.
IrDAEndPoint	Establishes connections to a server and provides infrared port information. This class is not supported in the desktop .NET Framework.
NetworkCredential	Provides credentials for password-based authentication schemes such as basic, digest, NTLM, and Kerberos.

Table A-16 Classes in the *System.Net* Namespace *(continued)*

Class	Description
ProtocolViolationException	The exception that is thrown when an error is made while using a network protocol.
ServicePoint	Provides connection management for HTTP connections.
ServicePointManager	Manages the collection of *ServicePoint* instances.
SocketAddress	Stores serialized information from *EndPoint*-derived classes.
SocketPermission	Not supported.
SocketPermissionAttribute	Not supported.
WebClient	Not supported.
WebException	The exception that is thrown when an error occurs while accessing the network through a pluggable protocol.
WebHeaderCollection	Contains protocol headers associated with a request or response.
WebPermission	Not supported.
WebPermissionAttribute	Not supported.
WebProxy	Contains HTTP proxy settings for the *WebRequest* class.
WebRequest	Makes a request to a Uniform Resource Identifier (URI). This is an abstract class (*MustInherit* in Visual Basic).
WebResponse	Provides a response from a Uniform Resource Identifier (URI). This is an abstract class (*MustInherit* in Visual Basic).

System.Net.Sockets Namespace

The *System.Net.Sockets* namespace provides a managed access to the Windows Sockets (Winsock) communications API. Most of this namespace is implemented in System.dll. However, the IrDA (Infrared) classes are in a separate assembly, System.Net.IrDA.dll. Table A-17 lists the classes in the *System.Net.Sockets* namespace.

Table A-17 Classes in the *System.Net.Sockets* Namespace

Class	Description
IPv6MulticastOption	Not supported.
IrDAClient	Provides connection information and creates client connection objects for opening and closing connections to a server. This class is not supported in the desktop .NET Framework.
IrDADeviceInfo	Provides information about available servers and ports obtained by the client during a discovery query. This class is not supported in the desktop .NET Framework.
IrDAListener	Places a socket in a listening state to monitor connections from a specified service or network address. This class is not supported in the desktop .NET Framework.
LingerOption	Contains information about a socket's linger time, which is the amount of time it will remain after closing if data remains to be sent.
MulticastOption	Contains IP address values for IP multicast packets.
NetworkStream	Provides the underlying stream of data for network access.
Socket	Implements the Berkeley sockets interface.
SocketException	The exception that is thrown when a socket error occurs.
TcpClient	Provides client connections for TCP network services.
TcpListener	Listens for connections from TCP network clients.
UdpClient	Provides User Datagram Protocol (UDP) network services.

System.Reflection Namespace

The *System.Reflection* namespace provides classes that allow you to declare attributes in assemblies. It also allows the run-time discovery of types and other characteristics in an assembly and has the ability to dynamically create and invoke types. It is implemented in the mscorlib.dll assembly. The related namespace *System.Reflection.Emit*, which provides classes that allow a compiler or tool to emit metadata and intermediate language (IL), is not supported in the .NET Compact Framework. Table A-18 lists the classes and structures in the *System.Reflection* namespace.

Table A-18 Classes and Structures in the *System.Reflection* Namespace

Class or Structure	Description
AmbiguousMatchException class	The exception that is thrown when binding to a method results in more than one method matching the binding criteria.
Assembly class	Defines an *Assembly*, which is a reusable, versionable, and self-describing building block of a common language runtime application.
AssemblyAlgorithmIdAttribute class	Specifies an algorithm to hash all files in an assembly.
AssemblyCompanyAttribute class	Defines a company name custom attribute for an assembly manifest.
AssemblyConfigurationAttribute class	Defines an assembly configuration custom attribute (such as retail or debug) for an assembly manifest.
AssemblyCopyrightAttribute class	Defines a copyright custom attribute for an assembly manifest.
AssemblyCultureAttribute class	Specifies which culture the assembly supports.
AssemblyDefaultAliasAttribute class	Defines a friendly default alias for an assembly manifest.
AssemblyDelaySignAttribute class	Specifies that the assembly is not fully signed when created.
AssemblyDescriptionAttribute class	Defines an assembly description custom attribute for an assembly manifest.
AssemblyFileVersionAttribute class	Not supported.
AssemblyFlagsAttribute class	Specifies whether an assembly supports side-by-side execution on the same machine, in the same process, or in the same application domain.
AssemblyInformationalVersionAttribute class	Defines an assembly informational version custom attribute for an assembly manifest.
AssemblyKeyFileAttribute class	Specifies the name of a file containing the key pair used to generate a shared name.
AssemblyKeyNameAttribute class	Specifies the name of a key container within the cryptography service provider (CSP) containing the key pair used to generate a strong name.

(continued)

Table A-18 Classes and Structures in the *System.Reflection* Namespace *(continued)*

Class or Structure	Description
AssemblyName class	Fully describes an assembly's unique identity.
AssemblyNameProxy class	Not supported.
AssemblyProductAttribute class	Defines a product name custom attribute for an assembly manifest.
AssemblyTitleAttribute class	Defines an assembly title custom attribute for an assembly manifest.
AssemblyTrademarkAttribute class	Defines a trademark custom attribute for an assembly manifest.
AssemblyVersionAttribute class	Specifies the version of the assembly being attributed.
Binder class	Selects a member from a list of candidates, and performs type conversion from actual argument type to formal argument type.
ConstructorInfo class	Discovers the attributes of a class constructor and provides access to constructor metadata.
CustomAttributeFormatException class	The exception that is thrown when the binary format of a custom attribute is invalid.
DefaultMemberAttribute class	Defines the member of a type that is the default member used by *InvokeMember*. The default member is a name given to a type.
EventInfo class	Discovers the attributes of an event and provides access to event metadata.
FieldInfo class	Discovers the attributes of a field and provides access to field metadata.
InterfaceMapping structure	Not supported.
InvalidFilterCriteriaException class	Not supported.
ManifestResourceInfo class	Not supported.
MemberInfo class	Discovers the attributes of a member and provides access to member metadata.
MethodBase class	Provides information about methods and constructors.
MethodInfo class	Discovers the attributes of a method and provides access to method metadata.

Table A-18 Classes and Structures in the *System.Reflection* Namespace *(continued)*

Class or Structure	Description
Missing class	Represents a missing *Object*.
Module class	Performs reflection on a module.
ParameterInfo class	Discovers the attributes of a parameter and provides access to parameter metadata.
ParameterModifier structure	Attaches a modifier to parameters so that binding can work with parameter signatures in which the types have been modified.
Pointer class	Not supported.
PropertyInfo class	Discovers the attributes of a property and provides access to property metadata.
ReflectionTypeLoadException class	Not supported.
StrongNameKeyPair class	Not supported.
TargetException class	Not supported.
TargetInvocationException class	The exception that is thrown by methods invoked through reflection.
TargetParameterCountException class	The exception that is thrown when the number of parameters for an invocation does not match the number expected.
TypeDelegator class	Not supported.

System.Resources Namespace

The *System.Resources* namespace contains classes that allow developers to manage culture-specific resources in an application. It is implemented in Mscorlib.dll. Table A-19 lists this namespace's classes.

Table A-19 Classes in the *System.Resources* Namespace

Class	Description
MissingManifestResourceException	The exception thrown if the main assembly does not contain the resources for the neutral culture, and they are required because of a missing appropriate satellite assembly.
NeutralResourcesLanguageAttribute	Informs the *ResourceManager* of the neutral culture of an assembly.

(continued)

Table A-19 Classes in the *System.Resources* Namespace *(continued)*

Class	Description
ResourceManager	Provides convenient access to culture-specific resources at run time.
ResourceReader	Enumerates .resources files and streams, reading sequential resource name and value pairs.
ResourceSet	Stores all the resources localized for one particular culture, ignoring all other cultures, including any fallback rules.
ResourceWriter	Not supported.
*ResX** classes	Not supported.
SatelliteContractVersionAttribute	Instructs the *ResourceManager* to ask for a particular version of a satellite assembly to simplify updates of the main assembly of an application.

System.Runtime.CompilerServices Namespace

The classes in the *System.Runtime.CompilerServices* namespace are for the compiler writer's use only. The following classes are implemented in the .NET Compact Framework: *AccessedThroughPropertyAttribute*, *CustomConstantAttribute*, *DateTimeConstantAttribute*, *DecimalConstantAttribute*, *IndexerNameAttribute*, *MethodImplAttribute*, and *RuntimeHelpers*. Full details are not given because these classes are not used by the majority of application developers.

System.Runtime.InteropServices Namespace

The *System.Runtime.InteropServices* namespace includes classes that allow the use of P/Invoke to call out to unmanaged code from a .NET Compact Framework application. The namespace is implemented in Mscorlib.dll. In the desktop implementation of this namespace, there is support for COM Interop, which is not supported in the .NET Compact Framework. The classes and structures of this namespace are listed in Table A-20.

Table A-20 Classes and Structures in the *System.Runtime.InteropServices* Namespace

Class or Structure	Description
ArrayWithOffset structure	Not supported.
AutomationProxyAttribute class	Not supported.

Table A-20 Classes and Structures in the *System.Runtime.InteropServices* Namespace *(continued)*

Class or Structure	Description
BestFitMappingAttribute class	Not supported.
BIND_OPTS structure	Not supported.
BINDPTR structure	Not supported.
ClassInterfaceAttribute class	Not supported.
CoClassAttribute class	Not supported.
All *Com** classes except the *ComVisibleAttribute* class	Not supported.
ComVisibleAttribute class	Controls COM visibility of an individual type or a member, or of all types within an assembly.
CONNECTDATA structure	Not supported.
CurrencyWrapper class	Not supported.
DispatchWrapper class	Not supported.
DispIdAttribute class	Specifies the COM *DispId* of a method, field, or property.
DISPPARAMS structure	Not supported.
DllImportAttribute class	Indicates that the attributed method is implemented as an export from an unmanaged DLL.
ELEMDESC structure	Not supported.
ErrorWrapper class	Not supported.
EXCEPINFO structure	Not supported.
ExtensibleClassFactory class	Not supported.
ExternalException class	The base exception type for all COM Interop exceptions and structured exception handling (SEH) exceptions.
FieldOffsetAttribute class	Not supported.
FILETIME structure	Not supported.
FUNCDESC structure	Not supported.
GCHandle structure	Provides a means for accessing a managed object from unmanaged memory.
GuidAttribute class	Supplies an explicit *Guid* when an automatic *Guid* is undesirable.
HandleRef structure	Not supported.
IDispatchImplAttribute class	Not supported.
IDLDESC structure	Not supported.

(continued)

Table A-20 Classes and Structures in the *System.Runtime.InteropServices* Namespace *(continued)*

Class or Structure	Description
ImportedFromTypeLibAttribute class	Not supported.
InAttribute class	Indicates that data should be marshaled from the caller to the callee.
InterfaceTypeAttribute class	Not supported.
InvalidComObjectException class	Not supported.
InvalidOleVariantTypeException class	Not supported.
LCIDConversionAttribute class	Not supported.
Marshal class	Provides a collection of methods pertaining to allocating unmanaged memory, copying unmanaged memory blocks, and converting managed to unmanaged types.
MarshalAsAttribute class	Not supported.
MarshalDirectiveException class	Not supported.
OptionalAttribute class	Not supported.
OutAttribute class	Indicates that data should be marshaled from callee back to caller.
PARAMDESC structure	Not supported.
PreserveSigAttribute class	Not supported.
PrimaryInteropAssemblyAttribute class	Not supported.
ProgIdAttribute class	Not supported.
RegistrationServices class	Not supported.
RuntimeEnvironment class	Not supported.
SafeArrayRankMismatchException class	Not supported.
SafeArrayTypeMismatchException class	Not supported.
SEHException class	Not supported.
STATSTG structure	Not supported.
StructLayoutAttribute class	Allows the user to control the physical layout of the data fields of a class or structure.
All *TYPE** structures	Not supported.
All *Type** classes	Not supported.
UnknownWrapper class	Not supported.
VARDESC structure	Not supported.
VARDESC.DESCUNION structure	Not supported.

System.Runtime.Remoting Namespaces

System.Runtime.Remoting comprises 13 different namespaces for remoting in the desktop .NET Framework version 1.1. .NET Remoting is not supported in the .NET Compact Framework.

System.Runtime.Serialization Namespaces

System.Runtime.Serialization comprises four namespaces in the .NET Framework version 1.1 that contain classes used for serializing and deserializing objects, using either the *BinaryFormatter* or the *SoapFormatter* class. These namespaces are not implemented in the .NET Compact Framework.

System.Security Namespace

The *System.Security* namespace provides the underlying structure of the .NET Framework security system. In version 1 of the .NET Compact Framework, only a limited implementation of the security system has been made. Consequently, the *System.Security.Cryptography*, *System.Security.Cryptography.Xml*, and *System.Security.Principal* namespaces have not been implemented. Table A-21 lists the classes in the *System.Security* namespace.

Table A-21 Classes in the *System.Security* Namespace

Class	Description
AllowPartiallyTrustedCallersAttribute	Not supported.
CodeAccessPermission	Not supported.
NamedPermissionSet	Not supported.
PermissionSet	Not supported.
SecurityElement	Not supported.
SecurityException	The exception that is thrown when a security error is detected.
SecurityManager	Not supported.
SuppressUnmanagedCodeSecurityAttribute	Not supported.
UnverifiableCodeAttribute	Not supported.
VerificationException	The exception that is thrown when the security policy requires code to be type safe and the verification process is unable to verify that the code is type safe.
XmlSyntaxException	Not supported.

System.Security.Cryptography.X509Certificates Namespace

The *System.Security.Cryptography.X509Certificates* namespace provides classes to represent an X.509 security certificate. Table A-22 lists the classes in this namespace.

Table A-22 Classes in the *System.Security.Cryptography .X509Certificates* Namespace

Class	Description
X509Certificate	Defines the common language runtime implementation of an X.509 version 3 certificate.
X509CertificateCollection	Not supported.
X509CertificateCollection.X509CertificateEnumerator	Not supported.

System.Security.Permissions Namespace

The *System.Security.Permissions* namespace defines classes that control access to operations and resources based on security policy. It is not supported in the .NET Compact Framework.

System.Security.Policy Namespace

The *System.Security.Policy* namespace contains the classes that govern the .NET Framework security policy system. Version 1 of the .NET Compact Framework has a fixed, non-configurable policy of "All code has full trust." Consequently, this namespace contains only the *Evidence* class.

System.ServiceProcess Namespace

The *System.ServiceProcess* namespace contains classes that allow you to implement, install, and control Windows service applications. It is not supported in the .NET Compact Framework.

System.Text Namespace

The *System.Text* namespace contains classes that represent ASCII, Unicode, UTF-7, and UTF-8 character encodings and classes that convert blocks of characters to and from blocks of bytes. This namespace is implemented in Mscorlib.dll. Table A-23 lists the classes in the *System.Text* namespace.

Table A-23 Classes in the *System.Text* Namespace

Class	Description
ASCIIEncoding	Represents an ASCII character encoding of Unicode characters.
Decoder	Converts encoded blocks of bytes into blocks of Unicode characters.
Encoder	Converts blocks of Unicode characters into encoded blocks of bytes.
Encoding	Represents a character encoding.
MLangCodePageEncoding	Represents a character encoding specified using a Code Page value. This class is not supported in the desktop .NET Framework.
StringBuilder	Represents a mutable string of characters.
UnicodeEncoding	Represents a UTF-16 encoding of Unicode characters.
UTF7Encoding	Represents a UTF-7 encoding of Unicode characters.
UTF8Encoding	Represents a UTF-8 encoding of Unicode characters.

System.Text.RegularExpressions Namespace

The *System.Text.RegularExpressions* namespace contains the .NET Framework regular expressions library. It is implemented in System.dll. Table A-24 lists the classes in this namespace.

Table A-24 Classes in the *System.Text.RegularExpressions* Namespace

Class	Description
Capture	Represents the results from a single subexpression capture. *Capture* represents one substring for a single successful capture.
CaptureCollection	Represents a sequence of capture substrings. *CaptureCollection* returns the set of captures done by a single capturing group.

(continued)

Table A-24 Classes in the *System.Text.RegularExpressions* Namespace *(continued)*

Class	Description
Group	Represents the results from a single capturing group. A capturing group can capture zero, one, or more strings in a single match because of quantifiers, so *Group* supplies a collection of *Capture* objects.
GroupCollection	Represents a collection of captured groups. *GroupCollection* returns the set of captured groups in a single match.
Match	Represents the results from a single regular expression match.
MatchCollection	Represents the set of successful matches found by iteratively applying a regular expression pattern to the input string.
Regex	Represents an immutable regular expression.
RegexCompilationInfo	Not supported.
RegexRunner	The *RegExRunner* type supports the .NET Framework infrastructure and is not intended to be used directly from your code.
RegexRunnerFactory	The *RegExRunnerFactory* type supports the .NET Framework infrastructure and is not intended to be used directly from your code.

System.Threading Namespace

The *System.Threading* namespace provides classes and structures that enable multithreaded programming. It is implemented in Mscorlib.dll. Table A-25 lists the classes and structures in this namespace.

Table A-25 Classes and Structures in the *System.Threading* Namespace

Class or Structure	Description
AutoResetEvent class	Notifies one or more waiting threads that an event has occurred.
Interlocked class	Provides atomic operations for variables that are shared by multiple threads.
LockCookie structure	Not supported.
ManualResetEvent class	Occurs when notifying one or more waiting threads that an event has occurred.

Table A-25 Classes and Structures in the *System.Threading* Namespace *(continued)*

Class or Structure	Description
Monitor class	Provides a mechanism that synchronizes access to objects.
Mutex class	A synchronization primitive than can also be used for interprocess synchronization.
NativeOverlapped structure	Not supported.
ReaderWriterLock class	Not supported.
RegisteredWaitHandle class	Not supported.
SynchronizationLockException class	Not supported.
Thread class	Creates and controls a thread, sets its priority, and gets its status.
ThreadAbortException class	Not supported.
ThreadExceptionEventArgs class	Not supported.
ThreadInterruptedException class	Not supported.
ThreadPool class	Provides a pool of threads that can be used to post work items, process asynchronous I/O, wait on behalf of other threads, and process timers.
ThreadStateException class	The exception that is thrown when a *Thread* is in an invalid *ThreadState* for the method call.
Timeout class	Contains a constant used to specify an infinite amount of time.
Timer class	Provides a mechanism for executing methods at specified intervals.
WaitHandle class	Encapsulates operating system–specific objects that wait for exclusive access to shared resources.

System.Timers Namespace

The *System.Timers* namespace contains the Timer component. This is not supported in the .NET Compact Framework. Instead, use the *System.Threading.Timer* or *System.Windows.Forms.Timer* classes.

System.Web Namespaces

The *System.Web*, *System.Web.Caching*, *System.Web.Configuration*, *System.Web.Handlers*, *System.Web.Hosting*, *System.Web.Mail*, *System.Web.Mobile*, *System.Web.RegularExpressions*, *System.Web.Security*, and *System.Web.SessionState* namespaces implement ASP.NET, the .NET Framework solution for Web server applications. The *System.Web.UI.** classes implement the controls used to build ASP.NET Web applications. None of these namespaces are supported in the .NET Compact Framework.

The *System.Web.Services.** classes implement support for hosting and accessing XML Web services. Of these, only classes in *System.Web.Services*, *System.Web.Services.Description*, and *System.Web.Services.Protocols* that are necessary for an application to act as an XML Web services client have been implemented in the .NET Compact Framework. *System.Web.Services.Discovery* and *System.Web.Services.Configuration* are not implemented in the .NET Compact Framework.

System.Web.Services Namespace

The *System.Web.Services* namespace consists of classes that enable you to create applications that are XML Web Services clients. It is implemented in System.Web.Services.dll. Table A-26 lists the classes in this namespace.

Table A-26 Classes in the *System.Web.Services* Namespace

Class	Description
WebMethodAttribute	Adding this attribute to a method within an XML Web service created using ASP.NET makes the method callable from remote Web clients.
WebService	Not supported.
WebServiceAttribute	Not supported.
WebServiceBindingAttribute	Declares the binding for one or more XML Web service methods implemented within the class implementing the XML Web service.

System.Web.Services.Description Namespace

In the desktop Framework, the *System.Web.Services.Description* namespace contains classes that allow you to publicly describe an XML Web service using

Web Services Description Language (WSDL). In the .NET Compact Framework, only the *SoapBindingUse* enumeration is implemented, which enables interpretation of WSDL in a client application.

System.Web.Services.Protocols Namespace

The *System.Web.Services.Protocols* namespace contains classes that enable communication between XML Web Services clients and servers. It is implemented in System.Web.Services.dll. Table A-27 lists the classes in this namespace.

Table A-27 Classes in the *System.Web.Services.Protocols* Namespace

Class	Description
HttpGetClientProtocol	Not supported.
HttpMethodAttribute	Not supported.
HttpPostClientProtocol	Not supported.
HttpSimpleClientProtocol	Not supported.
HttpWebClientProtocol	The base class for all XML Web service client proxies that use the HTTP transport protocol.
LogicalMethodInfo	Represents the attributes and metadata for an XML Web service method.
MatchAttribute	Not supported.
SoapClientMessage	Represents the data in a SOAP request sent or a SOAP response received by an XML Web service client at a specific SoapMessageStage.
SoapDocumentMethodAttribute	Applying the *SoapDocumentMethodAttribute* to a method specifies that SOAP messages to and from the method use Document formatting.
SoapDocumentServiceAttribute	Applying the optional *SoapDocumentServiceAttribute* to an XML Web service sets the default format of SOAP requests and responses sent to and from XML Web service methods within the XML Web service.
SoapException	The exception that is thrown when an XML Web service method is called over SOAP and an exception occurs.
SoapExtension	The base class for SOAP extensions for XML Web services created using ASP.NET.

(continued)

Table A-27 Classes in the *System.Web.Services.Protocols* Namespace *(continued)*

Class	Description
SoapExtensionAttribute	When overridden in a derived class, specifies a SOAP extension should run with an XML Web service method.
SoapHeader	When overridden in a derived class, represents the content of a SOAP header.
SoapHeaderAttribute	This attribute is applied to an XML Web service method or an XML Web service client to specify a SOAP header that an XML Web service method or an XML Web service client can process.
SoapHeaderCollection	Contains a collection of instances of the *SoapHeader* class.
SoapHeaderException	The exception that is thrown when an XML Web service method is called over SOAP and an exception occurs during processing of the SOAP header.
SoapHttpClientProtocol	Specifies what the class client proxies derive from when using SOAP.
SoapMessage	Holds the names and types of parameters required during serialization of a SOAP RPC. Note that this class is implemented in the *System.Runtime.Serialization.Formatters* namespace in the desktop .NET Framework.
SoapRpcMethodAttribute	Applying the *SoapRpcMethodAttribute* to a method specifies that SOAP messages sent to and from the method use RPC formatting.
SoapRpcServiceAttribute	Not supported.
SoapServerMessage	Not supported.
SoapUnknownHeader	Represents the data received from a SOAP header that was not understood by the recipient XML Web service or XML Web service client.
WebClientAsyncResult	Provides an implementation of *IAsyncResult* for use by XML Web service proxies to implement the standard asynchronous method pattern.
WebClientProtocol	Specifies the base class for all XML Web service client proxies created using ASP.NET.

System.Windows.Forms Namespace

The *System.Windows.Forms* namespace contains classes and structures that enable the construction of rich client applications using the Windows user interface. It is implemented in System.Windows.Forms.dll. Table A-28 lists the classes and structures in this namespace.

Table A-28 Classes and Structures in the *System.Windows.Forms* Namespace

Class or Structure	Description
AccessibleObject class	Not supported.
AmbientProperties class	Not supported.
Application class	Provides static methods (*Shared* in Visual Basic) and properties to manage an application, such as methods to start and stop an application and to process Windows messages; and properties to get information about an application.
ApplicationContext class	Not supported.
AxHost class and child classes	Not supported.
BaseCollection class	Provides the base functionality for creating data-related collections in the *System.Windows.Forms* namespace.
Binding class	Represents the simple binding between the property value of an object and the property value of a control.
BindingContext class	Manages the collection of *BindingManagerBase* objects for any object that inherits from the *Control* class.
BindingManagerBase class	Manages all *Binding* objects that are bound to the same data source and data member. This class is abstract.
BindingMemberInfo structure	Contains information that enables a *Binding* to resolve a data binding to either the property of an object or the property of the current object in a list of objects.
BindingsCollection class	Represents a collection of *Binding* objects for a control.
Button class	Represents a Windows button control.

(continued)

Table A-28 Classes and Structures in the *System.Windows.Forms* Namespace *(continued)*

Class or Structure	Description
ButtonBase class	Implements the basic functionality common to button controls.
CheckBox class	Represents a Windows check box.
CheckedListBox class and child classes	Not supported.
Clipboard class	Not supported.
ColorDialog class	Not supported.
ColumnClickEventArgs class	Provides data for the *ColumnClick* event.
ColumnHeader class	Displays a single column header in a *ListView* control.
ComboBox class	Represents a Windows combo box control.
ComboBox.ObjectCollection class	Represents the collection of items in a *ComboBox*.
CommonDialog class	Specifies the base class used for displaying dialog boxes on the screen.
ContainerControl class	Provides focus management functionality for controls that can function as a container for other controls.
ContentsResizedEventArgs class	Not supported.
ContextMenu class	Represents a shortcut menu.
Control class	Defines the base class for controls, which are components with visual representation.
Control.ControlAccessibleObject class	Not supported.
Control.ControlCollection class	Represents a collection of *Control* objects.
ControlBindingsCollection class	Represents the collection of data bindings for a control.
ControlEventArgs class	Not supported.
ControlPaint class	Not supported.
ConvertEventArgs class	Provides data for the *Format* and *Parse* events.
CreateParams class	Not supported.
CurrencyManager class	Manages a list of *Binding* objects.
Cursor class	Represents the image used to paint the mouse cursor.
CursorConverter class	Not supported.

Table A-28 Classes and Structures in the *System.Windows.Forms* Namespace *(continued)*

Class or Structure	Description
Cursors class	Provides a collection of *Cursor* objects for use by a Windows Forms application.
DataFormats class	Not supported.
DataFormats.Format class	Not supported.
DataGrid class	A data bound list control that displays the items from a data source in a table.
DataGrid.HitTestInfo class	Contains information about a part of the DataGrid control at a specified coordinate.
DataGridBoolColumn class	Not supported.
DataGridCell structure	Identifies a cell in the DataGrid control.
DataGridColumnStyle class	Specifies the appearance, text formatting, and behavior of a DataGrid control column. This class is abstract.
DataGridPreferredColumnWidthTypeConverter class	Not supported.
DataGridTableStyle class	Represents the table drawn by the DataGrid control at run time.
DataGridTextBox class	Not supported.
DataGridTextBoxColumn class	Hosts a TextBox control in a cell of a *DataGridColumnStyle* object for editing strings.
DataObject class	Not supported.
DateRangeEventArgs class	Not supported.
DateTimePicker class	Not supported.
DomainUpDown class	Represents a Windows up-down control that displays string values.
DomainUpDown.DomainUpDownItemCollection class	Encapsulates a collection of objects for use by the *DomainUpDown* class.
DragEventArgs class	Not supported.
DrawItemEventArgs class	Not supported.
ErrorProvider class	Not supported.
FeatureSupport class	Not supported.
FileDialog class	Displays a dialog window from which the user can select a file.
FolderBrowserDialog class	Not supported.
FontDialog class	Not supported.

(continued)

Table A-28 Classes and Structures in the *System.Windows.Forms* Namespace *(continued)*

Class or Structure	Description
Form class	Represents a window or a dialog box that makes up an application's user interface.
Form.ControlCollection class	Not supported.
GiveFeedbackEventArgs class	Not supported.
GridColumnStylesCollection class	Represents a collection of *DataGridColumnStyle* objects in the DataGrid control.
GridItem class	Not supported.
GridItemCollection class	Not supported.
GridTableStylesCollection class	Represents a collection of *DataGridTableStyle* objects in the DataGrid control.
GroupBox class	Not supported.
Help class	Not supported.
HelpEventArgs class	Not supported.
HelpProvider class	Not supported.
HScrollBar class	Represents a standard Windows horizontal scroll bar.
ImageIndexConverter class	Not supported.
ImageList class	Provides methods to manage a collection of *Image* objects.
ImageList.ImageCollection class	Encapsulates the collection of *Image* objects in an *ImageList*.
ImageListStreamer class	Not supported.
*InputLanguage** classes	Not supported.
InvalidateEventArgs class	Not supported.
ItemChangedEventArgs class	Provides data for the *ItemChanged* event.
ItemCheckEventArgs class	Provides data for the *ItemCheck* event of the ListView control.
ItemDragEventArgs class	Not supported.
KeyEventArgs class	Provides data for the *KeyDown* or *KeyUp* event.
KeyPressEventArgs class	Provides data for the *KeyPress* event.
KeysConverter class	Not supported.
Label class	Represents a standard Windows label.
LabelEditEventArgs class	Not supported.

Table A-28 Classes and Structures in the *System.Windows.Forms* Namespace *(continued)*

Class or Structure	Description
LayoutEventArgs class	Not supported.
LinkArea structure	Not supported.
LinkArea.LinkAreaConverter class	Not supported.
LinkClickedEventArgs class	Not supported.
*LinkLabel** classes	Not supported.
ListBindingConverter class	Not supported.
ListBox class	Represents a Windows list box control.
ListBox.ObjectCollection class	Represents the collection of items in a ListBox control.
ListBox.SelectedIndexCollection class	Not supported.
ListBox.SelectedObjectCollection class	Not supported.
ListControl class	Provides a common implementation of members for the *ListBox* and *ComboBox* classes.
ListView class	Represents a Windows list view control, which displays a collection of items that can be displayed using different views.
ListView.CheckedIndexCollection class	Not supported.
ListView.CheckedListViewItemCollection class	Not supported.
ListView.ColumnHeaderCollection class	Represents the collection of column headers in a ListView control.
ListView.ListViewItemCollection class	Represents the collection of items in a ListView control.
ListView.SelectedIndexCollection class	Represents the collection containing the indexes to the selected items in a list view control.
ListView.SelectedListViewItemCollection class	Not supported.
ListViewItem class	Represents an item in a ListView control.
ListViewItem.ListViewSubItem class	Represents a subitem of a *ListViewItem* control.
ListViewItem.ListViewSubItemCollection class	Represents a collection of *ListViewItem.ListViewSubItem* objects stored in a *ListViewItem* control.
ListViewItemConverter class	Not supported.

(continued)

Table A-28 Classes and Structures in the *System.Windows.Forms* Namespace *(continued)*

Class or Structure	Description
MainMenu class	Represents the menu structure of a form.
MeasureItemEventArgs class	Not supported.
Menu class	Represents the base functionality for all menus.
Menu.MenuItemCollection class	Represents a collection of *MenuItem* objects.
MenuItem class	Represents an individual item that is displayed within a *MainMenu* or *ContextMenu* object.
Message structure	Not supported.
MessageBox class	Displays a message box that can contain text, buttons, and symbols that inform and instruct the user.
MonthCalendar class	Not supported.
MouseEventArgs class	Provides data for the *MouseUp*, *MouseDown*, and *MouseMove* events.
NativeWindow class	Not supported.
NavigateEventArgs class	Not supported.
NodeLabelEditEventArgs class	Not supported.
NotifyIcon class	Not supported.
NumericUpDown class	Represents a Windows up-down control that displays numeric values.
OpacityConverter class	Not supported.
OpenFileDialog class	Represents a common dialog box that displays the control that allows the user to open a file.
OSFeature class	Not supported.
PageSetupDialog class	Not supported.
PaintEventArgs class	Provides data for the *Paint* event.
Panel class	Represents a Windows panel control.
PictureBox class	Represents a Windows picture box control for displaying an image.
PrintControllerWithStatusDialog class	Not supported.
*Print** classes	Not supported.
ProgressBar class	Represents a Windows progress bar control.

Table A-28 Classes and Structures in the *System.Windows.Forms* Namespace *(continued)*

Class or Structure	Description
PropertyGrid class	Not supported.
PropertyManager class	Maintains a *Binding* between an object's property and a data-bound control property.
PropertyTabChangedEventArgs class	Not supported.
PropertyValueChangedEventArgs class	Not supported.
QueryAccessibilityHelpEventArgs class	Not supported.
QueryContinueDragEventArgs class	Not supported.
RadioButton class	Represents a Windows radio button.
RichTextBox class	Not supported.
SaveFileDialog class	Represents a common dialog box that allows the user to specify options for saving a file.
Screen class	Represents a display device or multiple display devices on a single system.
ScrollableControl class	Defines a base class for controls that support auto-scrolling behavior.
ScrollableControl.DockPaddingEdges class	Not supported.
ScrollBar class	Implements the basic functionality of a scroll bar control.
ScrollEventArgs class	Not supported.
SelectedGridItemChangedEventArgs class	Not supported.
SelectionRange class	Not supported.
SelectionRangeConverter class	Not supported.
SendKeys class	Not supported.
Splitter class	Not supported.
SplitterEventArgs class	Not supported.
StatusBar class	Represents a Windows status bar control.
StatusBar.StatusBarPanelCollection class	Not supported.
StatusBarDrawItemEventArgs class	Not supported.
StatusBarPanel class	Not supported.
StatusBarPanelClickEventArgs class	Not supported.

(continued)

Table A-28 Classes and Structures in the *System.Windows.Forms* Namespace *(continued)*

Class or Structure	Description
SystemInformation class	Provides information about the operating system.
TabControl class	Manages a related set of tab pages.
TabControl.ControlCollection class	Not supported.
TabControl.TabPageCollection class	Contains a collection of *TabPage* objects.
TabPage class	Represents a single tab page in a *TabControl*.
TabPage.TabPageControlCollection class	Not supported.
TextBox class	Represents a Windows text box control.
TextBoxBase class	Implements the basic functionality required by text controls.
Timer class	Implements a timer that raises an event at user-defined intervals. This timer is optimized for use in Windows Forms applications and must be used in a window.
ToolBar class	Represents a Windows toolbar.
ToolBar.ToolBarButtonCollection class	Encapsulates a collection of *ToolBarButton* controls for use by the *ToolBar* class.
ToolBarButton class	Represents a Windows toolbar button.
ToolBarButtonClickEventArgs class	Provides data for the *ButtonClick* event.
ToolTip class	Not supported.
TrackBar class	Represents a standard Windows trackbar.
TreeNode class	Represents a node of a TreeView object.
TreeNodeCollection class	Represents a collection of *TreeNode* objects.
TreeNodeConverter class	Not supported.
TreeView class	Displays a hierarchical collection of labeled items, each represented by a *TreeNode* object.
TreeViewCancelEventArgs class	Provides data for the *BeforeCheck*, *BeforeCollapse*, *BeforeExpand*, or *BeforeSelect* events of a TreeView control.
TreeViewEventArgs class	Provides data for the *AfterCheck*, *AfterCollapse*, *AfterExpand*, or *AfterSelect* events of a TreeView control.

Table A-28 Classes and Structures in the *System.Windows.Forms* Namespace *(continued)*

Class or Structure	Description
TreeViewImageIndexConverter class	Not supported.
UICuesEventArgs class	Not supported.
UpDownBase class	Implements the basic functionality required by an up-down control.
UserControl class	Not supported.
VScrollBar class	Represents a standard Windows vertical scroll bar.

System.Windows.Forms.Design Namespace

The *System.Windows.Forms.Design* namespace contains classes that can be used to extend design-time support for Windows Forms. It is not supported in the .NET Compact Framework.

System.Xml Namespace

The *System.Xml* namespace provides support for processing XML. It is implemented in System.Xml.dll. Table A-29 lists the classes in this namespace.

Table A-29 Classes in the *System.Xml* Namespace

Class	Description
NameTable	Implements a single-threaded *XmlNameTable* object.
XmlAttribute	Represents an attribute. Valid and default values for the attribute are defined in a document type definition (DTD) or schema.
XmlAttributeCollection	Represents a collection of attributes that can be accessed by name or index.
XmlCDataSection	Represents a CDATA section.
XmlCharacterData	Provides text manipulation methods that are used by several classes.
XmlComment	Represents the content of an XML comment.

(continued)

Table A-29 Classes in the *System.Xml* Namespace *(continued)*

Class	Description
XmlConvert	Encodes and decodes XML names and provides methods for converting between common language runtime types and XML Schema definition (XSD) language types. When converting data types, the values returned are locale independent.
XmlDataDocument	Not supported.
XmlDeclaration	Represents this XML declaration node: *<?xml version='1.0' ...?>*.
XmlDocument	Represents an XML document.
XmlDocumentFragment	Represents a lightweight object that is useful for tree insert operations.
XmlDocumentType	Not supported.
XmlElement	Represents an element.
XmlEntity	Not supported.
XmlEntityReference	Represents an entity reference node.
XmlException	Returns detailed information about the last exception.
XmlImplementation	Defines the context for a set of *XmlDocument* objects.
XmlLinkedNode	Gets the node immediately preceding or following this node.
XmlNamedNodeMap	Represents a collection of nodes that can be accessed by name or index.
XmlNamespaceManager	Resolves, adds, and removes namespaces to a collection and provides scope management for these namespaces. This class is used by the *XmlReader* class.
XmlNameTable	Table of atomized string objects.
XmlNode	Represents a single node in the XML document.
XmlNodeChangedEventArgs	Provides data for the *NodeChanged*, *NodeChanging*, *NodeInserted*, *NodeInserting*, *NodeRemoved*, and *NodeRemoving* events.
XmlNodeList	Represents an ordered collection of nodes.
XmlNodeReader	Represents a reader that provides fast, non-cached forward-only access to XML data in an *XmlNode* object.
XmlNotation	Not supported.
XmlParserContext	Provides all the context information required by *XmlTextReader* to parse an XML fragment.

Table A-29 Classes in the *System.Xml* Namespace *(continued)*

Class	Description
XmlProcessingInstruction	Represents a processing instruction, which XML defines to keep processor-specific information in the text of the document.
XmlQualifiedName	Represents an XML qualified name.
XmlReader	Represents a reader that provides fast, non-cached, forward-only access to XML data.
XmlResolver	Resolves external XML resources named by a URI.
XmlSecureResolver	Not supported.
XmlSignificantWhitespace	Represents white space between markup in a mixed content mode or white space within an *xml:space='preserve'* scope. This is also referred to as significant white space.
XmlText	Represents the text content of an element or an attribute.
XmlTextReader	Represents a reader that provides fast, non-cached, forward-only access to XML data.
XmlTextWriter	Represents a writer that provides a fast, non-cached, forward-only way of generating streams or files containing XML data that conforms to the W3C Extensible Markup Language (XML) 1 and the Namespaces in XML recommendations.
XmlUrlResolver	Resolves external XML resources named by a URI.
XmlValidatingReader	Not supported.
XmlWhitespace	Represents white space in element content.
XmlWriter	Represents a writer that provides a fast, non-cached, forward-only means of generating streams or files containing XML data that conforms to the W3C Extensible Markup Language (XML) 1 and the Namespaces in XML recommendations.

System.Xml.Schema Namespace

The *System.Xml.Schema* namespace provides standards-based support for XML Schemas. The .NET Compact Framework does not support XML Schema validation; it supports only the *XmlSchema*, *XmlSchemaException*, and *XmlSchemaObject* classes, instead of the large number of classes found in the desktop implementation. This namespace is implemented in System.Xml.dll.

System.Xml.Serialization Namespace

The *System.Xml.Serialization* namespace contains classes used to serialize objects into XML format documents or streams. Note that this namespace is included only to support the handling of XML format streams by the base class libraries that implement XML Web service client functionality. The *XmlSerializer* class used by desktop developers to serialize objects as XML is not exposed to developers in the .NET Compact Framework. This namespace is implemented in System.Xml.dll. Table A-30 lists the classes of the *System.Xml.Serialization* namespace.

Table A-30 Classes in the *System.Xml.Serialization* Namespace

Class	Description
SoapAttributeAttribute	Specifies that the *XmlSerializer* class should serialize the class member as an encoded SOAP attribute.
SoapAttributeOverrides	Not supported.
SoapAttributes	Not supported.
SoapElementAttribute	Specifies that the public member value be serialized by the *XmlSerializer* class as an encoded SOAP XML element.
SoapEnumAttribute	Controls how the *XmlSerializer* class serializes an enumeration member.
SoapIgnoreAttribute	Instructs the *XmlSerializer* class not to serialize the public field or public read/write property value.
SoapIncludeAttribute	Allows the *XmlSerializer* class to recognize a type when it serializes or deserializes an object as encoded SOAP XML.
SoapTypeAttribute	Controls the schema generated by the *XmlSerializer* class when a class instance is serialized as SOAP encoded XML.
UnreferencedObjectEventArgs	Not supported.
XmlAnyAttributeAttribute	Specifies that the member (a field that returns an array of *XmlAttribute* objects) can contain any XML attributes.

Table A-30 Classes in the *System.Xml.Serialization* Namespace *(continued)*

Class	Description
XmlAnyElementAttribute	Specifies that the member (a field that returns an array of *XmlElement* or *XmlNode* objects) can contain objects that represent any XML element that has no corresponding member in the object being serialized or deserialized.
XmlAnyElementAttributes	Not supported.
XmlArrayAttribute	Specifies that the *XmlSerializer* class should serialize a particular class member as an array of XML elements.
XmlArrayItemAttribute	Specifies the derived types that the *XmlSerializer* class can place in a serialized array.
XmlArrayItemAttributes	Not supported.
XmlAttributeAttribute	Specifies that the *XmlSerializer* class should serialize the class member as an XML attribute.
XmlAttributeEventArgs	Not supported.
XmlAttributeOverrides	Not supported.
XmlAttributes	Not supported.
XmlChoiceIdentifierAttribute	Specifies that the member can be further disambiguated by using an enumeration.
XmlElementAttribute	Indicates that a public field or property represents an XML element when the *XmlSerializer* class serializes or deserializes the containing object.
XmlElementAttributes	Not supported.
XmlElementEventArgs	Not supported.
XmlEnumAttribute	Controls how the *XmlSerializer* class serializes an enumeration member.
XmlIgnoreAttribute	Instructs the *Serialize* method of the *XmlSerializer* class not to serialize the public field or public read/write property value.
XmlIncludeAttribute	Allows the *XmlSerializer* class to recognize a type when it serializes or deserializes an object.

(continued)

Table A-30 Classes in the *System.Xml.Serialization* Namespace *(continued)*

Class	Description
XmlNamespaceDeclarationsAttribute	Specifies that the target property, parameter, return value, or class member contain prefixes associated with namespaces that are used within an XML document.
XmlNodeEventArgs	Not supported.
XmlRootAttribute	Identifies a class, structure, enumeration, or interface as the root (or top-level) element of an XML-document instance.
XmlSerializer	Not supported.
XmlSerializerNamespaces	Contains the XML namespaces and prefixes that the *XmlSerializer* class uses to generate qualified names in an XML-document instance.
XmlTextAttribute	Indicates to the *XmlSerializer* class that the member should be treated as XML text when the containing class is serialized or deserialized.
XmlTypeAttribute	Controls the XML schema generated when the attribute target is serialized by the *XmlSerializer* class.
XmlTypeMapping	Not supported.

System.Xml.XPath Namespace

The *System.Xml.XPath* namespace contains the XML Path Language (XPath) parser and evaluation engine. It is not supported in the .NET Compact Framework.

System.Xml.Xsl Namespace

The *System.Xml.Xsl* namespace provides support for Extensible Stylesheet Language Transformations (XSLT). It is not supported in the .NET Compact Framework.

Index

Symbols and Numbers

A

B

C

D

E

G

H

I

J

K

L

M

N

O

P

Q

R

S

T

U

V

W

X

Y

About the Authors

Andy Wigley

Andy is a Principal Technologist at the U.K. technical authoring and consultancy company Content Master, focusing on mobile technologies. He has contributed to MSDN and other publications and regularly appears at conferences, presenting on applications of mobile technology. He has been involved in software engineering for nearly 20 years, working on projects as diverse as high-performance messaging, electronic document exchange, computer-integrated manufacturing, and laboratory robotics.

He is the coauthor of *Building .NET Applications for Mobile Devices* (Microsoft Press), which focuses on building mobile Web applications with Microsoft ASP.NET Mobile Controls.

Andy lives with his wife, Caroline, and their two daughters in North Wales, a location that allows him to pursue his passion for rock climbing.

Stephen Wheelwright

Stephen is a Senior Technologist at Content Master. He has been in the IT industry for more than 19 years and has written software solutions on a variety of systems. He has also written MSDN presentations and MOC courseware for Microsoft. Stephen lives in Worcestershire, England, with his wife, Melanie, and his two children. He is currently working through his jujitsu grades.

Robert Burbidge

Robert is an experienced software developer and trainer living in Swindon, in the west of England. He has been working for Content Master for two years and has development expertise in a variety of environments ranging from 8-bit assembly language and BCPL to Microsoft Visual Basic, C, and C# on today's PC platforms. He holds a B.Sc. degree in Electronics from the University of Southampton, although these days, when it comes to electrons, he rarely attempts anything more complex than changing a fuse. When not working with technology, Robert can usually be found working in amateur theater in his hometown as an actor or a director. He would like to thank his wife, Tina, and son, Andrew, for their patience while this book was being written!

Rory MacLeod

Rory did most of his programming in the scientific and technical areas before moving on to become a trainer and more recently a writer and developer for Content Master. Training and speaking engagements take him from home in Scotland a lot, so any spare time he gets is spent with his family, his old acoustic guitar, and his cats.

Mark D. Sutton

Mark is a technology specialist working for Content Master, providing consultancy and training in data access, ASP.NET applications, and SQL Server. He is particularly interested in producing intuitive, visually appealing, and easy to use software using state-of-the-art techniques and tools. Off duty will find him heading to the water for some sailing.

Feeler Gauge

You can use a **feeler gauge** to measure clearances in machinery, engines, or even musical instruments, such as the gear wear in a transmission, the clearance between a cam and a valve-actuating rocker arm, or the distance between the string and the fret on the neck of a guitar. The individual blades in the feeler gauge come in different thicknesses, often measured in thousandths of an inch or fractions of a millimeter. Keep inserting blades until you find one that fits snugly, and then read its thickness to determine the clearance.

At Microsoft Press, we use tools to illustrate our books for software developers and IT professionals. Tools very simply and powerfully symbolize human inventiveness. They're a metaphor for people extending their capabilities, precision, and reach. From simple calipers and pliers to digital micrometers and lasers, these stylized illustrations give each book a visual identity, and a personality to the series. With tools and knowledge, there's no limit to creativity and innovation. Our tag line says it all: *the tools you need to put technology to work.*

The manuscript for this book was prepared and galleyed using Microsoft Word. Pages were composed by Microsoft Press using Adobe FrameMaker+SGML for Windows, with text in Garamond and display type in Helvetica Condensed. Composed pages were delivered to the printer as electronic prepress files.

Cover Designer:	Methodologie, Inc.
Interior Graphic Designer:	James D. Kramer
Principal Compositor:	Dan Latimer
Electronic Artist:	Michael Kloepfer
Principal Copyeditor:	Holly M. Viola
Indexer:	Richard Shrout

MICROSOFT LICENSE AGREEMENT

Book Companion CD

IMPORTANT—READ CAREFULLY: This Microsoft End-User License Agreement ("EULA") is a legal agreement between you (either an individual or an entity) and Microsoft Corporation for the Microsoft product identified above, which includes computer software and may include associated media, printed materials, and "online" or electronic documentation ("SOFTWARE PRODUCT"). Any component included within the SOFTWARE PRODUCT that is accompanied by a separate End-User License Agreement shall be governed by such agreement and not the terms set forth below. By installing, copying, or otherwise using the SOFTWARE PRODUCT, you agree to be bound by the terms of this EULA. If you do not agree to the terms of this EULA, you are not authorized to install, copy, or otherwise use the SOFTWARE PRODUCT; you may, however, return the SOFTWARE PRODUCT, along with all printed materials and other items that form a part of the Microsoft product that includes the SOFTWARE PRODUCT, to the place you obtained them for a full refund.

SOFTWARE PRODUCT LICENSE

The SOFTWARE PRODUCT is protected by United States copyright laws and international copyright treaties, as well as other intellectual property laws and treaties. The SOFTWARE PRODUCT is licensed, not sold.

1. **GRANT OF LICENSE.** This EULA grants you the following rights:

   a. **Software Product.** You may install and use one copy of the SOFTWARE PRODUCT on a single computer. The primary user of the computer on which the SOFTWARE PRODUCT is installed may make a second copy for his or her exclusive use on a portable computer.

   b. **Storage/Network Use.** You may also store or install a copy of the SOFTWARE PRODUCT on a storage device, such as a network server, used only to install or run the SOFTWARE PRODUCT on your other computers over an internal network; however, you must acquire and dedicate a license for each separate computer on which the SOFTWARE PRODUCT is installed or run from the storage device. A license for the SOFTWARE PRODUCT may not be shared or used concurrently on different computers.

   c. **License Pak.** If you have acquired this EULA in a Microsoft License Pak, you may make the number of additional copies of the computer software portion of the SOFTWARE PRODUCT authorized on the printed copy of this EULA, and you may use each copy in the manner specified above. You are also entitled to make a corresponding number of secondary copies for portable computer use as specified above.

   d. **Sample Code.** Solely with respect to portions, if any, of the SOFTWARE PRODUCT that are identified within the SOFTWARE PRODUCT as sample code (the "SAMPLE CODE"):

      i. **Use and Modification.** Microsoft grants you the right to use and modify the source code version of the SAMPLE CODE, *provided* you comply with subsection (d)(iii) below. You may not distribute the SAMPLE CODE, or any modified version of the SAMPLE CODE, in source code form.

      ii. **Redistributable Files.** Provided you comply with subsection (d)(iii) below, Microsoft grants you a nonexclusive, royalty-free right to reproduce and distribute the object code version of the SAMPLE CODE and of any modified SAMPLE CODE, other than SAMPLE CODE, or any modified version thereof, designated as not redistributable in the Readme file that forms a part of the SOFTWARE PRODUCT (the "Non-Redistributable Sample Code"). All SAMPLE CODE other than the Non-Redistributable Sample Code is collectively referred to as the "REDISTRIBUTABLES."

      iii. **Redistribution Requirements.** If you redistribute the REDISTRIBUTABLES, you agree to: (i) distribute the REDISTRIBUTABLES in object code form only in conjunction with and as a part of your software application product; (ii) not use Microsoft's name, logo, or trademarks to market your software application product; (iii) include a valid copyright notice on your software application product; (iv) indemnify, hold harmless, and defend Microsoft from and against any claims or lawsuits, including attorney's fees, that arise or result from the use or distribution of your software application product; and (v) not permit further distribution of the REDISTRIBUTABLES by your end user. Contact Microsoft for the applicable royalties due and other licensing terms for all other uses and/or distribution of the REDISTRIBUTABLES.

2. **DESCRIPTION OF OTHER RIGHTS AND LIMITATIONS.**

   - **Limitations on Reverse Engineering, Decompilation, and Disassembly.** You may not reverse engineer, decompile, or disassemble the SOFTWARE PRODUCT, except and only to the extent that such activity is expressly permitted by applicable law notwithstanding this limitation.
   - **Separation of Components.** The SOFTWARE PRODUCT is licensed as a single product. Its component parts may not be separated for use on more than one computer.
   - **Rental.** You may not rent, lease, or lend the SOFTWARE PRODUCT.

- **Support Services.** Microsoft may, but is not obligated to, provide you with support services related to the SOFTWARE PRODUCT ("Support Services"). Use of Support Services is governed by the Microsoft policies and programs described in the user manual, in "online" documentation, and/or in other Microsoft-provided materials. Any supplemental software code provided to you as part of the Support Services shall be considered part of the SOFTWARE PRODUCT and subject to the terms and conditions of this EULA. With respect to technical information you provide to Microsoft as part of the Support Services, Microsoft may use such information for its business purposes, including for product support and development. Microsoft will not utilize such technical information in a form that personally identifies you.
- **Software Transfer.** You may permanently transfer all of your rights under this EULA, provided you retain no copies, you transfer all of the SOFTWARE PRODUCT (including all component parts, the media and printed materials, any upgrades, this EULA, and, if applicable, the Certificate of Authenticity), **and** the recipient agrees to the terms of this EULA.
- **Termination.** Without prejudice to any other rights, Microsoft may terminate this EULA if you fail to comply with the terms and conditions of this EULA. In such event, you must destroy all copies of the SOFTWARE PRODUCT and all of its component parts.

3. **COPYRIGHT.** All title and copyrights in and to the SOFTWARE PRODUCT (including but not limited to any images, photographs, animations, video, audio, music, text, SAMPLE CODE, REDISTRIBUTABLES, and "applets" incorporated into the SOFTWARE PRODUCT) and any copies of the SOFTWARE PRODUCT are owned by Microsoft or its suppliers. The SOFTWARE PRODUCT is protected by copyright laws and international treaty provisions. Therefore, you must treat the SOFTWARE PRODUCT like any other copyrighted material **except** that you may install the SOFTWARE PRODUCT on a single computer provided you keep the original solely for backup or archival purposes. You may not copy the printed materials accompanying the SOFTWARE PRODUCT.

4. **U.S. GOVERNMENT RESTRICTED RIGHTS.** The SOFTWARE PRODUCT and documentation are provided with RESTRICTED RIGHTS. Use, duplication, or disclosure by the Government is subject to restrictions as set forth in subparagraph (c)(1)(ii) of the Rights in Technical Data and Computer Software clause at DFARS 252.227-7013 or subparagraphs (c)(1) and (2) of the Commercial Computer Software—Restricted Rights at 48 CFR 52.227-19, as applicable. Manufacturer is Microsoft Corporation/One Microsoft Way/Redmond, WA 98052-6399.

5. **EXPORT RESTRICTIONS.** You agree that you will not export or re-export the SOFTWARE PRODUCT, any part thereof, or any process or service that is the direct product of the SOFTWARE PRODUCT (the foregoing collectively referred to as the "Restricted Components"), to any country, person, entity, or end user subject to U.S. export restrictions. You specifically agree not to export or re-export any of the Restricted Components (i) to any country to which the U.S. has embargoed or restricted the export of goods or services, which currently include, but are not necessarily limited to, Cuba, Iran, Iraq, Libya, North Korea, Sudan, and Syria, or to any national of any such country, wherever located, who intends to transmit or transport the Restricted Components back to such country; (ii) to any end user who you know or have reason to know will utilize the Restricted Components in the design, development, or production of nuclear, chemical, or biological weapons; or (iii) to any end user who has been prohibited from participating in U.S. export transactions by any federal agency of the U.S. government. You warrant and represent that neither the BXA nor any other U.S. federal agency has suspended, revoked, or denied your export privileges.

DISCLAIMER OF WARRANTY

NO WARRANTIES OR CONDITIONS. MICROSOFT EXPRESSLY DISCLAIMS ANY WARRANTY OR CONDITION FOR THE SOFTWARE PRODUCT. THE SOFTWARE PRODUCT AND ANY RELATED DOCUMENTATION ARE PROVIDED "AS IS" WITHOUT WARRANTY OR CONDITION OF ANY KIND, EITHER EXPRESS OR IMPLIED, INCLUDING, WITHOUT LIMITATION, THE IMPLIED WARRANTIES OF MERCHANTABILITY, FITNESS FOR A PARTICULAR PURPOSE, OR NONINFRINGEMENT. THE ENTIRE RISK ARISING OUT OF USE OR PERFORMANCE OF THE SOFTWARE PRODUCT REMAINS WITH YOU.

LIMITATION OF LIABILITY. TO THE MAXIMUM EXTENT PERMITTED BY APPLICABLE LAW, IN NO EVENT SHALL MICROSOFT OR ITS SUPPLIERS BE LIABLE FOR ANY SPECIAL, INCIDENTAL, INDIRECT, OR CONSEQUENTIAL DAMAGES WHATSOEVER (INCLUDING, WITHOUT LIMITATION, DAMAGES FOR LOSS OF BUSINESS PROFITS, BUSINESS INTERRUPTION, LOSS OF BUSINESS INFORMATION, OR ANY OTHER PECUNIARY LOSS) ARISING OUT OF THE USE OF OR INABILITY TO USE THE SOFTWARE PRODUCT OR THE PROVISION OF OR FAILURE TO PROVIDE SUPPORT SERVICES, EVEN IF MICROSOFT HAS BEEN ADVISED OF THE POSSIBILITY OF SUCH DAMAGES. IN ANY CASE, MICROSOFT'S ENTIRE LIABILITY UNDER ANY PROVISION OF THIS EULA SHALL BE LIMITED TO THE GREATER OF THE AMOUNT ACTUALLY PAID BY YOU FOR THE SOFTWARE PRODUCT OR US$5.00; PROVIDED, HOWEVER, IF YOU HAVE ENTERED INTO A MICROSOFT SUPPORT SERVICES AGREEMENT, MICROSOFT'S ENTIRE LIABILITY REGARDING SUPPORT SERVICES SHALL BE GOVERNED BY THE TERMS OF THAT AGREEMENT. BECAUSE SOME STATES AND JURISDICTIONS DO NOT ALLOW THE EXCLUSION OR LIMITATION OF LIABILITY, THE ABOVE LIMITATION MAY NOT APPLY TO YOU.

MISCELLANEOUS

This EULA is governed by the laws of the State of Washington USA, except and only to the extent that applicable law mandates governing law of a different jurisdiction.

Should you have any questions concerning this EULA, or if you desire to contact Microsoft for any reason, please contact the Microsoft subsidiary serving your country, or write: Microsoft Sales Information Center/One Microsoft Way/Redmond, WA 98052-6399.

PN 097-0002296

Proof of Purchase

Use this page as proof of purchase if participating in a promotion or rebate offer on this title. Proof of purchase must be used in conjunction with other proof(s) of payment such as your dated sales receipt—see offer details.

Microsoft® .NET Compact Framework (Core Reference)
0-7356-1725-2

____
CUSTOMER NAME

Microsoft Press, PO Box 97017, Redmond, WA 98073-9830